UNDERSTANDING FAMILY LAW

SECOND EDITION

By

John De Witt Gregory
Sidney & Walter Siben Distinguished Professor of Family Law
Hofstra University

Peter N. Swisher
Professor of Law
University of Richmond

Sheryl L. Wolf
Professor of Law
University of New Mexico

LexisNexis™

QUESTIONS ABOUT THIS PUBLICATION?

For questions about the **Editorial Content** appearing in these volumes or reprint permission, please call:

Raquel Bristol, J.D. at .... (800) 252-9257 (ext. 2151)
Outside the United States and Canada please call .... (973) 820-2000

For assistance with replacement pages, shipments, billing or other customer service matters, please call:

Customer Services Department at .... (800) 833-9844
Outside the United States and Canada, please call .... (518) 487-3000
Fax number .... (518) 487-3584

For information on other Matthew Bender publications, please call
Your account manager or .... (800) 223-1940
Outside the United States and Canada, please call .... (518) 487-3000

Library of Congress Cataloging-in-Publication Data
Gregory, John DeWitt
  Understanding Family Law / John De Witt Gregory, Peter N. Swisher, Sheryl L. Wolf.-
-2nd ed.
    p. cm. --(Legal text series)
  Includes index.
  ISBN 0-8205-5211-9 (softbound)
    1. Domestic relations--United States. I. Swisher, Peter N., 1944-II. Wolf, Sheryl
  L. (Sheryl Lynn), 1948-III. Title. IV. Series.
  KF505.G734 2001
  346.7301'5--dc21

TABLE OF CONTENTS

CHAPTER 1
AN INTRODUCTION TO FAMILY LAW

CHAPTER 2
MARRIAGE AND MARRIAGE ALTERNATIVES

CHAPTER 3
PROPERTY AND SUPPORT RIGHTS DURING MARRIAGE

CHAPTER 4
MARITAL CONTRACTS AND AGREEMENTS

CHAPTER 5
PROCREATION

CHAPTER 6
ADOPTION

CHAPTER 7
UNIQUE FAMILY ISSUES

CHAPTER 8
DIVORCE GROUNDS AND DEFENSES

CHAPTER 9
SPOUSAL AND CHILD SUPPORT ON DIVORCE

CHAPTER 10
EQUITABLE DISTRIBUTION OF PROPERTY

CHAPTER 11
CHILD CUSTODY AND VISITATION

Chapter 1

AN INTRODUCTION TO FAMILY LAW

§ 1.01 General Introduction

In its traditional sense, family law, also called domestic relations law, involves the legal relationships between husband and wife and parent and child as a social, political, and economic unit. In recent years, the boundaries of family law have grown to encompass legal relationships among persons who live together but are not married— so-called nontraditional families. The legal aspects of family relationships, whether traditional[1] or nontraditional,[2] necessarily include principles of constitutional law, property law, contract law, tort law, civil procedure, statutory regulations, equitable remedies, and, of course, marital property and support rights.

Increasingly, the theoretical and practical implications of family law have been shifting from moral to economic issues, and accordingly, a general practitioner or business lawyer must now understand and master important family law concepts and principles, separate and apart from any divorce litigation. For example, the validity or invalidity of a marriage has far-reaching social, legal, and economic implications in wrongful death actions, since most state wrongful death statutes limit economic recovery to the legal spouse as statutory beneficiary, rather than the de facto spouse.[3] Other areas of the law, including intestate succession and probate law, workers' compensation awards, social security benefits, pensions and retirement plans, medical benefits, insurance payments, loss of consortium actions, state and federal tax law, and marital property and support rights, are also directly affected by the validity or invalidity of a marriage,[4] although some of these benefits are also being covered through domestic partnership legislation in some states and municipalities.[5] American family law currently is in a state of flux and transition based upon the dynamic interplay of three interrelated factors: (1) state and federal legislatures that regulate by statute many important family relationships; (2) courts that interpret these statutes or determine equitable remedies in the absence of such statutes; and (3) family law practitioners who must ultimately decide what strategic alternatives exist in favor of their clients, and who must persuasively plead and prove these alternate remedies before the courts, and increasingly before the legislatures, based upon the law, facts, and social need in each particular case.

---

[1] *See infra* § 1.02[A].

[2] *See infra* § 1.02[B].

[3] *See generally infra* § 2.05[D].

[4] *See generally infra* §§ 2.05[D], 2.10[C], and 3.01 to 3.14.

[5] *See infra* Sec. 2.02[C].

[A] Legislative Regulation of Family Law

State legislatures traditionally have regulated important family law relationships such as marriage and divorce based upon the state's important nexus with the family unit, and based upon the general welfare of its citizens. As the United States Supreme Court stated in *Maynard v. Hill*:

> Marriage, as creating the most important relation in life, as having more to do with the morals and civilization of a people than any other institution, has always been subject to the control of the legislature. That body prescribes the age at which the parties may contract to marry, the procedure or form essential to constitute marriage, the duties and obligations it creates, its effects upon the property rights of both . . . and the acts which may constitute grounds for its dissolution.[6]

However, since marriage and divorce are fundamental rights subject to constitutional protection, a state cannot arbitrarily prohibit or interfere with the exercise of these marital rights without a compelling reason for doing so.[7] Additionally, although the state legislatures continue to regulate many important family law relationships, Congress in its federal capacity has also entered the field of family law regulation, especially in the areas of child custody[8] and child support[9] enforcement remedies, and federal domestic violence legislation.[10]

[B] Judicial Regulation of Family Law

State courts, on the other hand, must interpret and apply state family law statutes to each particular legal controversy, or attempt to find equitable remedies in the absence of such statutory remedies.

Most family law statutes are drafted as general guidelines. Consequently, state court judges normally have broad discretion in resolving many family law disputes, including spousal support and the division of marital property on divorce, and in child custody litigation. However, the *extent* of such judicial discretion in family law matters has come under increased scrutiny

---

[6] 125 U.S. 190, 205 (1888). Implicit throughout *Maynard* is the traditional view that marriage is a status relationship involving three parties: Husband, Wife, and the State. *See also Simms v. Simms*, 175 U.S. 162, 167 (1899) ("The whole subject of the domestic relations of husband and wife, parent and child, belongs to the laws of the State, and not the laws of the United States."). *See generally infra* § 1.03.

[7] *See, e.g., Skinner v. Oklahoma*, 316 U.S. 535 (1942) (protecting the fundamental freedom to procreate from state infringement); *Loving v. Virginia*, 388 U.S. 1 (1967) (declaring state statutes prohibiting interracial marriages to be unconstitutional); *Zablocki v. Redhail*, 434 U.S. 374 (1978) (requiring less onerous state enforcement means than prohibiting the marriage of a father who had not paid child support). *See generally infra* § 1.05.

[8] *See, e.g.*, The Federal Parental Kidnapping Prevention Act of 1980, 28 U.S.C. § 1738A. *See generally infra* § 11.02[C].

[9] *See, e.g.*, The Child Support Enforcement Amendments of 1984, 42 U.S.C. §§ 651–667. *See generally infra* §§ 3.14[C], 8.06[F].

[10] *See, e.g.*, The Violence Against Women Act (VAWA), Publ L. No. 103-322 (1994). *See generally infra* Sec. 7.08[A].

in recent years. For example, family court judges, from their equity heritage as triers of both law and fact, traditionally possess very wide discretion in adjudicating many family law disputes.[11] However, the American Law Institute's recently proposed *Principles of the Law of Family Dissolution*[12] argues that since judicial discretion in family law matters can be "inherently limitless", a major theme of the *Principles* is an effort to improve the consistency and predictability of such trial court decisions.[13]

Moreover, a particular judge's interpretation of family law issues will be guided by the law of the state whose family law governs a particular case, and the underlying law is by no means uniform from state to state. A judge, for example, may be bound to apply a particular state's "traditional" family law statutes and judicial precedents, a more "modern" approach, or a "centrist" combination of the two.[14] A family court judge's analysis of the relevant facts and law may also be influenced by whether he or she is a judicial "formalist" or a judicial "functionalist."

Under the theory of legal formalism, also known as legal positivism, correct legal decisions are determined by pre-existing legislative and judicial precedents, and the court must reach its decision based upon a logical application of the facts to these pre-existing rules. The formalist judge, embracing the principle of judicial restraint, must apply the existing law to the particular facts and remain socially neutral. Judging under this formalistic theory is thus a matter of logical necessity rather than a matter of choice.[15]

Under the countervailing theory of legal functionalism, also referred to as legal realism or legal pragmatism, the formalistic view of legal certainty

---

[11] *See, e.g.*, H. Clark, The Law of Domestic Relations in the United States 644–645 (2d ed. 1988):

> It is axiomatic that the trial courts have wide discretion in determining the propriety and the amount of [spousal support]. The relevant factors are so numerous and their influence so incapable of precise evaluation that the trial court's decision in a particular case will be affirmed unless it amounts to an abuse of discretion or is based upon an erroneous application of legal principles. . . As a result, claims for [spousal support] are won or lost in the trial courts, which have a corresponding heavy responsibility to deal fairly with the spouses in such cases. . . .

This broad judicial discretion also applies to the classification, valuation, and distribution of marital property on divorce, *see Id.* at 589–594; and to child custody determinations as well, *see Id.* at 796–797:

> In most states the award of [child] custody is held to be a matter for the discretion of the trial court, to be upset on appeal only where an abuse of that discretion is shown. . . Certainly any appellate court should be reluctant to substitute its judgment for that of a trial court in cases so entirely dependent upon particular facts and the subtle differences to be drawn from those facts.

[12] *See generally* ALI, *Principles of the Law of Family Dissolution: Analysis and Recommendations* (2000).

[13] *Id.* at 69–70, 83, and 259.

[14] *See, e.g.*, Hobbs & Mulligan, *Centrist Judging and Traditional Family Values*, 49 Wash. & Lee L. Rev. 345 (1992).

[15] *See, e.g.*, G. Paton & D.Dorham, Jurisprudence 3–14 (3d ed. 1972); Weinrib, *Legal Formalism: On the Imminent Rationality of Law*, 97 Yale L.J. 949 (1988). *See generally* M. Jori, Legal Positivism (1992).

and uniformity is viewed as rarely attainable, and perhaps even undesirable, in a changing society. Thus, the paramount concern of the legal functionalists is not logical and legal consistency, as the formalists believe, but socially desirable consequences.[16]

Put another way, where legal formalism is logically-based and precedent-oriented, legal functionalism is sociologically-based and result-oriented to validate society's needs and expectations. According to various commentators, the current transition in family law theory and practice is based upon the need to make American family law more rational and less harsh concerning the reasonable expectations of contemporary society.[17]

It remains open to debate whether state legislatures should remain preeminent in determining current family law needs and goals, as the formalists generally believe, or whether the judiciary should take a more active role in determining current family law goals and remedies, as the functionalists generally believe.[18] Moreover, disagreement persists as to which family law principles should be retained, and which should be changed to meet the needs of contemporary American society.

These questions are of more than academic importance, since although legal functionalism has been the dominant legal theory of American jurisprudence for most of the twentieth century,[19] legal formalism is far from a dead issue, and seems to be enjoying a remarkable resurgence:

> Not since the late 1920s and 1930s has there been such widespread interest in American jurisprudence. But it is no longer the [legal functionalists] who are challenging established norms. The victories at the polls of political conservatives like Richard Nixon and Ronald Reagan [and George Bush and a Republican-controlled Congress], and the corresponding ideological commitments of many recent appointments to the [state and] federal bench, now threaten the continued prominence of a theory of judicial interpretation first

---

[16] *See, e.g.*, W. Rumble, American Legal Realism (1968); G. Aichele, Legal Realism and Twentieth Century American Jurisprudence (1990).

There is yet a third school of American legal theory, the Critical Legal Studies Movement, which generally calls for the dismantling of existing political and legal institutions in favor of newly empowered forms of social democracy. *See, e.g.*, White, *From Realism to Critical Legal Studies*, 40 Sw. U. L. Rev. 819 (1986); Comment, *Round and Round the Bramble Bush: From Legal Realism to Critical Legal Scholarship*, 95 Harv. L. Rev. 1669 (1982); Tushnet, *Critical Legal Studies: A Political History*, 100 Yale L. J. 1515 (1991).

[17] *See, e.g.*, M. Glendon, The New Family and the New Property (1981); M. Glendon, The Transformation of Family Law: State, Law, and Family in the United States and Western Europe (1990); Schneider, *The New Step: Definition, Generalization, and Theory of American Family Law*, 18 U. Mich. J.L. Ref. 1039 (1985).

[18] *Compare Hewitt v. Hewitt*, 394 N.E.2d 1204 (Ill. 1979) ("We believe that [family law] questions are appropriately within the province of the legislature, and that, if there is to be a change in the law of this State on this matter, it is for the legislature and not the courts to bring about that change.") *with Frey v. Frey*, 471 A.2d 705 (Md. 1984) ("it is within the power of this court to change the common law").

[19] *See generally* K. Llewellyn, Jurisprudence: Realism in Theory and Practice (1962); W. Rumble, American Legal Realism (1968); G. Aichele, Legal Realism and Twentieth Century American Jurisprudence (1990).

articulated and advanced by the [legal functionalists]. Impossible only a decade ago, "mechanical jurisprudence" has made a remarkable comeback, and a new legal formalism may yet triumph as the principal mode of judicial interpretation.[20]

Thus, a family law student and practitioner must be aware of both the dichotomy between "traditional" and "modern" family law statutes and judicial opinions, and how these statutes and opinions will be interpreted by a formalist or a functionalist family court judge.

The role of the federal judiciary in family law matters is discussed later in this chapter.[21]

[C] The Role of the Family Law Practitioner

The ultimate client-representation role of the family law practitioner is to argue the client's case persuasively before the court. In the court setting, the attorney will employ various alternate remedies and legal strategies to advance the client's interests. Presentation of the client's position, as well as the analysis that went into preparation for court proceedings, will often find the attorney confronting, and deciding upon, an amalgam of theories best suited to the client's case. In each case, the family law practitioner must determine what "traditional" family law principles ought to be retained or abolished, what "modern" family law trends ought to be adopted or rejected, and what ultimate public policy goals are to be achieved through these various laws.

This process of analysis, repeated on behalf of various clients, can ultimately lead the practitioner to pronounced views of how the law should be structured and, once structured, how it should be implemented. In a very real sense, then, the family law practitioner is in the forefront of any movements for reform of the substance and procedure of American family law.[22]

These interrelated family law problems facing the legislator, the jurist, and the family law practitioner resist easy solution. For example, to remove some of the worst vestiges of long-standing fault-based divorce statutes, most jurisdictions have enacted "no-fault" divorce legislation and marital property distribution statutes. These no-fault divorce statutes currently allow divorces to be granted without regard to fault if the marriage has become insupportable because of discord or irreconcilable differences that destroy the legitimate ends of the marriage relationship and prevent any

---

[20] G. Aichele, Legal Realism and Twentieth Century American Jurisprudence x (1990). *See also* Schaier, *Formalism*, 97 Yale L.J. 509 (1988) (discussing how legal formalism still serves a useful function in limiting judicial discretion and judicial activism); and Weinrib, *Legal Formalism: On the Imminent Rationality of Law*, 97 Yale L.J. 949 (1988) (questioning whether the law is essentially rational as the formalists believe, or whether law is essentially political as the functionalists believe). *See generally* Symposium, *Formalism Revisited*, 66 U. Chi. L. Rev. 527–942 (1999).

[21] *See generally infra* §§ 1.04, 1.05.

[22] *See, e.g.,* Monroe Inker, *Changes in Family Law: A Practitioner's Perspective*, 33 Fam. L. Q. 515 (1999). *See also* Louise Raggio, *Women Lawyers in Family Law*, 33 Fam. L. Q. 501 (1999).

reasonable expectation of reconciliation. Modern property distribution statutes likewise focus on establishing a roughly equitable "no fault" distribution of marital property based on each party's contribution to the marriage. Although these no-fault procedures arguably are more efficient, and these marital property distribution guidelines have a ring of fairness to them, some commentators have argued that divorced wives and their children may actually be more economically disadvantaged under this "modern" family law legislation than under a more "traditional" approach.[23] Likewise, there is still continuing controversy involving what role (if any) marital fault should play in a "no fault" divorce regime.[24] Indeed, some commentators have concluded that the no-fault divorce revolution in America "has failed".[25]

---

[23] *See, e.g.*, L. Weitzman, The Divorce Revolution in America: The Unexpected Social and Economic Consequences for Women and Children in America (1985). Although the accuracy of Professor Weitzman's statistical studies have been questioned, other studies have corroborated this "feminization of poverty" resulting from divorce. *See* McLindon, *Separate but Unequal: The Economic Disaster of Divorce for Women and Children*, 21 Fam. L.Q. 351 (1987); K. Winner, Divorced from Justice: The Abuse of Women and Children by Divorce Lawyers and Judges (1996). Minor children also suffer from divorce:

> Two-thirds of all divorces involve minor children, and according to Columbia law professor Martha Fineman, author of *The Illusion of Equality*, the average annual child support payment is only around $3,000. "Equality is being applied with a vengeance against women", she says. Ultimately, the average household income for children of divorce drops thirty percent, while the poverty rate for children living with single mothers is five times as high as for those in intact families.

Elizabeth Gleick, *Hell Hath No Fury.* Time Magazine, Oct. 7, 1996 at 84. *See also* Scott, *Rational Decision-Making About Marriage and Divorce*, 76 Va. L. Rev. 9, 29 (1990) ("There is substantial evidence that the process of going through their parents' divorce and resulting changes in their lives are psychologically costly for most children"); Judith Wallerstein, The Unexpected Legacy of Divorce: A Twenty Five Year Landmark Study (2000); Judith Wallerstein and Sandra Blakeslee, Second Chances: Men, Women, and Children a Decade After Divorce (1989) (both discussing the long-term negative effects of divorce on children).

[24] *Compare* the ALI *Principles of the Law of Family Dissolution : Analysis and Recommendations* (2000) and Ellman, *The Place of Fault in Modern Divorce* Law, 28 Ariz. St. L.J. 773 (1996) (both arguing for the total abolition of all fault-based factors in marital dissolution or divorce) *with* Woodhouse, *Sex, Lies, and Dissipation: The Discourse of Fault in a No-Fault Era*, 82 Geo. L.J. 2525 (1994); and Swisher, *Reassessing Fault Factors in No-Fault Divorce*, 31 Fam. L. Q. 269(1997) (both arguing that fault factors on divorce still have a legitimate purpose to counteract egregious marital fault). See *also* Wardle, *No-Fault Divorce and the Divorce Conundrum,* 1991 B.Y.U. L. Rev. 79 (1991); and DiFonzo, Beneath the Fault Line: The Popular and Legal Culture of Divorce in Twentieth Century America (1997).

[25] *See, e.g.,* Council on Families in America, *Marriage in America: A Report to the Nation* (1995):

> The divorce revolution-the steady displacement of a marriage culture by a culture of divorce and unwed parenthood-has failed. It has created terrible hardships for children, incurred unsupportable social costs, and failed to deliver on its promise of greater adult happiness. The time has come to shift the focus of national attention from divorce to marriage and to rebuild a family culture based on enduring marital relationships.

But see also Divorce Reform at the Crossroads (Sugarman & Hill ed. 1990) (arguing that serious problems within a no-fault divorce regime need to be corrected, but without abandoning no-fault divorce *per se*).

Thus the quest continues to determine which family law principles are obsolete and which family law principles are relevant to the changing needs of our contemporary society. But while embarking on this legitimate quest, the legislator, jurist, scholar, and family law practitioner ought not be too hasty, in the absence of sound empirical evidence, to "throw the baby out with the bath water" in assessing and reassessing present and future family law needs and goals.

§ 1.02   What is a Family?

In order to understand the legal relationships existing in a family law context, we must first define what a "family" is. Narrowly defined, "family" can mean a group related by blood or by marriage, such as a traditional family involving a husband and wife or a parent and child.[26] Broadly defined, a "family" may include a nontraditional family, meaning one of a group living in the same household.[27]

A "family" can also be analyzed under an "organic" model or under an "individualistic" model. An organic family model emphasizes the good of the family unit at the expense of its individual members, and it is frequently associated with a hierarchically-ordered "traditional" family unit. An individualistic family model, on the other hand, views the family as composed of discrete and separate individuals, who are basically complete apart from the family unit.[28]

Regardless of how it has been defined, however, the remarkable resilience of the family unit has been primarily related to its role in the raising and socialization of children, and in the mutual social and economic support of its members.[29]

Arguably, a family is also morally justifiable under a "community" model, where the family finds its justification not only in its function of raising children and contributing to the economic well-being of its members, but also in the benevolence and the psychological satisfactions a family brings. Thus, family law finds its ultimate justification in reducing the uncertainties and inequities that are associated with conjugal relationships without rules, in establishing custody of children, in preventing harm to children, in providing economic rights and obligations for family members, and in

---

[26] See, e.g., Village of Belle Terre v. Boraas, 416 U.S. 1 (1974) (holding that a single family dwelling for zoning purposes, under a village ordinance, was limited to persons related by blood, adoption, or marriage).

[27] See, e.g., Braschi v. Stahl Associates, 543 N.E.2d 49 (N.Y. 1989) (for rent control purposes, a family included "two adult lifetime partners whose relationship is long-term and characterized by an emotional and financial commitment and interdependence"). See also Note, Legal Rights of Unmarried Heterosexual and Homosexual Couples and the Evolving Definitions of "Family", 29 J. Fam. L. 417 (1990–1991); and Chambers & Polikoff, Family Law and Gay and Lesbian Family Issues in the Twentieth Century, 33 Fam. L. Q. 523 (1999). And see notes 51 and 69 infra and accompanying text.

[28] See generally L. Houlgate, Family and State: The Philosophy of Family Law (1988).

[29] J. Eekelaar, Family Law and Social Policy 20–23 (2d ed. 1984).

establishing rules that will optimize human happiness within a family relationship. [30]

[A] The Traditional Family

Marriage, or the public bonding of a man and a woman to give legitimacy to their conjugal relationship, has existed since Biblical times. The nature of the marital union and the rights and obligations arising from this familial relationship have undergone a long, but surprisingly resilient, evolutionary process.

Unlike most other branches of the law, the evolution of family law has experienced the intertwining of secular and religious principles, and has carried forward elements of both. From the ancient Hebrew ceremonial requirement of a marriage contract or *Ketubah*, [31] to the Medieval Church's ecclesiastical canon law [32] which treated marriage as a holy sacrament rather than as a civil contract, [33] marriage and family law principles have come down through the centuries as an enduring and conservative body of law.

A more recent example of the Roman Catholic Church's attitude toward marriage is illustrated in a 1930 Encyclical by Pope Pius XI:

> . . .[L]et it be repeated as an immutable and inviolable fundamental doctrine that matrimony was not instituted or restored by man but by God; not by man were the laws to strengthen and confirm and elevate it but by God. . . . [T]his is the constant tradition of the Universal Church. . . .

> . . .Yet, although matrimony is of its very nature of divine institution, the human will, too, enters into it and performs a most noble part. For each individual marriage, inasmuch as it is a conjugal union of a particular man and woman, arises only from the free consent of each of the spouses; and this free act of the will, by each party hands over and accepts those rights proper to the state of marriage. . . . [A]mongst the blessings of marriage, the child holds the first place. [34]

Marriage requirements thus remained remarkably unchanged through the centuries leading up to the Protestant Reformation. However, when Henry VIII and the English Reformation transformed the Roman Catholic Church into an English Church, the regulation of the ecclesiastical courts in family law matters was transferred to the English civil courts, and to Parliament. [35]

---

[30] L. Houlgate, Family and State: The Philosophy of Family Law 49 (1988).

[31] *See generally* L. Epstein, The Jewish Marriage Contract (1927).

[32] *See* O'Connor, *The Origin and Development of Canon Law*, 4 Jurist 54 (1944).

[33] *See, e.g., Matthew* 19:6 "What therefore God hath joined together, let no man put asunder."

[34] Pope Pius XI, *Encyclical Letter on Christian Marriage* (1930).

[35] *See generally* S. Green & J. Long, Marriage and Family Law Agreements 8–12 (1984); T. Plucknett, A Concise History of the Common Law 628–629 (5th ed. 1956).

In 1753, Parliament enacted Lord Hardwicke's Act which required that all marriages must be celebrated in accordance with the rules of the Church of England: that there be a publication of the marriage announcement, that a marriage license be obtained, and that there be two witnesses to the ceremony. [36]

English law concerning marriage and family law generally was largely adopted by the American colonies, and was later readopted by most American states. However, there were no counterparts to the English ecclesiastical courts to resolve disputes regarding the validity of marriage and the application of other family law concepts. Also, after the seventeenth century, there was the increasing recognition of the concept of divorce in America. The ultimate result in America was the assignment of legal issues concerning marriage and divorce to the state legislatures and to the equity jurisdiction of state courts. [37]

By the turn of the twentieth century, European and American legal systems had come to share a common set of traditional assumptions regarding marriage and the traditional family unit as a basic social institution: (1) marriage was a primary support institution and a decisive determinant of the social, economic, and legal status of the spouses and children; (2) marriage in principle was to last until the death of a spouse, and would be terminated during the lives of the spouses only for serious cause; (3) the community aspect of marriage and the family was to be emphasized over the individualistic personalities of each member; (4) within the family, the standard pattern of authority and role allocation was that the husband-father was predominant in decision-making and was to provide for the material needs of the family, while the wife-mother cared for the household and the children; and (5) procreation and child rearing were assumed to be major purposes of marriage. [38]

However, as women began entering the salaried work force in increasing numbers, and their economic vulnerability lessened, it became easier for both men and women to dissolve their marriage. Thus, as a result of recent social and economic developments, "two paycheck" families have now become the norm, rather than the exception, and the modern American family is now being redefined by gender-neutral laws, new lifestyles, new realities, and new expectations— with a resulting decrease in the number of children per family, and a resulting increase in the divorce rate. [39]

---

[36] J. Davies & R. Lawry, Institutions and Methods of Law 72–74 (1982).

[37] See 1 H. Clark, Law of Domestic Relations in the United States 72 (2d ed. 1987); S. Green & J. Long, Marriage and Family Law Agreements 12–13 (1984); B. Whitehead, The Divorce Culture (1997).

[38] See M. Glendon, The New Family and the New Property 1–35 (1981).

[39] See, e.g., Orr v. Orr, 440 U.S. 268, 279–80 (1979) (holding that old notions that "generally it is the man's primary responsibility to provide a home and its essentials" can no longer justify family laws that discriminate on the basis of gender, and no longer "is the female destined solely for the home and the rearing of family, and only the male for the marketplace and the world of ideas"). See also Minow, *Toward a History of Family Law*, 1985 Wis. L. Rev. 819 (1985); Mather, *Evolution and Revolution in Family Law*, 25 St. Mary's L. J. 405 (1993). However, true gender equality in American family law and social policy is not yet a reality. See, e.g., Fineman, *Implementing Equality*, 1983 Wis. L. Rev. 789 (1983); Minow, *Toward a History of Family Law, supra.*

Concurrently, according to Professor Glendon, the notion is beginning to appear that now "the family exists for the benefit of the individual, rather than the individual existing for the benefit of the family."[40]

The traditional concept of marriage and the family has been further questioned by various feminist writers who claim that the traditional family structure was originally perpetuated to maintain male dominance,[41] and by various Marxists who argued that the laws supporting these marital institutions were exploitive instruments by which the ruling class maintained its economic and political power.[42]

But even those Marxist and former Marxist societies once committed to radical social change have been unable to alter the traditional family structure significantly. For example, the hope of early Soviet Communists was to weaken family ties and promote equality in sexual roles by allowing either spouse to escape marriage by a single *ex parte* application at a registrar's office, or alternately, it was not necessary to enter into a formal marriage, since Soviet *de facto* cohabitation was also recognized. However, subsequent Soviet legislation found it necessary to restore state supervision over entering marriage, and to put formidable obstacles in the way of divorce,[43] and a similar progression of events has been evident in other Marxist, and former Marxist, countries as well.[44]

Likewise, the United Nations, in its Universal Declaration of Human Rights, also recognizes that the family "is the natural and fundamental group unit of society and is entitled to protection by society and the State."[45]

Yet the present-day traditional American family, even with an increased pattern among husbands and wives of dual decision-making and dual economic support, has been battered by current social and economic developments. For example, according to the U.S. Census Bureau, where in 1970 about 12 percent of children lived with only one parent, by 1990 about one in four, more than sixteen million children, lived with only one parent. Currently one in four children is now born outside of marriage, compared to one in twenty in 1960. Moreover, children living with only one

---

[40] M. Glendon, The New Family and the New Property 33 (1981).

[41] *See, e.g.,* Rifkin, *Toward a Theory of Law and Patriarchy*, 3 Harv. Women's L.J. 83 (1980); Stark, *Divorce Law, Feminism, and Psychoanalysis: In Dreams Begin Responsibilities*, 38 U.C.L.A.L. Rev. 1483 (1991); Carbone & Brinig, *Rethinking Marriage: Feminist Ideology, Economic Chance, and Divorce Reform*, 65 Tulane L. Rev. 953 (1991); Bartlett, *Feminism and Family Law*, 33 Fam. L. Q. 475 (1999).

[42] *See generally* Marxism and Law (P. Beirne & R. Quinny, eds. 1982).

[43] *See generally* J. Eekelaar, Family Law and Social Policy 20–23 (2d ed. 1984) ("There are striking similarities between [the Soviet experience] and the position into which modern Western family law is moving."). *See also* Dyuzheva, *International Marriage and Divorce Regulation and Recognition in Russia*, 29 Fam. L. Q. 645, 646–648 (1995).

[44] *See, e.g.,* Palmer, *The People's Republic of China: New Marriage Regulations*, 26 J. Fam. L. 39 (1987–88); Soltesz, *Hungary: Toward a Strengthening of Marriage*, 26 J. Fam. L. 113 (1987–88); Zace, *Albania: Family Law Under the Dictatorship of the Proletariat*, 33 U. Louisville J. Fam. L. 259 (1995); Gec-Korosec & Rijavec, *Slovenia: Post-Independence Changes in Family Law*, 33 U. Louisville J. Fam. L. 485 (1995).

[45] U.N. General Assembly, *Universal Declaration of Human Rights* Article 16(3).

parent, usually the mother, are six times more likely to be poor as those living with both parents.[46]

These statistics suggest that the traditional American family may be at risk. The trend towards nontraditional family arrangements has already generated high-level reevaluation of the premises underlying the traditional family, resulting in strong endorsements of a rededicated commitment to the traditional structure. For example, a 1991 Report issued by the bipartisan National Commission on Children concluded that "Families formed by marriage, where two caring adults are committed to one another and to their children, provide the best environment for bringing children into the world and supporting their growth and development."[47] What most Americans do not realize, stresses this Report, is that various public regulatory policies actually discourage marriage. The most vivid examples of policies at odds with preservation of the traditional family unit are (1) the "marriage penalty" in income taxes that, in effect, rewards people for living together instead of marrying; and (2) the welfare system, which, with few exceptions, only applies to unwed mothers, not to two-parent families. The Report calls on leaders in the public and private sectors to "make conscious efforts to promote family values and to support the formation and functioning of healthy families"[48] Another Report by the centrist Progressive Policy Institute argues that any new state or federal governmental programs for children also will be largely ineffective without strengthening the two-parent family. This Report criticizes both liberals and conservatives alike for failing to address adequately the current strains on American family life:

> Traditional conservative support for families is largely rhetorical. Their disregard for the new economic realities engenders a policy of unresponsive neglect — expressed, for example, in President Bush's misguided veto of the Family Leave Act [later signed into law by President Clinton]. Conversely, traditional liberals' unwillingness to acknowledge that intact two-parent families are the most effective units for raising children has led them into a series of policy cul-de-sacs. . . . Given all the money in the world, government programs will not be able to instill self-esteem, good study habits, advanced language skills or sound moral values in children as effectively as can strong families.[49]

---

[46] 1990 U.S. Census Bureau Reports.

[47] National Commission on Children, Beyond Rhetoric (1990).

[48] Id. On August 5, 2000, President Clinton vetoed a Republican-sponsored tax cut for married couples, describing it as "the first installment of a fiscally reckless tax strategy" that would allegedly erase projected budget surpluses. George W. Bush, Republican presidential nominee, criticized Clinton's veto. The legislation, he said, "was the right thing to do. What kind of tax code is it that penalizes marriage? It's a bad tax code". Associated Press, *Clinton Vetoes Marriage-Tax Relief*, August 6, 2000.

[49] Kamarch & Gallston, Progressive Policy Institute Report, Putting Children First (1990). The centerpiece of this Report is a call to increase the personal income tax exemption for children from $2000 per dependent to at least $6,000, with a cut in Social Security taxes which hit especially hard at middle-income families. The Report also urges that divorce laws be reformed to take into account the cost of motherhood to women's earning capacity, and that child support programs be federalized.

These studies, among many others, suggest that the traditional family unit still continues to play an important role in our present-day society, and the traditional family unit therefore should continue to function as, and be legally protected as, a valuable social and institutional structure. Accordingly, a number of states have begun to enact bipartisan legislative measures to "reinstitutionalize" marriage and the traditional family structure, primarily by: (1) changing state laws that would make it harder for couples to divorce through so-called "covenant marriage" statutes; and (2) encouraging or mandating couples to participate in premarital education and counseling prior to marriage.[50] To date, the success or failure of these legislative initiatives have not yet been ascertained.

[B] The Nontraditional Family

An analysis of contemporary American family law, however, cannot be limited solely to the traditional family structure. As Professor Marjorie Schultz aptly observes:

> Marriage has undergone tremendous change in recent decades. . . . Only a small percentage of American families still have all the characteristics associated with the nuclear family ideal. In place of a single socially approved ideal we have compelling demands for autonomy and privacy, and multiple levels of intimacy: single parents, working wives, house husbands, homosexual couples, living together arrangements without marriage, serial marriage, stepchildren. The changes are legion, and their message is clear: the destruction of traditional marriage as the sole model for adult intimacy is irreversible.[51]

Accordingly, this treatise will also analyze various nontraditional family law concepts including: nonmarital cohabitation;[52] domestic partnership legislation;[53] same sex marriage;[54] de facto "marriage";[55] "marriage" by estoppel;[56] paternity and legitimacy issues;[57] single parent adoption;[58]

---

[50] See, e.g., Stanley & Markman, Can Government Rescue Marriages? (The University of Denver Center for Marital and Family Studies, 1997). See generally Chapter 2.03 infra.

[51] Schultz, Contractual Ordering of Marriage: A New Model for State Policy, 70 Cal. L. Rev. 204, 207 (1982); see also Minow, Redefining Families: Who's In and Who's Out, 62 U. Colo. L. Rev. 269 (1991); Treuthart, Adopting a More Realistic Definition of "Family", 26 Gonz. L. Rev. 91 (1990–91); Post, The Question of Family: Lesbians and Gay Men Reflecting a Redefined Society, 19 Fordham Urb. L.J. 747 (1992); Fineman, Intimacy Outside the Natural Family: the Limits of Privacy, 23 Conn. L. Rev. 955 (1991) (discussing single mother families); Note, Looking for a Family Resemblance: The Limits of the Functional Approach to the Legal Definition of Family, 104 Harv. L. Rev. 1640 (1991). The 21st Century Family, Newsweek, Winter/Spring 1990, at 15–46; Family Law Symposium, A More Perfect Union? Marriage and Marriage-Like Relationships in Family Law, 30 N.M. L. Rev. 1 (2000).

[52] See infra § 2.02.

[53] See infra 2.02[C]

[54] See infra § 2.08[B].

[55] See infra § 2.05[D].

[56] See infra § 2.05[E].

[57] See infra § 5.02.

[58] See infra § 6.01[H].

homosexual parent adoption;[59] and sexual preference issues related to child custody determinations on divorce.[60]

For example, unmarried heterosexual and homosexual cohabitants in many states may now contractually agree to define their property and support rights separate and apart from any marital rights and obligations;[61] and a growing number of American cities and states have recently passed various "domestic partnership" ordinances and statutes[62] that recognize an unmarried domestic partnership status for municipal and state purposes.[63] Although some other countries have recognized a legal status for unmarried domestic partners,[64] only a few American jurisdictions to date, including Hawaii and Vermont, have fully recognized a nonmarital domestic partnership status on a state-wide basis.[65]

As a result of this societal change in lifestyles found in the rapid growth of nontraditional families, commentators such as Professor Lenore Weitzman have questioned the continuing viability of traditional families per se:

> [O]ur society has undergone profound transformations in the past century, and the long-standing legal structure of marriage may now be anachronistic. The state's interest in preserving the traditional family may not be important enough to offset new societal and individual needs which require more flexibility and choice in family forms.[66]

Nevertheless, it seems unlikely that the majority of state legislatures will abolish these "anachronistic" marriage requirements in the foreseeable future.[67] And even if the parties were able to contract privately free from

---

[59] See infra § 6.01[I].

[60] See infra § 11.05[C].

[61] See generally infra §§ 2.02[A], 2.02[B], and 2.05[D].

[62] E.g., Seattle, Washington; Madison, Wisconsin; New York City; Takoma Park, Maryland; Berkeley, West Hollywood, Santa Cruz, and San Francisco, California among many other muncipalities. Hawaii and Vermont have enacted state-wide domestic partnership legislation. See Chapter 2.02[C] infra.

[63] See, e.g., Note, Domestic Partnership Recognition in the Workplace: Equitable Employee Benefits for Gay Couples (and Others), 51 Ohio St. L.J. 1067 (1990); Note, Legal Rights of Unmarried Heterosexual and Homosexual Couples and the Evolving Definitions of "Family", 29 J. Fam. L. 497 (1990–91); Note, A Legal and Social Analysis of Domestic Partnership Ordinances, 92 Colum. L. Rev. 1164 (1992); O"Brien, Domestic Partnership: Recognition and Responsibility, 32 San Diego L. Rev. 163 (1995). See generally Chapter 2.02[C] infra.

[64] See, e.g., Fawcett, Taking the Middle Path: Recent Swedish Legislation Grants Minimal Property Rights to Unmarried Cohabitants, 24 Fam. L.Q. 179 (1990); Bradley, Unmarried Cohabitants in Sweden: A Renewed Social Institution, 11 J. Legal Hist. 300 (1990). Norway, Denmark, and France have also passed similar legislation.

[65] See generally infra §§ 2.02[C].

[66] Weitzman, Legal Regulation of Marriage: Tradition and Change, A Proposal for Individual Contracts and Contracts in Lieu of Marriage, 62 Cal. L. Rev. 1169, 1170 (1974); see also L. Weitzman, The Marriage Contract — Spouses, Lovers, and the Law (1981).

[67] See 1 H. Clark, Law of Domestic Relations 75 (2d ed. 1987) ("Notwithstanding these developments, a majority of Americans still marry in the traditional way and continue to regard marriage as the most important relationship in their lives."). See also Chapters 2.03 to 2.05 infra.

all state regulation of marriage, what legal protection would be afforded to prevent the possible exploitation of one contracting party by the other contracting party?[68]

Finally, is present family law only a "patchwork attempt" stretching "old law to deal with modern realities" as Professor Weitzman argues, or can American family law adequately address, rectify, and subsume many of Professor Weitzman's legitimate concerns?

In conclusion, it is becoming clear that the preferable approach is for state legislatures and courts to recognize and protect the legal rights and obligations of *both* traditional *and* nontraditional families as they currently coexist in American society, by providing alternative legal rights and remedies for each social structure according to the public policy of each state, and based upon the present and future needs of its citizens.[69]

§ 1.03 State Regulation of Family Law

Historically in the United States, the marital relationship has always been controlled and regulated by the individual states. Marriage is therefore more than a mere contractual relationship between a man and a woman. It is a status, based on contract, and established by law. It

---

[68] *See* Glendon, *Marriage and the State: The Withering Away of Marriage*, 62 Va. L. Rev. 663, 666 (1976) ("If the state is in the process of divesting itself of its marriage regulation business, then, of course, it is not likely to set up shop as an enforcer to heretofore unenforceable contracts."). However, it seems unlikely that many states today will choose to legislate themselves out of the marriage regulation business. *See, e.g.,* Chapter 2.03 *infra.* Nevertheless, the parties may still privately order many of their marital rights and obligations through marital contracts and agreements, as long as they are not unconscionable to the parties or the state. *See generally* Chapter 4 *infra.*

[69] *See, e.g.,* Fawcett, *Taking the Middle Path: Recent Swedish Legislation Grants Minimal Property Rights to Unmarried Cohabitants*, 24 Fam. L.Q. 179 (1990). This article analyzes the unique approach of the Swedish government to cohabitation and marriage. The Swedish government, through different protective statutes, has attempted to accommodate cohabiting couples without disturbing the position of marriage as the preferred form of cohabitation in Sweden. The author makes the argument that these alternate Swedish laws can be beneficial to American courts and lawmakers in resolving disputes between unmarried cohabitants in the United States. *See also* Blumberg, *Cohabitation Without Marriage: A Different Perspective*, 28 U.C.L.A.L. Rev. 1125 (1981), where the author argues that a publicly created legal status is a much more suitable vehicle for handling support and property claims of unmarried and married cohabitants than is a contract theory.

See generally Comment, *Prohibiting Marital Status Discrimination: A Proposal for the Protection of Unmarried Couples*, 42 Hastings L.J. 1415 (1991); Minow, *Redefining Families*, 62 U. Colo. L. Rev. 269 (1991); Treuthart, *Adopting a More Realistic Definition of "Family,"* 26 Gonz. L. Rev. 91 (1990–91); Note, *Looking for a Family Resemblance: The Limits of the Functional Approach to the Legal Definition of Family*, 104 Harv. L. Rev. 1640 (1991); Note, *Family Law—Expansion of the Term "Family" to include Nontraditional Relationships*, 20 Mem. St. U. L. Rev. 135 (1989); Note, *Legal rights of Unmarried Heterosexual and Homosexual Couples and the Evolving Definitions of "Family"*, 29 J. Fam. L. 417 (1990–91); O'Brien, *Domestic Partnership: Recognition and Responsibility*, 32 San Diego L. Rev. 163 (1995); Family Law Symposium, *A More Perfect Union? Marriage and Marriage-Like Relationships in Family Law*, 30 N.M. L. Rev. 1 (2000).

To date, Hawaii and Vermont have enacted state-wide domestic partnership legislation, and a number of other states are considering similar legislative action. *See* Chapter 2.02[C] *infra.*

constitutes an institution involving the highest interests of society, and it is therefore subject to state regulation based upon the general welfare of its citizens.[70]

Since the prevailing view is that marriage is a status based on contract, even when a court is faced with a purely economic or contractual issue within the marital relationship, there is the continuing recognition of a state's power to regulate a marital relationship, and all the incidents of that marital relationship.[71]

The state may therefore prescribe the age at which parties may contract to marry, the procedure or form essential to constitute marriage, the duties and obligations created by marriage, the effect of marriage on the parties' property and support rights and obligations, and the acts which may constitute grounds for the dissolution of marriage.[72]

Various commentators, however, have questioned some of these traditional assumptions involving state regulation of marriage. They have questioned whether the legal *status* of marriage has now become obsolete, and whether the incidents of marriage should now move from *status* to *contract* implications, with a corresponding de-emphasis in the state's regulation of marriage.[73]

To date, however, the majority of states have *not* adopted this contractual approach, and most jurisdictions continue to regulate marriage and divorce as a status relationship consisting of three parties: husband, wife, and the state.[74]

---

[70] *See, e.g., Maynard v. Hill*, 125 U.S. 190, 205 (1888); *Griswold v. Connecticut*, 381 U.S. 479, 486 (1965); *Boddie v. Connecticut*, 401 U.S. 371, 376 (1971); *see also Simms v. Simms*, 175 U.S. 162, 167 (1899) (family law is normally subject to the laws of the states, not federal law); Restatement (Second) of Conflicts, § 283 (1969).

[71] *See, e.g., Boddie v. Connecticut*, 401 U.S. 371, 376 (1971) ("Without a prior judicial imprimatur, individuals may fully enter into and rescind commercial contracts, for example, but we are unaware of any jurisdiction where private citizens may covenant for or dissolve marriages without state approval."), quoted with approval in *Cramer v. Commonwealth*, 202 S.E.2d 911, 915 (Va. 1974).

[72] *Maynard v. Hill*, 125 U.S. 190, 205 (1888).

[73] *See, e.g.,* Schultz, *Contractual Ordering of Marriage: A New Model for State Policy*, 70 Cal. L. Rev. 204 (1982); Wright, *Marriage: From Status to Contract?* 13 Anglo-Am. L. Rev. 17 (1984); Comment, *Marriage as a Contract: Toward a Functional Redefinition of the Marital Status*, 9 Colum. J. L. & Soc. Probs. 607 (1973); Singer, *The Privatization of Family Law*, 1992 Wis. L. Rev. 1443 (1992).

See also Ponder v. Graham, 4 Fla. 23 (1851); *Ryan v. Ryan*, 277 So. 2d 266 (Fla. 1973), where two Florida courts viewed marriage more in terms of a contract than a status relationship, and questioned whether state legislation regulating marriage might arguably impair the parties' contractual rights if it detrimentally affected their vested property or support rights. *See generally* W. O'Donnell & D. Jones, The Law of Marriage and Marital Alternatives 1–4 (1982).

[74] *See, e.g., Sosna v. Iowa*, 419 U.S. 393, 404 (1975) (the inception and termination of marriage "has long been regarded as a virtually exclusive province of the State" within constitutional limitations). *See also* Sugarman, Divorce Reform at the Crossroads 138 (1990) ("Marriage, at least in this century, is typically said to be best understood as a status, rather than as a contractual relationship"). However, the parties may still privately order many of their marital rights and obligations through marital agreements, *see generally* Chapter 4, *infra*; or through nonmarital agreements, *see* Chapter 2.02[A] *infra*.

Although American state legislatures and state courts have traditionally regulated family law relationships such as marriage and divorce based upon a state's strong public policy involving the general welfare of its citizens, the state's right to regulate such marital relationships is not absolute, and cannot be arbitrary, unreasonable, or capricious. Because marriage has been recognized by the United States Supreme Court to be a fundamental right, a state cannot prohibit certain marital rights and obligations without demonstrating a compelling state interest for doing so.[75]

§ 1.04   Federal Regulation of Family Law

As discussed above, the individual states traditionally have regulated important family law relationships such as marriage and divorce.[76] Accordingly, on various occasions, the United States Supreme Court has reiterated the "domestic relations exception" rule— that federal courts do *not* have the jurisdiction to grant divorces, award spousal support, or determine child custody issues, even though there may in fact be diversity of citizenship, and even though the required amount in controversy for federal jurisdiction is met.[77]

One rationale for this "domestic relations exception" rule to federal diversity jurisdiction in family law matters has been that divorce was not a suit "of a civil nature at common law or equity" at the time the original Judiciary Act, which conferred jurisdiction on the federal courts, was passed.[78] Although this rationale has been criticized by some federal courts as "not convincing" and "dubious,"[79] the Supreme Court only recently has limited its scope in *Akenbrandt v. Richards*,[80] and Congress has not amended

---

[75] *See, e.g., Griswold v. Connecticut,* 381 U.S. 479 (1965) (striking down a state law prohibiting contraceptives to married couples and recognizing a fundamental right of privacy within the marital relationship free from state interference); *Loving v. Virginia,* 388 U.S. 1 (1967) (holding that under a constitutional right to marry, any state prohibition of interracial marriage violated the Equal Protection and Due Process Clauses of the Fourteenth Amendment of the Constitution); *Zablocki v. Redhail,* 434 U.S. 374 (1978) (holding that a state statute prohibiting a person from marrying if he had an unpaid child support obligation was unconstitutional since there were less onerous means of enforcing the child support obligation other than prohibiting the marriage per se); *see also infra* § 1.05.

[76] *See supra* § 1.03; *see also Simms v. Simms,* 175 U.S. 162, 167 (1899) ("The whole subject of the domestic relations of husband and wife, parent and child, belongs to the laws of the State, and not the laws of the United States.").

[77] *See, e.g., Barber v. Barber,* 62 U.S. 582 (1858); *Ex parte Burrus,* 136 U.S. 586 (1890); *Simms v. Simms,* 175 U.S. 162 (1899); *Ohio ex rel. Popovici v. Agler,* 280 U.S. 379 (1930). *See generally* C. Wright et al., Federal Practice and Procedure § 3609 (1975).

[78] *See, e.g.,* 28 U.S.C. § 1332(a), Revisor's Note. *See generally* 1 H. Clark, Law of Domestic Relations 705–713 (2d ed. 1987).

[79] *See, e.g., Spindel v. Spindel,* 283 F. Supp. 797(E.D.N.Y. 1968); *Lloyd v. Loeffler,* 694 F.2d 489 (7th Cir. 1982).

[80] 112 S. Ct. 2202 (1992), discussed *infra* § 8.02 at notes 34–38 and accompanying text. *But see Spindel v. Spindel,* 283 F. Supp. 797 (E.D.N.Y. 1968), where a federal court held that it *did* have jurisdiction to hear a case to invalidate a husband's Mexican divorce and award the wife damages for an alleged fraudulent inducement to marry action. *See also Vann v. Vann,* 294 F. Supp. 193 (E.D. Tenn. 1968) (federal jurisdiction found to determine the validity of a divorce decree attacked for fraud).

the statute.[81]

Nevertheless, important inroads have been made toward overcoming this "domestic relations exception" obstacle, and significant monetary recoveries in federal court have been recognized for family-related *tortious* conduct, including child enticement actions,[82] and the unlawful taking of a child.[83]

For example, in *Cole v. Cole*,[84] it was held that federal diversity cases having intrafamily aspects could not be dismissed merely upon that basis alone. In *Cole*, the husband brought a claim against his ex-wife for malicious prosecution, abuse of process, arson, conspiracy, and conversion. Noting that such claims could have arisen between strangers with no marital relationship whatever, and noting that this case did not require an adjustment of family status, the court found that the federal domestic relations exception was inapplicable in this particular case.[85]

Likewise, a federal court may take diversity jurisdiction whenever a cause of action sounds in tort or contract, even though there are important interrelated family law issues that must be resolved by the court in order to properly adjudicate the case. For example, in *Hewitt v. Firestone Tire & Rubber Co.*,[86] a federal district court took diversity jurisdiction in a wrongful death action dealing with the underlying issue of which of two women was the legal wife, qualifying her as beneficiary under a state wrongful death statute.[87] And in *Metropolitan Life Ins. Co. v. Holding*,[88] a federal court had to determine the validity of a marriage in order to ascertain the legal beneficiary of a life insurance policy.[89]

Federal courts, of course, also have jurisdiction to adjudicate the constitutionality of state statutes regulating the marital relationship.[90] Federal regulation of family law may also be found in federal statutory enactments, particularly in the field of child support[91] and child custody[92] enforcement remedies.[93]

---

[81] 28 U.S.C. § 1332(a).

[82] *See, e.g.*, W. Keeton, Prosser & Keeton on the Law of Torts 925–926 (5th ed. 1984).

[83] *See, e.g.*, Restatement (Second) of Torts, § 700 (1979).

[84] 633 F.2d 1083 (4th Cir. 1980).

[85] *Id.*; *see also Wasserman v. Wasserman*, 671 F.2d 832 (4th Cir. 1982) (federal diversity action for child enticement, intentional infliction of mental distress, and civil conspiracy in a child custody dispute was upheld).

[86] 490 F. Supp. 1358 (E.D. Va. 1980).

[87] *Id.*

[88] 293 F. Supp. 854 (E.D. Va. 1968).

[89] *Id.*; *see also Renshaw v. Heckler*, 787 F.2d 50 (2d Cir. 1986) (also determining the validity of an underlying common law marriage).

[90] *See generally infra* § 1.05.

[91] *See, e.g.*, The federal Child Support Enforcement Amendments of 1984, 42 U.S.C. §§ 651–667. *See generally infra* §§ 3.12[C], 9.06[F].

[92] *See, e.g.*, The Federal Parental Kidnapping Prevention Act of 1980, 28 U.S.C. § 1738A. *See generally infra* § 11.02[C].

[93] *See generally* K. Redden, Federal Regulation of Family Law (1982).

§ 1.05   Constitutional Parameters to Family Law Regulation

Although family law relationships involving marriage and divorce traditionally have been regulated by the individual states,[94] the state's right to regulate such marital relations is not absolute, and is subject to constitutional limitations if the state regulation is arbitrary, unreasonable, or capricious.[95]

In 1923, for example, the Supreme Court in *Meyer v. Nebraska*[96] recognized that the right to marry was a liberty guaranteed by the Due Process Clause of the Fourteenth Amendment of the United States Constitution.[97] The *Meyer* case, citing earlier Supreme Court precedent, justified this constitutional protection of the marital relationship based upon the importance of marriage to society in general. However, more recent Supreme Court cases have emphasized the importance of the marital relationship to the individual as well,[98] and many important Supreme Court cases beginning in the 1960s have evidenced a growing concern for the constitutional protection of the marital relationship from unreasonable state intrusion.

For example, in *Griswold v. Connecticut*,[99] the Supreme Court held that marriage is a "relationship lying within the zone of privacy created by several fundamental constitutional guarantees,"[100] and therefore a Connecticut state law forbidding the use of contraceptives to married couples was found to violate the constitutional right to marital privacy.[101]

Although this constitutional right to privacy, as enunciated in *Griswold*, is not mentioned in the Constitution, seven justices nevertheless found that there was constitutional protection for the right to privacy, although they could not agree as to where they found it. Justice Douglas, writing for the Court, found the right to privacy in a "penumbra" of other fundamental and enumerated rights. Justice Goldberg found protection for the right to privacy in the inherent fabric of the Constitution, specifically in the Ninth Amendment concept of reserved rights. And Justice Harlan utilized a *Meyer*-type constitutional analysis by finding that the Connecticut statute violated the Due Process Clause of the Fourteenth Amendment by violating

---

[94] *See supra* §§ 1.01, 1.03.

[95] *See generally* Strickman, *Marriage, Divorce and the Constitution*, 15 Fam. L.Q. 259 (1982); Note, *The Constitution and the Family*, 93 Harv. L. Rev. 1156 (1980).

[96] 262 U.S. 390 (1923).

[97] *Id.* at 399–400 (1923); *see also Skinner v. Oklahoma*, 316 U.S. 535 (1941) (marriage and procreation "involves one of the basic civil rights of man" which is "fundamental to the very existence and survival of the race").

[98] *See, e.g.*, M. Glendon, The New Family and the New Property 32 (1981) (the emphasis of family law is now that the family exists for the benefit of the individual, rather than that the individual exists for the benefit of the family); *see also* Strickman, *Marriage, Divorce and the Constitution* 15 Fam. L.Q. 259 (1982).

[99] 381 U.S. 479 (1965).

[100] *Id.* at 485 (1965).

[101] *Id.* at 486 (1965).

"basic values implicit in the concept of ordered liberty."[102] Two justices, however, Black and Stewart, applied a more formalistic judicial analysis[103] and declined to rule that the Connecticut statute was unconstitutional because they could find no express provision of the Constitution that it violated, although both found the statute to be personally repugnant.[104]

This important constitutional debate over the right to privacy in *Griswold* might be moot today if it were only limited to the use of contraceptives.[105] However, the constitutional debate found in *Griswold* remains crucially important today since the landmark abortion case of *Roe v. Wade*[106] also rests upon a constitutional right to privacy argument.[107]

Constitutional protection of the marital relationship against arbitrary and unreasonable state infringement was again reaffirmed by the Supreme Court in *Loving v. Virginia*,[108] where the Court held that Virginia's miscegenation laws violated the Equal Protection and Due Process Clauses of the Fourteenth Amendment. And in *Zablocki v. Redhail*[109] the Court held that a Wisconsin state statute prohibiting a person from marrying if he had an unpaid child support obligation was unconstitutional since there were less onerous means of enforcing the child support obligation other than prohibiting the marriage per se.

Thus, in both *Loving* and *Zablocki* the Supreme Court reiterated that the right to marry is a fundamental constitutional right subject to strict judicial scrutiny, and the state would have the burden of demonstrating a compelling state interest in order to prohibit such marriages.

However, when a state is merely regulating, rather than prohibiting, certain marital rights and obligations, then the state ordinarily must only show a rational reason, rather than a compelling state interest, for its actions. For example, in *Moe v. Dinkins*,[110] a New York federal district court upheld a New York marriage statute which required that applicants under the age of 18 obtain parental consent. The court reasoned that the statute's rational purpose was to protect minors from making immature decisions, and thereby prevent unstable marriages. The court also held that the New York statute only delayed the minors' decision to marry, and did not prohibit that fundamental right per se.[111]

---

[102] 381 U.S. 479 (1965).

[103] *See supra* § 1.01[B].

[104] 381 U.S. 479 (1965).

[105] *See also Eisenstadt v. Baird*, 405 U.S. 438 (1972) (striking down a Massachusetts statute that prohibited supplying contraceptives to unmarried persons). *See generally infra* § 5.04.

[106] 410 U.S. 113 (1973).

[107] *See generally infra* § 5.05.

[108] 388 U.S. 1 (1967).

[109] 434 U.S. 374 (1978).

[110] 533 F. Supp. 623 (S.D.N.Y. 1981) *affirmed* 669 F.2d 67 (2d Cir. 1981), *cert. denied* 459 U.S. 827 (1982).

[111] *Id.*

Chapter 2

MARRIAGE AND MARRIAGE ALTERNATIVES

§ 2.01 Introduction

Marriage is more than a personal relationship between a man and a woman. It is a legal status, founded on contract, and established by law.[1] It constitutes a social institution involving the highest interests of society, and therefore is subject to state regulation based upon the general welfare of the people of the state.[2]

The validity or invalidity of a marriage has far-reaching social, legal, and economic implications in such diverse areas as wrongful death actions, intestate succession and probate law, real property law, contract law, criminal law, constitutional law, social security benefits, worker's compensation awards, insurance coverage, pension plans, loss of consortium actions, state and federal tax law and, of course, marital property and support rights.[3]

Despite the growing diversity of family relationships and alternative family forms in contemporary American society, marriage still remains an important legal and social institution. A significant majority of Americans will marry at some point in their lives, and most Americans still regard marriage as an important part of their life plan.[4] Moreover, the law continues to encourage, support, and regulate the institution of marriage in contemporary American society as an important criterion for allocating a wide range of social and economic benefits. Indeed, contemporary debates over "family values" often center on the question of who may marry, and what legal and economic consequences should follow from the decision to marry.[5] Thus, decisions about who may marry, what relationships will be recognized as valid marriages, and what economic, social, political, and legal rights should devolve upon the parties through marriage, continue

---

[1] *See infra* § 2.03.

[2] *See, e.g., Maynard v. Hill*, 125 U.S. 190, 205 (1888); *Griswold v. Connecticut*, 381 U.S. 479, 486 (1965); *Boddie v. Connecticut*, 401 U.S. 371, 376 (1971); *see also supra* §§ 1.01[A], 1.03.

[3] *See generally infra* Chapters 3, 6, 8, 9.

[4] *See* Homer Clark, The Law of Domestic Relations in the United States 26 (2d ed. 1988) ("Notwithstanding [consensual alternatives to marriage], a majority of Americans still marry in the traditional way and continue to regard marriage as the most important relationship in their lives").

[5] *See, e.g.,* Weyrauch, *Metamorphoses in Marriage*, 13 Fam. L. Q. 415 (1980) (discussing the changing role of formal and informal marriages in the United States); Whitehead, The Divorce Culture (1997); and *Symposium, Law and the New American Family*, 73 Ind. L. J. 393 (1998). Historical evidence also suggests that access to marriage was at the core of the values that motivated those who fought for, and framed, the Fourteenth Amendment of the U.S. Constitution. *See* Davis, Neglected Stories: Family Values and the Constitution (1997).

to be of significant importance to legislators, jurists, scholars, family law practitioners, and the vast majority of Americans today.

Yet although marriage remains a central legal and social institution in America, an increasing number of Americans are establishing family relations outside of marriage. According to the U.S. Census Bureau, there were more than four million unmarried couple households in the United States in 1997, more than twice as many as in 1980, and almost eight times as many as in 1970. Because the Census Bureau defines an unmarried couple household as two adults of the opposite sex who share a housekeeping unit, this figure does not include same-sex partners, and the Census Bureau estimates that same-sex domestic partners account for an additional 1.8 million American households.[6]

The reasons for the rise in nonmarital cohabitation are as varied as the couples themselves. For same-sex couples, formal marriage is not currently a legal option. Surveys suggest, however, that a large number of American adults who identify themselves as lesbian or gay live with another person of the same sex and regard that person as their life partner.[7] For younger heterosexual couples, cohabitation is often a prelude to marriage, which tends to occur later today than in the past, both for women and men.[8] And for older heterosexual Americans, many of whom have been previously divorced and are cautious about recommitting to marriage again, long-term nonmarital cohabitation is often viewed as a viable alternative to marriage for a number of practical and philosophical reasons.[9]

State courts and legislatures therefore are increasingly asked to determine the legal rights and obligations of nonmarital cohabitants or domestic partners in the same manner as they would determine the legal rights and obligations of married spouses. Accordingly, this Chapter will analyze and discuss the essential characteristics of marriage and marriage-like relationships including: nonmarital cohabitation and domestic partnerships as alternatives to marriage; formal statutory marriages; informal marriages; the last-in-time marriage presumption; proof of marriage; the capacity and intent to marry; marital conflicts of law; and annulment of marriage.

§ 2.02 Consensual Alternatives to Marriage

Nonmarital cohabitation, as an American social development, has experienced an eight-fold increase from 1970–1990,[10] and there are strong

---

[6] Bureau of the Census, U. S. Dept. of Commerce, *Current Population Reports, Series P20-506, Marital Status and Living Arrangements* (March, 1997).

[7] *See, e.g.,* Chambers, *What If? The Legal Consequences of Marriage and the Legal Needs of Lesbian and Gay Male Couples,* 95 Mich. L. Rev. 447, 449 (1996).

[8] In 1997, the median age of first marriage for men was 26.8 years, up from 23.2 years in 1970. For women, the median age for first marriage was 25.0 years, compared to 20.8 years in 1970. Bureau of the Census, U.S. Dept. of Commerce, *Current Population Reports, Series P20–506, Marital Status and Living Arrangements* (March, 1997) (Table 1).

[9] *See, e.g.,* Parks, *Middle Age Couples: Committed, Unmarried,* Dallas Morning News, Sept. 11, 1994 at F-1; Steinhauer, *More Older Couples Move in Together,* Dallas Morning News, July 15, 1995 at C-11.

[10] *See, e.g.,* Bureau of the Census, U.S. Department of Commerce, Current Population Reports Series P-20, No. 445 "Marital Status and Living Arrangements" (1990).

indications that this trend may continue in the future.[11] Unlike marriage, where marital property and support rights are legally recognized and protected through state legislative and judicial authority,[12] a nonmarital relationship or domestic partnership between unmarried heterosexual or homosexual couples, in the vast majority of states, traditionally lacked any legal recognition based upon the legal status of the unmarried cohabitants, although this traditional rule has begun to moderate somewhat.[13] In the absence of state recognition of nonmarital cohabitation as a legal status, however, the parties might still have certain contractual rights and other equitable remedies based upon their nonmarital cohabitation.[14]

American legal treatment of nonmarital cohabitation has changed significantly over the past 25 years. Traditionally, the law viewed unmarried cohabitation relationships with disfavor, characterizing them as meretricious, and often criminal as well. Couples engaged in such relationships could not look to the courts to define their legal rights and obligations, nor to resolve their disputes in the event their relationship failed. Nor were unmarried cohabitants entitled to any of the statutory or common law benefits traditionally accorded to married couples. More recently, however, this traditional view has been replaced by an increased willingness on the part of the courts to resolve financial and property disputes between unmarried cohabitants. These judicial approaches to such disputes still vary considerably, however, and disagreement exists as to the extent to which nonmarital cohabitation should be analogized to marriage for the purpose of determining the unmarried partners' legal rights and obligations toward one another. Courts, in particular, disagree about whether the relationship between unmarried cohabitants should be governed primarily by principles of contract law, or whether the law should treat nonmarital cohabitation as a status relationship.[15]

In disputes between unmarried cohabitants and third parties, however, courts have been reluctant to extend to cohabitants many of the legal and economic benefits traditionally associated with marriage, although there have been some judicial exceptions to this general rule. Many courts have suggested that decisions regarding the extension of benefits to unmarried cohabitants are more properly made in the legislative area, rather than by the courts; and recently some state and local legislative bodies have responded to this need by passing "domestic partnership" statutes and ordinances designed to grant to unmarried cohabitants some, but not all, of the legal rights and benefits traditionally available to married couples. A number of public and private employers also have extended some employment-related benefits to unmarried couples, both heterosexual and

---

[11] *See, e.g.,* Bureau of the Census, U.S. Department of Commerce, Current Population Reports Series P-20 No. 506 "Marital Status and Living Arrangements" (1997).

[12] *See generally infra* Chapters 4, 8, 9.

[13] *See generally infra* § 2.02[C].

[14] *See generally infra* § 2.02[A].

[15] *See generally* Swisher, Miller & Singer, Family Law: Cases, Materials and Problems 189–233, 190 (2d ed. 1998)

homosexual.[16] These measures, in turn, have engendered debate about the appropriate definition of family, and about the role of the law in regulating and channeling intimate behavior.

[A] Nonmarital Cohabitation: Contract Implications

Since the widely publicized case of *Marvin v. Marvin*,[17] numerous state courts increasingly have been asked to evaluate and enforce nonmarital contracts, oral or written, express or implied, which purportedly cover the contractual rights and obligations of unmarried cohabiting heterosexual or homosexual couples.

The *Marvin* cases involved actor Lee Marvin and singer Michelle Triola Marvin, who cohabited together for approximately six years. Although Michelle legally changed her last name to Marvin, the parties were never married. After the couple's cohabiting relationship broke up, Michelle sued Lee in a contract action, alleging that Lee contractually had promised to support her in consideration of her companionship services during their cohabiting relationship, and Michelle argued that even if this alleged agreement was not an express contract, then it should be actionable as an implied contract.

The California Supreme Court in *Marvin I*[18] held that an express or implied contractual cause of action based upon a cohabiting nonmarital relationship was actionable in California, and in the absence of a contractual action the courts could also employ other equitable remedies:

> We conclude: (1) The Provisions of the Family Law Act do *not* govern the distribution of property acquired during a nonmarital relationship; such a relationship remains subject solely to [contractual] judicial decision. (2) The courts should enforce express contracts between nonmarital partners except to the extent that the contract is explicitly founded on the consideration of meretricious sexual services. (3) In the absence of an express contract, the courts should inquire into the conduct of the parties to determine whether that conduct demonstrates an implied contract, agreement of partnership or joint venture, or some other tacit understanding between the parties. The courts may also employ the doctrine of quantum meruit, or equitable remedies such as constructive or resulting trusts, when warranted by the facts of the case.[19]

However, a subsequent trial court in *Marvin II*,[20] and an appellate court in *Marvin III*,[21] both held that Michelle had not met her factual burden

---

[16] *Id.* at 191. *See generally* Cox, *Alternative Families: Obtaining Traditional Family Benefits Through Litigation, Legislation, and Collective Bargaining*, 15 Wis. Women's L.J. 93 (2000).

[17] *Marvin v. Marvin [Marvin I]*, 557 P.2d 106 (Cal. 1976); *Marvin v. Marvin [Marvin II]*, Case C23303, 5 Fam. L. Rep. (1979); *Marvin v. Marvin [Marvin III]*, 176 Cal. Rptr. 555 (Cal. Ct. App. 1981).

[18] *Marvin v. Marvin*, 557 P.2d 106 (Cal. 1976).

[19] *Id.*

[20] *Marvin v. Marvin*, Case C23303, 5 Fam. L. Rep. 3079 (1979).

[21] *Marvin v. Marvin*, 176 Cal. Rptr. 555 (Cal. Ct. App. 1981).

of proof in demonstrating that any implied or express contract existed in her particular case, nor was the trial court justified in giving Michelle any type of equitable rehabilitative award under California law.[22]

Although the general public has largely misinterpreted the *Marvin* decision as creating a type of quasi-marriage alternative,[23] in reality the *Marvin* decision was a basic contract case, and was decided utilizing a basic contractual analysis.[24] The *Marvin* decision was also important in illustrating the "severance" doctrine, which separates any meretricious sexual activities that generally would constitute illegal consideration in nonmarital cohabitation agreements, from legally recognized contractual consideration such as companionship and homemaking services.[25]

There were some dire predictions that *Marvin* would "open the door" to a flood of nonmarital contractual claims, that it would change the way society looks at marriage, and that it would put marital rights and obligations in jeopardy. In general, however, post-*Marvin* judicial decisions have taken a more conservative approach to nonmarital cohabitation agreements; and most courts have dealt only with contractual issues, and have basically ignored the larger social policy issues of the nonmarital relationship per se.

For example, in the case of *Morone v. Morone*,[26] the New York Court of Appeals rejected the concept of an implied nonmarital contract as recognized in *Marvin*, and held that it would only recognize express nonmarital contracts not based upon sexual conduct. The *Morone* court justified its decision based upon the fact that there would be difficulties of proof and risk of fraud in recognizing implied nonmarital contracts. The problem for the *Morone* court, therefore, was not one of failure to recognize a nonmarital relationship, but the difficulty in quantifying the remedy. A number of other state courts have followed this New York limitation to *Marvin*.[27]

---

[22] Michelle Marvin's attorney had, for some reason, dismissed her quantum meruit cause of action in *Marvin II*, thereby removing that equitable remedy from the court's consideration.

[23] Indicative of this common misunderstanding is the widespread use of the term "palimony" by the press and lay public when discussing *Marvin*-type cases.

[24] *See generally* Marital and Nonmarital Contracts: Preventative Law for the Family (J. Krauskopf ed., ABA 1979). *See also* Prince, *Public Policy Limitations on Cohabitation Agreements: Unruly Horse or Circus Pony?*, 70 Minn. L. Rev. 163 (1986); Comment, *Property Rights Upon Termination of Unmarried Cohabitation: Marvin v. Marvin*, 90 Harv. L. Rev. 1708 (1977).

A number of cases predating *Marvin* dealt with a similar nonmarital contractual analysis. *See, e.g., Tyranski v. Piggins*, 205 N.W.2d 595 (Mich. Ct. App. 1973); *Walker v. Walker*, 47 N.W.2d 633 (Mich. 1951). *But see* Comment, *Applying Marvin v. Marvin to Same-Sex Couples: A Proposal for a Sex-Preference Neutral Cohabitation Contract Statute*, 25 U.C. Davis L. Rev. 1029 (1992).

[25] Some other cases recognizing this "severance" doctrine as applied to nonmarital cohabitation contracts include: *Kozlowski v. Kozlowski*, 395 A.2d 913 (N.J. Super. Ct.), *aff'd*, 403 A.2d 902 (N.J. 1979); *Hierholzer v. Sardy*, 340 N.W.2d 91 (Mich. Ct. App. 1983); *Cook v. Cook*, 691 P.2d 664 (Ariz. 1984).

[26] 413 N.E.2d 1154 (N.Y. 1980).

[27] *See, e.g., Carnes v. Sheldon*, 311 N.W.2d 747 (Mich. Ct. App. 1981); *Merrill v. Davis*, 673 P.2d 1285 (N.M. 1983); *In re Estate of Alexander*, 445 So. 2d 836 (Miss. 1984). Minnesota, by state statute, requires an express written nonmarital agreement before it will be enforced. Minn. Stat. Ann. §§ 513.075, 513.076.

Still other states have totally rejected the *Marvin* rationale, either because nonmarital contracts purportedly violate state public policy, or because the "severance" doctrine regarding meretricious sexual relationships is not recognized in those jurisdictions. For example in *Hewitt v. Hewitt*[28] the Illinois Supreme Court stated that nonmarital cohabitation cases cannot be characterized solely in terms of contract law, since major public policy questions are involved in determining whether, under what circumstances, and to what extent it is desirable to accord some type of legal status to claims arising from nonmarital relationships.

The *Hewitt* court conceded that traditional public policy prohibitions on contracts based in whole or in part on illicit sexual intercourse[29] would not necessarily prevent the parties from forming valid contracts regarding independent matters for which sexual relations do *not* form any part of the consideration.[30] Nevertheless, the court held that "we believe that these questions are appropriately within the province of the legislature, and that, if there is to be a change in the law of this State on this matter, it is for the legislature and not the courts to bring about that change."[31] A number of other courts have followed the *Hewitt* rationale, holding that nonmarital contracts are unenforceable.[32]

A better reasoned approach, however, is found in *Watts v. Watts*,[33] where the Wisconsin Supreme Court expressly rejected the *Hewitt* rationale, holding that since courts regularly settle contract and property disputes between unmarried persons, some of whom have cohabited, they should also do the same for people who specifically indicate the existence of such a nonmarital cohabitation relationship.[34]

[B] Nonmarital Cohabitation: Property Issues

Although the *Marvin* decisions[35] rested primarily, though not exclusively, on principles derived from contract law, in other more recent unmarried cohabitation cases, litigants also have invoked property and

---

[28] 394 N.E.2d 1204 (Ill. 1979).

[29] *See, e.g., Wallace v. Rappleye*, 103 Ill. 229, 249 (1882) ("An agreement in consideration of future illicit cohabitation between the plaintiffs is void."); Restatement of Contracts § 589 (1932) ("a bargain in whole or in part for or in consideration of illicit sexual intercourse or a promise thereof is illegal").

[30] *See, e.g.,* Restatement of Contracts §§ 589, 597 (1932); 6A Corbin on Contracts § 1476 (1962).

[31] *Hewitt v. Hewitt*, 394 N.E.2d 1204 (Ill. 1979) (citing with approval *Mogged v. Mogged*, 302 N.E.2d 293, 295 (Ill. 1973)).

[32] *See, e.g., Rehak v. Mathis*, 238 S.E.2d 81 (Ga. 1977); *Roach v. Buttons*, 6 Fam. L. Rep. 2355 (Tenn. 1980); *Thomas v. LaRosa*, 400 S.E.2d 809 (1990).

[33] 405 N.W.2d 303 (Wis. 1987).

[34] *Id.*, holding, therefore, that a party's allegations were sufficient to state a cause of action for a breach of express or implied contract, unjust enrichment, and statutory or common law partition. *See generally* Burch, *Cohabitation in the Common Law Countries a Decade After Marvin: Settled In or Moving Ahead?* 22 U.C. Davis L. Rev. 717 (1989).

[35] *See* Chapter 2.02[A] *supra*.

partnership theories. Another important issue regarding nonmarital cohabitation therefore involves property rights acquired during a nonmarital cohabitation period, after the parties later marry one another, and then sue for divorce. As discussed in a subsequent chapter, on divorce most jurisdictions allow a family court judge to divide and distribute certain property acquired during the marriage which is classified as either "marital property" or "community property."[36] However, a family court judge in most states cannot divide or distribute property acquired prior to the marriage, which is still classified as "separate property" in most states.[37] Nevertheless, some courts have held that a "legal merger" may have taken place upon the marriage of nonmarital cohabitants, thus allowing a family court judge to consider both premarital *and* postmarital property in an equitable distribution of property award on divorce.[38]

Conversely, if unmarried cohabitants do not subsequently marry each other, the courts are split on whether or not state marriage-related property statutes ought to apply by analogy in adjudicating property claims between unmarried cohabitants as well. Some courts have held in the affirmative.[39] A majority of courts to date, however, have held in the negative.[40] And in contexts other than property division, the courts generally have refused to allow unmarried cohabitants to invoke statutory remedies generally available to divorcing couples.[41] Consequently, several commentators have suggested the creation of a legal status known as nonmarital cohabitation. When such a status is established, by the state courts or legislatures, the courts could then proceed to apportion the assets of the members of that status according to traditional principles of community property or equitable distribution.[42]

[C] Nonmarital Cohabitation: Status Implications

Although nonmarital cohabiting couples traditionally had few, if any, legal rights and obligations other than private contractual remedies,[43] a

---

[36] *See generally* §§ 10.02, 10.03 *infra.*.

[37] *See generally* § 10.03 *infra. See also In re. Marriage of Lindsey*, 676 P.2d 328 (Wash. 1984).

[38] *See, e.g., Chestnut v. Chestnut*, 499 N.E.2d 783 (Ind. App. 1986); *Easton v.* Johnson, 681 P.2d 606 (Kan. 1984). *But see contra Wilen v. Wilen*, 486 A.2d 775 (Md. Ct. App. 1985); *Crouch v. Crouch*, 410 N.E.2d 580 (Ill. Ct. App. 1980).

[39] *See. e.g., Connell v. Francisco*, 898 P.2d 831 (Wash. 1995); *W. State Constr. Co. v. Michoff*, 840 P.2d 1220 (Nev. 1992); *Shuraleff v. Donnelly*, 817 P.2d 764 (Or. Ct. App. 1991).

[40] *See, e.g., Davis v. Davis*, 643 So. 2d 931 (Miss. 1994).

[41] *See, e.g., Friedman v. Friedman*, 24 Cal. Rptr. 2d 892, 898 (Cal. Ct. App. 1993) (holding that a trial court lacks authority to award temporary support to a disabled cohabitant pending trial of her express and implied contract claims, since such temporary relief was available only in the context of marriage and divorce); *Crowe v. DeGioia*, 495 A.2d 889 (N.J. Super. Ct. App. Div. 1985) *aff'd* 505 A.2d 591 (N.J. 1986) (ruling that a state statute permitting an award of attorneys' fees on divorce was inapplicable to an action to distribute property following a nonmarital cohabitation relationship).

[42] *See, e.g.,* Blumberg, *Cohabitation Without Marriage: A Different Perspective*, 28 UCLA L. Rev. 1125 (1981); Bruch, *Property Rights of De Facto Spouses Including Thoughts on the Value of Homemakers' Services*, 10 Fam. L. Q. 101 (1976).

[43] *See generally supra* § 2.02[A].

growing number of cities [44] have enacted domestic partnership ordinances. These ordinances extend various municipal benefits to an individual's spousal equivalent without regard to sex, as though the two persons were legally married, and as an effective means for conferring certain legally recognized *status* benefits on unmarried heterosexual and homosexual domestic partners. [45] As one commentator has explained:

> In its simplicity, domestic partnership is one step more than cohabitation, but one step less than marriage. Its essential ingredient is a business or government recognition of benefits conferred on a nonmarital adult couple of the same or opposite sex because of conformity with a procedure established by the business or government. [46]

Likewise, various corporations recently have made employment benefits applicable not only to married spouses of their employees, but also to unmarried cohabiting domestic partners as well. [47] Although these modest initiatives have not yet enjoyed substantial support from the majority of other American cities or states, they nevertheless constitute a first major step in the recognition of nonmarital cohabitation as a legally protected status. [48]

Some critics, however, have opposed any legal recognition of nonmarital cohabitation on the ground that de jure legal recognition of nonmarital cohabitation would have a destabilizing effect on the traditional family unit, which is already at risk. [49] But whatever these theoretical rationales may

---

[44] *See, e.g.*, Berkeley, San Francisco, Los Angeles, Santa Cruz, and West Hollywood, California; New York City; Chicago: Boston; Seattle; Madison, Wisconsin; and Takoma Park, Maryland; among numerous other municipalities.

[45] *See, e.g.*, Berger, *Domestic Partnership Initiatives*, 40 DePaul L. Rev. 417 (1991); Bowman & Cornish, *A Legal and Social Analysis of Domestic Partnership Ordinances*, 92 Colum. L. Rev. 1164 (1992); Note, *Legal Rights of Unmarried Heterosexual and Homosexual Couples and the Evolving Definition of "Family"*, 29 J. Fam. L. 497 (1990–1991).

[46] O'Brien, *Domestic Partnership: Recognition and Responsibility*, 32 San Diego L. Rev. 163, 165 (1995).

[47] *See, e.g.*, Note, *Domestic Partnership Recognition in the Workplace: Equitable Employee Benefits for Gay Couples (and Others)*, 51 Ohio St. L. J. 1067 (1990). Among the employers offering domestic partnership benefits are more than 100 colleges and universities, as well as an increasing number of law firms, particularly in major cities. *See* Barge, *More Firms Offer Benefits for Gay Couples*, ABA J. June, 1995, at 81.

[48] *See generally* Blumberg, *Cohabitation Without Marriage: A Different Perspective*, 28 UCLA L. Rev. 1125 (1981); Minow, *Redefining Families*, 62 U. Colo. L. Rev. 269 (1991); Note, *Expansion of the Term "Family" to include Nontraditional Relationships*, 20 Mem. St. U. L. Rev. 135 (1989); Comment, *Prohibiting Marital Status Discrimination: A Proposal for the Protection of Unmarried Couples*, 42 Hastings L.J. 1415 (1991); Christensen, *Legal Ordering of Family Values: The Case for Gay and Lesbian Families*, 18 Cardozo L. Rev. 1299 (1997); Ertman, *Contractual Purgatory for Sexual Marginorities: Not Heaven, but Not Hell Either*, 73 Denver U. L. Rev. 1107 (1996); Family Law Symposium, *A More Perfect Union? Marriage and Marriage-Like Relationships in Family Law*, 30 N. M. L. Rev. 1 (2000).

[49] *See, e.g.*, Sullivan, *Here Comes the Groom*, New Republic, August 28, 1989 at 20: Society has good reason to extend legal advantages to heterosexuals who marry. . . . They make a deeper commitment to one another and to society; in exchange, society extends certain benefits to them. . . . We rig the law in its favor not because we disparage all forms of

be, American society today consists of approximately 30% of households that are composed of traditional families, defined as two heterosexual parents living with their children.[50] The remaining 70% of American households now constitute nontraditional families, defined as one parent families (approximately 30% of all households), single persons, and unmarried heterosexual and homosexual couples.[51]

Consequently, a number of American courts are now granting more legal recognition to unmarried domestic cohabitation on a statewide level, as well as on a municipal level, in loss of consortium actions, workers' compensation actions, and zoning or rental disputes involving real property.[52]

A better reasoned approach would be for more state legislatures and courts to recognize and protect the legal rights and obligations of *both* traditional *and* nontraditional families, as they currently coexist in American society today, by providing alternative legal rights and remedies for each social structure, according to the public policy of each state, and based upon the present and future needs of all its citizens.

For example, the Swedish government has established such a realistic approach that legally recognizes both marriage *and* nonmarital cohabitation through different protective statutes. These alternate statutes provide legal recognition and protection to cohabiting couples in durable long-term relationships, without disturbing the position of marriage as the preferred form of cohabitation in Sweden.[53] A statutory model based upon this

---

relationships other than the nuclear family, but because we recognize that not to promote marriage would be to ask too much of human virtue. . . . Enshrining in the law a vague principle like domestic partnership is an invitation to qualify at little personal cost for entitlement. . . .

[50] *See* Berger, *Domestic Partner Initiatives*, 40 DePaul L. Rev. 417 (1991).

[51] Gutis, *What Is a Family?* New York Times, August 31, 1989, at C6.

[52] For example, although a loss of consortium action traditionally depends upon proof of a valid marriage, *Curry v. Caterpillar Tractor Co.*, 577 F. Supp. 991 (E.D. Pa. 1984), some courts have allowed loss of consortium claims to be filed by unmarried cohabitants as well. *See, e.g., Bullock v. United States*, 487 F. Supp. 1078 (D.N.J. 1980). *See generally infra* § 3.05[D].

And although the prevailing traditional view is that state workers compensation statutes generally exclude unmarried cohabitants from any statutory benefits, a minority of states have awarded worker's compensation benefits to dependent unmarried de facto spouses as well. *See, e.g., Kempf v. State Accident Ins. Fund*, 580 P.2d 1032 (Or. Ct. App. 1978). *See generally infra* § 3.05[D].

Finally, the renting or purchasing of a home that is zoned or covenanted as a "family residence" has traditionally presented many legal problems for unmarried cohabitants. *See, e.g., Maryland Comm'n on Human Rights v. Greenbelt Homes*, 475 A.2d 1192 (Md. 1984), holding that enforcement of a cooperative housing regulation that prohibited unmarried couples did not constitute discrimination based upon marital status. However, on the other hand, the case of *Braschi v. Stahl Assocs.*, 543 N.E.2d 49 (N.Y. 1989), held that, for rent control purposes, a family would include "two adult lifetime partners whose relationship is long-term and characterized by an emotional and financial commitment and interdependence."

[53] *See* Fawcett, *Taking the Middle Path: Recent Swedish Legislation Grants Minimal Property Rights to Unmarried Cohabitants*, 24 Fam. L.Q. 179 (1990); Bradley, *Unmarried Cohabitation in Sweden: A Renewed Social Institution*, 11 J. Legal Hist. 300 (1990). Norway, Demark, France, and Canada, among a number of other countries, recently enacted similar domestic partnership statutes. *See, e.g.*, Sloan, *A Rose by Any Other Name: Marriage and the Danish Registered Partnership Act*, 5 Cardozo J. Int'l & Comp. Law 189 (1997).

Swedish experience may thus be beneficial to American courts and lawmakers in resolving disputes between unmarried cohabitants in the United States, without being limited to an often inadequate contractual remedy.[54]

In July of 1997, Hawaii became the first state in the United States to enact comprehensive, state-wide domestic partnership legislation. The Hawaii statute allows same-sex couples, and others who are legally prohibited from marrying, to register with the state as "reciprocal beneficiaries". Once registered, reciprocal beneficiaries are eligible for a wide range of benefits previously reserved for married couples. These benefits include: health insurance, retirement benefits, inheritance rights, workers' compensation benefits, family and funeral leave, joint automobile insurance, property rights, and legal standing relating to wrongful death benefits and victims' rights.[55] This legislation was passed in response to the Hawaii Supreme Court's decision in *Baehr v. Lewin*,[56] , suggesting that restricting marriage to opposite sex couples in Hawaii may be in violation of the Hawaii constitution.[57]

Likewise in 1999, the Vermont Supreme Court held in *Baker v. State*,[58] that Vermont "is constitutionally required to extend to same-sex couples the common benefits and protections that flow from marriage under Vermont law", but whether "this takes the form of inclusion within the marriage laws themselves or a parallel domestic partnership system or some equivalent statutory alternative, rests with the Legislature".[59] Consequently, a year later the Vermont legislature passed state legislation recognizing a "civil union" alternative to marriage. Under this domestic partnership legislation, partners in a civil union would be eligible for hundreds of state benefits normally given to married couples. They could transfer property, make medical decision for each other, inherit estates, and oversee burials. They would be required to accept the joint debt of their partners, and dissolve their civil union in Family Court in a proceeding equivalent to divorce.[60]

It is therefore likely that a number of other states may enact similar domestic partnership legislation, based on the statutory models found in Hawaii and Vermont, in the near future.[61] Indeed, the American Law

---

[54] *See, e.g.,* Henson, *A Comparative Analysis of Same-Sex Partnership Protections: Recommendations for American Reform,* 7 Int'l J. L. & Fam. 282 (1993).

[55] 1997 Hawaii H.B. 118 (July, 1997).

[56] 852 P.2d 44 (Haw. 1993).

[57] In the wake of the *Baehr* decision, a number of Hawaiian legislators in 1997 proposed a state constitutional amendment banning same-sex marriages in Hawaii, which was subsequently approved by the Hawaiian voters.

[58] 744 A.2d 864 (Vt. 1999).

[59] *Id.* at 867.

[60] *See. e.g.,* Ferdinand, *Gay Civil Unions Near Legality,* The Washington Post, April 19, 2000 at A-3.

[61] The Hawaii and Vermont experience, as well as public opinion polls in other states, suggest that while many Americans support the concept of domestic partnership legislation and other legal remedies for same-sex couples, they still remain opposed to same-sex marriage. *See, e.g.,* Garcia, *Californians Accepting Gay Rights, But Poll Finds Opposition to Same-Sex Marriages,* San Francisco Chronicle, March 3, 1997 at A-1. *See also* Chapter 2.08[B] *infra.*

Institute's *Principles of the Law of Family Dissolution,*[62] recently proposed a number of statutory recommendations relating to domestic partnership law for the possible adoption and enactment by state legislatures.[63] The scope of these proposed family law principles is to govern the financial claims of domestic partners against one another at the termination of their relationship.[64] Domestic partners are defined under the *Principles* as two persons of the same sex or opposite sex, not married to one another, who for a significant period of time share a primary residence and a life together as a couple.[65] "Domestic partnership property" is defined under the *Principles* as that property which would have been marital property had the domestic partners been married to one another during their domestic partnership period,[66] but nothing in the *Principles* would foreclose contract claims between such persons who have formed a contract that is enforceable under applicable state law.[67]

§ 2.03　Marriage: A Status or Contract?

The vast majority of states have held that marriage constitutes a legal *status* based upon contract. Accordingly, there are three parties to any marriage: Husband, Wife, and the State; and the public policy of the State is to regulate marriage based upon the general welfare of its citizens.[68]

The states therefore can prescribe the age at which parties may contract to marry, the procedures essential to constitute a valid marriage under state law, the duties and obligations created by the marriage, the effect of marriage on the parties' property and support rights and obligations, and the acts which may constitute grounds for the dissolution of marriage.[69] Thus, even when a court is faced with a purely economic or contractual issue within the marital relationship, there is a continuing recognition of the state's power to regulate *all* the incidents of the marital relationship.[70]

Some commentators, however, have questioned these traditional assumptions involving the state's regulation of marriage, and they have argued that the legal *status* of marriage has now become obsolete, and the incidents of marriage should therefore move from *status* to *contract* implications, with

---

[62] American Law Institute, *Principles of the Law of Family Dissolution: Analysis and Recommendations* (Tentative Draft No. 4, April 10, 2000).

[63] *Id.* Chapter 6, *Domestic Partners.*

[64] *Id.* Section 6.01(1)

[65] *Id.* Section 6.03.

[66] *Id.* Section 6.04, 6.05.

[67] *Id.* Section 6.01(3)

[68] *See, e.g., Maynard v. Hill,* 125 U.S. 190, 205 (1888); *Boddie v. Connecticut,* 401 U.S. 371, 276 (1971). *See also supra* § 1.03.

[69] *Id.; see also Fearon v. Treanor,* 5 N.E.2d 815, 816 (N.Y. 1936); *Cramer v. Commonwealth,* 202 S.E.2d 911, 915 (Va. 1974).

[70] *See, e.g., Boddie v. Connecticut,* 401 U.S. 371, 376 (1971) ("Without a prior judicial imprimatur, individuals may fully enter into and rescind commercial contracts, for example, but we are unaware of any jurisdiction where private citizens may covenant for or dissolve marriage without state approval.").

a corresponding de-emphasis in the state's regulation of marriage.[71] To date, however, only a small minority of jurisdictions have viewed marriage more in terms of a contract than a legal status.[72]

Nevertheless, the current statutory regulation of marriage has a number of critics. Professor Lenore Weitzman, for example, argues that "prospective spouses are neither informed of the terms of a [marriage] contract, nor are they allowed any options about these terms. . . .[O]ur society has undergone profound transformations in the past century, and the long-standing legal structure of marriage may now be anachronistic. The state's interest in preserving the traditional family may not be important enough to offset new societal and individual needs which require more flexibility and choice in family forms".[73] Marriage and the traditional nuclear family have been battered by current social and economic factors, and one commentator believes that "our society [may be] moving in the direction of a post-marriage or post-nuclear family system, where the married couple, father-mother unit will no longer be held up as the dominant cultural ideal and will no longer refect the empirical reality for all, or even most, children."[74] Some feminist writers have argued for the uncoupling of marriage and child rearing[75], while other commentators believe that many of our current social ills are caused in large part by father absence.[76] Writes Professor David Blankenhorn:

---

[71] *See, e.g.,* Wright, *Marriage: From Status to Contract?* 13 Anglo-Am. L. Rev. 17 (1984); Schultz, *Contractual Ordering of Marriage: A New Model for State Policy,* 70 Cal. L. Rev. 204 (1982); Singer, *The Privatization of Family Law,* 1992 Wis. L. Rev. 1443; Comment, *Marriage as a Contact: Toward a Functional Redefinition of the Marital Status,* 9 Colum. J. L. & Soc. Probs. 607 (1973); *see also* W. O'Donnell & D. Jones, The Law of Marriage and Marriage Alternatives 1–4 (1982).

[72] *See, e.g., Ponder v. Graham,* 4 Fla. 23 (1851); *Ryan v. Ryan,* 277 So. 2d 266 (Fla. 1973). *See also Seizer v. Sessions,* 915 P.2d 553, 561 (Wash. Ct. App. 1996) *rev'd on other grounds* 940 P.2d 261 (Wash. 1997) (comparing Washington and Texas law and pointing out that under Washington State law "the spouses by mutual consent can terminate a marriage, or can mutually treat the community property presumptions as terminated by agreeing to live separate and apart" whereas under Texas law "the institution of marriage is a status, more than a mere contract").

See also Stephen Sugarman, Divorce Reform at the Crossroads, 138 (1990) ("Marriage, at least in this century, is typically said to be best understood as a status, rather than as a contractual relationship").

[73] Weitzman, *Legal Regulation of Marriage: Tradition and Change, A Proposal for Individual Contract and Contracts in Lieu of Marriage,* 62 Cal. L. Rev. 1169, 1170 (1974). *See also* Shultz, *Contractual Ordering of Marriage: A New Model for State Policy,* 70 Cal. L. Rev. 204, 207 (1982) ("Marriage has undergone tremendous change in recent decades. . .only a small percentage of American families still have all the characteristics associated with the nuclear family ideal. In place of a single socially approved ideal we have competing demands for autonomy and privacy, and multiple models of intimacy: single parents, working wives, house husbands, homosexual couples, living together arrangements without marriage, serial marriage, and stepchildren. The changes are legion, and their message is clear: the destruction of traditional marriage as the sole model for adult intimacy is irreversible").

[74] Blankenhorn, *The State of the Family and the Family Law Debate,* 36 Santa Clara L. Rev. 431, 431–32 (1996).

[75] *See, e.g.,* Carbone & Brinig, *Rethinking Marriage: Feminist Ideology, Economic Change, and Divorce,* 65 Tulane L. Rev. 953 (1991); Martha Fineman, The Neutered Mother (1995).

[76] *See, e.g.,* David Blankenhorn, Fatherless America (1995).

> What is society going to do about this state of affairs? Given the increasing recognition of the trend toward the post-marriage, post-nuclear family and the obviously negative consequences of this trend, especially for children, a new family debate is now emerging. . . . There are two fault lines that I believe will characterize this new debate in the coming months and years. On one side of the fault line will be those who argue that we cannot reverse the trend-that is, that we cannot reinstitutionalize marriage. Therefore, we must instead deal with the consequences of the weakening of marriage, especially the economic consequences, recognizing the reality that more and more of our children are simply not going to be growing up with their two married parents. . . Those on the other side of this fault line will insist that we must seek to reverse this trend. They will direct their efforts to strengthening the institution of marriage and seeking to create cultural change in favor of the idea that unwed childbearing is wrong, that our divorce rate is far too high, and that every child deserves a father.[77]

Consequently, some states have attempted to "reinstitutionalize" or strengthen marriage through so-called "covenant marriage" legislation as an alternative to "regular" marriage.[78] Under a Louisiana "covenant" marriage, for example, the parties consensually agree not to obtain a no-fault divorce, and can only dissolve their marriage based upon traditional fault grounds or a separation for two years or more. The couple also agrees to obtain premarital counseling from a clergy member or marital counselor prior to marriage.[79] A number of other states have expressed interest in this Louisiana approach.[80] In 1998, the Florida state legislature, by a bipartisan vote of 91 to 16 in the House and a unanimous vote in the Senate, enacted a "Marriage Preparation and Preservation Act" providing that: (1) all Florida high school students must take a required course in "marriage and relationship skill based education"; (2) engaged couples are encouraged (but not required) to take a "premarital preparation course" of at least four hours in length, which may include instruction in conflict resolution, communication skills, financial responsibilities, children and parenting, and data on problems that married couples face—and those who take this premarital preparation course from a religious or secular marriage counselor are entitled to a reduction in the cost of their marriage license; (3) each couple applying for a marriage license will also be given a handbook prepared by the Florida Bar Association, informing couples of "the rights

---

[77] Blankenhorn, *The State of the Family and the Family Law Debate*, 36 Santa Clara L. Rev. 431, 436–37 (1996).

[78] *See, e.g.*, LA. REV. CODE Sec. 9-224 *et seq*; and ARIZ. REV. STAT. Sec. 25-901 *et seq.*

[79] *See generally* Louisiana House Bill 756 (1997).

[80] *See* Jeter, *Covenant Marriages Tie the Knot Tightly*, The Washington Post, August 15, 1997 at A-1; ("I don't think there's any question that you're going to see a lot of activity around the country as other state legislatures will be studying the concept and trying to adopt it", said Jeff Atkinson, a University of Chicago law professor and a member of the American Bar Association's Family Law Council"); Corey, *States Explore Making Breaking Up Hard to Do*, Baltimore Sun, May 19, 1997 at A-1 (reporting that legislators in at least 20 states have introduced bills to modify no-fault divorce).

and responsibilities under Florida law of marital partners to each other and to their children, both during marriage and upon dissolution"; and (4) couples with children who file for divorce must take a "Parent Education and Family Stabilization Course" that covers the legal and emotional impact of divorce on adults and children, financial responsibility, laws regarding child abuse and neglect, and conflict resolution skills.[81]

This recent legislative trend to "reinstitutionalize" and strengthen marriage—and to discourage divorce— has not been without its critics:

> The notion that the public has a vested interest in seeing families succeed is hardly a point of contention. Rather, the issue for opponents of [these legislative measures] is whether discouraging divorce is enough to improve the quality of marriage, either for parents or their children. . . "It's a laudable goal," says [Professor] Atkinson of the ABA. "But is divorce automatically worse than every alternative? I don't think these kinds of measures are going to be adding to the happiness or longevity of marriage."[82]

Although the evidence is not yet in whether this legislative trend to strengthen and "reinstitutionalize" marriage will be successful or not, it is nevertheless true that the vast majority of Americans today still support the institution of marriage,[83] and that the state legislatures and courts, while providing a number of legal rights and remedies for unmarried cohabitants,[84] currently show no sign of abandoning state regulation of marriage in the foreseeable future.[85]

---

[81] *See, e.g.,* McManus, *Florida Passes Nation's Most Sweeping Reform of Marriage Laws,* Ethics and Religion Advance (May 16, 1998) (predicting that this law will inspire many other states to pass similar laws).

Other legislators, sociologists, and clergy have also argued that more states should require premarital counseling prior to marriage. *See, e.g.,* Time Magazine, October 7, 1996 at 84 ("Marriage is a commitment," says Brian Willats, a spokesman for the Michigan Family Forum, which supports premarital counseling. "It's not just notarized dating.") And in an August, 1997 Time Magazine/CNN national poll, over two-thirds of those Americans poslled favored mandatory premarital counseling.

[82] Jeter, *Covenant Marriages Tie the Knot Tightly,* The Washington Post, August 15, 1997 at A-19. *See also* Bradford, *The Counterrevolution: A Critique of Recent Proposals to Reform No-Fault Divorce Laws,* 49 Stanford L. Rev. 607 (1997) (predicting that such legislative proposals "will not increase moral behavior" and that fault-based divorce regimes may have a negative impact on women); Ellman, *Divorce Rates, Marriage Rates, and the Problematic Persistence of Traditional Marital Roles,* 34 Fam. L. Q. 1–2 (2000) ("The evidence certainly offers little reason to believe that divorce rates are much affected by divorce laws. The same may prove true about the law's impact on marriage formation").

[83] *See, e.g.,* Homer Clark, The Law of Domestic Relations in the United States 26 (1988) ("Notwithstanding these developments, a majority of Americans still marry in the traditional way and continue to regard marriage as the most important relationship in their lives"); Elman, *Divorce Rates, Marriage Rates, and the Problematic Persistence of Traditional Marital Roles,* 34 Fam. L. Q. 1, 2 (2000) ("I conclude that women's improved economic position, relative to men, may indeed contribute to declining marital rates, but only because of the surprising persistence of traditional marital roles. This persistence in Americans' adherence to traditional marital roles is itself relevant to policy choices governing the law of divorce and cohabitation").

[84] *See* Chapter 2.02 *supra.*

[85] *See, e.g.,* Stanley & Markman, *Can Government Rescue Marriages?* (The University of

§ 2.04   Formal Statutory Marriage

Marriage traditionally has been defined as the "voluntary union of a man and a woman to the exclusion of all others"[86] and the vast majority of states therefore prohibit same-sex marriages.[87]

Most Americans who marry do so in a formal statutory marriage in accordance with applicable state statutes. Each state generally requires that: (1) the parties obtain a license prior to the marriage; and (2) the parties be married by an authorized priest, rabbi, minister, or other authorized religious, judicial, or civil officer according to state statute. A blood test for sexually transmitted diseases is also required in many states, and in other states a test for rubella (German measles) is required for women of child-bearing years.[88]

Depending upon the particular state, marriage licenses are valid from 30 to 60 days before they must be renewed; and there is a waiting period in the majority of states averaging from three to five days before the parties can be married. The marriage license is normally issued by a clerk of court or a county clerk where the parties, or either of them, reside, or where the marriage ceremony is to be celebrated. But since a residency or domiciliary requirement is not required for marriage in the vast majority of states, the parties may also be married in another state of their choice.[89]

The marrying official must be duly authorized by the state, and he or she must comply with the applicable state statutes. If the parties wish to be married according to the tenets of a religious denomination that does not have an acknowledged minister or celebrant, then so-called "Quaker statutes" in many states will recognize such a marriage if performed according to the tenets of that particular religious denomination. Other state

---

Denver Center for Marital and Family Studies, 1997) at 1–2: ("There is a trend sweeping the country to make changes in legal codes to strengthen and stabilize marriages. There are two key thrusts emerging in state legislatures: the first involves changes in laws that would make it harder for couples to divorce; the second involves efforts to encourage or mandate couples to participate in premarital counseling . . . While strange bedfellows, there is a growing consensus among both liberal and conservative political and religious leaders that something must be done. . . [Recent empirical studies] strongly suggest that couples can learn skills and enhance ways of thinking-prior to marriage-that significantly improves their odds of having good marriages. . . . With a growing national consensus, a large scale public health education campaign could bring together educators, clergy, mental health professionals, and politicians to focus on two key goals: 1) To extol strong and happy marriages as a high value and a high priority, and 2) to encourage couples to take advantage of effective tools to make their marriages not just more stable, but truly better. . . We are talking about values here. Values that say marriage is important. Values that say working to resolve differences is good. Values that say preparing for marriage is wise. Values that lead to increased dedication for the task of building strong and happy marriages. These things can be done if we have the collective will. Let's get to it.")

[86] *See, e.g., Hyde v. Hyde,* L.R. 1 P & D 130 (1866).

[87] See generally infra § 2.08[B]

[88] *See, e.g., infra,* Appendix A, The Uniform Marriage and Divorce Act, §§ 201 to 206. *See generally* 1 H. Clark, Law of Domestic Relations 85–100 (2d ed. 1987); S. Green & J. Long, Marriage and Family Law Agreements 18–20 (1984).

[89] *Id.*

statutes will recognize the marriage of native American Indians if performed according to tribal custom or law.[90]

If the parties do not fully comply with these statutory requirements for marriage— for example, if the marriage license is invalid, or if the celebrant is not authorized by state law to perform the marriage—such a marriage may be valid or invalid. A majority of states, in order to promote marriage and to validate the marital expectations of the parties, provide that state marital statutes are only *directory* statues, requiring only substantial compliance to constitute a valid marriage.[91]

A minority of states, however, have held that state marital statutes are *mandatory* statutes, requiring strict compliance to constitute a valid marriage.[92] However, these mandatory statute jurisdictions often include a curative or "savings" statute, providing that if there is a defect in the license, or a defect in the marrying official, but the parties consummate their marriage with a good faith belief that they have been lawfully joined in marriage, then the marriage is valid, despite their statutory noncompliance.[93]

A party who knew that an impediment existed in the marriage license or the marrying official at the time of the marriage may also be estopped from asserting such a marital impediment at a later date.[94]

§ 2.05 Informal Marriages

An alternative to formal statutory marriage,[95] and to nonmarital cohabitation,[96] is informal marriage which may include common law marriage, putative marriage, marriage by proxy, de facto "marriage," and "marriage" by estoppel.

Although some courts have traditionally viewed informal marriages with suspicion and mistrust, other courts have recognized the validity of such marriages under the public policy rationale of promoting marriage in general, and of validating the marital expectations of the parties in

---

[90] *Id.*

[91] *See, e.g., Picarella v. Picarella*, 316 A.2d 826 (Md. Ct. Spec. App. 1974); *Carabetta v. Carabetta*, 438 A.2d 109 (Conn. 1980); *Wright v. Vales*, 613 S.W.2d 850 (Ark. Ct. App. 1981); *Maxwell v. Maxwell*, 273 N.Y.S.2d 728 (N.Y. Sup. Ct. 1966). See *also* Annot., 61 A.L.R.2d 847 (1958) and Later Case Service.

[92] *See, e.g.*, Minn. Stat. Ann. § 517.01; Va. Code Ann. § 20-13; *See also Williams v. Williams*, 460 N.E.2d 1226 (Ind. App.1984); *Nelson v. Marshall*, 869 S.W.2d 132 (Mo. Ct. App. 1993); Annot., 61 A.L.R.2d 847 (1958) and Later Case Service.

[93] *See, e.g.*, Va. Code Ann. § 20-31. Consummation, or sexual intercourse, is *not* generally required for a valid marriage. But it *is* often required under various "curative" statutes.

[94] *See infra* § 2.05[E]. *See generally* 1 H. Clark, Law of Domestic Relations 94–96 (2d ed. 1987).

[95] *See supra* § 2.04.

[96] *See infra* § 3.02.

particular, especially with respect to the parties' marital property and support rights and obligations.[97]

[A] Common Law Marriage

A so-called common law marriage is an informal marriage that does not meet the requirements of a formal statutory marriage. All that is required for a common law marriage is a present intent and agreement of the parties to enter into a matrimonial relationship. In the absence of any express evidence of this present intent and agreement, most courts will infer such present intent and agreement through cohabitation and community repute as husband and wife.[98] Thus, common law marriages are as valid as formal statutory marriages in the 14 American jurisdictions where common law marriages are legally recognized.[99]

Moreover, even if most other American jurisdictions do not recognize common law marriages if contracted within their own state, nevertheless they will recognize common law marriages if contracted in one of the jurisdictions that do recognize such marriages.[100] The rationale for this recognition of sister state common law marriages is the doctrine that a marriage valid where celebrated is valid everywhere, unless such a marriage is against a state's strong public policy;[101] and that common law marriages which validate the present marital expectations of the parties do *not* violate a sister state's strong public policy, which is to promote and protect marriages generally.[102]

Some courts have held that the party claiming a common law marriage must have resided in, or must have established a significant relationship

---

[97] *See, e.g.,* Weyrauch, *Informal and Formal Marriage-An Appraisal of Trends in Family Organization,* 28 U. Chi. L. Rev. 88 (1960); Weyrauch, *Metamorphoses of Marriage,* 13 Fam. L.Q. 415 (1980).

[98] *See, e.g., Adams v. Adams,* 559 So.2d 1084 (Ala. 1990); *Crosson v. Crosson,* 668 So.2d 868 (Ala. Ct. App. 1995); *In re Estate of Fischer,* 176 N.W.2d 801 (Iowa 1970). *See generally* Stein, *Common Law Marriage: Its History and Certain Contemporary Problems,* 9 J. Fam. L. 271 (1969); Hall, *Common Law Marriage,* 46 Cambridge L.J. 106 (1987).

[99] According to S. Green & J. Long, Marriage and Family Law Agreements 80–86 (1984), the following jurisdictions still recognize common law marriages if contracted within that state: Alabama, Colorado, Georgia [until 1997], Idaho, Iowa, Kansas, Montana, Ohio [until 1991], Oklahoma, Pennsylvania, Rhode Island, South Carolina, Texas, and the District of Columbia. *See, e.g., Smereczynski v. Dep't of Health & Human Services,* 944 F.2d 296 (6th Cir. 1991) (applying Ohio law). Ohio, however, subsequently abolished common law marriage by statute in 1991.

[100] *See, e.g., In re Estate of Burroughs,* 486 N.W.2d 113 (Mich. Ct. App. 1992); *Blaw-Knox Constr. Co. v. Morris,* 596 A.2d 679 (Md. 1991); *Farrah v. Farrah,* 429 S.E.2d 626 (Va. Ct. App. 1993); *Michelli v. Michelli,* 527 So. 2d 359 (Fla. Dist. Ct. App. 1991); *Brack v. Brack,* 329 N.W.2d 432 (Mich. Ct. App. 1983); *Chatman v. Ribicoff,* 169 F. Supp. 931 (N.D. Cal. 1961); *Weisel v. National Trans. Co.,* 218 N.Y.S.2d 725 (N.Y. App. Div. 1961).

[101] *See, e.g.,* Restatement, Conflict of Laws, §§ 121–123 (1934); Restatement (Second) Conflict of Laws, § 283(2) (1971); *see also infra* § 2.09.

[102] *Id.; see also Metropolitan Life Ins. Co. v. Holding,* 293 F. Supp. 854 (E.D. Va. 1968); *Kersey v. Gardner,* 264 F. Supp. 887 (M.D. Ga. 1967).

with, the common law marriage state.[103] Other courts, however, have held that visits of short duration to a common law marriage state, where the parties held themselves out as husband and wife, would suffice to create a legally valid common law marriage.[104] This latter approach arguably validates the reasonable expectations of the parties in the marriage, as well as reaffirming state public policy of promoting and protecting marriages in general.[105]

The courts generally require that proof of a common law marriage be established by clear and convincing evidence in order to prevent any fraudulent claims.[106]

Another problem often arises in the context of a common law marriage when the purported husband and wife attempt to contract a common law marriage at a time when a legal impediment exists in their common law marriage. For example, a man and a woman begin to live together in a purported common law relationship when one or both of the parties have not yet been legally divorced from a prior spouse. In this situation, some courts have held that the initial meretricious relationship -when the marital impediment still existed -*cannot* ripen into a valid common law marriage, absent proof of a *new* agreement to marry after the impediment is removed.[107] The better reasoned view, however, to validate the marital expectations of the parties, is to hold that the common law marriage still exists after the legal impediment to marriage is removed, under a "continuing agreement" rationale.[108]

Although some courts have traditionally viewed common law marriage with suspicion and mistrust, and although -until recently -the recognition of common law marriage in the United States seemed to be on a decline, now with more cohabiting couples and alternate lifestyles, the recognition and enforcement of common law marriages by various courts may reverse this trend.[109]

---

[103] *See, e.g., Hesington v. Estate of Hesington*, 640 S.W.2d 824 (Mo. Ct. App. 1982); *Kennedy v. Damron*, 268 S.W.2d 22 (Ky. 1954); *Kelderhaus v. Kelderhaus*, 467 S.E.2d 303 (Va. Ct. App. 1996).

[104] *See, e.g., Renshaw v. Heckler*, 787 F.2d 50 (2d Cir. 1986); *Metropolitan Life Ins. Co. v. Holding*, 293 F. Supp. 854 (E.D. Va. 1968); *Ventura v. Ventura*, 280 N.Y.S.2d 5 (N.Y. Sup. Ct. 1967).

[105] *Id.* These sister state common law marriages are most often found to exist when the parties, in good faith, have been cohabiting as husband and wife for a number of years.

[106] *See, e.g., In re Estate of Fischer*, 176 N.W.2d 801 (Iowa 1970).

[107] *See, e.g., Dandy v. Dandy*, 324 So. 2d 728 (Fla. Dist. Ct. App. 1970); *Byers v. Mount Vernon Mills, Inc.*, 231 S.E.2d 699 (S.C. 1977).

[108] *See, e.g., Richard v. Trousdale*, 508 So. 2d 260 (Ala. 1987); *Parker v. Parker*, 265 S.E.2d 237 (N.C. Ct. App. 1980); *see also Travers v. Rinehart*, 205 U.S. 423 (1907).

[109] *See, e.g.*, Note, *Common Law Marriage and Unmarried Cohabitators: An Old Solution to a New Problem*, 39 U. Pitt. L. Rev. 579 (1978); Caudill, *Legal Recognition of Unmarried Cohabitation: A Proposal to Update and Reconsider Common Law Marriage*, 49 Tenn. L. Rev. 537 (1982).

For example, common law marriage actions have been brought against such celebrities as actor William Hurt and New York Yankee outfielder Dave Winfield. *See* Newsweek, July 24, 1989 at 46–47. The claim against Hurt was later dismissed, *see Jennings v. Hurt*, 554 N.Y.S.2d 220 (N.Y. App. Div. 1990), but the claim against Winfield was held to be actionable.

[B] Putative Marriage

A putative marriage is an informal "curative" marriage when one or both of the parties were ignorant of an impediment that made their formal statutory marriage invalid. This concept was well explained in an 1847 decision of the Texas Supreme Court:

> Putative matrimony is defined to be a marriage, which being null on account of some dissolving impediment, is held, notwithstanding, for a true marriage, because of its having been contracted in good faith, by both or one of the spouses being ignorant of the impediment. Good faith is always presumed, and he who would impede its effects, must prove that it did not exist.[110] A putative marriage must be contracted with a good faith belief of one or both of the parties that their formal statutory marriage was valid. But unlike common law marriages, cohabitation of the parties is not always required.[111]

The putative marriage doctrine is most frequently found in those states following a French or Spanish civil law tradition, such as California, Louisiana, and Texas, but various other states following an English common law tradition have also adopted the putative marriage concept by statute.[112] The federal government has also adopted a putative spouse test regarding social security benefits.[113] Like a spouse in any other marriage, a putative spouse may claim marital property and support rights, loss of consortium and personal injury awards, wrongful death benefits, and he or she may inherit from the other putative spouse.[114]

A state that does not recognize the putative marriage doctrine within its own jurisdiction would probably recognize a putative marriage contracted within another state under the well-established conflict of laws doctrine that a marriage valid where celebrated ought to be valid everywhere, unless it is against a state's strong public policy.[115] Accordingly, any imperfection in the marriage license or marrying official probably would not invalidate the putative marriage in most other states, either under a directory marriage statute,[116] or under a mandatory state "curative" statute.[117]

---

[110] *Smith v. Smith*, 1 Tex. 621 (1847). *See also In re Foy's Estate*, 240 P.2d 685 (Cal. Dist. Ct. App. 1952); *Wilkinson v. Wilkinson*, 91 Cal. Rptr. 372 (Cal. Dist. Ct. App. 1970).

[111] *See, e.g., Vyonis v. Vyonis*, 248 Cal. Rptr. 807 (Cal. Ct. App. 1988); *Garduno v. Garduno*, 760 S.W.2d 735 (Tex. Civ. App. 1988); *Rebouche v. Anderson*, 505 So. 2d 808 (La. Ct. App. 1987); *Hicklin v. Hicklin*, 509 N.W.2d 627 (Neb. 1994). See also Annot., 34 A.L.R.2d 1255 and Later Case Service.

[112] *E.g.*, Illinois, Minnesota, and Wisconsin. The Uniform Marriage and Divorce Act, § 209 also recognizes putative marriages.

[113] *See* 42 U.S.C. § 416(h)(1)(B).

[114] *See generally* Blakesley, *The Putative Marriage Doctrine*, 60 Tul. L. Rev. 1 (1985); Luther & Luther, *Support and Property Rights of the putative Spouse*, 24 Hastings L. J. 311 (1973); Note, *Rights of the Putative Spouse*, 1978 S. Ill. U. L. J. 423 (1978). *See also* Annot., 34 A.L.R.2d 1255, 1291 and Later Case Service.

[115] *See, e.g.*, Restatement, Conflict of Laws, §§ 121–123 (1934); Restatement (Second) Conflict of Laws, § 283(2) (1971); *see also infra* § 2.09.

[116] *See supra* note 14 and accompanying text.

[117] *See supra* note 15 and accompanying text.

However, some states recognizing the putative marriage doctrine have also held that a putative bigamous or polygamous marriage would also constitute a valid marriage.[118] But in states where bigamous or incestuous marriages are held to be *void ab initio* marriages and against a state's strong public policy,[119] such bigamous putative marriages may *not* be recognized irrespective of their recognition in the sister state.[120]

[C] Marriage by Proxy

A marriage by proxy is an attempt to comply with state statutory marriage requirements by designating a "stand in" who appears for the absent prospective spouse or, alternately, where the absent party "participates" in the ceremony via telephone or another similar form of communication.[121] The validity of a marriage by proxy is normally governed by the law of the jurisdiction where the ceremony takes place.[122]

Although a marriage by proxy is not uncommon in countries following a Spanish or French civil law tradition,[123] there is remarkably little case authority on the validity of proxy marriages contracted in American states.[124] Even within these cases there is a split of authority.

Some courts, for example, have construed state marriage statutes to require that both parties be present in person, either at the time the marriage license is obtained, or at the time of the marriage ceremony.[125] The better reasoned view, however, would be to recognize a marriage by proxy in order to validate the parties' marital expectations, and promote, rather than discourage, marriage in general.[126]

If a marriage by proxy takes place while an absent spouse is in another country, however, federal immigration law will not recognize such a

---

[118] *See, e.g., In re Dalip Singh Bir's Estate*, 188 P.2d 499 (Cal. Dist. Ct. App. 1948).

[119] *See infra* §§ 2.08[C], 2.08[D].

[120] *Cf. Hager v. Hager*, 349 S.E.2d 908 (Va. Ct. App. 1986) (*void ab initio* marriages, such as a bigamous South Carolina marriage, cannot be affirmed in Virginia). *But see In re Estate of Shippy*, 678 P.2d 848 (Wash. Ct. App. 1984) (the Washington court, in recognizing a *nunc pro tunc* California divorce decree, in effect *was* recognizing a bigamous putative marriage, that under Alaska law would *not* be recognized). *See generally* Annot., 19 A.L.R.3d 648 (1968); Fine, *The Rights of Putative Spouses: Choice of Law Issues and Comparative Insights*, 32 Int'l & Comp. L.Q. 708 (1983).

[121] *See, e.g.,* Comment, *Validity of Proxy Marriages*, 25 S. Cal. L. Rev. 181 (1952); Howery, *Marriage by Proxy and Other Informal Marriages*, 13 UMKC L. Rev. 48 (1944). *See also* Annot., 170 A.L.R. 947 (1947).

[122] *Id.*

[123] *See, e.g., Torres v. Torres*, 366 A.2d 713 (N.J. Super. Ct. Ch. Div. 1976) (New Jersey recognition of a Cuban marriage by proxy). Explorers Christopher Columbus and Vasco de Balboa were both married by proxy, but not presumably while en route to America.

[124] *See, e.g.,* 1 H. Clark, Law of Domestic Relations 124–125 (2d ed. 1987).

[125] *See, e.g., Blankenship v. Blankenship*, 133 B.R. 398 (N.D. Ohio W.D. 1991) (applying Ohio law); *Respole v. Respole*, 70 N.E.2d 465 (Ohio Ct. C.P. 1946) (purportedly applying W. Va. law).

[126] *See, e.g., Barrons v. United States*, 191 F.2d 92 (9th Cir. 1951) (discussing Texas, California, Nevada, West Virginia, and D.C. law, and upholding a marriage by proxy); *see also* Moore, *The Case for Marriage by Proxy*, 11 Clev. Mar. L. Rev. 313 (1962).

"spouse, wife, or husband by reason of any marriage ceremony where the contracting parties thereto are not physically present in the presence of each other, unless the marriage shall have been consummated."[127]

[D]　De Facto "Marriage"

A de facto "marriage," or a relationship between unmarried cohabitants, traditionally lacks any legal recognition as a valid marriage, because: (1) it does not comply with state statutory requirements for a formal marriage;[128] (2) it does not possess the present intent and agreement requirement, nor the community repute requirement for a common law marriage;[129] and (3) it lacks the good faith belief requirement needed for a putative marriage.[130] Thus, in the absence of a contractual nonmarital agreement,[131] or another nonmarital remedy,[132] the de facto "spouse" had few, if any, legal remedies.

For example, in the vast majority of states, only a legal spouse, and *not* a de facto "spouse," would qualify as a beneficiary under state wrongful death statutes,[133] and the prevailing view is likewise that a loss of consortium action[134] depends upon proof of a valid marriage.[135] However, a minority of states have held that loss of consortium actions *may* be brought by unmarried de facto "spouses."[136]

Likewise, the prevailing traditional view is that state workers' compensation statutes are only for the benefit of legal spouses; unmarried de facto "spouses" are therefore excluded from any statutory benefits.[137] However, a minority of jurisdictions have awarded workers' compensation benefits to dependent unmarried de facto "spouses."[138] The rationale for the

---

[127] 8 U.S.C. § 1101(a)(35).

[128] *See supra* § 2.04.

[129] *See supra* § 2.05[A].

[130] *See supra* § 2.05[B].

[131] *See supra* § 2.02[A].

[132] *See supra* § 2.02[B], [C].

[133] *See, e.g., Nieto v. Los Angeles*, 188 Cal. Rptr. 31 (Cal. Ct. App. 1982); *Hewitt v. Firestone Tire & Rubber Co.*, 490 F. Supp. 1358 (E.D. Va. 1980).

[134] *See infra* § 3.13.

[135] *See, e.g., Felch v. Air Florida*, 562 F. Supp. 383 (D.D.C. 1983); *Curry v. Caterpillar Tractor Co.*, 577 F. Supp. 991 (E.D. Pa. 1984).

[136] *See, e.g., Bullock v. United States*, 487 F. Supp. 1078 (D.N.J. 1980). In *Bullock*, the court did recognize a loss of consortium claim by an unmarried de facto "spouse," but on unique factual grounds. The cohabitants in this case had been married for 23 years and were then divorced. They began cohabiting again, but were not remarried when the former husband was injured and rendered impotent.
See also Butcher v. Superior Court, 188 Cal. Rptr. 503 (Cal. Ct. App. 1983) (the nonmarital relationship was both "stable and significant" and "possessed the characteristics of marriage"). But the *Butcher* rationale was expressly rejected in *Elden v. Sheldon*, 210 Cal. Rptr. 755 (Cal. Ct. App. 1985) (the *Butcher* decision adopts a "vague, indefinite standard that would be incapable of a just or predictable application").

[137] *See, e.g., Caudle-Hyatt, Inc. v. Mixon*, 260 S.E.2d 193 (Va. 1979).

[138] *See, e.g., Kempf v. State Accident Ins. Fund*, 580 P.2d 1032 (Or. Ct. App. 1978); *West v. Marton Marlow Co.*, 230 N.W.2d 545 (Mich. 1975).

minority view is that state workers' compensation statutes should be liberally construed, including the words "family" and "dependents" under an "elastic" view that would *not* exclude unmarried de facto "spouses."[139]

The renting or purchasing of a home that is zoned or covenanted as a single family residence has also presented legal problems to unmarried cohabitants and de facto "spouses".[140] On the other hand, the New York Court of Appeals has recently held that a homosexual couple who had lived together for ten years could be considered a "family," at least for purposes of avoiding eviction under New York City's rent control regulations.[141] The Court held that "In the context of eviction, a realistic, and certainly valid, view of a family includes two adult life-time partners whose relationship is long-term and characterized by an emotional and financial commitment and interdependence."[142]

Whether these initial decisions will be expanded to provide more legal recognition and protection for unmarried cohabitants and de facto "spouses" in the future, or whether these cases will be limited on their facts in a minority of states, remains to be seen. It is clear, however, that the legal rights and obligations of the nontraditional family[143] need to be addressed in a realistic manner by the courts, and needs to be decisively addressed by the state and federal legislatures.[144]

[E] "Marriage" by Estoppel

A so-called "marriage" by estoppel is most frequently found when a husband or wife has obtained an invalid divorce from a prior spouse and then remarries. Since the prior divorce is legally invalid, the second bigamous marriage is also invalid.[145]

If, however, the parties knew about, or had participated in, the invalid prior divorce and invalid second marriage, they may be estopped by their conduct from questioning the legal validity of the second marriage. Thus,

---

[139] *Id.*

[140] *See, e.g., Maryland Comm'n on Human Relations v. Greenbelt Homes*, 475 A.2d 1192 (Md. 1984) (a cooperative housing regulation that prohibited unmarried couples did not constitute discrimination based upon marital status); *Village of Belle Terre v. Boraas*, 416 U.S. 1 (1974) (a zoning ordinance restricting land use only to single family dwellings was held not to be unconstitutional). *See generally* Smith, *The Wages of Living in Sin: Discrimination in Housing against Unmarried Couples*, 25 U.C. Davis L. Rev. 1055 (1992).

[141] *See, e.g., Braschi v. Stahl Assocs.*, 543 N.E.2d 49 (N.Y. 1989).

[142] *Id.*

[143] *See supra* §§ 1.02[B], 2.02.

[144] *See generally* S. Green & J. Long, Marriage and Family Law Agreements 158–210 (1984); Wade, *Void and De Facto Marriages*, 9 Sydney L. Rev. 356 (1981). *See also* Minow, *Redefining Families*, 62 U. Colo. L. Rev. 269 (1991); Treuthart, *Adopting a More Realistic Definition of "Family"*, 26 Gonz. L. Rev. 91 (1990–91); Note, *Looking for a Family Resemblance: The Limits of the Functional Approach to the Legal Definition of Family*, 104 Harv. L. Rev. 1640 (1991); *supra* §§ 1.02, 2.02.

[145] *See infra* § 2.08[C].

they are still "married" by estoppel principles, even though they are *not legally* married.[146]

The equitable estoppel theory in family law is a way to validate the parties' present expectations in the contested "marriage." It is based upon a personal disability of the party attacking the void divorce decree and the subsequent invalid marriage under the theory that one who has taken a prior position regarding the divorce and subsequent marriage, and who has obtained a benefit from it, cannot later take an inconsistent position which would prejudice the other party.[147]

This "marriage" by estoppel doctrine is broader than a traditional estoppel theory in that one party does not necessarily have to rely to his or her detriment upon factual representations made by the other party. It is sufficient, in many cases, that a court find only that it would be unfair to let a party take advantage of the legal invalidity of a divorce decree and the invalidity of the subsequent marriage.[148]

The doctrine of "marriage" by estoppel is further complicated because there are no less than three different rules regarding the validity or invalidity of a "marriage" by estoppel, especially when it involves a void migratory divorce. The courts are often split as to which of these three rules should govern, even within the same jurisdiction.

Under the "traditional" rule, the domiciliary state and the parties are *not* bound by any estoppel defense in collaterally attacking a void divorce and subsequent remarriage.[149] The rationale behind this traditional rule is that estoppel, even for a limited purpose, ultimately results in the de facto recognition of a void divorce, usually granted by a court lacking any jurisdiction whatever, and therefore violates the domiciliary state's strong public policy.[150]

Under the "sociological" or "Restatement" rule of "marriage" by estoppel, a court will attempt to validate the parties' "real" expectations of divorce and remarriage, rather than relying on a purely theoretical, and perhaps "unreal" legal basis.[151] The Second Restatement of Conflict of Laws, § 74, states the general rule that "A person may be precluded from attacking the

---

[146] *See, e.g., In re Marriage of Recknor*, 187 Cal. Rptr. 887 (Cal. Ct. App. 1982). *But see Crosby v. Crosby*, 769 F. Supp. 197 (D. Md. 1991) (in Maryland, silence in the absence of a duty to speak will not give rise to estoppel). *See also* Clark, *Estoppel Against Jurisdictional Attack on Decrees of Divorce*, 70 Yale L.J. 45 (1960); Rosenberg, *How Void is a Void Decree, or the Estoppel Effect of Invalid Divorce Decrees*, 8 Fam. L.Q. 207 (1974); and Annot., 81 A.L.R.3d 110 (1977).

[147] *Id.*

[148] *Id.* Clark, *supra* note 143, at 46–49; Rosenberg, *supra*, note 143, at 208–209.

[149] *See, e.g., Everett v. Everett*, 345 So. 2d 857 (La. Ct. App. 1977); *In re Estate of Steffke*, 222 N.W.2d 628 (Wis. 1974).

[150] *Id.*

[151] *See* Clark, *Estoppel Against Jurisdictional Attack on Decrees of Divorce*, 70 Yale L.J. 45, 56–57 (1960).

validity of a foreign divorce decree if, under the circumstances, it would be inequitable for him [or her] to do so."[152]

Although this "sociological" or "Restatement" rule of "marriage" by estoppel appears to be the majority view in a growing number of jurisdictions, it has been criticized by one commentator for resulting in "uncertainty and ambiguity as to a person's marital status and his capacity to marry. . . . Then, too, estoppel can prevent a valid dissolution of a prior dead marriage and, consequently, the regularization of a bigamous marriage that has been attempted."[153]

A third rule of "marriage" by estoppel is called the "status vs. property right" rule. Under this rule, if the action deals with the marital status, including actions to declare the nullity of a void marriage, separation, or divorce; then estoppel is not appropriate since the parties are trying to clarify their legal status -who is married to whom. But if the action deals with a property right, such as taking against a deceased spouse's will, or enforcing an alleged right to support, then estoppel may apply.[154]

Whatever specific rule a court utilizes, however, "the application of the principles of equitable estoppel cannot be subjected to fixed and settled rules of universal application, but rests largely on the facts and circumstances of each particular case."[155]

Finally, even if husband and wife may be estopped from collaterally attacking a void migratory divorce and a subsequent remarriage, under the traditional majority rule, the state itself would not be estopped from prosecuting a bigamy or unlawful cohabitation action.[156] Some commentators believe, however, that the state should not be able to challenge a void out-of-state divorce.[157]

§ 2.06   The Last-in-Time Marriage Presumption

The typical scenario for a last-in-time marriage presumption is not as uncommon as one might suppose: A husband or wife has unexpectedly died, and the bereaved surviving spouse is in the process of bringing a legal

---

[152] Restatement (Second) Conflict of Laws, § 74 (1971). The First Restatement of Conflict of Laws, § 112 (1934) also prohibits the questioning of an invalid divorce "either by the spouse who has obtained such decree of divorce from a court which has no jurisdiction, or by a spouse who takes advantage of such decree by remarrying."

[153] See Phillips, *Equitable Preclusion of Jurisdictional Attacks on Void Divorces*, 37 Fordham L. Rev. 355, 365–366 (1969).

[154] See, e.g., Caldwell v. Caldwell, 81 N.E.2d 60 (N.Y. 1948); Rabourn v. Rabourn, 385 P.2d 581 (Alaska 1963).

[155] Weber v. Weber, 265 N.W.2d 436, 441 (Neb. 1978). See also Swisher, *Foreign Migratory Divorces: A Reappraisal*, 21 J. Fam. L. 9, 37–48 (1982–83).

[156] See, e.g., State v. DeMeo, 118 A.2d 1 (N.J. 1955); see also Von Mehren, *The Validity of Foreign Divorces*, 45 Mass. L.Q. 23, 29 (1960); Currie, *Suitcase Divorce in the Conflict of Laws*, 34 U. Chi. L. Rev. 26, 54–55 (1966).

[157] See, e.g., A. Ehrenzweig, Conflict of Laws 253 (1962); Goodrich, Handbook on the Conflict of Laws 259 (1964); see also infra § 8.02[E].

proceeding that may include a wrongful death action, a suit for social security benefits, workers' compensation benefits, other insurance benefits, or a probate action. During the pendency of such an action, however, a former wife (or husband) comes forward, claiming that she has never been divorced from the deceased spouse, and that she, rather than the subsequent wife, should recover in any legal proceedings as the legal wife. *Query*: Which wife should prevail?

To many lawyers and lay persons, the initial conclusion might be that because American family law in the vast majority of jurisdictions prohibits bigamy and other plural marriages,[158] the first-in-time wife should recover all the proceeds. But this conclusion would be wrong.

The last-in-time marriage presumption is based upon "one of the strongest presumptions of law" that an existing marriage, once shown, is valid. A subsequent marriage therefore raises the strong presumption that any former marriage was terminated by divorce, and the *former* spouse has the burden of proving that there was no divorce. Thus, if the former spouse fails to rebut this last-in-time marriage presumption, then the subsequent spouse will prevail.[159] An earlier spouse will only be able to rebut this last-in-time marriage presumption by searching all the divorce records where the deceased resided, or might have resided, in order to prove that no divorce decree was ever granted to the deceased spouse. Otherwise, the presumption will not be rebutted.[160] However, if the prior wife does present evidence that no divorce proceedings were instituted in any jurisdiction where the husband might reasonably have pursued them, then the presumption would be rebutted.[161]

Nevertheless, this last-in-time marriage presumption in the vast majority of American jurisdictions continues to exist as "one of the strongest presumptions known to the law" since "the law presumes morality and legitimacy, not immorality and bastardy."[162] Accordingly, this last-in-time marriage presumption applies with equal force to valid common law marriages,[163] as well as to valid statutory marriages.[164]

---

[158] *See infra* § 2.08[C].

[159] *See generally* Swisher & Jones, *The Last-in-Time Marriage Presumption*, 29 Fam. L. Q. 409 (1995); Annot., *Presumption as to the Validity of Second Marriage*, 14 A.L.R.2d 7 and Later Case Service.

[160] *See, e.g., Hewitt v. Firestone Tire & Rubber Co.*, 490 F. Supp. 1358 (E.D. Va. 1980); *Miller v. Harley-Davidson Motor Co.*, 328 N.W.2d 348 (Iowa Ct. App. 1982). This is the majority view. There is a minority view in a small number of states, however, that all the prior spouse has to do to rebut the last-in-time marriage presumption is offer evidence of a valid marriage, and the burden of proof then shifts to the subsequent spouse to demonstrate that there *was* a divorce. *See, e.g., Tatum v. Tatum*, 241 F.2d 401 (9th Cir. 1957) (applying Cal. law); *Glover v. Glover*, 322 S.E.2d 755 (Ga. Ct. App. 1984). The *Glover* rationale, however, is criticized in 21 Mercer L. Rev. 465.

[161] *See, e.g., Davis v. Davis*, 521 S.W.2d 603 (Tex. 1975).

[162] *See, e.g., Parker v. Am. Lumber Co.*, 56 S.E.2d 214 (Va. 1949).

[163] *See supra* § 2.05[A].

[164] *See supra* § 2.04. *See generally* Swisher & Jones, *The Last-in-Time Marriage Presumption*, 29 Fam. L. Q. 409 (1995).

§ 2.07   Proof of Marriage

A valid marriage license or a certified copy of the marriage record will normally constitute prima facie evidence of such a marriage. Also, a presumption of marriage is based upon marital cohabitation and repute, and this strong presumption can be overcome only by cogent and satisfactory proof that there was *no* valid marriage.[165] According to *Wigmore on Evidence*, a valid marriage may be proven by: (1) offering a valid marriage certificate or a record of the marriage;[166] (2) offering testimony of eyewitnesses who were present at the marriage ceremony;[167] or (3) offering evidence of matrimonial cohabitation and community repute.[168]

§ 2.08   Capacity and Intent to Marry

Assuming that the parties have met the legal requirements for a formal[169] or informal[170] marriage, they still must possess the legal *capacity* and *intent* to marry. If either the husband or the wife lacks this legal capacity or intent to marry, then the marriage may be *void* (also referred to as *void ab initio* or absolutely void), or *voidable*, depending on the seriousness of the marital impediment.[171] These marital impediments may therefore constitute grounds to *annul* the marriage.[172]

[A]   Void and Voidable Marriages

The historical distinction between void and voidable marriages, based upon a lack of capacity or intent to marry, arose as a result of jurisdictional conflicts between English ecclesiastical courts and English civil courts: If the marriage could be attacked after the death of one of the spouses, then it was a void *ab initio* marriage. But if the marriage could *not* be attacked after the death of either spouse, even though it was invalid under canon law, then the marriage was voidable only, and the surviving spouse was entitled to all marital property and support rights. When Henry VIII and the Church of England broke away from the Roman Catholic Church, however, no annulment of marriage-including Henry's-could be appealed

---

[165] *See, e.g., McClaugherty v. McClaugherty*, 21 S.E.2d 761 (Va. 1942) ("In the interest of morality and decency the law presumes marriage between a man and a woman when they live together as man and wife. . . . While it is true, however, that cohabitation and repute do not constitute marriage, they do constitute strong evidence tending to raise a presumption of marriage, and the burden is on him who denies the marriage to offer countervailing evidence."). *See also* Swisher, *Proving the Validity of a Marriage*, 43 Virginia Lawyer 29 (December, 1994).

[166] 5 Wigmore on Evidence § 1645 (1974 ed.)

[167] 7 Wigmore on Evidence §§ 2082–2088 (1978 ed.)

[168] 9 Wigmore on Evidence, § 2505 (1981 ed.). This would constitute evidence of a common law marriage, but it would only raise a *presumption* of a formal statutory marriage.

[169] *See supra* § 2.04.

[170] *See supra* § 2.05.

[171] *See infra* § 2.08[A].

[172] *See infra* § 2.10.

to the Pope in Rome, and thus void and voidable marriages both came under English common law jurisdiction. Under present-day American family law, a defective marriage is classified as either *void ab initio* or *voidable* based upon the seriousness of the marital defect.[173]

A void *ab initio* marriage is a legal nullity, incapable of possessing any marital consequences. Thus, the parties to a void *ab initio* marriage can never ratify it, and such marriages may be collaterally attacked by either "spouse," by any interested third party, or by the State—even after the death of either "spouse."[174]

Examples of void *ab initio* marriages in the majority of states are: same sex marriage; bigamous or polygamous marriage; and incestuous marriage. In a minority of states, underage marriage is also void *ab initio*. Since a void *ab initio* marriage is a legal nullity from its inception, no formal annulment action is necessary, but an annulment action may still be brought to establish a legal record of the void *ab initio* marriage.[175]

A voidable marriage, on the other hand, is valid for all civil purposes unless it is annulled[176] in a direct proceeding by either the husband or the wife. The marital defect in a voidable marriage may therefore be condoned and ratified by the parties, and when one of the spouses dies, an annulment action cannot be brought by the other spouse. Likewise, interested third parties and the State generally cannot attack a voidable marriage.[177] Examples of voidable marriages in most jurisdictions are: underage marriage; fraudulent marriage; marriage under duress; marriage to a mental incompetent; sham marriage; and marriage in jest. In some states a voidable marriage may also be annulled for: natural and incurable impotency of the body; marriage to a felon or prostitute; or marriage to a spouse who is pregnant by another man, or who has at a time close to the marriage impregnated another woman. When a voidable marriage is annulled in a formal proceeding, this voidable marriage then becomes a void marriage.

This traditional common law distinction between void and voidable marriages is therefore of crucial importance in determining any spousal support or marital property rights, because with a void *ab initio* marriage there are no marital rights, but with a voidable marriage, in the absence of a formal annulment action, both spouses still retain all property and support rights that normally devolve upon them by reason of their marriage.[178]

---

[173] *See generally* Goda, *The Historical Evolution of the Concepts of Void and Voidable Marriages,* 7 J. Fam. L. 297 (1967); Note, *The Void and Voidable Marriage: A Study in Judicial Method,* 7 Stan. L. Rev. 529 (1955); Wrenn, *In Search of a Balanced Procedural Law for Marriage and Nullity Cases,* 46 Jurist 602 (1986).

[174] *Id.*

[175] *Id. But see supra* § 2.05[E].

[176] *See infra* § 2.10.

[177] *Id.*

[178] *See generally infra* § 2.10[C].

[B] Same Sex Marriage

Historically, marriage has been defined as the voluntary union of one man and one woman to the exclusion of all others, and most states therefore have refused to permit marriages between two persons of the same sex.[179] Thus, same sex marriages are held to be void *ab initio* in the vast majority of states, since state prohibitions against marriages between persons of the same sex were held not to offend state or federal constitutional due process rights or equal protection rights.[180] For example, in a family law context, a constitutional right to privacy has been applied to married couples,[181] and to unmarried heterosexuals.[182] But such a right to privacy had not yet been recognized to include a consensual homosexual relationship.[183]

However in the 1993 case of *Baehr v. Lewin*,[184] the Hawaii Supreme Court found that sex was a suspect category for purposes of equal protection analysis under the Hawaii Constitution, and therefore any prohibition of same-sex marriage in Hawaii must be subject to a strict scrutiny constitutional analysis.[185] The Hawaii Supreme Court remanded the case back to the trial court, which subsequently held that the State of Hawaii had *not* established a compelling state interest to prohibit same-sex marriages in Hawaii, and thus the trial court recognized the validity of same-sex marriages in Hawaii.[186]

In the wake of the *Baehr* decision, a number of states enacted legislation providing that they would not recognize same-sex marriages if validly

---

[179] *See generally* Homer Clark, The Law of Domestic Relations in the United States 75–80 (1988).

[180] *See, e.g., In re Estate of Cooper*, 564 N.Y.S.2d 684 (N.Y. Sur. Ct. 1990); *Baker v. Nelson*, 191 N.W.2d 185 (Minn. 1971); *Dean v. District of Columbia*, 653 A.2d 307 (D.C. Ct. App. 1995); *Jones v. Hallahan*, 501 S.W.2d 588 (Ky. Ct. App. 1973); *De Santo v. Barnsley*, 476 A.2d 952 (Pa. Super. Ct. 1982); *Slayton v. State*, 633 S.W.2d 934 (Tex. Ct. App. 1982). But *see also M.T. v. J.T.*, 355 A.2d 204 (N.J. Super Ct. App. Div. 1976) (transsexual marriage held to be valid).

[181] *See, e.g., Griswold v. Connecticut*, 381 U.S. 479 (1965).

[182] *See, e.g., Eisenstadt v. Baird*, 405 U.S. 438 (1972).

[183] *See, e.g., Bowers v. Hardwick*, 418 U.S. 186 (1986) (upholding a Georgia sodomy statute). Justice Powell, the swing vote in this 5-4 decision, later admitted that he had probably erred in voting to uphold the constitutionality of the state sodomy statute. *See, e.g.,* John Jeffries Jr., Justice Lewis F. Powell Jr., 530 (1994) ("I think I probably made a mistake on that one," Powell said of *Bowers*. . . "When I had the opportunity to reread the opinions a few months later, I thought the dissent had the better of the arguments.")

[184] *Baehr v. Lewin*, 852 P.2d 44 (Haw. 1993).

[185] *Id.*

Baehr et al. v. Miike, No. 91-1394, 1996 Westlaw 69235 (Haw. Cir. Ct. 1996) Not surprisingly, the *Baehr* case has received both support and criticism from a number of legal scholars. *See, e.g.,* Coolridge, *Same-Sex Marriage? Baehr v. Miike and the Meaning of Marriage*, 38 S. Tex. L. Rev. 1 (1997); Wardle, *The Potential Impact of Homosexual Parenting on Children*, 1997 U. Ill. L. Rev. 8, 884–891 (1997) (arguing that the decision "leaves much to be desired in terms of fair summarization of the evidence, and thorough legasl analysis"). For a rather spirited dialogue, pro and con, on same-sex marriage, *see* Kendle, *Principles and Prejudice: Lesbian and Gay Civil Marriage and the Realization of Equality*, 22 J. Comp. L. 81 (1996); and Kohm, *A Reply to "Principles and Prejudice": Marriage and the Realization that Principles Win Over Political Will*, 22 J. Comp. L. 293 (1996).

[186] *Baehr et al. v. Miike*, No. 91-1394, 1996 Westlaw 694235 (Haw. Cir. Ct. 1996).

contracted in another state (such as Hawaii) under the rationale that same-sex marriages would be against the state's strong public policy.[187] Congress further enacted a so-called Defense of Marriage Act,[188] which amended 28 U.S.C. Section 1738C to provide that no state, territory, or possession of the United States shall be required to give full faith and credit to any sister state same-sex marriage.[189] Some commentators, however, have questions whether these state and federal legislators have the constitutional power to enact such laws.[190] The *Baehr* decision was rendered moot when the Hawaiian voters subsequently passed a constitutional amendment prohibiting same-sex marriages in Hawaii, although the Hawaiian legislature also passed corresponding domestic partnership legislation relating to homosexual and heterosexual cohabiting couples.[191]

In 1999, the Vermont Supreme Court in the case of *Baker v. State*[192] declared that the State of Vermont was constitutionally required to extend to same-sex couples "the common benefits and protections that flow from marriage under Vermont law," but "whether this ultimately takes the form of inclusion within the marriage laws themselves or a parallel domestic partnership system or some equivalent statutory alternative, rests with the Legislature."[193] The Vermont legislature subsequently enacted "civil union" domestic partnership legislation in lieu of recognizing same-sex marriage in Vermont.[194]

Thus it appears that although a large number of legal scholars and other commentators support the principle of same-sex marriage on legal, social, and constitutional grounds,[195] a large number of Americans and most state

---

[187] *See, e.g.,* Ariz. Rev. Stat. Ann. 25-101[C] (1996); Conn. Gen. Stat. Ann. 46a-81r (1995); Ill. Comp. Stat. Ann. 5/213.1 (1996); Utah Code Ann. 30-1-2 (1995); Va. Code Ann. 20-45.2 (1997).

[188] 110 Stat. 2419 (1996).

[189] *Id.* The Act also amended 1 U.S.C. Sec. 7 by adding a definition of "marriage" and "spouse" that would affect any ruling, regulation, or interpretation made by any federal bureau or administrative agency in the United States. The term *marriage* under the statute means only a legal union between one man and one woman as husband and wife, and the term *spouse* refers only to a member of the opposite sex who is either a husband or wife.

[190] *See, e.g.,* Kramer, *Same Sex Marriage, Conflict of Laws, and the Unconstitutional Public Policy Exception,* 106 Yale L.J. 1965, 2008 (1997) (arguing that "if states cannot selectively discriminate against each other's laws, Congress cannot authorize them to do it"). *See also* Guillerman, *Comment, The Defense of Marriage Act: The Latest Maneuver in the Continuing Battle to Legalize Same-Sex Marriage,* 34 Houston L. Rev. 425 (1997); Note, *The Defense of Marriage Act and the Overextension of Congressional Authority,* 97 Colum. L. Rev. 1435 (1997).

[191] *See generally* Chapter 2.02[C] *supra.*

[192] *Baker v. State,* 744 A.2d 864 (Vt. 1999)

[193] *Id.* at 867.

[194] *See generally* Chapter 2.02[C] *supra.*

[195] *See, e.g.,* Friedman, *The Necessity for State Recognition of Same Sex Marriage,* 3 Berkeley Women's L.J. 134 (1987–88); Buchanan, *Same Sex Marriage: The Linchpin Issue,* 10 U. Dayton L. Rev. 541 (1985); Note, *From This Day Forward: A Feminine Moral Discourse on Homosexual Marriage,* 97 Yale L.J. 1783 (1988); Note, *Homosexual's Right to Marry: A Constitutional Text and a Legislative Solution,* 128 U. Pa. L. Rev. 193 (1979); Note, *The Legality of Homosexual Marriage,* 82 Yale L.J. 573 (1973). *See generally* Same Sex Marriage: Pro and Con (Andrew

and federal legislators remain opposed to the recognition of same-sex marriage. Why this apparent dichotomy? Professor William Galston, speaking of American family law reform generally, observes: :

> [I]n a democratic society, we are compelled to reflect on the public culture of that society. We can, of course, draw moral principles from our scholarly work and from our philosophical speculation, which is entirely appropriate. But there are also moral principles at work in the culture as a whole. The balance that is to be struck between our private philosophical and scholarly conceptions of what is just, or where responsibility lies, for example, and what the public culture of society believes, about those same issues is an important question. I would submit that in a democracy, we are not free to ignore the public culture in which people believe. We cannot end our more and practical reflection with that, but we must take it into account.[196]

[C] Bigamous and Polygamous Marriage

Bigamous, polygamous, or plural marriages are void *ab initio* in the vast majority of American jurisdictions, and are further proscribed by state bigamy statutes.[197]

Polygamy has been defined as having several spouses at the same time, while bigamy has been defined as contracting a second marriage while the first marriage is still subsisting. Traditionally, state bigamy statutes do not require specific intent for a criminal conviction, but the Model Penal Code and a few recent judicial cases now require a guilty intent for a bigamy conviction.[198]

Sullivan, ed. 1997); and William Eskridge, The Case for Same Sex Marriage: From Sexual Liberty to Civilized Commitment (1997).

Not all advocates of gay and lesbian rights, however, support the concept of same-sex marriage. *See, e.g.*, Polikoff, *We Will Get What We Ask For: Why Legalizing Gay and Lesbian Marriage Will Not Dismantle the Legal Structure of Gender in Every Marriage*, 79 Va. L. Rev. 1535, 1549 (1993) ("Advocating lesbian and gay marriage will detract from, even contradict, efforts to unhook economic benefits from marriage and make basic health care and other necessities available to all"). *See also* Homer, *Against Marriage*, 29 Harv. C. Rts-C. L. L. Rev. 505, 515–516 (1994); and Ettelbrick, *Wedlock Alert: A Comment on Lesbian and Gay Family Recognition*, 5 J. L. & Policy 107 (1996) (favoring the attempt to broaden a definition of family to include gay and lesbian relationships, but rejecting any efforts to bring such relationships within a marriage rubric).

[196] Galston, *Public Morality and Public Policy: The Case of Children and Family Policy*, 36 Santa Clara L. Rev. 313, 314–315 (1996). *See also* Posner, *Should There be Homosexual Marriage? And If So, Who Should Decide?* 95 Mich. L. Rev. 1578 (1997) (critiquing William Eskridge's *The Case for Same Sex Marriage: From Sexual Liberty to Civilized Commitment* (1997) and finding Eskridge's argument for state legislative reform to be persuasive and compelling, but rejecting Eskridge's contention that the Constitution should be interpreted as granting the right to same-sex marriage).

[197] *See, e.g., Reynold v. United States*, 98 U.S. 145 (1878); Potter *v. Murray City*, 760 F.2d 1065 (10th Cir. 1985) (applying Utah law); *Rance v. Rance*, 587 N.E.2d 150 (Ind. Ct. App. 1992); *see also* Slovenko, *The De Facto Decriminalization of Bigamy*, 17 J. Fam. L. 297 (1978).

[198] *See generally* S. Green & J. Long, Marriage and Family Law Agreements 37–40 (1984).

To prevent an innocent spouse who in good faith erroneously believes the other spouse to be dead, and remarries, from being found guilty of violating a state's traditional bigamy statute, many states have adopted a so-called "Enoch Arden" statute.[199] "Enoch Arden" statutes establish a time period — normally five to seven years— after which a spouse may remarry with a good faith belief that the absent spouse is dead. However, it is important to note that "Enoch Arden" statutes do *not* validate the subsequent marriage; they only prevent a criminal prosecution for bigamy.[200]

Although bigamous or polygamous marriages are prohibited in the vast majority of American states, such marriages are legally recognized in many African, Asian, and Muslim countries, and although the practice of polygamy is in a decline throughout the Muslim world due to various social and economic factors, arguments in favor of its legality and morality are still being made. Four most commonly advanced arguments supporting polygamy are as follows:

(1) The Koran, like the Old Testament of the Bible, gives religious authority to a man having more than one wife;

(2) Polygamy is justified when the wife is barren or unwell, allowing the husband to have children without divorcing his first wife or leaving her illprovided for;

(3) Polygamy helps to prevent immorality, such as prostitution, rape, fornication, adultery, and the high divorce rate found in many Western monogamous societies; and

(4) Polygamy protects widows and orphans by catering to the possibility of a greater excess of women over men in time of war or other disasters.[201]

Similar arguments have been made supporting plural marriages in the United States, including the rising incidence of extra-marital sex, and a soaring American divorce rate.[202] Other commentators have suggested that judicial decisions subsequent to *Reynolds v. United States* that have upheld an individual's fundamental right to the free exercise of religion[203] might now make the *Reynolds* prohibition against plural marriage a candidate for judicial reconsideration.[204]

---

[199] So named after Alfred Lord Tennyson's 1864 poem entitled *Enoch Arden*.

[200] *See, e.g., Anonymous v. Anonymous*, 62 N.Y.S.2d 130 (N.Y. Sup. Ct. 1946); *see also* Fenton & Kaufman, *Enoch Arden Revisited*, 13 J. Fam. L. 245 (1973–74). *But see infra* § 2.06.

[201] *See generally* K. Hodkinson, Muslim Family Law: A Sourcebook 107–108 (1981).

[202] *See, e.g.,* Nedrow, *Polygamy and the Right to Marry: New Life for an Old Lifestyle*, 11 Mem. St. U. L. Rev. 303 (1981).

[203] *See, e.g., Sherbert v. Verner*, 374 U.S. 398 (1963) (involving the wrongful discharge of a Seventh Day Adventist from her state job for refusing to work on Saturdays, the Sabbath Day of her faith); *Wisconsin v. Yoder*, 406 U.S. 205 (1972) (involving Amish whose religious beliefs exempted them from attending public schools beyond the eighth grade).

[204] In a concurring and dissenting opinion to *Yoder*, Justice Douglas noted that *Yoder* opened the way to give religious beliefs a broader base than previously recognized, and he opined that in time *Reynolds* would be overruled. 406 U.S. 205, 247. Professor Lawrence Tribe has suggested that after *Sherbert* the *Reynolds* case may be a candidate for constitutional

Finally, even though most American jurisdictions will not recognize a bigamous or polygamous marriage, even though it may be valid in the country where the plural marriage was celebrated, some states nevertheless may recognize such a bigamous or polygamous marriage as a putative marriage.[205]

[D] Incestuous Marriage: Prohibited Degrees of Kinship

Incestuous marriages are proscribed in Biblical teachings,[206] and they are prohibited in a majority of states as void *ab initio* marriages. The problem, however, is ascertaining what particular degrees of kinship are prohibited by state statute.

Incestuous marriages can be prohibited either by consanguinity (relationship through bloodlines, such as marrying one's parent or one's sibling) or by legal affinity (relationship by marriage, such as marrying one's mother-in-law). An example of a traditional statute is found in a provision of the Annotated Laws of Massachusetts (1983) that was first enacted in 1785:

> (1) No man may marry his mother, grandmother, daughter, granddaughter, sister, stepmother, grandfather's wife, grandson's wife, wife's mother, wife's grandmother, wife's daughter, wife's granddaughter, brother's daughter, sister's daughter, father's sister, or mother's sister. (In 1983, son's wife was deleted.)

> (2) No woman shall marry her father, grandfather, son, grandson, brother, stepfather, grandmother's husband, daughter's husband, granddaughter's husband, husband's grandfather, husband's son, husband's grandson, brother's son, sister's son, father's brother, or mother's brother. (In 1983, husband's father was deleted.)[207]

In approximately half the states, first-cousin marriages are also prohibited.[208]

A growing number of states, however, have adopted a less restrictive and better reasoned approach to incestuous marriage based upon section 207 of the Uniform Marriage and Divorce Act. With minor amendments, these statutes generally provide that a marriage is incestuous and void only if it is between: (1) an ancestor and descendent; (2) a brother and sister of either half or whole blood, or, in some states, by adoption; or (3) an uncle and niece, or aunt and nephew.[209]

---

reconsideration. L. Tribe, American Constitutional Law 853–854 (1978). To date, however, few courts have seriously questioned the *Reynolds* rationale for prohibiting bigamous or polygamous marriage. *See also* Davis, *Plural Marriage and Religious Freedom: The Impact of Reynolds v. United States*, 15 Ariz. L. Rev. 287 (1973).

[205] *See, e.g., In re Dalip Singh Bir's Estate*, 188 P.2d 499 (Cal. Ct. App. 1948); *see also* 1 H. Clark, Law of Domestic Relations 134–135 (2d ed. 1987); *see infra* 2.05[B].

[206] *See Leviticus* 18:6-24.

[207] Mass. Ann. Laws ch. 207, §§ 1-2 (1983).

[208] *See, e.g., In re Marriage of Adams*, 604 P.2d 332 (Mont. 1979). *But see* Moore, *A Defense of First Cousin Marriage*, 10 Clev. Mar. L. Rev. 139 (1961).

[209] *See, e.g.,* Cal. Civ. Code § 4400 (1970); N.Y. Dom. Rel. Law § 5 (McKinney 1971); Va. Code Ann. § 20-38.1 (Michie 1975).

In addition to its religious proscription, incest prohibitions have also been justified based upon genetic and eugenics grounds, but this rationale has been seriously questioned by various writers.[210] Perhaps the strongest basis for justifying a prohibition against such marriages is the historical and sociological incest taboo, where survival of family harmony is dependent on prohibiting sexual rivalries.[211]

In some instances, close relatives, such as first cousins, procure an evasionary incestuous marriage in a sister state that legally recognizes such marriages, and then return to their domiciliary state. Some domiciliary states will not recognize such an evasionary incestuous marriage, on the grounds that it is against the domiciliary state's strong public policy.[212] Other states, however, would recognize such an evasionary marriage in order to validate the parties' marital expectations.[213]

Professor Carolyn Bratt has questioned many of the moral and legal difficulties in defining and justifying various statutory prohibitions against incestuous marriages. She writes:

> The mere word "incest" triggers strong feelings of revulsion in most people. Therefore, any *a priori* labeling of a marriage as incestuous tends to preclude objective thought about the permissibility of the particular form of the marriage prohibition at issue. Such revulsion stems largely from the confusion of incest with sexual abuse of children. This confusion is not limited to the general public, but extends to the courts as well. . . . Nevertheless, one must understand the distinction between state incest statutes as a vehicle for prohibiting and punishing sexual abuse of minors and state incest statutes as a marriage prohibition for adults. The rightful condemnation of the intrinsically abusive nature of adult-child sexual relationships must not be used to shield incest statutes prohibiting marriage between certain adults from an objective evaluation. . . . Once one recognizes these analytical difficulties-reflexive fears, shifting definitions of incest itself, ambivalent attitudes, and facile underlying generalizations-one can begin to rationally evaluate the validity of state incest statutes in the light of the constitutional right to marry. After making such an analysis, this author has concluded that neither the civil marriage bar nor the criminal bar against incestuous acts serves any valid purpose which cannot be better served by statutes which do not impinge on the constitutional right to marry.[214]

---

[210] *See, e.g.,* C. Stem, Principles of Human Genetics (3d ed. 1973); H. Maisch, Incest (1972).

[211] *See, e.g.,* Murdock, Social Structure 292–313 (1949). *See generally* Storke, *The Incestuous Marriage -Relic of the Past,* 36 U. Colo. L. Rev. 473 (1964); Bratt, *Incest Statutes and the Fundamental Right to Marry: Is Oedipus Free to Marry?* 18 Fam. L.Q. 257 (1984); Annot., 72 A.L.R.2d 706 and Later Case Service.

[212] *See, e.g., In re Estate of Stiles,* 391 N.E.2d 1026 (Ohio 1979); *In re Marriage of Adams,* 604 P.2d 332 (Mont. 1979); *see also infra* § 2.09.

[213] *See, e.g., Etheridge v. Shaddock,* 706 S.W.2d 395 (Ark. 1986) (first-cousin marriage); *In re May's Estate,* 114 N.E.2d 4 (N.Y. 1953) (uncle-niece marriage); *see also infra* § 2.09.

[214] Bratt, *Incest Statutes and the Fundamental Right to Marry: Is Oedipus Free to Marry?* 18 Fam. L. Q. 257, 257–258 (1984).

[E] Underage Marriage

Under the early common law, a marriage before the age of discretion rendered that marriage void *ab initio*. However, a majority of American jurisdictions now treat an underage marriage as merely voidable.[215] Statutory age restrictions for marriage are widely considered necessary to prevent minor, immature persons from entering into unstable marriages that are likely to fail. Accordingly, in most American jurisdictions, a man and a woman are free to marry without parental consent at the age of majority, normally 18 years of age, or older. The consent of a parent or a parent substitute, however, is required for certain underage marriages, most often for 16-and 17-year-olds, and a majority of states also provide for additional "exceptional circumstances," such as when the expectant bride is pregnant.[216]

Age restrictions to marriage have been held to be constitutional. In the case of *Moe v. Dinkins*,[217] a federal court judge, applying New York law, held that although the right to marry is a fundamental constitutional right, nevertheless there was no total deprivation of a minor's right to marry without parental consent, only a delay. Therefore the judge applied a rational relationship test in light of the state interest in protecting minors in particular and marriage in general.[218]

The courts have split on the issue of whether an underage spouse is able to annul his or her own marriage. Some courts have held that the minor's fraudulent misrepresentation of age bars such an annulment action based upon estoppel, or an "unclean hands," argument.[219]

Should a domiciliary state recognize an underage evasionary marriage of its citizens in a sister state? Again, the courts have split on this issue. On one hand, some courts have granted an annulment based upon the fact that such an evasionary underage marriage was against the domiciliary state's strong public policy.[220] But other courts have held that a domiciliary state has no strong public policy that would require the court to invalidate a sister state underage evasionary marriage, even though that marriage was contrary to the domiciliary state's law.[221]

---

[215] *See, e.g., Holbert v. West*, 710 F. Supp. 50 (E.D. Ky. 1990) (applying Ky. law).

[216] *See generally* Wardle, *Rethinking Marital Age Restrictions*, 22 J. Fam. L. 1 (1983–84); Comment, *Capacity, Parental Power, and a Minor's Right to Remain Married*, 22 Santa Clara L. Rev. 447 (1982). Prof. Wardle argues, however, that although legal policy should still discourage underage marriages, once the underage marriage has occurred, it ought to be vindicated, rather than annulled under an "escape valve" annulment proceeding.

[217] 533 F. Supp. 623 (S.D.N.Y. 1981).

[218] *Id.*

[219] *Compare Ruiz v. Ruiz*, 85 Cal. Rptr. 674 (Cal. Ct. App. 1970) (annulment was granted to the parent, acting as the minor's guardian ad litem, who was not a party to the minor's fraudulent misrepresentation of his age) *with Duley v. Duley*, 151 A.2d 826 (D.C. 1959) (the petition for annulment was denied, apparently based on an "unclean hands" defense).

[220] *See, e.g., Wilkins v. Zelichowski*, 140 A.2d 65 (N.J. 1958); *see also infra* § 2.09.

[221] *See, e.g., State v. Graves*, 307 S.W.2d 545 (Ark. 1957); *see also infra* § 2.09.

[F] Mental and Physical Incapacity

[1] Mental Incapacity

Under the common law, marriage to a mentally incompetent person was held to be void *ab initio*, and this view is still recognized in a minority of states. An increasing number of jurisdictions, however, by statutory or case law, have treated marriage to a mentally incapacitated person as voidable, rather than void *ab initio*. For example, Section 208 of the Uniform Marriage and Divorce Act provides in part that:

> (a) The . . . court shall enter its decree declaring the invalidity of a marriage entered into under the following circumstances: (1) a party lacked capacity to consent to the marriage at the time the marriage was solemnized, either because of mental incapacity or infirmity or because of the influence of alcohol, drugs, or other incapacitating substances. . . .

The test for mental capacity to consent at the time the marriage is performed has been defined by some courts as a capacity to understand the nature of the marital contract, as well as a capacity to understand the duties and responsibilities of marriage.[222] Other courts, however, have held that the only legal requirement is the ability to consent at the time of the marriage, without any additional duties or responsibilities test, in order to validate the marital expectations of the parties.[223]

Indeed, a number of courts have held that even though a person might have been previously adjudged to be legally incompetent to handle his or her business affairs, nevertheless such a person might still be competent to marry, by applying a lesser test of competency for marriage than for other business purposes, again to validate the public policy of promoting marriage in general, and to validate the marital expectations of the parties in particular.[224]

[2] Physical Incapacity

Physical incapacity, defined as the natural and incurable impotency of the body, also generally results in a voidable marriage whenever a party lacks the physical capacity to consummate the marriage by sexual intercourse, and at the time the marriage was solemnized the other party did not know of the incapacity.[225]

---

[222] *See, e.g., Kerckhoff v. Kerckhoff*, 805 S.W.2d 937 (Tex. Civ. App. 1991); *Homan v. Homan*, 147 N.W.2d 630 (Neb. 1967); *Forbis v. Forbis*, 274 S.W.2d 800 (Mo. 1955).

[223] *See, e.g., Young v. Colorado Nat'l Bank*, 365 P.2d 701 (Colo. 1961).

[224] *See, e.g., Geitner v. Geitner*, 312 S.E.2d 235 (N.C. Ct. App. 1984); *Edwards v. Edwards*, 287 N.W.2d 420 (Neb. 1980). *See generally* Shaman, *Persons who are Mentally Retarded: Their Right to Marry and Have Children*, 12 Fam. L.Q. 61 (1978); Linn & Bowers, *Historical Fallacies Behind Legal Prohibitions of Marriage Involving Mentally Retarded Persons*, 13 Gonz. L. Rev. 625 (1978); Note, *The Right of the Mentally Disabled to Marry*, 15 J. Fam. L. 463 (1977).

[225] Uniform Marriage and Divorce Act, § 208(a)(2).

It has been held that "incurable impotency" under a state annulment statute includes the inability to copulate, whether such inability arose from a physical or mental defect.[226] Moreover, under a common law doctrine of triennial cohabitation, if the couple lived together for three years or more, but the wife is still a virgin, the husband will be presumed to be impotent, and he would have the burden of proving that he was not at fault.[227]

A wife may be impotent, even though she had become pregnant and miscarried, according to the case of *T. v. M.*,[228] where a New Jersey judge held that a wife may be incurably impotent, due to vaginismus, a vaginal disorder preventing intercourse, despite her ability to conceive. Thus, impotence is not necessarily equated to sterility.[229]

[G] Fraudulent Marriage

A marriage procured by fraud is a voidable marriage according to case and statutory law in most states. The problem, however, is to ascertain the *degree* of fraud necessary to annul such a marriage.

The influential early case of *Reynolds v. Reynolds*[230] established a two-prong test for determining a fraudulent marriage: (1) there must be material fraud; and (2) the fraud must affect the essentials of the present marriage. Material fraud generally means "but for" the fraud, there would have been no marriage. The "essentials of the present marriage" test is harder to define, because the fraud must adversely affect "the *possibility* of normal marital cohabitation."[231] Thus, examples of material fraud that *do* affect the essentials of the marriage have included: lying about an intent not to have sexual intercourse, or not to have children during the marriage; concealment of impotency or venereal disease; concealment of pregnancy by another person; and lying about one's religious beliefs. However, examples of material fraud that do not affect the essentials of the marriage under the traditional rule have included lying about a party's character, chastity, age, health, wealth, citizenship, ancestry, number of prior marriages and divorces, or lack of love and affection.[232]

---

[226] *See, e.g., Rickards v. Rickards,* 166 A.2d 425 (Del. 1960).

[227] *See, e.g., Tompkins v. Tompkins,* 111 A. 599 (N.J. Ch. Ct. 1920). *See also* Annot., 28 A.L.R.2d 499 and Later Case Service.

[228] 242 A.2d 670 (N.J. Super Ct. Ch. Div. 1968).

[229] *Id. See generally* Annot., *Incapacity for Sexual Intercourse as a Ground for Annulment,* 52 A.L.R.3d 589 (1973).

[230] 85 Mass. 605 (1862). The *Reynolds* case was commented upon in 13 Harv. L. Rev. 110 (1899).

[231] *See* Kingsley, *What are the Proper Grounds for Granting Annulments?* 18 Law & Contemp. Probs. 39 (1953).

[232] *See, e.g., V.J.S. v. M.J.B.,* 592 A.2d 328 (N.J. Super. Ct. Ch. Div. 1991); *E.D.M. v. T.A.M.,* 415 S.E.2d 812 (S.C. 1992); *Haacke v. Glenn,* 814 P.2d 1157 (Utah 1991); *see also* Kingsley, *Fraud as a Ground for Annulment of Marriage,* 18 S. Cal. L. Rev. 213 (1945); Vanmeman, *Annulment of Marriage for Fraud,* 9 Minn. L. Rev. 497 (1925).

A more modern approach to fraudulent marriage, primarily adopted by the courts in New York, encompasses this material fraud test, but rejects the essentials of the present marriage test.[233]

If the wife misrepresents to the husband that she is pregnant at the time of the marriage, when in fact she is not pregnant, the majority of courts have held that the marriage is not fraudulent. Under a traditional majority rule, the courts have generally held that the representation of false pregnancy does *not* go to the "essentials" of the marriage, since the wife is not prevented from performing her other marital duties.[234] Nor will the courts extricate the husband who has created his "own dilemma" based upon his illicit premarital intercourse, and he is therefore barred from bringing an annulment action based on such fraud under the *in pari delicto* or "unclean hands" doctrine.[235]

Other courts, however, have adopted an opposing view, holding that a misrepresentation of pregnancy would indeed constitute material fraud, and that the gravity of such fraud should *not* be barred by any *in pari delicto* or "unclean hands" defense.[236]

[H] Marriage under Duress

In most states, by case or statutory law, a marriage where the consent of one of the parties was obtained by duress is a voidable marriage. Duress must have existed at the time of the marriage, where the complaining party could not act as a free agent in entering into the marriage due to coercive force or fear from another person. Moreover, many courts have held that the test for duress is a subjective test, rather than being based on the reasonable person of ordinary prudence standard.[237]

There have been various situations where a young man seduces a young woman, and she becomes pregnant. The judge then threatens to prosecute

---

[233] *See, e.g., Tacchi v. Tacchi*, 195 N.Y.S.2d 892 (N.Y. Sup. Ct. 1959) (misrepresentation of age); *Schinken v. Schinken*, 68 N.Y.S.2d 470 (N.Y. App. Div. 1947) (misrepresentation of love and affection). *But see Sangimino v. Sangimino*, 575 N.Y.S.2d 515 (N.Y. App. Div. 1991) (annulment action brought on the basis of fraud was denied since husband's alleged fraud did not evince a high degree of moral turpitude). Most cases following this "modern" approach to fraudulent marriage come from New York, and some commentators have pointed out that due to the extreme difficulty of getting a divorce in New York prior to 1970, far more New Yorkers sued for annulment to end their marriage, or obtained a migratory divorce in another state. *See* Note, *Annulments for Fraud -New York's Answer to Reno?* 48 Colum. L. Rev. 900 (1948).

[234] *See, e.g., Hill v. Hill*, 398 N.E.2d 1048 (Ill. App. Ct. 1979); *Husband v. Wife*, 262 A.2d 656 (Del. Super. Ct. 1970); *see also* Annot., 15 A.L.R.2d 706 and Later Case Service.

[235] *See, e.g., Tyminski v. Tyminski*, 221 N.E.2d 486 (Ohio Ct. C.P. 1966); *Brandt v. Brandt*, 167 So. 524 (Fla. 1936).

[236] *See, e.g., Parks v. Parks*, 418 S.W.2d 726 (Ky. Ct. App. 1967); *Masters v. Masters*, 108 N.W.2d 674 (Wis. 1961). For fraudulent inducement to marry actions, see *supra* § 3.02[B].

[237] *See, e.g., Stakelum v. Terral*, 126 So. 2d 689 (La. Ct. App. 1961); *Worthington v. Worthington*, 352 S.W.2d 80 (Ark. 1962). *See also* Kingsley, *Duress as a Ground for Annulment of Marriage*, 33 S. Cal. L. Rev. 1 (1959); Brown, *The Shotgun Marriage*, 42 Tul. L. Rev. 837 (1968); Bradley, *Duress and Arranged Marriages*, 46 Mod. L. Rev. 499 (1983); Annot., 16 A.L.R.2d 1430 and Later Case Service.

the young man under a state criminal seduction statute, under a state fornication statute, and contributing to the delinquency of a minor. Alternately, the court gives the young man the option of marrying the young woman in lieu of going to jail. Most courts have held that such a scenario would *not* constitute duress, since the young man still has a choice.[238]

[I] Sham Marriage

A sham marriage is a marriage for limited purposes and with a limited intent, such as a man marrying a pregnant woman only to legitimize their child, but without intending to consent to any of the other normal essentials of marriage. In this situation, many courts have held that such a marriage with limited intent and for a limited purpose is valid for *all* purposes, regardless of the parties' motive for marriage, and therefore no annulment of marriage may be granted.[239]

Sham marriages have also been utilized by various foreign nationals who marry American citizens in order to circumvent American immigration laws, and these so-called "green card" marriages may also constitute voidable sham marriages.[240] Accordingly, some courts have held that "green card" sham marriages for immigration purposes are invalid marriages.[241] Other courts, however, have held that the validity or invalidity of a "green card" sham marriage is irrelevant, since the foreign national can still be deported by the Immigration and Naturalization Service based upon the fraudulent purpose of the marriage.[242]

The confusion resulting from these conflicting court decisions regarding "green card" sham marriages has resulted in federal legislation and investigatory procedures that now cover all such marriages. Under the Immigration Marriage Fraud Amendments Act of 1986,[243] the granting of permanent residency based upon marital status now provides for a "conditional" permanent residency of two years before the alien attains "permanent" residence status. This provision of the Immigration Marriage Fraud

---

[238] *See, e.g., Figueroa v. Figueroa*, 110 N.Y.S.2d 550 (N.Y. Sup. Ct. 1952); *Jones v. Jones*, 314 S.W.2d 448 (Tex. Civ. App. 1958); *see also* Wadlington, *Shotgun Marriage by Operation of Law*, 1 Ga. L. Rev. 183 (1967); Note, *Coercive Power of the Criminal Seduction Statute*, 16 S.D. L. Rev. 166 (1971).

[239] *See, e.g., Schibi v. Schibi*, 69 A.2d 831 (Conn. 1949); *Bishop v. Bishop*, 308 N.Y.S.2d 998 (N.Y. Sup. Ct. 1970). *See generally* Wade, *Limited Purpose Marriages*, 45 Mod. L. Rev. 259 (1982); Comment, *Sham Marriages*, 20 U. Chi. L. Rev. 710 (1953); Annot., 14 A.L.R.2d 624 and Later Case Service.

[240] Indeed, House Report No. 99-906 (1986) stated that approximately 30% of all petitions for immigrant visas involve suspect marital relationships. *Id.* at 6.

[241] *See, e.g., United States v. Rubenstein*, 151 F.2d 915 (2d Cir. 1945), *cert. denied*, 326 U.S. 766 (1945); *United States v. Lutwak*, 195 F.2d 748 (7th Cir. 1952), *aff'd*, 344 U.S. 604 (1953). *But see United States v. Diogo*, 320 F.2d 898 (2d Cir. 1968) (two consummated "green card" marriages were held to be valid marriages).

[242] *See, e.g., Johl v. United States*, 370 F.2d 174 (9th Cir. 1967); *Roe v. Immigration & Naturalization Serv.*, 711 F.2d 1328 (9th Cir. 1985).

[243] Pub.L. No. 99-639, 100 Stat. 3537 (1986).

Act thus only affects aliens who have been married for less than two years. [244]

[J] Marriage in Jest

A marriage in jest, although it is based upon the apparent consent of the parties, actually involves no consent, since at least one of the parties realizes the marriage is no more than a "joke". However, because a marriage is presumed to be valid and possess the necessary element of mutual consent, the burden is on the party attempting to annul this voidable marriage to demonstrate that it was in fact a marriage in jest. [245]

The fact situation involving marriages in jest typically involves young people who, after a tennis match, dance, or another social engagement, dare each other to get married, and do so. In the relatively small number of reported cases, if such marriages remain unconsummated and the parties do not cohabit after the marriage, then the courts generally will be inclined to grant an annulment based upon the lack of voluntary consent, and based upon the parties' relative immaturity. [246]

However, other courts have taken the marriage relationship more seriously, and will not annul any marriage in jest, absent clear proof of fraud, duress, or mental incapacity. For example, in the case of *Hand v. Berry*, [247] a young couple dared each other to marry "in a spirit of hilarity and without serious intent," "in a spirit of fun, braggadocio, and levity," and "in a spirit of misguided fun and jest." The Georgia court was not amused, found no fraud, and held that the marriage was valid. [248]

§ 2.09   Conflict of Laws: Which Marriage Laws Govern?

Americans, as a migratory people, often move from state to state. Due to the large number and variety of differing state statutes that regulate marriage, [249] it becomes necessary to determine which particular law will govern the solemnization of marriage under applicable conflict of laws principles.

The traditional *lex loci contractus* rule states that the law of the place of celebration governs the legal requirements for marriage: that is to say, a marriage valid where celebrated is valid everywhere, unless that marriage violates a forum state's strong public policy. [250]

---

[244] *See generally* Note, *Immigration Marriage Fraud Amendments of 1986: Till Congress Do Us Part*, 41 U. Miami L. Rev. 1087 (1987).

[245] *See generally* Annot., 14 A.L.R.2d 624 and Later Case Service.

[246] *Id. See also Meredith v. Shakespeare*, 122 S.E.2d 520 (W. Va. 1924); *Davis v. Davis*, 175 A. 574 (Conn. 1934).

[247] 154 S.E. 239 (Ga. 1930).

[248] *Id. See also Lannamann v. Lannamann*, 89 A.2d 897, 898 (Pa. Super. Ct. 1952) ("since there was no fraud, duress, or lack of mental capacity, the marriage is valid").

[249] *See supra* § 1.03.

[250] *See, e.g.*, Restatement, Conflict of Laws §§ 121–123 (1934).

The more recent Restatement (Second) Conflict of Laws approach, adopted in a majority of the states, holds that the validity of a marriage is to be determined by the local law of the state which has the "most significant relationship" to the spouses and the marriage.[251] Section 283 (2) of the Second Restatement also provides that a marriage "which satisfies the requirements of the state where the marriage was contracted will everywhere be recognized as valid unless it violates the strong public policy of another state which has the most significant relationship to the spouses and the marriage."[252]

The corollary to this general rule that a marriage valid where contracted is valid everywhere would seem to be that a marriage not valid where contracted is not valid everywhere else, and a number of courts have adopted this corollary rule.[253] Other courts, however, in order to uphold marriage in general, and in order to validate the present expectations of the parties in particular, will look to the best of several possible forum rules to validate the marriage, even if such a marriage was invalid where contracted.[254]

§ 2.10 Annulment of Marriage

[A] Annulment Jurisdiction

Annulment is the legal determination that a void or voidable marriage was a legal nullity from its inception. An annulment action thus differs from a divorce action in that divorce is the dissolution of a legally valid marriage, where annulment is the legal declaration that a marriage never existed in the first place.

In order to annul a voidable marriage,[255] or in order to create a judicial record of a void *ab initio* marriage,[256] a court must have valid jurisdiction over the parties in the annulment proceeding.

The traditional minority rule is that the state where the marriage was contracted should have jurisdiction in an annulment action, unless the parties were domiciled in another state at the time of the marriage, in which case that domiciliary state should have jurisdiction.[257]

---

[251] *See* Restatement (Second) Conflict of Laws § 283(1) (1971).

[252] Restatement (Second) Conflict of Laws § 283(2) (1971). *See also* Restatement (Second) Conflict of Laws § 6 (1971).

[253] *See, e.g., Randall v. Randall*, 345 N.W.2d 319 (Neb. 1984); *Singh v. Singh*, 325 N.Y.S.2d 590 (N.Y. Sup. Ct. 1971). *See generally* Maddaugh, *Validity of Marriage and the Conflict of Laws*, 23 U. Toronto L. Rev. 117 (1973); Da Costa, *The Formalities of Marriage in the Conflict of Laws*, 7 Int'l & Comp. L.Q. 217 (1958).

[254] *See generally* 1 H. Clark, Law of Domestic Relations 98–100 (2d ed. 1987).

[255] *See supra* § 2.08[A].

[256] *See supra* § 2.08[A].

[257] *See, e.g.*, Goodrich, *Jurisdiction to Annul a Marriage*, 32 Harv. L. Rev. 806 (1919); *see also Worthington v. Worthington*, 352 S.W.2d 80 (Ark. 1962).

The modern majority view, however, is that the state where the parties, or either of them, are domiciled at the time of the annulment proceeding would have jurisdiction. Thus, a number of states now have jurisdictional statutes applying both to divorce and annulment, and effective at the time the action is actually brought. [258]

Another problem with annulment jurisdiction is whether it must be a bilateral proceeding, or whether it can also be an ex parte proceeding. Traditionally, under a "relation back" doctrine, since an annulment meant that no marriage existed, such an annulment action could not be based upon the nonexistent marriage for any subject matter jurisdiction *in rem*, and *in personam* bilateral jurisdiction over both the parties was therefore required for any annulment action. [259]

The landmark annulment case of *Perlstein v. Perlstein*, [260] however, attacked this traditional legal fiction that a judgment in an annulment case should "relate back" to the inception of the marriage. Rather, the *Perlstein* court made a persuasive analogy to the ex parte divorce case of *Williams v. North Carolina [I]*, [261] stating that annulment actions may also be ex parte as well as bilateral, based upon the petitioner's domicile and the questionable marriage as the dual basis for annulment jurisdiction. [262]

The *Perlstein* rationale has been adopted in the vast majority of American jurisdictions.

[B] Annulment Grounds and Defenses

Annulment is the legal determination that a void or voidable marriage was a nullity from its inception. An annulment action thus differs from a divorce action in that divorce is the dissolution of a legally valid marriage, whereas annulment is the legal declaration that a marriage never existed in the first place. [263]

A void *ab initio* marriage, [264] such as a same sex marriage, [265] a bigamous or polygamous marriage, [266] or an incestuous marriage, [267] does *not* require a formal annulment proceeding, but a party may still petition the court for a formal judicial record that such a marriage was void *ab initio*.

A voidable marriage, [268] on the other hand, is legally valid for all civil purposes unless it is annulled by the parties themselves. Thus, voidable

---

[258] *See, e.g.*, Vernon, *Labyrinthine Ways: Jurisdiction to Annul*, 10 J. Pub. L. 47 (1961); 1 H. Clark, Law of Domestic Relations 222–237 (2d ed. 1987).

[259] *See generally* 2 Bishop, Marriage, Divorce and Separation 2–14 (1891).

[260] 204 A.2d 909 (Conn. 1964).

[261] 317 U.S. 287 (1942).

[262] *Perlstein v. Perlstein*, 204 A.2d 909 (Conn. 1964). *See also Whealton v. Whealton*, 432 P.2d 979 (Cal. 1967).

[263] *See generally* 1 H. Clark, Law of Domestic Relations, 219–277 (2d ed. 1987).

[264] *See supra* § 2.08[A].

[265] *See supra* § 2.08[B].

[266] *See supra* § 2.08[C].

[267] *See supra* § 2.08[D].

[268] *See supra* § 2.08[A].

marriages *do* require a formal annulment proceeding, and a voidable marriage may include: an underage marriage,[269] a marriage to a spouse who is mentally or physically incompetent,[270] a fraudulent marriage,[271] a marriage under duress,[272] a sham marriage,[273] and a marriage in jest.[274]

There are certain defenses to annulment actions. First, if the parties fail to bring an annulment action for a voidable marriage during the lifetime of either party, or within a reasonable period of time, they are deemed to have condoned and ratified any marital imperfection, and the marriage remains a legally valid marriage.[275] However, the parties can *never* ratify a void *ab initio* marriage, which is a legal nullity from its inception based upon a state's strong public policy rationale.

A number of states have enacted a specific statute of limitations affecting annulment actions.[276] Other courts have held that in the absence of a specific annulment statute, a general statute of limitations would apply.[277] In the absence of any statute of limitations defense, a defense may also be raised based upon the unreasonable delay in bringing an annulment action under the equitable doctrine of laches.[278]

Estoppel by judgment or res judicata may also constitute another defense to annulment. For example, in *Statter v. Statter*,[279] the court dismissed the wife's annulment action on bigamy grounds based upon a prior divorce action where the court found the Statter's marriage to be a valid marriage. Therefore, res judicata principles will generally override any mistake of law or mistake of fact, as long as the parties had their day in court on the merits of the case.[280] Estoppel by conduct may also bar the parties from contesting the validity of their marriage based upon a prior invalid divorce.[281]

Finally, are children born into a void *ab initio* marriage, or born into a voidable marriage that is annulled, legitimate or illegitimate under the law? Under the common law, such children were deemed to be illegitimate since, under a traditional "relation back" doctrine the marriage was a nullity, and anything depending on the void marriage would also be void.[282] However,

---

[269] *See supra* § 2.08[E].

[270] *See supra* § 2.08[F].

[271] *See supra* § 2.08[G].

[272] *See supra* § 2.08[H].

[273] *See supra* § 2.08[I].

[274] *See supra* § 2.08[J].

[275] *See, e.g., Woods v. Woods*, 638 S.W.2d 403 (Tenn. Ct. App. 1982).

[276] *See, e.g.,* Va. Code Ann. § 20-89.1(c) (a two-year statute of limitations for voidable marriages from the date of the marriage); Cal. Fam. Code § 4425(d) (a four-year statute of limitations after discovery of fraud).

[277] *See, e.g., Witt v. Witt*, 72 N.W.2d 748 (Wis. 1955) (the statute begins to run from the time the marital defect is discovered). *But see Munger v. Munger*, 95 A.2d 153 (N.J. Super. Ct. App. Div. 1953). *See also* Annot., 52 A.L.R.2d 1163 and Later Case Service.

[278] *See, e.g.,* Annot. 34 A.L.R.2d 1306 and Later Case Service.

[279] 143 N.E.2d 10 (N.J. 1957).

[280] *C.f. Aldrich v. Aldrich*, 378 U.S. 540 (1964) (divorce case).

[281] *See supra* § 2.05[E].

[282] *See* 1 Bishop, Marriage, Divorce and Separation 313 (1891); *see also* Note, *Status of the Issue of Void Marriages*, 56 Harv. L. Rev. 624 (1943).

this unfortunate common law rule has now been abrogated by statute in almost every state, providing that children of void or voidable marriages are legitimate by statute.[283]

[C] Property and Support Rights on Annulment

If a marriage is void *ab initio*, or if a voidable marriage is annulled, then the marriage is a nullity. Thus, a majority of jurisdictions have held that permanent spousal support and marital property rights *cannot* be granted on annulment, absent specific statutory authority to the contrary.[284] Lacking such marital property and support rights on annulment, a needy "spouse" in these traditional jurisdictions would only have very limited contractual or equitable remedies.[285]

Fortunately, a growing number of states have recognized this financial plight of a needy "spouse" at the time of annulment, and have enacted legislation allowing permanent spousal support and marital property division to be granted on annulment, similar to divorce legislation.[286]

Another recurring problem with spousal support and annulment is based upon the following scenario: Husband and wife are divorced and the divorce decree provides that the payor spouse will pay spousal support to the needy spouse until the payor or payee dies, or until the payee remarries. The payee spouse then remarries, but this second marriage is subsequently annulled.

The states are split as to the effect of the annulment on the payor's initial spousal support obligation. Some courts, applying a traditional "relation back" annulment doctrine to both void *ab initio* and voidable marriages, hold that the prior spousal support obligation is *not* terminated, since there has been no second marriage.[287] Other courts would deny spousal support payments to the payee spouse when the second marriage was voidable, but not void *ab initio*.[288] Still other courts would terminate the prior spousal support obligation whether the remarriage was voidable or void *ab initio*.[289]

---

[283] *See, e.g.*, N.Y. Dom. Rel. Law § 24; Pa. Stat. Ann. tit. 48, § 169.1; Wis. Stat. Ann. § 767.60.

[284] *See generally* Annot., 54 A.L.R.2d 1410 and Later Case Service.

[285] *See, e.g., In re Estate of Thorton*, 499 P.2d 864 (Wash. 1972) (property awarded on an "implied partnership" theory); *Marvin v. Marvin*, 557 P.2d 106 (Cal. 1976) (cause of action based on expressed or implied contractual basis); *Walker v. Walker*, 47 N.W.2d 633 (Mich. 1951) (monetary award based upon equitable principle of unjust enrichment); *see also supra* §§ 2.02, 2.05[D].

[286] *See, e.g.*, Conn. Gen. Stat. Ann. § 46b-60; N.Y. Dom. Rel. Law § 236; Va. Code Ann. §§ 20-107.1 to 107.3; Wis. Stat. Ann. § 767.26; *see also* 1 H. Clark, Law of Domestic Relations 245–246 (2d ed. 1987) ("It is difficult to understand why more states have not enacted these statutes."). *See generally* Comment, *The Aftereffects of Annulment: Alimony, Property Division, Provision for Children*, 1968 Wash. U. L. Rev.148 (1968).

[287] *See, e.g., Sutton v. Leib*, 199 F.2d 163 (7th Cir. 1952); *Redmann v. Redmann*, 376 N.W.2d 803 (N.D. 1985).

[288] *See, e.g., McConkey v. McConkey*, 215 S.E.2d 640 (Va. 1975) (annulment for fraud terminated spousal support from the prior husband); *Johnston v. Johnston*, 592 P.2d 132 (Kan. Ct. App. 1979) (void *ab initio* marriage did not terminate spousal support payments, but a voidable marriage would).

[289] *See, e.g., Glass v. Glass*, 546 S.W.2d 738, 742 (Mo. Ct. App. 1977) ("We conclude . . .

A number of courts have granted temporary spousal support to a needy spouse during the pendency of an annulment action when that spouse was attempting to protect and validate the marriage. These courts often have denied temporary spousal support *pendente lite* if the spouse requesting support was the one bringing the annulment action in order to invalidate the marriage. [290] However, this traditional approach normally is not applied in those states where spousal support and marital property rights are recoverable in annulment actions by statutory authority. [291]

that remarriage . . . refers to the ceremony of marriage and not to the status or relationship -invalid, voidable, or void -which actually results."); *Gaines v. Jacobsen*, 124 N.E.2d 290 (N.Y. 1954); *Sefton v. Sefton*, 291 P.2d 439 (Cal. 1955). However, the *Sefton* court held that spousal support may be reinstated in certain situations for the protection of innocent parties; *see also Weintraub v. Weintraub*, 213 Cal. Rptr. 159 (Cal. Ct. App. 1985). *See generally* Annot., 45 A.L.R.3d 1033 (1972); Note, *The Annulment Controversy: Revival of Prior Alimony Payments*, 13 Tulsa L.J. 127 (1977).

[290] *See generally* Comment, *The Aftereffects of Annulment: Alimony, Property Division, Provision for Children*, 1968 Wash. U.L. Rev. 148 (1968).

[291] *See* footnote 193 *supra*, and accompanying text.

Chapter 3

PROPERTY AND SUPPORT RIGHTS DURING MARRIAGE

§ 3.01 Introduction

The legal status of marriage gives rise to various property and support rights and obligations affecting the spouses while they remain married. The concept of property rights relates to the parties' ownership interests in assets, while the idea of support involves the on-going provision of the goods and services necessary for daily living. These incidents of marriage involve a variety of concepts relating to the economic relationship of the spouses, both between each other and with respect to third parties.

Two systems of marital property co-exist in the United States: (1) the common law title system, which is followed by the majority of states, and (2) the community property system, recognized by a minority of jurisdictions. While the two regimes currently overlap upon dissolution of marriage under equitable distribution principles, they remain distinct during the existence of marriage, and have unique applications on the death of a spouse.

Traditionally, the common law regarded a married couple as one legal entity and the husband as the head of the household. Accordingly, it allocated the duty of protection and support of the wife and children to the husband and granted him the right to their services and most of their property.

During the 1970's, the United States Supreme Court struck down many gender-based laws which unconstitutionally distinguished between males and females under the Equal Protection Clause of the Fourteenth Amendment of the federal Constitution.[1] In *Orr v. Orr*[2] the Supreme Court held that a Georgia statute authorizing alimony for women, but not for men, was unconstitutional. *Orr* signaled the demise of many gender-based statutes regulating family support and property matters.[3] Since *Orr*, the Supreme Court has made it clear that statutory differences based on gender as must satisfy "an exceedingly persuasive justification."[4] To withstand

---

[1] *See, e.g., Reed v. Reed*, 404 U.S. 71 (1971) (Idaho statutory classifications that preferred men over women in appointment of administrators for decedents' estates violate Equal Protection Clause of the Fourteenth Amendment); *Stanton v. Stanton*, 421 U.S. 7 (1975) (Utah statute fixing age of majority at twenty-one for males and eighteen for females for purposes of child support violates equal protection).

[2] 440 U.S. 268 (1979).

[3] *See, e.g.*, Cal. Civ. Code § 204(5) (West 1990). *See generally* G. Michael Bridge, Note, *Uniform Probate Code Section 2-202: A Proposal to Include Life Insurance Assets Within the Augmented Estate*, 74 Cornell L. Rev. 511, 543, n.26 (1989).

[4] *Mississippi University for Women v. Hogan*, 458 U.S. 718, 724 (1982); *United States v. Virginia*, 518 U.S. 515, 515 (1996).

constitutional scrutiny, gender-based classifications must at least serve "important governmental objectives," and must be "substantially related to the achievement of those objectives."[5] Although statutory classifications based on gender may be justified, in limited circumstances, to compensate women "for particular economic disabilities [they have] suffered,"[6] the same heightened scrutiny applies, even where a statute's objective is to compensate for past discrimination or to balance the burdens borne by males and females.[7]

Nonetheless, both spousal support and child support rights and obligations now generally are regarded as gender-neutral concepts, imposing support obligations on both spouses or parents regardless of sex.[8] Property ownership during marriage, however, continues to be allocated under title theory principles in common law jurisdictions.[9]

§ 3.02   The Common Law Theory of Property Rights

During marriage, common law states adhere to a "title theory" of property, allocating ownership to the spouse who holds title to, or who has otherwise acquired, the asset in question. The owner of property may manage, control, and dispose of the asset without the consent of, or notice to, the other spouse. Unless transformed by gift, contract, or court decree, title to a marital asset is held by the party who earned the funds used to purchase the asset. Usually title can be traced to the primary wage earner who in the past was, and to a significant extent today remains, the husband.

Common law generally regarded any services rendered by one spouse to the other as either obligatory or gratuitous. Spousal services, therefore, did not entitle the spouse who rendered those services to any rights to the property of the other spouse. The presumption of a gift could be rebutted by factual evidence demonstrating that the services were *not* intended to be gratuitous.[10] Thus, a spouse was permitted to prove that certain property of the marriage was held in partnership, quasi-partnership, joint venture, or trust, or that a constructive trust should be imposed to prevent unjust enrichment of the title-holding spouse.[11]

---

[5] *Hogan*, 456 U.S. at 724; *see also J.E.B. v. Alabama*, 511 U.S. 127, 131–46 (1994).

[6] *Califano v. Webster*, 430 U.S. 313 (1977).

[7] *Hogan*, 458 U.S. at 728.

[8] *See infra* § 9.01.

[9] *Compare with infra* § 3.06.

[10] *See, e.g., Eggleston v. Eggleston*, 47 S.E.2d 243 (N.C. 1948).

[11] *See, e.g., McGehee v. McGehee*, 85 So. 2d 799 (Miss. 1956) (upholding formal, written partnership agreement between spouses relating to ownership of business assets). *But see Chaachou v. Chaachou*, 135 So. 2d 206 (Fla. 1961). In *Chaachou*, where the couple had no written partnership agreement with respect to business property, the court held that any partnership that may have been agreed to "became merged in their larger partnership of marriage and its terms are now too indistinct to be specifically enforced as such." *Id.* at 214. The court concluded, however, that the husband would be unjustly enriched if he were allowed to retain all the business assets without compensating the wife, and the wife was awarded a ³⁄₂₀ value of four hotel properties, as well as permanent alimony, a residence, and attorney fees.

§ 3.03   The *"Feme Sole* Estate" and the Married Women's Property Acts

Married women suffered severe economic disabilities under early common law, while no corresponding disabilities were imposed on husbands. Upon marriage, the husband acquired title to all the wife's personal property, except for her incidental personal "paraphernalia," such as clothing and ornaments. He also was granted possession of her real property, including the rents and profits, and the rights to manage, control, alienate, and encumber that property. The disabilities imposed on married women included the legal incapacity to contract, to execute wills, to vote, and to sue or be sued. According to Blackstone, the reason for the married woman's legal incapacity was the "unity" theory of marriage: the husband and wife "became one," and that "one" was the husband, who acted as "guardian" of the wife.[12] The husband, in turn, was required to support and protect the wife.

[A]   The *"Feme Sole* Estate"

As early as the 1600 and 1700s, courts of equity began to ameliorate the harsh common law disabilities by allowing specific property to be held in trust for the wife's "sole and separate use." This equitable trust arrangement created what was known as the *"feme sole* estate," or the "equitable separate estate." The *feme sole* estate accorded married women the same property rights enjoyed by their single female counterparts, enabling them to own and manage their own assets. The early *feme sole* estate was in the form of a trust and was often created by the wife's father, but could also be established by her husband or others.[13] This equitable doctrine permitted any type of property to be transferred into trust, thereby allowing the wife to retain her property rights after marriage and to contract, convey, devise, and sue or be sued with respect to that property, while safeguarding her from exposure to the claims of her husband or his creditors.[14]

American courts later adopted the English Chancery Courts' method of creating separate estates for married women without the use of trustees. Married women who held such separate property, therefore, were free to manage some of their own financial affairs. However, the separate estate without a trust still generally was created by the woman's male relatives, who frequently did not give her complete managerial authority over those assets.[15] The *feme sole* estate had gained considerable popularity in this country by the mid-nineteenth century.

---

[12] *See* 1 William Blackstone, Commentaries on the Laws of England 445 (3d ed. 1884).

[13] *See* 1 Homer Clark, Law of Domestic Relations 288-89 (2d. ed. 1987).

[14] *Id.* at 289.

[15] *See* Richard Chused, Cases, Materials and Problems in Property 252 (1988); *see also* Richard Chused, *Married Women's Property Law: 1800–1850,* 71 Geo. L.J. 1359 (1983).

[B]   The Married Women's Property Acts

By the late 1800s, state legislatures began to enact a series of statutes collectively known as the Married Women's Property Acts. Like the privately created *feme sole* estate, these statutes were intended to reduce or eliminate the economic disabilities imposed on wives under common law. Commentators have disagreed as to whether the Married Women's Property Acts have rendered the separate equitable *feme sole* estate obsolete.[16]

Although the Married Women's Property Acts varied in detail from one state to another, in general, they extended further than the *feme sole* estate. The Acts not only granted wives the rights to acquire, own, and transfer all types of real and personal property to the same extent as unmarried women, but many Acts further allowed married women to enter into contracts in their own names, to engage in business or employment and retain their own earnings, to make wills, to sue and be sued, and to be fully responsible for their own tortious and criminal conduct.[17] Typically, the Married Women's Property Acts shielded the woman's assets from the creditors of the husband.[18] The Acts had no effect, however, on the husband's position as head of the household, his duty to support the wife, or her reciprocal duty to provide him with household services. Nor did they give her any interests in property owned or earned by the husband. Therefore, because the typical wife was not employed outside the home and brought little, if any, property into the marriage, the economic position of married women in general was not greatly improved.

Because most family law doctrines are now gender neutral, features of the *feme sole* equitable estate and the Married Women's Property Acts which give women greater economic rights than men are subject to constitutional attack. The vast majority of states have amended their statutes, or judicially reinterpreted them, to apply marital support and property rights equally to husbands and wives.

§ 3.04   Tenancy by the Entirety

The common law recognized the estate of tenancy by the entirety, a form of concurrent property ownership available exclusively to married couples. The tenancy by the entirety has never been recognized in states adhering to the community property system.

The tenancy by the entirety is a means of protecting a married couple's property, both from each other and from their creditors. In a tenancy by the entirety, each spouse holds an equal, undivided interest in the property during the lifetimes of both parties. The estate incorporates a survivorship

---

[16] *Compare* 1 American Law of Property §§ 5.55–5.56 (1952) *with* Jack Rappeport, *The Equitable Separate Estate and Restraints on Anticipation*, 11 Miami L.Q. 85 (1956). *See also Anders v. Roller*, 37 S.E. 297 (Va. 1900) (the separate equitable *feme sole* estate continues to have an independent existence distinct from the Married Women's Property Acts).

[17] *See generally* Homer Clark, *supra* note 13, at 290, 293–304.

[18] *See supra* Richard Chused, note 15, at 259.

interest which gives the surviving spouse sole ownership of the whole property at the death of the other spouse.[19]

Neither spouse can unilaterally transfer, encumber, sever, or partition property held in tenancy by the entirety, nor destroy the other spouse's right of survivorship. Historically, the individual creditors of one spouse could not reach that spouse's interest in entirety property.[20] The husband, as head of the marital unit, however, had the power to manage the property held in tenancy by the entirety.

Traditionally, a tenancy by the entirety was created whenever property was conveyed simultaneously to a husband and wife,[21] although some states now require it to be expressly created. Originally, the tenancy by the entirety estate was limited to real property, but some states expanded it to include personal property, and some presumed a tenancy by the entirety whenever spouses acquired property together.[22]

Currently, fewer than half the common law property states recognize the tenancy by the entirety estate.[23] Where it is recognized, both spouses now have equal rights to property held in the entirety. The majority of states which continue to recognize the entirety estate shield the entirety property both from the unilateral acts of either spouse and from their individual creditors.[24] A few jurisdictions allow either spouse to transfer his or her individual interest and allow separate creditors to reach that spouse's interest, while preserving both the present interest and the survivorship right of the other spouse.[25] Because only married couples may hold property as tenants by the entirety, the estate generally is converted into a tenancy in common if the parties divorce.[26]

§ 3.05 Common Law Property Rights on Death of a Spouse

At death, subject to certain restrictions, a spouse may transfer by will any property that he or she owns individually. Under the common law title theory of marital property ownership,[27] because husbands traditionally owned most or all of a married couple's assets, a wife could be left without

[19] See Paul Haskell, Preface to Wills, Trusts and Administration 118 (1987).

[20] See id. at 118–19.

[21] See Homer Clark, supra note 13, at 295.

[22] See Jesse Dukeminier & James Krier, Property 334 (2d ed. 1988).

[23] Tenancy by the entireties is still recognized in Alaska, Delaware, District of Columbia, Florida, Hawaii, Kentucky, Maryland, Massachusetts, Michigan, New Jersey, North Carolina, Ohio, Oklahoma, Oregon, Tennessee, and Wyoming. Restatement (Second) of Property § 34.1 note 1 (1990).

[24] See, e.g., Sawada v. Endo, 561 P.2d 1291 (Haw. 1977) (reviewing present state of tenancy by the entirety law and adopting majority position).

[25] See Paul Haskell, supra note 19, at 118–19.

[26] See, e.g., Union Grove Milling & Mfg. Co. v. Faw, 404 S.E.2d 508 (N.C. Ct. App. 1991); V.R.W., Inc. v. Klein, 503 N.E.2d 496 (N.Y. 1986).

[27] See supra § 3.02.

any property or means of support if the husband died first and left his estate to someone other than his widow. Furthermore, spouses were not designated as each other's heirs at earlier common law, although today all American states recognize a surviving spouse as an heir, who will inherit a portion of property passing by intestacy. To alleviate the possibility that a surviving spouse would be left destitute, the common law developed methods of protecting surviving spouses in the form of dower, curtesy, and, during this century, the statutory elective share.

[A] Common Law Dower and Curtesy

Although the common law afforded wives no rights in their husbands' property during marriage, it did protect wives from total disinheritance on the husbands' death in the form of dower. Dower entitled a widow to possession of a life estate in one-third of certain real property that the husband owned at any time during the marriage, regardless of when or how the husband had acquired the property. Even if the husband had disposed of the property during his lifetime, unless she released those rights by voluntarily joining in the deed, the widow's dower rights attached to that land and became possessory at the husband's death.[28]

Common law dower was limited to inheritable real property which the husband held as a possessory freehold estate. Thus, dower did not attach to personal property, nor to land in which the husband had merely a leasehold estate, a life estate, a future interest, or a joint tenancy.[29] Dower gave the wife no rights during the husband's lifetime, during which time her dower interest was regarded as "inchoate." Nor did it grant her a property interest that she could transfer to her heirs or devisees if she predeceased him. Once dower became choate on the husband's death, the court assigned to the widow a specific one-third portion of each parcel of land to which dower had attached for her lifetime use. If such assignment was impractical, some courts awarded her one-third of the income from that land for her lifetime.[30] At the wife's death, her dower interest expired.

Although the common law already gave the husband the right to manage and control the wife's real property during the marriage,[31] it further granted the husband a continued interest upon her death in the form of curtesy. Like dower, curtesy was limited to the wife's inheritable freehold real property interests. Curtesy, however, gave the husband a life estate in *all* the wife's qualified property, although the husband's curtesy rights only attached once a child of the marriage was born alive.

During the past century, as people more commonly began to hold their accumulated wealth in the form of financial investments rather than in real property, dower and curtesy became a largely ineffective means for providing protection to a surviving spouse. Most states have abolished both dower

---

[28] *See* 1 American Law of Property §§ 5.1-76 (Casner ed. 1952); Paul Haskell, *supra* note 19, at 134–5.

[29] *See* 1 American Law of Property § 5.23.

[30] Paul Haskell, *supra* note 19, at 134.

[31] *See supra* § 3.03.

and curtesy, and where they still exist, usually in a statutory form, equivalent rights are accorded to both husbands and wives. Dower and curtesy have been replaced or supplemented in most common law states with some variation of an "elective" or "forced" share statute. [32]

[B] Elective Share Statutes

Elective share statutes entitle a surviving spouse to a statutorily prescribed minimum fraction of the decedent spouse's property owned at death. Typically, the fraction is one-third to one-half of the decedent's probate estate, but may vary depending on whether the decedent spouse left descendants or parents. [33] Although the statutes are sometimes referred to as "forced share" statutes, because the surviving spouse can renounce the will and demand a minimum portion of the deceased spouse's estate, the survivor must affirmatively assert this right during a specified time period or it will expire; hence, the term "elective share," as used by the Uniform Probate Code, is more appropriate. [34]

Unlike common law dower and curtesy, elective share statutes apply to both real and personal property. While a spouse still obtains no property interests in the other's property during the marriage, nor any devisable or inheritable interests if the non-owning spouse dies first, the elective share property is awarded outright to the surviving spouse, rather than as a life estate. However, the elective share generally only applies to property which the decedent spouse disposes of by will, although some states subject certain lifetime transfers to the spouse's elective share as well. [35] Furthermore, if the decedent spouse dies without a will that effectively devises all of his or her property, the intestacy statutes of every state designate a surviving spouse as an heir, entitling that spouse to a specified portion of the estate.

The Uniform Probate Code (UPC) sets out a more thorough and complex approach known as the "augmented estate" elective share, [36] which several states have adopted. [37] In its original version, the UPC included in the value of the estate certain enumerated lifetime transfers made by the decedent in which the decedent had retained some economic benefits, and allocated a one-third share of that amount to the surviving spouse. It then deducted from that sum any intervivos gifts from the decedent spouse to the surviving spouse and any non-testamentary benefits passing to the surviving spouse due to the decedent's death. [38] It satisfied the one-third share of an electing

---

[32] Paul Haskell, *supra* note 19, at 135–6.

[33] *Id.* at 136.

[34] *See* Lawrence Waggoner, et al., Family Property Law 473 (1991).

[35] *See, e.g.*, Elias Clark, *The Recapture of Testamentary Substitutes to Preserve the Spouse's Elective Share: An Appraisal of Recent Statutory Reforms*, 2 Conn. L. Rev. 513 (1970); Rena C. Seplowitz, *Transfers Prior to Marriage and the Uniform Probate Code's Redesigned Elective Share -Why the Partnership Is Not Yet Complete*, 25 Ind. L. Rev. 1, 13–18 (1991).

[36] Unif. Probate Code § 2-202, 8 U.L.A. 75 (1983) (amended 1990).

[37] *See, e.g.*, Colo. Rev. Stat. Ann. § 15-11-202 (West 1989); Neb. Rev. Stat. § 30-2314 (1989).

[38] Unif. Probate Code §§ 2-201, 2-202, 8 U.L.A. 74 (1983).

spouse first from property already transferred by the decedent spouse to the surviving spouse before distributing funds from the decedent's probate estate. Thus, the augmented estate approach reaches not only the decedents' probate estate, but accounts for certain intervivos transfers, while deducting from the spouse's share most economic benefits already transferred by the decedent to the surviving spouse. [39]

The 1990 Uniform Probate Code redesigned the elective share, attempting to better correlate the elective share with the partnership theory of marriage. [40] The new version retains and expands the augmented estate approach by combining the assets of both spouses in calculating the augmented estate. Further, it adjusts the percentage of the surviving spouse's entitlement according to the length of the couple's marriage, reaching a maximum of fifty percent after fifteen years of marriage. Moreover, it takes into account the surviving spouse's own separate assets, which are counted first in calculating the final amount to be awarded. [41]

§ 3.06   The Community Property System

Eight American states historically have followed the community property principles developed in Spain and France, rather than the common law property title theory imported from England. These eight states are Arizona, California, Idaho, Louisiana, New Mexico, Nevada, Texas, and Washington. Since its adoption of the Uniform Marital Property Act[42] in 1983, Wisconsin, traditionally a common law property jurisdiction, now also is generally regarded as a community property state. [43]

The community property system is based on a sharing or partnership theory of marriage, which presumes that each spouse contributes equally, in a direct or indirect manner, to the accumulation of assets during the marriage. [44] Equal ownership interests are allocated to homemaker or intangible contributions to the marriage relationship, as well as to income-producing activity. Although details vary considerably from one community property state to another, the system, in general, regards most property acquired through the efforts of either spouse during marriage as owned equally by both spouses as community property.

Spouses in community property jurisdictions also are permitted to hold separate property. Separate property generally includes assets that a spouse acquired prior to marriage or after its dissolution, by individual gift or inheritance during marriage, by designation as separate property by

---

[39] Unif. Probate Code § 2-202 (1983) (amended 1990). *See generally* J. Thomas Oldham, *Should the Surviving Spouse's Forced Share Be Retained?*, 38 Case W. Rev. L. Rev. 223 (1988).

[40] Unif. Probate Code § 2-202 (1991).

[41] *See generally* Lawrence Waggoner, et al., Family Property Law 80-113 (2d ed. 1997); Rena C. Seplowitz, *Transfers Prior to Marriage and the Uniform Probate Code's Redesigned Elective Share -Why the Partnership Is Not Yet Complete*, 25 Ind. L. Rev. 1 (1991).

[42] 9A U.L.A. 97 (1987).

[43] Wis. Stat. Ann. § 766 (West 1986).

[44] *See also infra* § 3.08.

valid contract between the spouses, or by a court decree.[45] Community property states differ with respect to classification of passive income and profits from separate property, but earnings attributable to the labor of either spouse and the assets procured with those earnings are equally owned as community property.[46]

Despite equality of ownership, the husband alone traditionally had the right to manage and control community property.[47] For example, in *Brown v. Boeing Co.*,[48] a wife argued that her deceased husband had breached his fiduciary duty to act in her best interest and had committed a constructive fraud upon her for electing an employee pension benefit option that did not include a survivor benefit, despite her objections. The Washington Court of Appeals held that under the state's community property statute, either spouse was entitled to manage and control community assets, such as the interest in the pension plan, subject to certain exceptions not applicable in this situation. Despite the fact that the wife ultimately received less money from the option selected than she would have under a joint and survivor option, the court held that the husband had not acted improperly, as his election did not attempt to make a bequest or gift of community property, nor did it transform the asset into the husband's separate property.

Under contemporary, gender-neutral community property principles developed during the 1970s, rights of management and control are allocated to either or both spouses, regardless of sex. The particulars of these management rights and powers differ considerably among community property states.[49]

Difficult tracing and characterization problems arise when assets are acquired with both separate property and community property funds and when separate property has been commingled with community property.[50] Therefore, community property law presumes that an asset acquired during marriage is community property unless the spouse claiming a separate property interest can rebut the presumption by proving that all or a portion

---

[45] *See, e.g.*, N.M. Stat. Ann. § 40-3-8 (Michie Cum. Supp. 1992); Nev. Rev. Stat. Ann § 123.130 (Michie 1986). *See generally* W. S. McClanahan, Community Property Law in the United States § 410 (1982).

[46] *See* Idaho Code § 32-906 (1983); La. Civ. Code Ann. art. 2338 (West 1985). *See generally* William DeFuniak & Michael Vaughn, Principles of Community Property § 67 (2d ed. 1971).

[47] *See, e.g.*, *Wilcox v. Wilcox*, 98 Cal. Rptr. 319 (Cal. Ct. App. 1971); *see also* Susan Prager, *The Persistence of Separate Concepts in California's Community Property System 1849 -1975*, 24 UCLA L. Rev. 1 (1976).

[48] 622 P.2d 1313 (Wash. Ct. App. 1980).

[49] *See, e.g.*, Ariz. Rev. Stat. Ann. § 25-214 (1988); Cal. Civ. Code § 5125 (West 1990); *see also* Carol Bruch, *Protecting the Rights of Spouses in Intact Marriages: The 1987 California Community Property Reform and Why It Was So Hard to Get*, 1990 Wis. L. Rev. 731 (1990); Carol Bruch, *Management Powers and Duties Under California's Community Property Laws: Recommendations for Reform*, 34 Hastings L.J. 227 (1982).

[50] *See* J. Thomas Oldham, Divorce, Separation and the Distribution of Property § 11.03 (1992); *see also infra* § 10.02.

of the asset falls within the definition of separate property and has not been transformed into community property by gift or transmutation.[51]

During marriage, an individual spouse's ownership interest in community property is undivided, but when the community dissolves, either by divorce or by death, the ownership interests in community property are severed and each spouse is entitled to an individual one-half. Thus, after termination of the marriage, each spouse owns his or her own separate property and one-half of the former community assets, although many community property states have modified property division on divorce with equitable distribution principles.[52]

Upon death, the decedent spouse may dispose of his or her one-half of the community property by will, along with his or her separate property, with no survivorship interest in that property accruing to the surviving spouse.[53] Because community property law, in theory, furnishes built-in protection for a non-wage-earning spouse, community property states do not recognize the tenancy by the entirety estate, nor provide for dower, curtesy, or an elective share.

§ 3.07 The Uniform Marital Property Act

The Uniform Marital Property Act [UMPA], promulgated in 1983, incorporates the partnership concept of marriage.[54] The UMPA was adopted, with some modifications, by Wisconsin in 1983[55] and has been considered by some other states.[56] Because the Act is based on principles of shared property ownership during marriage, it is generally regarded as a community property law.[57] The UMPA is not a typical community property act,

---

[51] See J. Thomas Oldham, *Tracing, Commingling, and Transmutation*, 23 Fam. L.Q. 219 (1989).

[52] Strict equality of community property division on divorce has been modified by equitable distribution statutes in all but three community property states, California, New Mexico, and Louisiana. See William A. Reppy, *Major Events in the Evolution of American Community Property Law and Their Import to Equitable Distribution States*, 23 Fam. L.Q. 163, 164 (1989). *See generally infra* Ch. 9.

[53] To the extent that a spouse dies intestate in a community property state, the surviving spouse will be entitled to a share of the decedent's separate and community property as an intestate heir. *See, e.g.*, Unif. Probate Code § 2-102A, 8 U.L.A. 73 (1992 Supp.). Additionally, both community and common law property states generally allow a surviving spouse a family allowance and personal property allotment from the decedent spouse's probate estate. *See, e.g.*, Unif. Probate Code § 2-403.

[54] 9A U.L.A. 97 (West 1987). *See generally* John DeWitt Gregory, The Law of Equitable Distribution ¶ 1.04 (1989).

[55] Wis. Stat. Ann. §§ 766.001-766.97 (West Supp. 1988–1989). *See generally* Howard Erlanger & June Weisberger, *From Common Law Property to Community Property: Wisconsin's Marital Property Act Four Years Later*, 1990 Wis. L. Rev. 769 (1990).

[56] Colorado, Illinois, Indiana, Michigan, and Missouri have deliberated variations of the UMPA. *See* Wendy A. Wake, Note, *Uniform Marital Property Act: Suggested Revisions for Equality Between Spouses*, 1987 U. Ill. L. Rev. 471, 474 n.11.

[57] See William Reppy, *The Uniform Marital Property Act: Some Suggested Revisions for a Basically Sound Act*, 21 Hous. L. Rev. 679 (1984).

however, because its drafters incorporated "the best solutions to various problems found among the eight community property states."[58]

The UMPA provides for a dual classification system of a married couple's property, which categorizes property as either marital property or individual property.[59] Each spouse has a present undivided one-half interest in marital property.[60] All property of spouses is presumed to be marital property,[61] and income from any source is designated marital property.[62] Individual property consists of property acquired prior to marriage[63] and property obtained during marriage by gift or inheritance by either spouse from a third party.[64] Individual property retains its character if it is exchanged for other assets.[65] Appreciation of individual property remains individual property unless substantial appreciation is attributed to the substantial uncompensated efforts of the other spouse.[66] If marital and individual property are commingled, the asset is classified as marital property unless the individual property interest can be traced.[67]

Management and control rights to property under the UMPA are based on title. A spouse may manage and control his or her individual property and, with some exceptions, marital property that is held in that spouse's name or not held in the name of the other spouse.[68] Property held in both spouses' names must be managed and controlled by the spouses together, unless it is held in their names alternatively, in which case either may act alone.[69] The UMPA imposes a duty on each spouse to act in good faith.[70]

The UMPA permits spouses to alter most of their property rights by marital property agreements.[71] Different fairness standards are set out for agreements made before and during marriage.[72] A spouse may not contractually impair certain creditors' or bona fide purchasers' rights,[73] nor adversely affect a child's right to support.[74]

---

[58] *Id.* at 683. *See generally* Howard Erlanger & June Weisberger, *supra* note 55, at 776–782.

[59] Unif. Marital Property Act § 4.

[60] Unif. Marital Property Act § 4(c).

[61] Unif. Marital Property Act § 4(b).

[62] Unif. Marital Property Act § 4(d).

[63] Unif. Marital Property Act § 4(f).

[64] Unif. Marital Property Act § 4(g)(1).

[65] Unif. Marital Property Act § 4(g)(2).

[66] Unif. Marital Property Act §§ 4(g)(3), 14(b).

[67] Unif. Marital Property Act § 14(a).

[68] Unif. Marital Property Act § 5.

[69] *Id.*

[70] Unif. Marital Property Act § 2

[71] Unif. Marital Property Act § 10.

[72] *Id.*

[73] Unif. Marital Property Act §§ 8, 9.

[74] Unif. Marital Property Act § 10(b).

The UMPA limits the amount of gifts of marital property to third parties by an individual spouse.[75] It further contains detailed provisions relating to life insurance policies and deferred employment benefits.[76]

While the UMPA regulates spousal property rights during marriage and at death,[77] it does not alter the law that governs property distribution on divorce.[78] The Wisconsin courts have held that the state's equitable distribution laws continue to apply to property division upon dissolution of marriage.[79]

§ 3.08   Marriage as an "Economic Partnership"

Dissatisfaction with the inequities inherent in the traditional common law concepts of property ownership during marriage[80] has resulted in a trend toward viewing marriage as ans economic partnership. In 1963, the Report of the Committee on Civil and Political Rights to the President's Commission on the Status of Women observed that:

> Marriage is a partnership to which each spouse makes a different but equally important contribution. This fact has become increasingly recognized in the realities of American family living. While the laws of other countries have reflected this trend, family laws in the United States have lagged behind. Accordingly, the Committee concludes that during marriage each spouse should have a legally defined and substantial right in the earnings of the other spouse and in the real and personal property acquired as a result of such earnings, as well as in the management of such earnings and property. Such right should survive the marriage and be legally recognized in the event of its termination by annulment, divorce, or death. This policy should be appropriately implemented by legislation which would safeguard either spouse against improper alienation of property by the other.[81]

This concept, based on principles of shared ownership of property during marriage embedded in community property law and incorporated into the Uniform Marital Property Act, have influenced the development of equitable distribution of property in common law states, but has not yet infiltrated the law governing property rights during marriage in those states.

Observing that the traditional common law view of marriage devaluates homemaker services and the law of spousal support inadequately protects wives, some scholars have advocated a theory of family partnership based

---

[75] Unif. Marital Property Act § 6.

[76] Unif. Marital Property Act §§ 12, 13.

[77] Unif. Marital Property Act § 18.

[78] *See* Unif. Marital Property Act § 17; *Prefatory Note*, Unif. Marital Property Act.

[79] *See Kuhlman v. Kuhlman*, 432 N.W.2d 295 (Wis. Ct. App. 1988).

[80] *See supra* § 3.02.

[81] Report of the Committee on Civil and Political Rights to the President's Commission on the Status of Women (1963), *quoted in Prefatory Note*, Unif. Marital Property Act, 9A U.L.A. 97 (1987).

on a modified version of the business partnership model and borrowing the fundamental tenets of community property law to assure the equality of both spouses' rights during marriage. [82] Although the parties would be free to tailor their property rights by contract prior to marriage, this proposal acknowledges equal rights and obligations of both husbands and wives with respect to services, management, property ownership, and creditors' rights during marriage. [83] Family roles would be made by the parties in accordance with their individual skills and interests, placing minimum restrictions on individual freedom. [84] The partnership model would allow married women to pursue careers or other activities outside the home, while protecting those who opt for a traditional role in the home or spend a portion of their lives rearing children. [85]

Over the past several decades, the structure of marriage and parenthood has changed considerably.

The traditional role-divided family, in which only the husband worked outside the home, and only the wife raised children, has become the exception, rather than the rule. Today, fewer than 10 percent of American families conform to the pattern of a sole, male wage earner married to a non-wage-earning female spouse. [86] In 1997, more than 70 percent of married mothers participated in the paid labor market, as compared to less than 40 percent in 1970. [87] This includes more than 60 percent of married mothers with children under three years old, and more than 55 percent of married mothers with children younger than one year. [88] In addition, the percentage of families maintained by a single parent has more than doubled since 1973, accounting for more than 30 percent of all families with children in 1997. [89]

Numerous commentaries have supported variations of the economic marital partnership ideal. [90] Its principles have been reflected in divorce reform legislation and judicial opinions relating to spousal support, property division, and other legal issues on divorce. [91]

---

[82] Joan Krauskopf & Rhonda Thomas, *Partnership Marriage: The Solution to an Ineffective and Inequitable Law of Support*, 35 Ohio St. L.J. 558 (1974).

[83] *Id.* at 587–588.

[84] *Id.* at 590–94.

[85] *Id.* at 594.

[86] *See* Sharon C. Nantell, *The Tax Paradigm of Child Care: Shifting Attitude Toward a Private/Parental/Public Alliance*, 80 Marq. L. Rev. 879, 894 (1997).

[87] *See* U.S. Department of Labor, Bureau of Labor Statistics, Employment Characteristics of Families in 1997 (stats.bls.gove/newsrels.htrm).

[88] *Id.* at Table 5.

[89] *See* Bureau of the Census, *Current Population Reports, Household and Family Characteristics: March, 1997*.

[90] *See, e.g.*, Grace Blumberg, *Marital Property Analysis*, 33 UCLA L. Rev. 1250 (1986); Marcia O'Kelly, *Entitlements to Spousal Support After Divorce*, 61 N.D. L. Rev. 225 (1985); Joan Krauskopf, *A Theory for "Just" Division of Marital Property in Missouri*, 41 Mo. L. Rev. 165 (1976); Susan Prager, *Sharing Principles and the Future of Marital Property Law*, 25 UCLA L. Rev. 1 (1977).

[91] *See, e.g.*, Unif. Marriage and Divorce Act, 9A U.L.A. 238–39 (1987); *Price v. Price*, 503 N.E.2d 684 (N.Y. 1986).

One scholar has criticized the partnership theory of marriage and equality models as "symbolic expression" which does not necessarily produce fair and just results when applied to women who have assumed traditional roles during marriage; she has urged unequal treatment to assure equitable economic results until the equality ideal is realized.[92] Other commentators have objected to equating the family relationship to a business, which may stimulate competition rather than sharing and encourage people to view marriage in financial terms.[93] Yet others have expressed concern that the partnership theory allows too much judicial discretion and places insufficient value on non-monetary marital contributions without promoting self-sufficiency after divorce.[94] Some have noted the continuing societal and legal assumptions regarding gender roles in marriage and child-rearing, and the decline of the importance of marriage as a forum for raising children.[95]

§ 3.09   Support Rights and Obligations

Although under the traditional common law system, wives had few, if any, property rights, to some extent, the common law protected wives by imposing a duty of support on their husbands. That duty arose solely from the status of marriage and required a man to support his wife. The wife, in exchange, had a corresponding duty to provide household and other services to the husband, although that duty was rarely, if ever, specifically defined or enforced.

The common law similarly imposed the duty on fathers to support their children. In return, the father had a right to control his children and was entitled to their services and income.

While the family unit remained intact, the courts seldom interfered with the standard of support provided by the husband or father. For example, in *McGuire v. McGuire*,[96] Lydia McGuire brought an action for maintenance and support against Charles, her husband of more than thirty years. The trial court ordered Charles to purchase a number of specific items for improving and repairing the home and a new automobile with an effective heater. It further granted Lydia a personal allowance and ordered Charles

---

[92] Martha Fineman, *Implementing Equality: Ideology, Contradiction and Social Change -A Study of Rhetoric and Results in the Regulation of the Consequences of Divorce*, 1983 Wis. L. Rev. 789 (1983). *See also* Joan William, *Is Coverture Dead? Beyond A New Theory of Alimony*, 82 Georgetown L. J. 2227, 2236–41, 2245–46 (1994).

[93] *See* Jane Rutherford, *Duty in Divorce: Shared Income as a Path to Equality*, 58 Fordham L. Rev. 539 (1990).

[94] Bea Ann Smith, *The Partnership Theory of Marriage: A Borrowed Solution Fails*, 68 Tex. L. Rev. 689 (1990).

[95] *See, e.g.*, Gary S. Becker, *Nobel Lecture: The Economic Way of Looking at Behavior*, 101 J. of Political Econ. 385, 397–98 (1993); Arlie Hochschild with Anne Machung, *The Second Shift* 11–13 (1989); June Carbone, *Morality, Public Policy and the Family: The Role of Marriage and the Public/Private Divide*, 36 Santa Clara L. Rev. 267, 267–69, 275–78 (1996); David Blankenhorn, *The State of the Family and the Family Policy Debate*, 36 Santa Clara L. Rev. 431, 436–37 (1996).

[96] 59 N.W.2d 336 (Neb. 1953).

to pay for Lydia's travel expenses to visit her daughters. The Nebraska Supreme Court reversed, recognizing a nonintervention policy and refusing to allow the courts to interfere in the husband's administration of the family's finances. It held that a couple must be separated or living apart before a court may set a precise standard of family support. The court reasoned:

> The living standards of a family are a matter of concern to the household and not for the courts to determine, even though the husband's attitude toward his wife, according to his wealth and circumstances, leaves little to be said in his behalf. As long as the home is maintained and the parties are living as husband and wife it may be said that the husband is legally supporting his wife and the purpose of the marriage relation is being carried out. Public policy requires such a holding.[97]

Cases similar to *McGuire*, in which the courts refuse to intervene in family governance except in extreme circumstances, rest not only on notions of family autonomy and privacy, but often express apprehensions that the courts would be over-burdened with "trivial" family matters if family members were provided a legal forum for airing their grievances against each other.[98]

Courts made exceptions to their attitude of non-interference in family support matters by applying the doctrines of necessaries[99] and separate maintenance,[100] and legislatures intervened by enacting family support statutes.[101] Similarly, the common law provided limited property rights to wives in the form of the tenancy by the entirety estate[102] and through the doctrine of dower.[103]

§ 3.10 The Doctrine of Necessaries

Although the common law rarely directly enforced the husband's duty to support his wife, or the father's duty to support his children, by dictating the level of support he must provide, it indirectly intervened with family autonomy through the doctrine of necessaries. Under the doctrine of necessaries, the wife and children could purchase any essential goods or services, including food, clothing, shelter, and medical and legal services, on the husband's credit and the husband became directly liable to the provider of these necessary items. Unlike agency law principles, the doctrine of necessaries held the husband responsible regardless of his consent to, or knowledge of, the purchases.[104]

---

[97] *Id.* at 342.

[98] *See, e.g., Commonwealth v. George*, 56 A.2d 228 (Pa. 1948).

[99] *See infra* § 3.10.

[100] *See infra* § 3.11.

[101] *See infra* § 3.12.

[102] *See supra* § 3.04.

[103] *See supra* § 3.05[A].

[104] *See generally* Margaret Mahoney, *Economic Sharing During Marriage: Equal Protection, Spousal Support and the Doctrine of Necessaries*, 22 J. Fam. L. 221 (1983–84); Note, *The Unnecessary Doctrine of Necessaries*, 82 Mich. L. Rev.1767 (1984).

In *State v. Clark*,[105] the Wisconsin Supreme Court held that a husband's assets could be considered in determining whether the wife could be declared indigent for the purpose of having her criminal appeal paid for at public expense. It further concluded that although the act giving rise to the conviction on a drug charge occurred prior to marriage, the husband was aware of the pending proceedings at the time of marriage, and the conviction occurred after marriage. Therefore, the husband was liable for necessary legal expenses of the wife.

The family's economic status and standard of living and the husband's ability to provide defined the scope of the necessaries doctrine. Thus, the application of the doctrine varied from one household to another and created uncertainty in an individual case.[106] In *Sharpe Furniture, Inc. v. Buckstaff*,[107] the wife purchased a sofa from the plaintiff, without her husband's knowledge. The family was economically prominent in the community and the husband had always provided the wife with necessaries, but had previously written to the credit bureau stating that he would not be responsible for any credit extended to his wife. The Wisconsin Supreme Court held that when any item or service is obtained for the benefit of the family, such as the sofa in this case, an implied-in-law contract exists and the husband is primarily liable. It further stated that refusal or neglect of the husband is not an essential element to recovery by the creditor. Justice Abrahamson, concurring, disagreed with the rule placing primary liability on the husband for necessaries, arguing that the rule denigrates the contribution of women and denies equal protection to husbands.

The necessaries doctrine denied recovery by the third-party when that party furnished money or necessary items gratuitously, when the husband had already supplied his dependents with necessaries, or when the wife wrongfully lived apart from the husband.[108] Consequently, the doctrine of necessaries had limited practical application because merchants and other providers were exposed to considerable risk when they relied on the husband's credit.

In recent years, the doctrine of necessaries has undergone reevaluation in response to assertions that imposing liability on husbands but not wives violates equal protection principles.[109] Some jurisdictions have reacted by expanding application of the doctrine equally to both spouses. For example, in *North Carolina Baptist Hospitals v. Harris*,[110] the North Carolina

---

[105] 563 P.2d 1253 (Wis. 1977).

[106] *Compare Gimbel Bros. v. Pinto*, 145 A.2d 865 (Pa. Super. Ct. 1958) (mink coat necessary); *Sharpe Furniture Co. v. Buckstaff*, 299 N.W.2d 219 (Wis. 1980) (sofa necessary) *with Chipp v. Murray*, 379 P.2d 297 (Kan. 1963) (private detective services not necessary); *Sharon Clinic v. Nelson*, 394 N.Y.S.2d 118 (N.Y. Sup. Ct. 1977) (no showing that abortion was necessary because of wife's medical condition).

[107] 299 N.W.2d 219 (Wis. 1980).

[108] *See* Note, *The Unnecessary Doctrine of Necessaries, supra* note 104, at 1767.

[109] *See generally* Karol Williams, Comment, *The Doctrine of Necessaries: Contemporary Application as a Support Remedy*, 19 Stetson L. Rev. 661 (1990).

[110] 354 S.E.2d 471 (N.C. 1987).

Supreme Court adopted a gender neutral application of the necessaries doctrine. In *Harris*, the court held that a wife could be held liable to a hospital for her husband's necessary medical expenses under the necessaries doctrine. It noted that, in light of the trend towards gender neutrality in other areas of the law, no contemporary reason existed for applying the doctrine only to husbands. Further, the court refused to abolish the doctrine, concluding that it continues to serve beneficial functions, including "the encouragement of health care providers and facilities to provide needed medical attention to married persons and the recognition that marriage involves shared wealth, expenses, rights, and duties."[111]

In a similar case, *Jersey Shore Medical Center-Fitkin Hospital v. Estate of Baum*,[112] the New Jersey Supreme Court took a different approach, adopting a rule of primary and secondary liability. In *Jersey Shores*, a hospital sued a wife for payment of her husband's medical expenses under the necessaries doctrine. In a limited extension of the doctrine to wives, the New Jersey Supreme Court stated:

> Interdependence is the hallmark of a modern marriage. The common law rule imposing liability on husbands, but not wives, is an anachronism that no longer fits contemporary society. Under the present rule, even a husband who is economically dependent on his wife would be liable for the necessary expenses of both spouses, while the wife would not be liable for either. In perpetuating additional benefits for a wife when the benefits may not be needed, the rule runs afoul of the equal protection clause.[113]

Although the court refused to apply the necessaries doctrine to the extent that it would impose "unqualified liability" on spouses for each other's debts, it concluded that, absent agreement with the creditor, "the income and property of one spouse should not be exposed to satisfy a debt incurred by the other spouse unless the assets of the spouse who incurred the debt are insufficient."[114] Thus, a spouse who incurs necessary expenses will be primarily liable for repayment of the debt, but the other spouse will be secondarily liable to the extent the incurring spouse is unable to pay.[115]

While a number of other courts have similarly held that the doctrine of necessaries applies equally to both spouses,[116] some courts have rejected the doctrine entirely.[117] For example, in *Connor v. Southwest Florida*

---

[111] *Id.* at 474.

[112] 417 A.2d 1003 (N.J. 1980).

[113] *Id.* at 1008.

[114] *Id.* at 1010.

[115] *See also Mem'l Hosp. v. Hahaj*, 430 N.E.2d 412 (Ind. Ct. App. 1982) (marital assets are held primarily for the benefit of the marital partnership and incidentally held for creditors who provide necessaries for either spouse); *Med. Bus. Associates v. Steiner*, 588 N.Y.S.2d 890 (N.Y. App. Div. 1992).

[116] *See, e.g., Jermunson v. Jermunson*, 592 P.2d 491 (Mont. 1979); *Richland Mem'l Hosp. v. Burton*, 318 S.E.2d 12 (S.C. 1984); *St. Mary's Hospital Med. Ctr. v. Brody*, 519 N.W.2d 706 (Wis. Ct. App. 1994).

[117] The Supreme Court of Virginia judicially abolished the doctrine as outdated and a viola-

Regional Medical Center,[118] the Supreme Court of Florida abrogated the necessaries doctrine, holding that its application to husbands, but not wives, constitutes a denial of equal protection. While the court acknowledged that it could have held the doctrine applicable to both spouses, it refused to impose a duty on wives where none had previously existed, absent a legislative mandate. The highest court of Vermont has adopted the same reasoning, abolishing the necessaries doctrine altogether.[119]

§ 3.11   Common Law Separate Maintenance

The common law suit for separate maintenance, sometimes referred to as alimony without divorce or separate support, provided another avenue for enforcing the duty of support. The equitable action for separate maintenance permitted a wife to sue her husband for non-support during the spouses' separation while they remained legally married.

In some states, the suit for separate maintenance was statutory. In some instances, it was combined with the divorce from bed and board, also designated divorce *a mensa et thoro* or judicial separation, although the two actions remain distinct. The action for separate maintenance was intended merely to provide support for the wife, while the divorce from bed and board technically decreed that the parties would live separate and apart. Little practical difference existed between the actions, as both suits left the parties legally married to each other, unable to remarry anyone else, and both ordered the husband to support the wife.[120]

However, in *Capodanno v. Commissioner of Internal Revenue*,[121] the court distinguished between a decree of separate maintenance and a divorce from bed and board for determining a wife's proper income tax filing status under New Jersey law. It noted that while a separate maintenance decree awarded to a wife recognizes a de facto separation based on the husband's fault, it merely enforces the husband's duty to continue supporting her financially. It does not legitimize their living apart but "favors a resumption of cohabitation."[122] The divorce from bed and board, however, "nullifies the marital obligation of cohabitation."[123] Therefore, regardless of the grounds for the separate maintenance decree, the couple remained "married" for tax purposes.

---

tion of equal protection in *Shilling v. Bedford County Mem'l Hosp.*, 303 S.E.2d 905 (Va. 1983), but the Virginia legislature reinstated the doctrine in gender-neutral terms. *See* Va. Code Ann. § 55-37 (1986). *See generally*, Elizabeth Jackson, *Equal Protection and Spousal Debt: Novel Application of Necessaries Doctrine*, 11 Stetson L. Rev. 173 (1981).

[118] 668 So. 2d 175 (Fla. 1995).

[119] *Med. Hosp. Ctr. of Vermont v. Lorrain*, 675 A.2d 1326 (Vt. 1996). *See also Medlock v. Fort Smith Serv. Fin. Corp.*, 803 S.W.2d 930 (Ark. 1991); *Condore v. Prince George's County*, 425 A.2d 1011 (Md. 1981).

[120] *See* Homer Clark, *supra*, note 13, at 266–67.

[121] 602 F.2d 64 (3d Cir. 1979).

[122] *Id.* at 67.

[123] *Id.*

Although the grounds for the two actions were comparable, they varied from state to state. Traditionally, under either a separate maintenance action or a divorce from bed and board, if the wife was guilty of marital fault, she forfeited her right to support.[124] An order for separate maintenance replaced the husband's common law duty of support,[125] and although reconciliation generally terminated a separate maintenance decree, it did not automatically terminate decrees for divorce from bed and board.[126] If the support recipient rejected a good faith offer to reconcile, she could lose the right to bring an action based on desertion if her support was based on a separate maintenance decree, although not if it had been ordered pursuant to a divorce from bed and board.[127]

In some jurisdictions, separate maintenance was intended to be a temporary remedy, while divorce from bed and board traditionally was regarded as permanent.[128] Modern statutes, however, require conversion of the divorce from bed and board into an absolute divorce after a specific period of time.[129]

The separate maintenance doctrine has been criticized for imposing the burdens, but not the benefits, of marriage, and some commentators have suggested its only purpose should be to provide relief when one spouse refuses to support the other or when absolute divorce is not an acceptable solution for religious or other reasons.[130] Under contemporary constitutional law principles, separate maintenance must be made available to husbands as well as wives or be subject to invalidation on equal protection grounds.[131]

§ 3.12 Statutory Support Obligations

[A] Spousal and Child Support Statutes

As an additional, but limited, means of enforcing the support obligation, most states have enacted a variety of family expense statutes that codify the spousal duty of support and statutes that impose criminal sanctions for non-support. Family expense and criminal non-support statutes also

---

[124] See Rosenthal v. Rosenthal, 107 N.W.2d 204 (Wis. 1961); Robert Coleman Brown, The Duty of the Husband to Support the Wife, 18 Va. L. Rev. 823, 846 (1932).

[125] See People ex rel. Comm'rs of Pub.Charities & Correction v. Cullen, 47 N.E. 894 (N.Y. 1897).

[126] Homer Clark, supra note 13, at 267–68 (noting that the parties may petition to have the divorce from bed and board vacated if they reconcile).

[127] Id.

[128] See, e.g., Chipman v. Chipman, 406 P.2d 150 (Or. 1965). But see Clifford v.Clifford, 42 Haw. 279 (Haw. 1958) (either party may convert divorce from bed and board into permanent divorce after thirty days).

[129] See, e.g., Unif. Marriage and Divorce Act § 314, 9A U.L.A. 180 (1979); N.Y. Dom. Rel. Law § 170(5) (McKinney 1988) (living apart for one or more years after grant of decree of judgment of separation is ground for divorce).

[130] Id. at 268–69.

[131] See Homer Clark, supra note 13, at 268.

apply to an equal, and sometimes greater, extent to child support. Equal protection principles now require that these statutes apply equally to both wives and husbands,[132] and federal legislation has significantly augmented child support remedies.[133]

Family expense statutes, often originally enacted in conjunction with the Married Women's Property Acts, provide an additional method for third parties to enforce support obligations.[134] These statutes typically allow a creditor to execute against either spouse's property to collect debts incurred for necessary family expenses.[135] Some statutes create personal liability against the spouse as well.[136] The statutes do not, however, provide a direct remedy for enforcing the duty of support by the spouses themselves.[137] Family expense statutes generally embrace the range of family expenditures included under the necessaries doctrine, although some are more limited. While the types of expenses encompassed by these statutes may vary, courts have found that funeral expenses, legal fees, and, most commonly, medical expenses, are included.[138]

One court recently held that its Family Expense Statute only applied to intact families and could not be asserted against a non-custodial father by a clinic that had provided medical treatment to his minor children after the parents were divorced.[139] The Court of Appeals of Washington has concluded that the state's family expense statute, which imposes a support obligation on stepparents, does not allow a foster parent to recover child support from the stepparent when the child is not living with him, nor does it allow recovery from the biological parent without establishing the amount of support actually furnished by the third party.[140]

[B] Criminal Non-Support Statutes

Most criminal non-support statutes are not as broad as the civil family expense statutes and apply only when a spouse is left completely without means of support or without necessary food, clothing, or housing.[141] Criminal non-support statutes typically require desertion, abandonment, or neglect in addition to non-support, and sometimes do not apply when

---

[132] See, e.g., Beers v. Public Health Trust of Dade County, 468 So. 2d 995 (Fla. Dist. Ct. App. 1985); In re Stanton-Rieger, 25 B.R. 650 (Bankr. Colo. 1982); Credit Bureau of Santa Monica Bay Dist. v. Terranova, 93 Cal. Rptr. 538 (Cal. Ct. App. 1971).

[133] See Chapter 8, infra.

[134] See Joan Krauskopf & Rhonda Thomas, Partnership Marriage: The Solution to an Ineffective and Inequitable Law of Support, 35 Ohio St. L.J. 558, 571 (1974).

[135] See, e.g., Mo. Rev. Stat. § 451.260 (1986).

[136] See, e.g., Ill. Ann. Stat. ch. 40, para. 1015 (West 1990).

[137] See supra Joan Krauskopf & Rhonda Thomas, note 134.

[138] Davis-Turner Funeral Home v. Chaney, 573 N.E.2d 1242 (Ohio Mun. Ct. 1991) (funeral expenses within statutory definition of necessaries); In re Dupont, 19 Bankr. 605, 607 (E.D.N.Y. 1982) (attorney fees are necessaries under New York law).

[139] Sentry Investigations, Inc. v. Davis, 841 P.2d 732 (Utah Ct. App. 1992).

[140] Brewer v. Spencer, 835 P.2d 267 (Wash. Ct. App. 1992).

[141] Homer Clark, supra note 13, at 271.

the spouses are living under the same roof. The purpose of these narrow criminal statutes is to protect the public, not the deserted spouse.[142] Other, more liberal criminal non-support statutes do not require the family to receive public assistance in order to prosecute for non-support.[143]

The defendant's conduct must be willful and a person cannot be convicted for non-support unless he or she is capable of providing that support.[144] Furthermore, a person cannot be prosecuted for non-support if the complaining spouse has refused to live with the other without cause or in other ways given the defendant "good excuse" for the failure to support.[145]

The use of criminal penalties for non-support has been criticized for creating undue hardship and for being self-defeating, because defendants will not be able to provide support for their families if they are jailed.[146] The statutes, however, have the dual purpose of punishing past behavior and acting as an incentive to the defendant to comply with support obligations in the future.[147]

[C] Pendente Lite Statutes

When spouses are separated but still married while an annulment or divorce action is pending, the needy spouse may petition the court in a *pendente lite*, or temporary support, action to obtain spousal or child support during the course of the divorce or annulment proceeding.[148] However, a court's determination of temporary spousal or child support is not binding in the final divorce or annulment decree.[149]

§ 3.13 Rights of Consortium

Traditional common law granted the husband rights collectively referred to as "rights of consortium". These "rights" included his wife's services, society, and companionship, and an entitlement to sexual relations with his wife.[150] Today, states now recognize a wife's corresponding rights of consortium with respect to her husband.[151] Contemporary rights of

---

[142] Joan Krauskopf & Rhonda Thomas, *supra* note 134, at 574.

[143] *See, e.g.,* Conn. Gen. Stat. Ann. § 53-304(a) (West 1990).

[144] *See, e.g., Burris v. State*, 382 N.E.2d 963 (Ind. Ct. App. 1978); *State v. Greer*, 144 N.W.2d 322 (Iowa 1966).

[145] *See* Homer Clark, *supra* note 13, at 273.

[146] *See* Michele Hermann & Shannon Donahue, *Fathers Behind Bars: The Right to Counsel in Civil Contempt Proceedings*, 14 N.M. L. Rev. 275 (1984).

[147] *See* Homer Clark, *supra*, note 13, at 270.

[148] *See, e.g.,* Cal Fam. Code § 3600 (1997); Fla. Stat. Ch. § 61.071 (1997); N.J. Dom. Rel. Law § 236 (1998).

[149] *See, e.g., Shepherd v. Shepherd*, 231 Ga. 257, 200 S.E.2d 893 (Ga. 1973).

[150] *See id.* at 391; *see also Carey v. Foster*, 221 F. Supp. 185 (E.D. Va. 1963), *aff'd*, 345 F.2d 772 (4th Cir. 1965) (no right of consortium in wife at common law).

[151] *See Am. Export Lines v. Alvez*, 446 U.S. 274 (1980) (41 states and District of Columbia allow either spouse to recover for loss of consortium); *see also* Kan. Stat. Ann. § 23-205 (1988); Va. Code Ann. § 55-36 (1986 Repl. Pam.).

consortium refer to "the total of tangible and intangible relationships prevailing between husbands and wives"[152] and encompass the love, affection, care, services, companionship and society of a spouse.[153]

To recover on a loss of consortium claim, most courts require proof that a third party intentionally or negligently harmed the spouse and caused physical injury,[154] although some courts have allowed recovery despite the absence of physical injury.[155] Punitive damages have sometimes been allowed as part of a claim for loss of consortium where the defendant's conduct was willful or malicious.[156]

Some courts have refused to recognize loss of consortium in wrongful death actions.[157] To avoid the potential double recovery, an increasing number of states require that a single suit combine the injured spouse's own claim for damages with the other spouse's claim for loss of consortium.[158]

Most courts recognize a claim for recovery for loss of consortium against a third party. The action is generally limited to legally married parties,[159]

---

[152] Homer Clark, *supra* note 13, at 382.

[153] *See Pickens Bond.Constr.Co. v. Case*, 584 S.W.2d 21 (Ark. 1979); *Clark v. Ark-La-Tex Auction, Inc.*, 593 So. 2d 870 (La. Ct. App. 1992); *Berger v. Weber*, 267 N.W.2d 124 (Mich. Ct. App. 1978).

[154] *See Johnson v. May*, 585 N.E.2d 224 (Ill. App. Ct. 1992) (spouse may recover from tortfeasor for losses incurred due to other spouse's injury); *Groat v. Town of Glenville*, 418 N.Y.S.2d 842 (N.Y. Sup. Ct. 1979) (physical injury or physical confinement away from other spouse necessary under tort principles governing loss of consortium damages); *see also* Kevin Lindsey, Note, *A More Equitable Approach to Loss of Spousal Consortium*, 75 Iowa L. Rev. 713 (1990).

[155] *See Molien v. Kaiser Found. Hosps.*, 606 P.2d 813 (Cal. 1980) (husband may recover for loss of consortium based on negligent infliction of emotional distress caused by hospital's erroneous diagnosis of syphilis in wife); *Habelow v. Travelers Ins. Co.*, 389 So. 2d 218 (Fla. Dist. Ct. App. 1980) (wife could maintain action on loss of consortium claim based on "malicious intent to inflict mental anguish" due to insults and abusive conduct directed toward husband).

[156] *See Butcher v. Robertshaw Controls Co.*, 550 F. Supp. 692 (D. Md. 1981). *But see Hammond v. N. Am. Asbestos Corp.*, 435 N.E.2d 540 (Ill. App. Ct. 1982), *aff'd*, 454 N.E.2d 210 (Ill. 1983) (allowing punitive damages for loss of consortium would involve important policy considerations that should be made by supreme court). *See also* Jo-Anne Baio, Note, *Loss of Consortium: A Derivative Injury Giving Rise to a Separate Cause of Action*, 50 Fordham L. Rev. 1344 (1982).

[157] *See Mullen v. Posada del Sol Health Care*, 819 P.2d 985 (Ariz. 1991) (allowable items of injury under wrongful death statute are loss of love, affection, companionship, consortium, personal anguish and suffering); *Liff v. Schildkrout*, 404 N.E.2d 1288 (N.Y. 1980) (recovery for loss of consortium prior to death permissible, but no statutory authority for such claim after death); *but see Elliot v. Willis*, 447 N.E.2d 1062 (Ill. App. Ct. 1983) (damages for loss of consortium allowable in wrongful death action); *In re Estate of Feld*, 582 N.Y.S.2d 922 (N.Y. Surr. Ct. 1992) (damages for loss of society not recoverable in wrongful death actions in New York).

[158] *See, e.g., Sharpenter v. Lynch*, 599 N.E.2d 464 (Ill. App. Ct. 1992) (loss of consortium claim accrued at same time husband was injured under sudden and traumatic event rule); *Mease v. Commonwealth*, 603 A.2d 679 (Pa. Commw. Ct. 1992) (widow of bystander who was killed by bullet was not entitled to obtain separate recovery for loss of consortium in wrongful death action); *Nicholson v. Chatham Mem'l Hosp.*, 266 S.E.2d 818 (N.C. 1980).

[159] *See, e.g., Johnson v. May*, 585 N.E.2d 224 (Ill. App. Ct. 1992) (must be married to injured spouse and prove damages); *Clinquennoi v. Michaels Group*, 577 N.Y.S.2d 550 (N.Y. App. Div. 1991) (wife did not have derivative cause of action for personal injuries suffered by her husband before their marriage).

and most courts do not allow recovery for injuries incurred prior to marriage or to unmarried cohabiting couples.[160] However, a few cases have recognized claims for loss of consortium by cohabiting couples or couples who were engaged but not yet married.[161]

In addition to the right of spousal consortium, a father traditionally could sue for the loss of a child's services and earnings;[162] today, either parent's interest in the society, companionship, and services of his or her child is compensable.[163] The law has been more reluctant, however, to extend loss of consortium actions to allow children to recover for injury to a parent.[164]

§ 3.14   Relative Responsibility Statutes

Under common law principles, and in the absence of statutory authority, an adult child has no legal duty to provide for his or her indigent parent's needs. However, a majority of states have enacted relative responsibility statutes, which are derived from the Elizabethan Poor Laws of the sixteenth and seventeenth centuries,[165] requiring adult children to contribute to the support of a needy parent. Some states also have statutes that create a crime of failure to support a parent in need.[166]

Relative responsibility statutes usually impose a joint and several duty upon any adult child with sufficient resources, after providing for his or her immediate family, to support parents who are destitute or in necessitous circumstances. A financial responsibility statute generally is enforceable by the parent, but more frequently is applied by an agency seeking reimbursement for services or by denying or altering an elderly person's eligibility for benefits.[167]

---

[160] See Curry v. Caterpillar Tractor Co., 577 F.Supp. 991 (E.D. Pa.1984) (no loss of consortium allowed to 15-year cohabitant and mother of injured party's three children); Anderson v. Eli Lilly & Co., 588 N.E.2d 66 (N.Y. 1991) (husband could not recover for loss of consortium for wife's exposure to DES and resultant injuries prior to marriage); Miller v. Davis, 433 N.Y.S.2d 974 (N.Y. Sup. Ct. 1980) (no loss of consortium allowed where injuries required that wedding be delayed).

[161] See Sutherland v. Auch Inter-Borough Transit Co., 366 F. Supp. 127 (E.D. Pa. 1973) (husband allowed damages for loss of consortium where marriage occurred after wife's accident).

[162] See Tinnerholm v. Parke-Davis & Co., 285 F. Supp. 432 (S.D.N.Y.), aff'd, 411 F.2d 48 (2d Cir. 1968); City of Dalton v. Webb, 206 S.E.2d 639 (Ga. Ct. App. 1974).

[163] See Kinsella v. Farmers Ins., 826 P.2d 433 (Colo. Ct. App. 1992); Rogers v. Donelson-Hermitage Chamber of Commerce, 807 S.W.2d 242 (Tenn. Ct. App. 1990); Glover v. Norick, 400 S.E.2d 816 (W. Va. 1990).

[164] See Murray v. Anthony J. Bertucci Constr. Co., 745 F. Supp. 373 (E.D. La. 1990) (child's action for loss of parent's consortium not available under general maritime law).

[165] 43 Eliz. 1 c. 2 (1601). See also Usha Narayan, The Government's Role in Fostering the Relationship Between Adult Children and Their Elder Parents: From Filial Responsibility Laws to . . . What?, A Cross-Cultural Perspective, 4 Elder L.J. 369, 372 (1996); Jacobus ten-Broek, California's Dual System of Family Law: Its Origin, Development, and Present Status, Part I, 16 Stan. L. Rev. 257, 257–58 (1964).

[166] See Ann Britton, America's Best Kept Secret: An Adult Child's Duty to Support Aged Parents, 26 Cal. W.L. Rev. 351, 354 (1990).

[167] See generally Terrance A. Kline, A Rationale Role for Filial Responsibility Laws in Modern Society?, 26 Fam. L.Q. 195 (1992); Walton Garrett, Filial Responsibility Laws, 28 J. Fam. L. 793, 813 (1980).

Relative responsibility statutes raise policy questions of whether family members or the state should assume responsibility for the elderly. The California Supreme Court addressed these issues in *Swoap v. Superior Court*,[168] a class action case attacking the constitutionality of statutes requiring adult children to reimburse the state for payments made to their elderly parents under a state public assistance program. The court in *Swoap* distinguished cases which had held that the cost of maintaining persons in state institutions could not be arbitrarily assessed to relatives who otherwise had no legal responsibility for the person's care and support,[169] and concluded that California law had long imposed a duty of support upon adult children who were capable of supporting their needy parents. Thus, that duty could be extended to require reimbursement to the state when the state had taken over the responsibility of supporting needy parents without constituting discrimination based on wealth. One justice dissented, arguing that the decision imposed "public expenses on a small class of citizens . . . plac[ing] disproportionate shares of public expenses on various minority groups . . . [and] sanction[ing] a perpetration of a dual system of family law which places special financial burdens on individuals simply because of the poverty of their families."[170]

One rationale supporting relative responsibility laws is the principle of reciprocity in the parent-child relationship. This reasoning, which implies an indebtedness to the parents for their previous support and care of their children, loses its strength when the children in question received disadvantages rather than benefits from their parents. Accordingly, some states' statutes do not impose liability on adult children whose parents wilfully neglected or deserted them while they were minors.[171]

Troublesome choice of law questions arise when support is sought on behalf of a needy parent living in a state that has a relative responsibility statute against an adult child who resides in a state without such a statute.[172] Similar problems arise when the defendant's state recognizes a defense, such as abandonment, that is not recognized in the plaintiff's state.[173]

It remains unclear whether a state may require adult children to support their parents without violating federal Medicaid or Medicare statutes and

---

[168] 516 P.2d 840 (Cal. 1973).

[169] *Dep't of Mental Hygiene v. Kirchner*, 388 P.2d 720 (Cal. 1964).

[170] 516 P.2d at 864 (Tobriner, J., dissenting).

[171] *See, e.g.*, Conn. Gen. Stat. Ann. § 326 (West Supp. 1987); Or. Rev. Stat. § 416.030(2)(c) (1999).

[172] *California v. Copus*, 309 S.W.2d 227 (Tex. 1958), *cert. denied*, 356 U.S. 967 (1958). *See also* George Indest, Comment, *Legal Aspects of HCFA's Decision to Allow Recovery from Children for Medicaid Benefits Delivered to their Parents Through State Financial Responsibility Statutes: A Case of Bad Rule Making Through Failure to Comply with the Administrative Procedure Act*, 28 Soc. Sec. Rep. Ser. 728 (1990).

[173] *See Commonwealth v. Mong*, 117 N.E.2d 32 (Ohio 1954).

regulations.[174] Largely because of this uncertainty, the number of states retaining and enacting relative responsibility legislation has fluctuated.[175]

Some commentators have questioned the wisdom of relative responsibility statutes and have recommended their repeal.[176] The underlying policy question of whether the state or adult children should be responsible for needy parents continues to be debated.

§ 3.15   Support Enforcement Remedies

Actions for contempt, with resulting imprisonment, and support enforcement remedies provided by the federal child support enforcement acts, may all be utilized when a person fails to support his or her dependents while the marriage remains intact. However, these remedies are most commonly applied in the context of divorce and are thus discussed in Section 8.06[F], *infra*.

In 1996, Congress passed the Personal Responsibility and Work Opportunity Act (PRWORA), also referred to as the 1996 Welfare Reform Act.[177] The PRWORA attempts to make payment of child support more certain and more predictable by processing these cases in bulk rather than individually, by providing greater access to related support information, and by creating automatic enforcement procedures.[178] Recent studies indicate that more stringent support enforcement measures are effective in increasing the amount of child support paid.[179] Because all of these enforcement remedies are most commonly applied in the context of divorced or never-married parents, they are addressed in more detail in Chapter 10.

---

[174] *See* Robin M. Jacobson, Note, *American Health Care Ctr. v. Randall: The Renaissance of Filial Responsibility*, 40 S.D. L. Rev. 518 (1995); Catherine Doscher Byrd, *Relative Responsibility Extended: Requirement of Adult Children to Pay for Their Indigent Parent's Medical Needs*, 22 Fam. L.Q. 87, 90 (1988).

[175] *See* Byrd., at 90; Lee Teitelbaum, *Intergenerational Responsibility and Family Obligations: On Sharing*, 1992 Utah L. Rev. 765; Renae Reed Patrick, *Honor Thy Father and Mother: Paying the Medical Bills of Elderly Parents*, 19 U. Rich. L. Rev. 69 (1984).

[176] *See, e.g.*, Robert Whitman & Diane Whitney, *Are Children Legally Responsible for the Support of their Parents?*, 123 Tr. & Est. L.J. 43 (1984).

[177] 42 U.S.C. § 601 (1996) et. seq.

[178] *See* Linda Elrod, *Child Support Reassessed: Federalization of Enforcement Nears Completion*, 1997 U. Ill. L. Rev. 695, 703 (1997).

[179] *Id.*; *see also* Paul K. Leglar, *The Coming Revolution in Child Support Policy: Implications of the 1996 Welfare Act,* 30 Fam. L.Q. 519 (1996).

Chapter 4
MARITAL CONTRACTS AND AGREEMENTS

§ 4.01 Introduction

Marital property rights and support obligations normally devolve upon the spouses by operation of law at the time of the marriage.[1] Likewise, property and support rights on divorce or dissolution of marriage are generally governed by state statutory and judicial authority at the time the marriage is dissolved.[2]

However, the parties may also create binding economic rights and obligations by contract or agreement: (1) prior to their marriage in the form of a premarital or antenuptial agreement; (2) when a marriage engagement is contracted for and subsequently broken in a minority of states; or (3) in the form of a separation agreement or property settlement agreement at the time of divorce or dissolution of marriage. Indeed, it is estimated that between 80 to 90 per cent of all divorces involve some form of a contractual agreement, which may affect the parties' spousal support rights (or the waiver of such rights), a division of the parties' marital property (or waiver of such rights), and child support and child custody issues (subject to court approval).[3]

The courts therefore have increasingly been asked by the parties to evaluate and enforce their marital contracts, either oral or written, actual or implied, that deal with the economic rights and obligations of the marital partners. For example, in the past, premarital agreements were primarily made by older couples-normally widows and widowers-who were about to be remarried, and who had acquired considerable property from a prior marriage that they wished to control and pass to the children of their first marriage.[4] Premarital agreements today, however, are increasingly being utilized by younger Americans who have acquired, or will acquire, substantial property and, due to a higher probability of divorce or marriage dissolution than in past decades, desire to retain such property as separate property rather than marital property.[5]

---

[1] *See generally* Chapter 3 *supra.*

[2] *See generally* Chapters 9 and 10 *infra.* Property and support rights for nonmarital relationships and domestic partnerships are discussed in Chapter 2.02 *supra.*

[3] *See* Green & Long, Marriage and Family Law Agreements 213 (1984); Mnookin & Kornhauser, *Bargaining in the Shadow of the Law: The Case for Divorce*, 88 Yale L.J. 950 (1979),

[4] *See generally,* Gamble, *The Antenuptial Agreement*, 26 U. Miami L. Rev. 692 (1972); Clark, *Antenuptial Contracts*, 50 U. Colo. L. Rev. 141 (1979)..

[5] *See, e.g.,* Swisher, *Divorce Planning in Antenuptial Agreements: Toward a New Objectivity*, 13 U. Rich. L. Rev. 175 (1979); Note, *For Better or For Worse. . .But Just in Case, Are Antenuptial Agreements Enforceable?* 1982 U. Ill. L. Rev. 531 (1982).

Premarital agreements may also be utilized by the prospective spouses to provide *more*— rather than less— sharing of income and assets during marriage, or after divorce, than state statutory rules would otherwise require.[6] In addition, some commentators have suggested that premarital contracts also have the potential to improve communication and enhance the commitment of the spouses, both before and during a couple's marriage.[7] For example, Professor Allison Marston states that:

> Prenuptials do not deserve their reputation as the bastion of greed and selfishness in marriage. They can offer more than protection against scheming second wives or social climbing husbands. Rather, prenuptial agreements can promote greater love, communication, and, ultimately, happiness in marriage. A legal framework incorporating an independent counsel requirement would promote fairness and full knowledge by both parties, which increases the potential for prenuptials to be a positive, relation-enhancing experience.[8]

Not all commentators, however, applaud the increased use of marital contracting. Some scholars, for example, oppose the "contractualization" of marriage and divorce because of "the unique nature of the marital relationship, the possibility of irrational and uninformed decision-making at the time of contracting, the likelihood of unforeseen changes in circumstances over the life of the marriage, and the real risk of disadvantage to the economically weaker spouse".[9] Moreover, some feminist scholars argue that premarital and separation agreements invariably harm women by waiving legal and financial protection afforded by state law, and by magnifying an unequal distribution of wealth along gender lines.[10] Other scholars have challenged this view, however, arguing that "emphasizing women's inferior status and bargaining power over women's autonomous right to structure their relations as they see fit reifies the perception that women are the weaker sex and justifies the view that the law--and men--need to protect women from themselves."[11] These scholars suggest that a better approach

---

[6] *See, e.g.,* Guggenheimer, *A Modest Proposal: The Feminomics of Drafting Premarital Agreements,* 17 Women's Rights L. Rep. 147, 204 (1996) (arguing that the drafting norms for premarital agreements should move away from an exclusive focus on competing interests and limiting claims and move "toward a vision of private ordering that is governed by conjoining interests and distributional needs"). *See also* Singer, *The Privatization of Family Law,* 1992 Wis. L. Rev. 1443 (discussing the advantages and disadvantages of a shift from public to private ordering of family law).

[7] *See, e.g.,* Marston, *Planning for Love: The Politics of Prenuptial Agreements,* 49 Stanford L. Rev. 887, 916 (1997).

[8] *Id.* at 916.

[9] Atwood, *Ten Years Later: Lingering Concerns About the Uniform Premarital Agreement Act,* 19 J. Legis. 127, 131 (1993). *See also* Sharp, *Fairness Standards and Separation Agreements: A Word of Caution on Contractual Freedom,* 132 U. Pa. L. Rev. 1399 (1984) (urging greater substantive and procedural fairness review for marital contracts).

[10] *See, e.g.,* Brod, *Premarital Agreements and Gender Justice,* 6 Yale J. L. & Feminism 229 (1994); Tidwell & Linzer, *The Flesh-Colored Band Aid Contracts: Feminism, Dialogue, and Norms,* 28 Houston L. Rev. 791 (1991).

[11] *See, e.g.,* Guggenheimer, *A Modest Proposal: The Feminomics of Drafting Premarital Agreements,* 17 Women's Rights L. Rep. 147, 155 (1996)

to empowering women would be to enact procedural and substantive reforms designed to make premarital agreements fairer from the outset, rather than allowing judges to invalidate such agreements on *ad hoc* grounds of fairness or equity.[12]

Likewise, separation agreements or property settlement agreements on divorce or dissolution of marriage that were once looked upon by various courts and commentators with mistrust and suspicion for allegedly being "in derogation of marriage", or for allegedly "promoting" the procurement of divorce,[13] are now highly favored by family law courts in almost all jurisdictions.[14] Like premarital agreements, separation agreements generally will be upheld by the courts if: (1) there is a full and fair disclosure of the parties' assets and liabilities at the time of contracting; and (2) there is independent legal advice and counsel for both parties, especially if one of the parties is educationally or economically less empowered, such as a traditional house spouse.[15]

Marital agreements—whether they be premarital, postmarital, or separation agreements-therefore allow the parties to agree upon, and privately control, many important aspects of their own marriage and divorce. While such agreements traditionally have been used to limit the parties' economic rights and obligations arising from marriage, they are increasingly being viewed as vehicles to enhance, as well as limit, both the economic and non-economic benefits of marriage. In assessing the desirability of such agreement, and evaluating their validity in any particular case, it may be useful to keep in mind the alternatives in relying on marital agreements as the private ordering of marriage and divorce. As Professors Michael Trebilcock and Rosemin Deshvani observe:

> Whatever the deficiencies of the private ordering process, in every context the hard question must be, compared to what? And the "what" with which actual private ordering regimes must be compared should not be some idealized alternative form of legal ordering, but the available alternative forms of legal ordering as they are actually likely to operate in the real world. . . . [T]he preferences of legislators, judges, bureaucrats, experts, and academics, with all their sundry biases and subjectivities, must be compared

---

[12] *Id.* at 204–207.

[13] *See, e.g.,* Madden, Handbook of the Law of Persons and Domestic Relations 331–335 (1931). *See also Dexter v. Dexter,* 371 S.E.2d 816 (Va. Ct. App. 1988) for a historical analysis of this traditional view, and its evolution into the current modern view of judicial promotion and encouragement of marital contracts in general, and separation agreements in particular.

[14] *See, e.g., Drawdy v. Drawdy,* 268 S.E.2d 30, 31 (S.C. 1980) (stating that marital agreements "are praiseworthy products of cooperation between parties seeking a divorce. They also serve to decrease the workload of family courts and thereby enhance judicial efficiency"); *Reynolds v. Reynolds,* 415 A.2d 535, 537 (D.C. 1980) ("This jurisdiction encourages the parties in any marital dispute to resolve by agreement their joint marital interests").

[15] *See generally* Lindey & Parley, Lindey on Separation Agreements and Antenuptial Contracts (1999 rev. ed.); Schlissel, Separation Agreements and Marital Contracts (1986); Green & Long, Marriage and Family Law Agreements (1984).

with the flawed self-understandings and preferences of individuals attempting to determine their life plans for themselves.[16]

§ 4.02   Marriage Promises and Premarital Gifts

[A]   Breach of Promise to Marry

An action for breach of promise to marry has existed under the common law for over 300 years. In a breach of promise action, the plaintiff was entitled to recover in contract or tort for injury to his or her feelings, health, and reputation; and damages could be awarded based upon the defendant's wealth, income, and social position. Seduction could also be argued as an "aggravation of damages."[17]

Proof of a broken promise to marry could be circumstantial in this highly emotional area, and thus it afforded "a fertile field for blackmail and extortion."[18] Accordingly, many critics over the past fifty years have advocated the abolition of this fault-based anachronistic action, especially in the era of no-fault divorce, and most states have now abolished breach of promise to marry actions through so-called state "anti-heart balm statutes."[19] Nevertheless, a minority of states still recognize a breach of promise to marry action under the common law.[20]

Although it is well settled under the law that inducing the breach of a business contract can be actionable in tort,[21] most courts have been unwilling to apply this legal theory to a third-party-induced breach of promise to marry. One rationale for denying such relief is that it would prevent parents, relatives, or friends from giving advice to the prospective spouse; another is that it would allow an unsuccessful suitor to sue his or her rival for damages.[22] Similarly, in the majority of jurisdictions, there is no longer an action for alienation of affections by a jilted suitor based upon the conduct of a third party.[23]

---

[16] Trebilcock & Keshvani, *The Role of Private Ordering in Family Law: A Law and Economics Perspective*, 41 U. Toronto L. Rev. 533, 589-90 (1991). *See also* Weisbrod, *The Way We Live Now: A Discussion of Contracts and Domestic Relations*, 1994 Utah L. Rev. 777 (1994); and Symposium, *Opportunities for and Limitations of Private Ordering in Family Law*, 73 Ind. L.J. 453 (1998).

[17] *See, e.g.*, Keeton et al., Prosser and Keeton on the Law of Torts § 124 (5th ed. 1984).

[18] *Id.*

[19] *See generally* 1 H. Clark, Law of Domestic Relations 1–30 (2d ed. 1987).

[20] According to Green & Long, Marriage and Family Law Agreements 102–107 (1984), the common law action for breach of promise to marry still exists today in a minority of jurisdictions, including: Georgia, Hawaii, Kansas, Nebraska, North Carolina, Texas, and Washington. Illinois retains this action by statute, but the statute limits recoverable damages only to actual damages. Ill. Ann. Stat.ch. 40 § 1801 *et seq. See generally Askew v. Askew*, 28 Cal. Rptr. 2d 284 (Cal. Ct. App. 1994) which provides and excellent background discussion of breach of promise to marry actions and state "anti-heart balm" statutes. *See, e.g., Stanard v. Bolin*, 565 P.2d 94 (Wash. 1977); *Wildey v. Springs*, 47 F.3f 1475 (7th Cir. 1995) (applying Ill. law).

[21] *See generally* Keeton et al, Prosser and Keeton on the Law of Torts § 129 (5th ed. 1984).

[22] *See generally*, 1 H. Clark, Law of Domestic Relations 33–34 (2d ed. 1987).

[23] *See generally* Brown, *The Action for Alienation of Affections*, 82 U. Pa. L. Rev. 472, 476 (1934). *But see Cannon v. Miller*, 322 S.E.2d 780 (N.C. Ct. App. 1984), *vacated*, 327 S.E.2d 888 (N.C. 1984).

[B] Fraudulent Inducement to Marry Actions

Even though the action for breach of promise to marry has been abolished in the vast majority of states, a party may still have an action against another party for a fraudulent inducement into a marriage contract. For example, if a man fraudulently conceals the existence of his prior marital status, and enters into a bigamous second marriage with another woman, that woman can seek compensatory and punitive damages against the man based upon his fraud; and damages can include her mental pain and suffering, as well as lost wages and other economic injuries. [24]

[C] Contracts Restraining or Promoting Marriage

A contract in general restraint of marriage is void as against public policy [25] for two reasons: (1) "the sanctity of the marriage relationship is at the foundation of the welfare of the State," [26] and (2) the right to marry is a fundamental right. [27]

However, the law will generally permit a partial restraint of marriage, if the specific restraint is shown to be "reasonable" under the circumstances. [28] The "reasonableness" of a restraint of marriage is illustrated by the following examples:

(1) A father promises his 25-year-old son that he will give the son $250,000 in return for the son's promise not to marry for at least ten years. This would be a general restraint of marriage, and not a reasonable one. [29]

(2) An ailing 70-year-old uncle promises to give his 45-year-old niece certain real and personal property in his will if she will remain unmarried, live with him, and take care of him. This would be a reasonable restraint of marriage, and constitute a valid contract. [30]

(3) A paragraph in a will gave a testator's niece "all my real and personal property so long as she remains single and unmarried." This has been held to be a "reasonable" restraint on marriage on the theory that the donee is provided with support or property rights until she marries a "new provider," and therefore it is not a general restraint on marriage. [31]

Contracts promoting marriage are likewise illegal, since marriage should be entered into freely, uninfluenced by third parties who are paid to bring

---

[24] *See, e.g., Holcomb v. Kincaid*, 406 So. 2d 650 (La. Ct. App. 1981); *Buckley v. Buckley*, 184 Cal. Rptr. 290 (Cal. Ct. App. 1982); *Humphreys v. Baird*, 90 S.E.2d 796 (Va. 1956). *See also* Annot., 72 A.L.R.2d 956, 981 and Later Case Service.

[25] Restatement (Second) of Contracts § 189 (1981).

[26] *See* 15 Williston on Contracts § 1741 (3d ed. 1972).

[27] *See, e.g., Zablocki v. Redhail*, 434 U.S. 374 (1978).

[28] *See, e.g.,* 6A Corbin on Contracts, § 1474 (1962).

[29] *See* Restatement (Second) of Contracts § 189, Illustration (1981).

[30] *Id. See also Gleason v. Mann*, 45 N.E.2d 280 (Mass. 1942).

[31] *See, e.g., Lewis v. Searles*, 452 S.W.2d 153 (Mo. 1970). *See also* Browder, *Conditions and Limitations in Restraint of Marriage*, 39 Mich. L. Rev. 1288 (1941). According to Annot., 122 A.L.R. 7 (1939), however, this rule has been "eaten out with exceptions."

it about. [32] Thus, no action would lie for the collection of any promised fees for procuring a husband or wife by a marriage broker, [33] or by a marriage service agency. [34]

[D] Premarital Gifts

Disputes frequently arise over who is entitled to an engagement ring or other premarital gifts conditioned on marriage when the engagement is broken. A number of courts follow the traditional rule that the donor of an engagement ring, or the donor of any other gift conditioned on marriage, can recover such a gift only if the engagement is dissolved by mutual agreement, or only if the engagement is unjustifiably broken off by the donee. [35]

Other courts, however, follow the modern view that in the absence of an agreement to the contrary, the engagement ring or other premarital gift conditioned on marriage must be returned to the donor upon the termination of the engagement, regardless of fault. [36] The rationale for this modern view, in the words of one court, is that:

> . . .in most broken engagements there is no real fault as such -one or both of the parties merely changes his [or her] mind about the desirability of the other as a marriage partner. Since the major purpose of the engagement period is to allow a couple time to test the permanency of their feelings, it would seem highly ironic to penalize the donor for taking steps to prevent a possibly unhappy marriage. Just as the question of fault or guilt has become largely irrelevant to modern divorce proceedings, so should it also be deemed irrelevant to the breaking of the engagement. [37]

However, if there is no persuasive evidence that a premarital gift was conditioned on marriage, then such a gift need not be returned to the donor once the engagement is broken off. [38]

---

[32] *See* 10 Williston on Contracts § 1289A (3d ed. 1967).

[33] *See, e.g., Jangraw v. Perkins,* 56 A. 532 (Vt. 1903); *Duvall v. Wellman,* 26 N.E. 343 (N.Y. 1891).

[34] *See, e.g., Attorney General v. Marital Endowment Corp.,* 242 N.W. 297 (Mich. 1932) (involving a quo warranto action brought against a company that was promoting marriage for profit).

[35] *See, e.g., White v. Finch,* 209 A.2d 199 (Conn. Cir. Ct. 1964); *DeCicco v. Barker,* 159 N.E.2d 534 (Mass. 1959); Restatement of Restitution § 58 cmt c (1937).

[36] *See, e.g., Lyle v. Durham,* 473 N.E.2d 1216 (Ohio Ct. App. 1984); *Brown v. Thomas,* 379 N.W.2d 868 (Wis. 1985).

[37] *Gaden v. Gaden,* 323 N.Y.S.2d 955, 961–962 (N.Y. 1971).

[38] *See, e.g., Gerard v. Costin,* 215 P. 1011 (Kan. 1923) (premarital gift of land was not conditioned on marriage); *Fortenberry v. Ellis,* 217 So. 2d 792 (La. Ct. App. 1969) (premarital gift of a stereo set was not conditioned on marriage).

However, if a premarital gift was induced by fraud, then it must be returned to the donor. *See, e.g., Earl v. Saks Co.,* 226 P.2d 340 (Cal. 1951) (premarital gift of a fur coat that was induced by fraud).

§ 4.03 Premarital Agreements

[A] Traditional versus Modern Approaches

Premarital agreements, also called antenuptial or prenuptial contracts, are most often utilized when prospective spouses wish to contractually vary, limit, or relinquish certain marital property and support rights that they would otherwise acquire by reason of their impending marriage.

In the past, premarital agreements were usually made by older couples who were about to be remarried, and who had acquired considerable property from a prior marriage that they wished to control. However, premarital agreements today are increasingly being used by younger Americans who have acquired, or will acquire, substantial property prior to, or during, their first or subsequent marriage -property that they desire to maintain as separate rather than as marital property.[39]

Traditionally, a premarital agreement could only affect property rights on the death of a spouse.[40] Typical premarital agreement provisions might include a release of the distributive shares in each other's estate; the mutual bar of dower and curtesy rights, or a statutory equivalent; the surrender of the right of election to take against the other's estate; and the transfer of money or property to the other, either before the marriage or after. Such an agreement would be judicially recognized as a valid contract only if (1) the premarital agreement provided for full disclosure of the parties' assets or, alternately, a "fair provision" was given to the needy spouse; and (2) independent legal advice of counsel was provided to the less empowered spouse, such as a traditional housewife.[41]

The rationale for this structured approach to determine the validity of a premarital agreement is that after the parties' engagement they are no longer contracting "at arm's length," because a fiduciary relationship has been established that requires full disclosure of the parties' assets, or a fair provision to the other spouse.[42] However, a premarital agreement does not

---

[39] *See generally* Gamble, *The Antenuptial Contract*, 26 U. Miami L. Rev. 692 (1972); Clark, *Antenuptial Contracts*, 50 U. Colo. L. Rev. 141 (1979); 3 Lindey, Separation Agreements and Antenuptial Contracts § 90 (1999 rev. ed.)

[40] *See, e.g., Crouch v. Crouch*, 385 S.W.2d 288 (Tenn. Ct. App. 1964); *see also* Annot., 57 A.L.R.2d 942 (1958) and Later Case Service.

[41] *See, e.g., In re Estate of Benker*, 331 N.W.2d 193 (Mich. 1982); *Friedlander v. Friedlander*, 494 P.2d 208 (Wash. 1972); *Battleman v. Rubin*, 98 S.E.2d 519 (Va. 1957) (a "fair provision" should be at least one-third of the husband's worth at the time of contracting, or the presumption of designed concealment is raised). However, the *Battleman* case holding was based upon common law dower and curtesy principles, before augmented estate statutes were enacted in a majority of states, including Virginia.
Under this general rule, the burden of proof is initially placed upon the party alleging the invalidity of a premarital agreement. But if there is evidence of nondisclosure of assets (also called overreaching or designed concealment) then the burden of proof shifts, and if this presumption of nondisclosure is not rebutted, then the premarital agreement may be invalidated. *See generally* 3 Lindey, Separation Agreements and Antenuptial Contracts §§ 90-52 to 90-58 (1999 rev. ed.).

[42] *Id.*

necessarily have to be "fair" to both parties, as long as full disclosure has been made to both parties.[43]

A less empowered traditional housewife may still require full disclosure of assets and representation by independent legal counsel.[44] However, if the prospective wife did not have full disclosure of the husband's assets, nor any independent legal advice, but learned of the prospective husband's assets independently, and she had the sophistication and business acumen to understand what she was signing, then the premarital agreement would not necessarily be declared invalid.[45]

Under this traditional approach, however, premarital agreements could not include any contingent divorce planning provisions, because such divorce planning provisions were thought to "encourage" or "promote" the procurement of divorce.[46] Moreover, this traditional rule prohibiting any divorce-planning provisions in premarital agreements resulted in the unfortunate judicial practice of invalidating any divorce planning contingency provisions in premarital agreements that *might* "encourage" or "promote" divorce,[47] which often resulted in voiding the entire premarital agreement itself.[48]

Accordingly, a modern view of divorce planning in premarital agreements began to evolve in some jurisdictions, where contingent divorce-planning provisions in premarital agreements were not judicially declared as invalid per se, but were to be tested by the objective intent of the contracting parties themselves.[49]

The rationale behind this modern rule, as explained in the case of *Posner v. Posner*,[50] was that:

---

[43] *See, e.g., Newman v. Newman*, 653 P.2d 728 (Colo. 1982) (once the tests of full disclosure and lack of fraud or overreaching are met, the parties are free to agree in a premarital agreement to any arrangement for the division of their property, including waiver of any claim to the property of the other); *see also Estate of Moss*, 263 N.W.2d 98 (Neb. 1978); *Del Vecchio v. Del Vecchio*, 143 So. 2d 17 (Fla. 1962). *See also Pardieck v. Pardieck*, 676 N.E. 2d 359, 363 (Ind. Ct. App. 1997) (holding that if a premarital agreement is clear on its terms, and is not unconscionable, it will be enforced as written); *Moore v. Gillis*, 391 S.E.2d 255, 256-57 (Va. 1990) (similar holding).

[44] *See, e.g., Matson v. Matson*, 705 P.2d 817 (Wash. Ct. App. 1985) (where a premarital agreement attempts to limit or eliminate martial property rights, "equity will zealously and scrupulously examine it for fairness").

[45] *See, e.g., Knoll v. Knoll*, 671 P.2d 718 (Or. Ct. App. 1983) (prospective wife was prospective husband's bookkeeper, and she knew, or should have known, what his assets actually were).

[46] *See, e.g., Mulford v. Mulford*, 320 N.W.2d 470 (Neb. 1982); *Duncan v. Duncan*, 652 S.W.2d 913 (Tenn. Ct. App. 1983).

[47] *See, e.g., Fricke v. Fricke*, 42 N.W. 500 (Wis. 1950); *In re Marriage of Gudenkauf*, 204 N.W.2d 586 (Iowa 1973). *See also* Annots., 70 A.L.R. 826 (1931), and 57 A.L.R.2d 942 (1958), and Later Case Service.

[48] *See generally* Swisher, *Divorce Planning in Antenuptial Agreements: Toward a New Objectivity*, 13 U.Rich. L. Rev. 175 (1979).

[49] *Id.; see also Posner v. Posner*, 233 So. 2d 381 (Fla. 1970); *Unander v. Unander*, 506 P.2d 109 (Or. 1973); *Frey v. Frey*, 471 A.2d 705 (Md. Ct. Spec. App. 1984).

[50] 233 So. 2d 381 (Fla. 1970).

> With divorce such a commonplace fact of life, it is fair to assume that many prospective marriage partners whose property and familial situation is such as to generate a valid antenuptial agreement settling their property rights upon the death of either, might want to consider and discuss also -and agree upon if possible -the disposition of their property and the alimony rights of the wife [and husband] in the event their marriage, despite their best efforts, should fail.[51]

Indeed, courts following this modern rule have repeatedly stated that there is little empirical evidence supporting the traditional view that such divorce planning provisions in premarital agreements actually invite dispute, encourage separation, or promote divorce. The possibility is equally arguable that such agreements promote rather than reduce marital stability by defining the expectations and responsibilities of the parties.[52]

There is also a second reason why some courts have refused to recognize divorce planning in premarital agreements, especially when it relates to contingent spousal support provisions or to a waiver of spousal support:

> The real reason for invalidating such antenuptial contracts seems to be that although the [spousal support] provisions may be fair at the time they are made, they may not be later when the separation or divorce occurs. The wife may thus be left with entirely inadequate support, or the husband with an excessively heavy liability to his wife [or vice versa]. . . . Thus, the difficulty of forecasting the parties' circumstances so far in the future has led [some] courts to disallow antenuptial contracts which attempt to do this with respect to support.[53]

An answer to this legitimate concern, however, is that by using an objective case-by-case evaluation, alimony or spousal support provisions in antenuptial agreements would be upheld by the court if (1) the contractual terms were fair, and (2) the contract was made with full disclosure of the parties' worth. Otherwise, as with separation agreements on divorce in most states, these provisions could be modified by the court using its equitable powers of judicial review. As the Oregon Supreme Court has stated this principle:

> We have now come to the conclusion that antenuptial agreements concerning alimony should be enforced unless enforcement deprives a spouse of support that he or she cannot otherwise secure. A provision providing that no alimony shall be paid will be enforced

---

[51] 233 So. 2d at 384; *see also Volid v. Volid*, 286 N.E.2d 42, 46 (Ill. App. Ct. 1972); *Unander v. Unander*, 506 P.2d 719, 720 (Or. 1973); *Osborne v. Osborne*, 428 N.E.2d 810 (Mass. 1981). Indeed, come commentators have urged that American family law should *require* couples to enter into premarital agreements. *See, e.g.,* Stake, *Mandatory Planning for Divorce*, 45 Vand. L. Rev. 397 (1992).

[52] *Unander v. Unander,* 506 P.2d 719, 720 (Ore. 1973). *See also Newman v. Newman*, 653 P.2d 728, 732 (Colo. 1982).

[53] *Reilling v. Reilling*, 474 P.2d 327, 328 (Or. 1970) (quoting H. Clark, Law of Domestic Relations 28–29 (1968)).

unless the spouse has no other reasonable source of support. If the circumstances of the parties change, the court can modify the decree just as it can modify a decree based upon [a separation] agreement made in contemplation of divorce which has a provision regarding payment of support. [54]

Consequently, with various courts continuing to apply either the traditional [55] or modern [56] view regarding divorce planning in premarital agreements, there has been a great deal of confusion in many American jurisdictions regarding when the courts *would* recognize certain premarital agreements as valid contracts, and when judicially they would *not*. [57] In an effort to resolve much of this judicial confusion regarding premarital agreements generally, a number of states have adopted the Uniform Premarital Agreement Act.

[B] The Uniform Premarital Agreement Act

Drafted in 1983, the Uniform Premarital Agreement Act [58] has been adopted by an increasing number of states. [59] The Uniform Premarital Agreement Act is intended to be relatively limited in scope, and does not deal with agreements between unmarried cohabitants, nor does it encompass postnuptial or separation agreements or oral agreements. [60]

Section 1 of the Act defines a premarital agreement as "an agreement between prospective spouses made in contemplation of marriage and to be effective upon marriage." [61]

Section 2 of the Act requires that a premarital agreement be in writing and signed by both parties. [62]

Section 3 of the Act deals with its content. Parties to a premarital agreement may contract with respect to: the property of either or both of

---

[54] *Unander v. Unander*, 506 P.2d 719, 721 (Or. 1973), *overruling in part Reiling v. Reiling, supra*.

[55] *See, e.g., Duncan v. Duncan*, 652 S.W.2d 913 (Tenn. Ct. App. 1983).

[56] *See, e.g., Newman v. Newman*, 653 P.2d 728 (Colo. 1982).

[57] *See, e.g.*, Note, *For Better or For Worse . . . But Just in Case, are Antenuptial Agreements Enforceable?* 1982 U. Ill. L. Rev. 531; Oldham, *Premarital Agreements are Now Enforceable Unless . . .* 21 Houston L. Rev. 757 (1984).

[58] Uniform Premarital Agreement Act (1983), 9B U.L.A. 369; reprinted in [Reference File] Family Law Reporter, 201:2001 (BNA, 1984) [hereafter referred to as the Act].

[59] To date, the Uniform Premarital Agreement Act has been adopted in 24 states including: Arizona, Arkansas, California, Hawaii, Idaho, Illinois, Indiana, Iowa, Kansas, Maine, Montana, Nevada, New Jersey, New Mexico, North Carolina, North Dakota, Oregon, Rhode Island, South Dakota, Texas, and Virginia. Additional states are likely to adopt this Act in the near future.

[60] 9B U.L.A. 369, Prefatory Note.

[61] *Id.* § 1. Some states subsequently have included postmarital agreements within their state Premarital Agreement Act as well. *See, e.g.,* Va. Code Ann. 20-155 (1987).

[62] *Id.* § 2. Nevertheless, an *oral* premarital agreement arguably may still be taken out of the Statute of Frauds through detrimental reliance and part performance under estoppel principles. *See, e.g., T. v. T.*, 224 S.E.2d 148 (Va. 1976); *In re Lord's Estate*, 602 P.2d 1030 (N. M. 1979).

the parties, whenever or wherever acquired or located; the disposition of property upon separation, marital dissolution, death, or the occurrence or nonoccurrence of any other event; the modification or elimination of spousal support; the making of a will, trust, or other arrangement; the ownership rights and disposition of death benefits from life insurance policies; the choice of law governing the agreement; and "any other matter . . . not in violation of public policy or a statute imposing a criminal penalty." Any child support rights, however, may not be adversely affected by a premarital agreement. [63]

Section 4 of the Act provides that an agreement becomes effective on marriage; and Section 5 states that after marriage, a premarital agreement may be amended or revoked only be a written agreement signed by the parties. [64]

Section 6 is the key operative section of the Act and sets forth the conditions under which a premarital agreement is not enforceable. [65] A premarital agreement is not enforceable if the party against whom enforcement is sought proves that: (1) the party did not execute the agreement voluntarily; or (2) the agreement was unconscionable when it was executed if a party: (i) was not provided with a fair and reasonable disclosure of the property or financial obligations of the other party; (ii) did not voluntarily and expressly waive, in writing, such disclosure; and (iii) did not have adequate knowledge of the property or financial obligations of the other party. [66]

Under the Act, if any provision in the premarital agreement modifies or eliminates spousal support, and causes one party to the agreement to be eligible for support under a program for public assistance at the time of separation or marital dissolution, a court, despite the terms of the agreement, may require the other party to provide support to the extent necessary to avoid that eligibility. [67] Furthermore, any issue of unconscionability of a premarital agreement shall be decided by the court as a matter of law. [68]

Although the Uniform Premarital Agreement Act does not expressly require independent legal counsel for the less empowered spouse, a Comment to Section 6 of the Act nevertheless states that:

> . . .Nothing in Section 6 makes the absence of assistance of independent legal counsel a condition for the unenforceability of a premarital agreement. However, lack of that assistance may well be a factor in determining whether the [unconscionability] conditions stated in Section 6 may have existed. [69]

---

[63] *Id.* § 3.

[64] *Id.* §§ 4, 5.

[65] *Id.* Prefatory Note.

[66] *Id.* § 6(a).

[67] *Id.* § 6(b).

[68] *Id.* § 6(c).

[69] *Id.* § 6 Comment, citing as authority *Del Vecchio v. Del Vecchio*, 143 So. 2d 17 (Fla. 1962).

§ 4.04   Contractual Agreements Between Husband and Wife

Since, under the common law, a husband and wife were considered to be one legal entity, spouses were prohibited from contracting with each other. The Married Women's Property Acts,[70] however, removed the wife's contractual incapacity and consequently, in most states today, husbands and wives are now capable of contracting with each other, and may recover for breach of contract against each other.[71] Spousal rights to sue each other also include actions in equity to enforce marital property rights.[72]

Despite this relaxation of the rules regarding interspousal contracts, however, the courts have been reluctant to enforce contracts that relate to altering the spousal duty of support during marriage. For example, courts have refused to enforce contracts in which a husband promised to pay his wife for her household services, under the legal rationale that a wife had a preexisting duty to render such services, and the contract thus failed for lack of consideration.[73] The courts have similarly invalidated spousal contracts where one spouse agreed to devise property to the other spouse in exchange for domestic services or care during the promisor spouse's lifetime.[74]

The common law therefore generally presumed that any services rendered by one spouse to the other spouse were either obligatory or gratuitous, but this presumption could be rebutted by factual evidence demonstrating that such spousal services were *not* intended to be gratuitous.[75] Thus, a spouse would be permitted to prove that certain property acquired during the marriage was held in partnership, quasi-partnership, joint venture, or in trust— or that a constructive trust should be imposed to prevent unjust enrichment of the title-holding spouse.[76]

Both spouses therefore have the right to enter into partnership agreements or any other business arrangements with each other, and creditors

---

[70] *See infra* § 3.03[B].

[71] *See, e.g., Hamilton v. Hamilton,* 51 So. 2d 13 (Ala. 1950).

[72] *See, e.g., Brobst v. Brobst,* 121 A.2d 178 (Pa. 1956); *see also* McCurdy, *Property Torts Between Spouses,* 2 Vill. L. Rev. 447 (1957).

[73] *See, e.g., Youngberg v. Holstrom,* 108 N.W.2d 498 (Iowa 1961).

[74] *See, e.g., In re Estate of Lord,* 602 P.2d 1030 (N.M. 1979).

[75] *See, e.g., Eggleston v. Eggleston,* 47 S.E.2d 243 (N.C. 1948); *Cooper v. Spencer,* 238 S.E.2d 805 (Va. 1977).

[76] *See, e.g., McGehee v. McGehee,* 85 So. 2d 799 (Miss. 1956) (upholding a formal, written partnership agreement between the spouses relating to ownership of business assets). *But see Chaachou v. Chaachou,* 135 So. 2d 206 (Fla. 1961). In *Chaachou,* where the couple had no formal partnership agreement with respect to their business property, the court held that any partnership that may have been agreed to "became merged in their larger partnership of marriage, and its terms are now too indistinct to be specifically enforced as such." *Id.* at 214. The court concluded, however, that the husband would be unjustly enriched if he were allowed to retain all the business assets without duly compensating the wife, and the wife was awarded a fraction of the value of the four hotel properties, as well as permanent alimony, a residence, and attorneys' fees.

may, or may not, be protected, depending upon the particular form of the business organization.[77]

§ 4.05 Postnuptial and Separation Agreements

After the parties are married, they may contractually agree to buy, sell, or exchange certain property, to dispose of property by will or trust, to determine certain insurance benefits, or to determine certain property and support rights in the event of death, separation, dissolution, or divorce.

If the contracting parties are not contemplating an immediate divorce, then they would be primarily concerned with existing marital property and support rights, wills and trusts, insurance benefits, or business agreements that normally would take effect during the marriage, or on the death of one or both of the spouses. Although relatively rare in the past, these postnuptial agreements are becoming more common as a result of the current economic climate in the United States, where one spouse may unexpectedly come into great wealth subsequent to the marriage, and may desire to alter the terms of his or her existing marital property and support rights and obligations.[78]

Like premarital agreements, postnuptial agreements can spell out what the dependent spouse claims or waives in the event of divorce or dissolution of marriage. However, although most states have specific laws that govern the creation and enforcement of premarital and separation agreements, only a few state courts and legislatures have adequately dealt with the relatively new concept of postnuptial agreements. New York and Florida, for example, have ruled that postnuptial agreements are enforceable to the same extent that premarital and separation agreements are enforceable; but North Carolina and Louisiana both require that postnuptial agreements be approved by a judge. And in Hawaii, postnuptial agreements are valid only if the judge deems the contractual terms are fair at the time of signing the agreement *and* at the time of divorce--meaning that a spouse whose wealth has grown substantially since the postnuptial was signed may have to renegotiate the terms of the agreement at the time of the parties' separation.[79] Clearly, this is an important area of marital contracting that

---

[77] *See, e.g., Northampton Brewery Corp. v. Lande,* 10 A.2d 583 (Pa. Super. Ct. 1939) (creditor recovered from a family restaurant business that creditor claimed was a partnership, but the wife claimed was held as tenancy by the entireties). *But see Kennedy v. Nelson,* 70 So. 2d 822 (Ala. Ct. App. 1954) (husband, as wife's tenant on her solely owned farm, could not bind his wife for improvements payable to the creditor on a theory of implied agency, despite husband's management of the farm).

However, when a spouse obtains the other spouse's interest in property held as tenants by the entireties during marriage, pursuant to an equitable distribution award on divorce, he or she takes such property subject to any preexisting creditor's interest on the property. *See, e.g., Union Grove Milling & Mfg. Co. v. Faw,* 404 S.E.2d 508 (N.C. Ct. App. 1991).

[78] *See, e.g.,* Desa Philadelphia, *Let's Remake a Deal: When one spouse gets rich, couples now often turn to postnuptial agreements. Are they fair?* TIME Magazine, April 24, 2000 at 56 ("veteran attorneys say the number of mid-marriage agreements has exploded in the last five years, perhaps as much as ten-fold").

[79] *Id.*

requires the serious attention of more state courts and legislatures in order to ensure that fundamental fairness exists within the contracting process; and that contractual oppression from a more empowered, wealthier, and overreaching spouse is thereby avoided.

Alternately, if the contracting parties were contemplating divorce, or the possibility of a divorce, then their postmarital agreement generally would be drafted in the form of a separation agreement.

[A] Separation Agreements: Necessary Elements

Separation agreements, also called property settlement agreements on divorce, were once looked upon by some courts with suspicion, since such agreements between the spouses to live separate and apart were believed to be in derogation of marriage, by allegedly "promoting" the procurement of divorce. [80]

Today, however, separation agreements are highly favored in almost all jurisdictions, [81] thus allowing a husband and a wife, with the help of their respective attorneys, to contractually agree on a division of the parties' marital property and other assets; to apportion marital debt; to agree on an amount of spousal support, or a waiver of spousal support; to agree on child support and child custody issues, subject to court approval; to determine the disposition of the family residence; to address various insurance coverages, pension plans, or retirement plans; to facilitate tax planning; and to contractually agree on any other related matters regarding the parties' pending divorce or dissolution of marriage. [82]

A voluntary separation agreement between husband and wife offers many benefits over an adversarial court-imposed order. First, the parties themselves know their own needs, assets, problems, and their children's needs much better than a divorce judge does. Second, a separation agreement drafted with a fair and reasonable compromise on both sides usually results in better compliance by both parties than a court-imposed adversarial solution. And third, an enormous amount of time and money can be saved

---

[80] For an historical analysis of this traditional rule questioning the validity of separation agreements, see *Dexter v. Dexter*, 371 S.E.2d 816 (Va. Ct. App. 1988). *See also* J. Madden, Handbook on the Law of Persons and Domestic Relations 331–335 (1931).

[81] *See, e.g., Reynolds v. Reynolds*, 415 A.2d 535, 537 (D.C. 1980) ("This jurisdiction encourages the parties in any marital dispute to resolve by agreement their joint marital interests."); *Drawdy v. Drawdy*, 268 S.E.2d 30, 31 (S.C. 1980) (Separation agreements "are praiseworthy products of cooperation between parties seeking a divorce. They also serve to decrease the workload on family courts and thereby enhance judicial efficiency.").

[82] *See, e.g.,* S. Green & J. Long, Marriage and Family Law Agreements (1984); S. Schlissel, Separation Agreements and Marital Contracts (1986); A. Lindey & L. Parley, Lindey on Separation Agreements and Antenuptial Contracts (1999 rev. ed.); *see also* Haas, *The Rationality and Enforceability of Contractual Restrictions on Divorce*, 66 N.C.L. Rev. 879 (1988).

in costly litigation expenses, including attorneys' fees, expert witness fees, and court costs, by using a separation agreement.[83]

Separation agreements, like other marital agreements, are generally recognized and encouraged under state statutory law,[84] and normally will be enforced by the courts.[85] But because the marital relationship imposes a fiduciary duty on each of the parties,[86] and because public policy dictates a requirement of essential fairness in the spouses' negotiations,[87] then most separation agreements require full disclosure by each party regarding his or her financial worth.[88]

However, when full disclosure of the parties' financial worth is *not* made, then the separation agreement may be invalidated due to fraud, overreaching [defined as conduct in taking unfair advantage of the other spouse], or designed concealment.[89] For example, in the case of *Selke v. Selke*,[90] a husband's failure to disclose the value of his pension plan to his unrepresented wife warranted voiding both their separation agreement and the divorce decree incorporating the separation agreement. It made no difference that the husband did not know the exact value of his pension plan, because he had access to information regarding its approximate value.[91]

---

[83] *See generally* S. Green & J. Long, Marriage and Family Law Agreements 213 (1984). *See also* Mnoookin & Kornhauser, *Bargaining in the Shadow of the Law: The Case of Divorce*, 88 Yale L.J. 950 (1979) (stating that divorce cases comprise a very high proportion of all civil cases, and that 80 to 90 percent of these cases are disposed of through separation agreements, with only administrative approval by the courts); 1 A. Lindey & L. Parley, Lindey on Separation Agreements and Antenuptial Contracts § 1.01 (1999 rev. ed.); and 1 S. Schlissel, Separation Agreements and Marital Contracts §§ 8.01–8.02 (1986).

[84] *See, e.g.*, N.Y. Dom. Rel. Law § 236 (separation agreements held valid and enforceable); and Va. Code Ann. § 20-109.1 (authorizing court approval of separation agreements); *see also* The Uniform Marriage and Divorce Act § 306, 9A U.L.A. 135 (authorizing separation agreements in order to promote the amicable settlement of disputes between spouses).

[85] *See, e.g.*, *LeBert-Francis v. LeBert-Francis*, 194 A.2d 662, 664 (D.C. 1963) (separation agreements should be encouraged, and when made they should be enforced); *see also Dominick v. Dominick*, 463 N.E.2d 564 (Mass. App. Ct. 1984) (a court should presumptively approve a separation agreement unless such an agreement is unconscionable).

[86] *See, e.g.*, Grisham, *A Fiduciary Relationship Between Divorcing Spouses: Impact on Property Settlements*, 13 Community Prop. J. 58 (1986).

[87] *See generally* Sharp, *Fairness Standards and Separation Agreements: A Word of Caution on Contractual Freedom*, 132 U. Pa. L. Rev. 1399 (1984). *See also Crawford v. Crawford*, 350 N.E.2d 103, 107 (Ill. App. Ct. 1976) (such agreements are enforceable based upon whether they are "reasonably fair and sufficient in light of the station in life and circumstances of the parties").

[88] *See e.g. O'Connor v. O'Connor*, 435 So. 2d 344 (Fla. Dist. Ct. App. 1983); *Golder v. Golder*, 714 P.2d 26 (Idaho 1986); *Williams v. Williams*, 508 A.2d 985 (Md. 1985); *Billington v. Billington*, 595 A.2d 1377 (Conn. 1991); *see also* 1 S. Schlissel, Separation Agreements and Marital Contracts §§ 8.03–8.04 (1986).

[89] *See, e.g.*, *Williams v. Williams*, 508 A.2d 985 (Md. 1985); *Koizim v. Koizim*, 435 A.2d 1030 (Conn. 1980).

[90] 569 N.E.2d 724 (Ind. Ct. App. 1991).

[91] *Id.*

A separation agreement may also be voided on grounds of unconscionability.[92]

In the absence of fraud, duress, concealment, overreaching, or unconscionability, a separation agreement normally will be binding on the parties, no matter how ill-reasoned or ill-advised a party may have been in executing it.[93] Thus, separation agreements are held by most courts to be presumptively valid if they are freely and understandingly signed by both parties, with full disclosure of the marital assets, regardless of any subsequent allegations of unfairness made by either party.[94] An otherwise valid agreement, therefore, will not be rejected merely because a party had a "change of heart" after the agreement was executed.[95]

Overreaching may occur when one of the parties signing the separation agreement is not represented by independent legal counsel.[96] Most courts and commentators strongly recommend that each party to a separation agreement should have independent legal advice before signing any separation agreement.[97]

---

[92] *See, e.g. Burke v. Sexton*, 814 S.W.2d 290 (Ky. Ct. App.1991) (a separation agreement requiring the wife to waive all her property interests and spousal support rights in order to receive child support was found to be unconscionable); *Derby v. Derby*, 378 S.E.2d 74 (Va. Ct. App. 1989) (while disagreeing with the trial court that a separation agreement was void due to fraud and duress, the appellate court found that a gross disparity in the parties' property division was shocking and unconscionable).

A separation agreement may also be unconscionable if a party was not provided a fair and reasonable disclosure of the other party's assets. *See e.g., Williams v. Williams*, 508 A.2d 985 (Md. 1985); *Koizim v. Koizim*, 435 A.2d 1030 (Conn. 1980). *But see In re Marriage of Turner*,803 S.W.2d 655 (Mo. Ct. App. 1991) (the parties' separation agreement was not unconscionable where the husband's representations about the status of his assets, although not entirely accurate, were not so awry as to be fraudulent, and the wife had legal counsel who could have investigated further, but did not).

[93] *See, e.g.,Reynolds v. Reynolds*, 415 A.2d 535 (D.C. 1980) (in the absence of fraud, duress, concealment or overreaching, an agreement is binding no matter how ill-advised a party may have been in executing it); *Lockhart v. Baxter*, 405 S.E.2d 434 (Va. Ct. App.1991) (the law will not invalidate a separation agreement contract merely because it was ill-reasoned or ill-advised).

[94] *See, e.g., Flora v. Flora*, 337 N.E.2d 846 (Ind. Ct. App. 1975); *Dominick v. Dominick*, 463 N.E.2d 564 (Mass. Ct. App.1984); *see also Jennings v. Jennings*, 409 S.E.2d 8 (Va. Ct. App. 1991), where the court found no unconscionability when the husband, in order to induce his wife to reconcile after she filed suit for divorce, offered to enter into a property settlement agreement which the wife's lawyer prepared and discussed with both parties. The husband signed the agreement after rejecting the recommendation by wife's lawyer that he seek independent legal counsel. After a brief reconciliation, the wife sought a divorce, and the court incorporated the agreement into the final divorce decree. The fact that the husband was an alcoholic and possessed some human frailties did not relieve him of his contractual obligations under the separation agreement.

[95] *See, e.g., Sontag v. Sontag*, 495 N.Y.S.2d 65 (N.Y. App. Div. 1985), *aff'd*, 498 N.Y.S.2d 133 (N.Y. 1986).

[96] *See, e.g., Compton v. Compton*, 612 P.2d 1175, 1183 (Idaho 1980); *Radigan v. Radigan*, 465 N.W.2d 483 (S.D. 1991).

[97] *See, e.g., Craft v. Craft*, 478 So. 2d 258 (Miss. 1985), where the court held that since both husband and wife were represented by independent legal counsel, that fact constituted strong evidence that each party was advised of his or her respective legal rights and responsibilities under the separation agreement, and that each party knowingly and voluntarily agreed to

However, the lack of independent legal counsel for either party in signing a separation agreement will not always render the agreement invalid and unenforceable. For example, the Washington Supreme Court in *Whitney v. Seattle First National Bank*[98] held that where the separation agreement was fair and reasonable, and where the petitioner had not shown fraud or overreaching, there was no absolute requirement that the wife or husband needed independent legal advice of counsel.[99]

The *Whitney* case notwithstanding, most courts still continue to examine the particular circumstances that led to a party not being represented by independent legal counsel. Such circumstances include the unrepresented party's awareness of the financial circumstances surrounding the agreement, and the unrepresented party's ability to understand the agreement and waive legal counsel.[100]

Another key issue involving separation agreements is whether or not an attorney may represent *both* parties in drafting a separation agreement. The answer is that if there are *any* disputes between the parties regarding spousal or child support, child custody matters, division of the marital assets or the like, then an attorney *cannot* ethically draft a separation agreement for both parties.[101] However, if an attorney is able to maintain his or her neutrality in the matter, and the separation agreement is fair and equitable to both parties, then some courts have held that the separation agreement would not be invalid per se if the attorney who drafted the agreement represented both parties.[102]

Finally, a dilemma may arise if an attorney attempts to represent one spouse in negotiating a separation agreement, but the other spouse refuses to retain independent legal counsel to represent his or her interests. According to one state bar advisory opinion,[103] the attorney for the

---

be bound by the agreement; *see also Murphy v. Murphy*, 239 S.E.2d 597 (N.C. Ct. App. 1977) (similar holding). *But see Smith v. Lewis*, 530 P.2d 589 (Cal. 1975); *Schauer v. Joyce*, 429 N.E.2d 83 (N.Y. 1981).

See also S. Green & J. Long, Marriage and Family Law Agreements 217 (1984) ("separate representation by retained counsel can go far to protect each side from a variety of possible claims advanced for the purpose of having a separation agreement set aside").

[98] 579 P.2d 937, 940 (Wash. 1978).

[99] *Id.*; *see also In re Marriage of Gerleman*, 741 P.2d 426 (Mont. 1987). *But see Eltzroth v. Eltzroth*, 679 P.2d 1369 (Or. Ct. App. 1984).

[100] *See, e.g., Levine v. Levine*, 451 N.Y.S.2d 26 (N.Y. 1982); *McClellan v. McClellan*, 451 A.2d 334 (Md. Ct. Spec. App. 1982) *cert. denied*, 462 U.S. 1135 (1982); *Longstreet v. Longstreet*, 566 N.E.2d 708 (Ohio Ct. App. 1989); *see also* 1 A. Lindey & L. Parley, Lindey on Separation Agreements and Antenuptial Contracts §§ 6.01–6.06 (1992 rev. ed.).

[101] *See, e.g.*, ABA Model Rules of Professional Conduct, Rule 1.7; ABA Code of Professional Responsibility Disciplinary Rule 5-105(C). *See generally infra* § 8.04.

[102] *See, e.g., Perry v. Perry*, 406 N.Y.S.2d 551, 552 (N.Y. App. Div. 1978) ("While the practice of one attorney representing both parties in the preparation of a separation agreement has been criticized, we agree with the trial court that, in this instance, the attorney managed to preserve neutrality and that the agreement was arrived at fairly, without overreaching by either spouse. Furthermore, the substantive provisions of the agreement are, in toto, fair and equitable."); *accord Levine v. Levine*, 436 N.E.2d 476 (N.Y. 1982); *see also infra* §§ 8.04[A], 8.05.

[103] Va. State Bar Committee on Legal Ethics, Opinion No. 876, reprinted in 13 Fam. L. Rep. 1284 (1987).

represented spouse has the following obligations: (1) advise the unrepresented spouse to secure independent counsel; (2) do not state or imply disinterest; (3) advise the unrepresented spouse that you represent the interests of your client only; and (4) advise the unrepresented spouse that his or her interests are, or may be, adverse to those of your client.[104]

[B] Separation Agreements: Application of Principles

Separation agreements, like other contracts, require valid consideration in order to be enforceable.[105] The exchange of mutual promises, creating bilateral legal rights and obligations between the parties, will normally suffice as consideration for separation agreements.[106]

Separation agreements are required to be in writing in most jurisdictions pursuant to state statutory authority,[107] but various courts have also upheld the enforceability of certain oral separation agreements under general principles of equity.[108] Because most separation agreements are in writing, extrinsic evidence of the parties' intent can only be offered if the agreement is ambiguous,[109] or if there is a mutual mistake of the parties that requires reformation of the contract.[110] The content of a separation agreement therefore is largely determined by the mutual intent of the parties, absent fraud, duress, designed concealment, overreaching, or unconscionability.[111]

Thus, a husband and wife may contractually agree in their separation agreement concerning the division -or waiver -of their respective property rights: whether real or personal, tangible or intangible, marital, community, or separate.[112] In the absence of such an agreement, however, the court would have to classify, value, and distribute the parties' property under applicable equitable distribution or community property statutes.[113]

---

[104] *Id.* It would also be a wise practice to give this advice to the unrepresented spouse orally *and* in writing, with a copy for the law office files. *See also Ayers v. Ayers*, 466 So. 2d 979 (Ala. Civ. App. 1985) (unrepresented wife held to the separation agreement drawn up by husband's attorney, which she read and which contained an acknowledgement that the attorney did not represent her).

[105] *See, e.g., Baggs v. Anderson*, 528 P.2d 141 (Utah 1974); *Barnes v. Barnes*, 226 S.E.2d 549 (N.C. Ct. App. 1976).

[106] *See, e.g., Sanchez v. Tilley*, 330 S.E.2d 319 (S.C. Ct. App. 1985); *B.T.L. v. H.A.L.*, 287 A.2d 413 (Del. 1972); *Capps v. Capps*, 219 S.E.2d 901 (Va. 1975).

[107] *See, e.g.*, Cal. Civ. Code § 4802; Conn. Gen. Stat. § 46b-66; N.Y. Dom. Rel. Law § 236(B)(3); Tex. Fam. Code § 3.631(a); Va. Code Ann. §§ 20-155, 20-149.

[108] *See, e.g., Richardson v. Richardson*, 392 S.E.2d 688 (Va. Ct. App. 1990); *Gangopadhyay v. Gangopadhyay*, 403 S.E.2d 712 (W. Va. 1991); *Kline v. Kline*, 284 N.W.2d 488 (Mich. Ct. App. 1979); *Kramer v. Kramer*, 339 A.2d 328 (Md. Ct. App. 1975).

[109] *See, e.g., Lohmann v. Piczon*, 487 A.2d 1386 (Pa. Super. Ct. 1985); *Richheimer v. Richheimer*, 292 N.E.2d 190 (Ill. App. Ct. 1972).

[110] *See, e.g., In re Marriage of Deines*, 608 P.2d 375 (Colo. 1980).

[111] *See supra* § 4.05[A].

[112] *See generally* 1 A. Lindey & L. Parley, Lindey on Separation Agreements and Antenuptial Contracts § 11.01–11.63 (1999 rev. ed.); 1 S. Schlissel, Separation Agreements and Marital Contracts §§ 20.01–22.29 (1986).

[113] *See generally infra* Chapter 9.

Likewise, the parties may also contract in their separation agreement regarding the payment -or waiver -of spousal support obligations.[114] And again, in the absence of such an agreement, the court would have to determine any spousal support obligations on divorce under applicable state statutes.[115]

However, contractual provisions regarding child support and child custody are interpreted by the courts in a very different manner from spousal support provisions and from marital property provisions in separation agreements.

Based upon the *parens patriae* power of the state, any child custody or child support provision, and any other provision in a separation agreement affecting the child's welfare, is *always* subject to court review and subject to court modification based upon the child's best interests, despite any provision to the contrary that may exist in a separation agreement.[116]

The parties' subsequent reconciliation may affect a prior separation agreement. In a majority of jurisdictions, the courts follow the general rule that a bona fide resumption of marital relations would terminate the executory provisions of a separation agreement, while all the executed provisions of a separation agreement would still remain valid.[117]

Although the theoretical underpinnings and practical techniques for drafting a separation agreement are beyond the scope of this treatise, there are a number of helpful resource books on the subject.[118]

---

[114] *See, e.g.*, 1 A. Lindey & L. Parley, Lindey on Separation Agreements and Antenuptial Contracts §§ 15A.01 to 15A.08 (1999 rev. ed.); 1 S. Schlissel, Separation Agreements and Marital Contracts §§ 19.01 to 19.35 (1986).

[115] *See generally infra* § 9.04.

[116] *See, e.g.*, Kan. Stat. Ann. § 60-1610(f) (separation agreements are not modifiable without the parties' consent, except for those provisions relating to children); Ky. Rev. Stat. Ann. § 403.180 (a separation agreement incorporated into a divorce decree is modifiable unless the parties state otherwise, excluding provisions relating to children which are always modifiable); Va. Code Ann. §§ 20-109.1, 20-108 (separation agreements are not modifiable unless the parties so stipulate, but child custody and child support provisions are always modifiable). *See generally* S. Schlissel, Separation Agreements and Marital Contracts §§ 12.01 to 12.16, 16.01 to 16.13 (1986).

[117] *See, e.g., Stegall v. Stegall*, 397 S.E.2d 306 (N.C. Ct. App. 1990); *Brazina v. Brazina*, 558 A.2d 69 (N.J. Super. Ct. 1989); *Kamansky v. Kamansky*, 364 S.E.2d 799 (W. Va. 1987); *see also Yeich v. Yeich*, 399 S.E.2d 170 (Va. Ct. App. 1990) (reconciliation abrogates the executory portions of a separation agreement, including the waiver of alimony). *But see Jennings v. Jennings*, 409 S.E.2d 8 (Va. Ct. App. 1991) (a separation agreement survived the parties' brief reconciliation).

[118] *See, e.g.*, A. Lindey & L. Parley, Lindey on Separation Agreements and Antenuptial Contracts (1999 rev. ed.); S. Schlissel, Separation Agreements and Marital Contracts (1986); S. Green & J. Long, Marriage and Family Law Agreements (1984); J. Krauskopf, ed. Marital and Nonmarital Contracts (1979); and numerous state-oriented publications; *see also* 7 West's Legal Forms 2d 308-719 (1983).

Separation agreements also appear in a number of reported cases, including *Greiner v. Greiner*, 399 N.E.2d 571 (Ohio Ct. App. 1979); *Roskein v. Roskein*, 96 A.2d 437 (N.J. Super. Ct. 1953).

Chapter 5

PROCREATION

§ 5.01 Introduction

The topics covered within this chapter address the legal issues involved with one of the most fundamental aspects of family life: procreation.

In some areas of procreation, the scientific and medical technology—and the legal response to such technology—is relatively new, such as in vitro fertilization and other forms of assisted conception.[1] In other areas of procreation the medical technology is relatively old, although the legal issues involved remain very controversial, such as abortion[2] and contraception.[3] Even in matters of paternity and legitimacy,[4] new methods of scientific testing in paternity matters now have a significant impact on the legal aspects of proving paternity, and providing support for nonmarital as well as marital children.

Although people have had the ability to prevent pregnancy and birth for hundreds of years, recent medical science has made a quantum leap in the efficacy and safety of these means. However, legal issues regarding contraception have led to the articulation of a fundamental right to privacy in matters of procreation which the Constitution does not specifically mention, but which has been judicially found to exist in the penumbra of other Constitutional rights.[5] In turn, this right of privacy serves as the legal basis for a limited freedom of choice regarding abortion, an area which has led to one of the greatest political and moral controversies confronting our society today.[6]

Improved means of sterilization, such as vasectomy, and tubal ligation via laparoscopy, have allowed individuals to have themselves voluntarily sterilized—and to propose the sterilization of others.[7] The eugenics movement, popular in the first half of the 20th century, and fueled by various geneticists and social Darwinists, led to laws which encouraged, or at least facilitated, widespread sterilization of the mentally ill and mentally incapacitated. These laws have for the most part been repealed in the vast majority of states, and yet a new concern is rising for the right of incompetent people to consent to sterilization, or have it judicially imposed upon them.[8]

---

[1] *See infra* § 5.07.

[2] *See infra* § 5.05

[3] *See infra* § 5.04.

[4] *See infra* § 5.02.

[5] *See infra* § 5.04.

[6] *See infra* § 5.05.

[7] *See infra* § 5.06.

[8] *Id.*

Artificial insemination and the newer medical technology of in vitro fertilization and other methods of artificially assisted conception allow many people who might otherwise be unable to procreate to have children,[9] but even these techniques are not in the forefront of medical science's capability. Fertilized ova have been successfully frozen and human cloning is scientifically feasible. These medical procedures raise difficult legal issues of paternity, and even maternity.[10] For example, what implications do such medical innovations have for the Rule Against Perpetuities?

Other pressing legal problems arise with surrogate parenting when a husband and wife contract with another woman to have a child by artificial insemination from the husband, or by in vitro fertilization from both the husband and the wife.[11] Issues include whether it is necessary for the father and his wife to adopt the child, whether the rights of the parents differ depending on whether artificial insemination or in vitro fertilization is utilized, the extent of the rights of the natural mother if she decides not to relinquish the child, and whether such contracts should be enforced as written or prohibited by state law.

Lastly, this chapter deals with adoption and the termination of parental rights.[12] The issues raised with adoption continue to include the legal standards involved in the termination of the natural parents' rights and the creation of a new legal relationship between the adoptive parents and the child.

Areas of recent concern with adoption have included ethical questions regarding the "supply" of adoptive children; rights of the unmarried biological father to prevent an adoption to which the biological mother has consented; custody rights for the unwed mother and father; rights of grand-parents; and the right of the adopted child to discover his or her biological parents.[13]

§ 5.02 Paternity and Legitimacy

[A] Historical Background and Current Perspectives

Under English and American common law, children born out of wedlock have long been subject to different laws and different rights from "legiti-mate" children. Under the common law, for example, the "illegitimate" child was regarded as *filius nullius*— the son or daughter of no one. Such a child

---

[9] *See infra* § 5.07.

[10] *See, e.g.*, Stanford P. Berenbaum, Note, *Frozen Embryos and the Thawing of Procreative Liberties*, 36 Wayne L. Rev. 1337 (1990); David P. Martin, Note, *A Cryopreserved in Vitro Embryo is a "Child" for Domestic Relations Purposes*, 13 U. Ark. Little Rock L.J. 95 (1990); *see also* Lisa Sowle Cahill, *In Vitro Fertilization: Ethical Issues in Judeo-Christian Perspective*, 32 Loyola L. Rev. 337 (1986); L. Thomas Styron, Note, *Artificial Insemination: A New Frontier for Medical Malpractice and Medical Products Liability*, 32 Loyola L. Rev. 411 (1986).

[11] *See infra* § 5.07

[12] *See infra* § 6.01.

[13] *Id.*

could therefore inherit from no one, and the common law did not impose upon the putative father any legal liability to support his offspring.[14] Indeed, William the Conqueror, who was formerly known as William the Bastard, might have conquered England in 1066, but under the law he had no rights of inheritance or support from either his father or his mother.[15]

In the United States, the laws governing illegitimacy, or bastardy as it was earlier called, generally followed the English common law. Thus, the historical treatment of nonmarital children in America was very harsh, without regard to the needs of the child, with the ultimate result of punishing the child, under the rationale of protecting the exclusivity of the marital unit and to punish adults (particularly women) who engaged in sex outside of marriage.[16]

However, a series of Supreme Court decisions between 1968 and 1983 eliminated as unconstitutional most of the categorical legal distinctions between marital and nonmarital children; thus, through a combination of legislative enactments and judicial opinions in America, this harsh common law treatment of the nonmarital child has moderated considerably. First, all states have now enacted statutes providing specific support rights to the nonmarital child upon proof of paternity.[17] Second, in almost all states, children born of void or voidable marriages are now deemed to be legitimate by statute.[18] And third, a nonmarital child may now inherit from both parents, once paternity has been clearly established.[19] Nevertheless, the legal rights of nonmarital children are not yet co-equal with those of marital children.

Finally, any discussion relating to illegitimacy and paternity matters must also relate to the current problems within our present society. According to various commentators, the rate of nonmarital births in the United States has more than tripled over the past 30 years, even with the greater availability of family planning information, contraceptive devices, and abortion. The number of nonmarital births in the United States has been estimated at over 500,000 per year, and in many of our major metropolitan areas, nonmarital births outnumber marital births.[20]

---

[14] *See, e.g.,* 1 William Blackstone, Commentaries on the Law of England 459 (4th ed. 1899).

[15] *See, e.g.,* 2 James Kent, Commentaries on American Law 212 (6th ed. 1856).

[16] *See, e.g.,* Jana Singer, *The Privatization of Family Law,* 1992 Wisc. L. Rev. 1443, 1447; Mary Becker, *The Rights of Unwed Parents: Feminist Approaches,* 63 Soc. Serv. Rev. 496 (1989).

[17] *See, e.g.,* The Uniform Parentage Act, 9B U.L.A. 287 (1987) (Supp. 2000), which has been adopted, with modifications, in a number of states including: Alabama, California, Colorado, Delaware, Hawaii, Illinois, Kansas, Minnesota, Missouri, Montana, Nevada, New Jersey, North Dakota, Ohio, Rhode Island, Washington, and Wyoming; *see also infra* § 5.02[E]. *See generally* Harry D. Krause, Illegitimacy 19–20 (1971).

[18] *See infra* § 5.02[C].

[19] *See infra* § 5.02[G].

[20] *See* Ralph C. Brashier, *Children and Inheritance in the Nontraditional Family,* 1996 Utah L. Rev. 93, 104; Amara Bachu, *Fertility of American Women;* June 1994 U.S. Bureau of the Census, Current Population Reports, P20-482 at v (1995). The leading paternity treatise is Sidney B. Schatkin, Disputed Paternity Proceedings (rev. ed. 1991). *See also* Harry D. Krause, Illegitimacy: Law and Social Policy (1971).

The underlying reasons for these sobering statistics are undoubtedly complex, but it will be up to the legislator, the jurist, and the family law practitioner to ensure that the nonmarital child's best interests and welfare continue to be legally protected, and to ensure that the social stigma of illegitimacy, which has never been the fault of the child, will no longer continue to be reinforced by archaic legal precedent.

[B] The Presumption of Legitimacy

During the eighteenth and nineteenth century, a common law rule, labeled Lord Mansfield's presumption, was recognized throughout England and America. Under Lord Mansfield's presumption, the "invariable rule" was that "a child born in lawful wedlock is presumed to be legitimate; unless a physical impossibility of procreation be proved, or there be strong evidence of non-access."[21] Thus, a child born in marriage is presumed to be the child of the mother's husband, absent extenuating circumstances.

The public policy behind Lord Mansfield's presumption, one of the strongest known in the law,[22] was to legally protect a recognized family, and any children born into that family.[23] Accordingly, the burden of proof was on the party claiming that a particular child was nonmarital; but proving a husband's non-access to his wife was extremely difficult under the common law because, under Lord Mansfield's presumption, a wife could not testify to the non-access of her husband.[24] But currently, under the law of most states, a wife is now permitted to testify to the non-access of her husband and, in effect, bastardize her child.[25] Therefore, a moving party

---

[21] See, e.g., Bowles v. Bingham, 16 Va. (2 Munf.) 442, 445 (1811) (quoting with approval 2 Blackstone, Commentaries on the Law of England, 446). Some courts, however, have held that this presumption could only be rebutted by proof that the mother's husband was impotent, or that he was out of the country or "beyond the four seas". See, e.g., In re Findley, 170 N.E. 471 (N.Y. 1930). See generally Harry D. Krause, Illegitimacy 9–21 (1971).

[22] See, e.g., Espree v. Guillory, 753 S.W.2d 722 (Tex. Civ. App. 1988) (the presumption of legitimacy is one of the strongest presumptions known to the law); In re Estate of Robertson, 520 So. 2d 99 (Fla. Dist. Ct. App. 1988) (to overcome this very strong presumption that a child born in wedlock is legitimate, the evidence must be clear, strong, and unequivocal).

[23] See Goodright ex dem Stevens v. Moss, 2 Cowp. 591, 98 Eng. Rep. 1257 (1777) (Mansfield, L.C.J.).

[24] See id. at 98 Eng. Rep. 1257, 1258 (1777) (Mansfield, L.C.J.) ("It is a rule founded in decency, morality and policy that [the husband and wife] shall not be permitted to say after marriage that they have had no connection and therefore that the offspring is spurious; more especially the mother who is the offending party.") See also Robert R. LaFortune, Comment, The Mansfield Rule of Nonaccess, 21 Wash. & Lee L. Rev. 146 (1964).

[25] See, e.g., B. v. O., 232 A.2d 401 (N.J. 1967); Gibson v. Gibson, 153 S.E.2d 189 (Va. 1967). Various courts, however, have held that a third-party putative father has no independent right to bring a paternity suit. See, e.g., Espree v. Guillory, 753 S.W.2d 722 (Tex. Civ. App. 1988) (The presumption of legitimacy of a child born during marriage is one of the strongest presumptions known to law, and unless the husband or wife deny the husband's paternity and seek and obtain a judgment nullifying the child's legitimate status, no one else may properly do so.) But see C.C. v. A.B., 550 N.E.2d 365 (Mass. 1990) (There is no longer any need for a presumption of legitimacy with regard to a child born to a married woman, and the putative father, who alleges he is the father of such a child, may prove paternity by clear and convincing evidence, instead of rebutting the presumption by proof beyond a reasonable doubt.).

today may attempt to rebut this presumption of legitimacy through factors such as lack of access, unavailability, physical impossibility, and blood tests.[26] However, in *Cleo A. E. v. Rickie Gene E.*,[27] on an appeal by the Child Advocate Office, the Court of Appeals of West Virginia refused to allow a couple to stipulate in their divorce decree that one of the children born during marriage was not the child of the husband on the basis that the child's best interests would not be served.

In *Michael H. V. Gerald D.*,[28] the United States Supreme Court upheld a California statute that provided, "the issue of a wife cohabiting with her husband, who is not impotent or sterile, is conclusively presumed to be a child of the marriage."[29] The presumption could be rebutted by blood tests only if a motion were made within two years from the child's birth by the husband, or if the biological father had filed an affidavit acknowledging paternity, by the wife. In *Michael H.*, Carole D. gave birth to a child, Victoria, while she was married to Gerald D., who was listed as the father on the birth certificate and held Victoria out as his daughter. Shortly after the child's birth, Carole informed Michael H., a neighbor with whom she had conducted an adulterous affair, that he was the father. For a several year period during Victoria's first three years, Carole and the child lived with Michael, and blood tests indicated a 98.07% probability that Michael was Victoria's father. Michael also held the child out as his own. After Carole parted with Michael, he filed a filiation action to establish his paternity and sought visitation with Victoria. Gerald, who had reconciled with Carole, intervened in the action, on the basis of the statutory conclusive presumption that he was Victoria's father.

At the United States Supreme Court, Michael argued that his substantive due process rights were violated because he had established a parental relationship that constituted a constitutionally protected liberty interest. The Court rejected his argument, concluding instead that the marital family is the unit to be protected from claims of third parties, such as Michael, and that the California legislature was free to select that entity as the one to protect. In a persuasive dissent, Justice Brennan, joined by Justices Marshall and Blackmun, argued that the plurality opinion conflicted with the Court's earlier opinions that protected established parent-child relationships between unmarried fathers and their children.[30]

---

[26] *See, e.g., N.P.A. v. W.P.A.*, 380 S.E.2d 178 (Va. Ct. App. 1989) (the presumption of legitimacy was rebutted by wife's admission that she had sexual intercourse with another man, plus husband's evidence of an HLA human leukocyte antigen blood grouping test that conclusively disproved his paternity); *In re Smith*, 534 N.E.2d 669 (Ill. App. Ct. 1989) (the presumption of legitimacy was overcome by blood test evidence showing 99.99% probability that the putative father, and not the mother's husband, was the father of the child). *See generally* Sidney B. Schatkin, Disputed Paternity Proceedings (1991 rev. ed.).

[27] 438 S.E.2d 886 (W. Va. 1993).

[28] 491 U.S. 110 (1989).

[29] Cal. Evid. Code Ann. § 621(a) (West Supp. 1989), *repealed by* Cal. Fam. Code §§ 7540–41 (1997)(establishing rebuttable presumption).

[30] 491 U.S. at 136-157, Brennan, J., dissenting.

Because the Supreme Court merely upheld the then-existing conclusive statutory presumption of paternity, but did not mandate it, the majority of states have adopted a rebuttable presumption of paternity based on marriage. [31] However, those states still face questions regarding the circumstances under which the presumption may be rebutted. Some states have required a putative father seeking to rebut the presumption to demonstrate that the best interests of the child would be served. [32]

Although biological paternity alone is currently a sufficient ground for imposing child support obligation, courts have been considerably more ambivalent about whether the *lack* of a biological connection necessarily precludes the imposition of a child support responsibility. For example, in *Pietros v. Pietros*, [33] the Supreme Court of Rhode Island held that a man who married his wife knowing that she was pregnant with another man's child, and assured her that he would treat the child as his own, was estopped from denying paternity during their subsequent divorce action.

[C] Children of Void and Voidable Marriages

Under the common law, children of void or voidable marriages [34] were illegitimate and, once again, such nonmarital children were deprived of their legal rights due to the parents' unmarried status, rather than due to any wrongdoing on the part of the child. [35] In reaction to this very harsh common law rule, all states have now enacted laws providing that children of void or voidable marriages are legitimate by statute.

These legitimization statutes are liberally construed for remedial purposes, [36] and they would therefore legitimize the children of invalid common law marriages, [37] or void bigamous marriages. [38] Likewise, if a marriage was invalidated based upon the husband's insanity, the children of that marriage nevertheless would be marital under the state statute. [39] However, most state legitimization statutes require a marriage of *some* kind, even though such a marriage is void or voidable. These statutes therefore cannot legitimize a child whose parents lived together in a cohabiting relationship without any pretense of a marriage of any kind. [40] A child who is legitimized

---

[31] 1 William Blackstone, Commentaries on the Law of England 454 (4th ed. 1899).

[32] *See, e.g., Weidenbacher v. Duclos*, 661 A.2d 988, 1000 (Conn. 1995); *In re Paternity of Adam*, 903 P.2d 207 (Mont. 1995), *cert. denied*, 116 S.Ct. 1544 (1996).

[33] 638 A.2d 545 (R.I. 1994).

[34] *See supra* § 2.08[A].

[35] The legal rationale for this severe law was "whatever depends on the void marriage is also void." 1 Joel Prentiss Bishop, Marriage, Divorce and Separation 313 (1891).

[36] *See, e.g., Kasey v. Richardson*, 462 F.2d 757 (4th Cir. 1972).

[37] *See, e.g., Murphy v. Holland*, 377 S.E.2d 363 (Va. 1989) (an invalid Virginia common law marriage nevertheless legitimized the parties' children under the state statute for inheritance purposes).

[38] *See, e.g., Rance v. Rance*, 587 N.E.2d 150 (Ind. Ct. App. 1992) (if a marriage is bigamous, the children of the marriage would still have the statutory means of obtaining child support).

[39] *See, e.g., Cornwall v. Cornwall*, 168 S.E. 439 (Va. 1933).

[40] *See, e.g., Kasey v. Richardson*, 462 F.2d 757 (4th Cir. 1972); *Grove v. Metropolitan Life Ins. Co.*, 271 F.2d 918 (4th Cir. 1959).

under such state statutes has all the rights of marital children including, but not limited to, inheritance rights, the right to participate under state wrongful death statutes, and the right to receive insurance proceeds.[41]

[D] Constitutional Protection of the Nonmarital Child

The legal status of the nonmarital child has been further normalized since 1968 by the United States Supreme Court, which brought many illegitimacy issues under the protection of federal constitutional law.

For example, in *Levy v. Louisiana*,[42] the court held that it was unconstitutional for a state to create a cause of action in favor of a marital child for the wrongful death of a parent, and exclude a nonmarital child from the same cause of action. The Supreme Court in *Levy* held that nonmarital children were clearly persons within the meaning of the Equal Protection Clause of the United States Constitution, and therefore it would be "invidious to discriminate against them when no action, conduct, or demeanor of theirs is possibly relevant to the harm that was done to [their] mother."[43]

In *Weber v. Aetna Casualty & Surety Co.*,[44] the Supreme Court held that a nonmarital child could also recover under state worker's compensation laws. The Court again invalidated a classification that burdened the nonmarital child for the sake of punishing the illicit relationship of the parents because "visiting this condemnation on the head of an infant is illogical and unjust."[45]

In the seminal case of *Gomez v. Perez*,[46] the Supreme Court held that there was a constitutional duty of *both* parents to support a nonmarital child, once paternity had been proved.[47] And in *Trimble v. Gordon*,[48] the Supreme Court held that a nonmarital child could inherit from the father as well as the mother once paternity had been proved.[49] Finally, in *Clark v. Jeter*,[50] the Supreme Court struck down a six-year Pennsylvania statute limiting the time to bring a support action for nonmarital children, because the statute did not withstand the heightened scrutiny test under the Equal Protection Clause when compared to support rights of marital children.[51]

---

[41] *See* Harry D. Krause, Legitimacy: Law and Social Policy 11–13 (1971).

[42] 391 U.S. 68 (1968).

[43] *Id.* Although the *Levy* court purportedly applied a rational reason test, arguably today laws that discriminate against nonmarital children must now meet a constitutional intermediate level of scrutiny test. *See, e.g., Clark v. Jeter*, 486 U.S. 456 (1988); *infra* notes 50-51 and accompanying text.

[44] 406 U.S. 164 (1972).

[45] 406 U.S. 164 at 175 (1972).

[46] 409 U.S. 535 (1973).

[47] *See infra* § 5.02[E].

[48] 430 U.S. 762 (1977).

[49] *See infra* § 5.02[G].

[50] 486 U.S. 456 (1988).

[51] *Id.* A more recently enacted 18-year Pennsylvania statute of limitations for paternity and support actions would undoubtedly withstand such heightened scrutiny, since it puts support actions for both nonmarital and marital children on a more equal footing.

These Supreme Court cases do not necessarily mean that *any* law which treats nonmarital children differently from marital children would be constitutionally invalid *per se*. For example, in the case of *Matthews v. Lucas*,[52] a Social Security requirement under applicable federal law[53] set out a two-prong test: dependent children could recover benefits only if: (1) they were marital or adopted children of the deceased; or (2) the children lived with the decedent and were dependents in the decedent's household at the time of his death. The nonmarital children of the decedent argued that the denial of benefits in this case violated constitutional due process and equal protection safeguards in that this federal law impermissibly discriminated against nonmarital children. The Supreme Court held otherwise and upheld the federal statute, on the grounds that the statute allowed nonmarital children the opportunity to prove their dependency, and this requirement was rationally related to the purpose of such a statute.[54]

Recently, in *Miller v. Allbright*,[55] the Supreme Court rejected an equal protection challenge to an immigration statute that imposed additional requirements for citizenship on nonmarital children born in another country, where the father, rather than the mother was an American citizen. While nonmarital children born abroad to an American mother and a non-American father automatically acquired citizenship at birth, the child born to an alien mother and an American father was required to provide formal proof of paternity before attaining the age of eighteen in order to qualify for U.S. citizenship. The court rejected the argument that the statute discriminated on the basis of sex, holding that the biological differences in proving relationship was a legitimate basis for the different rules.

[E] Paternity Grounds and Actions

One of the primary purposes of establishing paternity is to provide for the financial support of nonmarital children. Paternity and support actions can be brought either by the child's mother or by a social service agency. The federal government has required mothers to cooperate with state authorities in establishing paternity, in order to obtain public assistance benefits under both the Aid to Families with Dependent Children (AFDC) program and the more recent Temporary Assistance to Needy Families (TANF) program.[56] Although a narrow "good cause" exception exists,[57]

---

[52] 427 U.S. 495 (1976).

[53] 42 U.S.C. § 402(d)(1) (2000).

[54] *Id.*; *see also Prudential Ins. Co. v. Moorhead*, 730 F. Supp. 727 (M.D.La. 1989) (A statute providing methods for determining inheritance rights of nonmarital children of servicemen was substantially related to important governmental interests of an orderly disposition of property and deterring spurious claims, and thus the statute did not deny due process to an nonmarital child of a serviceman who died before acknowledging paternity.).

[55] 523 U.S. 420 (1998).

[56] *See* 42 U.S.C. § 408(a)(3) (1997 Supp.); 42 U.S.C. § 654(29) (1998)(replacing 42 U.S.C. § 602(a)(26) (1985).

[57] 42 U.S.C. § 654 (29)(1998); 45 C.F.R. § 232.42 (1995).

primarily for domestic abuse cases, advocates for low-income women have criticized the scope and intrusiveness of the cooperation requirement.[58]

Defenses to paternity and support actions are limited. An unmarried father may not be relieved of his child support obligation because the child's mother became pregnant by deceiving him. In *Murphy v. Meyers*[59], the Minnesota Court of Appeals denied a putative father's attempt to raise fraud and misrepresentation as affirmative defenses to a paternity and child support action. Although the defendant argued that the child's mother had deceived him by claiming she had been sterilized, the court held that "[t]he purpose of a paternity action is not to punish the father, but rather to impose a duty on the father to support the child, to ensure [that] the mother does not bear full financial responsibility for the child, and to protect the public by preventing the child from becoming a public charge."[60] The court noted that other states had unanimously barred fraud and misrepresentation defenses to such actions. Similarly, in *Matter of L. Pamela P. V. Frank S.*,[61] the court rejected the unwed father's argument that his constitutional right to decide whether or not to be a father was violated because the child's mother misrepresented to him that she was using birth control. The court held that the needs of the child and the means of the parent are the relevant factors in assigning child support, and noted that the father was not prevented from using contraception himself. However, actions by a nonmarital child against the father in tort or contract, based on breach of a promise to marry, have been unsuccessful. In *Zepeda v. Zepeda,*[62] the court rejected the child's suit, despite noting that the father's actions were morally wrong and perhaps criminally punishable, holding that such a sweeping change in the law was the function of the legislature.

The Supreme Court, in *Rivera v. Minnich*,[63] upheld the constitutionality of a preponderance of the evidence standard for determining paternity, distinguishing such actions from proceedings to terminate parental rights, which constitutionally require the clear and convincing evidence standard.[64] A few states still require that paternity be proved by clear and convincing evidence standard, viewing such actions as quasi-criminal.[65]

---

[58] *See, e.g.*, Lisa Kelly, *If Anybody AsksYou Who I Am: An Outsider's Story of the Duty To Establish Paternity*, 3 Am. U. J. Gender & Law 247 (1995); Paula Roberts, *The Family Law Implications of the 1996 Welfare Legislation*, 30 Clearinghouse Rev. 988, 997–1003 (1997).

[59] 560 N.W.2d 752 (Minn.Ct. App. 1997).

[60] *Id*. at 754.

[61] 499 N.E.2d 713 (N.Y. 1983).

[62] 190 N.E.2d 849 (Ill.Ct.App. 1963).

[63] 483 U.S. 574 (1987).

[64] *See Santosky v. Kramer*, 455 U.S. 745 (1982).

[65] *See, e.g., County Dep't of Soc. Services v. Williams*, 468 N.E. 2d 705 (N.Y. 1984). Others states have required the higher standard in paternity determinations that take place after the alleged father's death. *See, e.g., Reed v. Flournoy*, 600 So.2d 565 (Ala. Civ. App. 1992); *Ross v. Moore*, 758 S.W. 2d 423 (Ark. Ct. App. 1998).

[1] The Uniform Parentage Act

Under the early common law a father did not have a legal obligation to support his nonmarital child.[66] However, since the U.S. Supreme Court case of *Gomez v. Perez*,[67] such support for a nonmarital child is now constitutionally mandated, once paternity has been proven. Accordingly, in all fifty states today, fathers as well as mothers are compelled to support their nonmarital children under state statutory law.[68]

Although there is a wide diversity of state parentage statutes, and although a detailed study of each state statute is beyond the scope of this treatise, nevertheless, one of the most effective parentage statutes, adopted by an increasing number of states,[69] is the Uniform Parentage Act.[70]

The Uniform Parentage Act addresses legitimation in a two-step process: First, the statute provides that the parent-child relationship extends to every child and every parent, regardless of the parent's marital status.[71] Second, the statute delineates the various methods for establishing paternity.

Paternity under the Act may be established either by a civil suit,[72] or by the existence of a rebuttable presumption of paternity based upon the marriage of the child's parents, plus the father's acknowledgment of paternity, by the father's reception of the child into his home, or by other enumerated methods of acknowledgment of paternity by the father.[73] A court may, and upon the request of a party shall, require the child, mother, or alleged father to submit to blood tests to determine paternity or non-paternity.[74]

Other evidence relating to paternity under the Uniform Parentage Act may include: (1) evidence of sexual intercourse between the mother and the alleged father at the possible time of conception; (2) an expert's opinion concerning the statistical probability of the alleged father's paternity based upon the duration of the mother's pregnancy; (3) blood test results, weighed in accordance with evidence, if available, of the statistical probability of the alleged father's paternity; (4) medical or anthropological evidence relating to the alleged father's paternity of the child based on tests performed by experts; and (5) all other evidence relevant to the issue of paternity of the child.[75]

---

[66] *See, e.g., Allen v. Hunnicutt*, 52 S.E.2d 18 (N.C. 1949).

[67] 409 U.S. 535 (1973).

[68] *See, e.g.*, Harry D. Krause, Illegitimacy 19–20 (1971). *See generally* 1 Homer Clark, Law of Domestic Relations 278–358 (2d ed. 1987).

[69] *See, e.g.*, with some modifications, Alabama, California, Colorado, Delaware, Hawaii, Illinois, Kansas, Minnesota, Missouri, Montana, Nevada, New Jersey, New Mexico, North Dakota, Ohio, Rhode Island, Washington, and Wyoming.

[70] Unif. Parentage Act, 9B U.L.A. 287 (1987)(Supp. 2000).

[71] *Id.* § 2.

[72] *Id.* § 6, 14–15.

[73] *Id.* § 4.

[74] *Id.* § 11; *see also infra* § 5.02[F].

[75] Unif. Parentage Act, § 12, 9B U.L.A. 317 (1987) (Supp. 2000).

It has also been held that the Uniform Parentage Act has no application in a legal dispute between parties involved in a homosexual relationship. [76]

[2] Jurisdictional Issues

Because a paternity proceeding is normally brought against a putative father for payment of child support, most cases hold that there must be personal jurisdiction over the defendant. [77] Jurisdiction in paternity proceedings may also be based upon a state long-arm statute; [78] and jurisdiction may also exist under the Revised Uniform Reciprocal Enforcement of Support Act [RURESA] [79] and the Uniform Interstate Family Support Act [UIFSA]. The Uniform Parentage Act also provides that a person who has sexual intercourse within the state thereby submits to the jurisdiction of that state's courts with respect to a child who may have been conceived thereby. [80]

[3] Private Promises and Contracts

It is also important to note that even if a putative father has not been determined to be legally liable for the support of a nonmarital child under the Uniform Parentage Act [81] or a similar state paternity statute, he might still be legally liable for child support under the doctrine of equitable estoppel. For example, in *T. v. T.*, [82] an unwed pregnant woman relied on her boyfriend's oral promise that he would marry her and would support

---

[76] *See, e.g., Curiale v. Reagan*, 272 Cal. Rptr. 520 (Cal. Ct. App. 1990) (the Uniform Parentage Act, which deals with the rights of children and the determination of parentage has no application where it was undisputed that a woman who had a homosexual relationship with the natural mother of the child, and who sought custody and visitation with the child, was not the natural mother).

[77] *See, e.g., Schilz v. Superior Court*, 695 P.2d 1103 (Ariz. 1985) (personal jurisdiction required); *see also State ex rel. Karr v. Shorey*, 575 P.2d 981 (Or. 1978) (personal jurisdiction could also be based on an agreement acknowledging paternity and providing for the payment of child support).

[78] *See, e.g.,* Va. Code Ann. § 8.01-328.1(A) (1950) (Virginia courts would have personal jurisdiction under the state long-arm statute over a defendant who conceived or fathered a child in Virginia); *see also Cochran v. Wallace*, 381 S.E.2d 853 (N.C. Ct. App. 1989) (state statute which subjects a person who participates in an act of sexual intercourse within the state to jurisdiction of the state courts in a paternity matter did not violate the Due Process Clause); *Barber v. Profit*, 576 So. 2d 1168 (La. Ct. App. 1991) (mother's allegation that a child was fathered by the putative father and the parties' stipulation that the child was conceived in the state were sufficient to establish minimum contacts necessary to assert personal jurisdiction pursuant to a state long-arm statute). *But see Garvey v. Mendenhall*, 404 S.E.2d 613 (Ga. Ct. App. 1991) (putative father did not "transact business" in Georgia, so as to subject him to personal jurisdiction under the state long-arm statute in a paternity action by making social visits to Georgia.)

[79] Revised Unif. Reciprocal Enforcement of Support at, 9B U.L.A. 523 (Supp. 2000) (If an obligor asserts nonpaternity as a defense in an action under RURESA, the court may adjudicate the paternity issue "in the same manner as if the issue arose in a support case initiated and tried in this State."). *See generally infra* § 9.02[C].

[80] Unif. Parentage Act, § 8, 9B U.L.A. 309 (1968) (Supp. 2000).

[81] Unif. Parentage Act, 9B U.L.A. 287 (1987)(Supp. 2000).

[82] 224 S.E.2d 148 (Va. 1976).

her child as though it were his own. Although this premarital promise to support the child was not in writing to comply with the state statute of frauds,[83] nevertheless the wife's detrimental reliance and partial performance on the husband's oral promise took his promise to support the child out of the statute of frauds, and the husband was estopped to deny it.[84]

Likewise, according to the law of most states, if the putative father privately contracts to make child support payments in consideration of the mother's forbearance from bringing a paternity action against him, such a private contract would be legally binding upon the parties, assuming, of course, that the child support contractual provisions are reasonable and adequate.[85] The Uniform Parentage Act[86] also recognizes and authorizes these contracts. However, such a contract may not be enforceable if the consideration for the contract is based upon illicit sexual intercourse which is not severable from other valid consideration.[87]

[F] Scientific Testing in Paternity Proceedings

The development of increasingly sophisticated scientific testing has significantly enhanced the ability to determine paternity. Traditionally, medical or anthropological evidence relating to the alleged parentage of the child was based on tests performed by experts,[88] often involving an alleged family resemblance[89] or blood tests.[90] These tests generally could be used only to *disprove* paternity. In the 1980s new types of blood and genetic testing, primarily HLA typing, emerged, which could exclude more than 90 percent of the male population in most cases, and the traditional limitations on scientific evidence began to erode.[91] New DNA tests make paternity testing even more accurate. Virtually all states now provide for the introduction of genetic and other blood test evidence for the purpose

---

[83] Va. Code Ann. § 11-2(5) (1950).

[84] *T. v. T.*, 224 S.E.2d 148 (Va. 1976).

[85] *See, e.g., Peterson v. Eritsland*, 419 P.2d 332 (Wash. 1966); *Fiege v. Boehm*, 123 A.2d 316 (Md. 1956); *Haag v. Barnes*, 175 N.E.2d 441 (N.Y. 1961). The holding in *Haag v. Barnes, supra*, however, has been criticized in Albert A. Ehrenzweig, *The Bastard in the Conflict of Laws*, 29 U. Chi. L. Rev. 498 (1962); *see also* Note, *The Illegitimate Child Support Contract: A Prophylactic*, 1970 Law & Social Order 641 (1970).

[86] Unif. Parentage Act, 9B U.L.A. 334 (1987) (Supp. 2000).

[87] *See, e.g., Naimo v. La Fianza*, 369 A.2d 987 (N.J. Super. Ct. Ch. Div. 1976).

[88] *See, e.g.*, Unif. Parentage Act § 12(c), 9B U.L.A. 317 (1987) (Supp. 2000).

[89] *See, e.g.*, Judge Marvin C.Holz, *The Trial of a Paternity Case*, 50 Marquette L. Rev. 450,489 (1966-67).

[90] *See, e.g.*, Harry D. Krause, *Scientific Evidence and the Ascertainment of Paternity*, 5 Fam. L.Q. 252, 270–273 (1971).

[91] *See, e.g., In re the Paternity of J.L.K.*, 445 N.W.2d 673 (Wis. 1989) (results of "DNA fingerprinting" are admissible in a paternity proceeding under a state statute providing for the admission of blood test results and other statistical probabilities of an alleged father's paternity). For a comprehensive discussion of DNA testing in paternity matters, see 1 Sidney B. Schatkin, Disputed Paternity Proceedings, Chapter 11B, *Scientific and Legal Aspects of DNA Typing* (1992 rev. ed.).

of affirmatively proving paternity, as well as for the purpose of excluding an alleged father.[92]

Briefly, the accuracy of DNA tests for paternity, called restriction enzyme fragment length polymorphisms (RFLP), is much higher than HLA blood tests,[93] but also much more expensive. The major difference between DNA and HLA tests is that DNA tests actually pinpoint the father, while HLA tests involve an exclusion-by-probability method that is often complicated and cumbersome. The sample necessary for a DNA test is also smaller and easier to obtain, and the results are much more accurate.[94]

Blood grouping tests have been admitted into evidence in all states to prove or disprove paternity.[95] There are two major blood grouping tests that may be used.[96] First, there is the traditional A, B, O, and AB blood grouping tests with their Rh and Hr factors, which examine red blood cell genetic markers,[97] and these tests can establish *nonpaternity* by clear and convincing evidence, but cannot clearly establish paternity.[98]

The most accurate blood grouping test in paternity actions, however, is the HLA (Human Leukocyte Antigen) blood grouping tests based upon tissue typing of white blood cells with a cumulative paternity exclusion rate exceeding 99 percent.[99] Moreover, the HLA blood grouping tests can establish a very high degree of probability of paternity inclusion, as well as nonpaternity exclusion.[100] There has been almost universal praise for

---

[92] *See* D.H. Kaye & Ronald Kanwischer, *Admissibility of Genetic Testing in Paternity Litigation: A Survey of State Statutes*, 22 Fam. L. Q. 109 (1988).

[93] *See infra* notes 82–84 and accompanying text.

[94] For example, in one paternity case utilizing DNA testing, it was established that the putative father was the father of a nonmarital child by a ratio of 8,077,911 to 1, which would definitely constitute either clear and convincing scientific evidence of paternity, or evidence of paternity beyond a reasonable doubt, under applicable state parentage statutes. *In re Baby Girl S.*, 532 N.Y.S.2d 634 (N.Y. Sur. Ct. 1988). *See generally*1 Sidney B. Schatkin, Disputed Paternity Proceedings, Chapter 11B, *Scientific and Legal Aspects of DNA Typing* (1991 rev. ed.).

[95] *See, e.g.*, Unif. Parentage Act §§ 11,12(3), 9B U.L.A. 316, 317 (1987) (Supp. 2000).

[96] *Id. See also* Joseph W. Williford, Comment, *The Use of Blood Tests in Actions to Determine Paternity*, 16 Wake Forest L. Rev. 591 (1980).

[97] *See generally* E.G. Reisner & T. A. Bolk, *A Layman's Guide to the Use of Blood Group Analysis in Paternity Testing*, 20 J. Fam. L. 657 (1981-82).

[98] *See generally* 1 Sidney B. Schatkin, Disputed Paternity Proceedings, Chapters 5–8 (1991 rev. ed.). The exclusion rate for these red blood cell tests is approximately 76 percent. *Id.* § 8.08.

[99] *See generally* Vera L. Sterlek & Lee M. Jacobson, *Paternity Testing with the Human Leukocyte Antigen System: A Medicolegal Breakthrough*, 20 Santa Clara L. Rev. 511 (1980); T. I. Terasaki, *Resolution by HLA Testing of 1000 Paternity Cases Not Excluded by ABO Testing*, 16 J. Fam. L. 543 (1975). *But see* Leonard R. Jaffee, *Comment on the Judicial Use of HLA Paternity Test Results and Other Statistical Evidence: A Response to Terasaki*, 17 J. Fam. L. 457 (1978-79). *See also* 1 Sidney B. Schatkin, Disputed Paternity Proceedings § 8.08 ("HLA is a super system compared with all the others").

[100] *See, e.g., Denbow v. Harris*, 583 A.2d 205 (Me. 1990) (a blood test showing a 99.97% probability of paternity was admissible in a paternity action); *Braden v. Nash*, 550 So. 2d 866 (La. Ct. App. 1989) (expert testimony about blood test results was admissible even though the expert did not actually perform the tests, and a paternity index of 99.90% was sufficiently reliable to be used to support a finding of paternity). *See generally* Vera L.Sterlek & Lee M.

the HLA paternity tests from state legislatures and courts, and there is also a strong trend toward the admissibility of HLA tests as inclusionary evidence, as well as exclusionary evidence.[101]

Despite the development of modern genetic and blood testing evidence, the statistical assumptions and scientific methodology used to assess and present this evidence have created a number difficulties for the courts. The Wisconsin case of *In re Paternity of M.J.B.*[102] illustrates some of these difficulties, holding that statistics regarding probability of paternity may be introduced only competent evidence of sexual intercourse occurred between the parties during the period of conception. After explaining the statistical evidence, the court noted that although it is preferable to call an expert witness to explain or attack the tests, the statute does not require such testimony. Other jurisdictions employ various other approaches to the presentation of scientific evidence of paternity. For example, the Oregon Supreme Court held in *Plemel v. Walter*[103] that a range of calculations based on an array of probabilities should be presented, rather than a single figure estimated the probability of paternity.

Most courts that have considered the admissibility of DNA evidence in paternity cases have allowed it.[104] Because it involves many of the same statistical techniques as other types of paternity testing, it raises the same evidentiary concerns, although the fact that each individual's DNA is unique makes the evidence considerably more powerful.[105] Because DNA testing uses molecules that remain stable and testable even after a person's death, it has raised the possibility of accurate paternity testing long after a putative father has died[106] and a number of courts have granted requests for exhumation of bodies to perform DNA tests.[107] Further, comparing the

---

Jacobson, *Paternity Testing with the Human Leukocyte Antigen System*, 20 Santa Clara L. Rev. 511, 523 (1980) ("if a putative father is not excluded by the HLA test, the resulting inclusion rate is very likely over ninety percent").

[101] *See supra* note 83 and accompanying text. HLA tests are currently admissible to determine paternity in more than 41 states and the District of Columbia. A growing number of states have changed their parentage laws to accept inclusionary evidence of paternity, as well as exclusionary evidence. *See generally* S. Joel Kolko, *Admissibility of HLA Test Results to Determine Paternity*, 9 Fam. L. Rep. 4009 (BNA 1983). *But see* 1 Sidney B. Schatkin, Disputed Paternity Proceedings, Chapter 11A, *Challenging the HLA Blood Tests* (1991 rev. ed.).

[102] 425 N.W.2d 404 (Wis. 1988).

[103] 735 P.2d 1209 (Or. 1987).

[104] *See, e.g.*, *Mastromatteo v. Harkins*, 615 A.2d 390 (Pa. Super. Ct. 1992); *Isabella County Dep't of Soc. Services v. Thompson*, 534 N.W.2d 132 (Mich. Ct. App. 1995); *Commonwealth ex. rel. Overby v. Flaneary*, 469 S.E.2d 79 (Va. Ct. App. 1996).

[105] *See generally* Nina M. Vitek, Disputed Paternity Proceedings, 5th ed. (Matthew Bender 1998).

[106] *See* Charles Nelson LeRay, *Implications of DNA Technology on Posthumous Paternity Determination: Deciding the Facts When Daddy Can't Give His Opinion*, 35 B.C. L. Rev. 747 (1994).

[107] *See, e.g.*, *Lach v. Welch*, 1997 WL 536330 (Conn. Super. Ct. 1997); *In re Estate of Rogers*, 583 A.2d 782 (N.J. Super. Ct. App. Div. 1990); *Batcheldor v. Boyd*, 423 S.E.2d 810 (N.C. Ct. App. 1992); *Wawrydow v. Simonich*, 652 A.2d 843 (Pa. Super. Ct. 1994).

DNA of a close relative of a deceased putative father can help establish paternity posthumously.[108]

The federal government has become increasingly involved in establishing paternity. In 1993, Congress enacted legislation that requires states participating in federal income security programs to adopt rebuttable or conclusive presumptions of paternity upon genetic testing[109] and requires states to provide for genetic testing of all parties in contested paternity actions, upon the request of any party.[110] Federally funded child support enforcement agencies must also have the power to order genetic tests in appropriate contested cases[111] and certain genetic tests results must be admissible as evidence.[112] Further, states must establish and implement a simplified civil process for voluntary acknowledgment of paternity.[113]

Paternity judgments often raise difficult issues of res judicata. One problem arises when an adjudicated father seeks to reopen a paternity judgment on the grounds that newly-available scientific evidence demonstrates that he is not the child's biological father. The Court of Appeals of Maryland addressed that issue in *Tandra S. v. Tyrone W.*,[114] which consolidated two cases in which previously acknowledged and adjudicated paternity actions were challenged after blood tests excluded the paternity of the men. The court held that absent extrinsic fraud that would have prevented an adversarial trial, the paternity judgments were res judicata and could not be vacated. A strong dissent noted that paternity actions, unlike other civil suits, call upon the court to "declare a scientific, biological fact," which has continuing ramifications, and declared that the majority holding "defies common sense."[115] Although the Maryland legislature later amended the paternity statutes to provide that a paternity declaration may be revised or modified upon scientific evidence,[116] the issue remains unresolved in many other jurisdictions.

An additional issue arises when a child who was the subject of an unsuccessful paternity action later seeks to relitigate the paternity question. Another Maryland appellate case, *Jessica G. v. Hector M.*,[117] held that a nonmarital child was not bound by a dismissal with prejudice of an earlier paternity action brought by her mother against the same defendant when blood tests had indicated a 99.97% probability of paternity. Noting the split of authority among state courts, the court held that, in light of the circumstances of this case, the state's strong public policy in according

---

[108] *See Sudwischer v. Estate of Hoffpauer*, 589 So. 2d 474 (La. 1991).

[109] 42 U.S.C. § 666(G) (1998).

[110] 42 U.S.C. § 666(a)(5)(B) (1998).

[111] 42 U.S.C. § 666(c)(1)(a) (1998).

[112] 42 U.S.C. § 666(a)(5)(F)(I) (1998).

[113] 42 U.S.C. § 666(a)(5) (1998).

[114] 648 A.2d 439 (Md. App. 1994).

[115] *Id.* at 450-52, Elridge, J., dissenting.

[116] Md. Fam. Law Code Ann. § 5-1038(a)(2) (1997).

[117] 653 A.2d 922 (Ct. App. Md. 1995), *cert. denied*, 116 S.Ct. 99 (1995).

rights to nonmarital children, comparable to those afforded marital children, would be thwarted.

[G] Inheritance Rights

Under the common law, the child born out of wedlock traditionally was not allowed to share in the estate of his or her putative father unless the putative father had included the nonmarital child in a testamentary document. Indeed, in 1971, one of the most important forms of discrimination against the nonmarital child—discrimination regarding the nonmarital child's rights of inheritance—was held *not* to violate the Equal Protection Clause of the United States Constitution in *Labine v. Vincent.*[118]

In *Labine*, the United States Supreme Court held that an acknowledged nonmarital child could not inherit anything from her father under Louisiana law, because where marital children's rights were "socially sanctioned and legally recognized," nonmarital children's relationships were characterized as "illicit and beyond the recognition of the law."[119] Various commentators have criticized the *Labine* decision as an illogical judicial step backward from *Levy v. Louisiana,*[120] on the basis that the Court in *Labine* once again punished the nonmarital child for the sins of the parents.[121]

Fortunately, the Supreme Court again revisited this inheritance rights issue regarding nonmarital children in the 1977 case of *Trimble v. Gordon.*[122] In *Trimble*, the Supreme Court invalidated an Illinois statute on equal protection grounds where the statute provided that an acknowledged nonmarital child could inherit only from his mother and not from his father, while a marital child could inherit from both parents.[123] Although *Trimble v. Gordon* did not expressly overrule *Labine v. Vincent*, it did seriously limit any subsequent application of *Labine*, especially when paternity has been established.[124]

However, it is also important to note that the courts have usually upheld state statutes which impose reasonable prerequisites upon a nonmarital child's inheritance rights. The rationale is that because there are no vested rights to succession, a nonmarital child would be subject to reasonable limitations and conditions to such an inheritance as the state legislature may prescribe.

---

[118] 401 U.S. 532 (1971), *reh'g denied*, 402 U.S. 990 (1971).

[119] 401 U.S. at 538.

[120] 391 U.S. 68 (1968); *see also supra* notes 37 and 38 and accompanying text.

[121] *See, e.g.*, David Hallissey, Note, *Nonmaritals and Equal Protection*, 10 U. Mich. J. L. Ref. 543 (1977).

[122] 430 U.S. 762 (1977).

[123] *Id.*

[124] Professor Clark believes that *Labine* should be taken as being substantially limited, if not overruled; and the most plausible view of these two cases is that state inheritance rights *may* pass muster if they bar the nonmarital child's inheritance only from and through the father, and then only in those cases in which paternity is in doubt. 1 Homer Clark, Law of Domestic Relations 290 (2d ed. 1987).

For example, in *Lalli v. Lalli*,[125] the Supreme Court upheld the constitutionality of a New York intestate succession statute that allowed a nonmarital child to inherit only if the father's paternity had been established in court. The Supreme Court conceded in *Lalli* that such a statute might be unfair to a nonmarital child who can produce ample evidence of his or her paternity, but has never had the paternity issue formally adjudicated in court. Nevertheless, the statute was held to be constitutional since it was substantially related to the important state interest of providing for a just and orderly disposition of property at death, and therefore did not violate the Equal Protection Clause.[126]

The Supreme Court extended this rationale in *Parham v. Hughes*,[127] when it upheld a Georgia statute that precluded a father who had not legitimated a child from maintaining a wrongful death action arising from the child's death. It concluded that the statute did not invidiously discriminate against men as a class, although mothers did not need to prove maternity. Further, that the state's "interest in avoiding fraudulent claims of paternity in order to maintain a fair and orderly system of a decedent's property distribution" under its wrongful death statute was similar to its legitimate interest in probate actions.[128]

The Court of Appeals for the 7th Circuit held, in *Bennemon v. Sullivan*,[129] that a nonmarital child is eligible for Social Security benefits on account of a deceased parent only if state law so provides, if a written acknowledgment of paternity had been executed, or if a determination by the Social Security Administration indicates that the deceased parent was living with the child at the time of death or was contributing regular and substantial support to the child. In *Bennemon*, the child's parents, George Williams and Betty Bennemon, had met one year before Williams's death, during which time Bennemon became pregnant. Testimony from friends stated that the couple was in love and that Williams was excited about becoming a father. Although the two lived separately, Williams subscribed to electrical and telephone service on Bennemon's behalf, as she had a bad credit record. When Bennemon was pregnant, Williams was killed. He had never been declared a parent, and the court held that his contribution to the utility

---

[125] 439 U.S. 259 (1978).

[126] *Id.* at 276; *see also In re Estate of Blumreich*, 267 N.W. 2d 870 (Wis. 1978) (a state statute conditioning inheritance rights for a nonmarital child on a prior paternity adjudication, or on a father's admission of paternity in court, served a legitimate state interest in providing efficient estate administration, and therefore met the constitutional standards of *Trimble v. Gordon*); *Estate of Scheller v. Pessetto*, 783 P.2d 70 (Utah Ct. App. 1989) (A statute permitting a mother to inherit from her nonmarital child under all circumstances, but requiring a father to meet additional criteria that he treated the child as his own child and supported the child, did not violate federal equal protection standards since the statute served a legitimate state interest of providing efficient estate administration, and the development of meaningful relationships between nonmarital children and their fathers.).

[127] 441 U.S. 347 (1979).

[128] *Id.* at 360. Georgia subsequently amended its inheritance statutes to provide additional methods for an unmarried father to establish paternity and become eligible to inherit from his nonmarital child. Ga. Code Ann. § 53-4-5 (1997).

[129] 914 F.2d 987 (7th Cir. 1990).

payments was insufficient to constitute regular and substantial support. Therefore, the child was denied survivorship benefits.

[H] Artificial Insemination

Artificial insemination is a widely accepted means of assisted conception where a wife, with the consent of her husband, is artificially inseminated by a physician with semen provided by a third-party donor.[130] In the absence of a statute, therefore, the resulting child would not be the marital issue of the husband, and the husband might therefore argue that the child was nonmarital and that he had no legal obligation to support the child. In cases such as these, however, whether the child is deemed to be marital or nonmarital, if the husband consented to the artificial insemination, he is normally estopped to deny his support obligations to the child.[131]

Accordingly, a majority of states have now passed statutes dealing with children born as a result of artificial insemination.[132] These statutes generally provide that any child born to a married woman who was conceived by means of artificial insemination performed by a licensed physician, and with the written consent of the husband, shall be presumed for all purposes to be the marital natural child of such husband and wife.[133]

Some courts have held that even when the husband's written consent to artificial insemination is statutorily required, the failure to obtain such written consent does not relieve the husband of the responsibilities of parentage. Therefore, the husband's consent to his wife's impregnation by artificial insemination may be express, or it may be implied from conduct

---

[130] Normally, state statutes generally exclude the anonymous semen donor from any legal rights or obligations with respect to the resulting child. However, a known semen donor may have additional legal rights and obligations to the child if that was the original intent of the parties. *See, e.g., McIntyre v. Crouch*, 780 P.2d 239 (Or. Ct. App. 1989) (a state statute excluding semen donors from parenting rights and obligations would violate a semen donor's constitutional due process rights if he could establish that he and the mother agreed that he should have such rights and responsibilities of fatherhood); *J.R. v. E.C.*, 775 P.2d 27 (Colo. 1989) (state statute providing that semen donors do not have parental rights does not apply when a known semen donor and an unmarried recipient agree that the donor will be treated as the father of the child).

[131] *See, e.g., Gursky v. Gursky*, 242 N.Y.S. 2d 406 (N.Y. Sup. Ct. 1963), commented on in 52 Georgetown L.J. 633 (1964); *People v. Sorensen*, 66 Cal. Rptr. 7 (Cal. 1968); *L.M.S. v. S.L.S.*, 312 N.W.2d 853 (Wis. Ct. App. 1981).

[132] *See, e.g.*, Cal. Fam. Code § 7613 (West 1994); The Uniform Parentage Act, 9A U.L.A. 301, § 5; *see also* Judith Bick & Lynn Rice, Comment, *The Need for Statutes Regulating Artificial Insemination by Donors*, 46 Ohio St. L.J. 1062 (1985). A majority of these statutes, however, do not address the legal status of children born by artificial insemination to unmarried mothers.

[133] *Id.* Many of these state artificial insemination statutes are currently being expanded to cover children conceived by artificial insemination, in vitro fertilization, and any other reproductive technology. *See, e.g.*, Va. Code Ann. § 20-156 (Michie 1994). *See generally infra* § 5.07.

which evidences his knowledge of the artificial insemination procedure and his failure to object.[134]

[I]　Custody Issues

Historically, custody of a nonmarital child was always awarded to the mother. In part this was due to an historical lack of interest on the part of the putative father, and in part to traditional social and moral values that precluded an unwed father from any custodial rights or obligations.

However, an unwed father's custodial right to his nonmarital child began to be recognized in a constitutional sense beginning in 1972 with *Stanley v. Illinois*.[135] In *Stanley*, the United States Supreme Court held that an unwed father could not be deprived of the opportunity to demonstrate his fitness to have custody of his nonmarital children without a due process hearing.

In 1978 in *Quilloin v. Walcott*,[136] the Court held that a putative father who, for eleven years, had not attempted to establish any relationship with his nonmarital child, could not thereafter exercise any veto power over the child's subsequent adoption by the mother's husband. The test in this case was the best interests of the child, rather than parental fitness.

A year later, in 1979, in *Caban v. Mohammed*,[137] the Court held a New York statute invalid on equal protection grounds that precluded an unwed father from adopting his own nonmarital children, or from vetoing the adoption of his nonmarital children by a third party. The Court reaffirmed that there must be an ongoing relationship between the unwed father and the nonmarital child in order for the father to exercise his adoption or veto rights.[138]

Finally, in *Lehr v. Robertson*,[139] the Supreme Court held that there is a finite time limitation for the putative father to establish an "opportunity interest" in his nonmarital child. If he fails to establish this interest before a third party begins to legalize a new father-child relationship, then the putative father may lose any legal rights he may have in his nonmarital child.[140]

---

[134] *See, e.g., In re Baby Doe*, 353 S.E.2d 877 (S.C. 1987); *R.S. v. R.S.*, 670 P.2d 923 (Kan. Ct. App. 1983). *But see K.B. v. N.B.*, 811 S.W.2d 634 (1991) (husband's oral consent to artificial insemination performed on his wife did not estop him from relying on a state statute requiring that such consent be in writing).

[135] 405 U.S. 645 (1972).

[136] 434 U.S. 246 (1978).

[137] 441 U.S. 380 (1979).

[138] *Id.* This ongoing relationship has been held to constitute an "opportunity interest" of the putative father in the nonmarital child.

[139] 463 U.S. 248 (1983).

[140] *Id.; see also Adoption of G*, 529 A.2d 809 (Me. 1987); *In re Adoption of Stawser*, 522 N.E.2d 1105 (Ohio Ct. App. 1987). *But see In re Baby Girl Eason*, 358 S.E.2d 459 (Ga. 1987) for a case where the putative father's interest in his nonmarital child was held to be protected under the law. *See also* Lara C. Betty & Yvette L. Miranda, Note, *In re Baby Girl Easton: Expanding the Constitutional Rights of Unwed Fathers*, 39 Mercer L. Rev. 997 (1988).

Lehr appears to mean that the biological relationship only gives the father an opportunity to obtain a constitutionally protected right, but does not address what the biological father must do to exercise that opportunity. The Supreme Court of California, in *In re Adoption of Kelsey S.*,[141] held that a father of a nonmarital child may not constitutionally be denied the right to withhold his consent to his child's adoption when he has not been shown to be unfit. In that case, the petitioner had attempted to establish a relationship and obtain custody of the child, but had been thwarted by the mother, who wanted to place the child for adoption. The court held that the California Code did not anticipate such "constructive" receiving of the child into his home to satisfy the statutory basis for the father's attaining the status of a "presumed father."[142] However, it concluded that there was no substantial relationship between the state's interest in protecting a child and allowing the mother sole control over its placement and denying the father the same right; therefore the father's constitutional rights to due process and equal protection were violated. It advised that courts should consider all the factors, including "[t]he father's conduct both *before and after* the child's birth,"[143] in assuming parental responsibilities, and emphasized that only fathers who have "sufficiently and timely demonstrated a full commitment to his parental responsibilities"[144] will be granted the power to veto an adoption. That same court, in *In re Adoption of Michael H.*,[145] denied the right to withhold consent to adoption of an unwed father who had initially agreed with the child's mother to place the child for adoption, and assisted in the arrangements, but changed his mind after the child was born and had been placed with the adoptive parents for several weeks.

These cases still do not resolve the unanswered question of *Lehr*, regarding the rights of an unwed father who is denied an opportunity, through no fault of his own, to develop a relationship with his child. Thus, according to the facts of a particular case, an unwed putative father may or may not be awarded custody or visitation rights of his nonmarital child based upon the best interests of the child.[146]

[J] Claims and Defenses in Paternity Actions

Numerous courts have held, under the doctrine of res judicata, that a final judgment in a paternity matter is generally conclusive on the same parties, and relating to the same issues, in a subsequent paternity

---

[141] 823 P.2d 1216 (1992).

[142] *Id.* at 622; Cal. Civ. Code § 8600 (West 1994).

[143] *Id.* at 636.

[144] *Id.*

[145] 898 P.2d 891 (Cal. 1995), *cert. denied,* 116 S. Ct. 1272 (1996).

[146] *See generally* William Weston, *Putative Father's Right to Custody: A Rocky Road at Best,* 10 Whittier L. Rev. 683 (1989); Daniel C. Zinman, *Father Knows Best: the Unwed Father's Right to Raise his Infant Surrendered for Adoption,* 60 Fordham L. Rev. 971 (1992); Kara L. Boucher & Ruthann M. Macolini, *The Parental Rights of Unwed Fathers: A Developmental Perspective,* 20 N.C. Cent. L.J. 45 (1992).

proceeding.[147] However, various courts have also held that this res judicata defense as to the mother's and father's interests will not necessarily bar a subsequent action based upon the *child's* interests, since these interests are not necessarily the same.[148]

A statute of limitations in paternity proceedings may also be an issue, since in the past a number of state courts have held that a paternity action may be barred for failure to comply with a state's statute of limitations in bringing such an action.[149] However, state statutes of limitations applied to paternity actions have come under constitutional attack for invidiously discriminating against nonmarital children for the purpose of establishing support or inheritance rights, when no such statute of limitations was applicable in a support or inheritance action for marital children.[150] In *Opinion of the Justices (Supreme Court of New Hampshire)*,[151] the Supreme Court of New Hampshire responded to an inquiry from the state senate regarding a proposed law that would allow child support proceedings when the previous statute of limitations had run. The court answered that the previous one and two year statutes of limitations violated equal protection and that the mere running of that period would not give putative fathers a vested right to assert limitations as a defense to paternity actions. However, where a putative father had already obtained a judgment based on the running of the statute of limitation, res judicata would prevent the state from litigating paternity. The 1983 federal Child Support Enforcement Amendments require states to adopt 18-year statutes of limitations for paternity cases.

The courts are also sharply divided on the issue of whether or not an indigent defendant in a paternity proceeding is entitled to the assistance of legal counsel at state expense. Some courts have held that the indigent putative father is *not* entitled to legal counsel at the state's expense.[152] The better reasoned view, however, is that fundamental fairness in such an important family law matter requires that an indigent defendant in a paternity proceeding should be provided with legal counsel at the state's

---

[147] *See, e.g., Espree v. Guillory*, 753 S.W.2d 722 (Tex. Civ. App. 1988) (a final divorce decree declaring the husband to be the child's father was res judicata on the legal issue 1991) (former husband's failure to raise a defense of nonpaternity during a divorce proceeding in which child support orders were issued barred him from collaterally attacking the determination of paternity which implicitly supported the award of child support incident to that proceeding); *see also State ex rel. Daniels v. Daniels*, 817 P.2d 632 (Colo. Ct. App.) *Dep't of Health*, 459 So. 2d 1140 (Fla. Dist. Ct. App. 1984); *State ex rel. Partlow v. Law*, 692 P.2d 863 (Wash. Ct. App. 1984).

[148] *See, e.g., Dep't of Soc. Services v. Johnson*, 376 S.E.2d 787 (Va. Ct. App. 1989).

[149] *See, e.g., Anderson v. Sheffield*, 455 A.2d 53 (Md. Ct. Spec. App. 1983); *Locke v. Zollicoffer*, 608 S.W.2d 54 (Ky. 1980).

[150] *See, e.g., Clark v. Jeter*, 486 U.S. 456 (1988) (invalidating a six-year Pennsylvania statute of limitations for paternity actions, and noting that Pennsylvania has now passed a new eighteen-year statute of limitations for such actions); *see also Abrams v. Wheeler*, 468 So. 2d 126 (Ala. 1985); *Dornfeld v. Julian*, 472 N.E.2d 431 (Ill. 1984).

[151] 558 A.2d 454 (N.H. 1989).

[152] *See, e.g., Franks v. Mercer*, 401 So. 2d 470 (La. Ct. App. 1981); *Tidwell v. Booker*, 225 S.E.2d 816 (N.C. 1976); *State v. Walker*, 553 P.2d 1093 (Wash. 1976).

expense, because a paternity action is quasi-criminal in nature and can result in consequences of great magnitude.[153]

The United States Supreme Court has held, in *Little v. Streater*,[154] that a Connecticut statute which required anyone seeking a blood test to pay for the test, regardless of indigency, was an unconstitutional denial of due process. The court concluded that because the mother may establish a prima facie showing of paternity based solely on her testimony, the father's testimony alone is insufficient to refute her testimony, thus a father who was indigent and incarcerated at the time of the action to establish paternity had a right to blood testing regardless of his inability to pay.[155]

A common law defense frequently used by putative fathers in a paternity action is called *exceptio plurium concubentium*, or the multiple intercourse defense. In order to assert this defense, the alleged putative father must produce evidence that the mother had sexual intercourse during the period of conception with a man or men other than himself. The mother then has the burden of proof to show that only the alleged father could be the biological father of her child.[156]

The multiple intercourse defense, however, has fallen into some disuse, not only due to recent scientific evidence rebutting this defense,[157] but also due to the increasing reluctance of other men to testify concerning their sexual activities with the mother that may make them equally liable in a paternity suit themselves, or criminally prosecuted under state fornication or adultery statutes.[158]

Although a paternity action is usually brought against an unwed putative parent, such an action may also be brought as part of a divorce, legal separation, or annulment action. Finally, in the past, the cases were almost unanimous that the death of a putative father normally precludes any paternity or child support action, although a number of more recent decisions have allowed paternity to be proven posthumously.[159]

---

[153] *See, e.g., Pruitt v. Pruitt*, 282 N.W.2d 785 (Mich. Ct. App. 1979); *DeMace v. Whittaker*, 493 A.2d 219 (Conn. 1985). *See also Gardner v. Gardner*, 538 A.2d 4 (Pa. Super. Ct. 1988) (only when there is a trial on a disputed issue of paternity is an indigent putative father entitled to legal counsel).

[154] 452 U.S. 1 (1981).

[155] The Supreme Court has also held that a state statute that allows establishment of paternity under a preponderance of the evidence standard affords sufficient due process to a putative father. *Rivera v. Minnich*, 483 U.S. 574 (1987).

[156] *See generally* Samuel Green & John V. Long, Marriage and Family Law Agreements 287–289 (1984). An HLA blood test or a DNA test would rebut this common law defense. *See supra* § 5.02[F].

[157] *Id.*

[158] *See generally* 1 Sidney B. Schatkin, Disputed Paternity Proceedings § 3.06 (1991 rev. ed.).

[159] *See, e.g. Harris v. Stewart*, 981 S.W.2d 122(Ky. App. 1998); *In re Estate of Wilkins*, 707 N.Y.S.2d 744 (N.Y. Surr. 2000).

§ 5.03 The Fundamental Right to Procreate

The importance of the family in American society has led the Supreme Court to acknowledge a number of individual rights involving procreation. Because the Constitution does not specifically address a right to family privacy or personal autonomy regarding an individual's decision whether or not to have children, the sources of these personal rights are controversial. While some justices have secured personal rights solely from the Due Process Clause, others have found a right to privacy existing by implication from other Constitutional rights. The right of privacy serves as the legal basis for a limited freedom of choice with respect to contraception, voluntary sterilization, abortion, and artificially aided conception, areas which continue to generate political and moral disputes.

The recognition of a fundamental right to procreate originated largely from a line of Supreme Court cases relating to parents' rights in raising their children. In 1923, the Court addressed parental decision-making regarding their children's education in *Meyer v. State of Nebraska*.[160] In *Meyer*, the Court struck down a Nebraska statute that prohibited instruction in certain foreign languages in private schools on the basis that the restriction materially interfered with the power of parents to control the education of their children, as well as with the opportunity of children to acquire knowledge. It found a liberty interest protected by the Fourteenth Amendment which encompasses the right "to marry, establish a home and bring up children."[161]

Two years later, in *Pierce v. Society of Sisters*,[162] the Court held that a state could not require children to attend public, rather than private, schools, finding no reasonable relationship between the statute and a legitimate state purpose. It again spoke in broad terms of, "the liberty of parents and guardians to direct the upbringing and education of children under their control."[163]

When the Court struck down a statute providing for the compulsory sterilization of certain criminals in *Skinner v. Oklahoma*,[164] it expanded the concepts of constitutional protection of families to include marriage and procreation as "fundamental to the very existence and survival of the race" and "involv[ing] one of the basic civil rights of man."[165] It later concluded, in *Stanley v. Illinois*,[166] that equal protection principles demanded that an unmarried father could not be deprived of custody of his children, with whom he had lived, after the mother's death, without a showing of unfitness. The Court declared, "The private interest here, that of a man in the children he has sired and raised, undeniably warrants deference and absent

---

[160] 262 U.S. 390 (1923).

[161] *Id.* at 399.

[162] 268 U.S. 510 (1925)

[163] *Id.* at 534–535.

[164] 316 U.S. 535 (1942); *see also infra* § 5.05[B].

[165] 316 U.S. at 541.

[166] 405 U.S. 645 (1972).

a powerful countervailing interest, protection."[167] Thus, family life and procreation has been recognized as one of the liberties protected by the Due Process Clause of the Fourteenth Amendment.[168]

While on occasion the Supreme Court has expanded the concept of family rights to include extended families,[169] its decisions deal primarily with family and procreative rights in the context of marriage and the traditional family. Some states continue to maintain cohabitation statutes that may restrict the rights of single persons.[170]

Bowers v. Hardwick,[171] decided by the Supreme Court in 1986, may delineate the limits of the right of privacy. In *Bowers*, the Court held that the right of privacy did not invalidate state criminal statutes prohibiting sodomy. The court reasoned that none of the cases dealing with family relationships, procreation, marriage, contraception, and abortion

> bears any resemblance to the claimed constitutional right of homo-
> sexuals to engage in acts of sodomy that is asserted in this case.
> No connection between family, marriage, or procreation on the one
> hand and homosexual activity on the other has been demon-
> strated. . . . Moreover, any claim that these cases nevertheless
> stand for the proposition that any kind of private sexual conduct
> between consenting adults is constitutionally insulated from state
> proscription is insupportable. . . . Precedent aside, however, re-
> spondent would have us announce, as the Court of Appeals did, a
> fundamental right to engage in homosexual sodomy. This we are
> quite unwilling to do.[172]

The Court further concluded that the state could legislate against homosexual conduct based on a presumed public belief that such behavior is "immoral and unacceptable."[173]

The dissent argued that what the decision in fact "refused to recognize is the fundamental interest all individuals have in controlling the nature of their intimate association with others."[174] It would have struck down the statutes under a privacy theory.

§ 5.04 Contraception

Constitutional recognition of a right to procreate led to the more contro-versial issue of whether a corresponding right *not* to procreate exists,

---

[167] *Id.* at 650.

[168] *See also Cleveland Bd. of Educ. v. LaFleur*, 414 U.S. 632 (1974); *Wisconsin v. Yoder*, 406 U.S. 205 (1972) (parents' fundamental interest in guiding the religious future and educating their children overrides interest of state in compulsory school attendance).

[169] *See Moore v. City of East Cleveland*, 431 U.S. 494 (1977).

[170] Ariz. Rev. Stat. Ann. § 13-1409 (1989); Fla. Stat. Ann. ch. 798.02 (Harrison 1991); Mich. Comp. Laws Ann. § 750.335 (West 1991).

[171] 478 U.S. 186 (1986).

[172] *Id.* at 190-1.

[173] *Id.* at 196.

[174] *Id.* at 206 (Blackmun, J., dissenting).

beginning with a line of cases addressing contraception. Although birth control has been practiced for centuries, scientific developments have improved the efficacy and increased the availability of contraception. While contraception was at one time a highly controversial issue on both the social and legal levels, today it is generally a well-accepted matter. Currently, contraceptives are commonly used, publicly sold and displayed, and are not prohibited in any state. While the birth control pill and intrauterine devices have generated some concern over health and safety issues, they, along with diaphragms and condoms, are widely accepted as means of birth control.

The Supreme Court first recognized a right of married people to use contraceptive devices, based on an individual's liberty interest protected by the due process clause, in *Griswold v. Connecticut*.[175] In *Griswold*, the Court invalidated Connecticut statutes that restricted the right of married people to use contraceptives by imposing criminal penalties on their use. The defendants, the director of the Planned Parenthood organization and a physician, had been arrested as accessories to the crime of giving birth control information and advice to married persons and prescribing contraceptives for them.

Although no right of privacy, or even the term "privacy," is mentioned in the Constitution, seven Justices in *Griswold* agreed that Constitutional protection for the right of privacy existed, although they could not agree to its source. Justice Douglas, writing for the Court, found specific guarantees in portions of the Bill of Rights that give rise to "zones of privacy," such as the right of freedom to associate and privacy in one's association. He found that the "penumbra"of these other fundamental and enumerated rights includes the "right of procreation," implicit in the other important decisions delegated to parents in the child-rearing process.[176] He viewed a law forbidding the use of contraceptives, as opposed to regulating their manufacture or sale, as destructive to the marriage relationship, and observed: "Would we allow the police to search the sacred precincts of marital bedrooms for telltale signs of the use of contraceptives? The very idea is repulsive to the notions of privacy surrounding the marriage relationship."[177]

Justice Goldberg, joined by Chief Justice Warren and Justice Brennan, in one of three concurring opinions, found protection for the right of privacy in the inherent nature of the Constitution, especially in the Ninth Amendment concept of reserved rights. Justice Goldberg argued that because of the Ninth Amendment, other rights which were not enumerated are retained by the people, a theory which ultimately rests on a very traditional, and today somewhat disfavored, concept of natural law.[178]

---

[175] 381 U.S. 479 (1965).

[176] *See supra* § 5.03.

[177] 381 U.S. at 485–486.

[178] For a discussion of the Ninth Amendment as it relates to the right of privacy, *see* Calvin R. Massey, *Federalism and Fundamental Rights: The Ninth Amendment*, 38 Hastings L.J. 305 (1987); Lawrence E. Mitchell, *The Ninth Amendment and the'Jurisprudence of Original Intention,'* 74 Geo. L.J. 1719 (1986).

In other concurring opinions, Justice White determined that the right of privacy between married persons is protected by the concept of liberty in the Fourteenth Amendment. Justice Harlan found that the Connecticut statute in question infringed on "the Fourteenth Amendment because the enactment violates basic values implicit in the concept of ordered liberty."[179] Two Justices, Black and Stewart, representing the strict constructionalist school of Constitutional interpretation, declined to rule the Connecticut statute unconstitutional because they could find no express provision of the Constitution that it violated. Both, however, found the statute to be personally repugnant.

In *Eisenstadt v. Baird*,[180] the Supreme Court extended the right to use contraceptives to unmarried persons, striking down a Massachusetts statute which prohibited distribution of contraceptives except upon a physician's prescription to a married person. The defendant in *Eisenstadt* was convicted of giving a woman a package of contraceptive foam following a lecture which he had delivered on the subject of contraception at Boston University. The Court held that the statute violated the equal protection rights of unmarried persons, stating, "If the right of privacy means anything, it is the right of the individual, married or single, to be free from unwarranted governmental intrusion into matters so fundamentally affecting a person as the decision whether to bear or beget a child."[181]

In *Carey v. Population Services International*,[182] the Court struck down a statute that made it a crime to display or advertise contraceptives, for anyone but a pharmacist to sell non-medical contraceptive devices to persons over 16 years of age, and banned the sale of contraceptives to persons under 16. Without prohibiting all regulation of the manufacture and sale of contraceptives, the Court held that the state was unable to demonstrate a compelling interest in limiting their distribution to pharmacists sufficient to justify the burden that the statute placed on an adult's freedom of choice. The restriction on sale of contraceptives to children was also struck, but without a majority opinion. Justice Brennan, writing for four members of the Court, implied that even minors have some rights to freedom of choice in the use of contraceptives. Further, the ban on advertising and display was invalidated because it completely suppressed dissemination of truthful information regarding a lawful activity.

In *Planned Parenthood Federation of America v. Heckler*,[183] the Court of Appeals for the D.C. Circuit invalidated a regulation issued by the Secretary of the Department of Health and Human Services. The regulation required recipients of certain federal funds to order providers to notify parents or guardians when prescribing contraceptives to unemancipated minors. It also required those providers to comply with state laws requiring parental notice or consent, and to consider the eligibility of minors who wish

---

[179] 381 U.S. at 1690 (quoting *Paloka v. Connecticut*, 302 U.S. 319, 325 (1937)).

[180] 405 U.S. 438 (1972).

[181] *Id.* at 453.

[182] 431 U.S. 678 (1977).

[183] 712 F.2d 650 (D.C. Cir. 1983).

to receive services on basis of their parents' financial resources, rather than their own. The court held that the regulation was invalid because it exceeded statutory authority. It noted that the statute encouraged family participation in their children's decisions, but did not require it. Nor could the Secretary delegate the authority to set eligibility requirements to the states.

The contraceptive issue has recently resurfaced in challenges by parents to condom distribution programs in junior and senior high schools. Parents have argued that these programs violate their rights to privacy and their free exercise of religion, and their substantive due process rights. In *Curtis v. School Committee Of Falmouth*,[184] the Supreme Judicial Court of Massachusetts held that a condom-availability program did not violate parents' constitutional rights, reasoning that while parents possess a fundamental liberty interest to be free from governmental intrusion in the raising of their children, they have "no right to tailor public school programs to meet their individual religious or moral preferences."[185]

Although the *Griswold* line of cases has concluded the legal debate over the use of contraceptives, the underlying theories of the right of privacy in matters of marriage and procreation remain vital in the continuing evolution of the abortion controversy.

§ 5.05 Abortion

[A] General Introduction

The issue of abortion has been a topic of constant debate in the United States. The underlying controversy stems from weighing the rights of the unborn against a woman's right to choose whether to bear a child. Historically, abortions were commonly permitted up until the time of "quickening," the time at which the mother first felt any movement of the fetus, usually during the fourth or fifth month of pregnancy.[186] Although the performance of an abortion after the quickening stage was a crime, the woman herself was not subject to prosecution.[187]

In 1821, Connecticut became the first state to enact a statute regulating abortion, prohibiting inducement of an abortion by poison, in order to protect the mother's health.[188] Physicians led the support for criminalizing abortion because of the high mortality rate of women subjected to abortion methods employed by non-physicians. As the medical profession became more knowledgeable about fetal development, focus shifted to whether a fetus had a right to life.[189] Although numerous statutes were enacted to

[184] 652 N.E.2d 580 (Mass. 1995).
[185] *Id.* at 589.
[186] *See* Lawrence H. Tribe, Abortion: The Clash of Absolutes 28 (1990).
[187] *Id.*
[188] *Id.* at 29.
[189] *Id.* at 30.

prohibit abortions during the nineteenth century, they were rarely enforced and illegal abortions were still frequently performed.[190]

Abortion laws were more rigorously enforced during the 1950s and early 1960s, until infant deformities caused by an outbreak of German measles and the use of the tranquilizer thalidomide brought the issue of abortion to the forefront, inciting medical and public demands for abortion law reform.[191]

By 1967, a number of states began to liberalize their criminal statutes to allow abortion when continuation of the pregnancy would seriously impair the mental or physical health of the mother; when the child was likely to be born with serious mental or physical defects; and when the pregnancy was the result of rape or incest.[192] Yet, legal abortions remained inaccessible to many women, because of continued restriction, bureaucracy, and lack of financial resources.[193]

[B]   Constitutional Parameters: *Roe v. Wade*

Until the United States Supreme Court first addressed the issue of abortion in 1973 in *Roe v. Wade*,[194] states had the authority to enact and enforce the conditions under which abortions could be performed. In *Roe*, the Supreme Court overturned a Texas criminal statute which banned abortion except when necessary to save the mother's life. The Court found that the statute unnecessarily infringed on a woman's right to privacy in violation of the Due Process Clause of the Fourteenth Amendment.

Justice Blackmun, writing for the majority, extended the earlier interpretation of the Due Process Clause, which already included a fundamental right to bear a child, to a fundamental right of privacy in deciding whether to terminate her pregnancy. He declared:

> This right of privacy, whether it be founded in the Fourteenth Amendment's concept of personal liberty and restrictions upon state action, as we feel it is, or as the District Court determined, in the Ninth Amendment's reservation of rights to the people, is broad enough to encompass a woman's decision whether or not to terminate her pregnancy. The detriment that the State would impose upon the pregnant woman by denying this choice altogether is apparent. Specific and direct harm medically diagnosable even in early pregnancy may be involved. Maternity, or additional offspring, may force upon the woman a distressful life and future. Psychological harm may be imminent. Mental and physical health may be taxed by child care. There is also the distress, for all concerned, associated with the unwanted child, and there is the problem of

---

[190] *See id.* at 34–35.

[191] *Id.* at 35–38.

[192] *Id.* at 42.

[193] *Id.*

[194] 410 U.S. 113 (1973).

bringing a child into a family already unable, psychologically and otherwise, to care for it. In other cases, as in this one, the additional difficulties and continuing stigma of unwed motherhood may be involved. All these are factors the woman and her responsible physician necessarily will consider in consultation.[195]

The Court concluded that the right to terminate a pregnancy is not absolute, however, but must be balanced against the state's important interests in safeguarding the mother's health, in maintaining medical standards, and in protecting potential life. The Court applied a two-pronged strict scrutiny test, requiring the state to justify an abortion regulation by first showing that the regulation was necessary and, second, that it was supported by a compelling state interest.

Justice Blackmun articulated a trimester system of balancing the competing interests based on the stage of the pregnancy involved. In the first trimester, the woman's decision whether to have an abortion is a medical decision between the woman and her physician, completely private and protected from state interference. During the second trimester, the state's interest in the mother's health becomes compelling and the state has limited authority to regulate abortions only to the extent reasonably related to preserve and protect the woman's health. Because the Court reasoned that the potential life was entitled to constitutional protection only upon viability, deemed to occur in the third trimester, the fetus becomes protected during that time and the state's interest in protecting the fetus then becomes compelling. The state may prohibit abortions during that final trimester unless the mother's life is at stake.

The *Roe v. Wade* decision did not fully satisfy either side of the abortion debate. The choice of viability as the point at which the state may prohibit abortion has been criticized by pro-choice advocates, because the availability of abortion procedures will be undermined as medical and scientific research move the point of viability back further towards the time of conception. Anti-abortion, or "pro-life," advocates, of course, condemn *Roe* for legalizing abortion at all, based on their belief that life begins at the moment of conception and that any abortion is a wrongful taking of a life.

The right of privacy is central to *Roe*. Without this right, a woman has no constitutionally protected interest to balance against the state's interest in protecting potential life. Despite its importance, the majority merely assumed that the right of privacy exists, but did little to establish a theory of constitutional interpretation to support its belief in the existence of the right. Although Justice Blackmun cited numerous cases supporting his view, he mentions the penumbra theory only in passing as it related to *Griswold* and the Ninth Amendment view only with respect to Justice Goldberg's concurring opinion in that case.[196]

The holding in *Roe v. Wade* did not provide a formal test for application by the lower courts when reviewing the constitutionality of an abortion

---

[195] *Id.* at 153.

[196] *See generally* Ronald M. Dworkin, *Unenumerated Rights: Whether and How Roe Should be Overruled,* 59 U. Chi. L. Rev. 381 (1992).

regulation. Instead, the *Roe* Court couched its holding in a rigid trimester analysis for determining whether the government had a compelling interest in protecting the health of the woman or fetus. Although the Court did not formally announce its abandonment of the trimester analysis until recently, it soon began modifying the *Roe* test and applying, instead, a reasonableness test for determining if an abortion regulation was constitutional.[197]

[C] Constitutional Parameters: The State Response

Subsequent to *Roe v. Wade*, the Supreme Court has had numerous occasions to refine the parameters of that holding in cases challenging state authority to restrict *Roe*'s impact. Legal emphasis largely has shifted from the religious and moral problems concerning abortions to delegation of certain decisions to the medical profession, the rights of minors to obtain abortions, and the use of public funding and facilities. The Court has struck down such statutory attempts to confine *Roe* in a number of cases and upheld them in others. On balance, the Court in recent decisions has retreated from its position in *Roe*.

[1] Rights of the Potential Father

The Supreme Court broadly construed a woman's right to obtain an abortion in 1976 in *Planned Parenthood of Central Missouri v. Danforth*.[198] In *Danforth*, the Court considered the interest of an additional party, the potential father. The dispute centered around a Missouri statute which required the prior written consent of the spouse of a woman seeking an abortion during the first trimester of pregnancy, unless the abortion was necessary to save the mother's life. The court recognized the father's interest:

> We are not unaware of the deep and proper concern and interest that a devoted and protective husband has in his wife's pregnancy and in the growth and development of the fetus she is carrying. Neither has this Court failed to appreciate the importance of the marital relationship in our society. Moreover, we recognize that the decision whether to undergo or to forego an abortion may have profound effects on the future of any marriage, effects that are both physical and mental, and possibly deleterious.[199]

However, as between the interest of the father and the privacy right of the mother, the Court ruled in favor of the mother: "Since it is the woman who physically bears the child and who is the more directly and immediately affected by the pregnancy, as between the two, the balance weighs in her favor."[200] In striking down the statute, the Court concluded: "[W]e cannot

---

[197] *See* Daniel A. Farber & John E. Nowak, *Beyond the Roe Debate: Judicial Experience with the 1980s "Reasonableness" Test*, 76 Va. L. Rev. 519, 520-21 (1990).

[198] 428 U.S. 52 (1976).

[199] *Id.* at 69–70.

[200] *Id.* at 71.

hold that the state has the constitutional authority to give the spouse unilaterally the ability to prohibit the wife from terminating her pregnancy, when the state itself lacks that right."[201]

[2] Rights of Minors

The Court in *Danforth* also extended the fundamental right to choose to have an abortion to minors, striking down a parental consent statute, although it recognized that states have broader powers to protect minors than adults. The Court again directly addressed a parental consent statute in *Bellotti v. Baird (Bellotti I)*,[202] holding that the Massachusetts parental consent statute was unclear with respect to the authority of parents to veto the decision of a minor child to have an abortion and the availability of a judicial by-pass procedure. In a plurality opinion in *Bellotti v. Baird (Bellotti II)*,[203] the Court invalidated the Massachusetts statute. Although observing that the constitutional rights of minors, including the right to obtain an abortion, are not co-extensive with the rights of adults, the plurality in *Bellotti II* found that a minor's right to obtain an abortion could be restricted by requiring the consent of a parent only if the state provided a procedure for by-passing the requirements. A minor is entitled to an alternative proceeding in order to show that she is mature and well-informed enough to make her own decision about abortion by consulting her physician, regardless of her parents' consent. Even if she is not able to decide for herself, the minor is entitled to show that the abortion would be in her best interest. Thus, a minor's consent statute must provide for an alternative to parental permission in order to pass constitutional muster.

Three years later, in *H.L. v. Matheson*,[204] the court dealt with a statute that required parental notification rather than consent. In *Matheson*, the Court upheld a statute that required a physician to notify a minor's parents, whenever possible, before performing an abortion for a minor. The majority opinion found that notification, "furthers a constitutionally permissible end by encouraging an unmarried pregnant minor to seek the help and advice of her parents in making the very important decision whether or not to bear a child."[205] The concurring opinion in *Matheson* stressed that a judicial by-pass procedure that followed the guidelines of *Bellotti II* must be included before a notification statute would be found constitutional.[206]

In 1990, in *Hodgson v. Minnesota*,[207] the Supreme Court upheld the most restrictive consent and notice statute it had yet addressed.[208] The

---

[201] *Id.* at 70.

[202] 428 U.S. 132 (1976).

[203] 443 U.S. 622 (1979).

[204] 450 U.S. 398 (1981).

[205] *Id.* at 409-10.

[206] 450 U.S. 398 (Powell, J. & Stewart, J. concurring).

[207] 497 U.S. 417 (1990).

[208] *See generally* Ronald F. Berestka, Jr., *Constitutional Law-What Ever Happened to a Woman's Fundamental Right to Privacy*, 25 Suffolk U. L. Rev. 192 (1990).

Minnesota statute in question required at least 48 hours notice to *both* parents of a minor who sought an abortion, or, in the alternative, a judicial bypass procedure to determine whether the minor was mature enough to give informed consent without parental notification. The majority first considered the two state interests involved: the welfare of pregnant minors and the interest in promoting the role of parents in the care and upbringing of their children. The Court found the two-parent notification portion of the statute constitutionally objectionable on the basis that no legitimate state interest was served; however, the majority held that the constitutional impediment was removed by the judicial by-pass option, concluding that the interests of immature minors therefore were protected. The Court also held that the 48-hour waiting period was constitutional because it allowed time for parents to consult with their daughters, while imposing only a minimal burden on the right of a minor to decide whether to terminate her pregnancy.

In a companion case to *Hodgson, Ohio v. Akron Center for Reproductive Health*,[209] the Court upheld the judicial bypass procedure of an Ohio abortion statute requiring parental notice and consent. The Court declined to address whether parental notice statutes must contain by-pass procedures comparable to those required for parental consent statutes, concluding that the statute in question satisfied the requisites for the more intrusive consent statute.

[3] Health and Safety Regulations

In *Roe v. Wade*'s companion case, *Doe v. Bolton*,[210] the Court struck down a provision of the Georgia abortion statute which required that an abortion found necessary by a physician must be performed in a hospital accredited by a particular private agency, that it must be approved by a hospital committee, and that at least two other doctors must concur with the patient's doctor that the abortion is needed. The Court deferred to the medical profession and individual physicians, focusing on the private nature of the physician-patient relationship, and invalidated overly-restrictive portions of the statute.

In 1983, the Court overturned a city ordinance requiring that a patient be informed that an "unborn child is a human life from the moment of conception" in *Akron v. Akron Center for Reproductive Health*.[211] In *Akron*, the Court also held unconstitutional an Ohio regulation requiring all abortions after the first trimester to be performed in a hospital. The Court found that the regulations failed to promote a woman's health, because certain types of abortions could be safely performed in less expensive clinics. The Court stated that while the regulation may further the state's interest in safe abortions, it actually prevented economically disadvantaged women from obtaining abortions. State legislatures could regulate abortions, but

[209] 497 U.S. 502 (1990).

[210] 410 U.S. 179 (1973).

[211] 462 U.S. 416 (1983).

could not depart from accepted medical practices. Justice O'Connor dissented with respect to the applicable constitutional standard, arguing that strict scrutiny only applies when a regulation is unduly burdensome. She argued that non-burdensome regulations are constitutional if they are rational and logically relate to a legitimate state objective, which would return policy-making authority on abortion issues back to the states.

In *Planned Parenthood Association v. Ashcroft*,[212] the Court again rejected a requirement that abortions take place in an accredited hospital, but upheld a restriction that a second physician be present during abortions in order to care for a possibly viable fetus. It further upheld a provision requiring the filing of a pathologist's tissue report for abortions.

[4] Funding and Facilities

In order to qualify for federal Medicaid funds, states must create plans establishing standards for determining the extent of medical assistance they will provide to indigents.[213] Several states established plans that would cover only medically required abortions. On several occasions, the Court has addressed the extent, if any, to which states must authorize the use of public funds or facilities to provide abortions to women unable to pay.[214]

In *Maher v. Roe*,[215] the Court addressed a claim that a state plan that would not fund non-therapeutic abortions through Medicaid was an unconstitutional barrier to the right to abortion. The Court upheld the state's decision, construing *Roe v. Wade* to guarantee the freedom to choose to have an abortion, not the right to obtain one. Retreating from a strict scrutiny analysis, the Court framed its decision in terms of protecting women from unduly burdensome interference with their freedom to decide whether to end a pregnancy. It held that the plan did not interfere with that freedom. Observing that states are not required to pay any medical expenses of indigents, the Court concluded that states are not prohibited from making value judgments favoring childbirth over abortion and may allocate public funds accordingly. Justice Brennan, dissenting, viewed the Court's opinion as revealing "a distressing insensitivity to the plight of impoverished pregnant women, resulting in the indigent having no realistic possibility of exercising their constitutional right to choose an abortion."[216]

The Court upheld similar restrictions in *Beal v. Doe*,[217] and *Poelker v. Doe*,[218] companion cases to *Maher*. In *Beal*, the Court concluded that states have broad discretion in deciding what medical treatment is reasonably

---

[212] 462 U.S. 476 (1983).

[213] *See* 42 U.S.C. §§ 300 to 300a-6 (1988).

[214] *See generally* Gayle Binion, *Reproductive Freedom and the Constitution: The Limits on Choice*, 4 Berkeley Women's L.J. 12, 14–20 (1988).

[215] 432 U.S. 464 (1977).

[216] *Id.* at 483 (Brennan, J., dissenting).

[217] 432 U.S. 438 (1977).

[218] 432 U.S. 519 (1977).

necessary and need not fund non-essential abortions. In *Poelker*, it held that a city hospital may refuse public hospital services for abortions. In *Harris v. McRae*,[219] the Court extended *Maher* to uphold the Hyde Amendment, which restricted federal Medicaid reimbursement to limited types of abortions, excluding some medically necessary abortions where the woman's health was endangered.[220] The Eighth Circuit, however, later distinguished *Poelker in Nyberg v. City of Virginia*,[221] noting a "fundamental difference between providing direct funding to affect the abortion decision and allowing staff physicians to perform abortions at an existing publicly owned hospital," and upheld an injunction compelling a city hospital to permit staff physicians to perform paid abortions if they so chose. In 1991, in *Rust v. Sullivan*,[222] Title X grantees and supervising physicians challenged the facial validity of new regulations limiting the ability of federal Title X fund recipients to engage in abortion-related activities.[223] The regulations prohibited Title X projects from providing counseling regarding abortion and from providing referrals for abortion as a method of family planning; broadly forbade Title X projects from engaging in any activities that "encourage, promote or advocate abortion as a method of family planning"; and required that Title X projects be "physically and financially separate" from these forbidden types of activities.[224] The Court refused to invalidate the regulations because they constituted a plausible construction of the statute and did not interfere with Congress' express intent.

The Court in *Rust* held that the regulations did not violate the First Amendment by impermissibly discriminating on the basis of opinion; rather, they were legitimate decisions on program funding intended to encourage activities to benefit the public. The Court noted that the regulations prohibited abortion-related activities only as a "method of family planning," and did not prevent Title X projects from otherwise engaging in such activities.[225] The Court distinguished between denying benefits and refusing to allocate public funds for a specific purpose. Finally, it held that a woman's right to choose to have an abortion was not impinged upon, because her lack of access to abortion counseling from a Title X project "leaves her in no different position than she would have been if the government had not enacted Title X."[226]

---

[219] 448 U.S. 297 (1980).

[220] Pub. L. No. 94-439, § 209, 90 Stat. 1434 (1976). The Hyde amendment has been further amended to limit federally funded abortions to circumstances where the mother's life would be endangered if the pregnancy went to term. *See* Pub. L. No. 97-377, § 204, 96 Stat. 1894 (1982).

[221] 667 F.2d 754, 758 (8th Cir. 1982).

[222] 500 U.S. 173 (1991).

[223] Title X of the Public Health Service Act, 84 Stat. 1506, as amended, 42 U.S.C. §§ 300–300a-6 (1970). Title X provides federal funding for family-planning services. Grants and contracts under Title X must be made pursuant to regulations that the Secretary of HHS issues. A portion of the act provides that "[n]one of the funds appropriated under this subchapter shall be used in programs where abortion is a method of family planning." 42 U.S.C. § 300a-6.

[224] 500 U.S. at 180.

[225] *Id.* at 1759.

[226] *Id.* at 1777.

Justice Blackmun, joined by Justice Marshall, and in part by Justices
Stevens and O'Connor, dissented. Justice Blackmun argued that the
regulations were "clearly viewpoint-based" and an unconstitutional condition upon public employment. [227] Justice O'Connor would have reversed
solely on the basis that the regulations were not a reasonable interpretation
of the statute. [228]

[5] Re-evaluation of *Roe v. Wade*

In 1989, the Supreme Court again directly addressed the right to
abortion, for the first time with a reconstituted bench, in *Webster v.
Reproductive Health Services*, [229] signaling a further retreat from *Roe v.
Wade*. [230] *Webster*, a class action case opposing a Missouri statute which
placed restrictions on abortions, addressed the constitutionality of a statute
containing a legislative declaration that a fetus has protectable interests
in life, health and well-being from the moment of conception. The statute
also included requirements that physicians perform tests to determine the
development of a fetus and to advise pregnant women of certain facts to
constitute informed consent prior to an abortion. It further enacted a
legislative ban on the use of public funds and facilities for counseling and
performing abortions.

The Supreme Court upheld all of these restrictions as constitutional and
repudiated the strict scrutiny standard. Chief Justice Rehnquist, announc-
ing the judgment and delivering the plurality opinion, attacked "the rigid
Roe framework [as] hardly consistent with the notion of a Constitution cast
in general terms," faulting *Roe* for the confusing and inconsistent subsequent decisions and legislation. Justice Rehnquist complained that "[t]he
key elements of the *Roe* framework—trimesters and viability—are not
found in the text of the Constitution or in any place else one would expect
to find a constitutional principle." [231] He further questioned the designation
of viability as the point at which the state's interest in protecting human
life becomes compelling, arguing that such an interest is equally compelling
throughout pregnancy. The Court acknowledged that its decision expanded
state authority to avoid the restrictions of the trimester analysis and to
enact additional abortion regulations. *Webster* thus severely narrowed the
application of *Roe v. Wade* without expressly overruling it, although the
plurality, joined by Justice Scalia, urged overruling it entirely.

In 1992, five members of the Supreme Court reaffirmed the central
principles of *Roe v. Wade*, while upholding most of a highly restrictive
Pennsylvania abortion statute in *Planned Parenthood of Southeastern Pennsylvania v. Casey*. [232] In an opinion co-authored by Justices O'Connor,

---

[227] *Id.* at 1780.

[228] *Id.* at 1789.

[229] 492 U.S. 490 (1989).

[230] *See generally* Walter Dellinger & Gene B. Sperling, *Abortion and the Supreme Court:
The Retreat from Roe v. Wade*, 138 U. Pa. L. Rev. 83 (1989).

[231] 492 U.S. at 494.

[232] 505 U.S. 833 (1992).

Kennedy, and Souter, the Court struck down a spousal notification provision, but upheld provisions that define "medical emergency" as a condition that requires an immediate abortion to prevent the woman's death or a serious risk of substantial and irreversible impairment of a major bodily function, provided that the definition is construed broadly enough to include several enumerated conditions. It further upheld a minimum 24-hour waiting period for informed consent after a physician advises the patient about the nature and risks of the procedure, estimated gestational age of the fetus, information describing the fetus, and alternatives to abortion. The Court also approved a parental consent provision, with judicial bypass, for minors seeking abortion, and a reporting requirement for abortion providers.

The Court in *Casey* reasoned that although the state may demonstrate concern for the life of the unborn, its interest in that life may only override the woman's right to terminate her pregnancy once the fetus is viable. It recognized "the urgent claims of the woman to retain the ultimate control over her destiny and her body, claims implicit in the meaning of liberty. . . . Liberty must not be extinguished for want of a line that is clear."[233] The court concluded that "the line should be drawn at viability,"[234] which it defined as "the time at which there is a realistic possibility of maintaining and nourishing a life outside the womb, so that the independent existence of the second life can in reason and all fairness be the object of the state protection that now overrides the rights of the woman."[235] However, it rejected the trimester framework as unnecessary to accomplish its objective.

While the Court reaffirmed "the essential holding" of *Roe*, forbidding states to prevent women from making their own final decisions about terminating their pregnancies before viability, it could not agree on the appropriate standard for judicial scrutiny of abortion restrictions. The Court based its opinion largely on the principle of *stare decisis*, fearing its own legitimacy at stake if it were to overrule *Roe* when the factual underpinnings of that case and society's understanding of it had not changed. Thus, although *Casey* reaffirmed *Roe*, it failed to provide any clear standards for the regulations of abortion.[236]

[6] Abortion Demonstrations

One of the results of the abortion debate has been demonstrations from both sides of the issue. Most of the litigation involving these demonstrations has involved anti-abortion demonstrations. The Supreme Court in *Bray v. Alexandria Women's Health Clinic*[237] overturned the decision of the Fourth Circuit Court of Appeals which held that blocking access to abortion clinics interfered with the right to interstate travel and constituted trespass and

---

[233] *Id.* at 2816.

[234] *Id.*

[235] *Id.* at 2817.

[236] *See generally* William G. Peterson, *Splintered Decisions, Implicit Reversals and Lower Federal Courts: Planned Parenthood v. Casey*, 1992 B.Y.U. L. Rev. 289 (1992).

[237] 506 U.S. 263 (1993).

public nuisance under Virginia law.[238] Writing for the majority, Justice Scalia rejected the right to travel argument on the basis that the only restriction of movement that would have resulted from the proposed demonstrations would have been in the limited area of the abortion clinics.[239]

In response to this decision, Congress enacted the Freedom of Access to Clinic Entrances Act of 1994 (FACE).[240] FACE criminalizes violence and the threat of violence at the entrances of abortion clinics, in an attempt to prevent violence generated by the abortion protest movement.[241]

Additionally, the Supreme Court has reaffirmed a woman's right to "unobstructed access to abortion services" in *Madsen v. Women's Health Center, Inc.*[242] Again, in 1997, in *Schenk v. Pro-Choice Network of W.N.Y.*,[243] the Court held that a preliminary injunction could be granted against demonstrations at an abortion clinic in order to guarantee free access and upheld a fixed 15-foot buffer zone from the entrance to the clinic, although it declined to uphold a similar floating buffer.

The more recent Supreme Court cases have encouraged states to adopt increasingly stringent abortion regulations. The abortion debate is far from ended, and lower court cases addressing the extent of permissible restrictions on abortion, the validity of parental notification and consent statutes, the implications of public funding, and other issues will continue to wind their way to the Supreme Court.

§ 5.06   Voluntary and Involuntary Sterilization

Like contraception and abortion, voluntary sterilization of a competent person involves the right to control one's reproductive capacity by not having children. Sterilization has become a commonly used method of birth control, but in contrast to other methods of contraception, sterilization should be considered permanent. Vasectomy of a male is a relatively simple operation performed by severing the canal which carries the sperm, preventing its inclusion in the semen, and thus preventing pregnancy. Female sterilization procedures are somewhat more complicated. Usually either tubal ligation, in which the fallopian tubes are tied, or salpingectomy, in which they are severed, is employed to prevent passage and fertilization of the ova. Both male and female procedures are relatively safe and do not interfere with the ability to engage in sexual intercourse.[244]

While contraception, abortion, and voluntary sterilization deal with the right to control one's reproductive capacity by not having children,

---

[238] *See Nat'l Org. for Women v. Operation Rescue*, 914 F.2d 582 (4th Cir. 1990).

[239] *Bray* at 277.

[240] Pub. L. No. 103–259, 108 Stat. 694 (1994).

[241] *See* Helen R. Franco, Comment, *Freedom of Access to Clinic Entrances Act of 1994: The Face of Things to Come?*, 19 Nova L. Rev. 1083 (1995).

[242] 512 U.S. 753 (1994).

[243] 519 U.S. 357 (1997).

[244] *See* Homer J. Clark, Jr., *supra* note 3, at 214.

involuntary sterilization addresses the right to reproduce despite state interests in medically terminating that ability. The problems in this area have arisen because of developments in medical technology to sterilize people cheaply and efficiently, and because of the scientific or pseudo-scientific view that the mentally handicapped, mentally ill, or those convicted of a crime will have offspring similar to themselves and that society can benefit from eugenically controlling reproduction.

[A] Voluntary Sterilization

The right of competent adults to be voluntarily sterilized presumably has been resolved by *Griswold v. Connecticut.*[245] Voluntary sterilization is legal in the vast majority of states, provided an informed consent is obtained from the patient. No state interest or interest of an unconceived child arise to balance the right of a competent adult to choose voluntary sterilization.

One case, *Hathaway v. Worcester City Hospital,*[246] involving a woman with eight children whose health would be endangered by further child-bearing, recognized a right to a "therapeutic sterilization" in a public hospital. However, the *Hathaway* rationale, based on *Roe v. Wade,*[247] may no longer be persuasive in light of the Supreme Court's holding in *Poelker v. Doe,*[248] that there is no constitutional right to obtain a non-therapeutic abortion in a public hospital which provides public care for childbirth.[249]

Most recent cases dealing with voluntary sterilization have been medical malpractice actions addressing the liability of a physician for negligent performance of a voluntary sterilization resulting in the birth of a child.[250] Causes of actions have been framed in terms of "wrongful conception" or "wrongful pregnancy," which claim that negligent sterilization resulted in the birth of an unplanned or unwanted child; "wrongful birth," which alleges that a physician's inadequate counseling failed to give parents the option of avoiding conception or terminating pregnancy to prevent the birth of a child with genetic defects; and "wrongful life" claims brought on behalf of the child born with an impairment.[251] When negligence is proven, most courts allow direct damages, such as expenses of pregnancy, lost wages, pain and suffering, medical expenses for child birth, and a second steriliza-tion procedure, but have denied recovery for the expenses of raising and

---

[245] *See supra* § 5.04.

[246] 475 F.2d 701 (1st Cir. 1973).

[247] 410 U.S. 113 (1973). *See supra* § 5.05[B].

[248] 432 U.S. 519 (1977). *See supra* note 176 and accompanying text.

[249] *But see Nyberg v. City of Virginia*, 667 F.2d 754 (8th Cir. 1982) (city could not prohibit staff physicians from performing abortions for paying patients at the sole hospital in the community).

[250] *See generally* Bopp, *et al., The "Rights" and "Wrongs" of Wrongful Birth and Wrongful Life: A Jurisprudential Analysis of Birth Related Torts*, 27 Duq. L. Rev. 461 (1989).

[251] *See Miller v. Rivard*, 585 N.Y.S.2d 523 (N.Y. App. Div. 1992); Romney & Duffy, *Medicine and Law: Recent Developments*, 25 Tort & Ins. L.J. 351, 356–359 (1990).

educating a normal child.[252] A few recent cases have additionally allowed parents to recover the costs of raising the child to adulthood.[253]

[B]   Involuntary Sterilization

Involuntary sterilization deals with the converse issue: whether a person has a constitutional right to maintain the ability to procreate, despite countervailing interests of the state in mandating sterilization. Legal challenges to involuntary sterilization initially arose in response to scientific or pseudo-scientific theories, most of which have been discredited, that the mentally handicapped, mentally ill, and certain convicted criminals will bear offspring with the same characteristics. Involuntary sterilization actions generally arise from requests by institutions or parents responsible for people who are incapable of caring for themselves but are capable of reproduction.

In the early 1900s the government began an effort to segregate those with mental retardation, mental illness, epilepsy and other "undesirable" conditions into state institutions.[254] Some states took even more drastic action, authorizing by statute sterilization of the genetically "unfit."[255] Use of governmental power to institutionalize and sterilize persons with disabilities was based largely on then-popular theories of heredity, such as positive eugenics, the science of improving the characteristics and qualities of the human race by careful selection of parents, and its corollary, negative eugenics, which advocates attempting to prevent the reproduction of unfavorable traits.[256] Indiana enacted the first sterilization law in 1907, and by 1921, thousands of sterilizations had been performed.[257]

The United States Supreme Court upheld a Virginia statute authorizing salpingectomy of institutionalized mentally retarded female residents and vasectomy of males in certain circumstances in the 1927 case of *Buck v. Bell*.[258] The plaintiff, eighteen-year-old Carrie Buck, was described in

---

[252] *See, e.g., Rouse v. Wesley*, 494 N.W.2d 7 (Mich. Ct. App. 1992); *Girdley v. Coats*, 825 S.W.2d 295 (Mo. 1992); *Johnson v. Univ. Hospitals*, 540 N.E.2d 1370 (Ohio 1990).

[253] *See Burke v. Rivo*, 551 N.E.2d 1 (Mass. 1990) (damages include costs of pregnancy, wife's lost earning capacity, medical expenses of delivery and care following birth, cost of care for other children while wife was incapacitated, cost of second sterilization procedure, husband's loss of consortium, wife's pain and suffering in connection with pregnancy, birth, second sterilization operation, and emotional distress sustained as a result of the unwanted pregnancy, where parents wished to avoid having more children for economic reasons); *Lovelace Med. Ctr. v. Mendez*, 805 P.2d 603 (N.M. 1991) (no offset for intangible emotional benefits which will be received in raising the child; parents not required to mitigate damages by either having an abortion or placing the child for adoption because neither is an "ordinary or reasonable measure" within the meaning of the law relating to mitigation of damages).

[254] *See Hakola & Lavey, Forty-Three Million Strong: An Overview of Civil Rights Protections for Persons with Disabilities*, 70 Mich. B.J. 548 (1991).

[255] *See Ferster, Eliminating theUnfit-Is Sterilization the Answer?*, 27 Ohio St. L.J. 591, 592–593 (1966).

[256] *See id.* at 591–592.

[257] *See id.* at 593–594. *See generally* P. Reilly, The Surgical Solution: A History of Involuntary Sterilization in the United States 164 (1991).

[258] 274 U.S. 200 (1927).

Justice Holmes's majority opinion as "a feeble-minded white woman who was committed to the State Colony. . . . . She is the daughter of a feeble-minded mother in the same institution and the mother of an illegitimate feeble-minded child."[259]

After noting that the plaintiff had been afforded ample procedural protections, the Court upheld the statute on the grounds that, like compulsory vaccination, involuntary sterilization of Carrie Buck advanced the public good:

> We have seen more than once that the public welfare may call upon the best citizens for their lives. It would be strange if it could not call upon those who already sap the strength of the State for these lesser sacrifices, often not felt to be such by those concerned, in order to prevent our being swamped with incompetence. It is better for all the world, if instead of waiting to execute degenerate offspring for crime or to let them starve for their imbecility, society can prevent those who are manifestly unfit from continuing their kind. The principle that sustains compulsory vaccination is broad enough to cover cutting the Fallopian tubes. . . . *Three generations of imbeciles are enough.*[260]

The dominant basis of the *Buck* decision was the eugenic theory, which has since been discredited.[261] Fortunately, more current social and medical thought has influenced modern courts to reject this view and replace it with a much greater concern for the handicapped.[262] *Buck* did not address a constitutional right to procreate because it was decided prior to the development of the fundamental rights theory and adoption of the strict scrutiny analysis. Today, the statute at issue in *Buck* would be viewed as an interference with the fundamental right of privacy regarding the individual's ability to reproduce and could only be justified by a compelling governmental interest.[263]

The Supreme Court opinion of *Skinner v. Oklahoma*,[264] written by Justice Douglas in 1942, exemplifies a change in position and the development of a fundamental right to procreate. The petitioner in *Skinner* was incarcerated for his third offense involving moral turpitude and the Attorney General of Oklahoma sought to have him sterilized under the state's Habitual Criminal Sterilization Act. The Court struck down the statute, basing its decision upon the Equal Protection Clause because it found that the statute differentiated based on the type of crime committed. Most

---

[259] *Id.* at 205.

[260] *Id.* at 207 (emphasis added).

[261] Evidence exists to indicate that *Buck* was a collusive suit intended to gain support for the Virginia statute and the eugenic movement. *See* Paul Lombardo, *Three Generations, No Imbeciles: New Light on Buck v. Bell*, 60 N.Y.U.L. Rev. 30 (1985).

[262] *See generally* Elizabeth Scott, *Sterilization of Mentally Retarded Persons: Reproductive Rights and Family Privacy*, 1986 Duke L.J. 806 (1986).

[263] *See* Craig L. McIvor, *Equitable Jurisdiction to Order Sterilizations*, 57 Wash. L. Rev. 373, 376 (1982); J. Nowak & R. Rotunda, Constitutional Law 758 (4th ed. 1991).

[264] 316 U.S. 535 (1942).

importantly, the classification was held to be subject to strict scrutiny because of the affected aspect of human life:

> We are dealing here with legislation which involves one of the basic civil rights of man. Marriage and procreation are fundamental to the very existence and survival of the race. The power to sterilize, if exercised, may have subtle, far-reaching and devastating effects. In evil or reckless hands it can cause races or types which are inimical to the dominant group to wither and disappear.[265]

Skinner recognized the individual's interest in the freedom to procreate, thus extending the right to privacy as it relates to sexual matters. *Skinner* did not, however, hold that all statutes authorizing involuntary sterilization are unconstitutional per se; it was decided under an equal protection analysis and held that statutes permitting sterilization would be subjected to strict scrutiny.[266]

Whether sterilization may ever be imposed as punishment for a crime remains uncertain. Although, for example, the California Penal Code retains a provision that a person who is found guilty of "carnal abuse of a female person under the age of ten years," may be ordered sterilized in addition to other penalties,[267] the constitutionality of the statute is questionable in light of *Skinner*, and its validity apparently has never been adjudicated. One California case has held that conditioning a woman's probation for conviction of robbery on her not becoming pregnant without being married was improper because the condition was not reasonably related to the crime nor to future criminal behavior.[268] A later California case held that a condition of probation for conviction of felony child abuse, prohibiting the defendant from conceiving a child, was overbroad, despite its relation to the crime committed. An alternative that was less subversive of the fundamental right to procreate must be imposed.[269]

The Arizona Supreme Court has held that conditioning a more lenient criminal punishment for child abuse on the defendants' sterilizations was impermissible absent statutory authority. It noted, however, that had the defendants voluntarily submitted to sterilization, the court could have considered that fact in sentencing.[270]

A number of states retain some form of statutory authorization for involuntary sterilization.[271] Although the trend among the states is to

---

[265] *Id.* at 541.

[266] Nowak & Rotunda, *supra* note 263, at 759.

[267] Cal. Penal Code § 645 (West 1988). ["Whenever any person shall be adjudged guilty of carnal abuse of a female person under the age of ten years, the court may, in addition to such other punishment or confinement as may be imposed, direct an operation to be performed upon such person, for the prevention of procreation."]

[268] *See People v. Dominquez*, 64 Cal. Rptr. 290 (Cal. Ct. App. 1967).

[269] *See People v. Pointer*, 199 Cal. Rptr. 357 (Cal. Ct. App. 1984).

[270] *Smith v. Superior Court*, 725 P.2d 1101 (Ariz. 1986).

[271] *See, e.g.*, Colo. Rev. Stat. Ann. § 13-22-103 (West 1989); Del. Code Ann. tit. 16, §§ 5701-16 (Supp. 1992); Ga. Code Ann. § 31-20-3 (Supp. 1992); Idaho Code § 39-3902 (1977).

abolish these statutes,[272] other states have judicially determined that sterilization may be ordered in appropriate cases.[273]

Sterilization of the mentally disabled or mentally ill remains an important legal issue. Because of *Skinner's* recognition of a right to procreate, as well as the discrediting of the eugenic theory and changing conceptions of mental retardation, most contemporary cases and commentary have concluded that sterilization of the mentally handicapped cannot be presumptively acceptable.[274] This view was reflected in *North Carolina Ass'n for Retarded Children v. State*:[275]

> Most competent geneticists now reject Social Darwinism and doubt the premise implicit in Mr. Justice Holmes' incantation that ". . . three generations of imbeciles is enough." . . . [P]revalent medical opinion views with distaste even voluntary sterilization for the mentally retarded and is inclined to sanction it only as a last resort and in relatively extreme cases. In short, the medical and genetical experts are no longer sold on sterilization to benefit either retarded patients or the future of the Republic.[276]

Handicapped persons are now entitled to the same fundamental procreative rights as others, and because of their mental disability, a higher burden of proof should be required before submitting them to sterilization.[277]

Although voluntary sterilization of the mentally handicapped or mentally ill is permissible if it is performed with informed consent, it is often difficult to assess an individual's capacity to consent and the nature of the information which must be given. A number of states have statutes establishing procedures for determining the circumstances in which sterilization of a handicapped individual is permissible.[278] In the absence of statutory authority, a number of courts have held that sterilization cannot be ordered,[279] although other courts have concluded that they possess equitable jurisdiction to order such sterilizations.[280]

---

[272] *See McKinney v. McKinney*, 805 S.W.2d 66 (Ark. 1991) (holding Arkansas involuntary sterilization statute unconstitutional).

[273] *See, e.g., In re Matejski*, 419 N.W.2d 576 (Iowa 1988); *In re Truesdell*, 304 S.E.2d 793 (N.C. Ct. App. 1983), *modified & aff'd*, 321 S.E.2d 630 (N.C. 1985); *see also Nowak & Rotunda, supra* note 215 at 759.

[274] *See* Scott, *supra* note 262 at 834-40.

[275] 420 F. Supp. 451 (M.D.N.C. 1976).

[276] *Id.* at 454; *quoted in* Robert L. Burgdorf & Marcia Pearce Burgdorf, *The Wicked Witch is Almost Dead: Buck v.Bell and the Sterilization of Handicapped Persons*, 50 Temp. L.Q. 995 (1977).

[277] *See, e.g., Conservatorship of Valerie N.*, 707 P.2d 760 (Cal. 1985) (conservators not entitled to demand sterilization because such proceedings impermissibly deprives developmentally disabled persons of privacy and liberty); *Motes v. Hall County Dept. of Family & Children Services*, 306 S.E.2d 260 (Ga. 1983) (due process requires "clear and convincing evidence" to authorize sterilization); *In re Debra B.*, 495 A.2d 781 (Me. 1985) (mother failed to prove clearly and convincingly that daughter was physiologically capable of procreation).

[278] *See supra* note 262.

[279] *See, e.g., In re S.C.E.*, 378 A.2d 144 (Del. Ch. 1977); *In re D.D.*, 408 N.Y.S.2d 104 (N.Y. App. Div. 1978), *appeal dismissed*, 405 N.E.2d 333 (N.Y. 1980).

[280] *See, e.g., In re Moe*, 432 N.E.2d 712 (Mass. 1982); *Wentzel v. Montgomery Gen. Hosp.*,

Several tests have been applied for determining when sterilization of the handicapped should be ordered, including the best interests test, the substituted judgment test, and the medical necessity test.[281] The best interests test sustains sterilization if it is in the best interest of the patient and of society.[282] Under the substituted judgment test, based on the belief that an incompetent's inability to exercise a fundamental right should not result in a loss of the person's constitutional interests, the court substitutes its judgment by determining what the incompetent would choose if he or she were competent.[283] The medical necessity test requires a medical expert to determine that sterilization is essential to preserve the life or health of the patient.[284]

The courts have applied these tests strictly. A compelling state interest should be established before interference with a person's bodily integrity and procreative rights is authorized.[285] If the person is a sexually active mentally disabled person who is unwilling to or incapable of controlling procreation by other contraceptive means and who is likely to produce a handicapped child or would be unable to care for the child because of the degree of retardation, authorization of sterilization has been held to be constitutional.[286]

The Washington Supreme Court asserted its equitable jurisdiction to order a nonconsensual sterilization in the absence of a controlling statute in *In re Guardianship of Hayes*.[287] It adopted a best interests analysis, which balances the court's power against the individual's right to procreate. However, the plurality in *Hayes* failed to reach a consensus regarding when the individual's best interests would be served, and held that the minor's mother failed to show by clear and convincing evidence that the child's best interests would be served by undergoing involuntary sterilization.[288]

---

447 A.2d 1244 (Md. 1982), *cert. denied*, 489 U.S. 1147 (1983); *In re C.D.M.*, 627 P.2d 607 (Alaska 1981); *In re Sallmaier*, 378 N.Y.S.2d 989 (N.Y. Sup. Ct. 1976); *see also Wyat v. Aderholt*, 368 F. Supp. 1383 (M.D. Ala. 1974); Craig L. McIvor, Comment, *Equitable Jurisdiction to Order Sterilizations*, 57 Wash. L. Rev. 373 (1982).

[281] *See generally* Scott, *supra* note 262.

[282] *See In re C.D.M.*, 627 P.2d 607 (Alaska 1981); *In re Hayes*, 608 P.2d 635 (Wash. 1980); *In re Eberhardy*, 307 N.W.2d 881 (Wis. 1981).

[283] *See In re Grady*, 405 A.2d 851 (N.J. Super. Ct. App. Div. 1979), *vacated and remanded on other grounds*, 426 A.2d 467 (N.J. 1981).

[284] *See In re A.W.*, 637 P.2d 366 (Colo. 1981); *In re Moe*, 432 N.E.2d 712 (Mass. 1982).

[285] *See* John A. Robertson, *Procreative Liberty and the Control of Conception, Pregnancy, and Childbirth*, 69 Va. L. Rev. 405, 415 (1983).

[286] *See N. Carolina Ass'n for Retarded Children v. N. Carolina*, 420 F. Supp. 451 (D.N.C. 1976).

[287] 608 P.2d 635 (Wash. 1982).

[288] The same type of analysis has been applied in cases dealing with mandated abortion when the risk of pregnancy and childbirth outweigh the risk of an abortion. For example, in *Application of A.D.*, 394 N.Y.S.2d 139 (N.J. Surr. Ct. 1977), the guardian of a severely mentally retarded woman sought authority for the court to consent to an abortion for the ward. The appellate court rejected a medical necessity test and applied a best interest analysis, holding that absent proof that the guardian was not acting in the best interests of the ward, the court had no basis for denying the requested authority for consent.

In *In re Grady*,[289] the New Jersey Supreme Court, exercising equitable jurisdiction in the absence of a controlling statute, adopted a substituted judgment test to authorize sterilization of a twenty-year-old woman afflicted with Down's Syndrome. The court recognized that exercise of its power to allow sterilization potentially violated the woman's right to procreate and it expressly disavowed the eugenic theory. After examining the United States Supreme Court decisions dealing with privacy and contraception, the court in *Grady* concluded that these decisions support a personal right to control contraception, including the right to choose *voluntary* sterilization. The court reasoned that an individual's incompetence should not prevent exercise of this right and held that the court may employ its judicial power to exercise a fundamental right in cases where limited mental capacity renders a person's own right to choose meaningless.

Similarly, in *In re Moe*,[290] the mother of an adult mentally retarded woman filed a petition seeking an order for sterilization of her daughter. The Supreme Court of Massachusetts, before exercising its equitable jurisdiction to order sterilization, held that a guardian cannot validly consent to sterilization because the operation irreversibly extinguishes the ward's fundamental right to procreate. However, the court found that the doctrine of substituted judgment requires it to determine whether the incompetent would have chosen sterilization if she were competent. The court stressed that the personal rights implicated in a parent's or guardian's petition for sterilization require the judge to exercise the utmost care in reviewing all the evidence when determining whether the ward would consent to sterilization if competent.

Most states have repealed their non-consensual sterilization statutes or held them unconstitutional over the past two decades. Only a handful of states retain statutes authorizing involuntary sterilization of particular individuals. Statutes compelling sterilization of the mentally retarded or criminal sex offenders may be constitutionally flawed,[291] although more cases have upheld sterilization statutes than have invalidated them. The issue of sterilization has generated extensive literature and most recent commentary reflects dissatisfaction with laws which promote sterilization.[292]

§ 5.07 Artificially Aided Conception

Artificially aided conception, including artificial insemination, in vitro fertilization, and surrogacy, pose great challenges to the legal system by

---

[289] 426 A.2d 467 (N.J. 1981).

[290] 432 N.E.2d 712 (Mass. 1982).

[291] *See, e.g., In re Thompson*, 169 N.Y.S. 638 (N.Y. Crim. Ct), *aff'd*, 171 N.Y.S. 1094 (1918) (violation of state's police power); *Davis v. Berry*, 216 F. 413 (D.C. Iowa 1914) (statute constituted cruel and unusual punishment and failed to provide adequate procedural due process protections), *rev'd as moot*, 242 U.S. 468 (1917); *Haynes v. Lapeer*, 168 N.W. 938 (Mich. 1918) (violation of equal protection standards).

[292] *See, e.g.*, Scott, *supra* note 262; Lombardo, *supra* note 213; Gould, *Procreation: A Choice for the Mentally Retarded*, 23 Washburn L.J. 359 (1984).

enabling people to have children when they might otherwise be unable.[293] It has been argued that legal protection should be afforded not only to conception and childbirth but also to the right to become pregnant and to be a parent.[294] On the other hand, some have contended that freedom to have sex without reproduction does not guarantee the freedom to reproduce without sex.[295]

While artificial insemination has been employed for several generations in this country, the past two decades have generated new medical technologies which signal the potential for even more advanced means of aiding procreation. Such technologies enable procedures such as in vitro fertilization [IVF], cryopreservation of embryos, gamete interfallopian transfer [GIFT], zygote intrafallopian transfer [ZIFT], gamete donation, embryo donation, surrogate motherhood and surrogate gestational motherhood.[296]

Alternative reproduction methods allow procreation without sexual intercourse. These procedures are used by infertile individuals, individuals who do not want to pass a genetic defect on to their offspring, and individuals who are fertile but not living in traditional heterosexual relationships. One reason for the growth of reproductive technology is the increased incidence of infertility, which has been attributed in part to increasing procreative age.[297] An additional reason for the expansion of reproductive technology is the desire of infertile persons and individuals living in non-traditional family relationships to have a child with a genetic or biological link to them.[298] Other major impetus for such research and practices include a decreased supply of adoptive children, caused in large part by "legal availability of abortion and contraceptives; diminished social and legal stigma accompanying illegitimacy; recognition of constitutional limits on legal discrimination predicated on illegitimate status; greater

[293] See, e.g., Berenbaum, Note, *Davis v. Davis: Frozen Embryos and the Thawing of Procreative Liberties*, 36 Wayne L. Rev. 1337 (1990); Martin, Note, *A Cryopreserved In Vitro Embryo is a "Child" for Domestic Relations Purposes*, 13 U. Ark. Little Rock L.J. 95 (1990); see also Cahill, *In Vitro Fertilization: Ethical Issues in Judeo-Christian Perspective*, 32 Loy. L. Rev. 337 (1986); Styron, Comment, *Artificial Insemination: A New Frontier for Medical Malpractice and Medical Products Liability*, 32 Loy. L. Rev. 411 (1986).

[294] See *Carey v. Population Services Int'l*, 431 U.S. 678, 685 (1977) (decision whether or not to bear a child is fundamental to individual autonomy); *Eisenstadt v. Baird*, 405 U.S. 438, 453 (1972) ("If the right of privacy means anything, it is the right of the *individual*, married or single, to be free from unwarranted governmental intrusion into matters so fundamentally affecting a person as the decision whether to bear or beget a child.") (emphasis in original); see also *Davis v. Davis*, 842 S.W.2d 588 (Tenn. 1992) (while the outer limits of the privacy right are not delineated, the decision whether or not to bear a child is at the heart of protected choices).

[295] See Robertson, *Procreative Liberty and the Control of Contraception, Pregnancy and Childbirth*, 69 Va. L. Rev. (1983) (also tracing history of procreative rights from birth control to women's decision whether to reproduce or not).

[296] See, Andrews & Douglass, Symposium on Biomedical Technology and Health Care: Social and Conceptual Transformations, *Alternative Reproduction*, 65 S. Cal. L. Rev. 623 (1991).

[297] See *id.*, at 626 (Almost one-quarter of all married women between thirty-five and thirty-nine had infertility problems; the rate of infertility increases with age.).

[298] *Id.*

economic opportunity and child care services for single women; and changing male attitudes about child raising roles."[299]

[A] Artificial Insemination

Artificial insemination may be accomplished by several relatively simple
medical procedures. Artificial Insemination Donor [AID] involves impregnation of a woman by syringe, using the semen of a donor who is not married
to the patient. AID is a potential solution for couples where the male partner is infertile. Both non-profit and commercial sperm banks have been
established to freeze and store semen for later use. Homologous artificial
insemination [AIH] entails a similar procedure using the semen of the
patient's husband, while "confused" or "combined" artificial insemination
[CAI] mixes the semen of the husband and a sperm donor.[300]

When sperm from a third-party donor is used in either AID or CAI, legal
questions concerning paternal responsibility and factual questions regarding identity of the donor arise.[301] The Uniform Parentage Act, promulgated
in 1973, provides that if a married woman is artificially inseminated with
a third-party donor's semen under the supervision of a licensed physician
and with consent of her husband, a child so conceived will be legally treated
as the natural child of the husband.[302] Although the Act requires formal
registration by the physician, failure to record properly does not affect the
relationship between the father and the child. The sperm donor in an authorized procedure is legally regarded not to be the natural father of a child
conceived pursuant to the Act.[303] The Act fails to address the parentage
issues which arise when parties use artificial insemination in less formal
settings. By 1985, a majority of states had enacted AID statutes, a number
of them modeled after the Uniform Parentage Act provisions.[304]

The status of the parties is also maintained through procedures and
consent forms aimed largely at preserving the donor's anonymity. Many
recipients prefer to use an anonymous donor to ensure that the donor will
not interfere in the parent-child relationship. The primary fear of sperm
donors, future financial responsibility for the child, has been ameliorated
in states that have adopted statutes providing that the husband of the
sperm recipient is the legal father. However, confidentiality poses risks to
children created with donor gametes who develop a genetic defect. The
American Fertility Society recommends that confidential records be kept
on gamete or embryo donors and be made available, on an anonymous basis,

---

[299] Walter Wadlington, *Artificial Conception: The Challenge for Family Law*, 69 Va. L. Rev.
465, 466–467 (1983).

[300] *See id.* at 469.

[301] *See supra* § 5.02[H].

[302] Unif. Parentage Act, *Artificial Insemination*, § 5, 9B U.L.A. 301, (1987); *see also R.S.
v. R.S.*, 670 P.2d 923 (Kan. Ct. App. 1983); *L.M.S. v. S.L.S.*, 312 N.W.2d 853 (Wis. 1981).

[303] Unif. Parentage Act, § 5(b), 9B U.L.A. 301 (1987).

[304] *See* Judith Lynn Bick Rice, *The Need For Statutes Regulating Artificial Insemination
by Donors*, 46 Ohio St. L.J. 1055 (1985).

to the recipient or child.[305] Because anonymity has the disadvantage, however, of depriving the child of its genetic history, including knowledge of potential health problems, one state adopting the Uniform Parentage Act allows release of a donor's identity upon a showing of good cause.[306]

Confidentiality of semen donors also presents the risk of incest between half siblings or between a sperm donor and his unknown daughter. Some commentators have recommended limiting donors to no more than three offspring,[307] while other authors feel the risk of future incest is minimal in our large, transient society.[308] Other concerns include apprehension about insufficient screening of donors, lack of regulation of facilities and documentation, and potential liability resulting from cursory medical screening of sperm donors leading to potential risk of AIDS, genetic disorders, and sexually transmitted diseases.[309]

Obtaining consent of the donee's husband is critical for assuring financial support for the child. In *In re Baby Doe*,[310] a wife was artificially inseminated with the knowledge of her husband, who was unable to father children. After conception, but before the birth of the child, the couple separated and the husband sought an order declaring that he was not the child's father in order to avoid child support obligations. Noting that most recent decisions have been relatively uniform in assigning paternal responsibility to the husband when his conduct evidences consent to the artificial insemination, the court stated that a husband's consent to his wife's impregnation by artificial insemination need not be express, but may be implied from conduct demonstrating his knowledge of the procedure and his failure to object. It held that "a husband who consents for his wife to conceive a child through artificial insemination, with the understanding that the child will be treated as their own, is the legal father of the child born as a result of the artificial insemination and will be charged with all the legal responsibilities of paternity, including support."[311] The husband was thus responsible for support of the child due to his knowledge of and assistance in his wife's efforts to conceive through artificial insemination.

The husband's consent estops him from later denying paternity and assures that children conceived through artificial insemination will have parents who remain responsible for them, especially financially. In *L.M.S. v. S.L.S.*,[312] the Wisconsin Court of Appeals held that where the husband had consented to his wife's impregnation by artificial insemination, he had the legal duties and responsibilities of a father, including support. It concluded that a person who participates in the arrangement for a child's

---

[305] American Fertility Society, *New Guidelines for the Use of Semen Donor Insemination: 1990, in* 1 Fertility and Sterility 1S, 4S–5S (Supp. 1990).

[306] N.M. Stat. Ann. § 40-11-6(c) (Michie 1978).

[307] A. Baran & R. Pannor, Lethal Secrets 167-72 (1989).

[308] Andrews, *supra* note 296, at 661.

[309] *Id.* at 656.

[310] 353 S.E.2d 877 (S.C. 1987).

[311] 353 S.E.2d at 878.

[312] 312 N.W.2d 853 (Wis. Ct. App. 1981).

birth cannot consider the subsequent relationship to be a temporary one that may be disclaimed at will; rather, such an arrangement imposes an obligation to support the child for whose existence he is responsible.

Similarly, when a husband consented orally, but not in writing, to his wife's insemination and had no contact with the treating physician immediately prior to successful insemination, the Kansas Court of Appeal, in *R.S. v. R.S.*,[313] held the husband responsible for support of and responsibility for the resulting child. The *R.S.* court concluded that a husband who consents to heterologous insemination of his wife is estopped from denying paternity, unless the husband establishes by clear and convincing evidence that such consent has been withdrawn prior to the time the wife becomes pregnant.

The question of paternity was raised in a less conventional setting in *Karin T. v. Michael T.*,[314] in which the respondent had been born a female but changed her identity to male, then married a woman. The couple had two children by artificial insemination prior to the parties' separation, after which the department of Social Services filed a support action on behalf of the children. The New York court held that, in view of the agreement that the respondent signed as father of the children, the children were the respondent's own marital children and the respondent had waived any rights to disclaim them.

The issue of consent has also arisen in the context of a criminal prosecution for non-support. In *People v. Sorenson*,[315] a father who had been convicted of criminal non-support defended on the basis that he was not the child's father because his wife had conceived the child through AID. The court stated:

> One who consents to the production of a child cannot create a temporary relation to be assumed and disclaimed at will, but the arrangement must be of such character as to impose an obligation of supporting those for whose existence he is directly responsible. . . . [I]t is safe to assume that without defendant's active participation and consent the child would not have been procreated.[316]

The legal father of a child conceived through AID obtains corresponding rights to custody and visitation. In *Adoption of Anonymous*,[317] a couple divorced after the birth of a child conceived through consensual heterologous artificial insemination. Their divorce decree declared the child to be a child of the marriage. After the wife's remarriage, her new husband petitioned to adopt the child and the former husband refused. The court held that a child born of consensual artificial insemination during a valid marriage is a legitimate child of the marriage, entitled to the same rights and privileges of a child naturally conceived during marriage. A husband

---

[313] 670 P.2d 923 (Kan. Ct. App. 1981).

[314] 484 N.Y.S.2d 780 (N.Y. Fam. Ct. 1985).

[315] 437 P.2d 495 (Cal. 1968).

[316] *Id.* at 499.

[317] 345 N.Y.S.2d 430 (N.Y. Sur. Ct. 1973).

who consents to his wife's artificial insemination by semen of a third-party donor is the parent of the child so conceived and his consent is required in order for the child to be adopted by another.

A statute that denies paternal rights to a sperm donor when artificial insemination is performed with the assistance of a licensed physician does not apply when a donor provides semen directly to the child's mother. A donor may, therefore, establish paternal rights. In *C.M. v. C.C.*,[318] a New Jersey court acknowledged the donor of semen, used by an unmarried woman to artificially inseminate herself, as the natural father of the child and granted him visitation rights. Similarly, in *Jhordan C. v. Mary K.*,[319] Mary and her female partner mutually agreed that Jhordan would be the sperm donor for artificial insemination of Mary and that the two women would raise the child. No written contract was executed concerning Jhordan's status, although he maintained continuous contact with Mary throughout her pregnancy and after the birth of child. When Jhordan requested visitation, Mary refused, and Jhordan brought an action to establish paternity and visitation rights. The trial court declared Jhordan the legal father, ordered him to pay child support, and granted him visitation, but denied him any input into decision-making for the child. Upon Mary's appeal, the California Court of Appeals affirmed, holding that a statute denying paternal rights to a sperm donor when artificial insemination is performed according to statutory procedures does not apply to sperm donors who provide the semen directly to the child's mother.

Custody issues of frozen sperm have also arisen. In *Hecht v. Superior Court*,[320] an attorney who committed suicide left his semen by will to his long time cohabitant, who wishes to be impregnated by the semen. The decedent's children opposed and wanted the sperm destroyed. The California Court of Appeals upheld the testamentary disposition, concluding that the decedent's interest in his cryogenically preserved sperm was property over which the probate court had jurisdiction and that public policy would not prohibit artificial insemination of an unmarried woman, nor would posthumous artificial insemination violate any public policy.

The courts have limited the procreative rights of prisoners. In *Goodwin v. Turner*,[321] an inmate sought habeas corpus relief after denial of his request to artificially inseminate his wife. Goodwin requested artificial insemination because of his concern that his wife's age at the time of his scheduled release date would increase her chances of bearing a child with birth defects.[322] The court first recognized that procreation has consistently been recognized as a fundamental right;[323] however, the court denied Goodwin's request by finding the prison regulation prohibiting inmate procreation was rationally related to legitimate penological interests. The

---

[318] 377 A.2d 821 (N.J. Super. Ct. App. Div. 1977).

[319] 224 Cal. Rptr. 530 (Cal. Ct. App. 1986).

[320] 16 Cal. App. 4th 836, 20 Cal. Rptr. 2d 275 (1993).

[321] 908 F.2d 1395 (8th Cir. 1990).

[322] *Id.* at 1397.

[323] *Id.* at 1398 (citations omitted).

Goodwin decision supports the proposition that artificial insemination is part of the constitutionally protected right to procreate and suggests that review of regulations governing artificial insemination should employ a standard of strict scrutiny in cases which do not involve prisoners.[324]

[B] Surrogate Motherhood

A woman who is unable to produce ova or is unable to carry a fetus may decide to use a surrogate. Two methods of surrogacy currently are utilized: traditional surrogacy and gestational surrogacy.[325] In traditional surrogacy, a surrogate mother is used when a woman cannot contribute genetically or gestationally to reproduction. In this case, her partner's sperm is used to inseminate a surrogate mother who agrees to bear the child and then give the child to the couple to raise. In contrast, surrogate gestational mothers are used by women who are able to provide an ovum but are unable to carry a fetus. In this case, the couple who plan to raise the child are both genetic parents, whose sperm and ova are fertilized in vitro. The fertilized ovum is then implanted in the surrogate mother, who has contracted with the genetic parents to carry the child through birth and then release the child to the genetic parents.

The technologies of artificial insemination and in vitro fertilization have transformed surrogacy into a business, although it possibly occurred covertly long before the technology existed. The surrogate mother may be motivated by the desire to help a childless couple, but more likely is enticed by the money she is paid for the service. Usually a corporate or professional intermediary facilitates the surrogacy contract, often with similarly mixed motives.

Despite its apparent simplicity, both the process and the contract involved are quite complex. Generally, the intermediary advertises for both surrogate mothers and potential parents, interviews both, and often offers legal and psychological counseling. It matches the parents with the mother, prepares contracts between the parties and between them and itself, sets the fees, and arranges for the artificial insemination and the transfer of the child.

The surrogacy contract, usually between the husband and the surrogate mother, is framed as a service contract, not a contract to provide a child, because contracts to sell children are void as against public policy.[326] For the same reason, the wife is excluded from the contract. The husband agrees to provide semen, to pay a fee to the surrogate mother and to the intermediary, and to accept the child with any birth defects that cannot be discovered by amniocentesis. The surrogate mother, whose husband may also be a

---

[324] *See* Turner, Note, *Constitutional Law-Prisoners' Rights-Prison Regulation Denying Inmate The Right to Artificially Inseminate Wife Held Constitutional, Goodwin v. Turner, 908 F.2d 1395 (8th Cir. 1990)*, 13 U. Ark. Little Rock L.J. 671 (1991).

[325] Andrews & Douglass, *supra* note 296, at 630-31.

[326] *See* Katz, *Surrogate Motherhood and the Baby Selling Laws*, 20 Colum. J. L. & Soc. Probs. 3, 8 (1986).

party to the contract, agrees to be artificially inseminated, to bear the child, to relinquish it upon birth, to forego all rights that she has to the child, and to consent to the child's adoption by the wife. The intermediary agrees to introduce the parties and make all the arrangements. The contract is usually a form prepared by the intermediary and the other parties may or may not have legal advice.

In *Surrogate Parenting v. Commissioner ex. rel. Armstrong*,[327] the Kentucky Supreme Court held that the surrogacy business does not violate the state's law prohibiting child brokering and refused to revoke the corporate charter of a surrogate motherhood intermediary. The court found "fundamental differences between the surrogate parenting procedure . . . and the buying and selling of children."[328] Although the statute was intended to prevent "baby brokers from overwhelming an expectant mother or the parents of a child with financial inducements to part with the child,"[329] the court held that the procedure in issue involved merely a contract to bear a yet unconceived child, which assists persons who are unable to conceive one in the ordinary manner. The court reasoned:

> The essential considerations for the surrogate mother when she agrees to the surrogate parenting procedure are *not* avoiding the consequences of an unwanted pregnancy or fear of the financial burden of child rearing. On the contrary, the essential consideration is to assist a person or couple who desperately want a child but are unable to conceive one in the customary manner to achieve a biologically related offspring.[330]

The court concluded that any ban on surrogate parenting procedures was a matter for the legislature.

Litigation involving surrogacy issues most commonly arises when one party seeks to avoid fulfilling the contractual terms. Special difficulties exist when the child has already been born or at least conceived. While problems of paternity and support would arise if the father attempted to breach the contract, the usual difficulty is that the surrogate mother refuses to relinquish the child. In resolving the matter, conflicts develop between contract law and the laws of custody and adoption which govern the parent-child relationship.

Proponents of a contractual approach advocate specific enforcement of surrogacy agreements in recognition that adults are free to contractually bind themselves, absent fraud, duress, unconscionability, or overreaching.[331] Refusing to enforce surrogacy contracts may be paternalistic and as offensive as denying married women the right to contract.[332]

---

[327] 704 S.W.2d 209 (Ky. 1986).

[328] *Id.* at 211.

[329] *Id.*

[330] *Id.* at 211-12.

[331] *See* Antoinette Sedillo Lopez, *Privacy and Regulation of the New Reproductive Technologies: A Decision-Making Approach*, 22 Fam. L.Q. 173, 190–191 (1988).

[332] *Id.* at 191.

Opponents argue that such contracts are illegal because they violate the public policy against child-selling.[333] They further allege that they tend to exploit the poor.[334] Adoption law suggests that the surrogate mother has all the rights of a natural mother, which cannot be terminated except under statutory grounds. If the surrogate mother's rights are not forfeited, the wife cannot adopt the child. Moreover, because the father does not lose his rights either, the issue becomes one of child custody, which applies the "best interests of the child" standard.[335] In ordinary custody disputes, if custody is granted to one natural parent, the other party is normally given visitation rights.

Surrogate motherhood drew national attention issue during the litigation of *In re Baby M.*[336] *Baby M.* exemplifies both the demand for surrogate motherhood and the legal problems which can arise under three areas of law: contracts, adoptions, and child custody.

In the *Baby M.* case, William Stern had entered into a formal surrogacy contract with Mary Beth Whitehead and her husband Richard, in which Ms. Whitehead agreed to be artificially inseminated with Stern's semen. In addition to numerous assurances relating to the potential pregnancy, Ms. Whitehead further agreed not to form a parent-child relationship with the child, to surrender custody to Stern immediately upon the child's birth, and to terminate her own parental rights. Richard Whitehead also agreed to relinquish any rights to the child and do anything necessary to rebut the presumption of paternity. Stern agreed to pay Ms. Whitehead $10,000 for her services, plus her uninsured medical expenses. He further contracted to pay $7,500 to a corporate intermediary.

After the birth of the child, whom Stern and his wife named Melissa, Mary Beth Whitehead became severely distraught over the prospect of turning the child over to the Sterns and terminating her own parental rights to allow Mrs. Stern to adopt the child. After a series of changes in physical custody of Melissa, both voluntary and forced, the Sterns brought a suit to enforce a surrogacy agreement and to compel Ms. Whitehead to surrender the infant to them, to restrain her from interfering with their custody, and to terminate her parental rights. The superior court upheld the contract, awarded William Stern sole custody, and authorized the adoption by Mrs. Stern. Mary Beth Whitehead appealed.

The New Jersey Supreme Court held the surrogacy contract invalid on both legal and public policy grounds. It found "the payment of money to a 'surrogate' mother illegal, perhaps criminal, and potentially degrading to women."[337] Despite the care taken to frame the contract as one for services, it conflicted with laws which strongly prohibit payment in conjunction with adoption cases. The court observed that laws prohibiting baby

---

[333] *See id.* at 191–193; *see also* Honig, *Baby's Desperate Cry: A Call for Legislative Regulation of Surrogate Mother Contracts*, 9:9 Probate L.J. 9, 15–26 (1989).

[334] *See* Sedillo Lopez, *supra* note 331, at 192.

[335] *See infra* § 11.03[A].

[336] 537 A.2d 1227 (N.J. 1988).

[337] *Id.* at 1234.

selling are intended to prevent the exploitation of all the parties involved and to advance the best interests of children.

The court also found that the agreement for termination of Mrs. Whitehead's parental rights conflicted with statutory provisions which require proof of unfitness or abandonment prior to termination of parental rights or an order of adoption. Additionally, the provision for irrevocable consent to surrender the child contravened state law with respect to private placement adoptions.

The contract also violated public policy by allocating custody prior to the child's birth, without regard to the child's best interests. Such contracts have the potential for exploiting the poor and detracting from the requisite voluntariness for a binding agreement. They also could have unknown adverse impacts on the natural and adoptive parents as well as the child.

Finally, the court held that the right of procreation did not entitle the natural father and his wife to custody of the child. However, in light of extensive expert testimony, it concluded that the best interests of Melissa justified a custody award to Stern, with Ms. Whitehead entitled to visitation, on terms to be determined on remand.

On remand, the trial court held that Melissa's best interests would be furthered by unsupervised, uninterrupted, liberal visitation with her natural mother, who had since divorced and remarried. The court found no credible evidence or expert opinion suggesting that the child would suffer any harm from continued and expanded visitation with her natural mother. The court found that Mary Beth Whitehead [now Gould] had attained family stability with her new husband and had accepted that she would never have custody of Melissa. Moreover, Melissa had a warm and loving relationship with her mother and had demonstrated no separation anxiety during supervised visitation. In order to promote communication and cooperation between the parties, the court decided to appoint a mental health professional and direct the parties to participate in counseling. Lastly, the court restrained and enjoined the parties from publicly discussing their relationships with the child, or her personal activities, or from selling any movie rights they may have concerning "Baby M" without prior approval of the court. [338]

Although the court in *Baby M.* would allow surrogate motherhood where the surrogate gratuitously volunteers to carry the child and is given the right to change her mind and assert her parenthood, such an arrangement would lack the consideration necessary for a valid contract.

Other jurisdictions similarly have concluded that non-gratuitous surrogacy contracts are invalid. In *Doe v. Kelly*, [339] the Michigan Court of Appeals held that the state's adoption law, which prohibited the payment of money other than for expenses in connection with adoption, applied to surrogacy contracts, despite any fundamental interest in bearing or begetting a child. Michigan has since enacted a Surrogate Parenting Act in 1988 which

---

[338] *In re Baby M*, 542 A.2d 52 (N.J. Super. Ct. App. Div. 1988).

[339] 307 N.W.2d 438 (Mich. Ct. App. 1981), *cert. denied,* 459 U.S. 1183 (1983).

declares surrogate contracts void, makes them unlawful when entered into for compensation, and provides for placement of children born pursuant to surrogacy arrangements.[340] In a declaratory action brought by infertile couples and potential surrogate mothers, the Michigan Court of Appeals recently held the Act constitutionally valid.[341] The Court of Appeals found that the due process clauses of the State and Federal Constitutions, together with penumbral rights emanating from specific guarantees in the Bill of Rights, protect individual decisions in matters of procreation from unjustified intrusion by the state. However, it concluded that the state had compelling interests sufficient to warrant intrusion into the protected matter of childbearing which justified the invalidation of surrogacy contracts.

A New York court concluded that the terms of a surrogacy contract regarding the surrogate mother's surrender of custody and termination of parental rights are not void, but merely voidable.[342] While expressing strong moral and ethical reservations about surrogacy contracts in general, the court upheld a contract which provided for a $10,000 payment to a surrogate mother and held that the best interests of the child take precedence over any agreement between the parties. It further urged the state legislature to review the question of surrogacy contracts. In a subsequent New York case, however, the court, noting that proposed legislation had not been passed, concluded that the state's adoption statutes prohibited payment in excess of actual medical and related expenses in connection with childbirth, and held that surrogacy contracts are void. It ruled that it would only accept surrender and termination of the natural mother's parental rights if she would swear under oath that she had not and would not request, accept, or receive the payment promised her pursuant to a surrogate parenting agreement. It further requires the prospective adoptive parents to likewise swear not to compensate any party in exchange for the child.

New York has recently enacted legislation that regulates surrogate parenting contracts, which declares such contracts "contrary to the public policy of this state, and are void and unenforceable."[343] It prohibits payment of any direct or indirect remuneration in connection with any surrogacy contract, including the assistance by a third party, while excepting otherwise authorized payments in connection with adoption or "reasonable and actual medical fees and hospital expenses for artificial insemination or in vitro fertilization services incurred by the mother in connection with the birth of the child."[344] The Act sets out civil penalties for violation of its terms.[345] The Act further establishes proceedings regarding parental rights, status, and obligations and includes a provision that forbids the

---

[340] Mich. Comp. Laws § 722.851 (1992).

[341] *Doe v. Attorney Gen'l*, 487 N.W.2d 484 (Mich. Ct. App. 1992).

[342] *In re Adoption of Baby Girl, L.J.*, 505 N.Y.S.2d 813 (N.Y. Surr. Ct. 1986).

[343] N.Y. Dom. Rel. § 122 (McKinney Supp.1993) (effective July 17, 1993).

[344] *Id.* § 123-1(b).

[345] *Id.* §§ 123-2(a), (b).

court from considering the birth mother's participation in a surrogacy contract adversely with respect to her claims to custody.[346]

The Virginia legislature also has adopted a comprehensive new statutory scheme dealing with broadly defined types of assisted conception and their implications.[347] It defines the parentage of a child so conceived, deals with death and divorce of a party prior to the child's birth,[348] and validates and establishes a procedure for court approval of surrogacy contracts,[349] as well as for termination of surrogacy contracts.[350] The statutes regulate the rights of parties to unapproved surrogacy contracts[351] and prohibit surrogacy brokers.[352]

Several other states have enacted legislation directed at some of the issues involved in surrogacy arrangements. While some states, such as Louisiana[353] and Nebraska,[354] have invalidated such contracts, others permit but regulate surrogate parenting.[355] The Nevada Code completely excepts surrogate contracts from its provisions prohibiting payment in adoptions. Some states' statutes have declared surrogacy contracts void;[356] others invalidate only surrogacy contracts for compensation;[357] and yet others criminalize contracting for surrogacy[358] or pronounce surrogacy arrangements as illegal baby buying or selling.[359] In *Soos v. Superior Court*,[360] the Arizona Court of Appeals struck down a statute prohibiting surrogacy and awarding the children of an illegal surrogacy arrangement to the surrogate mother. A number of states permit surrogacy contracts,[361] and some jurisdictions apply their general artificial insemination statutes to surrogacy situations.[362] The Uniform Status of Children of Assisted

---

[346] *Id.* § 124.

[347] Va. Code Ann. §§ 20-156 to 20-165 (Michie 1991) (effective July 1, 1993).

[348] *Id.* § 20-158.

[349] *Id.* §§ 20-159, 20-160.

[350] *Id.* § 20-161.

[351] *Id.* § 20-162

[352] *Id.* § 20-165.

[353] La. Rev. Stat. Ann. § 9:2713 (West 1991).

[354] Neb. Rev. St. § 25–21, 200 (1989).

[355] *See, e.g.,* Ark. Code Ann. § 9-10-201 (Michie 1991) (creating a presumption of parentage in surrogacy arrangements).

[356] *See, e.g.,* N.Y. Dom. Rel. Law §§ 121–124 (Consol. 1993 & Supp. 1996); N.D. Cent. Code §§ 14-18-01 to -07 (1991 & Supp. 1995); Utah Code Ann. § 76-7-204 (1995).

[357] *See, e.g.,* Ky. Rev. Stat. Ann. § 199.590(2)-199.990 (Michie 1995); La. Rev. Stat. Ann. § 9:2713 (West 1991); Neb. Rev. Stat. § 24-21.200 (1996); Wash. Rev. Code Ann. §§ 26.26.210-26.26.260 (West 1989 & Supp. 1996).

[358] *See, e.g.,* Mich. Comp. Laws Ann. §§ 722.851–722.863 (West 1993)

[359] *See, e.g.,* Ala. Code §§ 26-10A-33 to 26-10A-34 (1990); W. Va. Code § 48-4-16 (1993).

[360] 897 P.2d 1356 (Ariz. Ct. App. 1995).

[361] *See, e.g.,* Fla. Stat. Ann. §§ 742.14 to 742.17 (West Supp. 1996); Nev. Rev. Stat. Ann. §§ 126.045, 127.287 (Michie 1993 & Supp. 1995). N.H. Rev. Stat. Ann. §§ 168-B:1 to 168-B:32 (1994 & Supp. 1995); Va. Code Ann. §§ 20-156 to 20-165 (Michie 1995).

[362] *See, e.g.,* Ark. Code Ann. §§ 9-10-201 to 9-10-202 (Michie 1993 & Supp. 1995); N.J. Rev. Stat. Ann. §§ 9:3041; 9:17-44 (West 1993 & Supp. 1996); Or. Rev. Stat. Ann. §§ 109.239, 109. 243, 109.247 (1990 & Supp. 1994).

Conception Act, promulgated in 1988, does not take a definitive position on the subject of surrogacy, but offers two alternatives, both of which take strong stands against open-market surrogacy.[363] Alternative A allows surrogacy if there has been judicial approval, and provides requirements for counseling, home study, and fitness.[364] Alternative B simply voids surrogacy contracts and favors the gestational mother if a child is conceived.[365]

Regardless of whether surrogacy contracts are deemed invalid, the courts have focused on the best interests of the child born through a surrogacy arrangement. The California Court of Appeals has held that a surrogate mother who had read and understood the contract is not entitled to withdraw her consent to adoption based on the illegality of the contract, as the parties had assumed the risk of illegality when they entered into the agreement.[366] It emphasized that the paramount consideration is the best interest of the child when determining custody.

If contract law is applied to resolve surrogacy issues, additional dilemmas arise if the father and his wife are found to be unfit or are discovered to possess qualities repugnant to the surrogate mother after the contract is signed.[367] Surrogate parenting agreements may also raise problems of paternity, which is comprehensively dealt with in other contexts by statutory schemes in most states, usually including procedures for establishing paternity and presumptions as to paternity.[368] The paternity issue could arise in a surrogacy context if the surrogate mother breached her promise to relinquish the child and sought to acquire child support or to establish the paternity of her husband or another man.

The biological father of the child also may attempt to establish paternity. A Michigan court addressed such a situation in *Syrkowski v. Appleyard*,[369] in which a married man with no other children sought a filiation order and entry of his name as natural and legal father of the child born through artificial insemination with his sperm. The surrogate mother cooperated in his action and her husband had consented in writing to the surrogacy arrangement. The Attorney General intervened, arguing that the Paternity Act, which allows a father to assert paternity of a child born out of wedlock, did not control because of the rebuttable presumption that the mother's husband was the father of the child. The trial court agreed, concluding that the Act was not intended to encompass monetary transactions of this nature. The Michigan Supreme Court reversed, deciding that the father could use the Act to establish paternity, that the presumption could be

---

[363] 9B U.L.A. (1998 Supp. at 190, 197).

[364] *Id.*, Alternative A.

[365] *Id.*, Alternative B.

[366] *In re Adoption of Matthew B.-M.*, 284 Cal. Rptr. 18 (Cal. Ct. App. 1991), *cert. denied*, 112 S. Ct. 1685 (1992).

[367] *See* Annas & Alias, *In Vitro Fertilization and Embryo Transfer: Medicolegal Aspects of a New Technique to Create a Family*, 17 Fam. L.Q. 199, 218 (1983).

[368] *See supra* §§ 5.02[B], [F].

[369] 362 N.W.2d 211 (Mich. 1985).

rebutted in a paternity action, and that the term "out of wedlock" included circumstances where the child resulted from a relationship of the wife and someone other than the husband, including a surrogacy arrangement.

Unresolved surrogacy issues will continue to develop, especially when surrogate parenthood and in vitro fertilization methods are used in conjunction with each other.

[C] In Vitro Fertilization

The first "test tube baby," Louise Brown, born in England in 1978, provoked medical, legal, and ethical debate over the implications of in vitro fertilization.[370] In vitro fertilization [IVF], along with embryo transfer, may facilitate child bearing for women otherwise unable to conceive or may allow the embryo of one couple to be carried by another woman who will deliver the child.[371]

In vitro fertilization with embryo transfer is widely used by women who have gynecological diseases which prevent conception and by couples with male factor or unexplained infertility.[372] IVF conception is accomplished by medically removing the ova of a woman and placing them in a sterile laboratory medium for fertilization with the sperm. Because the rate of pregnancy following IVF is related to the number of embryos placed in the uterus, most clinics stimulate the ovary with drugs in order to produce multiple ova for fertilization. After the ova and sperm are fertilized and the embryos reach the proper stage of development, they are implanted in the uterus of the woman who will carry the child until birth.[373]

Medical progress has occurred more rapidly than legal response to and regulation of IVF procedures, and IVF continues to pose many unanswered questions relating to paternity, maternity, and the rights and obligations of the various parties involved. One court has cautioned,

> In this era of artificial insemination, surrogate parenting and in-vitro fertilization, legal rights of a non-biological parent may become fixed by virtue of the parties' action and the developmental relationship of the child with the parent. To permit one parent to revoke the parentage of the other parent, once those rights have been legally determined, in the absence of fraud, by invoking a blood test invites chaos to the child's emotional well-being and legal status.[374]

The legality of the in vitro fertilization procedure was raised in *Smith v. Hartigan*.[375] In *Smith*, the Smiths had discussed the possibility of in vitro fertilization with a physician who determined that the procedure was the

---

[370] *See* Wadlington, *supra* note 299.

[371] *See id.* at 488.

[372] *See generally* W. Droegemueller et al., Comprehensive Gynecology (1987).

[373] *See Smith v. Hartigan*, 556 F. Supp. 157, 159 n.4 (N.D. Ill. 1983).

[374] *Com. ex rel. Coburn v. Coburn*, 558 A.2d 548 (Pa. Super. Ct. 1989).

[375] 556 F. Supp.157 (N.D. Ill. 1983).

only means available for Mrs. Smith to conceive children. Because of concern that the Illinois abortion statute contained a prohibition relating to in vitro fertilization, the doctor was reluctant to perform the procedure. The Smiths and the physician filed a suit challenging the constitutionality of the section which stated that "any person who intentionally caused the fertilization of a human ovum by human sperm outside the body of a living human female shall be deemed to have the care and custody of a child,"[376] subject to prosecution for child abuse if harm ensued, with an exception for lawful termination of pregnancy. The plaintiffs claimed that the in vitro provision failed to give adequate notice to physicians of the type of conduct that was prohibited, violating their constitutional rights to privacy, and was void for vagueness.

Partially in reliance on the State's concession that it had never initiated nor intended to pursue any prosecution against the doctor for engaging in such a procedure, the court dismissed the action for lack of controversy, concluding that it would be inappropriate for it to render a decision on the constitutionality of the challenged provision. The court held that the in vitro provision did not absolutely prohibit the act of causing in vitro fertilization because the procedure sought by the plaintiffs was not prohibited by the statute.

A class action by a group of physicians engaged in reproductive technology later challenged the Illinois abortion statute in *Lifchez v. Hartigan*,[377] and a portion of the statute was declared unconstitutional. The statute's prohibition against intentional experimentation upon human fetuses, unless the experimentation was therapeutic to the fetus, was held to be void for vagueness for failing to define "experimentation" and "therapeutic." Furthermore, because the statute prohibited embryo transfer and chorionic villi sampling, the court held that the statute interfered with a woman's right to attempt to bear a child or become informed of potential birth defects, activities protected under the right to privacy.

Because of its lack of specificity, the *Smith* court's position may place such a burden on physicians that they will be less likely to perform IVF, especially because the decision did not address other issues such as the treatment of multiple embryos or implantation into the uterus of another woman.[378] Commentators have noted that in a multiple embryo situation, a physician's options include (a) re-implanting all the fertilized embryos to enhance the possibility of pregnancy, (b) freezing them to use in the future if the initial transplantation fails, or (c) making them available to another couple, rather than destroying the excess embryos and risking prosecution.[379]

---

[376] *Id.* at 159.

[377] 735 F. Supp. 1361 (N.D. Ill. 1990).

[378] The Illinois abortion statute was amended to specifically exclude the performance of in vitro fertilization. Ill. Rev. Stat., ch. 38 para. 81-26, § 6(I) (1989). The statute continued to prohibit experimentation on a fetus produced by IVF "unless such experimentation is therapeutic to the fetus thereby produced," and criminalized intentional violation.

[379] *See* Annas, *supra* note 367, at 208.

Multiple fertilized ova that had not yet been implanted caused the controversy in *Davis v. Davis*. [380] In *Davis*, a married couple, Mary Sue and Junior Davis, decided to have children by in vitro fertilization and nine of the wife's ova were fertilized with the husband's sperm. Efforts to implant two of the ova were unsuccessful and seven fertilized ova were frozen for prospective future implantation. At the time, neither spouse anticipated their forthcoming divorce action, which commenced a "custody" battle over the preserved embryos.

The trial court found that the frozen embryos were "human beings" from the moment of fertilization and awarded custody of the seven fertilized ova to Mary Sue. It directed that she be afforded the opportunity to bring the children to term through implantation. The Tennessee Court of Appeals reversed, finding a constitutionally protected right in Junior Davis not to father a child when no pregnancy had yet occurred. On remand, it ordered the trial court to award joint custody and an equal right to disposition of the embryos to the parties, who had both since remarried. [381]

Upon Mary Sue's request for review, the Tennessee Supreme Court agreed that the parties had the sole decision-making authority over the embryos. Because they could not agree, the court balanced their interests and decided that the woman's interest in donating the embryos to a childless couple was outweighed by the man's constitutionally protected right to avoid procreation. [382] The court added that if the woman herself sought to use the embryos and was unable to achieve parenthood by any other means, the balancing of their relative interests would be closer. The court stated that while each case must be decided on its own merits, the party objecting to procreation should usually prevail, if the other party has a reasonable possibility of becoming a parent by other means. Absent an agreement regarding the disposition of the embryos, the court concluded that the clinic where the embryos were stored should dispose of them. [383]

The issues of in vitro fertilization have already intersected with those involving surrogacy. The California case, *Johnson v. Calvert*, [384] may be the first case to explore how to determine a child's mother to the same degree that courts have been determining paternity. In *Johnson*, Anna Johnson had offered herself as a surrogate mother to Mark Calvert and his wife Crispina, who had undergone a hysterectomy but retained intact ovaries. Anna, Mark, and Crispina signed a contract stating that an embryo created by Mark and Crispina would be implanted in Anna and the child born would be given to Mark and Crispina as their child. After Anna agreed to relinquish all parental rights in return for $10,000 plus a $200,000 life insurance policy, the couple's fertilized ova was implanted in Anna.

---

[380] 842 S.W.2d 588 (Tenn. 1992).

[381] *Id.* at 595.

[382] By this time, Mary Sue had shifted her earlier position of wanting to use the embryos herself. *Id.* at 590.

[383] *Id., cert. denied*, 113 S. Ct. 1259 (1993).

[384] 851 P.2d 776 (Cal. 1993).

After several disputes among the parties, Anna threatened to refuse to give up the child if the balance of the payments was not made, and Mark and Crispina sought a declaration that they were the legal parents. As a result of blood tests after the child's birth, the trial court found Mark and Crispina to be the genetic, biological, and natural parents. It held that the contract was legal and enforceable, precluding any parental and visitation rights in Anna. The Court of Appeal affirmed, and the Supreme Court of California granted review. Rejecting a constitutional or policy analysis, the court decided the issue under the Uniform Parentage Act. Noting that the Act recognizes both genetic relationship and the act of giving birth as methods of establishing maternity, the court held that where both were undisputed, the parties' intentions as expressed in the surrogacy contract should control. It rejected Anna's arguments that the contract was invalid under either the adoption laws or public policy grounds, holding that the contract was for Anna's services, not the sale of a child and that Anna had entered the contract knowingly and intelligently. The court concluded that concern that surrogacy contracts tend to exploit or dehumanize women, especially those of lower economic means, would be more appropriately addressed by the legislature. A strong dissent by Justice Kennard urged the application of a best interests of the child standard.

A New York court arrived at the opposite conclusion under similar facts in *Andres A. v. Judith N.*[385] A married woman, Luz Elena A., sought a determination that she was the biological mother of twins born to Judith N. pursuant to a surrogacy arrangement in which Judith agreed to become pregnant with Luz Elena's ova which had been fertilized by the sperm of Luz Elena's husband, Andres A. The parties agreed that Luz Elena and Andres were the biological parents of the children, but, in an uncontested filiation proceeding, the court held that the state's artificial insemination law precluded it from declaring Luz Elena the mother of the children.[386] It noted that she was not without a remedy, however, since she could seek to adopt the children.

Some commentators have emphasized that legislative action regarding new bio-medical techniques for conception should focus primarily on the interest of the children who will be conceived.[387] Professor Harry Krause has asserted that "the most important question goes to the child's legal status."[388] He further recommends that respect should be conferred to the interests of the adult parties involved, who may include the donor of the semen, the donor of the ovum, the woman who carries the child to term, and the husband of a married woman who bears the child.[389] Some commentators have favored the gestational mother;[390] others advocate the

---

[385] 591 N.Y.S.2d 946 (N.Y. Fam. Ct. 1992).

[386] The court found that the presumption of paternity of Judith N.'s husband had been successfully rebutted and declared Andres the father of the children. *Id.* at 3.

[387] *See, e.g.,* Yvonne M. Warlen, *The Renting of the Womb: An Analysis of Gestational Surrogacy Contracts Under Missouri Contract Law,* 62 U.M.K.C. L. Rev. 583, 617 (1994).

[388] Harry D. Krause, *Artificial Conception: Legislative Approaches,* 19 Fam.L.Q. 185 (1985).

[389] *Id.*

[390] *See, e.g.,* Goodwin, *Determination of Legal Parentage in Egg Donation, Embryo Transplantation, and Gestational Surrogacy Arrangements,* 26 Fam. L. Q. 275, 291 (1992).

intent test;[391] and while still others argue for or against the genetic relationship itself is a sufficient basis for allocating parenthood.[392]

In vitro fertilization has generated litigation in a number of other contexts.[393] *York v. Jones*[394] concerned the determination of the rights and duties of medical facilities and personnel involved in IVF. In *York*, a husband and wife successfully brought a breach of contract action against a medical college to obtain possession of their potential child, which had been cryo-preserved at a pre-zygote stage, after the college had refused to consent to a transfer to a different institution. The federal district court held that the parties' agreement constituted a bailment which limited the college's rights to exercise control over the fertilized ova.

As the new technologies are refined, additional issues inevitably will surface. Medical malpractice cases and potential suits based on theories of products liability are likely if ovum, sperm, or embryos are defective, and possible warranty claims or strict liability in tort actions may also be initiated.[395]

---

[391] *See, e.g.*, Fergus, Note, *An Interpretation of Ohio Law On Maternal Status in Gestational Surrogacy Disputes: Belsito v. Clark,* 644 N.E.2d 760, 21 U. Dayton L. Rev. 229, 247 (1995).

[392] *See, e.g.*, Place, *Gestational Surrogacy and the Meaning of "Mother,": Johnson v. Calvert, 851 P.2d 776 (Cal. 1993)*, 17 Harv. J. L. & Pub. Pol'y 907, 908 (1994) ("a genetic definition of motherhood is best suited for surrogacy cases"); Hill, *What Does It Mean to Be A "Parent,"?: The Claims of Biology as the Basis For Parental Rights,* 66 N.Y.U.L. Rev. 353, 418 (1991) ("the genetic relationship, in itself, should be accorded very little moral weight in the determination of parental status").

[393] *See, e.g., Egert v. Connecticut Gen. Life Ins. Co.,* 900 F.2d 1032 (7th Cir. 1990) (challenging carrier's decision that insured's in vitro fertilization was not covered under employee health insurance plan); *Official Comm. of Equity Sec. Holders v. Mabey,* 832 F.2d 299 (4th Cir. 1987), *cert. denied,* 485 U.S. 962 (1988) (holding that order to create emergency treatment for reconstructive surgery or in vitro fertilization for Dalkon Shield claimants violates Bankruptcy Code provisions governing preferential treatment of unsecured creditors).

[394] 717 F. Supp. 421 (E.D. Va. 1989).

[395] *See* Styron, Comment, *Artificial Insemination: A New Frontier for Medical Malpractice and Medical Products Liability,* 32 Loy. L. Rev. 411 (1986).

Chapter 6

ADOPTION

§ 6.01 Adoption and Termination of Parental Rights

[A] Introduction and Overview

Adoption is the statutory process by which existing parental rights and responsibilities with respect to a child are extinguished and a new parent-child relationship is created. Adoption is best understood as a two step process, although both steps may be accomplished in the same proceeding. The first step involves termination of all rights in the child of the parent or anyone else having a legal relationship with the child. The second and final step is the creation of a new parent-child relationship with its attendant rights and responsibilities.

Generally, termination of parental rights will occur in one of two ways. A natural parent may voluntarily relinquish parental rights, most often through the execution of a surrender to a licensed child care agency or consent to a private or independent adoption. Alternatively, a state agency may seek termination of parental rights in a judicial proceeding. In this latter case, most states require a showing of unfitness, such as abandonment, abuse or persistent neglect.

In some relatively rare instances, termination of the rights of a biological mother has been found unnecessary. Illustrative is the opinion and decision of the Supreme Court of Vermont in *B.L.V.B. v. E.L.V.B.*,[1] a case involving two women who had lived together as partners in a monogamous and committed relationship for several years. One of the parties gave birth after artificial insemination with the sperm of an anonymous donor. The probate court, despite lack of opposition, refused to approve the adoption of the child by the mother's partner under the conventional statutory mandate that required termination of the biological parent's rights. Thus, the issue before the court was "whether Vermont law requires the termination of a natural mother's parental rights if her children are adopted by a person to whom she is not married."[2] The court pointed out that the primary concern of the state's adoption statute is promotion of the welfare of children, and held that "when the family unit is comprised of the natural mother and her partner, and the adoption is in the best interests of the children, terminating the natural mother's rights is unreasonable and unnecessary."[3]

---

[1] 628 A. 2d 1271 (Vt. 1993).

[2] *Id.* at 1272.

[3] *Id.*

[B] Involuntary Termination of Parental Rights

[1] Introduction

Termination of parental rights, whether consensually or involuntarily is, like adoption, a creature of statute. Even in cases where adoption is not contemplated or possible, statutes authorizing involuntary termination enable the courts to sever the ties between children and parents who harm them.[4] Typical statutory grounds for termination of parental rights include abandonment, child abuse, neglect or dependency, non-support, incarceration of the parent, and a parent's mental illness. Generally, termination of parental rights will require a showing of the parent's unfitness in one form or another, although some statutes purport to authorize severance of the parent-child relationship based on the best interests of the child.

[2] Statutory Requirements

At first glance, variations in the language of statutes authorizing termination of parental rights appear bewildering. A close examination of the statutes reveals, however, that the requirements in many jurisdictions are similar. The grounds for involuntary termination set out in the Uniform Adoption Act are illustrative and typical, and provide:

> In addition to any other proceeding provided by law, the relationship of parent and child may be terminated by a court order issued in connection with an adoption proceeding under this Act on any ground provided by other law for termination of the relationship, and in any event on the ground (1) that the minor has been abandoned by the parent, (2) that by reason of the misconduct, faults, or habits of the parent or the repeated and continuous control, or subsistence, education, or other care or control necessary for his physical, mental, or emotional health or morals, or, by reason of physical or mental incapacity the parent is unable to provide necessary parental care for the minor, and the court finds that the conditions and causes of the behavior, neglect or incapacity are irremediable or will not be remedied by the parent, and that by reason thereof the minor is suffering or probably will suffer serious physical, mental, moral, or emotional harm, or (3) that in the case of a parent not having custody of a minor, his consent is being unreasonably withheld contrary to the best interest of the minor.[5]

[3] Constitutional Considerations

In 1981 and in 1982, the United States Supreme Court addressed two related questions that involved termination of parental rights. In the earlier case, *Lassiter v. Department of Social Services*,[6] the Court held that there was no requirement under the Constitution that counsel be appointed for

---

[4] *See* H. Clark, The Law of Domestic Relations 631 (1987).

[5] Unif. Adoption Act § 19(c) 9 U.L.A. 72 (1971).

[6] 452 U.S. 18 (1981).

an indigent parent in every proceeding for termination of parental rights. Rather, the Court held, the decision whether due process requires the appointment of counsel for parents in proceedings for the termination of parental rights should be left to the trial court, subject to appellate review.

In deciding whether the due process requirement of fundamental fairness required appointment of counsel in these proceedings, the Court gleaned from its earlier holdings the principle that the presumption that counsel must be appointed for an indigent litigant arises only when deprivation of physical liberty may result. The court then reviewed the other elements of due process, as reflected in its decision in *Mathews v. Eldridge*,[7] namely, the private interest at stake, the interest of the government, and the risk that the procedures used will lead to erroneous decisions. Having balanced these interests against each other and weighed them against the presumption, the Court concluded that the trial court's failure to appoint counsel in the case before it did not violate due process.

State courts have not slavishly adhered to the teaching of *Lassiter*. In *V.F. v. State*,[8] for example, the Supreme Court of Alaska held that in proceedings for the termination of parental rights, the due process clause of the Alaska Constitution guarantees to indigent parents the right to court appointed counsel. The court further held that whenever the state's Constitution guarantees the right to counsel in a proceeding, effective assistance of counsel also is required.

In *Santosky v. Kramer*,[9] the Court considered the standard of proof required in proceedings for termination of parental rights. Applying the factors in *Mathews v. Eldridge*,[10] the Court held that New York's fair preponderance of the evidence standard in termination proceedings violated the Due Process Clause, and that the constitutionally required standard is clear and convincing evidence.

In *Adoption of Kelsey S.*,[11] the petitioner was the undisputed natural father of an out-of-wedlock child. After the child's birth, the father initiated an action in the superior court to establish his parental relationship with the child and to obtain custody. Under California statutory law, a man who meets certain conditions is the presumed father, a status critical for the exercise of parental rights. The court held that the California statutory scheme was violative of federal constitutional guarantees of equal protection and due process to the extent that it permitted the mother unilaterally to preclude the biological father from achieving the status of presumed father.

---

[7] 424 U.S. 319 (1976).

[8] 666 P.2d 42 (Alaska 1983).

[9] 455 U.S. 745 (1982).

[10] 424 U.S. 319, 335.

[11] 823 P. 2d 1216 (Cal 1992).

[4] Grounds for Termination of Parental Rights

[a] Abandonment

Statutes that govern termination of parental rights generally list abandonment as one of the grounds. Frequently, there is a requirement of failure to communicate with the child for a specified period of time, failure to provide support, or other evidence of an intent to relinquish parental claims to the child. The elements of the California statute are typical. The statute authorizes an action to free from parental custody a person

> [who] has been left without provision for his identification by his parent or parents . . . in the care and custody of another for a period of six months or by one parent in the care and custody of the other parent for a period of one year without any provision for his support, or without communication from such parent or parents, with the intent on the part of such parent or parents to abandon the child. [12]

> The statute explicitly authorizes the court to declare a child abandoned when the evidence shows only token efforts by a parent to support or communicate with the child. [13]

The Minnesota statute similarly authorizes the court to terminate a parent's right to an abandoned child. The statute presumes abandonment when a parent has no contact or incidental contact for six months when the child is under age six, or for a year if the child is between six years and eleven years old. [14] Also, for the presumption of abandonment to obtain, the social service agency must have made "reasonable efforts to facilitate contact, unless the parent establishes that an extreme financial or physical hardship or treatment for mental disability or chemical dependency or other good cause prevented the parent from making contact with the child." [15]

Lack of parental contact might not constitute abandonment if its cause is not within the parent's control. In *In re T.R.M.*,[16] for example, the California Court of Appeal acknowledged that sporadic efforts at communication or communications in the face of threatened legal action may be considered only token. Nevertheless, the court reversed the trial court's order terminating the parental rights of a mother who was incarcerated. The court noted that the mother wrote to the children twice a month and sent them birthday and Christmas cards, the only means of communication available to her.

In a similar vein, the Supreme Court of Alaska in *R.N.T. v. J.R.G.*[17] reversed a determination that an imprisoned father need not consent to the adoption of his two children because of failure to communicate with

---

[12] Cal. Fam. Code § 7808 (West 2001).

[13] *Id.*

[14] Minn. Stat. Ann. § 260(c).301(b)(1) (West 2001).

[15] *Id.*

[16] 116 Cal. Rptr. 292 (Cal. Ct. App. 1974).

[17] 666 P.2d 1036 (Alaska 1983).

them for the statutory period of one year.[18] The court, citing the generally recognized principle that "parental conduct which causes loss of a parent's right to consent to adoption must be wilful," found that the circumstances of the father's imprisonment and parole barred him from communicating with the children.

In *In re Adoption of Baby E.A.W.,*[19] the Supreme Court of Florida addressed the certified question whether an out-of-wedlock father had abandoned the child, which would free her for adoption without parental consent. The question before the court was whether the trial court could consider lack of emotional support or emotional abuse in evaluating the statutory factor or "conduct of the father toward's the child's mother during the pregnancy."[20] The court answered the question in the affirmative and affirmed the trial court's finding of abandonment.

[b]   Child Abuse, Neglect and Dependency

Termination of parental rights may result from abuse or persistent neglect of a child. The opinion of the Colorado Court of Appeals in *People ex rel. C.R.*[21] sets out a scenario that is not atypical. At the time of the termination proceeding in *C.R.*, the children were in the custody of the county department of social services, the three youngest children having been adjudicated as neglected or dependent because of child abuse, and the mother having been found incompetent to care for the oldest child. The finding of neglect or dependency was based on evidence that a man with whom the mother was cohabiting had inflicted injuries on the children over an extended time period, and that she did not seek medical or other assistance for the children.

The court affirmed the trial court's termination of the mother's parental rights in a subsequent dispositional hearing. The court held:

> In decreeing termination of parental rights, a trial court must find that the conditions which resulted in the earlier determination of dependency will in all probability continue into the future, and that under no reasonable circumstances would the welfare of the children be served by a continuation of the parent-child relationship.[22]

The court in *C.R.* also noted that a trial court properly may infer that a non-abused child lacks proper care from evidence of the mistreatment of the other children. The decision of the Wyoming Supreme Court in *In re M.L.M.*[23] reflects this principle, observing that abuse by a stepfather or some other person is evidence of a mother's neglect if she takes no steps to stop the abuse or remove the child from the abusive environment.[24]

---

[18] See Alaska Stat. § 25.23.050(a)(2) (1991).

[19] 658 So. 2d 961 (Fla. 1995).

[20] *See* FLA. STAT. § 63.032(14)(Supp. 1992).

[21] 557 P.2d 1225 (Colo. Ct. App. 1976).

[22] *Id.* at 1228.

[23] 682 P.2d 982 (Wyo. 1984).

[24] *Id.* at 987.

[c] Failure to Provide Child Support

The failure of a parent to provide support is frequently a ground for involuntary termination of parental rights. The influential Uniform Adoption Act lists among those whose consent is not required for adoption of a child "a parent of a child in the custody of another, if the parent for a period of at least a year has failed significantly without justifiable cause . . . to provide for the care and support of the child as required by law or judicial decree."[25] The Minnesota statute, while its language is more elaborate, is to the same effect, authorizing termination of parental rights upon the finding of the following condition:

> That the parent has substantially, continuously, or repeatedly refused or neglected to comply with the duties imposed upon that parent by the parent and child relationship, including but not limited to providing the child with necessary food, clothing, shelter, education and other care and control necessary for the child's physical, mental, or emotional health and development, if the parent is physically and financially able, and reasonable efforts by the social service agency have failed to correct the conditions that formed the basis of the petition.[26]

The decision of the Supreme Court of Alaska in *In re J.J.J.*,[27] a leading case, is frequently cited as an illustration of the elements required for involuntary termination of parental rights on the ground of non-support. The trial court in *J.J.J.* held that under the controlling statute the stepfather could adopt a 7-year-old boy without the biological father's consent because the father had for a twelve month period "failed significantly without justifiable cause to provide support required by judicial decree."[28]

In its affirmance, the court held that the father's sporadic partial payments of court ordered support did not preclude the finding of significant failure to provide support, and that child support payments should be substantial or regular and constitute a material factor in child support. The resistance of the former wife to the father's interest in visitation with the boy did not excuse failure to support him.

[d] Unfitness

Unfitness as a ground for termination of parental rights encompasses a vast array of parental conduct. In *In re Adoption of Michael J.C.*,[29] the prospective adoptive parents sought termination of the parental rights of the mother of an infant girl who sought to withdraw consent to adoption. The court reviewed evidence in the record that the child's mother had

---

[25] Unif. Adoption Act § 6(a)(2), 9 U.L.A. 28 (1988).

[26] Minn. Stat. Ann. § 260.221(1)(b)(2) (West 1992).

[27] 718 P.2d 948 (Alaska 1986).

[28] *Id.*

[29] 486 A.2d 371 (Pa. 1984).

physically abused her own mother and children for whom she was a baby sitter. There was also evidence of alcohol abuse and illegal drug use, including hospitalization for a drug overdose, and treatment in a mental hospital after suicide threats.

Furthermore, she had engaged in promiscuous sexual intercourse at the age of sixteen, and had a history of violent exhibitions of temper toward friends and family members. She maintained an insanitary apartment that her landlord described as uninhabitable. The court concluded:

> "[W]hen a parent has demonstrated a continued inability to conduct his or her life in a fashion that would provide a safe environment for a child, whether that child is living with the parent or not, and the behavior of the parent is irremediable as supported by clear and convincing evidence, the termination of parental rights is justified. [30]

In *New Jersey Division of Youth and Family Services v. A.W.*,[31] the New Jersey Supreme Court cautioned that a court analyzing parents' ability to care for their children should determine only whether the parents foresee-ably can cease to harm their children, rather than determining that the parents are themselves unfit or "the victims of social circumstances beyond their control."[32] The court observed that "[p]arents are not to be adjudged unfit because they lack resources or intelligence, but only by reason of conduct detrimental to the physical or mental health of the child, specifi-cally in the form of actual or imminent harm."[33] Absent such a showing, children may not be removed from their parents.

[e] Mental or Physical Disability of the Parent

In some jurisdictions, statutes authorize termination of parental rights when a parent is unable to care for a child because of mental illness or retardation. The Uniform Adoption Act permits a court to dispense with parental consent to adoption by "a parent judicially declared incompetent or mentally defective if the Court dispenses with the parent's consent."[34] The California statute is of similar effect, authorizing the court to declare free from parental custody and control a child

> [w]hose parent or parents have been declared by a court of compe-tent jurisdiction . . . to be developmentally disabled or mentally ill
> . . ..[35]

In *In re K.F.*,[36] Iowa's Supreme Court affirmed a judgment terminating the parental rights of a mother who suffered from paranoid schizophrenia. The court noted that mental disability alone will not suffice for terminating

---

[30] *Id.* at 375.

[31] 512 A.2d 438 (N.J. 1986).

[32] *Id.* at 447.

[33] *Id.* at 451.

[34] Unif. Adoption Act § 6(a)(6), 9 U.L.A. 28–29 (1988).

[35] Cal. Fam. Code § 7826(a) (West 2001).

[36] 437 N.W.2d 559 (Iowa 1989).

the parent and child relationship. It is, however, a proper factor for consideration, and when it contributes to one's inability to act as a parent, mental disability may determine whether the child's best interests require termination of parental rights.

[f] Best Interests of the Child

Although the cases do not always say it explicitly, it is obvious that termination of parental rights and adoption should be in the best interests of the child. At the same time, however, the cases make it clear that conduct that is harmful to the child or that reflects what may be deemed "unfitness" will be weighed in the determination of what constitutes the child's best interest. The Supreme Court of Rhode Island, in *In re Kristina L.*,[37] set out the generally prevailing principle:

> Parental unfitness and the best interest of the child are not unre-
> lated concepts. Concern for the best interests of the child is "not
> inconsistent with a respect for parental rights with which no agency
> of the state may interfere on arbitrary or irrational grounds." . . .
> The inability of parents to provide the basic necessities for their
> children is certainly not in the child's best interest. However, even
> though it may be in a child's best interest to live with a family of
> comfortable means rather than a poorer family, this standard may
> not justify the state's intervention absent a finding of parental
> unfitness.[38]

In sum, it is only after a determination of parental unfitness that the best interests of the child will outweigh other considerations in a proceeding for termination of parental rights.

[C] Independent or Private Adoption

The adoption of children may be accomplished in every jurisdiction through state licensed child care agencies. In a number of states, however, adoptions occur independent of agencies licensed to care for and place children. In such independent adoptions, the child's birth parent and prospective adoptive parents may know each other prior to adoption and arrange for the adoption through direct placement without an intermediary. More frequently, however, an adoption intermediary brings together the birth parent and the prospective adoptive parents, culminating in a private placement adoption.[39]

Independent adoptions sometimes are referred to as "gray market" adoptions, a term that purportedly is meant "to indicate that independent adoptions often fall into a gray area of the law, somewhere between the highly regulated agency adoptions and the patently illegal baby selling of

---

[37] 520 A.2d 574 (R.I. 1987).

[38] *Id.* at 581 (citations omitted).

[39] *See* Gustafson, Note, *Regulating Adoption Intermediaries: Ensuring that the Solutions Are No Worse than the Problem*, 3 Geo. J. Legal Ethics 837, 842 (1990).

black market adoptions."[40] As one commentator has succinctly and correctly observed:

> A black market adoption differs from a legal private placement or gray market adoption only in that the intermediary receives a disallowable fee. Since it is so easy to cross the line between a permitted private placement and an illegal black market sale of a child, the threat of a black market adoption is greater with independent adoptions.[41]

As is generally the case with adoption and termination of parental rights, the states take a variety of approaches to independent adoptions. In the vast majority of jurisdictions, a parent may place a child with unrelated prospective adoptive parents either directly or with an intermediary's assistance. Only six states bar independent adoptions and limit authorization for adoption placements to state agencies or state licensed private agencies.[42]

Those states in the majority that permit private placement have sought to prevent profiteering in adoption placements by the enactment of laws or regulations that limit compensation payable to intermediaries who arrange adoption placements.[43] In some instances, states have prescribed criminal sanctions for the violation of statutory procedures governing adoption placement.[44]

An array of regulations, often conflicting, govern independent adoptions in the several states. Some states, for example, require a home study to be conducted by an approved social worker, while others require no such study.[45] There are also conflicting approaches among the states with respect to such issues as whether the birth mother must receive mandatory counseling; whether prospective adoptive parents may advertise that they wish to adopt a child; whether birth parents and adoptive parents may share identifying information; and the time within which a consent may be signed or revoked.[46]

Without exception, states that permit independent adoption placement do not permit a person to profit from the placement.[47] As one commentator has noted, "if the attorney, physician, or other intermediary who arranges an independent adoption were permitted to profit from the transaction, the

---

[40] Hartfield, *The Role of the Interstate Compact on the Placement of Children in Interstate Adoption*, 68 Neb. L. Rev. 292, 304 (1989).

[41] Atwell, *Surrogacy and Adoption: A Case of Incompatibility*, 20 Colum. Hum. Rights L. Rev. 1, 13–14, n.62 (1988).

[42] Blair, *Lifting the Genealogical Veil: A Blueprint for Legislative Reform of the Disclosure of Health-Related Information in Adoption*, 70 N.C.L. Rev. 681, 720, n.212 (1992).

[43] Jonet, *Legal Measures to Eliminate Transnational Trading of Infants for Adoption: An Analysis of Anti-Infant Trading Statutes in the United States*, 13 Loyola L.A. Int'l & Comp. L.J. 305, 307 (1990).

[44] *Id.* at 307.

[45] *See* Gufstason, *supra* note 39, at 843.

[46] *Id.*

[47] *See* Atwell, *supra* note 41, at 27-29.

temptation would arise to place the child with adoptive parents who would pay the highest price for the child rather than with the parents who would act in the child's best interest."[48]

There is general agreement that it is ethically improper for a lawyer to represent both the birth parent and the prospective adoptive parents in a private placement adoption. In *Matter of Petrie*,[49] the Supreme Court of Arizona upheld disciplinary sanctions imposed on a lawyer who violated conflict of interest rules by representing multiple clients in a private adoption. The lawyer in *Petrie* established an attorney-client relationship with the child's natural mother, and subsequently with two different prospective adoptive couples. The court noted that while the parties to an independent adoption proceeding generally do not have an adversary relationship, there is nevertheless the potential for conflicts of interest. The court stated:

> Despite the spirit of cooperation often present in an adoption, conflict of interest situations are likely to arise for an attorney involved in the proceedings. First, the interests of potential adoptive parents of the same child are always adverse to one another. . . .
>
> Second, and perhaps less apparent, the interests of the adoptive parents may be adverse to the interests of the natural parents. The decision to give the baby up for adoption is often a difficult one to make. The natural parents' attorney has a duty to provide them with counsel about such matters as paternity issues, economic matters, and the legal effect of signing the consent to adopt.[50]

Criminal sanctions may also apply to unauthorized private placement adoptions. For example, in *Galison v. District of Columbia*,[51] the appellant was a New York lawyer whose associate was contacted by a Florida lawyer who stated that he had not been able to arrange for an adoption in Florida of the expected child of a Florida resident. The expectant mother was willing to travel only as far as the District of Columbia, where Galison met her. After the woman's change of heart, Galison persuaded her to proceed with the adoption and that she would be paid $2000 in addition to her medical and living expenses. Ultimately, Galison was convicted of the District statute that proscribed placement of children by other than a licensed child-placing agency.

[D] Agency Adoption

In every state, children may be placed for adoption by either state agencies or by private agencies licensed by the state to undertake child care and child placement. Ordinarily, children will come into the care and custody of an authorized agency through either involuntary termination of

---

[48] *Id.* at 29.

[49] 742 P.2d 796 (Ariz. 1987).

[50] *Id.* at 800.

[51] 402 A. 2d 1263 (D.C. Ct. App. 1979).

parental rights in a judicial proceeding, or voluntary relinquishment of parental rights through execution of a document commonly known as a surrender. Under either method of placement, the child generally will be eligible for adoption.

As a leading commentator has pointed out, adoption statutes contain few restrictions as to what persons are eligible to adopt, including age and residence requirements in some states, and generally requiring only that they be adults, and for married persons that both husband and wife join in the adoption petition.[52] The rationale offered for this state of affairs is the intent to rely on adoption agencies to screen out prospective adoptive parents who are unsuitable.[53] The writer concludes:

> Since particular adoption agencies may have many standards or rules of thumb respecting the qualifications of prospective adoptive parents, this gives the agencies considerable legal power over the grant or denial of adoptions. The agency's refusal to place a child with prospective adoptive parents, although it may theoretically be reviewable by the courts, as a practical matter will seldom be challenged.[54]

In *Scott v. Family Ministries*,[55] a prospective adoptive parent mounted a successful challenge to the policies of an authorized adoption agency. Richard Scott, a physician, sought to adopt a Cambodian child who was in the custody of Family Ministries, a California licensed adoption agency that served the evangelical Protestant community and placed children only in evangelical Protestant homes. Although he signed the agency's required statement of faith, he was informed that he was not qualified to adopt because he was an Episcopalian, and not an evangelical Protestant.

The California Court of Appeal affirmed the trial court's judgment granting injunctive relief. In the course of its opinion the court noted that the adoption laws of almost all states embody religious considerations. The California statute, like those in a number of other states, provides for religious matching, which "requires or gives preference to adoption by parents of the same faith as that of the natural parents of the child or of a religion for which the natural parents express a preference."[56] The court observed:

> The process preserves constitutionality by placing the state in a neutral position in which parentage or parents and not the state determines the religion of the home into which the child is to be adopted. . . . It recognizes the common law right of a natural parent to control the religious upbringing of his child.[57]

---

[52] H. Clark, The Law of Domestic Relations in the United States 908 (1988).

[53] *Id.*

[54] *Id.*

[55] 135 Cal. Rptr. 430 (Cal. Ct. App. 1976).

[56] *Id.* at 437; *see also Dickens v. Ernesto*, 281 N.E.2d 153 (N.Y. 1972).

[57] *Id.* at 437.

The court noted that because of the significant role that private licensed adoption agencies play under the California statutory scheme and the extent to which the state delegates to those agencies the governmental function of performing tasks leading to judicially approved adoptions, the activities of the agencies constitutes state action. Accordingly, the court held that in order to make the California statute constitutional, it must be interpreted as precluding the imposition of religious requirements upon prospective adoptive parents beyond the religious matching provisions of the applicable statute.

[E] Consent

[1] Who Must Give Consent?

In every state, the statute governing adoption requires the consent of the mother of a minor child before a petition to adopt is granted. Also required is the consent of the father of the child if he was married to the child's mother at the time of the child's conception or birth. Such persons whose consent is required may, of course, relinquish their parental rights voluntarily, or may have those rights terminated involuntarily in a judicial proceeding.[58]

Historically, the consent of the father of a child born out of wedlock was not required. Following a series of decisions by the Supreme Court of the United States, however, it is now well established that the consent of the father of an out of wedlock child is required in a variety of circumstances. Unlike birth mothers, these fathers must establish their right to consent. Among the ways of doing so are formal acknowledgement or judicial establishment of paternity, or by showing under the applicable statute that they have established a relationship with the child that is entitled to recognition.

[2] Consent of the Unwed Father

In a series of four cases, the United States Supreme Court has established the contours of the rights of fathers of children born out of wedlock to consent to their adoption. In the seminal case, *Stanley v. Illinois*,[59] the court considered the constitutionality of an Illinois statutory scheme that presumed that every father of a child born out of wedlock was unfit to have custody of his children. The father in *Stanley* had lived with the children for all of their lives, and had lived with their mother intermittently for 18 years. When the mother died, the children were declared wards of the state.

The Court held that under the due process clause, Stanley was entitled to a hearing as to his fitness, and that the state could not presume that he, and unwed fathers generally, were neglectful and unsuitable parents. The Court also held that denying a hearing for unwed fathers while

---

[58] *See supra* § 6.01[B].

[59] 405 U.S. 645 (1972).

extending that right to all other parents whose custody of their children was challenged violated the equal protection clause of the Constitution.

Although adoption was not involved in *Stanley*, the Court made a brief reference to the subject in footnote 9 to its opinion:

> We note in passing that the incremental cost of offering unwed fathers an opportunity for individualized hearings on fitness appears to be minimal. If unwed fathers, in the main, do not care about the disposition of their children, they will not appear to demand hearings. If they do care, under the scheme here held invalid, Illinois would admittedly at some later time have to afford them a properly focused hearing in a custody or adoption proceeding.

> Extending opportunity for hearing to unwed fathers who desire and claim competence to care for their children creates no constitutional or procedural obstacle to foreclosing those unwed fathers who are not so inclined. The Illinois law governing procedure in adoption cases . . . provides for personal service, notice by certified mail, or for notice by publication when personal or certified mail service cannot be had or when notice is directed to unknown respondents under the style of "All whom it may Concern." Unwed fathers who do not promptly respond cannot complain if their children are declared wards of the State. Those who do respond retain the burden of proving their fatherhood. [60]

Largely in response to this footnote, a number of states amended their adoption statutes to require notice to unwed fathers.

Some six years after *Stanley*, the court addressed an unwed father's rights in the adoption context, ruling on the constitutionality of a Georgia statute that authorized adoption of a child born out of wedlock over the objection of the natural father. The statute in question required only the mother's consent to adoption of an out of wedlock child, but permitted the father to veto the adoption if he had legitimated the child in accordance with Georgia law. After the mother and her new husband had filed an adoption petition, the father attempted to block the adoption, secure visitation rights, and legitimate the child. The Georgia courts ruled that the adoption was in the best interests of the child.

The Court held that application of a "best interests of the child standard did not violate due process or equal protection. On the question of due process, Mr. Justice Marshall, writing for a unanimous Court, observed:

> [T]his is not a case in which the unwed father at any time had, or sought, actual or legal custody of his child. Nor is this a case in which the proposed adoption would place the child with a new set of parents with whom the child had never before lived. Rather, the result of the adoption in this case is to give full recognition to a family unit already in existence, a result desired by all concerned,

---

[60] 405 U.S. at 657, n. 9.

except appellant. Whatever might be required in other situations, we cannot say that the State was required in this situation to find anything more than that the adoption, and denial of legitimation, were in the "best interests of the child."[61]

The Court also rejected the appellant's equal protection challenge to the statute, holding that the state could properly recognize the differences in commitment to a child's welfare between an unwed father like appellant and a divorced father who bore responsibility to the child during marriage.

The parties in *Caban v. Mohammed*[62] lived together and held themselves out as husband and wife for more than five years, although they were never legally married. Two children were born during the relationship and the father, whose name was on the birth certificate, lived with them and contributed to their support. When the parties separated, the mother took the children and married another man. For the next two years the father visited or maintained contact with the children. Subsequently, the New York Surrogate's court granted a petition by the mother and her new husband, over the father's objection, to adopt the children. The Court acted pursuant to the New York statutory scheme, which permitted an unwed mother, but not an unwed father, to withhold consent to a child's adoption.

The Supreme Court upheld the father's equal protection challenge to the statute, holding that its gender based distinction bore no substantial relation to an important governmental interest. In support of its conclusion, the Court observed that "maternal and paternal roles are not invariably different in importance," and pointed out that "[e]ven if unwed mothers as a class were closer than unwed fathers to their newborn infants, this generalization concerning parent-child relations would become less acceptable as a basis for legislative distinctions as the age of the child increased."[63] Further, where the father has not participated in the rearing of his child, the equal protection clause does not preclude the state from withholding his power to veto his child's adoption.

The unwed father in *Lehr v. Robertson*[64] had lived with the mother prior to the child's birth but not afterward, and did not provide financial support. Subsequently, she married another man, and when the child was two years old, the mother and her new husband commenced adoption proceedings. A month later, the father filed a petition seeking a declaration of his paternity and orders for support and visitation. Soon afterward, he learned of the pending adoption proceeding and immediately sought to have it stayed pending determination of his paternity action. The state court informed him that it had signed the adoption order, and then dismissed the paternity petition.

The Supreme Court in *Lehr* rejected the unwed father's due process claim. After reviewing and discussing its earlier holdings in the area, the Court stated:

---

[61] *Quilloin v. Walcott*, 434 U.S. 246, 255 (1978).

[62] 441 U.S. 380 (1979).

[63] *Id.* at 389.

[64] 463 U.S. 248 (1983).

The difference between the developed parent-child relationship that was implicated in *Stanley* and *Caban*, and the potential relationship involved in *Quilloin* and this case, is both clear and significant. When an unwed father demonstrates a full commitment to the responsibilities of parenthood by "com[ing] forward to participate in the rearing of his child," . . . his interest in personal contact with his child acquires substantial protection under the Due Process Clause. At that point, it may be said that he "act[s] as a father toward his children." . . . But the mere existence of a biological link does not merit equivalent constitutional protection.[65]

The Court pointed out that after *Stanley* New York had enacted a statutory scheme that gives notice automatically to seven categories of unwed fathers likely to have assumed responsibility for their children's care. The father in *Caban*, if he had sent a postcard to the state's putative father registry, could have guaranteed that he would receive notice of the adoption proceeding.

The Court in *Lehr* also rejected the unwed father's equal protection claim, factually distinguishing the case before it from *Caban*. The court noted that in *Lehr* the child's mother had continuous custody of the child and the father did not establish a custodial, personal, or financial relationship. The Court concluded that "[i]f one parent has an established custodial relationship with the child and the other parent has either abandoned or never established a relationship, the Equal Protection Clause does not prevent a State from according the two parents different legal rights.[66]

[3] Consent of Minor Parent

Ordinarily, the fact that the biological parent of a child is a minor is of no consequence with respect to the ability to give valid consent. State adoption statutes typically validate the consent of minor parents in the absence of fraud or duress. The Virginia statute, for example, provides that "[a] parent who has not reached the age of eighteen shall have legal capacity to give consent to adoption and shall be as fully bound thereby as if the parent had attained the age of eighteen years."[67] In *Norfolk Division of Social Services v. Unknown Father*,[68] the Court of Appeals of Virginia upheld a minor's agreement that surrendered her child to an agency for adoption, holding that there was not the requisite clear and convincing evidence of fraud or duress.

In *Kathy O. v. Counseling & Family Services*,[69] fifteen-year-old parents filed a habeas corpus petition seeking the return of their child whom they had surrendered for adoption. The Appellate Court of Illinois upheld the surrender, noting that the evidence was clear and convincing that the

---

[65] *Id.* at 261 (citations omitted).

[66] *Id.* at 267–268 (citations omitted).

[67] Va. Code Ann. § 63.1-219.10 (2001).

[68] 345 S.E.2d 533 (Va. Ct. App. 1986).

[69] 438 N.E.2d 695 (Ill. App. Ct. 1982).

parents knew the legal effect of the document they signed and that there was neither fraud nor duress by the agency.

While status as a minor will not impair the ability to consent to adoption of one's child, some states also require the consent of the minor's parents. The Michigan statute is illustrative. In the section describing persons who are authorized to consent to adoption, the statute provides: "If the parent of the child to be adopted is an unemancipated minor, that parent's consent is not valid unless a parent, guardian, or guardian ad litem of the minor parent has also executed the consent."[70]

[4] Revocation of Consent

The law relating to revocation of consent to adoption is not easily summarized. The subject is addressed in some, but by no means all state adoption statutes. The Virginia statute, for example, provides as follows: "Parental consent to an adoption . . . shall be revocable prior to the final order of adoption (i) upon proof of fraud or duress, or (ii) after placement of the child in an adoptive home, upon written, mutual consent of the birth parents and proposed adoptive parents."[71]

The Uniform Adoption Act provides that

> a relinquishment of parental rights with respect to a child, executed under this section, may be withdrawn by the parent, and a decree of a court terminating the parent and child relationship . . . may be vacated by the Court upon motion of the parent, if the child is not on placement for adoption and the person having custody of the child consents in writing to a withdrawal or vacation of the decree.[72]

In some jurisdictions, the statute provides for a time within which there may be revocation. The Georgia statute, for example, states: "A person signing a surrender shall have the right to withdraw the surrender by written notice within ten days after signing; and the surrender document shall not be valid unless it so states. . . . After ten days, a surrender may not be withdrawn."[73] *Yopp v. Batt*[74] is also illustrative of typical principles relating to revocation of consent. In this case, the Supreme Court of Nebraska examined relinquishment of consent in a closed private adoption. The court noted that the rights of the relinquishing parent are not entirely extinguished until the formal adoption of the child, and that an adoption in Nebraska cannot take place until at least six months after the child is relinquished. Also, the court conceded that the law was not clear with respect to who has legal rights to the child during the period between relinquishment and adoption. Nevertheless, in the case before it, the court concluded that the mother, even before the child's birth, had firmly stated

---

[70] Mich. Comp. Laws Ann. § 710.43(4) (West 1993).

[71] Va. Code Ann. § 63.1-225[3] (2001).

[72] Unif. Adoption Act § 19(g), 9 U.L.A. 11, 72 (1988).

[73] Ga. Code Ann. § 19-8-9(b) (1999).

[74] 467 N.W. 2d 868 (Neb. 1991).

that she did not want to keep the child. Also, she made her decision independently and without influence by any other person. Accordingly, her relinquishment was valid.

[F]　Subsidized Adoptions and Children With Special Needs

Federal legislation has driven state legislation that encourages the adoption of those prospective adoptees who are frequently referred to as hard-to-place children. Under the applicable federal statute, in order for a state to qualify for federal payments for foster care and adoption assistance, the state must provide financial assistance to adoptive parents of children with special needs.[75] For a child to be considered a child with special needs, the State must determine, among other things,

> that there exists with respect to the child a specific factor or condition (such as his ethnic background, age or membership in a minority or sibling group, or the presence of factors such as medical conditions or physical, mental or emotional handicaps) because of which it is reasonable to conclude that such child cannot be placed with adoptive parents without providing adoption assistance . . . or medical assistance. . . .[76]

The Model Act for Adoption of Children With Special Needs,[77] published by the Department of Health and Human Services in 1981, notes in its introduction that because of barriers to adoption, thousands of children remain in institutional or foster care. The Act describes among its express purposes identification of children with special needs and removal of barriers to their adoption, and recruitment of adoptive families for such treatment.

The District of Columbia Subsidized Adoption Statute is illustrative of state legislation pursuant to the federal initiative. The statute authorizes the payment of adoption subsidies to adoptive families, defined to include single persons, for children with special needs who would otherwise in all likelihood not be adopted.[78] The statute further provides:

> The amount and duration of adoption subsidy payments may vary according to the special needs of the child, and may include maintenance costs, medical dental and surgical expenses, psychiatric and psychological expenses, and other costs necessary for his care and well-being.[79]

The New York statute authorizing subsidies for the adoption of children provides for monthly payments for the care of handicapped or hard to place

---

[75] *See* 42 U.S.C.A. §§ 670, 671, 673 (1991).

[76] *Id.* § 673(c)(2).

[77] 46 Fed. Reg. 50,022 (1981).

[78] D.C. Code § 3-115(b).

[79] *Id.* § 3-115(e).

children who have been placed for adoption or adopted.[80] The statute also permits payments for non-recurring adoption expenses of adoptive parents of a child with special needs who adopts through an authorized agency,[81] and for medical subsidies.[82]

[G] Adult Adoption

In *In re Adoption of Robert Paul P.*,[83] the New York Court of Appeals affirmed a judgment denying the petition of a 57-year-old homosexual male to adopt a 50-year-old male with whom he shared a relationship. The Court discussed at some length the purpose of adult adoptions. The court began with the fundamental proposition that in New York, as in other states, the parent and child relationship may be established by law under an adoption statute, resulting in the adopted child enjoying all the incidents of that relationship as would a natural child, despite the absence of blood ties.

The court firmly rejected the use of adoption as a "quasi-matrimonial vehicle to provide nonmarried partners with a legal imprimatur for their sexual relationship, be it heterosexual or homosexual."[84] Among the reasons an adult adoption would be appropriate in the eye of the Court are perpetuation of the family name by a childless individual, ties of filial affection, or the desire of a stepparent to adopt the adult children of a spouse.[85]

Cases concerning adult adoption most often involve the effect of such an adoption on the disposition of estates, and typically require a parent and child relationship when approving the adoption of an adult.[86]

[H] Equitable Adoption

Equitable adoption does not involve a lawful adoption pursuant to state statute resulting in a parent and child relationship for all purposes. One commentary has provided the following serviceable definition: "Equitable adoption is the term used to describe the willingness of courts to recognize the inheritance rights of children who have been taken into the home of the deceased who cares for and treats the child as if he or she were adopted."[87] In *Kisamore v. Coakley,*[88] the Supreme Court of Appeals of

---

[80] N.Y. Soc. Serv. Law § 453 (McKinney 1992).

[81] *Id.* § 453-a.

[82] *Id.* § 454.

[83] 471 N.E.2d 424 (N.Y. 1984).

[84] *Id.* at 425.

[85] *See generally* Wadlington, *Adoption of Adults: A Family Law Anomaly*, 54 Cornell L. Rev. 566 (1969).

[86] *See, e.g., In re Adoption of John A.S.*, 1992 WL 361416 (Del. Fam. Ct. 1992); *In re Adoption of an Adult by G.V.C.*, 581 A.2d 123 (N.J. Super. Ct. Ch. Div. 1990).

[87] P. Swisher, H. Miller, & W. Weston, Family Law: Cases, Materials and Problems 616 (1990). For an in-depth exploration of the concept of equitable adoption, see Note, *They Took Him into Their Home and Called Him Fred*, 58 Va. L. Rev.727 (1972). *See also Long v. Willey*, 391 S.W.2d 301 (Mo. 1965).

[88] 437 S.E. 2d 585 (W. Va. 1993).

West Virginia held that the appellant had failed to meet the criteria for equitable adoption and was, therefore, not an heir to an estate. In the course of its decision, the court pointed out that equitable adoption requires proof by clear and convincing evidence that the claimant's status, except for lack of a formal adoption order, is identical to that of a formally adopted child.

[I]   Effects of Adoption

Simply stated, the general rule today is that the law will treat the parent and child relationship between an adopted child and the adoptive parent precisely as it would if the child were the parent's natural or birth child. In *In re Estate of Rose Zestrow*,[89] the Wisconsin Supreme Court reviewed the provisions of a Wisconsin adoption statute, which, in language typical of such statutes, provided:

> After the order of adoption is entered the relationship of parent and child between the adopted person and his natural parents, unless the natural parent is the spouse of the adoptive parent, shall be completely altered and all the rights, duties and other legal consequences of the relationship shall cease to exist.[90]

The court read the language literally as changing the status of an adopted person, but held that it did not bar a testatrix from transferring property by will to her grandnephews, as she had intended. In *In re Estate of Holt*,[91] a testamentary disposition was not involved, but the issue was whether an adopted child could inherit from her natural grandmother. The Supreme Court of New Mexico held that because the child's natural father had predeceased the grandmother, and the adoption by her stepfather occurred prior to the grandmother's death, the adopted child could not inherit from her grandmother. Similarly, in *In re Estate of Carlson*,[92] the Court of Appeals of Minnesota held that two brothers who were adopted after the death of their parents could not inherit from the estate of a third brother who died intestate and who was not adopted, because the adoption statute cut off inheritance rights of blood relatives.

---

[89] 166 N.W.2d 251 (Wis. 1969).

[90] *Id.* at 253.

[91] 622 P.2d 1032 (N.M. 1981).

[92] 457 N.W.2d 789 (Minn 1990).

Chapter 7

UNIQUE FAMILY ISSUES

§ 7.01 Introduction

Once a family unit has been established, some troubling legal questions still remain concerning the proper roles of, and interrelationships between, the parents and the state in regulating the supervision, education, medical care, and upbringing of children and providing for their general welfare. For example, assuming that there is a constitutionally protected right of privacy within the American family, should the parents always serve as the ultimate authority for their child's welfare, or at some point must the State intervene when this parenting function is perceived to be inadequate or harmful to the child?[1] And assuming that the State does in fact have a legitimate role in protecting the best interests of the child, at what point should this state interest be manifested, and at what point should this state interest be limited or curtailed?[2] Additionally, what are the legal rights of an abused spouse or child, and what legal remedies are available to a family member who has been injured through the tortious or criminal action of another family member?

This Chapter will analyze these important family law issues, exploring the interplay and tensions involving parental authority to raise children, children's rights as individuals, and state responsibility to protect spouses and children.[3]

---

[1] *See, e.g., Darryl H. v. Coler*, 801 F.2d 893 (7th Cir. 1986), where the court was attempting to resolve and reconcile the "fundamental constitutional values of the privacy rights of the child; the privacy rights of the family in the important area of childrearing; and the obligation and right of responsible government to deal effectively with the stark reality of child abuse in our society."

[2] *See, e.g.*, L. Tribe, American Constitutional Law 988 (1978) ("Once the State, whether acting through its courts or otherwise, has "liberated" the child-and the adult-from the shackles of such intermediate groups as the family, what is to defend the individual against the combined tyranny of the State and her own alienation?"); *see also* McCarthy, *Parents, Children, and the Courts: The Confused Constitutional Status and Meaning of Parental Rights*, 22 Ga. L. Rev. 975 (1988).

[3] *See also* Woodhouse, *Who Owns the Child? Meyer and Pierce and the Child as Property*, 33 Wm. & Mary L. Rev. 995 (1992) (arguing that it makes sense to locate the parental right to control children in the liberty clause of the Fourteenth Amendment only if children are viewed as the "property" of their parents); and Scott & Scott, *Parents as Fiduciaries*, 81 Va. L. Rev. 2401 (1995) (arguing that granting parents broad authority over their children is justified as a way of encouraging parents to invest the effort necessary to fulfill the obligations of child-rearing).

§ 7.02   Intrafamily Tort Immunity and Liability

[A]   Interspousal Tort Actions

Under the early common law, because a wife's legal identity merged into that of her husband under a "unity of person" doctrine,[4] neither spouse was able to bring a tort action against the other. By the late 1800s, however, all states had adopted the Married Women's Property Acts,[5] which allowed the wife to bring an action against her husband for tortious acts against her *property* interests, including recoveries based upon wrongful conversion, trespass to land, fraud, and negligent injury to her property. And because this "unity of person" doctrine was abolished for property interests under the Married Women's Property Acts, the husband also possessed these same property rights against his wife.[6]

The Married Women's Property Acts, however, did *not* destroy the spousal immunity doctrine when it came to *personal*, rather than property, torts.[7] The rationale for this interspousal tort immunity doctrine generally was based upon two major premises: (1) that such an action would destroy the "peace and harmony" of the marital home; and (2) that such an action might encourage fraud and collusion between the spouses when the tort injury was covered by insurance.[8]

However, over the past three decades, the interspousal tort immunity doctrine has come under increasing criticism from various commentators,[9] largely based upon an inflexible judicial application of the interspousal tort immunity rule to the detriment of many injured spouses.[10] A majority of

---

[4] *See, e.g.,* 1 Blackstone, Commentaries on the Law of England 445 (3d ed. 1884).

[5] *See supra,* § 3.02[B], 4.03.

[6] *See, e.g., Hubbard v. Ruff,* 103 S.E.2d 134 (Ga. Ct. App. 1958); *Vigilant Ins. Co. v. Bennett,* 89 S.E.2d 69 (Va. 1955). *See generally* W. Keeton, Prosser & Keeton on Torts 900–904 (5th ed. 1984).

[7] *See, e.g., Thompson v. Thompson,* 218 U.S. 611 (1910). A criminal act, however, by one spouse against the other spouse or children, may still be prosecuted as long as the action is criminal rather than civil in nature. *See, e.g., Goode v. Martinis,* 361 P.2d 941 (Wash. 1961).

[8] *See, e.g., Bonkowsky v. Bonkowsky,* 431 N.E.2d 998 (Ohio 1982), *cert. denied,* 457 U.S. 1135 (1982); *Robeson v. International Indem. Co.,* 282 S.E.2d 896 (Ga. 1981); *Shoemake v. Shoemake,* 407 S.E.2d 134 (Ga. Ct. App. 1991). *See generally* Moore, *The Case for Retention of Interspousal Tort Immunity,* 7 Ohio N.U. L. Rev. 943 (1980).

[9] *See, e.g.,* 1 Clark, Law of Domestic Relations 631–639, 632 (2d ed. 1987) ("the kindest thing to be said about these policy arguments is that they are frivolous"); *see also* Johnson, *Interspousal Tort Immunity: The Rule Becoming the Exception,* 27 Howard L.J. 995 (1984); Barker, *Spousal Immunity and Domestic Torts,* 15 Am. J. Trial Advoc. 625 (1992).

[10] For example, in *Counts v. Counts,* 266 S.E.2d 895 (Va. 1980), a husband was seriously injured in an unsuccessful murder-for-hire scheme instituted by his wife. His tort action against the wife, however, was barred by the interspousal tort immunity doctrine since it "could well destroy the marriage." Negative reaction to the *Counts* case, and to interspousal tort immunity in general, culminated a year later in a Virginia statute that abolished the doctrine completely. Va. Code Ann. § 8.01-220.1 (Michie 1981). However, various courts in other states have held that a spouse may still maintain a tort action against the other spouse for damages arising out of an outrageous intentional act, even though a simple negligence action would still be barred under the state's interspousal tort immunity doctrine. *See, e.g., Waite v. Waite,* 593 So. 2d 222 (Fla. Dist. Ct. App. 1991); *Lusby v. Lusby,* 390 A.2d 77 (Md. 1978); *Windauer v. O'Conner,* 485 P.2d 1157 (Ariz. 1971); *see also* Note, 13 St. Mary's L.J. 443 (1981).

jurisdictions today therefore have abrogated the doctrine of interspousal tort immunity, either wholly or partially, especially when applied to motor vehicle accidents.[11]

Interspousal tort liability actions have also been brought for the infliction of sexually transmitted diseases[12] and for victims of domestic violence.[13] Courts and commentators, however, are divided on the desirability of recognizing tort claims based on the infliction of emotional distress during marriage and other intimate relationships.[14]

The abolition of interspousal tort immunity in many states has prompted many insurance companies to insert a "family exclusion clause" in their liability insurance policies, with particular application to automobile and homeowner's liability insurance. These "family exclusion clauses" generally provide that liability insurance coverage will *not* apply to any member of the insured's family living in the same household.[15]

Some courts have held that such a "family exclusion clause" is a valid exercise of an insurer's legitimate contractual right to limit its liability, and therefore is not contrary to state public policy.[16] Other courts, however, have held that a "family exclusion clause" is contrary to public policy since all victims of negligence, including family members, should be able to recover from a tortfeasor.[17]

---

[11] *See, e.g., Asplin v. Amica Mut. Ins. Co.*, 394 A.2d 1353 (R.I. 1978) (the rule is abrogated for motor vehicle torts; and when the death of either spouse occurs, there is no longer any family harmony to disrupt); *see also Merenoff v. Merenoff*, 388 A.2d 951 (N.J. 1978) (there is no danger of domestic tranquility being disturbed by a negligence action brought by one spouse against the other spouse who carries indemnity insurance, and the courts already have the means to deal with the real or asserted spectre of insurance fraud in marital tort claims without having to ban the claim entirely); *Burns v. Burns*, 518 So. 2d 1205 (Miss. 1988) (interspousal tort immunity abolished in a tort suit arising out of damages for husband beating wife); *Boblitz v. Boblitz*, 462 A.2d 506 (Md.1983) (this case includes a detailed appendix on how all 50 states have held regarding interspousal tort immunity actions). *See generally* Tobias, *Interspousal Tort Immunity in America*, 23 Ga. L. Rev. 359 (1989); Annot., 92 A.L.R.3d 901 (1979).

[12] *See generally* Oyler, *Interspousal Tort Liability for Infliction of a Sexually Transmitted Disease*, 29 J. Fam. L.519 (1990–1991); Note, *To Have and to Hold: The Tort Liability for the Interspousal Transmission of Aids*, 23 New Eng. L. Rev. 887 (1988–1989); Note, *Homeowner's Insurance Coverage of Negligent Transmission of Sexually Transmitted Disease*, 31 B.C.L. Rev. 1209 (1990).

[13] *See generally* Scherer, *Tort Remedies for Victims of Domestic Abuse*, 43 S.C.L. Rev. 543 (1992). *See also infra* § 6.08.

[14] *See, e.g., Twyman v.* Twyman, 855 S.W.2d 619 (Tex. 1993). See *also* Cole, *Intentional Infliction of Emotional Distress Among Family Members*, 61 Denver L.J. 553 (1984) (arguing in favor of recognizing tort claims for outrageous marital conduct that leads to emotional injury; and Ellman & Sugarman, *Spousal Emotional Abuse as a Tort?* 55 Md. L. Rev. 1268 (1996) (exploring arguments pro and con for recognition of such a tort action, and arguing that spousal abuse not be recognized as a tort unless the abusive behavior is also criminal). *See generally* Spector, *Marital Torts: The Current Legal Landscape*, 33 Fam. L. Q. 745 (1999).

[15] *See generally* Ashdown, *Intrafamily Immunity, Pure Compensation, and the Family Exclusion Clause*, 60 Iowa L. Rev. 239 (1974).

[16] *See, e.g., Linehan v. Alkabbaz*, 398 So. 2d 989 (Fla. Dist. Ct. App. 1981); *Allstate Ins. Co. v. Boles*, 481 N.E.2d 1096 (Ind. 1985); *see also* Annot., 46 A.L.R.3d 1024 (1972).

[17] *See, e.g., Jennings v. GEICO*, 488 A.2d 166 (Md. 1985); *Bishop v. Allstate Ins. Co.*, 623 S.W.2d 865 (Ky. 1981); *see also* Annot., 52 A.L.R. 4th 18 (1987).

If, for example, a husband and wife are domiciled in one state, which has abolished interspousal tort immunity, and they are involved in an automobile accident caused by the negligence of one spouse and the other spouse is seriously injured in a state that still recognizes the doctrine of interspousal tort immunity, complex choice of law issues may arise. Under traditional conflict of laws principles, whether one spouse can sue the other in tort is generally determined by the law of the state where the injury took place,[18] and a minority of states still follow this rule.[19] A majority of states, however, in determining whether or not the spouses can sue one another in tort, often apply the law of the state of the parties' domicile or the state which has the "most significant relationship" with the action.[20]

[B] Child and Parent Tort Actions

Although the early common law recognized a "unity of identity" doctrine between a husband and wife, no such doctrine applied to a parent and minor child. Accordingly, a child—emancipated or not—could sue his or her parent for breach of contract or for torts affecting property, and an emancipated child could sue his or her parent for personal injury torts.[21]

Personal injury tort actions brought by unemancipated minors, however, historically have been subject to a parent-child tort immunity doctrine which was recognized throughout the United States beginning in the late 1800s, and which was based on the rationale of preserving family harmony. But, once again, this parent-child tort immunity doctrine tended to be inflexibly applied by the courts. For example, in the 1905 case of *Roller v. State*,[22] the Washington Supreme Court held that a daughter could not sue her father for rape under the doctrine of the parent-child tort immunity, since such a suit would "impair the family harmony."

As a result of many subsequent court decisions similar to the *Roller* case, increasing criticism of the parent-child tort immunity doctrine was expressed by various courts[23] and commentators.[24] Accordingly, a growing number of jurisdictions today have abolished or greatly limited the parent-child tort

---

[18] Restatement of Conflict of Laws § 384 (1934).

[19] *See, e.g., McMillan v. McMillan*, 253 S.E.2d 662 (Va. 1979); *Yates v. Lowe*, 348 S.E.2d 113 (Ga. Ct. App. 1986). *See generally* Annot., 96 A.L.R.2d 973 (1964) and Later Case Service.

[20] *See* Restatement (Second) of Conflict of Laws, §§ 145, 169 (1971); *see also Henry v. Henry*, 229 S.E.2d 158 (N.C. 1976); *Brooks v. Sturiano*, 497 So.2d 976 (Fla. Dist. Ct. App. 1986).

[21] *See, e.g.*, W. Keeton, Prosser & Keeton on Torts 904–911 (5th ed. 1984); McCurdy, *Torts Between Parent and Child*, 5 Vill. L. Rev. 521 (1960); Annot., 41 A.L.R.3d 904 (1972).

[22] 79 P. 788 (Wash. 1905).

[23] *See, e.g., Karam v. Allstate Ins. Co.*, 436 N.E.2d 1014 (Ohio 1982), *cert. denied*, 459 U.S. 1070 (1982); *Rousey v. Rousey*, 528 A.2d 416 (D.C. 1987).

[24] *See, e.g.*, Hollister, *Parent-Child Immunity: A Doctrine in Search of Justification*, 50 Fordham L. Rev. 489 (1981-82); Note, *The Parental Tort Immunity Doctrine Applied to Wrongful Death Actions: A Rule Without Reason*, 13 S. Ill. U. L.J. 175 (1988); Dean, *It's Time to Abolish North Carolina's Parent-Child Immunity, But Who's Going to Do It?* 68 N.C. L.Rev. 1317 (1990); Haley, *The Parental Tort Immunity Doctrine: Is It A Defensible Defense?* 30 U. Rich. L. Rev. 575 (1996).

immunity doctrine,[25] although a significant minority of states still adhere to the doctrine, at least in the context of negligence actions.[26]

Even those states that have abolished or limited the parent-child tort immunity doctrine have done so in varying degrees. Some states, for example, have totally abolished the parent-child tort immunity doctrine in favor of a "reasonable parent" standard.[27] Other states maintain a distinction between torts occurring in the exercise of parental discretion and authority, where the parent-child immunity doctrine would continue to exist, and other kinds of tortious parental activity which would not be immune to a tort suit by the child.[28] For example, if a child is injured in an automobile accident caused by the negligence of a parent, because such a negligent act does *not* involve parental discretion or authority, the parent *can* be held liable for the child's injuries.[29] However, if the child is injured while the parent is exercising parental discretion and authority, even in the realm of a parent's negligent supervision of the child, then the parent would *not* be held liable for the child's injuries.[30] Some courts still recognizing the parent-child tort immunity doctrine have nevertheless found that when parental conduct is so outrageous, egregious, and intentional, as going far beyond mere negligence, a tort action by the child against the parent is justified and should be actionable.[31]

Whether the parent-child immunity doctrine applies to a grandparent or other person acting *in loco parentis* usually depends on whether or not there was a true *in loco parentis* relationship,[32] or whether the defendants were only temporary custodians of the child.[33]

If a child is injured by the negligence of a parent while the parent is acting within the course of his or her employment, and the child is barred from

---

[25] *See, e.g., Broadbent v. Broadbent,* 907 P.2d 43 (Ariz. 1995). *See generally* Annot., 6 A.L.R.4th 1066 (1981).

[26] *See, e.g., Mitchell v. Mitchell,* 598 So. 2d 801 (Ala. 1992); *Warren v. Warren,* 650 A.2d 252 (Md. 1994); *Mohorn v. Ross,* 422 S.E.2d 290 (Ga. Ct. App. 1992).

[27] *See, e.g., Armstrong v. Armstrong,* 821 S.W.2d 852 (Mo. 1991); *Rousey v. Rousey,* 528 A.2d 416 (D.C. 1987); *Gibson v. Gibson,* 479 P.2d 648 (Cal. 1971); *see also* Restatement (Second) of Torts, § 895G (1979); Note, *Defining the Parent's Duty After Rejection of Parent-Child Immunity,* 33 Vand. L. Rev. 775 (1980).

[28] *See, e.g., Holodook v. Spencer,* 324 N.E.2d 338 (N.Y. 1974).

[29] *See, e.g., Unah v. Martin,* 676 P.2d 1366 (Okla. 1984); *Ard v. Ard,* 414 So. 2d 1066 (Fla. 1982); *Black v. Solmitz,* 409 A.2d 634 (Me. 1979).

[30] *See, e.g., Haddrill v. Damon,* 386 N.W.2d 643 (Mich. Ct. App. 1986); *Wagner v. Smith,* 340 N.W.2d 255 (Iowa 1983).

[31] *See, e.g., Doe v. Holt,* 418 S.E.2d 511 (N.C. 1992) (parent-child immunity doctrine does not bar recovery for injuries suffered as a result of a parent's wilful and malicious conduct); *Calhoun v. Eagan,* 681 A.2d 609 (Md. Ct. App. 1996) (applying this exception to allow a wrongful death suit on behalf of the children against the father, based on allegations that the father deliberately or recklessly killed the children's mother).

[32] *See, e.g., Lawber v. Doil,* 547 N.E.2d 752 (Ill. App. Ct. 1989) (stepfather stood *in loco parentis* and was immune from suit); *Maddox v. Queen,* 257 S.E.2d 919 (Ga. Ct. App. 1979) (grandparents stood *in loco parentis* and were immune under the doctrine).

[33] *See, e.g., Gulledge v. Gulledge,* 367 N.E.2d 429 (Ill. App. Ct. 1977) (grandparents, as mere custodians of the child, did not come under the parent-child immunity doctrine).

suing the parent in tort under the parent-child immunity doctrine, the courts are split as to whether the child may sue the parent's employer. Some courts hold that if a child cannot sue the parent, then the child would not be able to sue the parent's employer, since the employer's liability is derivative.[34] Other courts, however, would allow a tort action against the employer based upon the doctrine of *respondent superior*, even if the parent was immune under the doctrine.[35]

The courts have been unable to reach agreement on whether or not a parent should be able to sue his or her children in tort.[36] Similarly, the courts are split as to whether minor brothers or sisters can sue each other for tortious injuries.[37]

Finally, conflict exists over whether a child may sue his or her mother for prenatal injuries brought about through the mother's negligence or other conduct. The traditional rule was that under a "unity of person" rationale, a child who was born alive did not have a cause of action for prenatal injuries.[38] However, the modern majority rule now allows a child to sue his or her mother for prenatal injuries;[39] and thus children born with drug addiction or fetal alcohol syndrome based upon the mother's prenatal actions increasingly are able to hold their mothers legally accountable.[40]

§ 7.03 Parental Discipline of a Child

A parent, or a person acting *in loco parentis*, has the legal right and authority to discipline, punish, or chastise his or her child, but such discipline or punishment cannot exceed due moderation, nor be used as a cloak for violence or malevolence on the part of the parent.[41] Thus, where a

---

[34] *See, e.g., Pullen v. Novak*, 99 N.W.2d 16 (Neb. 1959); *Sherby v. Western Bros. Trans. Co.*, 421 F.2d 1243 (4th Cir. 1970) (applying Md. law).

[35] *See, e.g., Begley v. Kohl & Madden Co.*, 254 A.2d 907 (Conn. 1969); *Littlejohn v. Jordan*, 428 S.W.2d 472 (Tex. Civ. App. 1968). *See generally* Annot., 1 A.L.R.3d 677, 699 (1965).

[36] *Compare Kirtz v. Kirtz*, 447 A.2d 492 (Md. Ct. Spec. App. 1982) *and Mauk v. Mauk*, 466 N.E.2d 166 (Ohio 1984) (as a corollary to the parent-child immunity doctrine, a parent cannot sue his or her child in tort) *with Silva v. Silva*, 446 A.2d 1013 (R.I. 1982) *and Ertl v. Ertl*, 141 N.W.2d 208 (Wis. 1966) (a parent is legally capable of suing his or her child in tort). *See also* Annot., 60 A.L.R.2d 1284 (1958) and Later Case Service.

[37] *See, e.g., Midkiff v. Midkiff*, 113 S.E.2d 857 (Va. 1960) (since an infant is generally liable for his or her own torts, it is not against public policy to permit an unemancipated minor to sue his or her minor sibling in tort). *But see Smith v. Sapienza*, 417 N.E.2d 530 (N.Y. 1981). *See also* Annot., 81 A.L.R.2d 1155 (1962) and Later Case Service.

[38] *See, e.g., Egbert v. Wenzl*, 260 N.W.2d 480 (Neb. 1977).

[39] *See, e.g., Grodin v. Grodin*, 301 N.W.2d 869 (Mich. Ct. App. 1980); *Bonte v. Bonte*, 616 A.2d 464 (N.H. 1992).

[40] *See generally* Beale, *Can I Sue Mommy? An Analysis of a Woman's Tort Liability for Prenatal Injuries to her Child Born Alive*, 21 San Diego L. Rev. 325 (1984); Oberman, *Rethinking the Problems of Pregnant Women Who Use Drugs*, 43 Hastings L.J. 505 (1992); Bopp & Gardner, *AIDS Babies, Crack Babies: Challenges to the Law*, 7 Issues L. & Med. 3 (1991). *See also infra* § 7.06.

[41] *See, e.g., Commonwealth v. Diehl*, 385 S.E.2d 228 (Va. Ct. App. 1989) (a parent becomes criminally liable for punishment to a child which exceeds due moderation, even though a parent has a right to discipline his or her child).

question is raised as to whether the parental discipline or punishment has been moderate or excessive, the trier of fact must make the ultimate determination, considering the age and conduct of the child; the nature of the child's misconduct; the means of punishment; and the damage inflicted upon the child.[42]

For example, in the case of *In re Edward C.*,[43] a California appellate court held that although the First Amendment to the United States Constitution severely limits the power of the State to interfere with parental rights in directing the upbringing of their children, nevertheless the parents' religious beliefs that God and the Bible ordained excessive discipline by beating and whipping children cannot jeopardize the health and safety of such children, nor be tolerated by the State.[44]

§ 7.04 Parental Liability for a Child's Act

Under the common law, a parent was not liable for his or her child's wrongful acts unless the child's tortious acts were authorized by the parent, such as in a vicarious master-servant relationship, or a principal-agent relationship.[45] Thus, in the absence of a state statute to the contrary, a parent would not be liable for any injury or damage inflicted upon a third party by his or her child.[46]

However, an increasing number of states have now passed specific statutes making the parents civilly liable in tort[47] if their child wilfully

---

[42] *See, e.g., Harbaugh v. Commonwealth*, 167 S.E.2d 329 (Va. 1969). *See generally* Annot., 89 A.L.R.2d 396 and Later Case Service. *See also* Strauss & Yodanis, *Corporal Punishment by Parents*, 2 U. Chi. L. School Roundtable 35, 37 (1995) (noting that most Americans believe that "a good spanking is sometimes necessary" to discipline children); and Gelles & Cornell, Intimate Violence in Families 44 (2d ed. 1990) (indicating that physical punishment is used by 84% to 97% of all parents at some time in their children's lives). Some commentators have defended the use of physical punishment by parents, arguing that such disciplinary measures are both effective and constitutionally protected. *See, e.g.,* John Rosemond, To Spank or Not to Spank 13 (1994). Other studies suggest that corporal punishment during childhood may be associated with higher levels of dysfunctional and aggressive behavior in adulthood, including adult domestic violence and physical abuse of children. *See, e.g.,* Chiancone, *Corporal Punishment: What Lawyers Need to Know*, 16 Child Law Practice 1 (1997); and Straus & Yodanis, *Corporal Punishment by Parents*, 2 U. Chi. L. Sch. Roundtable 35 (1995).

However, the distinction between reasonable physical punishment and actionable child abuse is not always so obvious. *See, e.g., In the Interest of J.P.*, 692 N.E.2d 338 (Ill. Ct. App. 1998).

[43] 178 Cal. Rptr. 694 (Cal. Ct. App. 1981).

[44] *Id.; see also infra* § 67.08[B].

[45] *See, e.g., Bell v. Hudgins*, 352 S.E.2d 332 (Va. 1987); *Lanterman v. Wilson*, 354 A.2d 432 (Md. 1976); *Ross v. Souter*, 464 P.2d 911 (N.M. 1970).

[46] *See generally* Annot., 54 A.L.R.3d 974 (1973).

[47] *See* Restatement (Second) of Torts § 316 (1979), which would hold parents liable for their own negligence, resulting in personal injury or property damage intentionally inflicted by their minor child on third parties.

causes personal injury,[48] or if their child wilfully destroys or vandalizes property,[49] up to a statutory limit.[50]

§ 7.05　Medical Care for the Child and the Spouse

The general rule with respect to medical and psychiatric care for children is that the parents ultimately decide whether medical care is to be provided for the child, and what that care is to be. This general rule, however, is not absolute. Parents still owe their minor children the legal duty of providing adequate medical care, and their failure to provide it could lead to prosecution for child abuse or manslaughter.[51]

Although parents have substantial authority to determine their child's medical care, the state under a *parens patriae* doctrine also is permitted, when the child's welfare and best interests demand it, to override certain parental decisions concerning medical care for the child. The difficult legal problem, however, is to determine at what point parental authority for the medical care of a child should cease, and at what point the state should take over the social and legal responsibility to protect the medical welfare of the child.[52]

Although most of these difficult judicial decisions are normally made on a case-by-case analysis, nevertheless there is general agreement that when the medical treatment involves little risk to the child, but a failure to provide such treatment would substantially endanger the child's life or health, then the state may step in, and a court may order such medical treatment over the parents' medical, ethical, or religious objections.[53]

---

[48] *See, e.g., Gilbert v. Floyd*, 168 S.E.2d 607 (Ga. Ct. App. 1969) (a child's malicious stabbing of a guest with a butcher knife made the parents liable under a Georgia statute). *But see Owens v. Ivey*, 525 N.Y.S.2d 508 (N.Y. City Ct., Rochester 1988) (New York's Parental Liability Act was held to be invalid on constitutional grounds as constituting a bill of attainder in an intentional assault action by the parents' daughter against another teenage girl).

[49] *See, e.g., Frost v. Taylor*, 649 S.W.2d 264 (Mo. Ct. App. 1983) (parents' 15-year-old shot and killed plaintiff's dog without provocation).

[50] *See, e.g., Buie v. Longspaugh*, 598 S.W.2d 673 (Tex. Civ. App. 1980) (the parents were liable under state statute for their son's vandalism up to $5,000 per act, for a total of $15,000). *See generally* Annot., 54 A.L.R.3d 974 (1973).

[51] *See, e.g., In the Matter of Hofbauer*, 393 N.E.2d 1009 (N.Y. 1979) (a child suffering from Hodgkin's disease was placed by the parents under the care of a physician who prescribed injections of laetrile rather than radiation or chemotherapy treatment); *Pennsylvania v. Barnhart*, 497 A.2d 616 (Pa. Super. Ct. 1985) (parents were convicted of manslaughter of their child by withholding medical treatment, despite their religious beliefs).

[52] *See generally* Vorys, *The Outer Limits of Parental Autonomy: Withholding Medical Treatment from Children*, 42 Ohio St. L.J. 813 (1981); Sdokolosky, *The Sick Child and the Reluctant Parent: A Framework for Judicial Intervention*, 20 J. Fam. L. 69 (1981).

[53] *See, e.g., Jehovah's Witnesses v. King County Hosp.*, 278 F. Supp. 488 (W.D. Wash. 1967), *aff'd*, 390 U.S. 598 (1968) (life saving blood transfusions ordered for children over the religious objections of their parents); *In re McCauley*, 565 N.E.2d 411 (Mass. 1991) (life saving blood transfusions for eight-year-old girl suffering from leukemia ordered over the religious objections of her parents); *Custody of a Minor*, 379 N.E.2d 1053 (Mass. 1978) (chemotherapy ordered for a child suffering from leukemia when the parents refused to have the child treated).

If the state does not intervene with medical treatment, and the child is seriously harmed or

On the other hand, the courts have been more reluctant to order medical treatment for a child over parental objections when the medical treatment does not involve a substantial risk to the child, or when the absence of treatment would not threaten a greater probability of harm to the child.[54] Similarly, it is unclear when, if ever, a state court should order a caesarean operation, purportedly to protect the life of the fetus, over the objections of the mother.[55]

Another legal, medical, and ethical problem involves the medical care of children who are born with serious birth defects. The law, on the books at least, makes no exception for the necessary medical treatment of a child with serious birth defects,[56] and a parent or physician who withholds such medical treatment may well risk criminal and civil sanctions.[57]

---

dies, then the parents may be held criminally responsible. *See, e.g., Walker v. Superior Court,* 763 P.2d 852 (Cal. 1988) (parents were convicted of manslaughter of their child by withholding medical treatment, despite their religious beliefs). *See also* Trescher & O'Neil, *Medical Care for Dependent Children: Manslaughter Liability for the Christian Scientist,* 109 U. Pa. L. Rev. 203 (1960); Ingram, *State Interference with Religiously Motivated Decisions on Medical Treatment,* 93 Dick. L. Rev. 41 (1988); Comment, *The Conflict Between a Parent's Right to Free Exercise of Religion versus His Child's Right to Life,* 19 Cumb. L. Rev. 585 (1989). A number of states have enacted faith healing exceptions to their criminal neglect statutes. In general, these exceptions protect parents from certain kinds of legal liability when they provide faith healing to their children in accordance with their good faith religious beliefs. However, the scope and effect of these faith healing exemptions varies significantly from state to state, especially when the child's life or health is at serious risk. *See generally* Rosato, *Putting Square Pegs in a Round Hole: Procedural Due Process and the Effect of Faith Healing Exemptions on the Prosecution of Faith Healing Parents,* 29 U.S.F. L. Rev. 43 (1994); and Monopoli, *Allocating the Costs of Parental Free Exercise: Striking a New Balance Between Sincere Religious Belief and a Child's Right to Medical Treatment,* 18 Pepperdine L. Rev. 319 (1993).

[54] *See, e.g., Commonwealth v. Barnhart,* 497 A.2d 616, 626 (Pa. Super. Ct. 1985). *See also* Annot., 52 A.L.R.3d 1118 (1973); Annot., 97 A.L.R.3d 421 (1980).

[55] *See, e.g.,* Williams, *In re A.C.: Foreshadowing the Unfortunate Expansion of Court-Ordered Caesarean Sections,* 74 Iowa L. Rev. 287 (1988); Finer, *Toward Guidelines for Compelling Caesarean Surgery: Of Rights, Responsibility, and Decisional Authenticity,* 76 Minn. L. Rev. 239 (1991).

In *In re A.C.,* 533 A.2d 611 (D.C. 1987), the lower court judge allowed a caesarian delivery of the fetus over the mother's objection, who was terminally ill *in extremis. In re A.C.* was subsequently reversed on appeal, however, because the judge did not properly apply a "substituted medical judgment test" to ascertain the mother's intent. *See also* Harmon, *Legal Fictions and the Doctrine of Substituted Judgment,* 100 Yale L.J. 1 (1990).

[56] *See generally* 29 U.S.C. § 794 (1973) (hospitals and health care programs cannot discriminate against the handicapped); 42 U.S.C. § 5103(b)(2)(k) (1984); 45 C.F.R. § 84.55 (1987).

[57] These federal statutes were largely enacted as a result of the Indiana Baby Doe case and the New York Baby Jane Doe case where the parents in both these controversial cases refused to consent to life saving medical treatment and surgery for their severely disabled newborn children. *See generally* Angell, *Handicapped Children: Baby Doe and Uncle Sam,* 309 New Eng. J. of Med. 443 (1983); Mathieu, *The Baby Doe Controversy,* 1984 Ariz. St. L.J. 605 (1984); Annas, *The Case of Baby Jane Doe: Child Abuse or Unlawful Federal Intervention?* 74 Am. J. Pub. H. 727 (1984); *see also* Shapiro, *Medical Discrimination against Children with Disabilities: A Report of the U.S. Commission on Civil Rights,* 6 Issues L. & Med. 285 (1990); Lind, *Medical Treatment Decisionmaking for Seriously Handicapped Infants: Is There a Role for the Federal Government?* 29 B.C.L. Rev. 715 (1988).

The duty of one spouse to pay the necessary medical expenses for his or her spouse is also recognized in the vast majority of states, either by state statute or under the common law doctrine of necessaries.[58]

In response to difficult questions regarding whether a state's interest in preserving life may override a competent adult's right to refuse medical treatment, a growing body of state law now allows a competent adult to refuse such medical treatment under "living will" statutes and Natural Death Acts.[59] In the absence of such legislation, uncertainty continues about the circumstances in which a spouse, parent, or other family member may remove medical life support systems from an incompetent loved one. This controversial legal, medical, and ethical dilemma continues to be debated from the earlier case involving Karen Ann Quinlan[60] to the more recent case involving Nancy Cruzan.[61]

In the *Cruzan* case, Nancy Cruzan was in a persistent vegetative state as a result of an automobile accident, and her parents sought to remove her nasogastric feeding tube and permit her to die of natural causes. In a sharply divided 4-3 decision, the Missouri Supreme Court held that a patient's right to privacy is not absolute, and the interest of the State of Missouri in preserving life could outweigh any privacy interest. In balancing these interests, and applying a clear and convincing evidence standard, the Missouri Supreme Court held that Nancy Cruzan's parents could not withdraw Nancy's food or water since they had not met Missouri's clear and convincing evidence standard that Nancy would have made such a decision herself.[62]

---

[58] *See, e.g.*, Va. Code Ann. § 55-37 (Michie 1998); *see also Mem'l Hosp. v. Hahaj*, 430 N.E.2d 412 (Ind. Ct. App. 1982); *Marshfield Clinic v. Discher*, 314 N.W.2d 326 (Wis. 1982); Annot., 20 A.L.R.4th 196 (1983). *But see Sharon Clinic v. Nelson*, 394 N.Y.S.2d 118 (N.Y. County Ct. 1977) (nontherapeutic elective abortion did not come under the doctrine of necessaries). *See also supra* § 3.10.

[59] *See, e.g., John F. Kennedy Mem'l Hosp. v. Bludworth*, 452 So. 2d 921 (Fla. 1984) (a terminally ill patient may consent to terminate extraordinary life support systems that are keeping him alive, and an incompetent person may further express this intent through a prior "living will"); *In re Conroy*, 486 A.2d 1209 (N.J. 1985) (a competent adult has the right to refuse medical treatment and be free from medical intervention even at the risk of death, and this right to an individual's self-determination, which outweighs any state interest in preserving life or safeguarding the integrity of the medical profession, should not be affected by the patient's medical condition or prognosis); *see also* Childress, *Refusal of Lifesaving Treatment by Adults*, 23 J. Fam. L. 191 (1984).

[60] *In re Quinlan*, 355 A.2d 647 (N.J. 1976), *cert. denied*, 429 U.S. 922 (1976). This case involved the parents of Karen Ann Quinlan who sought to remove extraordinary medical life support systems from their unconscious adult daughter, who was in an irreversible coma. Refusal of medical treatment may now include the removal of artificial life-prolonging devices such as a respirator or a nasogastric feeding tube. *See, e.g., Corbett v. D'Alessandro*, 487 So. 2d 368 (Fla. Dist. Ct. App. 1986).

[61] *Cruzan v. Director, Mo. Dept. of Health*, 760 S.W.2d 408 (Mo. 1988), *aff'd*, 497 U.S. 261 (1990).

[62] *Id.* The Missouri Supreme Court criticized the New Jersey *Quinlan* decision, *supra*, as allegedly "departing from previous accepted norms." *But see* Weinberg, *Whose Right is it Anyway? Individualism, Community, and the Right to Die: A Commentary on the New Jersey Experience*, 40 Hastings L.J. 119 (1988).

The United States Supreme Court affirmed *Cruzan*, but with two important qualifications. First, the Court ruled that artificial feeding is a form of medical treatment that may be terminated to fulfill a person's desire to die with dignity. Second, the Court held that Missouri's requirement that a patient's desire to have medical treatment withdrawn needed to be proved by clear and convincing evidence was not facially unconstitutional.[63] Nevertheless, the Supreme Court did not *require* a clear and convincing evidentiary standard, and in fact most states today do not apply this higher Missouri evidentiary standard to surrogate medical decisionmaking.[64]

§ 7.06   Wrongful Death, Wrongful Birth, and Wrongful Life

Under state wrongful death statutes, the surviving spouse and children of the deceased would normally qualify as the primary class of beneficiaries, and if there were none in that class, then the parents, brothers, and sisters of the deceased would qualify as the statutory beneficiaries.[65]

Regarding the term "deceased," a majority of states now recognize that a viable fetus constitutes a "person" under state wrongful death statutes.[66] The traditional common law rule, however, did not recognize a viable unborn child as a "person" under state wrongful death statutes.[67]

In a majority of states a tort remedy for "wrongful birth" is also actionable if a child is born with a severe illness, handicap, or genetic abnormality that was negligently misdiagnosed by the attending physician. The recoverable damages may include medical expenses for the child, and damages for the parents' mental distress.[68]

---

[63] *Id.*

[64] *See, e.g., In re Conroy,* 486 A.2d 1209 (N.J. 1985); *see also* Stewart, *Right to Die, But . . .* 76 A.B.A. J. 36–40 (Sept. 1990), where even legal counsel for the Missouri Attorney General's Office described the Missouri clear and convincing evidentiary rule in *Cruzan* as "an aberration," and opined that most other states will *not* follow its example. *Id.* at 40. Accordingly, the vast majority of states have now enacted important surrogate medical decision making statutes in this area utilizing a preponderance of the evidence test, rather than a clear and convincing evidence standard. *See generally* Symposium, *Cruzan and the Right to Die,* 25 Ga. L. Rev. 1253 (1991); Grant & Cleaver, *Cruzan and the Looming Debate over Active Euthanasia,* 2 Md. J. Contemp. Legal Issues 99 (1991); Peters, *The State's Interest in the Preservation of Life: From Quinlan to Cruzan,* 50 Ohio St. L.J. 891 (1989); Fentiman, *A New Framework for Substitute Decision Making for Incompetent, Incurably Ill Adults,* 57 Geo. Wash. L. Rev. 801 (1989).

[65] *See generally* 3 M. Minzer, et al., Damages in Tort Actions, chs. 20, 22 (1981); Speiser, Recovery for Wrongful Death (2d ed. 1975). *See also* Annot., 95 A.L.R.2d 585 and Later Case Service; 13 A.L.R.4th 1060.

[66] *See generally* Starczewski, *Wrongful Death of a Fetus: Does a Cause of Action Arise When There is no Live Birth?* 31 Villanova L. Rev. 669 (1986); Annot., 84 A.L.R. 3d 411.

[67] *See, e.g., Lawrence v. Craven Tire Co.,* 169 S.E.2d 440 (Va. 1969); Note, 4 U. Rich. L. Rev. 322 (1970). *See also supra* § 5.05[A].

[68] *See, e.g., Procanik v. Cillo,* 478 A.2d 755 (N.J. 1985) (In this case a child was born with congenital birth defects caused by rubella, which had not been properly diagnosed by the physician. The claim of the parents for extraordinary medical care and emotional distress was found to be actionable.); *Naccash v. Burger,* 290 S.E.2d 825 (Va. 1982) (Medical damages, and damages for the parents' emotional distress, were actionable against a physician who had negligently failed to discover that the fetus was affected with Tay-Sachs disease.).

Some states have imposed liability for "wrongful life."[69] For example, if a doctor negligently performs a voluntary sterilization,[70] such as a vasectomy on the husband or a salpingectomy or tubal ligation on the wife, and the result is a healthy, bouncing baby, the doctor may be liable for negligence.

In some states, such "wrongful life" damages have included the cost of raising the healthy child until he or she reaches the age of majority.[71] Other states, however, have held that these damages are generally limited only to medical expenses for the child and emotional distress damages for the parents, and would *not* include the cost of raising a healthy child until the age of majority, under the dual rationale that healthy children are a foreseeable part of most families, and the extent of such a third party support obligation cannot be reasonably ascertained.[72]

§ 7.07 Regulation of a Child's Education

The conflicting interests of parents, their children, and the state are very much in evidence with compulsory education laws, which have been enacted in all states, and which require children to be sent to school, usually between the ages of five and seventeen.[73] Generally, these state compulsory education statutes require that a minor child attend a public school or be provided with appropriate equivalent education, such as a state approved private school[74] or approved home schooling instruction.[75]

See generally Note, *Birth Related Torts: Can They Fit the Malpractice Mold?* 56 Mo. L. Rev. 175 (1991); Note, *The Question of Prospective Damage Claims for Genetic Injury in Wrongful Life Cases*, 23 Ind. L. Rev. 753 (1990); 3 M. Minzer, et al., Damages in Tort Actions, ch. 18 (1981).

[69] Where "wrongful birth" cases normally involve children who are born with a severe illness or handicap that has been negligently misdiagnosed by a physician, "wrongful life" cases normally involve the negligent birth of a healthy child.

[70] See also supra § 5.06.

[71] See, e.g., Sherlock v. Stillwater Clinic, 260 N.W.2d 169 (Minn. 1977). For other "wrongful life" cases that were held to be actionable, see *Turpin v. Sortini*, 643 P.2d 954 (Cal. 1982); *Harbeson v. Parke-Davis*, 656 P.2d 483 (Wash. 1983). See also Kelly, *The Rightful Position in "Wrongful Life" Actions*, 42 Hastings L.J. 505 (1991); Tucker, *Wrongful Life: A New Generation*, 27 J. Fam. L. 673 (1989); 3 M. Minzer, et al., Damages in Tort Actions, ch. 18 (1981).

[72] See, e.g., Berman v. Allan, 404 A.2d 8 (N.J. 1979); *Miller v. Johnson*, 343 S.E.2d 301 (Va. 1986). See generally Tucker, *Wrongful Life: A New Generation*, 27 J. Fam. L. 673 (1989); Bopp, Bostrom & McKinney, *The "Rights" and "Wrongs" of Wrongful Birth and Wrongful Life: A Jurisprudential Analysis of Birth Related Torts*, 27 Duq. L. Rev. 461 (1989); Roberts, *Distinguishing "Wrongful" from "Rightful" Life*, 6 J. Contemp. Health L. & Policy 59 (1990); Berenson, *The Wrongful Life Claim*, 64 Tulane L. Rev. 895 (1990).

[73] See generally Van Geel, The Courts and American Education Law (1987).

[74] In *Pierce v. Society of Sisters*, 268 U.S. 510, 534 (1925), the Supreme Court ruled that a state cannot compel all its students to be educated in public schools. Nevertheless, it did recognize "the power of the state reasonably to regulate all schools, to inspect, supervise, and examine them, their teachers and pupils; [and] to require that all children of proper age attend some school. . . ."

[75] See generally Burgess, *The Constitutionality of Home Education Statutes*, 55 UMKC L. Rev. 69 (1986–87); Knight, *The Case for Allowing Home Education*, 18 Tex. Tech L. Rev. 1261

Noncompliance with state compulsory education laws may lead to the filing of misdemeanor charges against the parents and the initiation of juvenile court proceedings against the children for their truancy.[76]

A related problem some courts have faced is that of parents attempting to exempt their children from compulsory state education laws for religious reasons, citing *Wisconsin v. Yoder*[77] as their authority. However, most courts have read and distinguished the *Yoder* case narrowly, as applying only to Amish children and other self-contained religious communities of long standing.[78]

Another legal issue addressed by the courts has been the issue of corporal punishment in the schools. For example, in *Ingraham v. Wright*,[79] the Supreme Court held that the paddling of a Florida junior high school student did not constitute cruel or unusual punishment, and the imposition of reasonably necessary corporal punishment for discipline and classroom control was not tortious, even without the consent of the child's parents. Moreover, notice or a hearing prior to any corporal punishment was not required under *Ingraham*.[80] However, if the corporeal punishment is so unnecessary, malicious, or atrocious as to amount to a brutal abuse of power, then the student may be able to recover for violation of his or her civil rights under 42 U.S.C. § 1983, and for violation of his or her substantive due process rights.[81]

Student free expression and school dress codes have also constituted a legal issue. For example, in *Tinker v. Des Moines Independent School*

(1987). As to whether or not parents have a constitutionally protected right to educate their children at home, the courts have reached varying conclusions. *Compare Mazaenic v. North Judson-San Pierre School Corp.*, 614 F. Supp. 1152, 1160 (N.D. Ind. 1985) *affirmed* 798 F.2d 230 (7th Cir. 1986) (holding that parents have "a constitutional right to educate [their] children in an educationally proper home environment") *with Null v. Board of Educ.*, 815 F.Supp. 937, 939–940 (S.D. W. Va. 1993) (holding that parents do *not* have a fundamental constitutional right to direct their children's education, but only a general liberty interest subject to reasonable state regulation). Today, however, all 50 states now allow home schooling, and the number of children educated at home has increased significantly over the past decade. *See* Likasik, *The Latest Home Education Challenge: The Relationship Between Home Schools and Public Schools*, 74 N.C. L. Rev. 1913 (1996). *See also* MacMullan, *The Constitutionality of State Home School Statutes*, 39 Vill. L. Rev. 1309 (1994) (discussing various types of state home schooling regulations).

[76] *See generally* 1 H. Clark, Law of Domestic Relations 571–580 (2d ed. 1987).

[77] 406 U.S. 205 (1972). In *Yoder*, the Supreme Court exempted Amish children from Wisconsin's compulsory education laws because post-eighth-grade education violated Amish religious tenants.

[78] *See, e.g., Duro v. District Attorney*, 712 F.2d 96 (4th Cir. 1983); *see also Burrow v. State*, 669 S.W.2d 441 (Ark. 1984); *State v. Morrow*, 343 N.W.2d 903 (Neb. 1984). State approved home schooling, however, is legally recognized in all 50 states. *See* footnote 75 supra.

[79] 430 U.S. 651 (1977).

[80] *Id.*; *see also* Note, *Ingraham v. Wright: The Supreme Court's Whipping Boy*, 78 Colum. L. Rev. 75 (1978).

[81] *See, e.g., Hall v. Tawney*, 621 F.2d 607 (4th Cir. 1980) (West Virginia student was severely paddled and subsequently hospitalized with permanent injuries to her lower back and spine). Corporal punishment of less severity that is still unreasonable may also result in a tort action by the student against the school officials for personal injuries. *See generally* M. McCarthy & N. Cambrone-McCabe, Public School Law: Teachers' and Students' Rights (3d ed. 1992).

District,[82] which involved children who wore black armbands to school in protest of the Vietnam War, the Supreme Court stated "It can hardly be argued that either students or teachers shed their constitutional rights to freedom of speech or expression at the schoolhouse gate."[83] Nevertheless, the courts have been hopelessly divided on how much proof the school system must demonstrate in order to uphold school dress codes governing student grooming policies and type of permitted dress.[84]

Search and seizure issues involving public schools have drawn increased attention in recent years, reflecting the unfortunate and pervasive problems of illegal drugs, weapons, and alcohol on school grounds. In several cases, students have asserted that warrantless searches conducted by school officials impaired their Fourth Amendment constitutional rights. However, in *New Jersey v. T.L.O.*,[85] the Supreme Court held that although the Fourth Amendment's prohibition against unreasonable search and seizures applied to school officials, nevertheless the school officials' substantial interest in maintaining discipline required an "easing" of warrant and probable cause requirements that are normally imposed on other public officials. Thus, the Court in *T.L.O.* held that the legality of school searches should depend on the "reasonableness, under all the circumstances, of the search" which is based upon a two-prong test: (1) Are there reasonable grounds for suspecting that the search will turn up evidence that the student has violated, or is violating, either the law or the rules of the school? and (2) Are the measures adopted reasonably related to the objectives of the search and not excessively intrusive in light of the age and sex of the student and the nature of the infraction?[86]

With respect to expulsion and suspension from school, the Supreme Court in *Goss v. Lopez*[87] held that minimum due process requirements must be met before a student can be suspended from school, even for a short period of time. The Court recognized that a student's state-created property right to an education is protected by the Fourteenth Amendment and cannot be impaired unless the student has notice of the charges and an opportunity to refute them.[88] *A fortiori* these same procedural safeguards should apply when a student is expelled from school.[89]

---

[82] 393 U.S. 503 (1969).

[83] *Id.* at 506 (1969).

[84] *Compare Massie v. Henry*, 455 F.2d 779 (4th Cir. 1972) *and Breen v. Kahl*, 419 F.2d 1034 (7th Cir. 1969) (dress codes held unconstitutional) *with Olff v. E. Side Union High Sch. Dist.*, 445 F.2d 932 (9th Cir. 1971) *and Jackson v. Dorrier*, 424 F.2d 213 (6th Cir. 1970) (dress codes held constitutional). The Supreme Court, wisely or unwisely, refused to grant certiorari in any of these cases.

[85] 469 U.S. 325 (1985).

[86] *Id.* at 341–342 (1985); *see also* M. McCarthy & N. Cambron-McCabe, Public School Law: Teachers' and Students' Rights (3d ed. 1992).

[87] 419 U.S. 565 (1975).

[88] *Id.*

[89] *See, e.g., Dunn v. Tyler Indep. Sch. Dist.*, 460 F.2d 137 (5th Cir. 1972).

The Supreme Court also has dealt with private, as well as public, schools that attempt to discriminate based upon race, gender, or religious beliefs. [90]

Courts have been reluctant to enforce private contractual agreements dealing with the religious education of children, such as a premarital, postmarital, or separation agreement providing that the children should be raised in a particular religious faith. If both parties mutually agree to a certain religious education and upbringing for their children, then there is no legal controversy to settle. But if the custodial parent subsequently decides not to honor his or her previous agreement, then the court normally cannot compel compliance with the prior agreement. [91] Therefore, religious education decisions concerning children are modifiable based upon the child's best interests, and they are normally left to the discretion of the custodial parent and the court even if the parents have, at a prior time, contractually agreed otherwise. [92]

§ 7.08   Domestic Violence

Under the early common law, a disciplinary "rule of thumb" allowed the husband a legal right to inflict "moderate personal chastisement" upon his wife and children, provided that he used a stick no larger around than his thumb. [93]

Although this archaic and outrageous common law rule is now prohibited under state law, [94] for many years allegations of domestic violence, which now includes any intentional or reckless act that causes physical injury to another family member, were largely ignored by both law enforcement officials and the courts. [95]

One traditional response to domestic abuse by a battered spouse or child was a tort action, but such an action did not constitute a legal remedy in those jurisdictions recognizing the doctrine of intrafamily tort immunity. [96]

---

[90] *See, e.g., Runyon v. McCrary*, 427 U.S. 160 (1976) (a private school case interpreting 42 U.S.C. § 1981, which states that all persons shall have the same right to make an enforce contracts as are enjoyed by white citizens); *Mississippi Univ. for Women v. Hogan*, 458 U.S. 718 (1982) (a male student desired to attend a state-supported all-female nursing school); *Bob Jones Univ. v. United States*, 461 U.S. 574 (1983) (a sectarian private school prohibited interracial dating and marriage); *see also* T. Van Geel, The Courts and American Education Law 15–63 (1987).

[91] *See, e.g., Hackett v. Hackett*, 150 N.E.2d 431 (Ohio Ct. App. 1958); *Stanton v. Stanton*, 100 S.E.2d 289 (Ga. 1957); *Lundeen v. Struminger*, 165 S.E.2d 285 (Va. 1969).

[92] *See generally* Comment, *You get the house. I get the car. You get the kids. I get their souls. The Impact of Spiritual Custody Awards on the Free Exercise Rights of Custodial Parents*, 138 U. Pa. L. Rev. 583 (1989).

[93] 3 Va. L. Reg. 241 (1917).

[94] *See infra* §§ 7.08[A], [B].

[95] *See generally* M. Straus et al., Behind Closed Doors: Violence in the American Family (1980). *See also* Gelles & Cornell, Intimate Violence in Families 11 (2d ed. 1990) ("People are more likely to be killed, physically assaulted, hit, beaten up, slapped, or spanked in their own homes by other family members than anywhere else, or by anyone else, in our society.")

[96] *See supra* § 7.02. *See also* Scherer, *Tort Remedies for Victims of Domestic Abuse*, 43 S.C. L. Rev. 543 (1992); and Dalton, *Domestic Violence, Domestic Torts, and Divorce Constraints and Possibilities*, 31 New Eng. L. Rev. 319 (1997).

Moreover, traditional tort remedies did not provide physical protection, nor immediate relief for the battered spouse or child in the midst of repeated violent acts.

Similarly, state criminal assault statutes also failed to adequately protect the battered spouse or child due to delayed police response to domestic violence calls, as well as the unfortunate de facto policy of many law enforcement agencies to treat victims of domestic assault differently than victims of non-domestic assaults.[97]

Since the mid 1970s, however, the vast majority of states have given increased attention to the serious implications of intrafamily violence, which currently affects an estimated one-fourth of all American families. Legal responses to family violence have changed dramatically over the past two decades, and the vast majority of states have responded to this domestic violence crisis by enacting serious domestic abuse legislation which provides, among other remedies, for a temporary restraining order against the abusive spouse.[98]

According to two leading scholars:

> In the last twenty years, litigation, legislation, activism, and, to a lesser extent, social services for battered women have proliferated. In that time society has moved from virtual denial of the existence of domestic violence to a somewhat grudging acknowledgment that it is a pervasive and serious problem with legal, sociological, and psychological dimensions. Fundamental changes in civil and criminal law and practice have resulted in battered women becoming more visible in the legal system: protective restraining orders are now available in every state; many states have amended their custody statutes to provide for consideration of domestic violence in custody cases; policies for arrest of batterers are increasingly common; prosecutors' offices have begun to prosecute domestic violence cases; and public defenders have begun to recognize the relevance of battering to some of their clients' defenses.[99]

[A] Spousal Abuse

The vast majority of states have now recognized that there had been inefficient enforcement of state criminal statutes dealing with spousal abuse or abuse of an intimate partner,[100] and these states therefore have

---

[97] *See, e.g.,* Oppenlander, *Coping or Copping Out: Police Service Delivery in Domestic Disputes,* 20 Criminology 449 (1982).

[98] *See generally* Cook, *Domestic Abuse Legislation in Illinois and Other States: A Survey and Suggestions for Reform,* 1983 U. Ill. L. Rev. 261 (1983).

[99] Cahn & Meier, *Domestic Violence and Feminist Jurisprudence: Toward a New Agenda,* 4 B.U. Pub. Int. L.J. 339, 339 (1995).

[100] Although spousal abuse problems are most commonly referred to in terms of the "battered wife," husbands are also assaulted by their wives. *See, e.g.,* M. Straus et al., Behind Closed Doors: Violence in the American Family 40–44 (1980); *and* Guerin, *The Battered Husband Defense,* 7 Crim. Just. J. 153 (Fall, 1983). National crime statistics, however, indicate that more than 90% of heterosexual partner violence reported to law enforcement authorities is perpetrated by men against women. *See, e.g.,* Kurz, *Physical Assaults by Husbands: A Major*

provided alternative civil remedies to deter what is essentially criminal behavior. Unlike tort actions against the abusive spouse, these civil protective restraining orders also protect the abused spouse from further violent acts, and often provide financial support as well as physical protection.[101] Civil protection orders thus grant immediate relief to victims of domestic abuse by enjoining batterers from further violence against their partners, and usually provide further relief by evicting the batterer from a shared residence, providing for temporary relief of children, limiting the batterer's visitation rights, ordering the payment of child and spousal support, and requiring the batterer to attend mandatory counseling sessions. In addition, a number of state protection order statutes authorize the award of monetary damages to compensate victims for the economic costs of domestic violence.[102]

The purpose of this domestic abuse legislation, therefore, is to provide immediate protection to an abused spouse or other intimate partner by allowing a court to enjoin the violent spouse or partner from further assaulting, molesting, or in any other way harming the abused victim. Violations of these court orders usually result in a contempt penalty ranging from six months to one year in prison.[103]

Many victims of domestic violence are often followed and threatened by their abusers, both before and after being attacked. Until recently, the law offered little recourse for these acts of intimidation. Since 1990, however, virtually all states have enacted statutes that criminalize such stalking behavior. These state anti-stalking statutes typically define stalking as the "wilful, malicious, and repeated following and harassing of another person", and most state anti-stalking statutes require both threatening behavior and a continuing course of conduct.[104]

Social Problem in Current Controversies on Family Violence 89–90 (1993) (Gelles & Loseke, ed.). Indeed, domestic violence has been identified as the single largest cause of injury to women in the United States—more significant than automobile accidents, rapes, and muggings combined. *See, e.g.,* Stark & Flitcraft, *Spouse Abuse* in Violence in America: A Public Health Approach 123, 139 (1991) (Rosenberg & Fenley, ed.).

[101] *See, e.g.,* Ariz. Rev. Stat. Ann. § 13-3602 (1981); Cal. Civ. Code §§ 545, 547 (West 1982); Va. Code Ann. § 16.1-279.1 (Michie 1984).

[102] *See, e.g., Stelski v. Stelski,* 604 A.2d 206 (N.J. Super. Ct. 1992); *Powell v. Powell,* 547 A.2d 973 (D.C. 1988). *See also* Klein & Orloff, *Providing Legal Protection for Battered Women: An Analysis of State Statutes and Case Law,* 21 Hofstra L. Rev. 801 (1993); Finn, *Statutory Authority in the Use and Enforcement of Civil Protection Orders Against Domestic Abuse,* 23 Fam. L. Q. 43 (1989).

[103] *See generally* Cook, *Domestic Abuse Legislation,* 1983 Ill. L. Rev. 261 (1983); Waits, *The Criminal Justice System's Response to Battering: Understanding the Problem and Forging the Solutions,* 60 Wash. L. Rev. 267 (1985). *But see also* Topliffe, *Why Civil Protection Orders are Effective Remedies for Domestic Violence but Mutual Protective Orders Are Not,* 67 Ind. L.J. 1039 (1992).

[104] *See* Klein & Orloff, *Providing Legal Protection for Battered Women: An Analysis of State Statutes and Case Law,* 21 Hofstra L. Rev. 801, 874–75 (1993). Some state anti-stalking statutes have been constitutionally challenged for vagueness or First Amendment overbreath. *Compare State v. Bryan,* 910 P.2d 212 (Kan. 1996) (state anti-stalking statute struck down as unconstitutionally vague because statutory terms lacked definition and there was no objective standard) and *Commonwealth v. Kwiatkowski,* 637 N.E.2d 854 (Mass. 1994) (use of

Unfortunately, no matter what spousal abuse remedy is sought, delayed police response to domestic violence calls is still a major problem. The belief that many police agencies respond to domestic violence calls with a minimum of intervention and arrests has been confirmed in various research studies.[105] Accordingly, a number of battered women have brought lawsuits against their local police departments, and if an injured spouse can prove an administrative pattern of police neglect in domestic violence cases, then a cause of action may lie against the local police department and the municipality pursuant to 42 U.S.C. Sec. 1983, as well as a violation of the Equal Protection Clause of the Fifth and Fourteenth Amendments to the Constitution based upon the nonperformance or malperformance of official duties by the defendant police officers.[106]

As a result of this delayed or trivialized police response to domestic violence, a growing number of advocates for battered women are demanding that more states and municipalities enact mandatory arrest and no-drop prosecution policies.[107] But mandatory arrest statutes and no-drop prosecution policies have generated controversy. Supporters of mandatory arrest policies argue that, by reducing police discretion, mandatory arrest policies ensure that police officers will not trivialize domestic violence or make decisions about arrests on a discriminatory or otherwise illegitimate basis. Moreover, by physically removing the abuser, arrest provides immediate protection for the victim, affords her time away from her batterer to evaluate her situation, and further empowers her by demonstrating that she can take effective action to stop the abuse.[108] Critics of mandatory arrest laws counter, however, that under a mandatory arrest regime, a victim's call to the police is tantamount to a request for arrest, and although some victims may be encouraged to summon help because they will be assured of at least

---

statutory phrase "repeatedly follows or harasses" was unconstitutionally vague) *with State v. Culmo*, 642 A.2d 90 (Conn. 1993) (state anti-stalking statutory language was upheld as constitutional since it was "narrowly tailored to serve significant governmental interests") *and State v. McGill*, 536 N.W.2d 89 (S.D. 1995) (also rejecting a vagueness challenge to a state anti-stalking statute). *And see* Bjerregaard, *Stalking and the First Amendment: A Constitutional Analysis of State Stalking Laws*, 32 Crim. Just. Bull. 3007 (1996).

[105] *See, e.g.*, Oppenlander, *Coping or Copping Out: Police Service Delivery in Domestic Disputes*, 20 Criminology 449, 451–463 (1982); *see also* Battered Women 13 (D. Moore, ed. 1979).

[106] *See, e.g., Thurman v. City of Torrington*, 595 F. Supp. 1521 (D. Conn. 1984); *Watson v. City of Kansas City*, 857 F.2d 690 (10th Cir. 1988); *Balisteri v. Pacifica Police Dept.*, 855 F.2d 1421 (9th Cir. 1988); *see also* Eppler, *Battered Women and the Equal Protection Clause: Will the Constitution Help Them When the Police Won't?* 95 Yale L.J. 788 (1986); Schuerman, *Establishing a Tort Duty for Police Failure to Respond to Domestic Violence*, 34 Ariz. L. Rev. 355 (1992); Buzawa & Buzawa, Domestic Violence: The Criminal Response 75 (1990).

[107] *See, e.g.*, Hoctor, *Domestic Violence as a Crime Against the State: The Need for Mandatory Arrest in California*, 85 Calif. L. Rev. 643 (1997) (arguing that domestic violence is not simply an assault on a particular intimate partner, but it is an offense against the state as well); and Walsh, *Domestic Violence and the Law: The Mandatory Arrest Law: Police Reaction*, 16 Pace L. Rev. 97 (1995) (observing that many police officers also favor mandatory arrest laws because of the clarity and predictability they provide). *But see also* Corsilles, *No-Drop Policies in the Prosecution of Domestic Violence Cases: Guarantee to Action or Dangerous Solution?* 63 Fordham L. Rev. 853 (1994).

[108] *See, e.g., Developments in the Law: Legal Responses to Domestic Violence*, 106 Harv. L. Rev. 1498, 1537–38 (1993).

temporary incarceration of their abuser, other victims who do not want their batterer arrested may be discouraged from calling the police.[109] In addition, when arrest is mandatory, women who strike their batterers in self-defense risk being arrested along with— or instead of— their abusers. This problem of dual arrest may be alleviated by instructing police officers to arrest only the primary physical aggressor, but it is not always so easy to determine who that is, particularly if spousal abuse is on-going. Some criminologists also have questioned whether arrest alone actually deters future battering.[110] But other observers urge the adoption of more—rather than less— vigorous law enforcement strategies, including a commitment to arrest, prosecution, and more severe sentencing practices.[111]

Until the mid-1990s, legal efforts to combat domestic violence took place almost exclusively at the state and local level, and federal involvement was limited to providing modest amounts of funding for battered women's shelters and other victim services. In 1994, however, Congress enacted a major domestic violence initiative—the Violence Against Women Act, or VAWA.[112] VAWA contains a wide range of provisions designed to enhance the enforcement of laws against domestic violence. In particular, VAWA's funding provisions encourage states to implement mandatory arrest or pro-arrest policies, and coordinate the enforcement, prosecution, and judicial responsibility for domestic violence cases.[113]

VAWA also established several new federal causes of action. First, the Act creates a new federal crime of interstate domestic violence, which punishes a person who travels across a state line with the intent of injuring, harassing, or intimidating a spouse or intimate partner, and who commits a crime of violence in the course of, or as a result of, such interstate travel. The Act also criminalizes travel across a state line with the intent to engage in conduct that violates the provisions of a protection order, and allows a person victimized by gender-motivated violence to obtain injunctive and monetary relief, including both compensatory and punitive damages from the perpetrator of the violence.[114]

---

[109] *Id.* at 1538.

[110] *See, e.g.,* Sherman, *The Influence of Criminology on Criminal Law: Evaluating Arrests for Misdemeanor Domestic Violence*, 83 J. Crim. L. & Criminology 1 (1992) (discussing various studies).

[111] *See, e.g.,* Lehrman, *The Decontextualization of Domestic Violence*, 83 J. Crim. L. 217 (1992); and Mitchell, *Contemporary Police Practice in Domestic Violence Cases: Arresting the Abuser: Is It Enough?* 83 J. Crim. L. & Criminology 241 (1992). *But see also* Hanna, *No Right to Choose: Mandated Victim Participation in Domestic Violence Prosecutions*, 109 Harv. L. Rev. 1849 (1996).

[112] Pub. L. No. 103–322, Title IV of the Violent Crime Control and Law Enforcement Act of 1994.

[113] *See generally* Goldfarb, *The Civil Rights Remedy of the Violence Against Women Act: Legislative History, Policy Implications and Litigation Strategy*, 4 J. Law & Policy 391 (1996); Norse, *Where Violence, Relationship, and Equality Meet: The Violence Against Women's Act Civil Rights Remedy*, 11 Wis. Women's L.J. 13 (1996).

[114] *See* 42 U.S.C.A. Sec. 13701 (West 1997). *See, e.g., U.S. v. Helem*, 186 F.3d 449 (4th Cir. 1999).

A number of commentators, however, have criticized VAWA's civil rights remedy as unnecessary and inconsistent with federalism principles. Opponents of the VAWA remedies have argued that defining gender-motivated violence as a civil rights violation raises serious questions about the federal courts' capacity to manage their caseload, the need for federalization of a traditional state responsibility, and the appropriate role that federal courts should play, with specific concerns about the "overfederalization" of domestic violence crimes, and the abililty of federal law enforcement to do "the kind of on-site policing that the federal system has never been very good at".[115]

The courts apparently have agreed with this criticism of VAWA. In the case of *Brzonkala v. Virginia Polytechnical Institute and State University*,[116] where a former university student brought a VAWA action against other students who allegedly raped her, the federal Fourth Circuit Court of Appeals found that the civil rights remedy contained in the Violence Against Women Act was unconstitutional in that Congress exceeded its powers under the Commerce Clause, and Section 5 of the Fourteenth Amendment.[117] This ruling was subsequently affirmed by the United States Supreme Court in the case of *U.S. v. Morrison*.[118]

Another legal problem relating to spousal abuse is whether or not a battered wife who subsequently kills her husband should be allowed to testify regarding a "battered women's syndrome" which produces severe stress and anxiety as a defense or to mitigate her criminal sentence. Not surprisingly, the courts have split on this controversial issue.[119]

---

[115] *See, e.g.,* Brassler, *The Federalization of Domestic Violence: An Exercise in Cooperative Federalism or A Misallocation of Federal Judicial Resources?* 48 Rutgers L. Rev. 1139, 1141–42 (1996); Kadish, *The Folly of Overfederalization,* 46 Hastings L.J. 1247, 1249 (1995). Chief Justice William Rehnquist expressed similar concerns in a Congressional hearing by criticizing VAWA's private right of action as so sweeping that it "could involve the federal courts in a whole host of domestic disputes". 138 Cong. Rec. 746, 747 (March 9, 1992).

[116] *Brzonkala v. Virginia Polytechnic Inst. and State University,* 169 F.3d 820 (4th Cir. 1999) (en banc).

[117] *Id.* This decision has been criticized in that the Fourth Circuit's opinion, which concluded that gender-based violence is "too remote" both from interstate commerce and state action to give Congress authority to act under the Commerce Clause or Section Five of the Fourteenth Amendment, "rests on an unwarranted adherence to traditional notions of privacy that are damaging to women". *See, e.g.,* Goldfarb, *Violence Against Women and the Persistence of Privacy,* 61 Ohio St. L. J. 1 (2000).

[118] *U.S. v. Morrison et al.,* 120 S.Ct. 1740 (2000) (Christy Brzonkala, Petitioner). In *Morrison,* Chief Justice Rehnquist held that: (1) the Commerce Clause did not provide Congress with the authority to enact the civil remedy provision of VAWA; and (2) the enforcement clause of the Fourteenth Amendment did not provide Congress with the authority to enact the civil remedy provision of VAWA either.

[119] *Compare Hawthorne v. State,* 408 So. 2d 801 (Fla. Dist. Ct. App. 1982), *Smith v. State,* 277 S.E.2d 678 (Ga. 1981) *and State v. Amaya,* 438 A.2d 892 (Me. 1981) (all admitting such evidence) *with State v. Griffiths,* 610 P.2d 522 (Idaho 1980), *People v. White,* 414 N.E.2d 196 (Ill. App. Ct. 1980) *and State v. Thomas,* 423 N.E.2d 137 (Ohio 1981) (refusing to admit such evidence).

See also Note, *The Use of Expert Testimony in the Defense of Battered Women,* 52 Colo. L. Rev. 587 (1981); Note, *Does Wife Abuse Justify Homicide,* 24 Wayne L. Rev. 1705 (1978); Note, *The Battered Wife Kills and Tells Why,* 34 Stan. L. Rev. 615 (1982). *But see also* Dowd, *Dispelling the Myths about the "Battered Woman's Syndrome": Toward a New Understanding,* 19 Fordham Urb. L.J. 567 (1992).

Although domestic violence is difficult to measure, various studies suggest that it is an extensive problem, and one which strikes American families regardless of their economic class, race, national origin, or educational background. And most commentators agree that those domestic abuse victims who do identify themselves are only the tip of the iceberg.[120]

[B] Child Abuse

Child abuse and neglect[121] has always existed in the United States, but important articles regarding battered children, written by concerned physicians in the 1960s,[122] brought widespread public attention to this serious and continuing problem.[123] Consequently, child abuse and neglect remedial statutes and protective services now exist in all states. However, because child abuse generally occurs in the privacy of the family home, these legal remedies can only become effective when evidence of the child's mistreatment comes to light through child abuse reporting acts, which have been adopted in all fifty states.[124]

The number of child abuse and neglect reports has risen steadily since the adoption of these child abuse reporting acts. In 1995, state child protective services agencies investigated approximately two million reports alleging the maltreatment of almost three million children.[125] More than half of these reports came from professionals, including educators, law enforcement and justice officials, medical and mental health professionals, social service professionals, and child care providers. Although a majority of these reports were not substantiated, agencies determined that over one million children were the victims of substantiated child abuse or neglect.[126]

---

[120] *See generally* U.S. Commission on Civil Rights, Battered Women: Issues of Public Policy (1978); and Domestic Violence: The Changing Criminal Justice Response (Buzawa & Buzawa ed. 1992).

[121] Child abuse and neglect has been defined broadly in some states as consisting of physical injury, sexual abuse, or mistreatment. *See, e.g.*, Kansas Stat. Ann. § 38–717. Other state statutes are more specific, where child abuse is defined as any physical injury inflicted on a child by other than accidental means including, but not limited to: severe bruising, lacerations, fractured bones, burns, internal injuries, sexual intercourse on contact, or any other injury constituting great bodily harm. *See, e.g.*, Wis. Stat. Ann. § 48.981.

[122] *See* Kempe et al., *The Battered Child Syndrome*, 181 JAMA 17 (1962); *see also* C. Kempe & R. Helfer, The Battered Child (3d ed. 1980); Gelles & Cornell, Intimate Violence in Families 33–35 (2d ed. 1990).

[123] *See, e.g.*, Davis, *Child Abuse: A Pervasive Problem of the 80s*, 61 N.D.L. Rev. 193 (1985); Meyers, *The Legal Response to Child Abuse: In the Best Interests of Children?* 24 J. Fam. L.149 (1986).

[124] *Compare* Va. Code Ann. 63.1-248.3-.4 (1998) (certain enumerated persons, including physicians, nurses, teachers, and law enforcement officials must report suspected child abuse; and any other person may report suspected child abuse) *with* Md. Family Law Code Ann. 5–705 (1997) (mandatory reporting requirements are expanded to include all persons).

[125] U.S. Dept. of Health & Human Services, National Center on Child Abuse and Neglect, *Child Maltreatment 1995: Reports from the States to the National Child Abuse and Neglect Data System* (1997).

[126] *Id.*

For some children, state intervention comes too late. According to the United States Advisory Board on Child Abuse and Neglect, approximately 2.000 infants and young children die each year at the hands of their parents or caretakers, approximately 18,000 children a year are permanently disabled, and approximately 142,000 children are seriously injured as a result of parental or caretaker maltreatment.[127]

Child abuse reporting acts generally provide that certain designated persons such as physicians, nurses, teachers, social workers, child care workers, and law enforcement officials have an affirmative duty to report any suspected child abuse or neglect to the proper state authorities. Any other person who suspects that a child is abused or neglected may also make a complaint, and such a person is normally immune from any civil or criminal liability if the complaint was made in good faith.[128]

Most state child abuse statutes also provide for the establishment of child protective services. They further allow a protective service worker, law enforcement official, or physician to take a child into protective custody for a certain period of time, without prior approval of the parents, whenever the circumstances of the child are such that remaining with the parent or other person responsible for the child's care appears to present an imminent danger to the child's life or health.[129]

Once the state takes a child into protective custody, it then acquires an affirmative obligation to look after that child's safety.[130] However, in the controversial case of *DeShaney v. Winnebago County*,[131] the Supreme Court held that there was no state liability when a child was *not* taken into state custody, even though a state social worker had feared for his life if he remained with his father at home.[132]

A parent still has the legal right to discipline his or her child for misbehavior,[133] but child abuse statutes become applicable in cases of excessive punishment, and overly severe discipline.[134]

---

[127] U. S. Dept. of Health & Human Services, *A Nation's Shame: Fatal Child Abuse and Neglect in the United States* 9 (1995).

[128] *See* 1 H. Clark, Law of Domestic Relations 594–616, 597–602 (2d ed. 1987).

[129] *See, e.g., State v. Poehnelt*, 772 P.2d 304 (Ariz. 1985); *People v. Schwartz*, 678 P.2d 1000 (Colo. 1984) (holding that child abuse reporting obligations generally take precedence over the physician/patient privilege). *See also* Mosteller, *Child Abuse Reporting Laws and Attorney Client Confidence: The Reality and the Specter of Lawyer as Informant*, 42 Duke L.J. 203 (1992).

[130] *See, e.g., Vonner v. State Dep't of Pub. Welfare*, 273 So. 2d 252 (La. 1973) (state agency was held vicariously liable when a foster child was beaten to death by the foster mother); *Doe v. New York City Dep't of Soc. Services*, 709 F.2d 782 (2d Cir. 1983) (state agency was liable under 42 U.S.C. § 1983 for negligently failing to supervise plaintiff child's placement in a foster home where she was sexually abused). *But see Langton v. Maloney*, 527 F. Supp. 538 (D. Conn. 1981) (state social workers are entitled to a good faith immunity in civil rights actions if they acted in good faith, both objectively and subjectively). *See generally* Davidson, *Legal Response to Abuse of Children in Out-of-Home Care*, 7 Children's Legal Rts.J. 2 (Fall 1986).

[131] 489 U.S. 189 (1989).

[132] *Id.*

[133] *See supra* § 7.03.

[134] *See, e.g., In re Edward C.*, 178 Cal.Rptr. 694 (Cal. Ct. App. 1981) (excessive discipline

Conversely, the non-violent parent who is able to prevent an injury to his or her child, but fails to do so, may also be guilty of child abuse and neglect. For example, in *Smith v. State*,[135] a mother watched as her boyfriend drowned, kicked, and beat her 4-year-old son Eric to death because Eric could not correctly spell the word "butterfly." Although she repeatedly pleaded for the boyfriend to stop, he did not respond. At her trial on child abuse and manslaughter charges, the mother's attorney argued that she was meek, timid, and dependent on her boyfriend, and was therefore unable to stop him. However, the court held that the mother had a duty to remove her child from any situation of danger; she had knowingly placed her son in that situation, and allowed him to remain in it. The mother was therefore convicted of child abuse and manslaughter.[136]

Finally, should drug abuse or alcohol abuse by a pregnant woman constitute child abuse when the child is born addicted to drugs, or is born with a fetal alcohol syndrome? Although some courts have held that the word "child" in child abuse and child endangerment statutes does not include an unborn child or fetus,[137] other courts have found that an unborn child is indeed a "person" under the Child Abuse Act,[138] and such a child therefore has a legal right to begin life with a sound mind and body under the protection of the state.[139]

---

by beating and whipping cannot jeopardize the health or safety of a child); *State v. Campbell*, 306 N.W.2d 272 (Wis. 1981) (throwing a baby against a wall constituted child abuse, even though no injury was alleged in the complaint).

[135] 408 N.E.2d 614 (Ind. Ct. App. 1980).

[136] *Id.*; *see also State v. Williams*, 670 P.2d 122 (N.M. 1983) (even if a mother could not stop her husband from beating their daughter, that did not prevent her from seeking help, and therefore the mother could be convicted of child abuse); *Commonwealth v. Cardwell*, 515 A.2d 311 (Pa. Super. Ct. 1986) (a mother was guilty of child abuse when she was aware that the husband had sexually abused the child over a period of time, and she took only feeble and ineffective actions to protect the child).

[137] *See, e.g., Reyes v. Superior Court*, 141 Cal. Rptr. 912 (Cal. Ct. App. 1977).

[138] *See, e.g., Matter of Smith*, 492 N.Y.S.2d 331 (N.Y. Fam. Ct. 1985).

[139] *See, e.g., Matter of Baby X*, 293 N.W.2d 736 (Mich. Ct. App. 1980); *Whitner v. State*, 492 S.E.2d 777 (S.C. 1977) *cert. denied* 118 S.Ct. 1857 (1998). *See generally* Note, *The Efficacy and Constitutionality of Criminal Punishment for Maternal Substance Abuse*, 64 S. Cal. L. Rev. 1103 (1991); Note, *Prosecuting Pregnant Addicts for Dealing to the Unborn*, 33 Ariz. L. Rev. 221 (1991); Smith, Bundy & Dabiri, *Prenatal Drug Exposure: The Constitutional Implications of Three Governmental Approaches*, 2 Seton Hall Const. L.J. 53 (1991); Oberman, *Sex, Drugs, Pregnancy, and the Law: Rethinking the Problems of Pregnant Women Who Use Drugs*, 43 Hastings L.J. 505 (1992).

Some commentators have argued that the state should intervene more aggressively *before* birth, to protect a developing fetus from serious or well-defined dangers. *See, e.g.,* Chan, *S.O.S. From the Womb: A Call for New York Legislation Criminalizing Drug Use During Pregnancy*, 21 Fordham Urb. L.J. 199 (1993); Dougherty, *The Right to Begin Life With Sound Body and Mind: Fetal Patients and Their Mothers*, 63 U. Det. L. Rev. 89 (1985).

Some recent medical studies suggest that long-term effects on children of prenatal exposure to cocaine may be less devastating than previously believed. *See* Fitzgerald, *"Crack Baby" Fears May Have Been Overstated*, The Washington Post, Sept. 16, 1997 at Z10, although evidence continues to mount that maternal alcohol abuse during pregnancy poses a significant threat to the health and well-being of a developing fetus. *See, e.g.,* U.S. Department of Commerce, *Fetal Alcohol Syndrome— Diagnosis, Epidemiology, Prevention, and Treatment* (1996).

[C] Spousal Rape

Under a common law rule, which is still the law in several states, a husband who forcibly rapes his wife could not be prosecuted for that crime. The origin of this common law rule apparently dates back to unsupported dicta of Lord Hale, who was Chief Justice of the Court of King's Bench from 1671 to 1675, and who made an extrajudicial declaration that by consenting to marry, a wife grants consent to intercourse with her husband "from which she cannot retreat."[140] Some commentators, however, have suggested that the marital rape exemption was derived from the traditional definition of rape as "unlawful" carnal knowledge without consent, while intercourse between a husband and wife is not unlawful, no matter what the surrounding circumstances may be.[141]

It was not until the early 1980s, however, that the questionable reasoning behind this common law rule came under critical scrutiny by legal commentators[142] and by the courts, specifically in the landmark *Smith* and *Chretien* cases.[143] A growing number of states have followed the *Smith* and *Chretien* precedents, holding that an estranged wife can now unilaterally revoke her implied consent to marital sex when she has manifested her intent to terminate the marital relationship by living separate and apart from her husband, and when she conducts herself in a manner that establishes a *de facto* end to the marriage, even though the parties have not yet obtained a divorce.[144]

Many states, however, still prohibit prosecution of a husband for the rape of his wife while they are still living together. Approximately eleven states now permit prosecution of husbands who rape their wives during the marriage while living apart, and at least eight states have abolished the marital rape exemption entirely.[145] Most states, therefore, now recognize

---

Other commentators have expressed concern that most women who have been prosecuted for using drugs during pregnancy have been poor and women of color. *See, e.g.,* Roberts, *Representing Race: Unshackling Black Motherhood,* 95 Mich. L. Rev. 938 (1997); Roberts, *Punishing Drug Addicts Who Have Babies: Women of Color, Equality, and the Right to Privacy,* 104 Harv. L. Rev. 1419 (1991).

[140] 1 Hale, Pleas of the Crown 629 (1847).

[141] *See, e.g.,* Model Penal Code § 213.1 which still defines the act of rape as sexual intercourse between a male and a female "not his wife"; *see also* Perkins & Boyce, Criminal Law 203 (3d ed. 1982); Annot., 24 A.L.R.4th 105, 108–111 (1983).

[142] *See generally* Pracher, *The Marital Rape Exemption: A Violation of a Woman's Right to Privacy,* 11 Golden Gate U. L. Rev. 717 (1981); Bearrows, *Abolishing the Marital Exemption for Rape: A Statutory Proposal,* 1983 U. Ill. L. Rev. 201 (1983); Note, *The Marital Rape Exemption,* 27 Loyola L. Rev. 597 (1981). *See also* Annot., 24 A.L.R.4th 105 (1983).

[143] *See Smith v. State,* 426 A.2d 38 (N.J. 1981) (husband was convicted of raping his estranged wife when the parties were living separate and apart at the time of the attack); *Commonwealth v. Chretien,* 417 N.E.2d 1203 (Mass. 1981) (husband was convinced of raping his wife where the attack occurred after the wife had been granted an interlocutory divorce, but before entry of the final divorce decree).

[144] *See, e.g., People v. Brown,* 632 P.2d 1025 (Colo. 1981); *Weishaupt v. Commonwealth,* 315 S.E.2d 847 (Va. 1984); *People v. Hawkins,* 407 N.W.2d 366 (Mich. 1987).

[145] *See* Note, *Sexism and the Common Law: Spousal Rape in Virginia,* 8 Geo. Mason L. Rev. 369, 370 (1986).

sexual assault of a spouse or intimate partner as a form of domestic violence.[146]

§ 7.09   Children in Need of Supervision

Most states have enacted statutes dealing with so-called "status offenses" that normally involve children under the age of eighteen who habitually disobey and disregard their parents' lawful guidance and discipline, who habitually run away from home, or who are habitually truant from school. State legislation concerning such "ungovernable" children gives a court jurisdiction over their conduct, even though such conduct does not specifically amount to a violation of state criminal law. These state statutes dealing with children in need of supervision (CHINS) therefore provide state support for parental authority over ungovernable children in non-criminal matters.[147]

Some commentators have criticized these CHINS statutes for permitting all kinds of harmless conduct to be prosecuted by the courts; for often failing to investigate the underlying reasons behind the child's conduct; and for allowing the courts to deal ineffectively with ungovernable children, when that role ought to be the responsibility of other community organizations.[148] Most state CHINS statutes, however, have withstood constitutional attacks for their alleged vagueness and overbreadth.[149]

Generally speaking, a child under the age of 18 will be considered to be "beyond the control" of his or her parents or legal guardian, and classified as a minor in need of supervision under state CHINS statutes if he is incorrigible, a frequent runaway, or his acts posed serious hazards to himself or others.[150] For example, in *In re Snyder*,[151] evidence that a minor was adamant about refusing to return home, had established a pattern of refusing to obey her parents, and on two occasions had fled her home, was

---

Subsequently, Virginia passed a new criminal statute providing that a person is guilty of rape if, by force, threat, or intimidation, he or she has sexual intercourse with his or her spouse against the spouse's will if, at the time of the offense, the spouses were living separate and apart, or the defendant caused serious physical injury to the spouse by the use of force or violence. Va. Code Ann. § 18.2-61(B) (Michie 1986).

[146] *See generally* West, *Marital Rape, Equality, Theory and the Promise of the Fourteenth Amendment*, 42 Fla. L. Rev. 45 (1990); Schelong, *Domestic Violence and the State: Responses to and Rationales for Spousal Battering, Marital Rape, and Stalking*, 78 Marq. L. Rev. 79 (1994).

[147] *See, e.g., L.A.M. v. State*, 547 P.2d 827 (Alaska 1976) (the purpose of CHINS is to vindicate the parents' right to custody to their child, and to protect the child against the harms resulting from running away or rejecting parental supervision); *see also* Gregory, *Juvenile Court Jurisdiction Over Noncriminal Behavior*, 39 Ohio St. L.J. 242 (1978).

[148] *See, e.g.*, Rosenberg & Rosenberg, *The Legacy of the Stubborn and Rebellious Son*, 74 Mich. L. Rev. 1097 (1976); Note, *Ungovernability: The Unjustifiable Jurisdiction*, 83 Yale L.J. 1383 (1974).

[149] *See, e.g., Blonheim v. State*, 529 P.2d 1096 (Wash. 1975).

[150] *See, e.g., In re Polovchak*, 454 N.E.2d 258 (Ill. 1983) (citing examples of a frequent runaway; a minor beyond her parents' control; and a habitually truant minor).

[151] 532 P.2d 278 (Wash. 1975).

sufficient to support a finding of loss of parental power and control, and subjecting the minor to state CHINS jurisdiction. But in *In re D.J.B.*,[152] the court held that, although evidence that a minor is beyond the control of his parents may be predicated on a single act if sufficiently serious, nevertheless evidence in this case that a minor left home without parental consent was *not* of such a nature as to be indicative of the loss of parental control.[153]

If a child is found to be in need of supervision under state CHINS jurisdiction, a number of remedies are available to the court including: leaving the child with his or her parents, with or without a protective order, or an order for medical or psychiatric treatment and counseling; placing the child on probation, or under the supervision of a social worker; placing the child in the custody of a relative or another suitable person; placing the child in a foster home; placing the child with a state agency; or committing the child to a state institution.[154] However, the courts have disagreed on whether or not a child in need of supervision, as a status offender, should be placed in the same state institutions housing juvenile delinquents who have committed serious crimes.[155]

§ 7.10 Family Rights versus Individual Rights

Throughout this chapter, and throughout this text, there is ample evidence of a dramatic and fundamental change in the way our society, and our courts, view the American family. Traditionally, the American family unit was highly valued as the fundamental cornerstone of our society,[156] and the state legislatures and courts therefore were reluctant to intervene in family affairs on behalf of individual family members. Two basic reasons have been suggested for this traditional opposition to state intervention in family matters. First, many courts perceived that such intervention would be ineffective. And second, the specter of governmental intrusion should not invade the traditional right to family privacy, which had been so deeply ingrained in American social and legal consciousness.[157]

---

[152] 96 Cal. Rptr. 146 (Cal. Ct. App. 1971).

[153] *Id. And compare Matter of Morrison*, 442 N.Y.S.2d 43 (N.Y. Fam. Ct. 1981) (repeated acts, or evidence of habitual conduct, is required to come under the statute) *with In re S*, 91 Cal. Rptr. 261 (Cal. Ct. App. 1970) (a single serious act, such as a 14-year-old boy running away 600 miles from home and attempting to cross the border into Mexico, may show that a child was beyond the control of his parents).

[154] *See* 1 H. Clark, Law of Domestic Relations 621–623 (2d ed. 1987).

[155] *See, e.g., State ex rel. Harris v. Calendine*, 233 S.E.2d 318 (W. Va. 1977) (juvenile status offenders must be helped and not punished, and incarceration of status offenders in prison-like facilities along with children guilty of criminal conduct would inflict a constitutionally disproportionate penalty upon status offenders). *But see contra Vann v. Scott*, 467 F.2d 1235 (7th Cir. 1972) (applying Illinois law) (incarceration of runaway juveniles in training schools with delinquents who had committed serious crimes was not unconstitutional under a Illinois law which authorized a finding of delinquency whenever a minor violated a lawful court order).

[156] *See, e.g., Maynard v. Hill*, 125 U.S. 190, 205 (1888); *see also supra* § § 1.02[A], 1.03.

[157] *See* Schneider, *Moral Discourse and the Transformation of the American Family*, 83 Mich. L. Rev. 1803, 1837–1838 (1985).

In 1965, the United States Supreme Court held that marital privacy was a constitutional right in *Griswold v. Connecticut*,[158] but this new constitutional right to marital privacy rapidly became not just a family right, but an individual right as well.[159]

Thus, according to Professor Jane Rutherford, despite the new commitment to the constitutional right to privacy, individualism prevailed when individualism and privacy conflicted, and the courts increasingly were willing to intrude on marital privacy rights to further the goal of individual independence.[160]

Professor Carl Schneider also agrees that the rise of individual legal rights over family rights means that when the law makes moral decisions, it now transfers them to individuals rather than to families, thus sustaining the image of the family as a collection of discrete individuals rather than a unified family entity.[161] Moreover, a major problem involved with the fundamental right to privacy is that although most Americans believe that this right should exist, they do not all agree on exactly what should be included within this right. For example, Professor Robert Mnookin gives the illustration that liberals generally consider sexuality to be a private sphere, but view economics as a public sphere; whereas conservatives generally believe in private economic enterprise, yet favor regulation of such sexual matters as abortion and homosexuality.[162]

In an attempt to incorporate and synthesize the traditional view of family privacy rights with a more recent judicial emphasis on individual rights, Professor Rutherford persuasively argues for a new theory of family rights. This theory recognizes: (1) that fundamental family rights belong both to the family as a group, and to each individual family member; and (2) that when competing rights need to be accommodated, the rights of the objectively weaker party should take priority over the privacy rights of the family. These competing rights, however, would only arise in an adversarial context against other people or against the government.[163] Thus, the modern American family, as a viable legal entity, could arguably continue to coexist with, and nurture, its individual family members under its mutually supportive legal and constitutional safeguards.

The alternative to a strong and viable family structure may be grave. As Professor Laurence Tribe warns, "Once the State, whether acting

---

[158] 381 U.S. 479 (1965) (overturning a Connecticut statute prohibiting contraceptives to married couples based upon a constitutional right to marital privacy).

[159] *See, e.g., Eisenstadt v. Baird*, 405 U.S. 438 (1972) (use of contraceptives by unmarried individuals); *Roe v. Wade*, 410 U.S. 113 (1973) (a woman's right to privacy of her body in abortion decisions).

[160] Rutherford, *Beyond Individual Privacy: A New Theory of Family Rights*, 39 U. Fla. L. Rev. 627, 636–637 (1987).

[161] Schneider, *Moral Discourse and the Transformation of American Family Law*, 83 Mich. L. Rev. 1803, 1858 (1985).

[162] Mnookin, *The Public/Private Dichotomy*, 130 U. Pa. L. Rev. 1430 (1982).

[163] Rutherford, *Beyond Individual Privacy: A New Theory of Family Rights*, 39 U. Fla. L. Rev. 627, 643–644 (1987).

through its courts or otherwise, has "liberated" the [individual] from the shackles of such intermediate groups as the family, what is to defend the individual against the combined tyranny of the State and [his or] her own alienation?"[164]

---

[164] L. Tribe, American Constitutional Law 988 (1978).

Chapter 8

DIVORCE GROUNDS AND DEFENSES

§ 8.01 Introduction

Divorce, or dissolution of marriage, is the legal termination of a valid marriage. Divorce actions not only affect the parties' legal status, but involve the resolution of the essentials of marriage, including the division of marital property, the continued support of dependent family members, and the custody of children.

[A] Historical Background

Early Hebrew, Greek, and Roman societies afforded a right to divorce only to the husband, who could repudiate and divorce his wife for no reason and without legal or public intervention.[1] However, after the Punic Wars, Roman divorce law was liberalized to permit either the husband or the wife to divorce at will. During that time, marriages for limited and temporary purposes were common, often solely for economic or political reasons, and the Roman divorce rate reached alarming proportions. In 18 B.C. Caesar Augustus attempted to restrict divorce by enacting the *Lex Julia de Adulteris*, making adultery a crime and requiring a divorcing party to execute a written statement renouncing the marriage. In that period, Roman law also required a mandatory property settlement on divorce. The settlement directed the husband to return the wife's dowry or other premarital property if he divorced his wife on minor grounds or was at fault himself, which discouraged husbands from divorcing wealthy wives. On divorce, the Roman husband was usually awarded custody of any children of the marriage.[2]

Divorce law in England, and subsequently in the United States, evolved from different sources. Early English law assimilated the rather informal Anglo-Saxon custom of bride purchase, along with the husband's sole right to divorce. The extremely influential Medieval Church doctrine later replaced these customs. Under the doctrine of the Roman Catholic Church and its ecclesiastical courts, and later the Church of England, marriage was regarded as a holy sacrament that created an indissoluble bond. Accordingly, absolute divorce, also designated divorce *a vinculo matrimonii* or a divorce from the bonds of marriage, was not permitted under canon law, although influential individuals sometimes were able to have their marriages annulled based on specific marital impediments.[3] Permanent

---

[1] *See* Joyce Green, et al., Dissolution of Marriage 6–7 (1986 & Supp. 1991).

[2] *Id.* at 7–10.

[3] *Id.* at 11–14. *See generally* Lawrence Stone, The Road to Divorce: England 1530–1987 (1990).

separation, or divorce *a mensa et thoro* (divorce from bed and board), was allowed upon certain fault grounds, but neither party could remarry under that type of decree.[4]

During the Protestant Reformation, activists rebelled against the many perceived abuses of, and inconsistencies in, divorce law under the canon law and its ecclesiastical courts. These reformers argued that marriage and divorce should be regulated by secular legislative authority and by courts of equity, rather than by the Church. They further contended that absolute divorce should be granted upon specified marital fault grounds such as adultery, cruelty, or desertion, in addition to recognizing those grounds as the basis for the traditional divorce *a mensa et thoro*.[5]

The English law has been a dominant force in the establishment of American divorce law. Influenced by these Protestant reformers, the American colonies refused to adopt an ecclesiastical court system. Primarily in the New England colonies, colonial legislatures were given the authority to establish divorce grounds. In other areas, mostly in the southern and middle colonies, this authority was granted to the courts of equity.[6] Today, every state in this country regulates its divorce grounds and procedures by statute and designates specific state courts as the forum for divorce proceedings.[7]

[B] Fault Grounds for Divorce and the No-Fault Revolution

Historically, public policy in the United States has placed considerable value on the institution of marriage and has discouraged divorce except in extreme circumstances. Regulation of both marriage and divorce in this country has reflected this perspective. A 1945 Virginia case, *Jacobs v. Jacobs*, illustrates the prevailing judicial philosophy of the mid-20th century. The Virginia supreme court declared that it could not guarantee a happy relationship, but would only cancel the parties' errors of judgment upon a serious, statutory marital breach.[8]

This country, as well as earlier societies, traditionally regarded divorce as a statutory remedy available exclusively to an innocent spouse whose partner has caused the breakdown of the marriage by committing some enumerated type of egregious marital fault. American law borrowed the traditional fault grounds which English law had developed for application in divorce *a mensa et thoro* and applied those grounds to absolute divorce. Under this system, a guilty spouse could not obtain a divorce, nor would

---

[4] *See infra* § 8.03[B][1].

[5] *See* Joyce Green, *supra* note 1, at 13–14.

[6] *Id.* at 14–15.

[7] *See generally* Nelson Blake, The Road to Reno (1962); Homer Clark, The Law of Domestic Relations in the United States § 15.1, p. 73 (2d ed. 1987); Joyce Green, *supra* note 1, at 4–53; Max Rheinstein, Marriage Stability, Divorce, and the Law (1972); Walter Wadlington, *Divorce Without Fault Without Perjury*, 52 Va. L. Rev. 32 (1966).

[8] 35 S.E.2d 119 (Va. 1945).

a court award a divorce when both spouses were found to have contributed to the marital breakdown. Accordingly, the grounds for marriage dissolution originally were narrow and few. Adultery, extreme cruelty, and desertion by a spouse commonly were considered by most state legislatures to constitute serious enough injuries for awarding the innocent spouse a divorce. The statutory lists of marital fault became expanded in many states to include insanity, conviction of a crime, habitual drunkenness and drug addiction, and other perceived evils.[9]

Because divorce itself was discouraged, very strict and specific proof of fault was required for dissolving a marriage. Unlike other civil actions, the plaintiff in a divorce case could not merely receive a default judgment without proof that the other spouse had in fact committed the enumerated wrongs. A divorce case could be dismissed for insufficient evidence, and many jurisdictions employed divorce referees to assure that the alleged facts had actually occurred. As a result, many couples in unhappy marriages fabricated fault grounds and resorted to perjury, often with the assistance of legal counsel. Others left the jurisdiction to obtain a divorce in a state with more liberal divorce laws.[10] The subversion of state divorce laws led to corruption of the legal system and disrespect for divorce attorneys and their practices.

Critics of the fault-based divorce system in the fields of both law and the social sciences long contended that divorce should be viewed as a regrettable but necessary legal consequence of a failed marriage. Furthermore, those critics argued, the breakdown of the marital relationship usually resulted from the incompatibility and irreconcilable differences of both spouses, rather than the unilateral "fault" of one "guilty" spouse. No convincing data existed to demonstrate that liberal divorce grounds would generate unstable marriages or that strict divorce laws prevented or reduced the incidence of marital discord. By the second half of this century, a strong movement had formed, demanding that the legal system allow failed marriages to be dissolved in a peaceful and honest manner.[11]

Widespread divorce law reform began in the United States in the 1960s and 1970s, culminating in what has been referred to as the "divorce revolution."[12] No-fault divorce legislation began in 1966 when a California Governor's Commission recommended that divorce grounds be limited to "irremediable breakdown" and insanity. That recommendation became the law of California in 1969.[13]

Noting a "virtual unanimity as to the urgent need for basic reform," and describing the fault-based divorce ground system as "an unfortunate device which adds to the bitterness and hostility of divorce proceedings,"[14] the

---

[9] See generally Chester Vernier, American Family Laws 70–71 (1932).

[10] See, e.g., Nelson Blake, supra note 3.

[11] See, e.g., Max Rheinstein, The Law of Divorce and the Problem of Marriage Stability, 9 Vand. L. Rev. 633 (1956); see also Max Rheinstein, supra note 7.

[12] See Lenore Weitzman, The Divorce Revolution (1985).

[13] Cal. Civ. Code § 2310 (West 1994).

[14] Prefatory Note, Unif. Marriage and Divorce Act, 9A part I U.L.A. 159 (1998).

National Conference of Commissioners on Uniform State Laws proposed the Uniform Marriage and Divorce Act [UMDA] in 1970.[15] The UMDA attempts to "reduce the adversary trappings of marital litigation" and encourages divorcing parties "to make amicable settlements of their financial affairs," in part by designating the no-fault ground of irretrievable breakdown of marriage as the sole ground for divorce.[16] The American Bar Association approved the UMDA and recommended its passage by the states in 1974.

Section 302 of the UMDA currently provides that a court shall enter a decree of dissolution of marriage when it finds that the marriage is "irretrievably broken." The Act mandates that legal conclusion when either the parties have lived separate and apart for more than 180 days or there exists "serious marital discord" adversely affecting the attitude of one or both of the parties toward the marriage.[17]

By 1985, all states had adopted some from of no-fault divorce, either by designating a no-fault ground as the exclusive basis for divorce or by adding such a provision to existing fault grounds. Currently, some 15 states have adopted irreconcilable differences or irretrievable breakdown as the sole ground for divorce, while an additional 20 states list one of those grounds in addition to traditional fault-based grounds. The remaining states provide for a no-fault type divorce based on living separate and apart for a stated period of time, in addition to traditional fault-based grounds.[18]

[C] Current Divorce Concerns and Statistics

Although divorce was once relatively rare in the United States, it is now commonplace. During the decade between 1970 and 1980, the divorce rate more than doubled, and more than a million divorces currently are granted each year,[19] a figure that has remained fairly constant throughout the 1980s and 1990s.[20] An estimated one-half or more of American marriages will end in divorce.[21] The average duration of marriage was seven years in 1987[22] and remarriage of divorced persons accounts for nearly one-half

---

[15] Unif. Marriage and Divorce Act, 9A part I U.L.A. 159 (1998).

[16] *Id.* at 147, 149.

[17] 9A U.L.A. § 302 (1987).

[18] *See* Timothy Walker, *Family Law in the Fifty States: An Overview*, 25 Fam. L.Q. 417, 439–440 (1992).

[19] Bureau of the Census, U.S. Dep't of Commerce, Statistical Abstract of the United States: 1991 at 86–89 (111th Ed. 1991).

[20] *See* Laura Gatland, *Putting the Blame on No-Fault*, 83 A.B.A. J. 50, 51 (April 1997).

[21] Statistical Abstract of the United States, Table No. 133, at 89 (1990); Bureau of Census, U.S. Dep't of Commerce, Studies in Marriage and the Family, Special Studies Series P-23, No. 162, at 4 (June 1989).

[22] Bureau of the Census, U.S. Dep't of Commerce, Statistical Abstract of the United States: 1991 at 88 (111th Ed. 1991).

of the marriages in this country.[23] The continuing high divorce rate is one of the most dramatic alternations in contemporary American family life.[24]

According to one judge, "Approximately half of all the civil cases heard in the major state courts involve domestic matters. . . . It is not surprising, therefore, that a state civil court's most important function, at least with respect to the number of lives touched, is in the resolution of family matters."[25]

With no-fault divorce now available in all states, divorce litigation has largely shifted from moral issues to economic controversies, primarily property division and child and spousal support, and to child custody disputes. Large law firms are increasingly involved in family law practice with their more prosperous clients, whose divorce actions often require corporate and tax advice as well as the more traditional aspects of family law.[26]

Most divorcing Americans, however, are not affluent, and some commentators have criticized the negative financial impact of no-fault divorce legislation on persons in lower economic brackets. Sociologist Lenore Weitzman, for example, has documented the severe economic impact of no-fault divorce on women and children. Weitzman concluded that gender-neutral rules have falsely assumed that women are equally capable of earning adequate livings as their former husbands following divorce. The results have deprived divorced women, especially older homemakers and those with small children, of the legal and financial benefits that the old law provided.[27] While Weitzman does not advocate a return to the traditional fault-based divorce system, she urges that the new law reflect "a continuous process of correction and refinement . . . to follow through on the road to fairness, equity, and equality in the legal process of divorce."[28]

Uncomplicated, no-fault divorce has also been charged with having a negative impact on children of divorced parents. Without significant safeguards, no-fault laws may contribute to long-term psychological damage to the children of divorce.[29]

---

[23] First time marriages for both the bride and groom represented fewer than 54% of all marriages in each year from 1981–1987. Bureau of the Census, U.S. Dep't of Commerce, Statistical Abstract of the United States: 1991 at 87 (111th Ed. 1991).

[24] Terry Arendell, Mothers and Divorce: Legal, Economic, and Social Dilemmas 1 (1986).

[25] Richard Neely, The Divorce Decision: The Legal and Human Consequences of Ending a Marriage 1 (1984).

[26] See Mark Diamond, *Big Firms Get in on Divorce Action*, 74 A.B.A. J. 60 (August 1988).

[27] Lenore Weitzman, *supra* note 12.

[28] *Id.* at 401; *See also* Michael Redman, *Coming Down Hard on No-Fault*, 10 Fam. Advoc. 6 (no. 2, 1987); Donald C. Schiller, *Dueling Over Issues of Fault-Fault Undercuts Equity*, 10 Fam. Advoc. 10 (no. 2, 1987).

[29] See Robert Cochran & Paul Vitz, *Child Protective Divorce Laws: A Response to the Effects of Parental Separation on Children*, 17 Fam. L.Q. 327 (1983); Judith Wallerstein & Sandra Blakeslee, Second Chances: Men, Women and Children A Decade After Divorce (1989); Elizabeth Scott, *Rational Decision-Making About Marriage and Divorce*, 76 Va. L. Rev. 9, 29 (1990)..

The American Law Institute has proposed a financially based "Principles of the Law of Family Dissolution: Analysis and Recommendations"[30] that argues for the total abolition of all fault-based factors in marital dissolution. Some recent commentators, on the other hand, have argued that fault factors still serve a legitimate function in contemporary society.[31]

In summary, the no-fault divorce revolution is still undergoing reassessment and modification in an attempt to meet the current and future needs of our changing society.

§ 8.02   Jurisdiction and Venue

[A]   Divorce Jurisdiction in General

Family law jurisdiction, including jurisdiction of divorce, is governed by state statutes and administered by state courts.[32] Under the "domestic relations exception" to federal subject matter jurisdiction, the federal courts have no jurisdiction over family law matters, despite the existence of diversity of citizenship. The domestic relations exception is a judicially created doctrine first pronounced by the United States Supreme Court in *Barber v. Barber*[33] in 1858 and developed through a long line of cases.[34] The courts have made some exceptions to the domestic relations exception on occasion.[35]

In *Jagiella v. Jagiella*,[36] the Court of Appeals for the Fifth Circuit held that the federal district court had jurisdiction to grant judgment for alimony and child support arrearages. It further held that the court had properly dismissed the former husband's counterclaim for modification of child support and visitation and damages for alienation of the children's affection and infliction of mental anguish by his former wife, because these claims would necessitate inquiry into the marital or parent-child relationship.

The United States Supreme Court limited the scope of the exception in *Ankenbrandt v. Richards*,[37] a 1992 case which dealt with a tort action based

---

[30] Ali, *Priniciples of the Law of Family Dissolution,* § 5.06 Comment e (1997) (proposed draft).

[31] *See, e.g.*, Barbara Bennett Woodhouse, *Sex, Lies, and Dissipation: The Discourse of Fault in a No-Fault Era*, 82 Geo. L. J. 2525 (1994); Jana Singer, *Husbands, Wives, and Human Capital: Why the Shoe Won't Fit*, 31 Fam. L. Q. 119 (1997); Peter Nash Swisher, *Reassessing Fault Factors in No-Fault Divorce*, 31 Fam. L.Q. 269 (1997).

[32] *See supra* § 1.03.

[33] 62 U.S. (21 How.) 582 (1858).

[34] *See, e.g., In re Burrus*, 136 U.S. 586, 593–94 (1890); *Solomon v. Solomon*, 516 F.2d 1018 (3d Cir. 1975).

[35] *See, e.g., Spindel v. Spindel*, 283 F. Supp.797 (E.D.N.Y. 1968) (federal court jurisdiction to resolve question of fraudulent divorce decree); *Lloyd v. Loeffler*, 694 F.2d 489 (7th Cir. 1982) (parent's claim for damages for concealment of child); *Crouch v. Crouch*, 566 F.2d 486 (5th Cir. 1978) (private contract to pay money between persons long since divorced).

[36] 647 F.2d 561 (5th Cir. 1981).

[37] 112 S. Ct. 2206 (1992).

on alleged child abuse. The Court reviewed the basis for the limitation of federal court jurisdiction, noting that no Constitutional restrictions existed. It questioned the historical rationale that because no ecclesiastical courts were recognized in the United States, divorce was not considered an action "of a civil nature at common law or equity" under the original Judiciary Act.[38] It acknowledge, however, that policy considerations continue to support the rule, such as a lack of family law expertise on the part of federal court judges and judicial economy. Although it expressed unwillingness to completely set aside a rule that has been recognized for over a century, the Court held that the domestic relations exception applied only to the traditional areas of family law: divorce, alimony, and child custody decrees.

In response to an alternative argument based on abstention, the Court also emphasized that federal abstention should rarely be invoked unless proceedings are pending in state courts or in a case involving "elements of the domestic relationship even when the parties do not seek divorce, alimony, or child custody."[39]

> This would be so when a case presents "difficult questions of state law bearing on policy problems of substantial public import whose importance transcends the result in the case then at bar." . . . Such might well be the case if a federal suit were filed prior to effectuation of a divorce, alimony, or child custody decree, and the suit depended on a determination of the status of the parties. Where, as here, the status of the domestic relationship has been determined as a matter of state law, and in any event has no bearing on the underlying torts alleged, we have no difficulty concluding that . . . abstention is inappropriate. . . .[40]

The *Ankenbrandt* decision is likely to generate considerable future litigation concerning the extent to which the domestic relations exception remains applicable.[41]

[B] The Domiciliary Requirement

Although divorce law is a state law matter, the United States Supreme Court has delineated some special rules for divorce jurisdiction, primarily to specify which divorce decrees must be afforded full faith and credit. The Court has held that domicile of one or both spouses is *sufficient* to confer divorce jurisdiction to a state court, stating that "each state, by virtue of its command over its domiciliaries and its large interest in the institution of marriage, can alter within its own borders the marriage status of the spouse domiciled there."[42] Nonetheless, other than by dicta in a series of

---

[38] *See Barber v. Barber*, 62 U.S. (21 How.) 582, 605 (1858) (dissenting opinion); *Ohio ex rel. Popovici v. Agler*, 280 U.S. 379 (1930).

[39] Ankenbrandt at 2208.

[40] *Id.* at 2216 (citation omitted).

[41] *See, e.g., Lannan v. Maul*, 979 F.2d 627 (8th Cir. 1992) (federal district court erred in dismissing child's claim against deceased father's estate to recover proceeds of life insurance policy according to terms of property settlement agreement).

[42] *Williams v. N. Carolina [Williams I]*, 317 U.S. 287, 299 (1942).

mid-twentieth century cases, it has never squarely held that domicile is *necessary*, nor that it is the *sole* basis for divorce jurisdiction.[43]

Because marriage is a status, based on contract, the Court has viewed divorce as essentially an *in rem* action, regarding the "marriage" itself as an entity present in the state whenever either of the spouses is present. Mere presence alone, however, is insufficient to confer divorce jurisdiction, and the state which regulates the marriage or terminates the status must have a substantial nexus with that marriage. State law generally requires that the nexus to be established by the domicile of one or both of the spouses as a requisite for proper assertion of divorce jurisdiction.

"Domicile" is generally defined as the place where a person is physically present with the intent of making that place his or her home.[44] While a person may have more than one "residence," or place where he or she resides, "domicile" connotes a subjective intent to remain more or less permanently or indefinitely.[45] Unnecessarily confusing the issue, many states use the term "residence" rather than "domicile" in their divorce jurisdiction statutes. However, in interpreting the jurisdictional requirements for divorce, a statutory reference to "residence" is usually construed to mean "domicile."[46]

In *In re Marriage of Kimura*,[47] both spouses were Japanese citizens. The husband came to the United States on a temporary visa, and the wife remained in Japan. The husband moved to Iowa, and after one year, filed for divorce in that state. The wife challenged the jurisdiction of the court and also argued that the matter should be dismissed on forum non conveniens grounds. The Iowa Supreme Court upheld the state's assertion of jurisdiction and concluded that the divorce could be granted on the basis of the husband's domicile within the state. It noted, however, that its jurisdiction was limited to terminating the marriage and did not extend to determination of the other issues related to the dissolution.

A state's jurisdictional requirement of domicile is a critical issue in any divorce action. As a general rule, divorce jurisdiction cannot be waived and may be asserted at any time during a divorce proceeding. Lack of jurisdiction may be the basis for a subsequent collateral attack on a prior divorce decree.[48] A valid divorce cannot be granted if the forum court does not have jurisdiction over the marriage or if the defendant did not receive notice sufficient to satisfy constitutional due process standards.[49] Similarly, if a

---

[43] See Williams v. N. Carolina [Williams II], 325 U.S. 226 (1945), rehearing denied, 325 U.S. 895 (1945); *Alton v. Alton*, 207 F.2d 667 (3d Cir.), dismissed as moot, 347 U.S. 610 (1954).

[44] *See Fiske v. Fiske*, 290 P.2d 725 (Wash. 1955).

[45] *See* Restatement (Second) of Conflict of Laws § 70–72 (1971).

[46] *See, e.g., Cooper v. Cooper*, 74 Cal. Rptr. 439 (Cal. Ct. App. 1969); *Raybin v. Raybin*, 430 A.2d 953 (N.J. Super. Ct. App. Div. 1981). *But see contra Garrison v. Garrison*, 246 N.E.2d 9 (Ill. App.Ct. 1969). *See generally* Willis Reese & Robert Green, *That Elusive Word "Residence"*, 6 Vand. L. Rev. 561 (1953).

[47] 471 N.W.2d 869 (1991).

[48] *See, e.g., Hartman v. Hartman*, 412 N.E.2d 711 (Ill. App. Ct. 1980); *see also* Restatement (Second) of Judgments §§ 11, 12, 69 (1982).

[49] *See supra* § 8.02.

divorce decree is entered without proper jurisdiction or upon insufficient notice, the decree is void and has no legal effect. Such a decree may be attacked at any time, although equitable defenses may apply.[50]

The domiciliary requirement for divorce jurisdiction has been criticized as obsolete and irrelevant in our current transient society with no-fault divorce options.[51] At the same time, because some form of no-fault divorce is presently available in all American jurisdictions, the problems that migratory divorces once posed are diminished. Therefore, it is questionable whether requiring merely physical presence rather than domicile would serve any compelling social need. Because significant connections continue to be required between an individual and the state with respect to state and local police protection, property rights, rights of inheritance, taxes, voting rights, education, and employment, such a nexus may be equally relevant with respect to the parties' marital status.[52]

Some legal commentators have contended that mere domicile as a basis for divorce jurisdiction in unilateral ex parte divorces is an insufficient nexus and may constitute an unconstitutional violation of the absent spouse's due process rights.[53] In *Shaffer v. Heitner*,[54] the Supreme Court stated that "in order to justify an exercise of jurisdiction *in rem*, the basis for jurisdiction must be sufficient to justify exercising jurisdiction over the interests of persons in a 'thing.'" However, Professor Clark has pointed out that while *Shaffer* stated that both *in rem* and *in personal* cases require minimum contacts to satisfy due process requirements, the Court disclaimed any intention of changing jurisdictional rules based upon status. Therefore, it is not likely that *Shaffer* and subsequent cases alter the jurisdictional rules for divorce.[55]

Although domicile provides a sufficient basis for a state court to assert jurisdiction in a divorce case, the United States Supreme Court has held that states may additionally impose a durational residency requirement without unconstitutionally discriminating against residents who have recently moved to the state and seek a divorce there. In *Sosna v. Iowa*,[56]

---

[50] *See supra* § 8.02[J].

[51] *See, e.g.*, Helen Garfield, *The Transitory Divorce Action: Jurisdiction in the No-Fault Era*, 58 Tex. L. Rev. 501, 544 (1980) (suggesting that "the problem today is not so much migratory divorce as migratory people," and recommending a proposed Uniform Divorce Jurisdiction Act which would provide as the basis for divorce jurisdiction the mere presence of both parties in a state for bilateral divorces, and a brief period of presence or simple residence in the forum state for ex parte, unilateral divorces).

[52] *See, e.g.*, *Boddie v. Connecticut*, 401 U.S. 371, 376 (1971).

[53] *See, e.g.*, Hawkens, *The Effect of Shaffer v. Heitner on the Jurisdictional Standard in Ex Parte Divorces*, 18 Fam. L.Q. 311 (1984); Sheila Cunningham, Note, *Jurisdiction in the Ex Parte Divorce: Do Absent Spouses Have a Protected Due Process Interest in Their Marital Status?*, 13 Memphis St. U.L. Rev. 205 (1983).

[54] 433 U.S. 186, 207 (1977).

[55] Homer Clark, *supra* note 7, at 424; *see also In re Marriage of Rinderknecht*, 367 N.E.2d 1128 (Ind. Ct. App. 1977) (domicile of one of the spouses in a state is a sufficient minimum contact to meet the requirements of Shaffer).

[56] 419 U.S. 393 (1975).

Carol Sosna had moved from New York, the marital domicile, to Iowa, where she sought dissolution of her marriage to Michael Sosna. Although Michael was personally served when he visited the couple's children in Iowa, the Iowa court dismissed the action for lack of jurisdiction under an Iowa statute that required a divorce petitioner to have been an Iowa resident for one year. Noting that the vast majority of states impose durational residency requirements for divorce, the Supreme Court upheld the statute.

> A decree of divorce is not a matter in which the only interested parties are the State as a sort of "grantor," and a plaintiff such as appellant in the role of "grantee." Both spouses are obviously interested in the proceedings, since it will affect their marital status and very likely their property rights. Where a married couple has minor children, a decree of divorce would usually include provisions for their custody and support. With consequences of such moment riding on a divorce decree issued by its courts, Iowa may insist that one seeking to initiate such a proceeding have the modicum of attachment to the State required here.[57]

The Court further recognized a state interest in "avoiding officious intermeddling in matters in which another State has a paramount interest, and minimizing the susceptibility of its own divorce decrees to collateral attack."[58] Furthermore, Ms. Sosna was not prevented from divorcing in Iowa, but was merely delayed in obtaining access to its courts until she fulfilled the durational residency requirement.

Although the concept of domicile as the exclusive basis for divorce jurisdiction remains open to debate,[59] state law currently considers domicile essential for divorce. While a few states have no durational requirement but require only a bona fide residency or domicile,[60] most states additionally impose a durational requirement ranging from six weeks[61] to one year.[62] The most common durational requirement for divorce is six months.[63]

An important exception to the general jurisdictional requirements for divorce involves military personnel and their spouses. Approximately twenty states, as well as the Uniform Marriage and Divorce Act, additionally confer divorce jurisdiction over members of the armed forces who are

---

[57] *Id.* at 406–407.

[58] *Id.* at 407.

[59] *See, e.g., Williams v. N. Carolina [Williams II]*, 325 U.S. 226, 239–260 (1945) (Rutledge, Black, & Douglas dissenting); Edward Stimson, *Jurisdiction in Divorce Cases: The Unsoundness of the Domiciliary Theory*, 42 A.B.A. J. 222 (1956); Russell Weintraub, *An Inquiry into the Utility of "Domicile" as a Concept in Conflicts Analysis*, 63 Mich. L. Rev. 961 (1965).

[60] *E.g.*, Alaska Stat. § 01.10.055 (1998); S.D. Codified Laws Ann. § 25-4-30 (1999).

[61] *E.g.*, Idaho Code § 32-701 (1996); Nev. Rev. Stat. Ann. § 125.020 (Michie 1998).

[62] *E.g.*, Conn. Gen. Stat. Ann. § 46b-44 (West 1995); Iowa Code Ann. § 598.6 (West 1996); N.Y. Dom. Rel. L. § 230 (McKinney 1999).

[63] *See* Timothy Walker, *Family Law in the Fifty States: An Overview*, 25 Fam. L.Q. 417, 441 (1992).

stationed in the state for a specified period of time.[64] Because of the mobile nature of the military, servicemen and women and their spouses might otherwise be unable to establish domicile or meet the residency requirements of the jurisdiction of their current station. Although the state of their pre-military domicile may continue to assert jurisdiction to grant divorces to absent military personnel, that state may have little current connection with the serviceperson may be a distant and inconvenient forum.[65] Although one state has declared its special military jurisdictional statute unconstitutional,[66] the United States Supreme Court has upheld other statutes that confer special benefits to veterans against equal protection attacks, based on the legitimate longstanding policy to compensation veterans for past contributions.[67]

Relatedly, the Soldiers' and Sailors' Civil Relief Act permits stay of continuance in any divorce and related family law matter to military personnel stay who are prevented from being present and participating in the scheduled proceedings due to their military service.[68]

Whether a court has jurisdiction to enter a divorce decree is especially important in determining whether other states must recognize the divorce as valid pursuant to full faith and credit principles. The validity of a decree may depend largely on whether the divorce was granted in a bilateral or ex parte proceeding.

[C] Venue

Jurisdictional rules for divorce determine whether any court in a particular state has authority to hear the case and to grant a valid divorce decree. Venue, on the other hand, governs the appropriate place *within* the state for bringing the divorce action. Venue statutes generally require filing a divorce action in the county of the parties' last marital domicile, in the county where the defendant resides, or, if the defendant's location is

---

[64] *See, e.g.*, Unif. Marriage and Divorce Act § 302(a), 9A part I U.L.A. 200 (1998); *see also* Pearson, Annotation, *Validity and Construction of Statutory Provisions Relating to Jurisdiction of Court for Purpose of Divorce for Servicemen*, 73 A.L.R. 3d 431 (1976 & Supp. 1992).

[65] *See Johnson v. Johnson*, 53 Cal. Rptr. 567 *(Cal. Ct.App. 1966) (change of residence required by military service will not change domicile, absent clear intent); see also In re Marriage of Thornton*, 185 Cal. Rptr. 338 *(Cal. Ct. App. 1982) (divorce jurisdictional requirements may be met without domicile of either spouse in unique circumstance by residency of one spouse, unavailability of better forum, property within the jurisdiction, and site of last marital home).*

[66] *Viernes v. Dist. Court of Fourth Judicial Dist.*, 509 P.2d 306 (Colo. 1973) (other "significant contacts" in addition to stationing in state necessary).

[67] *See Regan v. Taxation with Representation*, 461 U.S. 540 (1983) (tax exemption for veterans' lobbying groups does not violate equal protection). *See also United States v. Hampshire*, 95 F.3d 999 (10th Cir. 1996) cert. denied, 117 S. Ct. 753 (1997) (state court order under Child Support Recovery Act did not violate soldier's due process rights or his right to attorney under Soldier's and Sailor's Relief Act, because father was absent without leave (AWOL)).

[68] 50 U.S.C.A. § § 501, 521; *see also Lackey v. Lackey*, 278 S.E.2d 811 (Va. 1981). *See generally* Annotation Soldiers' and Sailors' Civil Relief Act of 1940 as Amended as Affecting Matrimonial Actions, 54 A.L.R.2d 390 (1957 & Supp. 1992).

unknown or is out-of-state, in the county where the plaintiff resides.[69] Other venue statutes provide for alternatives, such as the county of the parties' last domicile, the county where the defendant resides, or, if the defendant is out of state or the defendant's whereabouts are unknown, the county where the plaintiff resides.[70]

While jurisdictional requirements may not be waived in a divorce proceeding, some states have held that venue rules may be waived.[71] However, in other states, venue statutes in divorce proceedings have been interpreted as mandatory and jurisdictional, thus not waivable.[72] If venue statutes may not be waived in a divorce action, the validity of the divorce decree may be affected.

[D] Service on the Defendant

Due process requires that service of process on the defendant in a divorce action be made in strict compliance with state statutes. If the defendant is not properly served in a manner reasonably calculated to give notice, the divorce may be attacked and invalidated for lack of adequate notice.[73]

A United States District Court applied this principle in *Breuer v. Sullivan*,[74] overturning an administrative law judge's conclusion that he must recognize a divorce decree valid for purposes of a woman's claim for widow's benefits under the Social Security Act. In light of the woman's testimony that she had never received a copy of the 1958 divorce summons or complaint, the District Court Judge held that, on remand, the administrative law judge must determine the claimant's marital status before deciding her eligibility for benefits.

A divorce plaintiff's false representations of lack of knowledge of the defendant's whereabouts may constitute a fraud sufficient to invalidate the divorce.[75] Similarly, if the notice to the defendant fails to indicate that the plaintiff is also seeking a division of marital property in the divorce action, the service may be adequate for granting the divorce but inadequate to confer jurisdiction to distribute property.[76]

[E] Bilateral Divorces

A bilateral divorce is a divorce proceeding in which both spouses are subject to the jurisdiction of the forum state court. A divorce is bilateral

---

[69] *See, e.g.*, Cal. Civ. Code § 2320 (West 1994); *In re Marriage of Dick*, 18 Cal Rptr. 2d 743 (Ct. App. 1993). *See also Dunn v. Dunn*, 577 So. 2d 378 (Miss. 1991).

[70] *See, e.g.*, Va. Code Ann. § 8.01-261 (Michie 1995).

[71] *See, e.g., Nelms v. Nelms*, 108 S.E.2d 529 (N.C. 1959); Kelley v. Kelley, 263 S.W.2d 505 (Tenn. 1953).

[72] *See, e.g., Gerdel v. Gerdel*, 313 A.2d 8 (Vt. 1973); *Netzer v. Reynolds*, 345 S.E.2d 291 (Va. 1986).

[73] *See* Homer Clark, *supra* note 7, at 421.

[74] 18 Fam. L. Rep. (BNA) 1439 (D.N.M. 1991).

[75] *See, e.g., Ford v. Whelan, 288 N.W. 737 (Wis. 1930).*

[76] *See In re Marriage of Campbell*, 683 P.2d 604 (Wash. Ct. App. 1984).

when both of the spouses the are domiciliaries of the forum state or when both are subject to the forum state's personal jurisdiction because of consent, appearance, or application of a long-arm statute. A bilateral divorce and decree may not be collaterally attacked by the parties themselves nor, generally, by third parties, including other states.[77] In a bilateral divorce actions the court may resolve all the incidents of the marriage as well as terminate the parties' marital status.[78]

[F] Ex Parte Divorces

An ex parte or unilateral divorce is a divorce proceeding in which the court of the forum state has personal jurisdiction in the over only one of the spouses. While the United States Supreme Court has held that the domicile of one spouse is sufficient for the forum court to litigate the status of marriage and to grant a divorce,[79] the forum state does not have jurisdiction to resolve the economic incidents of the marriage without personal jurisdiction over the party whose rights are to be affected.[80] Problems involving ex parte divorces most commonly arise in the context of migratory divorces, although the same problems may be encountered when one or both parties have moved from the state of the last marital domicile for purposes other than obtaining a divorce.

[G] Migratory Divorces

The classic migratory divorce cases, in which one spouse leaves the state of the marital domicile to obtain a divorce in another jurisdiction, serve as useful examples of the structure of divorce jurisdiction and the principles controlling recognition of divorce decrees by other states. Although the availability of no-fault divorce in all 50 states has greatly decreased the incentive for a spouse to go out-of-state to procure a divorce, some individuals still may attempt to obtain a divorce in another state or a foreign country that has more lenient jurisdictional requirements, a shorter waiting period, or less stringent substantive standards, or to avoid the publicity that may arise in the forum state.[81]

[1] Sister State Divorces

The Full Faith and Credit Clause of the United States Constitution requires states to recognize valid divorce decrees entered by the courts of other states.[82] However, because each state has developed specific divorce

---

[77] *See infra* § 8.02[J].

[78] *See infra* § 8.02[F].

[79] *Williams v. N. Carolina [Williams I]*, 317 U.S. 287 (1942); *see supra* § 8.02[B].

[80] *See infra* § 8.02[F].

[81] *See* Philip Adams & Stephen Adams, *Ethical Problems in Advising Migratory Divorce*, 16 Hastings L.J. 60, 99 (1964).

[82] Article IV § 1, U.S. Constitution (requiring states to give full faith and credit to the public acts, records, and judicial proceedings of every other state).

laws based on its own public policy, confusion historically resulted as to the circumstances in which one state must recognize a divorce decree from a sister state and when that state may legally refuse to recognize such a decree. Because many parties who obtain migratory divorces subsequently remarry, and because substantial property and support rights are determined on divorce, both the parties and the states themselves have a strong interest in ensuring that their divorce decrees will be recognized in all states.

The United States Supreme Court first addressed the issue of migratory divorce in the 1906 case of *Haddock v. Haddock*.[83] In *Haddock*, the husband had obtained a divorce in a state where he had established a bona fide domicile after wrongfully leaving his wife in the state of the marital domicile. The Court held that the state of the marital domicile was not obligated to recognize the ex parte divorce decree. The *Haddock* decision remained the law until 1942, when the Supreme Court decided the seminal ex parte divorce case of *Williams v. North Carolina [Williams I]*.[84]

In *Williams*, Mr. Williams and Mrs. Hendrix left their respective spouses in North Carolina and traveled to Las Vegas, Nevada, where, after fulfilling Nevada's six weeks residency requirement, they both obtained divorces. Although neither of their North Carolina spouses was personally served in Nevada nor entered an appearance there, they received notice of the divorce complaints and summonses in North Carolina. Mr. Williams and Mrs. Hendrix then married each other in Nevada and returned to North Carolina. Relying on *Haddock*, the State of North Carolina tried and convicted them of bigamous cohabitation, despite their argument that the Nevada divorce decree and remarriage should be recognized in North Carolina.[85]

In *Williams I*, an opinion written by Justice Douglas, the Supreme Court overruled *Haddock* and held that an ex parte divorce, based on proper jurisdiction and with adequate due process notice to the other spouse, must be given full faith and credit by another state, even though the public policies of the two states might conflict. Moreover, the Court held that domicile of the plaintiff would supply the basis for jurisdiction in an ex parte divorce. Because no evidence in the record in the North Carolina proceeding indicated that Mr. Williams and Mrs. Hendrix were *not* domiciled in Nevada, Justice Douglas stated that the Court "must assume that petitioners had a bona fide domicile in Nevada, not that the Nevada domicile was a sham."[86] The case was reversed and remanded back to the North Carolina court.

Upon remand, North Carolina again upheld the bigamy convictions on the basis that the petitioners had not in fact been domiciled in Nevada,

---

[83] 201 U.S. 562 (1906).

[84] 317 U.S. 287 (1942).

[85] *See generally* Thomas Reed Powell, *And Repent at Leisure: An Inquiry into the Unhappy Lot of Those Whom Nevada Hath Joined Together and North Carolina Hath Put Asunder*, 58 Harv. L. Rev. 930 (1945).

[86] 317 U.S. 287, 302.

therefore the divorces had no legal validity in North Carolina. In 1945, the appeal again reached the Supreme Court in *Williams v. North Carolina* [*Williams II*].[87] In a decision written by Justice Frankfurter, the Court reaffirmed the *Williams I* doctrine that an ex parte divorce based upon the domicile of only one spouse, with proper due process to the non-appearing spouse, must be recognized by other states under the Full Faith and Credit Clause. However, although the Nevada court's finding of a Nevada domicile "was entitled to respect and more," the Court held that North Carolina was not bound by the Nevada jurisdictional finding of domicile[88] and could subsequently reexamine the facts to determine whether the parties had actually acquired a Nevada domicile. Thus, under *Williams II*, a sister state court may inquire into the factual basis for jurisdiction and refuse to recognize an ex parte divorce if it concludes that the divorcing court did not have adequate jurisdiction to grant the divorce because no true domicile had been established.[89] The Williams' conviction of bigamous cohabitation was therefore affirmed.

The Iowa Supreme Court applied the *Williams II* doctrine in *Cooper v. Cooper*,[90] when it determined that an ex parte Nevada divorce decree was based on proper jurisdiction. The husband in *Cooper* had left Iowa, the marital domicile, after a lengthy marriage and moved to Nevada where he lived for three months, obtained a license to practice medicine, worked at a medical center, rented an apartment, opened a bank account, and obtained a driver's license. A Nevada court granted him a default judgment of divorce, after which he moved back to Iowa, remarried, and subsequently died. Denying the first wife's claim that the divorce and remarriage were invalid, the court held that she had failed to prove by clear, satisfactory, and convincing evidence that the husband did not have the requisite intent to establish a domicile in Nevada.

A state court's determination regarding the validity of another state's divorce decree under the *Williams II* doctrine may not bind subsequent states. Subsequent states may re-examine the factual issue of domicile, resulting in a divorce decree that is considered valid in some states but not in others.[91]

On occasion, courts have issued injunctions against a spouse's obtaining a divorce in another state when it appears likely that the spouse does not intend to establish domicile in the new state.[92]

---

[87] 325 U.S. 226 (1945).

[88] *Id.* at 233.

[89] *See, e.g., Manasseri v. Manasseri*, 504 N.Y.S.2d 140 (N.Y. App. Div. 1986) (finding husband's move to Nevada a sham when he moved with only two suitcases and golf clubs soon after dismissal of New York divorce action, despite his registering to vote and acquiring driver's license in Nevada).

[90] 217 N.W.2d 584 (Iowa 1974).

[91] *See Colby v. Colby*, 369 P.2d 1019 (Nev. 1962), cert. denied, 371 U.S. 888 (1962); see also Recent Developments, 15 Stanford L. Rev. 331 (1963); Restatement (Second) of Judgments § 15 (1982). *But see, e.g., Sutton v. Leib*, 342 U.S. 402 (1952); *Layton v. Layton*, 538 S.W.2d 642 (Tex. Civ. App. 1976).

[92] *See Monihan v. Monihan*, 264 A.2d 653 (Pa. 1970); *Stambaugh v. Stambaugh*, 329 A.2d 483 (Pa. 1974); *see also* Annotation, *Injunction Against Suit in Another State or Country for Divorce or Separation*, 54 A.L.R.2d 1240 (1957 & Supp. 1992).

While the *Williams I* and *Williams II* doctrines apply generally to ex parte divorces, bilateral migratory divorces involve some different concerns. A new issue arises when neither spouse is domiciled in the divorcing state, but both submit to the court's jurisdiction by personal or general appearance. The Supreme Court first dealt with the issue of bilateral migratory divorce in the 1948 case of *Sherrer v. Sherrer*.[93]

The *Sherrer* case involved a husband and wife who both had been Massachusetts domiciliary before Mrs. Sherrer moved to Florida and commenced a divorce action there. Mr. Sherrer, through his attorney, made a general appearance in the Florida divorce action, but did not challenge his wife's allegations that she was a Florida domiciliary during the proceedings. The Florida court found that Mrs. Sherrer was a Florida domiciliary and Mr. Sherrer did not appeal the divorce in a Florida appellate court.

Subsequently, Mr. Sherrer attacked the validity of the Florida divorce in a Massachusetts court, alleging that Mrs. Sherrer's domicile in Florida was a sham and that the Florida court did not have jurisdiction to grant a valid divorce. Despite his argument that Massachusetts should not recognize the decree under the *Williams II* doctrine, the Supreme Court upheld the validity of the Florida divorce and stated that Massachusetts must recognize the decree.

The distinction between *Sherrer* and the *Williams* cases is that Mr. Sherrer had submitted to the jurisdiction of the Florida court by entering an appearance in the divorce action, making it a bilateral, rather than an ex parte, divorce. He had therefore participated in the bilateral Florida divorce proceeding and had the opportunity to dispute the jurisdictional issue, which he failed to do. The Supreme Court held that because Mr. Sherrer had his day in court on the merits of the case, he was precluded from relitigating the issue under the doctrine of res judicata or estoppel by judgment.[94] The practical effect of the *Sherrer* decision was to limit the scope of the *Williams II* decision to jurisdictional challenges of ex parte divorces.[95]

The Court in *Sherrer* did not hold that divorces are valid without domicile of either party, but rather foreclosed collateral attack by a party who participated in a bilateral divorce. It remains uncertain, therefore, whether the domicile state of one or both of the divorcing parties may itself collaterally attack a bilateral migratory divorce in a proceeding such as a bigamy or adultery prosecution.[96]

---

[93] 334 U.S. 343 (1948).

[94] 334 U.S. at 352.

[95] *See also Aldrich v. Aldrich*, 378 U.S. 540 (1964) (relitigation of a mistake of law or a mistake of fact in divorce decree barred by res judicata). *See generally* John R. McDonough, Jr., *Mr. Justice Jackson and Full Faith and Credit on Divorce Decrees: A Critique*, 56 Colum. L. Rev. (1956).

[96] *See infra* § 8.02[J].

[2] Foreign Country Divorces

Although the Full Faith and Credit Clause requires recognition of valid sister state migratory divorce decrees,[97] migratory divorces granted in foreign countries are not shielded by this constitutional mandate. Instead, state courts apply the discretionary principle of comity in determining whether to recognize such divorces. The Supreme Court has defined comity as:

> neither a matter of absolute obligation, on the one hand, nor of mere courtesy and good will, upon the other. But it is a recognition which one nation allows within its territory to legislative, executive, or judicial acts of another nation, having due regard both to international duty and convenience, and to the rights of its own citizens or of other persons who are under the protection of its laws.[98]

Comity is generally interpreted to mean merely that a state is not obligated to apply foreign law.[99] Consequentially, a state may decide not to afford comity to a foreign divorce when it is contrary to the state's public policy or prejudicial to its interests.[100] Circumstances in which state courts typically refuse to grant comity to foreign divorce decrees include insufficient proof or lack of finality of a foreign judgment; lack of subject matter or personal jurisdiction or insufficient notice or opportunity to be heard; clear mistake of fact or law made by the foreign court or procurement of the foreign judgment by fraud; and contravention of the public policy of the recognition forum.[101]

In *Mayer v. Mayer*,[102] the North Carolina Court of Appeals analyzed whether foreign country migratory divorces should be recognized under comity principles. In *Mayer*, a husband seeking to avoid alimony challenged the validity of his marriage by attacking his wife's Dominican divorce from her first husband. Although the court ultimately held that the second husband, who had assisted the wife in procuring the foreign divorce, was estopped from attacking the decree,[103] it denounced foreign divorces that are not based on sufficient jurisdiction.

The *Mayer* court found that the divorce decree offended the state's public policy "against hasty dissolution of marriages" and rejected the wife's contention that the Dominican ground of "irreconcilable differences" was substantially equivalent to North Carolina's divorce ground based on a one year's separation. It refused to

> . . . sanction a procedure by which citizens of this State with sufficient funds to finance a trip to the Caribbean can avoid our

---

[97] *See supra* § 8.02[E][1].

[98] *Hilton v. Guyot*, 159 U.S. 113, 163–64 (1895).

[99] *See Growe v. Growe*, 138 N.W.2d 537 (Mich. Ct. App. 1965).

[100] *See, e.g., Watson v. Blakely*, 748 P.2d 984 (N.M. Ct. App. 1987).

[101] *See* Courtland H. Peterson, *Res Judicata and Foreign Country Judgments*, 24 Ohio St. L.J. 291, 308–310 (1963).

[102] 311 S.E.2d 659 (N.C. Ct. App. 1984), appeal denied, 321 S.E.2d 140 (N.C. 1984).

[103] *See infra* § 8.02[J].

legislature's judgment on the question of divorce. To hold otherwise would be to flout our law; it would permit domiciliaries of North Carolina to submit their marital rights and obligations to the contrary policies and judgments of a foreign nation with which they have no connection.[104]

Similar reasoning has led the overwhelming majority of American states to refuse to recognize foreign divorce decrees. A court is likely to deny recognition, regardless of the purported validity of the divorce in the country awarding it, unless at least one of the spouses was a good-faith domiciliary of that country at the time the divorce was rendered, and regardless of whether the foreign divorce was procured bilaterally, ex parte, or by mail order.[105]

Although no states recognize ex parte or mail-order migratory foreign divorces, a few American jurisdictions have recognized bilateral foreign divorces based solely on both parties' physical presence in the foreign jurisdiction, despite a lack of domicile.[106] For example, in the New York case of *Rosenstiel v. Rosenstiel*,[107] New York couples were allowed to evade the then strict New York divorce laws by obtaining foreign divorces. The *Rosenstiel* decision has been strongly criticized by commentators as overriding state public policy as declared by the New York legislature.[108]

On the other hand, the Connecticut court, in *Yoder v. Yoder*,[109] found "no repugnancy" between Mexican and Connecticut divorce grounds and granted comity to a Mexican divorce based on irretrievable breakdown in the marriage. However, *Yoder* did not involve a claim that the Mexican court lacked jurisdiction to enter the divorce decree.[110]

In the past, Americans frequently procured easy, 24-hour divorces in Mexico.[111] In 1971, however, Mexican law was amended to require aliens to become residents for at least six months prior to obtaining a divorce, making Mexican divorces less available to American citizens. Nevertheless, Mexican divorces continue to generate litigation because of the distinction between "residence" and "domicile" and because of the potential for forged Mexican residency certificates.[112]

---

[104] 311 S.E.2d at 666.

[105] Peter Nash Swisher, *Foreign Migratory Divorces: A Reappraisal*, 21 J. Fam. L. 9, 22–33 (1982–83). *See also Kugler v. Haitian Tours Inc.*, 293 A.2d 706 (N.J. Super. Ct. Ch. Div. 1972) (Haitian divorce); *Basiouny v. Basiouny, 445 So. 2d 916 (Ala. Civ. App. 1984) (Egyptian divorce).*

[106] *See, e.g., Yoder v. Yoder*, 330 A.2d 825 (Conn. Super. Ct. 1974) (Mexican divorce); *Hyde v. Hyde*, 562 S.W.2d 194 (Tenn. 1978) (Dominican Republic divorce).

[107] 209 N.E.2d 709 (N.Y. 1965), cert. denied, 384 U.S. 971 (1966).

[108] *See David P. Currie, Suitcase Divorce in the Conflict of Laws: Simmons, Rosensteil and Borax*, 34 U. Chi. L. Rev. 26, 57–62 (1966); Comment, *Mexican Bilateral Divorce*, 61 Nw. U. L. Rev. 584, 608 (1966).

[109] 330 A.2d 825 (Conn. Super. Ct. 1974).

[110] *See also Bruneau v. Bruneau*, 489 A.2d 1049 (Conn. App. Ct. 1985).

[111] *See, e.g.*, David P. Currie, *supra* note 94; W. Barton Leach, *Divorce by Plane Ticket in the Affluent Society-With a Side Order of Jurisprudence*, 14 Kans. L. Rev. 549 (1966).

[112] *See* J. Gareth Miller, *Mexican Divorces Revisited*, 84 Case & Com., No. 4 at 43 (1979).

The Dominican Republic and Haiti have now replaced Mexico as favored locations for Americans seeking quick divorces. Neither country has either a residency or domicile requirement.[113] "Divorce tour packages" are advertised in prominent periodicals, and solicitations by Haitian and Dominican divorce lawyers are sometimes mailed directly to American attorneys.[114]

These practices were successfully attacked in *Kugler v. Haitian Tours*[115] when the New Jersey attorney general brought an action under the Consumer Fraud Act against Haitian Tours, Inc., for selling travel packages to Haiti for the purpose of assisting clients to obtain a divorce in that country, which did not require domicile of either party. Although the package did not express any views as to the validity or recognition of the Haitian divorce in this country, the court held that their sale constituted a fraud, because the divorces were worthless and did not accomplish the purpose for which they were purchased.

Various countries have attempted to alleviate the problems involved in the recognition of foreign country divorces by adopting the Hague Convention on the Recognition of Divorce and Legal Separations.[116] The Hague Convention authorizes jurisdiction for divorce or legal separation based upon the "habitual residence" (including, but not limited to "domicile") of either spouse or when the petitioner is a national of that state. Approximately 14 countries, including the United Kingdom, have adopted the Hague Convention. However, the United States is not a signatory to this Convention, which, therefore, is not binding law in this country.[117]

[H] The Divisible Divorce Doctrine

Although a valid ex parte divorce is entitled to full faith and credit in all sister states with respect to termination of the marital status of the parties,[118] a court may not create, extinguish, or modify the financial incidents of marriage, such as spousal and child support and marital property division, without personal jurisdiction over the defendant.[119] The Supreme Court limited the *Williams I* doctrine when it announced the principle of "divisible divorce" in *Estin v. Estin*[120] in 1948.

---

[113] *See Blair v. Blair*, 643 N.E.2d 933 (Ind. Ct. App. 1994) (refusing to recognize husband's ex parte Dominican divorce).

[114] *See generally* Peter Nash Swisher, *supra* note 91; Robert Steuk, Note, *Isle of Hispaniola: American Divorce Haven?*, 5 Case W. Res. J. Int'l L. 198 (1973); James Fulton, Note, *Caribbean Divorce for Americans: Useful Alternative or Obsolescent Institution?*, 10 Cornell Int'l L.J. 116 (1976).

[115] 293 A.2d 706 (N.J. Super. Ct. App. Div. 1972).

[116] 978 U.N.T.S. 399 (1975).

[117] *See* John Nichols, *Recognition and Enforcement: American Courts Look at Foreign Decrees*, 9 Fam. Advoc. 9 (Spring 1987); David Cavers, *Habitual Residence: A Useful Concept?*, 21 Am. U. L. Rev. 475 (1972).

[118] *See supra* § 8.02[D].

[119] Jurisdictional rules pertaining to child custody are different. *See infra* § 10.02.

[120] 334 U.S. 541 (1948).

In *Estin*, Mrs. Estin, a New York domiciliary, had been awarded a decree of legal separation, including an order for spousal support, in 1943, one year after her husband had left her. In 1945, Mr. Estin obtained an ex parte Nevada divorce, which made no provision for spousal support. When Mr. Estin ceased making support payments, Mrs. Estin brought an action in New York for support arrearages against Mr. Estin. Mr. Estin appeared in the New York action and argued that under the *Williams I* doctrine the subsequent Nevada ex parte divorce decree legally extinguished the earlier New York separation decree.

After examining the conflicting interests of Nevada and New York, the Supreme Court held that although a divorcing state has a valid interest in determining the legal status of the marriage, the state of the former marital domicile also has an interest in preventing an abandoned spouse from becoming a public charge. The Court reconciled these interests by holding that although an ex parte divorce may terminate the marital status, it does not necessarily result in the termination of all the financial incidents of the marriage. It held that Mrs. Estin's prior New York judgment was a property interest that could not be affected by a Nevada court without personal jurisdiction over Mrs. Estin.[121] Hence, the Court created the concept of "divisible divorce," validating ex parte divorces as to the parties' status, but refusing to allow marital support or property rights to be altered without personal jurisdiction over both parties.[122]

In 1957, in *Vanderbilt v. Vanderbilt*,[123] the Supreme Court extended the concept of divisible divorce to situations in which one spouse obtains an ex parte divorce when the other does not have a pre-existing support order. In *Vanderbilt*, the couple had separated in California after a four-year marriage; the wife moved to New York, and the husband subsequently obtained an ex parte Nevada divorce decree which declared that both parties were "freed and released from the bonds of matrimony *and all the duties and obligations thereof.*"[124] The next year, the wife instituted an action in New York, seeking a separation and alimony from Mr. Vanderbilt. The husband contended that the Nevada decree both terminated the marriage and extinguished any duty of support.

The Supreme Court held that it was not material that the wife did not have a preexisting support order, as the wife in *Estin* had. The Nevada court had no power to extinguish any of the wife's rights to support without personal jurisdiction over her, nor could a court without jurisdiction over the husband order him to pay support. Thus, the Nevada decree was void to the extent that it purported to terminate the non-appearing party's support rights.

The Supreme Court constrained the divisible divorce doctrine to some extent in *Simons v. Miami Beach First National Bank*[125] in 1965. In

---

[121] 334 U.S. at 548.

[122] *See also* Joyce Green, *supra* note 1, at 163–64.

[123] 354 U.S. 416 (1957).

[124] 354 U.S. at 416 (emphasis added).

[125] 381 U.S. 81 (1965).

Simons, the husband had moved to Florida where he obtained an ex parte divorce after Mrs. Simons had obtained a New York legal separation decree which included spousal support. Mr. Simons continued to pay the spousal support until his death in Florida some years later. When Mrs. Simons filed an election to take dower rights as a surviving spouse in the Florida probate proceedings, the Supreme Court held that under Florida law, dower rights in Florida property may be legally extinguished by an ex parte divorce under the divisible divorce doctrine. The distinction was that the wife in *Simons* sought property benefits granted to surviving spouses, which were created by the law of the divorcing state and depended on the claimant's marital status.

The United States District Court for the Southern District of New York reached a similar conclusion in *Kahn v. Kahn*.[126] It held that a former wife could not challenge an ex parte sister state divorce decree in order to obtain retirement benefits under her former husband's pension plan. The court noted that although the divorce court could not directly deprive the wife of property rights without personal jurisdiction, it could terminate her spousal status, upon which her claim to the pension benefits depended.

Most states have interpreted the divisible divorce doctrine to mean that neither marital support nor property rights can be modified or extinguished without personal jurisdiction over both parties,[127] although a court may refuse to order spousal support if the petitioner moved to the forum state after the divorce.[128] In *Newport v. Newport*,[129] the Supreme Court of Virginia held that a Virginia court with jurisdiction over the husband could awarded the wife alimony after the husband's ex parte Nevada divorce. It noted that although spousal support is a duty incident to marriage, it survives an absolute ex parte divorce and may be granted in an independent suit. A minority of states, however, have held that an ex parte divorce granted in another state may extinguish spousal support that a spouse might ordinarily be able to assert on divorce, because the duty of spousal support and the power to order a continuation of that duty via alimony derives from a valid marriage. Once that marital status is terminated, the court has no authority to order support.[130]

[I]　Long-Arm Statutes

To minimize the problems associated with the concept of divisible divorce, many states have enacted long-arm statutes specifically designed to enable

---

[126] 801 F. Supp. 1237 (S.D.N.Y. 1992).

[127] *See, e.g., Newport v. Newport*, 245 S.E.2d 134 (Va. 1978); Unif. Marriage and Divorce Act § 208(1) (1987); *see also* Homer Clark, *supra* note 7, at 452.

[128] *See Loeb v. Loeb*, 152 N.E.2d 36 (N.Y. 1958).

[129] 245 S.E.2d 134 (Va. 1978).

[130] *See, e.g., Hudson v. Hudson*, 344 P.2d 295 (Cal. 1959); *Stambaugh v. Stambaugh*, 329 A.2d 483 (Pa. 1974); *Morphet v. Morphet*, 502 P.2d 255 (Or. 1972); *Burton v. Burton*, 376 S.W.2d 504 (Tenn. Ct. App. 1963). Also compare Restatement (Second) of Conflict of Laws § 77 Comment f (1971) with Homer Clark, *supra* note 7, at 452–53.

assertion of personal jurisdiction over both spouses in divorce actions.[131] These statutes are intended to enable the forum court to determine related marital support and property rights in a divorce action even when the defendant spouse no longer resides in the state at the time of the divorce.

To assure constitutional "minimum contacts" necessary for a valid assertion of such long-arm jurisdiction, many of these statutes require the spouses to have maintained a marital domicile within the state at the time of their separation. Thus, a brief stay in the state during any period of time will not be sufficient for valid assertion of long-arm jurisdiction.[132]

In *Hine v. Clendenning*,[133] the Supreme Court of Oklahoma held that personal jurisdiction could be exercised over an absent husband in an action for divorce, support and attorney fees, pursuant to the state's long-arm statute. The couple had been married in Oklahoma and had resided in the state during two periods of their marriage, and the husband had obtained a medical license and registered to vote in Oklahoma. Although the couple later moved to California when the husband entered the Air Force, the husband continued to vote in Oklahoma. He later demanded that the wife return to her parents' home in Oklahoma and refused to allow her to return to California. In light of these facts and the interest of the state in assuring financial relief for its residents in divorce actions, the court concluded that the husband had maintained sufficient minimum contacts to satisfy the constitutional requirements for assertion of jurisdiction.

Even when a state long-arm statute does not specifically apply to divorce, states have sometimes applied more general long-arm statutes to assert jurisdiction in divorce or related family law matters.[134] To avoid constitutional challenges, however, the defendant's connections with the forum state must not only fall within the actions described in the state's long-arm statute, but must fulfill the constitutional "minimum contacts" requirements.[135]

[J] Collateral Attack and Estoppel

Whether a divorce decree may be collaterally attacked may depend on whether the divorce action was ex parte or bilateral and on the identity

---

[131] *See, e.g.*, Me. Rev. Stat. tit. 14 § 704-A(2)(G) (1980); Va. Code Ann. § 8.01-328.1(A)(9) (1992); Wis. Stat. Ann. § 801.05(11) (West 1994).

[132] *See, e.g., Thompson v. Thompson*, 657 S.W.2d 629 (Mo. 1983); see also Kulko v. Superior Court, 436 U.S. 84 (1978), *discussed infra*, § 9.02[E].

[133] 465 P.2d 460 (Okla. 1970).

[134] *See, e.g., Ross v. Ross*, 358 N.E.2d 437 (Mass. 1976) (execution of separation agreement constitutes purposefully availing oneself of privilege of conducting activities in state); *Poindexter v. Willis*, 231 N.E.2d 1 (Ill. App. Ct. 1967) (support for non-marital child). *But see Janni v. Janni*, 611 S.W.2d 785 (Ark. 1981) (long-arm statute did not extend to confer jurisdiction over child support on divorce when acts of husband occurred in other state, despite commission of act which caused harmful consequences in Arkansas); *Boyer v. Boyer*, 383 N.E.2d 223 (Ill. 1978) (failure of defendant to make alimony payments ordered by foreign decree not commission of tortious act in Illinois). *See also* Joyce Green, *supra* note 1, at 141–143; Homer Clark, *supra* note 7, at 448.

[135] *See infra* § 9.02[E].

of the person challenging that decree in a subsequent action. If an ex parte divorce is invalid under the *Williams I* or *Williams II* doctrine,[136] the party who obtained the invalid decree may be estopped by his or her conduct to deny its invalidity. The non-appearing defendant, however, is not estopped from attacking the invalid ex parte decree unless he or she remarried in reliance on the decree or benefitted in other ways from assuming the validity of that decree.[137] Under the *Sherrer* doctrine of res judicata or estoppel by judgment, neither party can thereafter collaterally attack a bilateral divorce, even if based on invalid jurisdiction, due to estoppel by conduct and estoppel by judgment.[138]

The overwhelming majority of American states refuse to recognize foreign country divorces, regardless of the decree's validity in the nation awarding it, unless at least one of the spouses was a bona fide domiciliary of that country at the time the divorce was rendered.[139] A minority of states recognize foreign country bilateral divorces not based on domicile under a theory of comity, but all states, on that same theory, refuse to recognize foreign country ex parte or mail-order divorces without a domicile requirement. However, even though these divorces are legally invalid, certain estoppel defenses may nevertheless bar the parties from collaterally attacking the decree.

Although courts in this country are likely to deny comity to a foreign country migratory divorce decree and consider the decree void, the spouse who obtained the foreign divorce generally will be estopped from denying its validity.[140] In *Perrin v. Perrin*,[141] a defendant husband appealed the decision of the District Court of the Virgin Islands that granted the wife a divorce and custody. The wife had obtained a divorce decree in Mexico six months earlier, where she had appeared personally and the husband appeared by a duly empowered attorney and filed a consenting answer. The appellate court reversed the District Court, holding that the husband's motion to dismiss for lack of subject matter jurisdiction, holding that there was no marriage to dissolve because it had already been dissolved in the Mexican proceeding. Recognizing that domicile of one of the spouses in the foreign country is usually required, such proceedings should be recognized as a matter of comity where no public policy is offended. Because the wife had initiated the earlier Mexican proceeding as a bilateral divorce, she was precluded from denying the validity of that proceeding.

Similarly, if a subsequent spouse of a party actively helps procure the invalid decree, estoppel by conduct may also prevent that spouse from later

---

[136] *See supra* § 8.02[E][1].

[137] *See* Restatement of Conflict of Laws § 112 (1934); Restatement (Second) of Conflict of Laws § 74 Comment b (1971).

[138] *See supra notes 79–82 and accompanying text.*

[139] *See supra* § 8.02[G][2].

[140] *See, e.g., Contra Costa Country ex rel. Petersen v. Petersen*, 451 N.W.2d 390 (Neb. 1990); *Lowenschuss v. Lowenschuss*, 579 A.2d 377 (Pa. Super. Ct. 1990).

[141] 408 F.2d 107 (3d Cir. 1969). *See also, e.g., Mayer v. Mayer*, 311 S.E.2d 659 (N.C. Ct. App. 1984), appeal denied, 321 S.E.2d 140 (N.C. 1984); *Spellens v. Spellens*, 317 P.2d 613 (Cal. 1957); *Bruneau v. Bruneau*, 489 A.2d 1049 (Conn. App. Ct. 1985).

repudiating the divorce.[142] For example, the court in *Mayer v. Mayer*,[143] applied the doctrine of "quasi-estoppel," or estoppel by conduct, to bar a husband from attacking his wife's earlier Dominican divorce which he had helped her obtain. It held that despite the state's strong policy against foreign divorces, "it would be even more inimical to our law and to our public policy, to permit [the husband] to avoid his marital obligations by acting inconsistently with his prior conduct."[144] The court emphasized that the estoppel did not validate the foreign divorce, rather

> [t]here is a difference, however, between declaring a marriage valid and preventing one from asserting its invalidity. The theory behind the equitable estoppel doctrine is not to make legally valid a void divorce or to make an invalid marriage valid, but rather, to prevent one from disrupting family relations by allowing one to avoid obligations as a spouse.[145]

Thus, the doctrine of equitable estoppel merely forecloses the attacking party from asserting its invalidity.[146] The same void divorce might still be collaterally attacked by the state or by another interested third party.

In many states, estoppel by conduct and other equitable doctrines, such as laches or unclean hands, may effectively bar the party attacking the decree from obtaining a judgment of invalidity. The result is the modern concept of "practical" recognition of a divorce decree which would otherwise have no legal effect. Similarly, if the person attacking a void divorce is "taking a position inconsistent with his past conduct, or if the parties to the action have relied on the divorce, and if, in addition, holding the divorce invalid will upset relationships or expectations formed in reliance upon the divorce, then estoppel will preclude calling the divorce in question."[147] Moreover, these same equitable principles may bar a third party, such as a subsequent spouse of a party who obtained a foreign divorce, from later attacking the decree and, consequently, the validity of the later marriage.[148]

Some states, however, have refused to follow this modern trend. A more conservative approach was taken by the Louisiana court in *Everett v. Everett*,[149] which rejected any estoppel defense in holding a bilateral

---

[142] *See, e.g., Mayer v. Mayer*, 311 S.E.2d 659 (N.C. Ct. App. 1984), appeal denied, 321 S.E.2d 140 (N.C. 1984); *Spellens v. Spellens*, 317 P.2d 613 (Cal. 1957); *Bruneau v. Bruneau*, 489 A.2d 1049 (Conn. App. Ct. 1985).

[143] 311 S.E.2d 659 (N.C. Ct. App. 1984), appeal denied, 321 S.E.2d 140 (N.C. 1984). *See supra* § 8.02[E][2].

[144] *Id.* at 669.

[145] *Id.* at 536, 311 S.E.2d at 663.

[146] *Accord Kazin v. Kazin*, 405 A.2d 360 (N.J. 1979).

[147] Homer H. Clark, Jr., *Estoppel Against Jurisdictional Attack on Decrees of Divorce*, 70 Yale L.J. 45, 57 (1960).

[148] *See, e.g., Zwerling v. Zwerling*, 244 S.E.2d 311 (S.C. 1978) (second husband, who knew of wife's bilateral Mexican divorce from first husband, could not attack validity of his subsequent marriage).

[149] 345 So. 2d 586 (La. Ct. App. 1977).

Dominican divorce invalid, thus permitting the wife to pursue a Louisiana divorce on adultery grounds.

Even within the same jurisdiction, courts have been inconsistent in their approaches to an estoppel defense. Three different estoppel theories have been used, often within the same jurisdiction. Under the "traditional" rule, neither the domiciliary state nor the parties themselves are bound by any estoppel defense.[150] Under the "practical recognition" or "sociological" view, a person who has obtained a void divorce, or who has assisted in obtaining a void divorce, will be precluded from attacking the validity of that divorce, if, under the circumstances, it would be inequitable to do so.[151] Under the "status versus property right" doctrine, an estoppel defense is denied in an action to determine marital status, but may apply when the action deals with a related marital property right or spousal support.[152]

Regardless of whether the parties themselves are estopped from challenging an invalid divorce decree, uncertainty remains whether the state of domicile itself may collaterally attack a void divorce, such as in a bigamy or adultery prosecution.[153] Most of the cases holding that the state was not barred were decided before the *Sherrer* case,[154] and some recent commentators now believe that the state may not collaterally attack a bilateral divorce decree, regardless of its actual lack of validity.[155]

Interested third parties, other than the spouses or the state, on occasion have attempted to collaterally attack an invalid divorce decree. For example, in *Johnson v. Muelberger*,[156] a daughter by a man's first marriage attacked the validity of her deceased father's Florida divorce from his second wife based on the latter's sham domicile in Florida. Had she been successful, the daughter, who was the sole beneficiary under her father's will, would have inherited his entire estate by establishing that his third marriage was bigamous and void, preventing his third wife from claiming a statutory share. The United States Supreme Court held that where the parties to the divorce themselves could not have collaterally attacked the decree, children or other strangers to the divorce proceedings were similarly barred by res judicata or estoppel by judgment under the *Sherrer* doctrine.[157]

[150] *See, e.g., Everett v. Everett*, 345 So. 2d 586 (La. Ct. App. 1977); *In re Estate of Steffke*, 222 N.W.2d 624 (Wis. 1974).

[151] *See, e.g., Sherrer v. Sherrer*, 334 U.S. 343 (1948); *Kazin v. Kazin*, 405 A.2d 360 (N.J. 1979); *see also supra* note 79 and accompanying text.

[152] *See, e.g., Caldwell v. Caldwell*, 81 N.E.2d 60 (N.Y. 1948); *Rabourn v. Rabourn*, 385 P.2d 581 (Alaska 1963).

[153] *See, e.g., Zenker v. Zenker, 72 N.W.2d 809 (Neb. 1955); State v. DeMeo, 118 A.2d 1 (N.J. 1995).* Also compare David Currie, *supra* note 94, at 54–55 n. 130, with Albert Ehrenzweig, Conflict of Laws 253 (1962).

[154] *See, e.g., Lipham v. State*, 22 S.E.2d 532 (Ga. Ct. App. 1942).

[155] *See* Eugene Scoles & Peter Hay, Conflict of Laws § 15.11 (1982).

[156] 340 U.S. 581 (1951).

[157] *See also Evans v. Asphalt Roads & Materials, Inc.*, 72 S.E.2d 321 (Va. 1952) (under common law rule, son of a deceased employee could not collaterally attack validity of his father's Nevada divorce unless son had a pre-existing interest at time of divorce; worker's

§ 8.03 Divorce Grounds and Defenses

[A] Introduction

The role of traditional fault grounds for divorce, as well as their impact on the economic incidents of marriage, has declined significantly since the adoption of no-fault statutory grounds for divorce in all states. Nevertheless, traditional fault grounds remain important for several reasons. First, no-fault grounds have been enacted as an alternative, not a replacement, to fault grounds in the majority of states. Second, fault remains a factor in awarding spousal support or dividing marital property in many states. And third, family law remains in transition, and although some commentators believe no-fault laws, with additional safeguards for dependent spouses and children, ultimately will prevail,[158] others maintain that fault still serves a legitimate role in some aspects of dissolution.[159] Each state's legislature must determine for itself what role, if any, marital fault should play in divorce proceedings in its state.[160]

[B] Fault Grounds for Divorce

[1] Bed and Board Divorces and Absolute Divorces

Although the grounds for divorce are completely statutory in the United States, those grounds evolved from the English ecclesiastical law and from equitable rules. Until recently, English law did not recognize absolute divorce, or divorce from the bonds of matrimony, which terminates the parties' marital status. Rather, when certain serious marital problems arose, the innocent party could be granted a divorce from bed and board, or divorce *a mensa et thoro*, which amounted to a legal separation.

The divorce from bed and board, still recognized in about half the American states today, is a judicial decree which orders the spouses to live separate and apart, but does not affect their marital status and, thus, neither spouse is free to remarry. Because the parties remain legally married, the marital duty of support continues, and in this respect the action for divorce from bed and board differs little from an action for separate maintenance or alimony without divorce.[161] In some states,

---

compensation benefits considered mere expectancy, not pre-existing interest). *But see Old Colony Trust v. Porter*, 88 N.E.2d 135 (Mass. 1949) (third-party interest does not always need to be pre-existing at time of divorce).

[158] *See, e.g.*, Ira Ellman, *The Place of Fault in a Modern Divorce Law*, 28 Ariz. St. L.J. 773 (1996); Norman Lichtenstein, *Marital Misconduct and the Allocation of Financial Resources at Divorce: A Farewell to Fault*, 54 UMKC L. Rev. 1 (1985); Herma Hill Kay, *Equality and Difference: A Perspective on No-Fault Divorce and its Aftermath*, 56 U. Cinn. L. Rev. 1 (1987).

[159] *See, e.g.*, Michael Redman, *Coming Down Hard on No-Fault: Why the Author Believes that No-Fault Divorce is an Experiment that Failed*, 10 Fam. Advoc. 7, 39 (Fall, 1987); Abrams, *The Effect of Marital Misconduct on Monetary Awards*, 57 Fla. Bar J. 95 (Feb. 1983).

[160] *See generally* Harvey Golden & Michael Taylor, *Fault Enforces Accountability*, 10 Fam.Advoc. 11, 12 (Fall 1987).

[161] *See supra* § 3.11. *See generally* Homer Clark, *supra* note 7, at 266.

statutes that authorize divorce from bed and board also allow the court to divide property and enter child custody decrees.[162]

If the parties reconcile, they may have the decree of divorce from bed and board terminated. Under some statutes, if the parties fail to reconcile, the decree for divorce from bed and board may be converted into an absolute divorce after a specific time has elapsed.[163]

American law, influenced by the Protestant reformers, has always taken a more liberal view of divorce than English law, and statutes permitting absolute divorce were enacted during the colonial period. Although judicial separations were not favored, they were sometimes allowed. Most importantly, however, American law borrowed the traditional English grounds of adultery, cruelty, and desertion, which had been developed in the actions of divorce from bed and board and separate maintenance, and applied those grounds to actions for absolute divorce. After the American Revolution, many states modified those traditional grounds and often added additional statutory grounds.[164]

[2] Adultery Grounds

Adultery, a traditional fault ground, is currently a ground for divorce in approximately 29 states.[165] Adultery is generally defined as sexual intercourse by either spouse with someone other than their spouse. Such actions may constitute adultery although the spouses are living separate and apart, as long as the marriage has not been legally dissolved.[166] Even in situations where the parties have entered into a separation agreement, adulterous behavior may provide grounds for divorce. For example, in *Hanger v. Hanger*,[167] the wife had admitted to her husband that she was having an affair. They thereafter entered into a separation agreement providing in pertinent part that the husband waived his right to sue for divorce on grounds of adultery. After the wife began to cohabit with another man, the husband had an adulterous affair, upon which the wife based an action for divorce. The court held that a separation agreement would not allow the parties to avoid claims of adultery because the adultery is an offense against the institution of marriage which the parties cannot contract away. Furthermore, the husband could not raise the wife's previous adultery because of the agreement, and the wife obtained a divorce based on grounds of the husband's adultery.

Some jurisdictions also regard sexual intercourse with a person of the same sex as adultery.[168] Some courts have held that sexual activities short

---

[162] Homer Clark, *supra* note 7, at 267.

[163] *See, e.g.*, Unif. Marriage & Divorce Act § 314, 9A part II U.L.A. 75 (1998); N.Y. Dom. Rel. L. § 170(5) (1977).

[164] *See* Homer Clark, *supra* note 7, at 406–409.

[165] *See* [Reference File — State Divorce Laws] Fam. L. Rep. (BNA) 400ii (1989).

[166] *See, e.g., Clark v. Clark*, 644 S.W.2d 681 (Tenn. Ct. App. 1982).

[167] Civ. No. D1382-74 (D.C. Super. Ct. Aug. 31, 1974).

[168] *See, e.g., Bales v. Hack*, 509 N.E.2d 95 (Ohio Ct. App. 1986) (although homosexuality

of intercourse may constitute adultery.[169]

Adultery cases frequently involve problems of proof because there are seldom any eyewitnesses to the act. Adultery may be proved by circumstantial evidence, but the standard of proof varies from a preponderance of the evidence in many states to clear and convincing evidence or beyond a reasonable doubt in others states.[170] In *Patzschke v. Patzschke*,[171] the Maryland Court of Appeals upheld a divorce granted to the husband on grounds of the wife's adultery.[172] The court held that circumstantial evidence which clearly establishes that the accused spouse had both the disposition and the opportunity to commit the offense is sufficient. In *Patzschke*, a pattern of unusual behavior by the wife, substantiated by private detectives' observations, although not wholly conclusive of adulterous behavior, was believable and adequate.

In addition to difficult problems of proof, many jurisdictions also recognize a complex assortment of defenses to adultery.[173] The fact that the spouse was intoxicated at the time of the adulterous acts, however, is not a defense to adultery.[174] Although the plaintiff in a divorce case may not have sufficient evidence to prove adultery, the same facts may constitute cruelty as a ground for divorce.[175]

[3] Cruelty Grounds

Prior to the enactment of no-fault statutes, the traditional fault ground of cruelty was the most commonly utilized ground for divorce in the United States. Cruelty, sometimes designated cruel and inhuman treatment, is

---

not a specifically enumerated ground for divorce, it could constitute adultery or extreme cruelty); *M.V.R. v. T.M.R.*, 454 N.Y.S.2d 779 (N.Y. Sup. Ct. 1982) (extramarital homosexual act may be grounds for divorce, but has no relevance in equitable distribution of property, where fault may not be introduced).

[169] *See, e.g., Menge v. Menge*, 491 So. 2d 700 (La. Ct. App. 1986) (wife's admission of having had oral sex but not coitus fell under definition of adultery).

[170] *Compare, e.g., Westervelt v. Westervelt*, 258 N.E.2d 98 (N.Y. 1970) (evidence of spouse's cohabitation with another insufficient to prove adultery); *Seeman v. Seeman*, 355 S.E.2d 884 (Va. 1987) (evidence that defendant wife had spent ten nights in room with adult male insufficient to prove adultery when wife testified that she had not slept with the man due to her strong religious beliefs) *with Everett v. Everett*, 345 So. 2d 586 (La. Ct. App. 1977) ("Courts are a bit more sophisticated today and infer that people do what comes naturally when they have the opportunity.").

[171] 238 A.2d 119 (Md. 1968).

[172] *See also Lickle v. Lickle*, 52 A.2d 910 (Md. 1947) (evidence that husband and another, married, woman, vacationed together and shared a hotel room registered to him and his family, that he visited her regularly at her home in four separate residences, spent the night with her several times a week and was at her house most of the time, in addition to her husband's testimony that he was serving in military duty overseas at the time and his wife had refused to have sexual relations with him for more than two years, was sufficient circumstantial evidence of adultery).

[173] *See, e.g., Surbey v. Surbey*, 360 S.E.2d 873 (Va. Ct. App. 1987), discussed infra § 8.03[F].

[174] *See Miller v. Miller*, 116 A. 840 (Md. 1922).

[175] *See, e.g., Bales v. Hack*, 509 N.E.2d 95 (Ohio Ct. App. 1986) (although homosexuality not specifically enumerated ground for divorce, it could constitute adultery or extreme cruelty).

currently a ground for divorce in about 28 states.[176] Cruelty typically has been defined as bodily harm, or reasonable apprehension of bodily harm, that endangers life, limb, or health, and renders marital cohabitation unsafe or improper.[177]

Traditionally, cruelty required successive acts of ill-treatment over an extended period of time. A single act of physical cruelty ordinarily did not provide a basis for divorce unless the act was so severe and atrocious that it endangered life or inflicted serious bodily harm, or caused reasonable apprehension of serious danger in the future.[178]

The ground of cruelty has been liberalized to a great extent over the past few decades. In states which retain cruelty as a ground for divorce, most courts today recognize mental, as well as physical, cruelty. In *Hughes v. Hughes*,[179] the Louisiana Court of Appeals considered the sufficiency of evidence necessary to sustain a separation from bed and board based on mental cruelty. The wife's allegations of the husband's cold and indifferent treatment, threats, and generally abusive behavior, were substantiated by the parties' only child, and the court found sufficient mental harassment to sustain her action and defeat the husband's counterclaim that the wife had abandoned him.

In *Brady v. Brady*,[180] the New York court concluded that the conduct constituting cruel and inhuman treatment may partially depend on the length of the marriage. It noted that although isolated acts of mistreatment might be considered substantial misconduct in a marriage of short duration, similar conduct might indicate only "transient discord" in a long-term marriage and a higher degree of proof would be demanded. The court found that such a standard was especially important when a spouse would be ineligible to receive alimony if he or she was at fault in the divorce. Although the law no longer precluded alimony because of marital misconduct, the court held that the duration of the marriage remained relevant and that the alleged actions must be viewed in the context of the entire marriage, including its duration, before deciding if those actions properly can be designated cruel and inhuman. Despite the broad discretion of the trial court, it cannot grant a divorce based on cruelty merely because it concludes that the marriage is "dead."

In *Muhammad v. Muhammad*,[181] however, the Mississippi Supreme Court determined that a divorce may be obtained on cruelty grounds without proof that intolerable conditions had been caused by the offending spouse, but rather that they were inseparable from the marital relationship itself. In *Muhammad*, the couple had converted to the Black Muslim religion and moved from Michigan to the University of Islam in Mississippi.

---

[176] *See* [Reference File — State Divorce Laws] Fam. L. Rep. (BNA) 400(ii) (1989).

[177] *See, e.g., Brady v. Brady*, 476 N.E.2d 290 (N.Y. 1985).

[178] *See, e.g., Gibson v. Gibson*, 322 S.E.2d 680 (S.C. App. 1984).

[179] 326 So. 2d 877 (La. Ct. App. 1976)

[180] 476 N.E.2d 290 (N.Y. 1985).

[181] 622 So. 2d 1239 (Miss. 1993).

The wife was extremely dissatisfied with the living conditions at the University, including the regulation of family relations, diet, personal mobility, and privacy, and returned to Michigan with the children after two years and sought a divorce. The court reasoned that one of the primary considerations in granting a divorce on cruelty grounds is whether the nonoffending spouse finds the situation in tolerable, with any change in those circumstances being unforeseeable.

Divorces based on cruelty have included such diverse acts as a spouse's insistence on "excessive, unnatural, or otherwise unreasonable" sexual intercourse,[182] refusal to engage in "reasonable" sexual intercourse,[183] mistreatment and abuse of children,[184] and transvestitism or transsexualism.[185] Similarly, verbal and physical abuse, non-support, homosexuality, drunkenness or use of drugs, false accusations of infidelity or criminal misconduct, and general marital unkindness have supported divorce actions based on cruelty.[186] If a spouse's cruelty forces the other spouse out of the marital home, the offending spouse may be guilty of constructive desertion as well as cruelty.[187]

Not all allegations of mistreatment rise to the level of cruelty, however. In *Benscoter v. Benscoter*,[188] the husband petitioned for divorce based on grounds of cruelty, alleging that his wife of 16 years, who had been diagnosed with multiple sclerosis a year earlier, had complained about, and blamed him for, their having four sons and no daughters, and was sporadically verbally abusive. The court found that because the husband had tolerated verbal abuse and complaints for many years prior to filing for divorce, his "condition could not have been intolerable nor his life so burdensome as he now alleges," and that the wife's alleged behavior was not the "course of conduct" required by law.[189] The court concluded that the wife's ill health explained and excused her actions. Further, evidence of the husband's extramarital affair made him a non-innocent party and, therefore, not entitled to a divorce on cruelty grounds.

[4] Desertion Grounds

Desertion, sometimes designated abandonment, is another traditional fault ground for divorce that is currently recognized in approximately 30 states.[190] The ground of desertion has been defined as the breaking off of

---

[182] *See Thomason v. Thomason*, 332 S.W.2d 148 (Tex. Civ. App. 1959).

[183] *See Mante v. Mante*, 309 N.Y.S.2d 944 (N.Y. App. Div. 1970).

[184] *See Halderman v. Halderman*, 326 A.2d 908 (Pa. Super. Ct. 1974).

[185] *See Steinke v. Steinke*, 357 A.2d 674 (Pa. Super. Ct. 1976). *See* James White, *Symposium: One Hundred Years of Uniform State Laws, Ex Proprio Vigore*, 89 Mich. L. Rev. 2096 (1991).

[186] *See* James White, *Symposium: One Hundred Years of Uniform State Laws, Ex Proprio Vigore*, 89 Mich. L. Rev. 2096 (1991).

[187] *See Day v. Day*, 501 So. 2d 353 (Miss. 1987); *Weatherspoon v. Weatherspoon*, 246 P.2d 581 (Or. 1952).

[188] 188 A.2d 859 (Pa. Super. Ct. 1963).

[189] *Id.* at 860.

[190] *See* [Reference File — State Divorce Laws] Fam. L. Rep. (BNA) 400ii (1989).

marital cohabitation with an intent to end the marriage on the part of the deserting spouse. It thus involves a voluntary separation by one spouse from the other, with the intent not to resume marital cohabitation, and without justification or the consent of the other spouse.[191] A separation by mutual consent is not desertion by either party.[192] In *Gottlieb v. Gottlieb*,[193] the Virginia Court of Appeals held that a spouse who reasonably fears for his or her life or health by remaining in the home and has unsuccessfully taken reasonable measures to eliminate the danger has not deserted the other spouse by leaving the household.

In the past, a husband could divorce his wife for desertion if she failed to accompany him wherever he chose to live. The Court of Appeals of Louisiana held that a statute defining desertion in this manner violates equal protection in *Crosby v. Crosby*,[194] a case in which a wife had been denied alimony for desertion under this statute.

In *Reid v. Reid*,[195] the Virginia Court of Appeals reversed the divorce court's conclusion that a wife, as a matter of law, had not intended to desert the marriage when she informed her husband that she wanted a separation and left the marital home. Although she claimed she wanted to show her husband the seriousness of their marital problems, stemming from sexual inactivity, lack of meaningful communication, and her husband's excessive work habits and lack of involvement with their children, the court held that her complaints were not attributable solely to the conduct of the husband, but rather to their different personalities and the husband's efforts to financially support his family. Additionally, the fact that the wife filed for divorce two months after leaving the marital home supported its conclusion that she had not intended only a temporary separation.

Actions that fall short of physically leaving the marital home may constitute constructive desertion. For example, one recent case held that the wife's wilful withdrawal of sexual privileges from her husband without just cause and her breach and neglect of her other marital duties, such as doing her husband's laundry, cleaning, preparing meals, and failing to help alleviate her husband's financial problems, which destroyed the couple's home life, gave the husband sufficient evidence of desertion.[196] Constructive desertion may also operate as a defense to the other spouse's divorce action.[197]

---

[191] *See, e.g., Bergeron v. Bergeron*, 372 So. 2d 731 (La. Ct. App. 1979); *In re Marriage of Jones*, 412 N.E.2d 1122 (Ill. App. Ct. 1980).

[192] *See, e.g., Day v. Day*, 501 So. 2d 353 (Miss. 1987) (living separate and apart prior to divorce did not constitute desertion).

[193] 448 S.E.2d 666 (Va. Ct. App. 1994).

[194] 434 So. 2d 162 (La. Ct. App. 1983).

[195] 375 S.E.2d 533 (Va. Ct. App. 1989).

[196] *See Jamison v. Jamison*, 352 S.E.2d 719 (Va. Ct. App. 1987).

[197] *Alphin v. Alphin*, 424 S.E.2d 572 (Va. Ct. App. 1992).

[5] Other Miscellaneous Fault Grounds

At various times, states have recognized numerous other statutory fault grounds for divorce, including conviction of a crime, drunkenness, or drug addiction. In *Husband D. v. Wife D.*,[198] the court construed the husband's allegations that the wife had been habitually drunk for over two years as a petition for divorce based on statutory grounds of "habitual intemperance . . . so destructive of the marriage relation that the petitioner cannot reasonably be expected to continue in that relation."[199] The trial court had found the parties were both alcoholics and granted the divorce. The appellate court reversed because the parties frequently drank together before and during the marriage and the difference between their drinking habits was one of degree only. Although it found that the defenses of condonation and connivance did not apply, it held that the doctrine of recrimination barred the divorce, because only an injured or innocent party may obtain a divorce. The court further found that the wife's behavior did not have a sufficiently adverse effect on the husband's life, as he admitted that she adequately maintained the household; therefore, it denied him a decree of divorce.

Some states have authorized divorce on grounds of insanity;[200] however, in others, insanity may constitute a defense to a fault-based divorce because of a lack of intent to commit a marital offense.[201] In *Anonymous v. Anonymous*,[202] a wife unsuccessfully defended her husband's divorce action on grounds of adultery based on her insanity. The wife's psychiatrist testified that the wife did not or could not appreciate the wrongfulness of her behavior because of her mental illness. The court held that the spouse asserting an insanity defense must overcome a presumption of sanity by a preponderance of the evidence. Although the wife had testified that she attempted to resist the adulterous affair, but felt compelled to continue, the court concluded that she appreciated the wrongfulness of her actions, and therefore had not overcome the presumption of sanity.

[C] Defenses to Fault-Based Divorce

The system of fault-based grounds for divorce generated a complex system of defenses to those grounds. The decline in the importance of fault-based grounds has led to a corresponding decrease in the relevance, and in some states, complete obsolescence, of the traditional defenses, even when fault grounds remain coexistent with no-fault grounds. Where they are recognized today, these defenses only apply to fault-based divorce grounds and have no application to no-fault divorces. To the extent that fault continues to play a role in divorce today, however, some of those defenses remain applicable.

---

[198] 383 A.2d 302 (Del. Fam. Ct. 1977)

[199] 13 Del. Code Ann. tit. 13, § 1503(5) (1999).

[200] *See* Idaho Code § 32-603(7) (1996).

[201] *See* Homer Clark, *supra* note 7, at 534.

[202] 236 N.Y.S.2d 288 (N.Y. Sup. Ct. 1962).

Four traditional defenses to fault-based divorce were commonly available: connivance, collusion, condonation, and recrimination. Some states recognized additional statutory or common law defenses. Justification also constituted a defense to the divorce ground of desertion. In some jurisdictions, certain types of marital fault were deemed more serious than others; in other states, particular defenses were available only with respect to specific fault grounds, but not to other grounds.

[1] Connivance

Connivance occurs when one spouse procures or consents to the other spouse's commission of a marital fault. The defense of connivance has also been based on the equitable clean hands doctrine.[203]

Connivance was primarily applied as a defense to a divorce brought on grounds of adultery, but could apply to other fault grounds as well.[204] For example, a husband and wife who mutually agreed that the husband would commit adultery or desert the wife to furnish grounds for the wife to bring a divorce action engaged in connivance. The wife would not be entitled to a divorce, as she could not complain of something to which she has consented.

Hiring an agent to seduce a defendant spouse also may constitute connivance.[205] Connivance has been broadly interpreted to include instances in which a spouse knows of the other's inclination to commit a marital offense but does nothing to prevent it. In the 1920 case of *Sargent v. Sargent*,[206] a defense of connivance was successfully raised against the husband's charges that his wife had engaged in adulterous behavior with their chauffeur. The court found that the petitioner had reason to suspect that his wife was inclined towards an illicit relationship with the chauffeur, but did nothing to prevent it. Rather, the husband continued to employ him, left the parties alone in the home at night, and engaged detectives to report to him. The court noted, "He did not even warn her against intimacy with Simmons, but he left her in danger, and did nothing whatever to withdraw her from Simmons' evil influence."[207] It concluded that the husband wanted the wife to commit the offense and, therefore, he had implicitly consented to it.[208]

[2] Collusion

Collusion is a fraud upon the divorce court by the husband and wife, committed by their alleging false evidence of a marital offense in order to

---

[203] *See, e.g., Fonger v. Fonger*, 154 A. 443 (Md. 1931).

[204] Homer Clark, *supra* note 7, at 521.

[205] *See generally* Marvin M. Moore, *An Analysis of Collusion and Connivance Bars to Divorce*, 36 UMKC L. Rev. 193 (1968).

[206] 114 A. 428 (N.J. Super. Ct. Ch. Div. 1920).

[207] *Id.* at 438.

[208] *See also Hollis v. Hollis*, 427 S.E.2d 233 (Va. Ct. App. 1993) (holding that wife's connivance in husband's adultery was established by her encouraging his extramarital affair).

obtain a divorce. The defense was related to the theory that, traditionally, only the injured spouse could be granted a divorce and that injury had to be established by the evidence.[209] However, while the parties' mutual desire for a divorce generally did not amount to collusion unless some fraud was actually perpetrated upon the court,[210] an agreement that one spouse would sue for divorce and the other would not defend has been deemed collusion.[211] In *Fuchs v. Fuchs*,[212] for example, the wife agreed to a default judgment of divorce in exchange for sole custody of the parties' child, then later moved to set aside the judgment. The court granted her motion, based on collusion, holding that the state has a strong interest in the regulation of divorce and a collusively obtained default judgment attempts to subvert the state's interest.

When collusion was discovered at trial, the court could simply deny the divorce and dismiss the case. When collusion was uncovered after a divorce had been finalized, the court could subsequently vacate the divorce decree.[213] If one of the parties had remarried or become dissatisfied with the economic aspects of the divorce, however, vacating the decree would effectively reward one of the wrongdoers, and courts have tended to refuse relief, invoking equitable theories of estoppel, clean hands, or *in pari delicto*.[214]

[3] Condonation and Cohabitation

Condonation is the conditional forgiveness of a marital fault by the aggrieved spouse, with the understanding that the offence will not be reported. Condonation, in effect, places the offending spouse on temporary probation. If the marital fault is repeated or the spouse exhibits conduct that indicates an intention not to perform the terms of the condonation in good faith, the defense is nullified and the divorce ground is revived, even if the later conduct would have been insufficient to provide grounds for divorce in and of itself.[215]

Although condonation may be express or implied, the general rule is that the innocent spouse's knowledge of the marital fault is necessary for a condonation defense to apply.[216] Continued or resumed cohabitation, or resumption of sexual intercourse, with knowledge of the marital offense, historically led to a presumption of condonation. A 1960 English case, *Willan v. Willan*,[217] employed this principle, denying a husband a divorce

---

[209] *See* Homer Clark, *supra* note 7, at 522.

[210] *See* Marvin M. Moore, *supra* note 193.

[211] Homer Clark, *supra* note 7, at 523.

[212] 64 N.Y.S.2d 487 (N.Y. Sup. Ct. 1946).

[213] *See generally* John S. Bradway, *Collusion and the Public Interest in the Law of Divorce*, 47 Cornell L.Q. 372 (1962); Note, 47 Cornell L.Q. 459 (1962).

[214] Homer Clark, *supra* note 7, at 524.

[215] *Wood v. Wood*, 495 So. 2d 503 (Miss. 1986).

[216] *See generally* F. Eugene Reader, *Knowledge or Belief as a Prerequisite for Condonation*, 21 Minn. L. Rev. 408 (1936).

[217] 2 All E.R. 463 (1960).

based on cruelty when he had sexual intercourse with his wife, allegedly at her insistence, on the day the couple separated. When applied to isolated acts of intercourse, condonation has been criticized as discouraging attempts at reconciliation.[218] The New York Appellate Division took this approach in *Haymes v. Haymes,*[219] concluding that a six week attempted reconciliation period was insufficient to preclude a wife from pursuing an otherwise valid claim of abandonment.

[4] Recrimination

Under the doctrine of recrimination, if *both* spouses are guilty of marital misconduct, then any fault-based divorce action must be dismissed, because traditionally a divorce could only be granted to an innocent spouse. Under the recrimination doctrine, both spouses are *in pari delicto* under the "clean hands" rule.[220]

Application of the doctrine of recrimination has led to egregious results. For example, in *Rankin v. Rankin,*[221] both parties had been physically and verbally abusive to each other. The husband presented evidence that the wife had threatened to kill him, both by car and by knife, had thrown hot water on him, called him names, refused to have children, and spit in his face, among other things; the wife claimed that the husband had kicked and beat her, causing serious injuries, and threatened to kill her. The court held that neither spouse was entitled to a divorce based on indignities to the person when neither party was innocent. It concluded:

> The fact that married people do not get along well together does not justify a divorce. Testimony which proves merely an unhappy union, the parties being high strung temperamentally and unsuited to each other and neither being wholly innocent of the causes which resulted in the failure of their marriage, is insufficient to sustain a decree.[222]

Similarly, in *Kucera v. Kucera,*[223] the North Dakota Supreme Court reversed the granting of a divorce on the basis of recrimination. The wife had been pregnant by another man at the time of the marriage, but contended that the husband knew, and adopted the baby at its birth. Both parties indicated that it was doubtful that the marriage would work, but married to give the child a name, and agreed to divorce after a year. After a second child was born, the parties did not engage in sexual relations for a two year period, and the wife resumed a relationship with the father of her first child. The trial court granted a divorce to the wife, on her allegations of grievous mental suffering, and held that insufficient evidence of the wife's adultery

---

[218] Homer Clark, *supra* note 7, at 526–527.

[219] 646 N.Y.S.2d 315 (App. Div. 1996).

[220] *See generally* J. G. Beamer, *Doctrine of Recrimination in Divorce Proceedings*, 10 UMKC L. Rev. 213 (1942).

[221] 124 A.2d 639 (Pa. Super. Ct. 1956).

[222] *Id.* at 644.

[223] 117 N.W.2d 810 (N.D. 1962).

existed. However, Supreme Court held that the husband's allegations did justify a claim of desertion on his behalf, and because both parties had demonstrated sound fault grounds for divorce, the doctrine of recrimination preclude the granting of a divorce to either party.

Under similar circumstances, where the wife had committed adultery after the parties had separated and was able to demonstrate the husband's cruel and inhuman treatment, including verbal abuse, excessive jealousy, apparent infidelity, and causing the closure of the wife's beauty shop, the Mississippi Supreme Court, in *Parker v. Parker*,[224] upheld the court's decision to grant the wife a divorce despite the doctrine of recrimination. The Court reasoned that the traditional justifications of the defense were not applicable in this chase, because marital stability could no longer be promoted and the wife's economic security had already been seriously undermined, and the denial of divorce would perpetuate a bad marriage.

Professor Clark has censured the doctrine of recrimination as an "outrageous legal principle" that "prevents the dissolution of those very marriages most appropriate for dissolution, insuring that warring spouses may never form happier attachments."[225] Fortunately, the doctrine of recrimination has been abolished in most states, and where it still officially exists, it is rarely applied.[226]

[5] Justification

A divorce action based on grounds of desertion may be defended against on the basis of justification. A spouse may be justified in leaving the marital home due to the misconduct of the other spouse. Although some courts have required this misconduct to be equivalent to a specific ground for divorce or "constructive desertion," other courts have simply demanded that the provoking conduct "is inconsistent with the marriage relationship or makes it impossible to continue cohabitation with due regard to safety, health, or self-respect."[227] Adultery and cruelty could never be defended by justification.

[6] Other Defenses

To prevent against the possibility of connivance and collusion of the parties, many states historically required third-party corroboration of the

---

[224] 519 So. 2d 1232 (Miss. 1988).

[225] Homer Clark, *supra* note 7, at 527.

[226] Homer Clark, *supra* note 7, at 528. *But see Merrick v. Merrick*, 627 N.Y.S.2d 884 (N.Y. Sup. Ct. 1995), aff'd, 636 N.Y.S.2d 1006 (N.Y. App. Div. 1995) (applying a recrimination defense to adultery grounds).

[227] Note, *Constructive Desertion—A Broader Basis for Breaking the Bond*, 51 Iowa L. Rev. 108, 120 (1965). *See also, Breschel v. Breschel*, 269 S.E. 2d 363 (Va. 1980) (spouse who reasonably believes health would be endangered by remaining in home, and has unsuccessfully taken reasonable measure to eliminate danger without breaking off cohabitation, not legally at fault in leaving).

divorce ground. [228] Today, in light of no-fault grounds for divorce, lack of corroboration rarely, if ever, bars a divorce.

In addition to the traditional ground of collusion, other types of fraud on the court may result in dismissal of the divorce action or subsequent invalidation of a divorce decree. Broadly speaking, any fraud that affects a judicial proceeding may be a fraud on the court. [229] For instance, the Ohio Supreme Court, in *Coulson v. Coulson*, [230] held that when an attorney's conduct and misrepresentations to the court and to the wife in a divorce action prevented the wife from adequately presenting her case, his conduct interfered with the functioning of the judicial system and constituted a fraud on the court, providing the basis for vacating the divorce decree. At the same time, a fraud between the parties themselves does not necessarily constitute a fraud on the court; in the situation, the defrauded party may need to seek redress from the other party or by a motion for relief from judgment. [231]

Insanity has sometimes been asserted as a defense to a fault grounds divorce, based on the argument that the defendant spouse lacked sufficient capacity to appreciate the wrongfulness of the conduct. In *Simpson v. Simpson*, [232] the Tennessee Supreme Court held that the testimony by the husband's physician, that the husband was suffering from paranoid schizophrenia when he verbally and physically assaulted his wife, was insufficient to demonstrate an insanity defense to her divorce brought on grounds of cruelty and inhuman treatment.

When a party had knowledge of a defense and could have raised it during the divorce proceeding itself, res judicata will prevent subsequent collateral attack. [233] Similarly, even jurisdictional defenses and issues relating to fraud upon the court may be barred by equitable defenses such as laches or estoppel. [234]

A minority of states have statutes of limitation for bringing a divorce based on specific fault grounds. [235] These statutes frequently apply only to divorces based on grounds of adultery.

[D]　Divorce Based upon Living Separate and Apart

Approximately half the states authorize divorce based on living separate and apart for a specified period of time. These statutes are generally

---

[228] 2 Chester G. Vernier, *American Family Laws: A Comparative Study of the Family Law of the Forty-eight American States, Alaska, the District of Columbia, and Hawaii*, note 22 at 142 (1932).

[229] *See* 11 Charles Alan Wright & Arthur Miller, Federal Practice and Procedure (1973) 253, § 2870.

[230] Coulson v. Coulson, 448 N.E.2d 809 (Ohio 1983).

[231] *See* Fed. R. Civ. P. 60(B).

[232] 716 S.W.2d 27 (Tenn. 1986).

[233] *See supra* § 8.02[C] (bilateral divorce).

[234] *See supra* § 8.02[J]; *See also* Homer Clark, *supra* note 7, at 551–559.

[235] *See, e.g.,* N.Y. Dom. Rel. L. § 171(3) (1999) (5 years for adultery actions); Va. Code Ann. § 20-94 (Michie 1995) (5 years for adultery, sodomy, or buggery).

regarded as a form of no-fault divorce because the parties are not required to prove the reasons for the separation. Some of these statutes preceded the widespread enactment of no-fault divorce grounds in general, although many of the earlier versions have since been liberalized.

The specified period of separation for divorce based on living separate and apart varies from sixty days to three years, although periods of six to eighteen months are the most frequently employed.[236] The Uniform Marriage and Divorce Act provides that a marriage may be dissolved if the parties have lived separate and apart for more than 180 days preceding the commencement of the suit.[237]

Mere physical separation alone is insufficient for obtaining a divorce based on grounds of living separate and apart; at least one of the parties must intend to dissolve the marital relationship and must clearly manifest or communicate this intention. In *Sinha v. Sinha*,[238] the husband originally came to the United States to pursue an advanced decree in 1976, while his wife remained in India because of her inability to obtain a visa. For the first two years of their separation, the couple corresponded regularly and the husband professed his love for his wife. In August 1979, three years after his arrival in this country, the husband filed for divorce. The first divorce action was dismissed due to the husband's relocation and he filed a new action, alleging that the parties had lived separate and apart for the requisite three years under Pennsylvania law. The court found that the husband first revealed his intention to terminate the marriage upon filing the initial divorce complaint, not when the couple became physically separated. The court noted, "The demands placed on marriage by modern society will often force a spouse to leave the marital abode for long periods of time. These separations should not to be interpreted as an intent to terminate the marriage."[239] Thus, to satisfy the statutory requirement of living separate and apart, the separation period will not commence until it is clear that at least one of the parties intends to dissolve the marriage. Otherwise, the other spouse would be denied a chance to attempt reconciliation.

The period of separation must be uninterrupted, and the parties may not cohabit during that period. Some older cases held that any voluntary resumption of sexual relations, even casual or isolated instances, during the statutory separation period interrupts the period of separation.[240] Because this approach thwarts attempts at reconciliation and risks manipulation, most modern decisions have concluded that resumption of the

---

[236] *See* Linda Elrod & Robert G. Spector, *A Review of the Year in Family Law*, 30 Fam. L.Q. 765, 807 (1997).

[237] Unif. Marriage and Divorce Act § 302, 9A part I U.L.A. 200 (1998).

[238] 526 A. 2d 765 (Pa. 1987).

[239] *Id.* at 766.

[240] *See Pitts v. Pitts*, 282 S.E.2d 488 (N.C. Ct. App. 1981) (overruled by N.C. Gen. Stat. § 52-10.2 (1999), which provides: "Isolated incidents of sexual intercourse . . . shall not constitute resumption of marital relations").

marital relationship itself, with its corresponding rights and responsibilities, must occur before the ground for divorce is destroyed.[241]

In some circumstances, living in separate dwellings will be insufficient to constitute living separate and apart if the couple in other respects continues their relationship as before. For example, in *Ellam v. Ellam*,[242] the court held that the husband was not entitled to a divorce on grounds of separation when the couple maintained the appearances of marriage. Although the husband slept at his mother's home every night and the couple did not have sexual intercourse during this time, the husband ate his meals, watched television, and kept his vehicle and dog at the marital residences. The court concluded that "the substantial number of the many elements and ties which go into and make up the marital relationship and bind the parties together" precluded them from living separate and apart within the meanings of the divorce statute.

Likewise, in *Bennington v. Bennington*,[243] the Ohio Court of Appeals held that the time during which the husband lived in a travel van located on the same premises as the marital home did not count toward the period of living separate and apart. During that time the husband had no intention of abandoning the marriage, and went regularly into the home to assist his disabled wife. He asserted that he moved into the van because the wife kept the home excessively hot and took 15 to 20 minutes to open the door for him when he returned from work. The court held that because there was no cessation of marital duties, the couple was not actually living separate and apart in the marital sense.

Conversely, some courts have concluded that when a husband and wife occupy separate portions of the same house and have little contact with each other, they may have been "constructively" separated for the requisite time period.[244] Constructive separation may be a sensible approach when the couple's financial circumstances make their living in separate households prohibitive.

A small minority of states provide that the separation required under living separate and apart divorce grounds must be voluntary and by mutual consent of the parties. Thus, if one spouse is mentally incapacitated at the time of separation, the requisite voluntariness for separation would not be present and a divorce on this ground could not be granted.[245] Furthermore, a lack of mutual consent to separate might result in the non-consenting spouse bringing an action for desertion against the separating spouse.

However, a majority of states that have a living separate and apart ground for divorce do not require that the separation be mutual and voluntary, and these statutes therefore approximate a no-fault alternative.

[241] *See Thomas v. Thomas*, 483 A.2d 945 (Pa. Super. Ct. 1984); *Petachenko v. Petachenko*, 350 S.E.2d 600 (Va. 1986).

[242] 333 A.2d 577 (N.J. Super. Ct. 1975).

[243] 381 N.E.2d 1355 (Ohio Ct. App. 1978).

[244] *See, e.g., In re Marriage of Uhls*, 549 S.W.2d 107 (Mo. Ct. App. 1977).

[245] *See, e.g., Adams v. Adams*, 402 So. 2d 300 (La. Ct. App. 1981).

Nevertheless, an *intent* to separate for purposes of ending the marriage must still be shown to avoid "instant to divorces" and to allow an opportunity for reconciliation.[246]

In *Bruce v. Bruce*,[247] the Court of Appeals of North Carolina held that the facts which constitute a separation ground for divorce must be pleaded and proved even though they are uncontested by the defendant spouse, because of the general rule prohibiting default judgments in divorce actions. That court further held that traditional defenses such as recrimination would not be applicable in an action for divorce on grounds of living separate and apart.

[E] No-Fault Divorce Grounds

Approximately 18 states have abolished all fault grounds for divorce and have substituted a no-fault statute as the sole and ground for divorce or dissolution of marriage; the remaining states have combined traditional fault grounds with statutes providing for no-fault divorce.[248] Some no-fault statutes are worded in terms of "irretrievable breakdown" of the marriage, while others are expressed in terms such as "irreconcilable differences," "incompatibility," "living separate and apart," or "mutual consent."[249]

Incompatibility was one of the first forms of no-fault divorce, although it was construed narrowly in earlier cases. The courts often struggled with the factual question of whether a couple was incompatible to the extent that a divorce was warranted. For example, in *Husband W. v. Wife W.*,[250] the Delaware Supreme Court reversed a trial court's refusal to grant a divorce to a husband who had presented evidence of a separation of almost one and a half years. The separation followed numerous violent quarrels involving personal injury, which frequently involved the police and the family court. The trial court found that the husband had not satisfied his burden of proving that no reasonable possibility of reconciliation existed.

Some states will not grant a no-fault divorce absent mutual consent of the parties. For example, in *Marriage of Mitchell*,[251] The Missouri Court of Appeals held that if one party denies under oath that the marriage is irretrievable broken the petitioner must satisfy the court that one of five alternative facts exist, relating to the respondent's behavior or that they have satisfied the provisions for living separate and apart. The Missouri Court of Appeals reiterated this position in *Nieters v. Nieters*,[252] concluding

---

[246] *See, e.g., Hooker v. Hooker*, 211 S.E.2d 34 (Va. 1975) (although couple physically separated earlier, husband was not entitled to divorce until two years after the time at which he could additionally prove intention to terminate marriage).

[247] 339 S.E.2d 855 (N.C. Ct. App. 1986).

[248] *See* [State Divorce Laws], Fam. L. Rep. (BNA) (1989).

[249] *See* Timothy Walker, *Family Law in the Fifty States: An Overview*, 25 Fam. L.Q. 417, 439–40 (1992).

[250] 297 A.2d 39 (Del. 1972).

[251] 545 S.W.2d 313 (Mo. App. 1976).

[252] 815 S.W.2d 124 (Mo. Ct. App. 1991).

that husband's unsubstantiated evidence of the couple's differences in child rearing attitudes and the wife's donation of money to television evangelists failed to establish that the marriage was irretrievably broken.

States vary as to whether a petitioner seeking a no-fault divorce must present factual evidence proving the no fault ground or whether a simple sworn allegation is sufficient. Some states apply a subjective test to determine whether the parties themselves believe that they cannot continue living together as husband and wife. In *Riley v. Riley*,[253] the Florida Court of Appeals interpreted the state's new "irretrievable breakdown" statute to require a judicial inquiry into the circumstances in order to ascertain that the parties could no longer live together and that no reasonable effort could effect a reconciliation. The court continued the proceedings for three months to enable an attempt at reconciliation or consultations with professional counselors before the dissolution would be granted.

Other jurisdictions implement an objective standard based on the court's perception of the facts.[254] In *Hagerty v. Hagerty*,[255] the Minnesota Court refused to engraft an exception onto its dissolution statute based on discord and irretrievable breakdown. The husband in *Hagerty* filed for divorce after the wife requested that he seek treatment for alcoholism and asked him to leave the marital home. The trial court granted the divorce, finding that the husband's alcoholism was the principle cause of the marital discord which had adversely affected the husband's attitude. The wife appealed, arguing that the marriage was salvageable if the husband obtained treatment. The appellate court affirmed, holding that because the statute did not contain a provision for a separate determination of the likelihood of reconciliation, nor did public policy require such an inquiry, the established fact of breakdown would not be defeated. In *Desrochers v. Desrochers*,[256] The New Hampshire Supreme Court stated that although inquiry into the particular circumstances of the couple's relationship is important in deciding whether to grand a divorce, based on irremedial break down, the length of separation and the determination and persistence of the party seeking the divorce is evidence to be considered.

Section 302 of the Uniform Marriage and Divorce Act provides that the marriage may be dissolved as "irretrievably broken" if there is an evidentiary finding that the parties have lived separate and apart for more than 180 days preceding the commencement of the suit *or* if there is "serious marital discord adversely affecting the attitude of one or both parties

---

[253] 271 So. 2d 181 (Fla. Dist. Ct. App. 1972).

[254] *See, e.g., Dunn v. Dunn*, 511 P.2d 427 (Or. Ct. Appl 1973). *Compare Grotelueschen v. Grotelueschen*, 318 N.W.2d 227 (Mich. Ct. App. 1982) (after moving out of home and living with another woman, husband argued that marriage was irretrievably broken and no reconciliation was possible, while wife believed that marriage could still be saved) with *In re Baier's Marriage*, 561 P.2d 20 (Colo. Ct. App. 1977) (wife stated she no longer like or trusted husband, but husband stated that the marriage was satisfactory and wife's problems could be overcome with counseling).

[255] 281 N.W.2d 386 (Minn. 1979).

[256] 347 A.2d 150 (N.H. 1975).

toward the marriage."[257] A marriage may be terminated under such a statute despite one spouse's opposition to absolute divorce or preference for a divorce from bed and board.[258]

In jurisdictions that have supplemented rather than replaced fault grounds with no-fault, conflicts may arise when one spouse seeks a divorce based on a no-fault statute and the other on a fault ground. The no-fault ground will not necessarily override the fault ground, and the courts may need to determine the cause of the marital breakdown and award the divorce accordingly.[259] *Williams v. Williams,*[260] a Virginia case, emphasizes that the trial court has extensive discretion in determining which of conflicting grounds should be the basis of a divorce degree. In *Williams* the husband argued on appeal that, in light of his proof of the wife's adultery, the court should not have granted the divorce on grounds of one year separation. The husband's motive was that adultery would bar the wife from permanent maintenance and support.[261] In addition to affirming the granting of the divorce on no fault grounds, the Virginia Court of Appeals noted that a finding of adultery in not an absolute bar on a spousal support award, not to a recovery of fees and costs.[262]

[F]   Effect of Fault on Property Division and Spousal Support

Obtaining a divorce based upon no-fault grounds does not automatically mean that marital property will be distributed and spousal support will be awarded on a no-fault basis.[263] Courts are almost equally divided on the question of whether legislation adopting no-fault grounds for divorce, as either an exclusive or an alternate ground, also requires that they adopt no-fault property distribution and spousal support principles. A total lack of uniformity exists among states as to whether fault continues to be a relevant factor in dividing marital property or awarding spousal support. While some jurisdictions permit or require consideration of fault or relative merits in formulating financial awards,[264] other states have expressly excluded fault as a factor in determining spousal support or dividing marital property.[265]

---

[257] 9A U.L.A. 96, 120 (1979).

[258] *See Husting v. Husting,* 194 N.W.2d 801 (Wis. 1972); *In re Halford's Marriage,* 528 P.2d 119 (Or. Ct. App. 1974); *Colabianchi V. Colabianchi,* 646 S.W.2d 61 (Mo. 1983). *But see* Tenn. Code Ann. § 36–4–103 (1984). *See also* Homer Clark, *Divorce Policy and Divorce Reform,* 42 U. Colo. L. Rev. 403 (1971).

[259] *See, e.g., Ebbert v. Ebbert,* 459 A.2d 282 (N.H. 1983); *Robertson v. Robertson,* 211 S.E.2d 41 (Va. 1975).

[260] 415 S.E.2d 252 (Va. Ct. App. 1992).

[261] Va. Code § 20–107.1 (listing adultery as the sole fault ground for precluding spousal support).

[262] *See also Hammonds v. Hammonds,* 597 So. 2d 653 (Miss. 1992) (alimony should not have been denied solely because of adulterous behavior).

[263] *See generally* Allen Parkman, *No-Fault Divorce-What Went Wrong* (1992).

[264] *See, e.g., Sparks v. Sparks,* 485 N.W.2d 893 (Mich. 1992); *see also* Timothy Walker, *supra* note 18, at *Table V,* 451–452.

[265] *See* Timothy Walker, *supra* note 18 at *Table V,* 451–452.

Some courts have held that when a divorce is granted on a no-fault ground, facts that might have supported an alternative fault ground are necessary to bar a dependent spouse from receiving alimony. For example, in the Virgin case of *Surbey v. Surbey*,[266] the husband filed for divorce, alleging that the wife's cruel conduct amounted to constructive desertion, which had forced him to leave the marital residence. The wife counter-claimed, arguing that the husband deserted her without causes and that he additionally was guilty of adultery prior to and after their separation. The husband denied the charges, pled condonation as a defense to adultery, and later alleged that the wife had also committed adultery, which she denied. The evidence, supported by detective reports on behalf of both parties, established misconduct by both the husband and the wife. The trial court concluded that because both parties were at fault and were guilty of adultery after their separation, recrimination barred each from using the ground of adultery as basis for divorce, and the divorce was granted on grounds of separation.

The husband in *Surbey* appealed the court's awarding spousal support to the wife, arguing that she should be barred because of her adultery. The Virginia Court of Appeals upheld the award, noting that while post-separation adultery may give a deserting party grounds for divorce, it is unnecessary to determine which party caused the separation which ultimately became the basis for the divorce. Furthermore, because both parties were guilty of adultery, the doctrine of recrimination prevented either from obtaining a divorce on that ground. Therefore, the wife was not barred from receiving spousal support, because neither party's duty of support would be affected absent a finding of fault that would have constituted independent grounds for divorce.

Subsequent to *Surbey*, the Virginia Code was amended to provide that divorces granted on grounds of cruelty, desertion, and conviction of a felony would not constitute an absolute bar to spousal support, but evidence supporting those grounds could be considered factors in determining the amount of support awarded. Adultery remains the only fault ground that would comprise an absolute bar to spousal support, unless "manifest injustice" would occur if support were denied.[267]

In *Tenner v. Tenner*,[268] a wife who committed adultery during marriage and would be barred from receiving maintenance raised the defense of the mental illness of Multiple Personality disorder as an excuse, claiming that it was not the same person who married her husband who had committed adultery, although they occupied the same body. The Kentucky Supreme Court reversed the appellate court, holding that the wife had not demonstrated by a preponderance of the evidence that she had not been able to appreciate the wrongfulness of her conduct, and reinstated the trial court's judgment denying her claim for maintenance.

---

[266] 360 S.E.2d 873 (Va. Ct. App. 1987).

[267] Va. Code Ann. § 20–107.1 (Michie 1995).

[268] 906 S.W.2d 322 (Ky. 1995).

A minority of courts have concluded that enactment of no-fault grounds for divorce has no effect on the traditional bases for awarding alimony, child support, custody, property division, or attorney's fees. Although a trial judge is not required to take fault into consideration in all cases, it may, in its discretion, regard all the facts and circumstances regarding the marriage and the causes for its dissolution. In *Grosskopf v. Grosskopf*,[269] the Wyoming Supreme Court aligned itself with this minority view and denied the wife alimony in light of the extent to which her actions contributed to the break-up of the marriage, despite the fact that the husband was awarded a no-fault divorce based on grounds of irreconcilable differences.

One rationale for considering marital fault relevant in determining spousal support and property division is that although divorce is governed by statute, it is essentially an equitable proceeding and, therefore, the conduct of the parties is always relevant.[270] Some courts regard marital fault as more relevant in awarding spousal support than in distributing marital property.[271]

Other jurisdictions refuse to consider marital fault in determining spousal support and property division on theory that the actual financial needs and abilities of the parties, rather than their marital conduct or misconduct, should control those awards.[272] Thus, in *In re Koch*[273] the court rejected a wife's claim for spousal support based on injuries sustained in a physical confrontation with her husband, absent an actual need arising from her physical condition. Some courts have made exceptions, however, when a spouse's conduct has been outrageous or egregious.[274]

[G] "Economic Fault"

Most states' statutes take into account both the economic and non-economic contributions of the parties to the marriage when equitably distributing marital property or awarding spousal support on divorce.[275] Even in jurisdictions where traditional types of marital fault are not to be considered in dividing property or awarding support, the waste or dissipation of marital assets, or "economic fault," usually is considered relevant in resolving the financial incidents of divorce, although it is often difficult to distinguish between marital fault and economic fault.

---

[269] 677 P.2d 814 (Wyo. 1984).

[270] *See, e.g., Robinson v. Robinson*, 444 A.2d 234, 236 (Conn. 1982) (a spouse "whose conduct has contributed substantially to the breakdown of the marriage should not expect to receive financial kudos for his or her misconduct"); *Williamson v. Williamson*, 367 So. 2d 1016, 1018 (Fla. Dist. Ct. App. 1979) ("A spouse who invokes the jurisdiction of a court of equity to resolve his or her marital difficulties must submit to the equitable doctrines that he who seeks equity must stand before the court with 'clean hands' . . .").

[271] *See* Timothy Walker, *supra* note 18, at *Table V*, 451–452.

[272] *See generally* Norman Lichtenstein, *Marital Misconduct and the Allocation of Financial Resources at Divorce: A Farewell to Fault*, 54 UMKC L. Rev. 1 (1985).

[273] 648 P.2d 406 (Or. Ct. App. 1982).

[274] *Compare D'Acr v. D'Acr*, 395 A.2d 1270 (N.J. Super. Ct. Ch. Div. 1978), *cert. denied*, 451 U.S. 971(1981) *with In re Marriage of Cihak*, 416 N.E.2d 701(Ill. App. Ct. 1981).

[275] *See infra* § 10.12.

Allegations of economic fault may arise when one spouse has "consumed, given away or otherwise transferred, mismanaged, converted or otherwise adversely affected property that, had it been before the court, would have been subject to equitable distribution."[276] Professor Lewis Becker has noted a conflict between the policy of protecting spouses from conduct of the other party that diminishes the amount of property available for equitable distribution and protecting spouses from undue restrictions on the use of their own property. He also warns of an increased risk of perjury if economic fault is considered a factor in property division.[277]

Some courts consider dissipation of marital assets as a factor in determining the shares of remaining property.[278] Dissipation may also be a factor supporting a larger share of marital property when the other spouse has squandered his or her own nonmarital property.[279] Some courts limit consideration of dissipation to actions occurring after the marital relationship has broken down;[280] others look to the motive or nature of the expenditures.[281] In light of the diversity of approaches applied by various courts and other deficiencies in the law, Professor Becker has recommended a nonrestrictive standard for evaluating dissipation, involving a general duty of good faith that does not include expenditures for family support unless a spouse secures an unfair benefit from the use of jointly held funds when he or she had individual funds. He further would except expenditures made with the consent or acquiescence of the other spouse.[282]

[H] Divorce Practice and Procedure

Although divorce law originated in equality and in the ecclesiastical courts, today it is primarily statutory. In general, divorce cases are treated like other civil cases, and, in the absence of a special statutory provisions or local rules, the rules of civil procedure apply. Considerable variation exists among jurisdictions as to the specific rules governing divorce procedure.[283]

The party petitioning for divorce must pay a filing fee and pay the costs of service of process on the defendant. In *Boddie v. Connecticut*,[284] the Supreme Court held that these fees must be waived if the plaintiff is indigent. *Boddie* left open the questions of what constitutes indigency and whether an indigent litigant has a constitutional right to counsel. States

---

[276] Lewis Becker, *Conduct of a Spouse That Dissipates Property Available for Equitable Property Distribution: A Suggested Analysis*, 52 Ohio St. L.J. 95, 96 (1991).

[277] *Id.* at 97.

[278] *See, e.g., Lenczycki v. Lenczycki*, 543 N.Y.S.2d 724 (N.Y. App. Div. 1989); *Booth v. Booth*, 371 S.E.2d 569 (Va. Ct. App. 1988).

[279] *See In re Marriage of Cecil*, 560 N.E.2d 374 (Ill. App. Ct. 1990).

[280] *See In re O'Neill*, 563 N.E.2d 494 (Ill. 1990).

[281] *See* Lewis Becker, *supra* note 253, at 106–111.

[282] *Id.* at 125–132.

[283] *See generally* Homer Clark, *supra* note 7, at 529–30.

[284] 401 U.S. 371(1971).

have varied as to when a party to a divorce proceeding is entitled to court appointed counsel.[285]

In general, only the spouses are appropriate parties to a divorce action, although third parties may be joined in issues other than the granting of the divorce itself if they have an interest in the case, such as the disposition of marital property.[286] Furthermore, a number of states authorize the appointment of a guardian ad litem to protect the interests of the parties' children in divorce actions.[287]

Most courts allow liberal discovery in divorce cases as long as the information is relevant.[288] Discovery may be particularly important in the property division stage of divorce, especially when the couple has considerable assets.

During pending divorce litigation, a divorce court may grant support pendente lite for a dependent spouse and children of the marriage, as well of attorneys' fees.[289] It may also order injunctions to protect the property interests of the spouses and to protect the spouses and children from physical abuse or interferences during the course of the divorce process.[290]

Despite the existence of no-fault divorce, most courts require the petitioner to appear before the court and will not grant a divorce based solely on affidavits. In *Manion v. Manion*[291] the New Jersey Supreme Court held that when the defendant husband neglected to answer or appear, the trial court erred in entering a default judgment of divorce, holding that it is essential that the non-defaulting party appear before the courts to answer any questions it must have. In *In re Marriage of McKim*,[292] the California Supreme Court held that although the general rule was to require appearance, in exceptional cases, an affidavit or the testimony of competent witnesses could be used to establish proof of irreconcilable difference. In this case, the court determined that it would be an unnecessary hardship to deny the wife's divorce because she was unaware that the trial court could, in its discretion, require her appearance, especially in light of the fact that the defaulting husband had appeared and gave sparse testimony that the couple had irreconcilable differences.

Approximately one-half of the states have statutes creating some form of court-ordered conciliation or mediation prior to divorce, in which the spouses meet with a third-party counselor to discuss their marital differences.[293] Under some statutes, this conciliation or mediation process is

---

[285] *See, e.g., Flores v. Flores,* 598 P.2d 893 (Alaska 1979) (denial of counsel to indigent party in child custody case would be fatal to mother's action; court appointed counsel from private bar).

[286] *See* Homer Clark, *supra* note 7, at 532.

[287] *See, e.g.,* Cal. Civ. Code § 4606 (1990); Wis. Stat. Ann. § 767.045 (1993).

[288] *See Roussos v. Roussos,* 434 N.Y.S.2d 600 (N.Y. Sup. Ct. 1980).

[289] *See infra* § 9.04[A], 9.06[B].

[290] *Id. See generally* Homer Clark, *supra* note 7, at 536–539.

[291] 363 A.2d 921 (N.J. Super. 1976).

[292] 493 P.2d 868 (Cal. 1972).

[293] *See infra,* § 8.05 [A].

wholly voluntary, while other statutes, empower the court to order mandatory participation by the spouses, especially when minor children are involved.[294]

In most jurisdictions, divorce cases are tried before a judge without a jury,[295] although a minority of states permit the parties to demand a jury trial.[296] The court may conduct the trial in private if necessary to protect the privacy of the parties and their children, as long as the parties are not deprived of a fair trial.[297]

A few states grant interlocutory decrees of divorce that do not become final until a specified time period has elapsed.[298] In some of these jurisdictions, the divorce automatically becomes final, while in others, the court must enter a final decree.[299] Because the parties remain married during this interlocutory period, problems arise if either spouse attempts to remarry or dies before the decree is finalized.[300]

Death of either party during the divorce action usually results in the automatic abatement of the action.[301] Some courts, however, have continued to divide property if the divorce action was bifurcated and the decree dissolving the marriage was already entered.[302]

[I] Appellate Review

The Rules of Civil Procedure establish the time limitation for filing an appeal from a divorce case, as well as other cases. Except for attacks on the courts' jurisdiction to enter the divorce decree,[303] once the time for appeal expires, the divorce itself and other related issues addressed by the divorce decree will be considered res judicata and not susceptible to later attack, unless appropriate motions are filed based on limited grounds available for reopening judgments such as fraud, mistake, or newly discovered evidence.[304]

---

[294] *See generally* Linda Silberman & Andrew Shepard, *Court-Ordered Mediation in Family Disputes: The New York Proposal*, 14 N.Y.U. Rev. L. & Soc. Change 741 (1986); Nancy Maxwell, *Keeping the Family Out of Court: Court-Ordered Mediation of Custody Disputes under the Kansas Statutes*, 25 Washburn L.J. 203 (1986); Lincoln Clark & Jane Orbeton, *Mandatory Mediation of Divorce: Maine's Experience*, 69 Judicature 310 (Feb.–Mar. 1986); Susan Kuhn, *Mandatory Mediation: California Civil Code Section 4607*, 33 Emory L.J. 733 (1984).

[295] *See, e.g.*, Unif. Marriage and Divorce Act § 302(a)(4), 9A part I U.L.A. 200 (1979); Mich. Com. Laws Ann. § 25.92 (1984).

[296] *See, e.g.*, N.Y. Dom. Rel. Law § 173 (1999); Texas Fam. Code Ann. § 6.703 (West 1998).

[297] *See* Homer Clark, *supra* note 7, at 541.

[298] *See, e.g.*, Cal. Civ. Code Ann. §§ 4512, 4514 (1997); Mass. Gen. Laws Ann. ch. 208, § 21(1998).

[299] *See* Homer Clark, *supra* note 7 at 545.

[300] *Id.* at 545–546.

[301] *See, e.g.*, *Howard v. Howard*, 364 N.E.2d 464 (Ill. App. Ct. 1977); *State ex rel. Rivera v. Conway*, 741 P.2d 1380 (N.M. 1987).

[302] *See, e.g.*, *In re Allen (Allen v. Graham)*, 10 Cal. Rptr. 2d 916 (Cal. Ct. App. 1992), *review granted*, 839 P.2d 983 (Cal. 1992); *Kinsler v. Superior Court*, 175 Cal. Rptr. 564 (Cal. Ct. App. 1981).

[303] *See supra* § 8.02.

[304] *See, e.g.*, Fed. R.Civ. P.60.

In general, the decision of the trial court in a divorce case will not be overturned absent an abuse of discretion or an error in the interpretation or application of law.[305] A few states, however, direct de novo consideration of the facts of specific issues in divorce cases.[306]

§ 8.04   Ethical Issues for the Family Lawyer

All the ethical obligations that otherwise pertain to the practice of law, such as the duty to exercise reasonable care, skill, and diligence, obviously apply equally to divorce practice.[307] However, a number of ethical issues particularly concern family law practitioners,[308] and the American Academy of Matrimonial Lawyers has recently adopted Standards of Conduct that exceed the ethical requirements of the ABA and state bar ethical codes.[309] Attorney misconduct in a divorce action may cause a court to vacate a divorce decree, and also may result in a substantial malpractice action and professional discipline, including suspension or disbarment.[310]

[A]   Dual Representation in Divorce Proceedings

Divorcing couples frequently request that one attorney represent both spouses in their divorce action. While their primary motive may be to avoid the expense of hiring separate counsel, they also may have agreed to the general terms of their divorce or anticipate no serious disagreements, or both may have a great deal of confidence in the attorney. Whether such dual representation is ethical depends primarily on whether any present or potential disputes exist between the spouses, regarding spousal or child support, child custody, division of marital property, or other matters.[311] Issues of confidentiality also make dual representation problematic.

---

[305] *See, e.g., Burhoop v. Burhoop,* 380 N.W.2d 254, (Neb. 1986); *Schwandt v. Schwandt,* 471 N.W.2d 176 (S.D. 1991).

[306] *See, e.g.,* Tenn. Code Ann. § 36–6–101 (1996) (authorizing de novo review of custody cases); Neb. Rev. Stat. § 42–366–(7) (reissue 1998) (decree can limit modification or prohibit review of terms, except for child custody and support).

[307] *See* Model Rules of Professional Conduct, Rule 1.1 (2d ed. 1982); *see also, e.g., Smith v. Lewis,* 530 P.2d 589 (Cal. 1975) (failure to research wife's interest in husband's pension benefits); *Morris v. Geer,* 720 P.2d 994 (Colo. Ct. App. 1986) (failure to properly value marital property and failure to reopen and prosecute after discovery of fraud); *Ziegelheim v. Apollo,* 607 A.2d 1298 (N.J. 1992) (attorney advising client on divorce settlement held to same standard of professional care required in other legal tasks); *Rodgers v. Davenport,* 331 S.E.2d 389 (Va. 1985) (client's allegations that attorney settled action for child support arrearages without her consent sufficient to overturn summary judgment for attorney).

[308] *See generally* Richard Crouch, *Ethics Aspects of Gamily Law Practice,* 25 Trial 63 (April 1989); Norman Robbins, *Family Law Ethics,* 4 Am. J. Fam. L. 117 (Summer 1990).

[309] American Academy of Matrimonial Lawyers, *Bounds of Advocacy: Standards of Conduct* (1991). A number of states continue to adhere to the ABA's Model Code of Professional Responsibility, although many have adopted the newer ABA Model Rules of Professional Conduct.

[310] *See generally* Nathan Crystal, *Ethical Problems in Marital Practice,* 30 S.C.L. Rev. 321 (1979); *Trend Analysis, The "Changed Landscape"S of Divorce Practice as Ethical Minefield,* 3 Fam. L. Rep. (BNA) 4031(1977).

[311] *See, e.g., Jensen v. Jensen,* 557 P.2d 200 (Idaho 1976) (attorney purporting to represent both parties must adequately protect the interests of each spouse).

The ABA Model Code of Professional Responsibility permits an attorney to represent multiple clients only if it is clear that the attorney can adequately and objectively represent the interest of each client.[312] The lawyer must fully explain the implications of representing both spouses to each and accept or continue employment only upon their consent.[313] Thus, if the interests of the clients conflict or if any dispute between the parties later arises, the attorney cannot adequately represent either party and must withdraw from the case.[314] In *Board of Overseers of the Bar v. Dineen*,[315] an attorney, Dineen, was suspended for failing to withdraw from a divorce case due to a conflict of interests. Dineen originally agreed to represent both parties so long as there were no contested issues. During the pendency of the action, the wife was hospitalized for alcoholism and asked Dineen to continue the proceedings. Dineen subsequently began representing the husband exclusively and requested that custody of the parties' children be awarded to the husband because of the wife's alcoholism. After the wife moved to have Dineen withdraw and he refused, the state bar brought disciplinary proceedings against him, resulting in his suspension. The Supreme Court Maine upheld the suspension, holding that his use of the information of the wife's alcoholism communicated by her Dineen during the existence of an attorney-client relationship, along with his refusal to withdraw from representing the husband, clearly violated a number of rules of professional ethics.

The majority of states consider divorce as inherently involving conflicting legal issues between the spouses and regard representation of both spouses as improper.[316] Some commentators have argued for an absolute prohibition of dual representation in divorce cases under the rationale that the "friendly" or "uncontested" divorce is actually a myth because all divorces have significant areas of disagreement.[317] *Lange v. Marshall*,[318] in which a jury awarded a former wife damages based on attorney negligence, illustrates this concern. In *Lange*, the attorney had agreed to represent both parties, who were his personal friends, if they could agree on the terms of the divorce. During the divorce discussions, the wife was admitted to a psychiatric ward and, upon her release, signed the settlement agreement which the defendant attorney had drafted for them. When the trial judge delayed judgment, the defendant attorney withdrew and both parties sought separate counsel. The wife later received a more favorable settlement and filed a negligence action against the first attorney, alleging that

---

[312] *See* Model Code of Professional Responsibility, EC 5–14–-BC–17 (1980); Disciplinary Rule 5–105(C), Model Rules of Professional Conduct, Rule 1.7.

[313] Model Code of Professional Responsibility, EC 5–16, Disciplinary Rule 5–105(c); Model Rules of Professional Conduct, Rule 1.7.

[314] Model Code of Professional Responsibility, EC 5–15 (1980). *See also* Model Rules of Professional Conduct, Rule 2.2.

[315] 500 A.2d 262 (Me. 1985), *cert. denied*, 476 U.S. 1141(1986).

[316] *See, e.g.*, Ethics Comm. of the Miss. State Bar, Op. 80 (1983); Comm. on Professional Ethics, State Bar of Wisconsin, Op. E–84–3 (1984).

[317] *See Trend Analysis, supra* note 285, at 4034–36.

[318] 622 S.W.2d 237 (Mo. Ct. App. 1981).

he had failed to inquire into her husband's financial status, to negotiate a better settlement or advise her that she could obtain a better settlement through litigation, and to fully and fairly disclose her marital property, custody, and maintenance rights. Although the appellate court reverse the jury award for failure to prove damages proximately caused by attorney's negligence, *Lange* illustrates the potential hazards of dual representation.

Even if no dispute arises during the divorce action itself, one may occur later. For example, in *Ishmael v. Millington* [319] an attorney who had previously represented the husband in other matters prepared a divorce complaint and a property settlement agreement for the wife. After the court approved the agreement and entered a divorce decree, the wife sued the attorney for malpractice for failing to properly ascertain the actual value of the property covered by the agreement. The court cautioned:

> Divorces are frequently uncontested; the parties may make their financial arrangements peaceably and honestly. . . . The husband may then seek out and pay an attorney to escort the wife through the formalities of adjudication,. . . . Even in that situation the attorney's professional obligations do not permit his descent to the level of a scrivener. The edge of danger gleams if the attorney has previously represented the husband. A husband and wife at the brink of division of their marital assets have an obvious divergence of interests. Representing the wife in an arm's length divorce, an attorney of ordinary professional skill would demand some verification of the husband's financial statement; or, at a minimum, [would] inform the wife that the husband statement was unconfirmed, that wives may be cheated, [and] that prudence called for investigation and verification. Deprived of such disclosure, the wife cannot make a free and intelligent choice. Representing both spouses in an uncontested divorce situation (whatever the ethical implications), the attorney's professional obligations demand no less. He may not set a shallow limit on the depth to which he will represent the wife.

Purporting to represent both parties in a divorce proceeding may also lead to allegations of fraud on the court and the vacating of a prior divorce decree. For example, in *Coulson v. Coulson* [320] the husband requested his corporate counsel to draft a separation agreement and handle his divorce. The attorney merely drafted the agreement as dictated to him, then purported to represent the wife, but never advised her or the court that his representation was limited. At the divorce hearing, the attorney advised the wife that the settlement was fair and reasonable, and the separation agreement was incorporated into the divorce decree. More than two years later, the wife filed a motion seeking relief from the judgment, alleging fraud on the court. Affirming that the judgment should be vacated, the Ohio Supreme Court held that:

> when an attorney files and signs a divorce complaint, purporting to represent the plaintiff in the action even though he drafted the complaint

---

[319] 50 Cal. Rptr. 592 (Cal. Ct. App. 1966).
[320] 448 N.E.2d 809 (Ohio 1983).

and accompanying separation agreement at the direction of and upon the terms dictated by the defendant in the same action, and he represents to the court that he is plaintiff's counsel and that the separation agreement, which he had not examined for fairness and equity, is fair and equitable, and the court, in reliance on these representations, proceeds to approve the divorce and incorporate the separation agreement into the judgment, which it would not have done hand it known of the arrangement between the attorney and the defendant, the attorney perpetrates a fraud upon the court, and a trial court does not abuse its discretion in granting relief from judgment. . .[321]

Thus, a divorce decree procured by an attorney's misrepresentations about his or her client may be set aside as a fraud on the court. An attorney's participation in a fraudulent divorce proceeding may also provide a ground for a disciplinary action for suspension or disbarment.[322]

If both spouses consent to dual representation, preferably in writing and after full disclosure of the dangers, some states do not consider dual representation in an uncontested divorce action to be unethical per se.[323] Some courts have also required that the attorney discuss the implications of a separation agreement and consider whether it fair to both parties.[324] In *Klemm v. Superior Court of Fresno County*,[325] an attorney, Bailey, had agreed to represent both parties pro bono because they were personal friends. The couple agreed to the terms of their divorce, and their agreement stated that the wife did not seek and that the husband did not want to pay child support. Upon a court-ordered investigation, the District Attorney's office recommended that the husband pay $50 a month child support, because the wife was receiving AFDC payments. Bailey attempted to represent both parties again at the support hearing; however, no written waivers of representation were filed, and the evidence conflicted as to whether the wife wished Bailey to continue representing her. At a subsequent support hearing, Bailey produced a written waiver from both the husband and wife, but the court refused Bailey's motion to allow her to represent both parties. The parties filed a writ of mandate to order the court to allow continued dual representation. The appellate court held that an attorney may represent both parties if they agree on all the issues and consent in writing to representation of both and there is no actual conflict. It remanded the case for determination of the validity of the waivers.

If either spouse is financially disadvantaged or dependent, that spouse should have independent legal counsel.[326] When the opposing party is

---

[321] *Id. at 813.*

[322] *See, e.g., In re Hockett*, 734 P.2d 877 (Or. 1987); *see also* Model Code of Professional Responsibility, DR 7–102(A)(4)–(7).

[323] *See, e.g., Levine V. Levine*, 436 N.E.2d 476 (N.Y. 1982); *Klemm v. Superior Court* 142 Cal. Rptr. 509 (Cal. Ct. App. 1977); *see also* Ethics Comm. of the Board of Professional Responsibility of the Supreme Ct. of Tennessee, Formal Ethics Opinion No.81–F–16 (1981).

[324] *See Blum v. Blum*, 477 A.2d 289 (Md. Ct. Spec. App. 1984); *In re Marriage of Eltzroth*, 679 P.2d 1369 (Or. Ct. App. 1984).

[325] 142 Cal. Rptr. 509 (Cal. Ct. App. 1977).

[326] *See* Nathan Crystal, *supra* note 310, at 329–30.

represented by a lawyer, an attorney must not communicate with that party on the subject matter without prior consent of that person's lawyer unless otherwise required by law.[327]

Representation of both spouses in a divorce action also raises problems of confidentiality. The parties must waive their attorney-client privilege and the attorney may later be forced to testify to damaging information if the divorce becomes contested.[328]

[B] Confidential Information

Both the Model Code and the Model Rules impose a high duty of confidentiality on attorneys in order to facilitate appropriate representation and to encourage persons to obtain necessary counsel.[329] Unless the client consents to disclosure, virtually anything the client tells the lawyer must be kept confidential, except for information necessary to respond to a client's allegations of the attorney's misconduct or ineffective representation and certain communications regarding the client's criminal or fraudulent intentions.[330] While the ABA Code permits the attorney to reveal confidential information relating to the client's intention to commit a crime and the information necessary to prevent the crime,[331] the Model Rules provide that "[a] lawyer may reveal such information to the extent the lawyer reasonably believes necessary: (1) to prevent the client from committing a criminal act that the lawyer believes is likely to result in imminent death or substantial bodily harm;. . ."[332] Because of the difficulty in demonstrating that the information is actually subject to disclosure, without actually revealing it, the court should conduct a preliminary *in camera* investigation of a limited nature before requiring disclosure.[333]

An ethical dilemma regarding privileged communications may arise if an attorney learns of a clients fraud or other misconduct through client communications, such as intentional concealment of substantial assets.[334] The ABA Code of Professional Responsibility provides that a lawyer who receives information clearly establishing that his or her client has perpetuated a fraud upon a person or tribunal shall promptly "call upon his client to rectify the same;" if the client refuses or is unable to do so, the attorney "shall reveal the fraud to the affected person or tribunal, except when the information is protected as a privileged communication."[335] Further, the

---

[327] Model Code of Professional Responsibility, DR 7–104(A)(1).

[328] *See* Model Rules of Professional Conduct, Rule 1.6; Nathan Crystal, *supra* note 310, at 325–332.

[329] *See* Model Code of Professional Responsibility, DR 4–101; Model Rules of Professional Conduct, Rule 1.6.

[330] *Id.*

[331] Model Code of Professional Responsibility, DR 4–101 (C)(3).

[332] Model Rules of Professional Conduct, Rule 1.6(b)(1).

[333] *See United States v. Zolin*, 491 U.S. 554 (1989); *In re Decker*, 606 N.E.2d 1094 (Ill. 1992) (attorney's refusal to disclose whereabouts of client who allegedly abducted child).

[334] *See generally* Nathan Crystal, *supra* note 310 at 348–53.

[335] Model Code of Professional Responsibility, DR 7–102(B)(1)(1974). *See also* Model Rules of Professional Conduct, Rule 3.3 and Comment.

attorney may be required to withdraw from continuing representation of the client. [336] Similarly, the attorney must reveal a fraud on the court committed by person other than the client. [337]

Confidentiality issues may also arise when a lawyer has previously represented one or both spouses in other legal matters. [338] If there is a substantial possibility that knowledge acquired in a earlier representation could be used against the former client in the subsequent divorce, the lawyer may be disqualified from representing either spouse in the divorce action. [339]

For example, in *Woods v. Superior Court of Tulare County*, [340] the California Court of Appeal held that, absent consent or waiver, an attorney who had represented the family business should be disqualified from representing one of the spouses in a divorce action, despite conflicting evidence concerning whether the attorney actually had obtained confidential information from the other spouse. The court emphasized that potential, as well as actual, adversity to a former client created a conflict and that an attorney for a family corporation must be impartial among all the shareholders and decline to represent either side to avoid the appearance of impropriety.

Similarly, in *In re Braun*, [341] an attorney was disciplined for representing the wife in divorce action after discussing a potential reconciliations with both parties and later conferring with the husband alone about possible representation. Although the attorney alleged that no confidential information was exchanged in his meeting with the husband and withdrew as the wife's counsel after the husband complained, the court held that attorneys may be disciplined for acts which give rise to the appearance of impropriety even if no confidential information was actually revealed.

On some occasion, courts have demanded termination of the attorney-client privilege when failure to disclose perpetrates a fraud on the court and when the best interest of children need to be considered. In *Bersani v. Bersani*, [342] the wife moved with the children and failed to tell the

---

[336] *See* Model Code of Professional Responsibility, DR 2–110.

[337] Model Code of Professional Responsibility, DR 7–102(B)(2).

[338] *Cf. In re Boyle*, 611 A.2d 618 (N.H. 1992) (attorney serving as guardian ad litem for children in custody action violated ethical rules by undertaking to represent children's father is criminal case).

[339] *See In re Conduct of Jayne*, 663 P.2d 405 (Or. 1983) (representation of husband in dissolution proceeding after previous representation of wife in various other matters constituted violation of ethical obligation to preserve confidences and secrets of clients and of duty to refuse to accept employment on behalf of client if exercise of independent professional judgment of lawyer on behalf of another client would be impaired; public reprimand warranted). *But See Rush v. Rush*, 574 So. 2d 808 (Ala. Civ. App. 1990) (attorney's previous representation of husband in another matter did not meet substantial relationship test for disqualification); *Gause v. Gause*, 613 P.2d 1257 (Alaska 1980) (wife's motion to disqualify husband's attorney's law firm in divorce action denied because two prior occasions of representation did not raise substantial possibility of knowledge being gained to detriment of wife).

[340] 197 Cal. Rptr. 185 (Cal. Ct. App. 1983).

[341] 227 A.2d 506 (N.J. 1967).

[342] 565 A.2d 1368 (Conn. 1989).

husband of her whereabouts. The wife's attorney knew of her location but would not disclose any information based on the attorney-client relationship. After the husband was granted custody of the children, the wife's counsel continued to argue the privilege, on the basis that the custody was a separate issue. The court held that the issue of custody was inextricably intertwined with the attorney-client privilege issue and counsel's withholding information constituted a fraud on the court, compelling counsel to reveal the whereabouts of the wife and children.

[C] Attorney Fees on Divorce

An attorney must not charge excessive fees in a divorce action. Whether a fee is reasonable depends on factors such as the time expended on the case, the attorney's individual skill and professional reputation, the nature and complexity of the case, the usual charges, and the benefit to the client.[343] When a fee is questioned, the trial court normally has the discretion to determine its reasonableness.[344]

In *Moses v. Moses*,[345] The Pennsylvania appellate court held that an attorney involved a divorce case must remain cognizant of how much of the time he is billing is actually necessary to achieve the desired results. An attorney cannot expect to be reimbursed by one spouse for an inordinate number of hours spent tending to the emotional need of the other spouse. In *Moses*, the bill reflected 121 hours spent over a period of 56 days, often at strange hours and involving discussions based on the attorney's personal relationship with the couple. The settlement reached through these efforts was a weekly support award of $275, and the couple did not divorce. The court held that an attorney must balance a number of factors in determining the number of hours to spend with a client, and that these facts did not necessitate such a fee.

The prevailing general rule is that contingent fee arrangements, in which the client agrees to pay a percentage the amount recovered, are not proper in divorce litigation.[346] Fees contingent upon obtaining a divorce, upon the amount of alimony, or a portion of a lump sum settlement in lieu of alimony are often considered to be void as against public policy, because an attorney would obtain an interest in discouraging the couple's reconciliation and because support payments may not be assigned.[347] It has also been suggested that because divorce clients are often distraught, they may be

---

[343] *See Reid v. Reid*, 562 N.Y.S.2d 981(N.Y. App. Div. 1990).

[344] *See, e.g., Ransom v. Ransom*, 429 N.E.2d 594 (Ill. App. Ct. 1981); *In re Matter of Kinast*, 357 N.W.2d 282 (Wis. 1984); *see also* Stuart Speiser, *Attorneys Fees § 8.2 (1973 & Supp. 1992)*.

[345] 1 Fam. L. Rep. (BNA) 2604 (July 22, 1975), aff'd, 344 A.2d 912 (Pa. Super. Ct. 1975).

[346] *See* ABA Code of Professional Responsibility EC 2–20; Model Rules of Professional conduct, Rule 1.5(d)(1); *Thompson v. Thompson*, 319 S.E.2d 315 (N.C. Ct. App. 1984), *rev'd on other grounds*, 328 S.E.2d 288 (N.C. 1985). *But see* Kathleen Southern, *Professional Responsibility-Contingent Fees in Domestic Relations Actions: Equal Freedom to Contract for Domestic Relations Bar*, 62 N.C.L. Rev. 381(1984).

[347] *See McCrary v. McCrary*, 764 P.2d 522 (Okla. 1988); *see also* Stuart Speiser, *supra* note 345 at § 2:6 (1973 & Supp. 1992).

more likely to allege that contingent fees were obtained through undue influence and overreaching, ultimately to the detriment of the legal profession.[348]

Contingent fee agreements in child support cases raise additional policy questions. In *Davis v. Taylor*,[349] the court held that the portion of an award of over $45,000 for attorneys' fees that was based on a contingent-fee contract was void because it "alters and disrupts the judicial formulation and structuring of the support award."[350] Statutes allowing the award of reasonable legal fees enable parties to bring support actions when they otherwise lack the financial means to employ counsel. Such statutes protect the best interests of the child by assuring that the opposing party will be met on fair terms. The court concluded, "To allow a contingent-fee contract based on a percentage of a child support award would upset the equilibrium between judicially-monitored support schedules and judicially-monitored awards of attorneys' fees for plaintiffs who could not otherwise afford adequate legal representation."[351]

The issue of contingent fees most commonly arises in connection with attempted collection of support or property division payments, often long after the divorce itself has been granted. The decisions on their appropriateness in this context are inconsistent.[352] In *Meyers v. Handlon*,[353] the Indiana Court of Appeals held that contingent fee agreements are not allowed in divorce cases, despite the fact that the defendant attorneys were hired after the divorce had been granted and they were not in a position to promote divorce. The court concluded that all questions relating to marriage and property rights arising therefrom are part of the divorce action, and the contingent fee arrangement was void and unenforceable as a violation of public policy.

[D]　Sexual Relations with Divorce Clients

The ethical implications of an attorney engaging in sexual relations with a divorce client recently have generated considerable concern. Courts have found that repeated attempts to exploit the attorney-client relationship and the resulting trust produced therein may take "particular advantage of clients whose matrimonial difficulties placed them in a highly vulnerable emotional state."[354] Engaging in a sexual relationship with a divorce client

---

[348] *See Thompson v. Thompson*, 319 S.E.2d 315 (N.C. Ct. App. 1984), *rev on other grounds*, 328 S.E.2d 288 (N.C. 1985).

[349] 344 S.E.2d 19 (N.C. Ct. App. 1986).

[350] *Id.* at 22.

[351] *Id.*

[352] *Compare Licciardi v. Collins*, 536 N.E.2d 840 (Ill. App. Ct. 1989) (contingency fee contract not valid in post-divorce modification of property divisions) *with Roberds v. Sweitzer*, 733 S.W.2d 444 (Mo. 1987) (contingent fee arrangement not improper in action to set aside property division); *Gross v. Lamb*, 437 N.E.2d 309 (Ohio Ct. App. 1980) (contingency fee not improper where client could not afford hourly fee of experienced domestic relations lawyer). *See also* Kathleen Southern, *supra* note 347.

[353] 479 N.E.2d 106 (Ind. App. 1985).

[354] *Matter of Bowen*, 542 N.Y.S.2d 45 (N.Y. App. Div. 1989).

may destroy the chance for reconciliation and may prevent the attorney from properly exercising independent judgment. [355]

However, in the absence of any specific ethical prohibition and lack of evidence that the attorney took advantage of the professional relationship, the court in *Edwards v. Edwards*, [356] held that an attorney is not compelled to withdraw from representation of a client with whom he is sexually involved. In *Edwards*, the attorney was nonetheless required to withdraw from the case once he was named as a witness in the husband's counter-claim for divorce based on the wife's adultery. [357]

The seriousness of an ethical issue posed by an attorney's sexual relations with a divorce client depends on the particular jurisdiction and the facts of each case. On one hand, for example, an Illinois court of appeals held that an attorney's sexual relationship with his divorce client did not constitute malpractice in the absence of allegations of inadequate represen-tation, exchange of sexual favors for legal services, or actual damages. [358] On the other hand, the Supreme Court of Rhode Island, in *In re DiSandro*, found that engaging in a consensual sexual relationship with a divorce client was unethical and would warrant public censure. That court noted,

> [A]ny attorney who practices in the area of domestic relations must be aware that the conduct of the divorcing parties, even in a divorced based on irreconcilable differences . . . may have a significant impact on that client's ability to secure child custody and/or may materially affect the client's rights regarding distribution of marital assets. An attorney who engages in sexual relations with his or her divorce client places that client's rights in jeopardy. The lawyer's own interest in maintaining the sexual relationship creates an inherent conflict with the obligation to represent the client properly.

More serious sanction may also be brought against an attorney who has sexual relations with his or her divorce client, as *Committee on Professional Ethics and Conduct of the Iowa State Bar v Hill*, [359] illustrates. In *Hill*, a client, K.C., who was unemployed and a drug addict, contacted attorney Hill for representation in a divorce and custody action. Hill agreed to represent her, although she had no money. K.C. offered to engage in sexual intercourse with Hill in exchange for money. Although Hill offered to extend K.C. a personal loan if she did not wish to engage sex, she declined because she had no means of repayment. Hill gave her money and they had sexual intercourse in his office.

K.C. later underwent treatment for chemical dependency, reconciled with her husband, and the divorce action was dismissed. Upon a complaint to

[355] *See Colorado v. Zeilinger*, 814 P.2d 808 (Colo. 1991).

[356] 567 N.Y.S.2d 645 (N.Y. App. Div. 1991).

[357] *See also Suppressed v. Suppressed*, 565 N.E.2d 101(Ill. App. Ct. 1990) (attorney's sexual relationship with divorce client not malpractice in absence of allegations of inadequate representation, exchange of sexual favors for legal services, or actual damages).

[358] *Suppressed v. Suppressed*, 565 N.E.2d 101(Ill. App. Ct. 1990).

[359] 436 N.W.2d 57 (1989).

the Grievance Commission, Hill was found to have violated his ethical obligations and the commission recommended that he be suspended from practice. The Supreme Court of Iowa, holding that Hill had violated the high standards of ethical conduct and that such conduct reflects negatively on the legal profession, and suspended Hill's license to practice indefinitely with no possibility of reinstatement for three months.

The California State Bar became the first in the country to enact rules forbidding attorney-client sexual relations in specified circumstances, although it refused to enact a complete ban[360] While neither the ABA Model Rules of Professional Conduct or the Model Code of Professional Responsibility forbid sexual relations with clients, the ABA Standing Committee on Ethics and Professional Responsibility has advised against such conduct, warning that the attorney may be lured into other conduct that may result in violation of other ethical rules.[361]

[E] Candor Toward the Court and Withdrawal from the Case

Both the ABA Model Rules and the Model Code of Professional Conduct contain various rules governing a lawyer's relationship with the court and behavior in court. Under various formulations, lawyers' obligations include duties not to make false statements of material law or fact to a court, to disclose material facts necessary to avoid assisting a criminal or fraudulent act by a client, and to not offer false evidence or perjured testimony.[362] A lawyer must withdraw from representing a client for any or no reason, and a client may hire and fire attorneys at will.[363] A lawyer who withdraws or is discharged must give reasonable notice to the client, allow time for the client to employ other counsel, deliver paperwork and property to which the client is entitled, and refund any advance but unearned fees.[364] Mandatory withdrawal is required when further representation will result in violation of rules of professional conduct, the law or when the lawyer's physical or mental health material impairs the ability to represent the client.[365] *Matza v. Matza*[366] illustrates a case where client misconduct justifies attorney withdrawal, where the attorney withdrew because he feared that his client would commit perjury or submit fraudulent documents in court.

Lawyers have also been disciplined for professional misconduct in the context of their own divorces, including failing to pay spousal or child support[367] and failing to make an adequate financial disclosure of marital

---

[360] Cal. Ethics Rule 3–120(B)(1992).

[361] ABA Comm. on Ethics and Professional Responsibility, Formal Op. 92–354 (1992).

[362] *See, e.g.*, Model Rule 3.3, Model Code of Professional Responsibility DR 7–102.

[363] *See, e.g.*, *In Re Cooperman*, 611 N.Y.S.2d 465, 468 (N.Y. 1994).

[364] *See* Model Code DR 2–110; Model Rules 1.16.

[365] *Id.*

[366] 627 A.2d 414 (Conn. 1993).

[367] *See, e.g.*, *In re Warren*, 888 S.W.2d 334, 336–37 (Mo. 1994).

property.[368] Similarly, a lawyer spouse who purports to represent both parties by convincing the other spouse that independent counsel is unnecessary may have breached a confidentiality fiduciary relationship and the divorce decree may be set aside.[369]

[F] Pro Se Divorces

Over the past two decades, the number of pro se litigants in divorce cases has grown rapidly. A 1993 ABA study of divorce filings in one Arizona county, known for its user-friendly court system, found that in almost 90% of divorce cases, at least one party was unrepresented and in more than 50% of the cases, both parties were unrepresented.[370]

If one spouse is not represented by counsel, the attorney must not give that person the impression that the attorney is disinterested and must make reasonable efforts to assure that the unrepresented party understands the attorney's role of representing the other spouse.[371] Other than advising the other party to obtain counsel, the lawyer must not give advice to the unrepresented party if that person's interests could conflict with the client's interests.[372] The lawyer must not make any inaccurate or misleading statements of law to the unrepresented spouse.[373]

An unrepresented spouse may later attack the validity of a divorce decree and the fairness of a separation agreement if the attorney violated these ethical principles. *Adkins v. Adkins*[374] depicts an egregious case of attorney misconduct against an unrepresented opposing party. In *Adkins* the wife had threatened her husband that she would get a lawyer who would force him out of the marital home, obtain all his property, and require him to pay her for the rest of his life if he refused to comply with her wishes regarding a divorce. The husband, who had little education or knowledge of his legal rights, believed her. The wife subsequently retained an attorney, Franchshessa Bixler, who requested that the husband come to her office. She discouraged the husband from hiring his own lawyer and misrepresented his legal rights, then induced him to sign a marital settlement agreement which gave the wife most of parties' property, created an obligation for the husband to pay alimony, and assessed him with the wife's attorney's fees and all outstanding debts. The husband signed the documents without the opportunity to read or understand them after Bixler convinced him he would do worse if litigation was necessary.

After the divorce decree was entered, the husband in *Adkins* received notification of a proceeding to hold him in contempt for failure to pay

---

[368] *See, e.g., In re Finnerty*, 641 N.E.2d 1323, 1327 (Mass. 1994).

[369] *See Webb v. Webb*, 431 S.E.2d 55, 61 (Va. Ct. App. 1993).

[370] ABA Standing Committee On Delivery of Legal Services, Self-Representation in Divorce Cases 33 (1993).

[371] Model Rules of Professional Conduct, Rule 4.3.

[372] *See* Model Code of Professional Responsibility, DR 7–104(A)(2).

[373] Model Rules of Professional Conduct, Rule 4.1.

[374] 186 Cal. Rptr. 818 (Cal. Ct. App. 1982).

spousal support. He then sought independent legal advice for the first time and instituted an action which resulted in vacating the judgment and rescinding the marital settlement agreement. In upholding the invalidation of the divorce and settlement agreement, the California Court of Appeals held that the documents had been obtained by fraud and that the wife and her attorney had deceived and prevented the husband from knowing his rights and asserting them in court.

In a similar case, *Tenneboe v. Tenneboe*,[375] the unrepresented husband filed a motion to set aside a property settlement agreement drafted by the wife's attorney, on grounds of misrepresentation and overreaching. The husband signed an agreement providing for alimony and child support payments of $700 per week when he netted just over $800 a week, working seven days a week. He later testified that when he signed the agreement, he protested that the payments were more than he could handle, but the wife's attorney told him he could go back to court at a future time to have the payments modified, but did not inform him he would need to show a substantial change in income. Additionally, the agreement gave the wife most of the couple's assets. The Florida Court of Appeals concluded that the agreement left the husband impoverished and the that unless separate counsel represents both parties, the parties relationship remains nonadversarial and each party has a fiduciary type responsibility to the other. The court held that the husband had provided enough evidence on misrepresentation and overreaching to allow him to have the property settlement set aside.

In response to the growth of pro se divorce litigants, a number of court systems have hired staff or developed programs designed to provide information and assistance to these self-represented parties. These programs range from simplified form pleading and instruction books to group classes and telephone hot-lines.[376]

While some have applauded the rise of pro se divorce as a necessary alternative to the high cost of attorney representation, others have voiced concern about the dangers of self-representation and about the quality of some of the programs developed to assist pro se litigants.[377] The increase in pro se divorce litigants also poses an ethical dilemma for attorneys, since individuals who self-represent may seek limited attorney services for specific issues or aspects of a case. Traditionally, the establishment of an attorney-client relationship encompassed full service representation for an entire matter and could result in significant malpractice exposure. Recently, several commentators have proposed for notion of unbundled legal services, or discrete task representation as an alternative to this traditional full-service model, under which clients could contract for specific tasks or aspects of the divorce.[378] Unfortunately, existing ethical and malpractice

---

[375] 558 So. 2d 470 (Fla. App. 1990).

[376] *See* Robert B. Yegge, *Divorce Litigants Without Lawyers*, 28 Fam. L.Q. 407, 412–16.

[377] *See* Elizabeth McCulloch, *Let Me Show You How: Pro Se Divorce Courses and Client Power*, 48 Fla. L. Rev. 481 (1996).

[378] *See* Forrest S. Mosten, *Unbundling of Legal Services and the Family Lawyer*, 28 Fam. L.Q. 421 (1994).

rules fail to address the situation of an attorney who handles only discrete parts of a case, making such unbundled representation a risky undertaking.

In response to the cost of attorneys' fees, do-it-yourself, pro se divorces have become increasingly popular, assisted with pre-packaged "divorce kits."[379] Because of simplification of divorce proceedings due to no-fault legislation, various groups, including "feminists, family law reformers, consumer activists, and entrepreneurs" have supported pro se divorce, largely to protest the pricing practices of the bar.[380] Bar associations have assailed pro se divorce kits on the basis that they may mislead the lay public and result in serious problems, especially with respect to marital support and property rights.[381]

Although some decisions have upheld the commercial sale of these divorce kits,[382] such methods have been successfully attacked as the unauthorized practice of law.[383] In *State Bar v. Cramer*,[384] a non-attorney was held in civil contempt of court for continuing to sell divorce kits after having been permanently enjoined from holding herself out to the public as qualified to render advice and services and from furnishing forms and documents. The court found that her advertising, conferring with and advising clients, and preparing and filing documents constituted the unauthorized practice of law.

[G] Representing Children

Most states permit, but do not require, the appointment of counsel to represent children in contested divorce or custody proceeding.[385] Considerable disagreement exists, however, regarding the appropriate role of a child's attorney. Conflict exists over whether the attorney should be a zealous of the child's wishes, or whether the attorney should make an independent assessment of the child's best interests and present that position to the court. The Supreme Court of Wyoming, in *Clark v. Alexander*,[386] examined the roles of guardian ad litem and acknowledge a hybrid

---

[379] *See* Project, *The Unauthorized Practice of Law and Pro Se Divorce: An Empirical Analysis* 86 Yale L.J. 104 (1976); Patricia Winks, *Divorce Mediation: A Nonadversary Procedure for the No-Fault Divorce*, 19 J.Fam. L. 615, 625 (1980–81).

[380] Project, *supra* note 381, at 109.

[381] *See, e.g., In re Marriage of Eller*, 552 P.2d 30 (Colo. Ct. App. 1976) (wife waived right to support in "divorce kit" separation agreement; later sought support from husband).

[382] *See Oregon State Bar v. Gilchrist*, 538 P.2d 913 (Or. 1975) (publishing, advertising, and sales of "divorce kits," without personal contact with customers, not "practice of law," although consultation, explanation, or advice does constitute such practice and may be enjoined).

[383] *See Delaware State Bar v. Alexander*, 386 A.2d 652 (Del. 1978) (injunction to prohibit divorce reform group from engaging in unauthorized practice of law); *Florida State Bar v. Stupica*, 300 So.2d 683 (Fla. 1974) (publication of "divorce kit" including explanations, instruction, and advice on use of forms to secure no-fault divorce constitutes unauthorized practice of law).

[384] 249 N.W.2d 1 (Mich. 1976).

[385] *See* Ann Haralambie, The Child's Attorney 2 (1993).

[386] 953 P.2d 145 (1998).

role, which necessitates a modification of the Rules of Professional Conduct. Some commentators have rejected the hybrid approach and advocate that the attorney's role is the same as with adult clients.[387]

§ 8.05   Alternative Dispute Resolution

Traditional adversarial divorce litigation often is an expensive, time-consuming, and emotionally-laden process. With the advent of no-fault divorce grounds, the use of alternative dispute resolution (ADR) techniques, particularly divorce mediation and arbitration, has greatly increased, largely because of their potential to reduce the emotional and financial burdens that so often accompany divorce. Especially when the parties have children, peaceful resolution of divorce issues is considered particularly important in avoiding any additional stress and psychological damage that children may suffer.[388]

Divorce mediation and arbitration allow the parties to resolve their differences regarding child and spousal support, division of marital property, and child custody in a private, cooperative and non-adversarial manner. Use of divorce mediation and arbitration, based on no-fault alternatives, therefore "reflects a preference for private ordering over public name calling, [and] for resolution over retribution."[389]

Nevertheless, although ADR is not necessarily appropriate in all situations, divorce mediation and arbitration may be valuable alternatives to traditional divorce litigation. Divorce mediation and arbitration techniques and processes continue to be refined and are gaining increasing understanding and acceptance by the practicing bar and the courts.[390]

[A]   Divorce Mediation

Divorce mediation is a process in which the parties to a divorce are assisted by an impartial, professional third party mediator in reaching an agreement with respect to divorce related matters such as spousal and child support, custody, and property division.[391] Divorce mediation differs from

---

[387] *See, e.g., Proceedings of the Conference on Ethical Issues in the Legal Representation of Children: Recommendations of the Conference,* 64 Ford. L. Rev. 1301(1996); *Representing Children:For Attorneys and Guardians Ad Litem in Custody or Visitation Proceedings (With Commentary),* 13 J. Am. Acad. Matrim. Law 1(1995). *See also* Peter Margulies, *The Lawyer As Caregiver: Child Client's Competence in Context,* 64 Ford. L. Rev. 1473 (1996).

[388] *See* Hugh McIsaac, *Reducing the Pain of a Child Custody Struggle,* 14 Fam. Advoc. 26 (Spring 1992).

[389] Patricia Winks, *Divorce Mediation: A Nonadversary Procedure for the No-Fault Divorce,* 19 J. Fam. L. 615, 615 (1980–81).

[390] *See, e.g.,* John Fiske, *Divorce Mediation: An Attractive Alternative to Advocacy,* 20 Suffolk U.L. Rev. 55 (1986); Debra Moss, *Enter the Divorce Mediator: Family Mediation is Gradually Gaining Acceptance,* 73 A.B.A. J.27 (August 1987); Richard Salem, *The Alternate Dispute Resolution Movement: An Overview,* 40 Arb. J. 3 (1985); Jessica Pearson & Nancy Thoennes, *Divorce Mediation: An Overview of Research Results,* 19 Colum. J.L. & Soc. Probs. 451 (1985).

[391] *See, e.g.,* Joan Kelly, *Who Should Be the Mediator?,* 14 Fam. Advoc. 19 (Spring 1992) (comparing three models of divorce mediation); Joan Blades, *Family Mediation: Cooperative Divorce Settlement* (1985).

conciliation in that the mediator does not attempt to reconcile the parties, but aids them in procuring a divorce settlement agreement with minimal adversarial hostility and economic expense. One commentator has described the basic features of mediation as "contracting, gathering and analyzing data, generating and evaluating options, negotiating, and drafting agreements."[392]

Several states mandate mediation in certain contexts, most commonly, in disputed child custody cases.[393] For instance, the California Civil Code expressly provides for mediation in child custody or visitation cases.[394] It further requires standards of practice which include providing for the best interests of the child and safeguarding the child's rights to frequent, continuing contact with both parents, easing the transition of the family by enumerating the factors be considered in decisions regarding the child's future, and conducting negotiations in a manner that will equalize the power relationships of the parties.[395]

Absent formal requirements for mediation in state statutes, local rules, or state supreme court rules, a court may order mediation, in its discretion, in a disputed custody case when a reasonable basis exists.[396] In most instances however, divorce mediation is a voluntary arrangement that requires the approval of both spouses.

As divorce and custody mediation has grown in popularity, it has also become increasingly professionalized. In the mid-1980s, both the Family Law Section of the American Bar Association and the Association of Family and Conciliation Courts issued model standards of practice for divorce and family mediators.[397] The standards require a mediator to define and describe the mediation process and its costs before beginning mediation, not to disclose voluntarily information acquired during mediation without the prior consent of both parties, to be impartial, and to assure that the parties have sufficient information and knowledge for making decisions. The mediator must discontinue or end mediation when continuation would injure or prejudice one or both participants, and advise each party to obtain independent legal review before reaching agreement.[398] A number of states have also adopted practice standards and/or minimum qualifications for mediators.[399]

---

[392] Joan Kelly, *supra* note 393, at 21.

[393] *See, e.g.*, Cal. Civ. code § 3155–77 (West supp. 1998); N.C. Gen. Stat. § 50–13.1 (1999). *See also* Dane E. Gashen, *Note & Comment, Mandatory Custody Mediation: The Debate Over Its Usefulness Continues*, 10 Ohio St. J. On Disp. Resol. 469, 469, 472–73 (1995).

[394] Cal. Civ. Code § 3155 (West Supp. 1998).

[395] Cal. Civ. Code § 3155 (West Supp. 1998).

[396] *See, e.g.*, *Biel v. Biel*, 336 N.W.2d 404 (Wis. 1983).

[397] Family Law Section of the ABA, *Standards of Practice for Family Mediators*, 17 Fam. L.Q. 455 (1984); AFCC Model Standards of Practice for Divorce and Family Mediators, *reprinted in* Divorce Mediation: Theory and Practice 403 (Jay Folberg & Ann Milne, eds. 1988).

[398] *See* Thomas Bishop, *Outside the Adversary System: An ADR Overview*, 14 Fam. Advoc. 16 (Spring 1992).

[399] *See* Stephen G. Bullock & Linda Rose Gallagher, *Surveying the State of the Mediative Art: A Guide to Institutionalizing Mediation in Louisiana*, 57 La. L. Rev. 885, 930–936 (1997) (reporting that as of 1993, twenty states had adopted qualifications for practicing as a mediator and that three states have recently adopted ethical rules for mediators).

Questions exist regarding whether divorce mediation is the practice of law, and, if so, whether non-lawyers are prohibited from mediating family disputes. If not, it is unclear what ethical rules and standards govern the conduct of lawyer-mediators.[400] If mediation does constitute the practice of law, then lawyer-mediators risk violating ethical rules, especially constraints on dual representation; although the ABA Model Rules of Professional Conduct recognize a professional role as "intermediary," and permit this role under certain conditions.[401]

Confidentiality remains a problem which statutes in only a minority of states have addressed.[402] The ABA Standards suggest that the parties agree in writing "not to require the mediator to disclose to any third party any statements made in the course of mediation."[403] If the mediation process breaks down, however, one of the parties may attempt to introduce such evidence in court in subsequent litigation and an agreement regarding confidentiality may be unenforceable.[404]

California enacted mandatory pre-hearing mediation in child custody and visitation disputes and permitted the mediator to make a recommendation to the court if the parties were unable to agree.[405] To implement the statute, the local court had adopted a rule or policy that required a mediator to make recommendations, but not to state the reasons for the recommendations, and prohibited cross-examination by the parties, in order to assure the confidentiality of the mediation proceedings. The California Court of Appeal held in *McLaughlin v. Superior Court for San Mateo County*[406] that the rule violated the parties' right to cross-examine witnesses. It concluded that the trial court should not receive a recommendation from a mediator on any contested issue on which agreement had not been reached unless the court first enters a protective order guaranteeing the parties the right to have the mediator testify and be cross-examined, unless those rights are waived.

Total neutrality, fairness, and impartiality of mediators may not always be realistically possible when one of spouses has superior educational and business knowledge or other strong negotiating advantages. The ABA Standards do not, however, equate impartiality with neutrality, and they stress that the mediator must be concerned with fairness in order to avoid an unreasonable result. Some commentators indicate that a mediator may need to balance the parties' negotiating skills, even while retaining an

---

[400] *See, e.g.*, Carrie Menkel-Meadow, *Is Mediation the Practice of Law?*, 14 Alternatives to the High Cost of Litis. 1, 60 (1996); Bruce Meyerson, *Lawyers Who Mediate Are Not Practicing Law*, 14 Alternatives to the High Cost of Litis. 74 (1996).

[401] A.B.A. Model Rule 2.2.

[402] *See, e.g.*, Cal. Fam. Code § 3177 (1994).

[403] Thomas Bishop, *The Standards of Practice for Family Mediators: An Individual Interpretation and Comments*, 17 Fam. L.Q. 455, 456 (1984).

[404] *See id.* at 465.

[405] Cal. Fam. Code § 3183 (1994).

[406] 189 Cal. Rptr. 479 (Cal. Ct. App. 1983).

appearance of neutrality.[407] Such balancing or "empowering" of the more vulnerable spouse might objectively constitute representation of multiple clients under the ABA Code of Professional Responsibility, and the divorce mediator may risk legal and ethical problems resulting from dual representation.[408]

The status and the duties of the mediator are not always entirely clear. In *Lange v. Marshall*[409] the court held that an attorney who had represented the plaintiff and her husband as a mediator rather than an advocate was not liable for negligence in failing to inquire into the financial position of the husband and negotiate a better settlement for the wife or advise her of her rights to marital property, custody and maintenance or to advise her that she would get a better settlement if she litigated. Because both spouses repudiated the mediated agreement, obtained separate counsel, and litigated the divorce action, the court held that the wife failed to establish any damages proximately by the lawyer-mediator's conduct.

One of the claimed advantages of mediation is its potential for reducing the costs of divorce. However, because a lawyer-mediator cannot represent either party in a subsequent divorce or other legal action and because each party should also obtain independent legal counsel before signing a mediated agreement, three lawyers, rather than the usual two, may be required.[410] Conversely, if mediation breaks down, each party will need to obtain individual counsel. Thus, mediation risks adding one more tier to the divorce process and increasing, rather than reducing, the expense.[411]

The role of attorneys and judges as mediators, as opposed to trained lay counselors and mental health professionals, remains controversial.[412] Using an interdisciplinary team of mental health professionals and lawyer mediators may prove beneficial in assisting the parties in dealing with the interrelationship of the legal, emotional, and economic issues involved in divorce.[413] Non-lawyer mediators may lack the background to understand the legal ramifications of decisions made by the spouses in areas such as spousal and child support rights, child custody issues tax implications, and property division.[414] The non-lawyer mediator risks charges of unauthorized practice of law and may be disadvantaged by the lack of a confidentiality privilege.

---

[407] *See, e.g.*, Joan Blades, *supra* note 20; *see also* Richard Crouch, *Divorce Mediation and Legal Ethics*, 16 Fam. L.Q. 219 (1982) (discussing differences in dual representation in mediated versus litigated divorce).

[408] *See supra* § 8.04[A].

[409] 622 S.W.2d 237 (Mo. Ct. App. 1981).

[410] *See* Kevin Mazza, *Divorce Mediation*, 14 Fam. Advoc.40, 42–43 (Spring 1992).

[411] *See* Richard Crouch, *Mediation and Divorce: The Dark Side is Still Unexplored,* 4 Fam. Advoc. 27, 33 (Winter 1982). *But see* Jessica Pearson & Nancy Thoennes, *Mediation and Divorce: The Benefits Outweigh the Costs,* 4 Fam. Advoc. 26 (Winter 1982).

[412] *See* Joan Kelly, *Who Should Be a Mediator?*, 14 Fam. Advoc. 19 (Spring 1992).

[413] *See* Linda Silberman, *Professional Responsibility Problems of Divorce Mediation*, 16 Fam. L.Q. 107, 128–31 (1982); Folberg, *Divorce Mediation-A Workable Alternative*, 1982 ABA Nat'l Conf. on Alternate Means of Family Dispute Resolution 39–40.

[414] *See* Linda Silberman, *supra* note 415, at 123.

ADR, however, has not been fully embraced without serious reservations and criticism.[415] The extent to which a mediator may give legal information or advice to either or both parties has raised ethical questions concerning conflicts of interest and confidentiality, and a lack of standards and guidelines regulating mediation has caused concern. Mediation has been criticized for forfeiting the protections of the adversarial process and for being less advantageous to a party who is more inclined to compromise or is in a weaker economic position.[416] Feminist commentators, in particular, have cautioned that mediation may disadvantage women.[417] Other scholars have suggested that the informality and emphasis on consensus that characterizes mediation may reinforce racial and ethnic hierarchies, as well as gender inequalities.[418] Many scholars and mediators believe that mediation is unsuited and dangerous for cases involving domestic violence.[419] Balancing both the advantages and disadvantages of divorce mediation, most commentators and a growing number of judges and practitioners recognize the mediation process as a valuable alternative to traditional adversarial divorce litigation in offering a workable resolution to an individual family's unique needs.[420] Supporters of mediation stress that it encourages parents to put their children's needs first, helps them to develop communication and problem solving skill that can facilitate post-divorce co-parenting, and avoid the trauma, bitterness, and costs associated with trial.[421]

[B] Arbitration

Approximately half the states have adopted the Uniform Arbitration Act.[422] Arbitration, which is widely used in settling various labor law and commercial law disputes, is also being used in many states to settle divorce disputes.

---

[415] *See, e.g.*, Penelope Bryan, *Killing Us Softly: Divorce Mediation and the Politics of Power*, 40 Buff. L. Rev. 441 (1992); Trina Grillo, *The Mediation Alternative: Process Dangers for Women*, 100 Yale L.J. 1545 (1991); Kevin Mazza, *Divorce Mediation*, 14 Fam. Advoc. 40 (Spring 1992).

[416] *See, e.g.*, Richard Crouch, *Mediation and Legal Ethics*, 16 Fam. L.Q. 219(1982); Richard Crouch, *Mediation and Divorce: The Dark Side is Still Unexplored*, 4 Fam. Advoc. 27 (Winter 1982); Andrew Morrison, *Is Divorce Mediation the Practice of Law? A Matter of Perspective*, 75 Cal. L. Rev. 1093 (1987); William Weston, *Divorce Mediation: Cheaper for Your Client But Dangerous for You*, 4 Compleat Law. 40 (Spring 1987).

[417] *See* Jana B. Singer, *The Privatization of Family Law*, 1992 Wis. L. Rev. 1443, 1540–48.

[418] *See, e.g.*, Isabelle R. Gunning, *Diversity Issues in Mediation: Controlling Negative Cultural Myths*, 1995 J. Disp. Resol. 55, 70; Richard Delgado, Chris Dunn, Pamela Brown, Helena Lee & David Hubbert, *Fairness and Formality: Minimizing the Risk of Prejudice in Alternative Dispute Resolution*, 1985 Wis. L. Rev. 1359.

[419] *See, e.g*, Mary Pat Treuthart, *In Harms Way? Family Mediation and the Role of the Attorney Advocate*, 23 Golden Gate U. L. Rev. 717 (1993).

[420] *See* Russell Coombs, *Noncourt-Connected Mediation and Counseling in Child Custody Disputes*, 17 Fam. L.Q. 469–495 (1984); Joshua Rosenberg, *In Defense of Mediation*, 33 Ariz. L. Rev. 467(1991).

[421] *See* Nancy S. Palmer & William D. Palmer, *Family Mediation: Good for Clients, Good for Lawyers*, the Compleat Lawyer 32, 33 (Fall 1996).

[422] 7 U.L.A. 201 (1985).

Arbitration resembles the adversarial judicial process to the extent that the parties voluntarily submit their disputes to an impartial decision-maker, but arbitration avoids the delay and expense often associated with using a traditional judicial forum. Arbitration awards are normally binding on the parties and are affirmed by a court, unless they were fraudulently procured or the arbitrator did not act in an impartial manner.[423] Although courts have approved agreements to arbitrate spousal support and property issues, arbitration of divorce issues relating to children remains controversial.

Arbitration may be conducted before a single arbitrator chosen by either the parties or a designated third party, or by an impartial tripartite board appointed under the guidelines of the American Arbitration Association (AAA), or by a panel consisting of two designees appointed by the parties and a third member chosen by the designees or a third party.[424] The AAA, one of numerous arbitration organizations, is a well-known national non-profit agency that conducts arbitration and mediation work throughout the United States. Judicare, another organization that conducts arbitration and "minitrials," uses retired judges for its work.

Most commonly, an agreement to arbitrate rather than litigate certain issues will be included in the parties' separation agreement, but a pre-marital agreement may also contain an arbitration provision. The agreement should specify that the arbitration will be final and binding, and set out the arbitration procedure. The agreement should def the procedure for selecting the arbitrator and scheduling the time and place of arbitration. The parties may also agree to enlarge their rights to review and appeal.

Arbitration affords procedural flexibility and may be quicker and less expensive than litigation. Clear definition of issues that may be arbitrated is crucial, however, because arbitration is based on the parties' agreement, and the arbitrator may not exceed the scope of the contractual authority.[425] Lack of specificity resulted in litigation in *Bowmer v. Bowmer*,[426] in which a former wife sought to stay arbitration on the issue of whether the husband's support obligation could be decreased. The Bowmer's separation agreement contained a clause reading: "Any claim. dispute or misunderstanding arising out of or in connection with this Agreement, or any breach hereof, or any default in payment by the Husband, or any matter herein made the subject matter of arbitration, shall be arbitrated." In deciding that the arbitration clause did not pertain to support modification, the New York Court of Appeals declared that "unless the agreement to arbitrate expressly and unequivocally encompasses the subject matter of the particular dispute, a party cannot be compelled to forego the right to seek judicial relief and

---

[423] *See, e.g.*, Unif. Arbitration Act §§ 12–13.

[424] *See generally* Joyce Green, note 1 at 187–192; 2 Alexander Lindey & Louis Parley, Separation Agreements and Antenuptial Contracts, § 29 (1992); Janet Maleson Spencer & Joseph P. Zammit, *Mediation-Arbitration*, 1976 Duke L.J. 911 (1976).

[425] *See* Allan Koritzinsky, et al., *The Benefits of Arbitration*, 14 Fam. Advoc. 45 (Spring 1992).

[426] 406 N.E.2d 760 (N.Y. 1980).

instead submit to arbitration."[427] Because the separation agreement specifically delineated other issues that were to be arbitrable and contained a detailed formula for calculating support, the court held that the arbitration clause was not intended to encompass support modification. Subsequent to *Bowmer*, the American Arbitration Association recommended inclusion of support modification and enforcement in its standard arbitration provision.[428]

Disadvantages of arbitration include the lack of discovery procedures and the inapplicability of the rules of evidence and other procedural safeguards. Arbitrators do not have the power to enforce their awards, nor to enter divorce decrees, although the Uniform Arbitration Act provides for confirmation by a court in a judgment or decree unless the court vacates or modifies the arbitration award.[429]

Although most courts have approved, in general, of arbitration provisions dealing with spousal support and property rights,[430] courts generally afford less weight to similar provisions concerning child support and custody.[431] Neither the parties nor the arbitrator may deprive the court of the power to enforce or modify orders for alimony, child support, or to hold a party in contempt.[432]

In *Faherty v. Faherty*,[433] the former wife sought a court order establishing the amount of past-due alimony, child support, and property division payments and compelling discovery of the husband's business records. The husband successfully filed a cross-motion to compel arbitration of the arrearages and to reduce future payments, pursuant to an arbitration agreement in the parties' separation agreement. After extensive arbitration, the arbitrator set the amount of the arrearages and denied the husband's request for reduction of future alimony and child support. When the court confirmed the arbitration award, the husband challenged the validity of the arbitration clause, arguing that arbitration of alimony and. child support violates public policy, and attempted to overturn confirmation of the award.

In upholding the confirmed arbitration award, the New Jersey Supreme Court found no reason to prohibit binding arbitration of spousal support, since parties are free to settle those matters by contract. It observed that arbitration has proven to be an effective and highly desirable method of resolving disputes:

---

[427] *Id.* at 762.

[428] *See also* Alexander Lindey, *supra* note 426 at § 29.

[429] Unif. Arbitration Act § 11, 7 U.L.A. 264 (1997); *see also* Allan Koritzinsky, et. al., *The Benefits of Arbitration*, 14 Fam. Advoc. 45, 46 (Spring 1992).

[430] *See Spencer v. Spencer*, 494 A.2d 1279 (D.C. 1985).

[431] *Compare Fence v. Fence*, 314 N.Y.S.2d 1016 (N.Y. Fam. Ct. 1970); *Nestel v. Nestel*, 331 N.Y.S.2d 241 (N.Y. Sup. Ct. 1972); *Biel v. Biel*, 336 N.W.2d 404 (Wis. 1983) *with Sheets v.Sheets*, 254 N.Y.S.2d 320 (N.Y. Sup. Ct. 1964); *Faherty v. Faherty*, 477 A.2d 1257 (N.J. 1984); *Crutchley v. Crutchley*, 293 S.E.2d 793 (N.C. 1982). *See also Unif. Arbitration Act § 12(a)*, 7 U.L.A.280 (1997).

[432] *See Fence v. Fence*, 314 N.Y.S.2d 1016 (N.Y. Fam. Ct. 1970).

[433] 477 A.2d 1257 (N.J. 1984).

the advantages of arbitration of domestic disputes include reduced court congestion, the opportunity for resolution of sensitive matters in a private and informal forum, reduction of the trauma and anxiety of marital litigation, minimization of the intense polarization of the parties that often occurs, and the ability to choose the arbitrator.[434]

It tempered its support of arbitration with public policy considerations involving child support and custody conflicts. Although it refused to prohibit arbitration of child support and custody matters entirely, it held that courts should review those arbitrated decisions more closely because of the courts' responsibility for protecting the best interest of children. In reviewing child support awards, the court should review any award that reduces or refuses to increase child support which affects the substantial best interests of the child. Without reaching the question of child custody, which was not before the court, it advised that the same reasoning may apply to those cases.

The Superior Court of Pennsylvania, in *Miller v. Miller*,[435] directly confronted the issue of an agreement to arbitrate child custody. In *Miller*, the parties had agreed that the father would have custody of the children and that if any dispute over the children could not be resolved by mediation, that they would submit to binding mediation. When the mother sought a modification of custody, the parties were unable to mediate the issue and the matter was submitted to arbitration, which was decided in favor of the mother. The father refused to relinquish custody and the mother attempted to have the arbitrators' decision enforced as a court order. The trial judge, who had originally entered the divorce decree which incorporated the parties agreement, struck the provisions calling for binding arbitration of custody and refused to enter the arbitrators' award. Upon appeal, the superior court agreed that arbitration is generally a favored remedy, but held that a custody determination is subject to court review based on its responsibility to examine the best interest of the child. Accordingly, it concluded that the trial court erred in striking the arbitration provisions as void as against public policy, but that court was not bound to confirm the arbitration.

One commentator has observed that the AAA rules do not require an arbitrator to determine child-related issues under the standard of the best interest of the child, and has encouraged parties to include such directions in the arbitration agreements.[436] With appropriate safeguards, arbitration may prove as effective in dealing with child support and custody issues as it has in other family law matters.

---

[434] *Id.* at 1262.

[435] 620 A.2d 1161 (Sup. Ct. Penn. 1993).

[436] Philbrick, *Agreements to Arbitrate Post-Divorce Custody Disputes*, 18 Col. J.L. & Soc. Prob. 419, 453–454 (1985).

Chapter 9

SPOUSAL AND CHILD SUPPORT ON DIVORCE

§ 9.01 Introduction

Spousal support or maintenance, traditionally called alimony, originally was based on a husband's duty to support his wife after a divorce from bed and board. In this country, alimony was later extended to absolute divorce as a continuation of the duty of support after the marriage ended. Alimony was based primarily on fault and was only available to innocent wives whose husbands had caused the marriage to fail. In this sense, alimony functioned as a type of damages remedy for breach of the marriage contract.[1] With the advent of no-fault divorce, the role of fault in alimony began to decline, although not entirely disappear,[2] as greater emphasis was placed on the needs of the wife and the husband's ability to pay. Because of this change in focus, many states replaced the term "alimony" with "support" or "maintenance," although the terminology is often used synonymously.

In 1979, the United States Supreme Court held In *Orr v. Orr*[3] that divorce statutes which authorized alimony payments only to needy wives, but not to needy husbands, constituted gender-based discrimination which violated the Equal Protection Clause of the Fourteenth Amendment. The *Orr* court held that the "old notion" that "generally it is the man's primary responsibility to provide a home and its essentials"could no longer justify a statute that discriminated on the basis of gender.[4] "No longer is the female destined solely for the home and the rearing of the family, and only the male for the marketplace and the world of ideas."[5] *Orr* thus extended alimony rights on divorce to needy or dependent spouses of either gender. As a practical matter, however, when alimony is granted at all, it is much more commonly awarded to wives than to husbands.

In practice, only a small percentage (14.6%) of divorced women are awarded alimony today, and even fewer (10.7%) actually receive alimony.[6] Many courts have been reluctant to award much, if any, alimony, believing

---

[1] *See* Jana B. Singer, *Divorce Reform and Gender Justice*, 67 N.C.L. Rev. 1103, 1106 (1989) (noting that statistics indicate that only a small minority of women were awarded alimony under the fault-based regime).

[2] *See supra* §§ 8.01[B], [C].

[3] 440 U.S. 268 (1979).

[4] *Id.* at 279.

[5] *Id.* at 280 (quoting with approval *Stanton v. Stanton*, 421 U.S. 7, 14–15 (1975)).

[6] U.S. Dept. of Commerce, Bureau of the Census, Current Population Reports, Child Support and Alimony, Tables G and I (1987).

they should encourage nonwage earning spouses to obtain work outside the home and become self-supporting. The traditional stereotype of an ex-wife who is "living in luxury" on the proceeds of her ex-husband's labor is rarely found in the real world.[7]

The impact of no-fault divorce has had a devastating impact on divorced women who have not worked outside the home during marriages of long duration and on mothers who have custody of small children. Sociologist Lenore Weitzman has documented that most divorcing couples do not have substantial assets, that the average alimony is too meager to constitute an adequate means of support, and that the average child support award pays for less than half the cost of raising children.[8]

The authority to grant spousal support or alimony on divorce is statutory in nature. All states except Texas authorize alimony or support awards upon divorces, although the statutory factors for both eligibility and amount vary considerably from state to state.

Statutory law in all states also authorizes the courts in divorce actions to provide for the support of the parties' minor children.[9] While generally both parents today are responsible for providing child support, fathers remain more likely to be ordered to pay child support than mothers. Numerous studies have documented that a large number of divorced fathers fail to comply with court-ordered child support obligations, causing much of the welfare dependency in female-headed households and impoverishment of children.[10] Studies have revealed that only about one-third of all eligible women actually receive some child support payments.[11] Such distressing statistics led to the enactment of federal and state remedies under the Child Support Enforcement Amendments of 1984, which apply to both recipients and non-recipients of Aid to Families with Dependent Children (AFDC).[12]

The family law practitioner must be familiar with all the available spousal and child support remedies on divorce, as well as their equally important enforcement mechanisms.

---

[7] *See, e.g., Grinold v. Grinold*, 348 A.2d 32 (Conn. Super. Ct. 1975). *See generally* Homer Clark, The Law of Domestic Relations In the United States (2d Ed. 1987), at 619–622.

[8] *See* Lenore Weitzman, *The Economics of Divorce: Social and Economic Consequences of Property, Alimony, and Child Support Awards*, 28 UCLA L. Rev. 1181, 1189–1256 (1981); Lenore Weitzman, The Divorce Revolution: The Unexpected Social and Economic Consequences for Women and Children In America (1985); *see also* James McLindon, *Separate but Unequal: The Economic Disaster of Divorce for Women and Children*, 21 Fam. L.Q. 351, 405 (1987).

[9] *See generally* Donna Schuele, *Origins and Development of the Law of Parental Child Support*, 27 J. Fam. L. 807 (1988–89).

[10] *See* Theresa Amott, *Working for Less: Single Mothers In the Workplace*, In *Women as Single Parents* 106–108 (Elizabeth Mulroy, ed. 1988); Jessica Pearson & Nancy Thoennes, *Supporting Children After Divorce*, 22 Fam. L.Q. 319 (1988), *quoting* Hoffman, Marital Instability and the Economic Status of Women, 14 Demography 67 (1977).

[11] *See* U.S. Dept. of Commerce, Bureau of the Census, Current Population Survey, Child Suport Payments Due and Actually Received, by Gender, Table 1 (1997) (60% of custodial mothers actually receive the child support payments due).

[12] *See* 42 U.S.C. § 654 (1996). *See infra* § 9.06[F][4].

§ 9.02   Jurisdiction for Spousal and Child Support

[A]   The Doctrine of Continuing Jurisdiction

A court must have personal jurisdiction over the defendant in order to create, modify, or extinguish marital support or property rights or obligations.[13] Once a court has asserted personal jurisdiction over the parties in an action for spousal or child support, most jurisdictions view any subsequent support actions as part of one continuing process which began in the original divorce or support decree.[14] Because the majority of jurisdictions recognize the doctrine of continuing jurisdiction, a court may subsequently modify an alimony award entered by another state if it has jurisdiction over both parties and if the award was modifiable in the jurisdiction that originally ordered support.[15]

[B]   The Doctrine of Divisible Divorce

Although a court only needs to have personal jurisdiction over one of the parties to validly terminate the marital status under the doctrine of divisible divorce,[16] it must have jurisdiction over both parties to determine any support or marital property rights.[17] Thus, a valid divorce decree may be entered without affecting the parties' rights and duties with respect to support.

A small minority of states, however, will not order spousal support once the marital status has been terminated, because the duty of support arises from marriage and continuation of that duty in the form of alimony presupposes an existing duty.[18] Child support, however, may be ordered at any time, because the parent-child relationship is not affected by the marital status of the parties.[19]

---

[13] *See, e.g., Auman v. Auman*, 653 P.2d 688 (Ariz. 1982); *Boyd v. Boyd*, 340 S.E.2d 578 (Va. Ct. App. 1986); Restatement (Second) Conflict of Laws § 77 (1971). *See generally* Robert Casad, *Jurisdiction In Civil Actions*, §§ 9-17 to 9-24 (1991). For discussion of jurisdiction on divorce, see *supra* § 8.02.

[14] *See, e.g., Campbell v. Campbell*, 357 So. 2d 129 (Miss. 1978); *Sauls v. Sauls*, 577 P.2d 771 (Colo. Ct. App. 1977). The Restatement (Second) of Conflict of Laws § 26 (1971) states: "If a state obtains judicial jurisdiction over a party to an action, the jurisdiction throughout all subsequent proceedings which arise out of the original cause of action. Reasonable notice and reasonable opportunity to be heard must be given the party at each new step in the process."

[15] *See, e.g., Brisco v. Brisco*, 355 So. 2d 506 (Fla. Dist. Ct. App. 1978); *Lumpkins v. Lumpkins*, 495 P.2d 371 (N.M. 1972)

[16] *See supra* § 8.02[H].

[17] *See, e.g., Vanderbilt v. Vanderbilt*, 354 U.S. 416 (1957). For full discussion of the divisible divorce doctrine, see *supra* § 8.02[F].

[18] *See* Homer Clark, *supra* note 7, at 452–454.

[19] *Id.* at 456, 711–713.

[C] URESA, RURESA, and UIFSA

The Uniform Reciprocal Enforcement of Support Act [URESA] or its modified version, the Revised Uniform Reciprocal Enforcement of Support Act [RURESA],[20] has been adopted by all American jurisdictions. URESA and RURESA offer an additional method for obtaining a support order when the obligor is in another jurisdiction and is not subject to the personal jurisdiction of the forum state. It also may be used when the parties are in different areas of the same state. URESA and RURESA allow a support action to be initiated against an absent obligor even without a previous court order for support.[21]

[D] State Long-Arm Statutes

In many states, a person seeking support may also utilize a state's long-arm statute to enforce spousal and child support obligations.[22] *Soule v. Soule*[23] was among the first cases to apply a long-arm statute to allow a spouse to obtain a divorce with alimony after the other spouse had moved to another state. Similarly, in *Lozinski v. Lozinski*,[24] the Supreme Court of West Virginia approved application of the state's long-arm statute on the basis that the father's failure to support his children qualified as a tortious act under the statute. Therefore, it concluded that service on the West Virginia Secretary of State was an acceptable form of process over the father who was then located in Florida. A number of states now have special long-arm statutes which authorize extending jurisdiction over an absent spouse for purposes of awarding support, although some of those statutes require continued residence by the spouse seeking such support.[25]

[E] Child Support Jurisdiction: The *Kulko* Case

Child support jurisdiction, like jurisdiction for spousal support is based on personal jurisdiction over the obligor. In *Kulko v. Superior Court*,[26] the United States Supreme Court held that the mere fact that the child is living in the forum state is insufficient for asserting personal jurisdiction over the parent, even if the parent sent the child or acquiesced into the child's moving to that state. In *Kulko*, the parties had lived in New York for most of their marriage and their two children were born there. The parties entered into a written separation agreement which provided that the children

---

[20] U.L.A. Enforcement Supp. § 1 (1987).

[21] For a complete discussion of URESA, see *infra* § 8.06[F][3][b]. *See also* Lisabeth Hughes, Note, *Interstate Enforcement of Support Obligations Through Long-Arm Statutes and URESA*, 18 J. Fam. L. 537, 543–563 (1980).

[22] For a complete discussion of the use of long-arm statutes in divorce actions, see *supra* § 8.02[G]. *See also* Lisabeth Hughes, *supra* note 21, at 543–563.

[23] 14 Cal. Rptr. 417 (Cal. Ct. App. 1961). *See, e.g.*, Mass. Gen. Laws Ann. ch. 223A, § 3(h) (West 1985 & Supp. 2000); Tex. Fam. Code Ann. § 6.305 (West 1998).

[24] 408 S.E.2d 310 (W.Va. 1991).

[25] *See, e.g.*, Mass. Gen. Laws Ann. ch. 223A, § 3(h) (West 1985 & Supp. 2000); Tex. Fam. Code Ann. § 3.26 (West Supp. 1992).

[26] 436 U.S. 84 (1978).

would remain in New York with their father during the school year, but would spend holidays and summer vacations with their mother, who had moved to California. The father agreed to pay child support for the periods when the mother had physical custody. The wife obtained a divorce in Haiti, which incorporated the separation agreement.

A year after the parents' divorce, one of the children requested that she be allowed to remain in California with her mother following the Christmas vacation. The father consented and bought her a one-way ticket. Several years later, the other child decided he also wanted to live with his mother; she sent him a plane ticket without consulting the father. After the second child's arrival in California, the mother brought an action in California to modify custody and increase the child support obligation. The father appeared specially to object to the state's assertion of personal jurisdiction over him; his motion was denied. On appeal, he renewed his argument only with respect to the child support action. The California Court of Appeals held that the court had jurisdiction based on its long-arm statute, finding that the father had "caused an effect" in the state. The California Supreme Court affirmed, holding that the exercise of jurisdiction was reasonable because the father had "purposely availed himself of the benefits and protection" of California's laws by consenting to his daughter's living in that state.[27]

The United States Supreme Court reversed, holding that when a state asserts jurisdiction to order or modify child support, the obligor must have sufficient contacts with the forum state to satisfy due process standards of fairness and substantial justice. The Court concluded that the father did not have sufficient minimum contacts with California and that allowing that state to enter a judgment against him would "sanction a result that is neither fair, just, nor reasonable."[28] The Court noted that the father's agreement to allow the children to live in California with their mother, "in the interest of family harmony and his children's preferences," could "hardly be said to have 'purposefully availed himself of the benefits and protection' of California's laws."[29] Nor was the exercise of jurisdiction warranted by the financial benefit he received from his daughter's presence in that state for a large portion of the year, as any decrease in his expenses was due to the child's absence from his household rather than her presence in California. Additionally noting that the mother was not without a remedy, since she could bring an action for modification of child support in the New York courts, the Court concluded that the father's single act of acquiescing in the child's choice of residence "is surely not one that a reasonable parent would expect to result in the substantial financial burden and personal strain of litigating a child-support suit in a forum 3,000 miles away. . . ."[30] *Kulko* thus limits the extent to which long-arm statutes may be applied to obtain jurisdiction for awarding or modifying child support orders.

---

[27] *Id.* at 93.

[28] *Id.* at 92.

[29] *Id.* at 94.

[30] *Id.* at 97

The Supreme Court later reaffirmed the rule that personal service on a defendant within the forum state continues to constitute a valid basis for personal jurisdiction, despite a defendant's lack of other connections with the state. In *Burnham v. Superior Court of California*,[31] the wife and children had moved to California, while the husband remained in New Jersey.[32] When the husband went to California on business, then visited the children in that state, he was served with a summons and divorce petition. The husband asserted that the California court lacked personal jurisdiction over him because he lacked sufficient contacts in that state. The Supreme Court held that the minimum contacts requirement applies only when jurisdiction is sought over a defendant who is not physically present within the forum state. It declared that jurisdiction over nonresidents who are physically present in a state is one of "the most firmly established principles of personal jurisdiction in American tradition."[33] Under the *Burnham* analysis, a parent who is personally served within the forum state may be required to litigate support issues in that state.

§ 9.03 Spousal Support Factors and Judicial Discretion

While alimony traditionally was based on fault concepts which extended the husband's duty to support his wife after the marriage ended due to his fault, the decline of the role of fault, along with the recognition of gender-neutral principles, has caused most states to shift their focus in awarding alimony. Today alimony, commonly designated spousal support or maintenance, is generally based on need and is regarded as a means for providing necessary support to dependent former spouses.[34] Even if a custodial parent must work outside the home after divorce, his or her earning power may not be sufficiently adequate to support both the ex-spouse and the children, and alimony may be an appropriate vehicle for supplementing that income. Alimony frequently is viewed as a temporary measure to allow a spouse to obtain the necessary education or work skills in order to re-enter the job market and become self-supporting.[35]

[A] General Factors

The statutory factors for determining spousal support differ considerably from state to state. Some states' statutes authorize alimony in broad terms, granting the judge discretion to award it when it is, for example, "equitable"

---

[31] 495 U.S. 604 (1990).

[32] Although the couple had agreed that the wife would file for divorce in California, the husband later filed in New Jersey, but the wife was not served in that action. After unsuccessfully demanding that the husband honor the agreement, the wife filed for divorce in California. *Id.* at 608.

[33] *Id.* at 610. *See generally* Peter Hay, *Transient Jurisdiction, Especially Over International Defendants: Critical Comments on Burnham v. Superior Court of California*, 1990 U. Ill. L. Rev. 593 (1990).

[34] *See generally* Joan Krauskopf, *Maintenance: A Decade of Development*, 50 Mo. L. Rev. 259 (1985).

[35] *See infra* § 9.04[C].

or "just and proper," and allow the courts to develop more precise standards.[36] Many other states, however, have statutes which list mandatory and permissible factors for consideration in alimony awards.[37]

A number of states require a two-step determination in awarding spousal support: first, the court must decide whether the spouse is *eligible* for support; and second, it must calculate the appropriate *amount* of support to be ordered.[38] The Uniform Marriage and Divorce Act limits eligibility to a spouse who lacks property sufficient for his or her reasonable needs *and* who is unable to support himself or herself through appropriate employment *or* is a custodian of a child such that it would be inappropriate for the parent to work outside the home.[39] In applying such a standard for eligibility, the court in *Neal v. Neal*[40] concluded that a spouse must not only demonstrate insufficient income, but also show that he or she is incapable of employment, in order to qualify for spousal maintenance. It held that because the wife, who had custody of two school-age children and worked part-time as a cleaning person, did not prove that she was physically unable to work full time, she failed to satisfy the requisites for receiving maintenance.

This approach may impose severe hardships on an older spouse who has never worked outside the home or who has been out of the labor force for many years.[41] Some states, while limiting support to a spouse who is "dependent" on the supporting spouse, have interpreted dependency to mean that the party must merely be incapable of maintaining the accustomed standard of living.[42]

If a spouse is qualified to receive alimony, various factors may be applied for determining the appropriate amount to be awarded. Those factors are generally based on the financial needs of the party seeking support; the earning capacity, assets, and ability of the defendant spouse to pay; and the standard of living established during the marriage. Typical factors include the duration of the marriage; the ability of the dependent spouse to secure job-related education and training; the age, physical and mental condition of both parties; and the contribution or dissipation by each party in preserving the marital assets, including homemaking services.[43]

In recent years, some states have recognized a "fairness objective" in addition to the "support objective" in the factors to be considered in fashioning maintenance awards. The court in the *In re Marriage of LaRocque*[44] held that the trial court had erred in awarding limited term alimony

---

[36] *See, e.g.,* Ala. Code § 98-105 § 2 (1999); N.M. Stat. Ann. § 40-4-7(A) (Michie 1999).

[37] *See, e.g.,* Alaska Stat. § 25.24.160 (1998); Cal. Fam. Code § 4320 (West 1994).

[38] *See, e.g.,* Unif. Marriage and Divorce Act, 9A U.L.A. 159 (1998).

[39] *Id.*

[40] 570 P.2d 758 (Ariz. 1977).

[41] *See, e.g., Abuzzahab v. Abuzzahab,* 359 N.W.2d 12, 14 (Minn. 1984) (Wahl, J., dissenting); *see also* Lenore Weitzman, The Divorce Revolution: The Unexpected Social and Economic Consequences for Women and Children In America (1985).

[42] *See Williams v. Williams,* 261 S.E.2d 849 (N.C. 1980).

[43] *See* Unif. Marriage and Divorce Act § 308, 9A U.L.A. 347–8 (1998).

[44] 406 N.W.2d 736 (Wis. 1987).

of $1,500 per month for five months, then $1,000 a month for 13 months. The wife had received a bachelor's degree the year of the couple's marriage and had been employed in several capacities including secretary, clerk, and teacher. During most of the parties' twenty-five-year marriage, however, she was a homemaker and cared for the couple's five children. The husband received a law degree during the marriage and was employed as an attorney and later a judge, earning $60,000 per year at the time of divorce.

The *LaRocque* court held that the state's alimony statute was intended to assure a fair and equitable financial arrangement, as well as to provide support according to the parties' needs and earning capacities. In addition, it held that the trial court should consider the feasibility of the spouse's becoming self-supporting at a standard of living reasonably comparable to that enjoyed during marriage, as well as the length of time necessary to acquire such ability. The court should measure a reasonable maintenance award in terms of the marital lifestyle rather than the average annual earnings of the parties over the duration of the marriage. A reasonable starting point is to consider an equal division of the parties' total income.

[B] Fault as a Factor In Spousal Support

Because of the decreased importance of marital fault in divorce and the corresponding emphasis on need in awarding spousal support, approximately half the states have entirely eliminated consideration of marital misconduct in ordering support.[45] The remaining half, however, still recognize marital fault either as a factor in determining the amount of spousal support or as an absolute bar to spousal support.[46]

Even when fault is not an enumerated factor for determining the appropriate amount of support, some courts have determined that misconduct should remain relevant. For example, in *Williams v. Williams*,[47] the North Carolina Supreme Court noted that despite the statutory omission of fault as a factor for determining a spouse's dependency or the amount of support to be ordered, the state retained statutes that conditioned receipt of alimony on the supporting spouse's committing one of ten specific acts. It further disqualified a dependent spouse from receiving alimony for committing any of those acts. The court concluded that because divorce works an economic hardship on both parties:

> the burden of contending with diminished assets should, in all fairness, fall on the party primarily responsible for the breakup of the economic unit. . . . Sound public policy would dictate that the party who violated that binding [marriage] contract should continue to bear its financial burden where he or she can reasonably do so and where that is necessary to prevent a relatively greater economic hardship on the party without fault.[48]

---

[45] *See* Timothy Walker, *Family Law In the Fifty States: An Overview*, 25 Fam. L.Q. 417, 462–463 (1990).

[46] *Id.* at 451; *see also supra* § 8.03[F].

[47] 261 S.E.2d 849 (N.C. 1980).

[48] *Id.* at 858–859.

Other courts have held that while fault may be properly considered to compensate a spouse for actual injuries incurred because of the other's misbehavior or to bear the economic burden of divorce, it may not be used to punish a spouse. In *Taylor v. Taylor*[49] the court held that alimony could not be used as a "substitute for a money judgment in a personal injury case," where the husband had physically abused the wife during their marriage, although he could be required to pay her medical and dental expenses resulting from his abuse.

Because a trial court has wide discretion in determining both a spouse's eligibility for spousal support and the amount to be awarded in an individual case, awards are often inconsistent and unpredictable. A trial court's alimony decision will not be overturned by an appellate court absent abuse of discretion or a misapplication of the statutory standards.[50]

§ 9.04   Forms of Spousal Support

[A]   Temporary Spousal Support *Pendente Lite*

During a period of separation, while a divorce action is pending but prior to a divorce decree, a dependent spouse may petition the court for temporary spousal support, or support *pendente lite*.[51] *Pendente lite* support may provide for daily necessities during the interim, preserve a spouse's assets, prevent the other spouse from controlling all the parties' income and assets, and decrease the financial burden of family, friends or the public, upon whom the dependent spouse may otherwise rely.[52] Disadvantages of seeking temporary support include limited time for discovery, lack of a hearing in some jurisdictions, and the potential that the amount of temporary support awarded may unduly influence a final award.[53] Courts have upheld temporary *pendente lite* support orders for payments to a spouse to continue her education which she had commenced prior to the filing of a divorce petition[54] and for making mortgage payments while the divorce is pending.[55]

In *In re Marriage of Burlini*,[56] the California Court of Appeals held that spousal support guidelines are to be used only for awarding temporary, not permanent, spousal support. The court observed that temporary support is intended to maintain the parties' standard of living as closely as possible

---

[49] 378 So. 2d 1352 (Fla. Dist. Ct. App. 1980).

[50] *See, e.g., Clark v. Clark*, 696 P.2d 1386 (Kan. 1985); *Rosenberg v. Rosenberg*, 497 A.2d 485 (Md. Ct. Spec. App. 1985); *Quick v. Quick*, 290 S.E.2d 653 (N.C. 1982).

[51] *See generally* Kathleen Kay, *Alimony Pendente Lite and Earning Capacity*, 45 La. L. Rev. 79 (1984).

[52] *See* Melvyn Frumkes, *Temporary Alimony — The Importance of Itemizing Daily Expenses*, 25 Trial 36, 37 (April 1989).

[53] *Id.*

[54] *See McNulty v. McNulty*, 500 A.2d 876 (Pa. Super. Ct. 1985).

[55] *See Taylor v. Taylor*, 364 S.E.2d 244 (Va. 1988).

[56] 191 Cal. Rptr. 541 (Cal. Ct. App. 1983).

to the status quo during the pendency of the divorce action. Permanent support, on the other hand, is meant to provide long-term financial assistance, when necessary, as determined after dissolution and division of property. The court encouraged the continued use of guidelines for temporary support orders, absent unusual facts, to promote consistency by proportionately dividing the family income.

[B] "Permanent" Spousal Support

Alimony following divorce traditionally was ordered as a series of specified periodic payments for an indefinite period of time. Periodic support or alimony, often called "permanent" alimony, is not literally, "permanent," because it generally terminates on the death of either former spouse and on the remarriage of the recipient, absent a separation agreement to the contrary.[57] It also can be modified upward or downward on motion of either party upon proof of a significant change of circumstances.[58]

A spouse is most likely to be awarded permanent alimony when the spouse is older, without significant job skills, and is unlikely to become self-supporting, especially when the marriage has been long term. The Arizona Court of Appeals addressed this concept in *Rainwater v. Rainwater*,[59] when the husband appealed an award granted to the wife of $1900 per month for 3 years or until one year after the wife completed her bachelor's degree, whichever occurred first, and then $1200 a month until her death or remarriage. The husband argued that Arizona law permitted spousal maintenance only for a finite, transitional, rehabilitative term unless the recipient is permanently unable to become self-sustaining. The court decided that although the policy goal of a fixed term maintenance award is to promote a diligent effort to become self-sustaining, this goal must be balanced with the likelihood that the receiving spouse will be able to support herself in a manner reasonably approximating the standard of living during marriage. The couple in *Rainwater* had been married for 22 years, the wife was now 42 and working as a secretary while she pursued a college degree. During much of the marriage she had worked full time outside the home, helping to support the husband while he worked toward an engineering degree. She had contributed socially and emotionally to the husband's career, while maintaining the home and raising their two now-grown children. At the time of divorce the husband earned more than $100,000 a year. The court concluded that the wife could not foreseeably expect to maintain her standard of living without ongoing support from the husband at a level reasonably within his ability to provide.

Later the same year, in *Hughes v. Hughes*,[60] the Arizona Court of Appeals applied the same standard it set out in *Rainwater* and denied permanent spousal maintenance because the wife presented no evidence that she would

---

[57] *See, e.g.*, Unif. Marriage and Divorce Act § 316(b), 9A U.L.A. 183 (1998).

[58] *See infra* § 9.05.

[59] 869 P.2d 176 (Ariz. App. 1993).

[60] 869 P.2d 198 (Ariz. App. 1993).

not be able eventually to be able to generate her own earnings. In addition, the marriage was relatively short, there was not evidence that their standard of living increased during the marriage, the wife made no contribution to the husband's education or earning capacity, and she received a half interest in the husband's business when the marriage ended.

Many states also authorize "lump sum" support payments, also referred to as "alimony in gross" or "alimony in solido."[61] Although lump sum alimony is defined in terms of a definite, specific sum, it may be payable in a series of installments for a designated time. Alimony payable in lump sum may closely resemble property division payments, and despite its different theoretical basis, difficult categorization problems may arise when enforcement is sought.[62]

[C] "Rehabilitative" Spousal Support

Because a large proportion of married women now work outside the home, courts currently tend to disfavor permanent alimony, regarding it as a "pension" to the recipient, and prefer to make spousal support awards, if at all, for a limited period of time.[63] Many states now have a presumption or a preference for "rehabilitative" or "transitional" alimony, limited to definite time periods in an attempt to encourage the recipient to become self-supporting or to re-adjust to single status.[64] Rehabilitative alimony is intended to provide both spouses with some measure of predictability concerning their present and future needs and obligations, as well as to encourage the recipient to find employment or to undertake the education or training that will lead to future employment.[65]

In *Phohl v. Phohl*,[66] both the wife and husband appealed from the trial court's awarding the husband $30,000 lump sum alimony when the husband had previously received $200,000 in assets as gifts from the wife. The wife had a net worth of $4,250,000, and the couple had enjoyed a high standard of living based on the wife's contributions during the nine-year marriage. Noting that Florida's no-fault divorce law permitted alimony to be awarded to a husband under the same criteria as to a wife, the court held that the husband had shown both the wife's ability to pay and his own need, in light of the standard of living enjoyed during the marriage. The husband was 37 years old and in good health, but was mentally impaired and unemployed, with limited skills. Furthermore, the wife had insisted

---

[61] *See, e.g., Winokur v. Winokur*, 365 S.E.2d 94 (Ga. 1988); *Washburn v. Washburn*, 677 P.2d 152 (Wash. 1984).

[62] *See infra* § 9.06[F].

[63] *See generally* Joan Krauskopf, *Rehabilitative Alimony: Uses and Abuses of Limited Duration Alimony*, 21 Fam. L.Q. 573 (1988).

[64] *See, e.g., Taylor v. Taylor*, 504 N.Y.S.2d 698 (N.Y. App. Div.1986); *Stevenson v. Stevenson*, 511 A.2d 961 (R.I. 1986); *see also* N.H. Rev. Stat. Ann. § 458.19 (1992 & Supp. 2000) (three-year limitation on alimony unless renewed).

[65] *See also Turner v. Turner*, 385 A.2d 1280 (N.J. Super. Ct. App. Div. 1978); *Kulakowski v. Kulakowski*, 468 A.2d 733 (N.J. Super. Ct. App. Div. 1982).

[66] 345 So. 2d 371 (Fla. Dist. Ct. App. 1977).

that the husband quit his job as a toy salesman so he could devote all his time to her and the family. Rehabilitative alimony was appropriate to supplement the husband's other means until he could become self-supporting.

The Missouri Court of Appeals reached a similar conclusion in *Michael v. Michael,*[67] a case in which the husband had worked outside of the home for only 5 years of the 15 year marriage, while the wife had outside employment during the entire marriage. While the husband was at home he did some housework, but preparation the couple's evening meal was the only task he performed with any regularity. When the trial court allotted only 24.4% of the marital assets and no maintenance to the husband, he appealed. The appellate court held that the trial court had abused its discretion and that the husband was entitled to a greater share of the marital assets, and that he should be awarded maintenance because he had detrimentally relied on the wife for monetary support. The court noted that he needed education for reentry into the field of journalism, and remanded for an award of rehabilitative maintenance.

Professor Clark regards the use of rehabilitative alimony as potentially dangerous because trial courts, "in their zeal to restrict alimony and under the influence of the notion that most married women today work outside the home, will award rehabilitative alimony when the wife has no realistic expectation of earning enough to support herself in an acceptable [manner]."[68] An example of this result is *Otis v. Otis,*[69] in which the court upheld an award of alimony that terminated after four years, despite the fact that the wife had not worked during the couple's 25-year marriage since the birth of their child. Quoting a 1978 law review article, the court observed that statutory changes in the state's law of alimony were a reflection that:

> traditionally spousal support was a permanent award because it was assumed that a wife had neither the ability nor the resources to become self-sustaining. However, with the mounting dissolution rate, the advent of no-fault dissolution, and the growth of the women's liberation movement, the focal point of spousal support determinations has shifted from the sex of the recipient to the individual's ability to become financially independent.[70]

Although the husband's income exceeded $120,000 per year, the court held that the limited alimony award satisfied the state's new statutory standards.

To safeguard against such unfortunate consequences, some courts have concluded that permanent, rather than rehabilitative, alimony must be awarded when the spouse is older, is without significant job skills or work history, has medical problems, or is otherwise unlikely to be able to become

---

[67] 791 S.W.2d 772 (Mo. Ct. App. 1990).

[68] *See* Homer Clark, *supra* note 7, at 265–266.

[69] 299 N.W.2d 114 (Minn. 1980).

[70] *Id.* at 116 (citation omitted).

self-supporting.[71] For example, in *Lash v. Lash*[72] the Florida Court of Appeals held that, in light of the husband's substantial salary as an executive, an award of rehabilitative, rather than permanent, alimony was improper when inequities would result because of the wife's medical problems and absence from the job market for most of the parties' 26-year marriage. Other courts have held that rehabilitative alimony is proper only when the recipient can obtain employment at compensation which provides a standard of living roughly commensurate to that established during marriage.[73]

The Supreme Court of North Dakota, in *Van Klootwyk v. Van Klootwyk*,[74] noted that two concepts of rehabilitative spousal support have been developed, a "minimalist" doctrine, which seeks to educate and retrain the recipient for minimal self-support, and an "equitable" doctrine, which attempts to enable the disadvantaged spouse to obtain "adequate" self-support, in light of the standard of living during the marriage. Under the latter, the recipient may be eligible for rehabilitative support despite whether she is employed full-time, and should not be disqualified because she began her economic self-rehabilitation by education or training during the marriage. This is especially true where the parties accumulated few assets during the marriage. A strong dissent would have denied the wife rehabilitative alimony because of her attainment of an education and career during marriage and because the husband's living expenses were higher.

At the same time, when a spouse has been awarded a large amount of marital property,[75] when the marriage was of short duration,[76] or when the spouse has the ability and desire to obtain additional education in order to eventually increase his or her earning power,[77] rehabilitative alimony may be more appropriate. In *In re Marriage of Wilson*[78] the court noted that limited-term alimony may be proper in a short term, second marriage when the spouse is incapable of becoming self-supporting due to an injury incurred during the marriage, affirming termination of alimony after 58 months following a 70-month marriage.

The Vermont Supreme Court, in *Clapp v. Clapp*,[79] upheld a one-year award of maintenance to the wife based on an equalization of the parties' incomes. Although that court had previously rejected a permanent maintenance award based on the equalization approach, it held that the trial court had acted in its discretion.

---

[71] *See In re Marriage of Morrison*, 573 P.2d 41 (Cal. 1978); *see also* Md. Code Ann. Fam. Law § 11-106(c) (1998).

[72] 307 So. 2d 241 (Fla. Dist. Ct. App. 1975).

[73] *See, e.g., Bagan v. Bagan*, 382 N.W.2d 645 (N.D. 1986); *In re Marriage of Carney*, 462 N.E.2d 596 (Ill. App. Ct. 1986).

[74] 563 N.W. 2d 377 (1997).

[75] *See Ingram v. Ingram*, 721 S.W.2d 262 (Tenn. Ct. App. 1986).

[76] *Carlson v. Carlson*, 722 P.2d 222 (Alaska 1986).

[77] *Tesch v. Tesch*, 399 N.W.2d 880 (S.D. 1987).

[78] 247 Cal. Rptr. 522 (Cal. Ct. App. 1988).

[79] 653 A.2d 72 (Vt. 1994).

[D] New or Hybrid Forms of Alimony

Because many modern alimony statutes authorize alimony only when a spouse can demonstrate need,[80] a number of states recently have recognized new forms of alimony to compensate a spouse for contributions to the other spouse's education or career development. These awards, based on statute,[81] contract, or equitable principles, allow compensation when little divisible property has been accumulated, but one spouse has obtained valuable career assets not categorized as property, partially attributable to the other's contributions.[82] These new awards, frequently denominated "reimbursement" or "restitutional" alimony, are hybrids of alimony and property division, as they combine features of both doctrines.

In *Pyeatte v. Pyeatte*,[83] the Arizona Court of Appeals rejected a wife's contract claim that she had put the husband through three years of law school based on his agreement that he would then put her through graduate school. When the husband sought a divorce after completing law school and entering the bar, the wife sought damages for breach of contract. The court denied her claim, holding that the agreement was insufficiently defined in terms of time, place, and cost of performance, and lacked other material provisions. However, it acknowledged that the wife could obtain restitution, based on an equitable theory of quasi-contract, to prevent the husband's unjust enrichment. It limited the award on remand to her financial contributions to the husband's living expenses and direct educational expenses, not to exceed the amount of benefit she had anticipated.

Some courts have authorized similar awards even when the contributing spouse does not intend to pursue further education. In *DeLa Rosa v. DeLa Rosa*,[84] the wife worked as a teacher and other jobs while the husband pursued his undergraduate and medical degrees. Before the husband completed his medical degree, he filed for dissolution of the marriage and the court awarded restitution to the wife for the financial support she had provided. The Minnesota Supreme Court approved the concept of reimbursement, but remanded the judgment for a reduction of the award after establishing a formula to calculate reimbursement based on the wife's actual contributions to the husband's living expenses and direct educational expenses, after subtracting her own living expenses and the husband's own contributions.

In *In re Marriage of Francis*,[85] the Iowa Supreme Court approved an award, framed in terms of "reimbursement" alimony, that allowed the wife some return on her investment in addition to her direct contributions. The

---

[80] *See, e.g., McDermott v. McDermott*, 628 P.2d 959 (Ariz. Ct. App. 1981) (wife unable to demonstrate need because she had supported couple as teacher while husband obtained education; court awarded her $500 per month for up to 33 months as matter of equity, provided that she attended school).

[81] *See, e.g.*, Ariz. Rev. Stat. § 25-319(A)(3)(1999); Cal. Civ. Code § 4801 (West Supp. 1997).

[82] *See infra* § 10.08, Licenses, Degrees and Enhanced Earnings.

[83] 661 P.2d 196 (Ariz. Ct. App. 1983).

[84] 309 N.W.2d 755 (Minn. 1981).

[85] 442 N.W.2d 59 (Iowa 1989).

court permitted consideration of the future earning capacity of the husband who had completed his medical degree and residency while the wife supported him and their two children by running an in-home day care business. The court stated:

> [A]limony has traditionally taken the place of support that would have been provided had the marriage continued. A calculation of future earning capacity, in a case like the present one, essentially represents a value placed on the income to be derived from the advanced degree achieved during the marriage. The amount that would have been the student spouse's contribution to the future earning capacity. Thus, the court's duty to look at the future earning capacity of the spouses tracks more closely with a concern for loss of anticipated support, reimbursable through alimony, than through division of as-yet-unrealized tangible assets. [86]

Professor Ira Mark Ellman has argued that because spouses often make sacrifices to their own earning capacity based on decisions to benefit the marital community, new principles of alimony should be developed in order to recompense the contributing spouse's reliance interests. He advocates recovery on divorce for losses in earning capacity in order to ensure that marital sharing principles result in sharing the costs, as well as the benefits of, marriage. [87]

The Supreme Court of Montana, in *In re Marriage of Williams*,[88] expressly approved a support award designed to compensate a spouse for foregone career opportunities. In *Williams*, the wife had a bachelor's degree at the time of marriage, but remained home to raise the couple's six children and had been out of the job market for eighteen years, while the husband was engaged in the practice of law. The court calculated the wife's career losses in terms of her lost retirement benefits and salary differential due to her absence from outside work, and held that these factors were appropriate in determining her reasonable needs and ability to support herself through appropriate employment. [89]

The Vermont Supreme Court considered an income sharing approach to alimony in *Delozier v. Delozier*.[90] In that case the family court had awarded permanent monthly maintenance to a wife in an undetermined amount to be calculated by annually dividing equally the parties' combined income. The court held that in some long term marriages, permanent alimony may be appropriate to approximate the parties' marital standard of living, but regarded the use of formulas with disfavor, in that they modify support

---

[86] *Id.* at 63.

[87] *See* Ira Ellman, *The Theory of Alimony*, 77 Cal. L. Rev. 3 (1989).

[88] 714 P.2d 548 (Mont. 1986).

[89] *See also* Joan Williams, *Is Coverture Dead? Beyond a New Theory of Alimony*, 82 Geo. L. J. 2227 (1994); Jana B. Singer, *Alimony and Efficiency: The Gendered Costs and Benefits of the Economic Justification for Alimony*, 82 Geo. L.J. 2433 (1994) (examining the economic opportunities forgone by a child-rearing spouse, and the corresponding enhancement of their partner's earning capacities).

[90] 640 A.2d 55 (Vt. 1994).

payments without regard to modification standards and are not responsive to the needs of the parties. In this case, in which the former wife was relatively young, in good health, and was pursuing a career as a registered nurse, the court determined that rehabilitative support and compensatory alimony was appropriate, and temporary income equalization was permissible, it authorized the trial court to leave the details of the equalization formula work out with an accountant.

§ 9.05   Modification of Spousal Support

Most states authorize modification of future payments of periodic spousal support or alimony by statute.[91] In general, the party seeking modification must show a change of circumstances that is sufficiently substantial or material to justify either an increase or decrease in the amount originally ordered. The Uniform Marriage and Divorce Act adopts a higher standard, which provides in part:

(a) . . . [T]he provisions of any [divorce] decree respecting maintenance or support may be modified only as to installments accruing subsequent to the motion for modification and only upon a showing of changed circumstances *so substantial and continuing as to make the terms unconscionable* . . .

(b) Unless otherwise agreed in writing or expressly provided in the decree, the obligation to pay future maintenance is terminated upon the death of either party or the remarriage of the party receiving maintenance. . . .[92]

Unless an order modifying spousal support has been entered, the majority of states regard each installment of alimony as final and non-modifiable when it becomes due. An alimony installment that is final and non-modifiable has the status of a final judgment and is entitled to full faith and credit in all other states.[93] Accrued alimony installments or arrearages cannot be modified retroactively, and future alimony payments may be modified prospectively only after a motion has been filed and the other party served with notice.

In a minority of jurisdictions, however, retroactive modification of alimony arrearages is permitted, either by statute or judicial decision.[94] If accrued alimony arrearages are retroactively modifiable, other states need not afford them full faith and credit because they are not final judgments. When full faith and credit does not prohibit modification, other state courts apply comity principles and consider modification issues under the standards of the state which originally granted the alimony.[95]

---

[91] *See, e.g.,* Cal. Civ. Code §§ 4801, 4801.5 (West Supp. 1997); Fla. Stat. Ann. ch. 61.14 (1994 & Harrison Supp. 1999).

[92] Unif. Marriage and Divorce Act, § 316, 9A U.L.A. 183 (1998) (emphasis added).

[93] *See, e.g., Sistare v. Sistare,* 218 U.S. 1 (1910); *Corliss v. Corliss,* 549 P.2d 1070 (N.M. 1976).

[94] *See, e.g.,* N.Y. Dom. Rel. Code § § 236, 244 (McKinney 1999 & Supp. 2000); *Fainberg v. Rosen,* 278 A.2d 630 (Md. Ct. Spec. App. 1971); *Rust v. Rust,* 177 N.W.2d 888 (Wis. 1970).

[95] *See Alig v. Alig,* 255 S.E.2d 494, 497 (Va. 1979).

When the original decree did not sufficiently provide for the spouse or children, most states permit modification of alimony, regardless of whether it arose in a written separation agreement or a court order, without a showing of changed circumstances.[96] Courts in a minority of jurisdictions have interpreted separation agreements under traditional contract principles and refused to allow modification of contractual spousal support unless the parties agree.[97] In *In re Marriage of Mass*,[98] the court distinguished between court ordered support and contractual support. It held that the husband's contractual agreement to pay alimony did not merge into the divorce decree and that his obligation would not terminate under statutory provisions that terminated alimony upon remarriage of the recipient. Child support, however, is always modifiable based on a bona fide change of circumstances when it is in the child's best interests, regardless of whether it is based on a court order or private agreement.[99]

The moving party must prove that the circumstances of either or both of the parties have substantially changed before a modification is justified. The alleged change in circumstances must have occurred since the last hearing. In *Herndon v. Herndon*,[100] the husband, a chiropractor, had previously been granted a reduction in both his child support and alimony obligations, based on the appreciation of the wife's assets and his own health problems involving his hands. His later petition for termination of alimony was denied because the trial court found no sufficient change of circumstances since the previous hearing, since the husband's hand condition had not changed and, although the wife's assets had appreciated, their increase in value was due to inflation, which had also affected her costs of raising the child. The husband was not currently practicing chiropracty, but maintained his licenses in Arizona and California, and had not shown he was unable to maintain a practice. The Supreme Court of South Dakota affirmed concluded that the trial court had not abused its discretion.

Determining a legitimate and sufficient change of circumstances that warrants an increase, decrease, or termination of spousal support has generated considerable litigation.[101] Modification generally will be authorized if the recipient's needs or the payor's ability to pay changes because of circumstances beyond the party's control, if the recipient remarries; or, in some states, cohabits with another; or when either party dies.[102]

A substantial increase in the recipient's cost of living, including additional expenses for the parties' children, may constitute grounds for an increase in spousal support.[103] Similarly, a recipient's continuing illness

---

[96] *See, e.g., Lepis v. Lepis*, 416 A.2d 45 (N.J. 1980); *Levitt v. Levitt*, 399 P.2d 33 (Cal. 1965).

[97] *See, e.g., Parrillo v. Parrillo*, 336 S.E.2d 23 (Va. 1985).

[98] 431 N.E.2d 1 (Ill. App. Ct. 1981).

[99] *Id.*; *Drummond v. Drummond*, 495 P.2d 994 (Kan. 1974); *see infra* § 9.06[E].

[100] 305 N.W.2d 917 (S.D. 1981).

[101] *See generally* James Higgins, Note, *Modification of Spousal Support: A Survey of a Confusing Area of Law*, 17 J. Fam. L. 711 (1979).

[102] *See, e.g., Lepis v. Lepis*, 416 A.2d 45 (N.J. 1980).

[103] *Naylor v. Naylor*, 700 P.2d 707 (Utah 1985); *Siegel v. Siegel*, 102 Cal. Rptr. 613 (Cal. Ct. App. 1972).

or a significant mental or physical impairment normally would comprise a bona fide change of circumstances. However, if the payee's elevated need was due to a voluntary change in lifestyle, courts are hesitant to increase support.[104]

Whether temporary or rehabilitative alimony may be extended when the recipient has not improved his or her earning capacity has troubled the courts. In *Hecker v. Hecker*,[105] the wife was awarded ten years temporary spousal maintenance. During those years, she worked part-time so she could retain flexibility to meet the needs of the children. When the maintenance was scheduled to end, the former wife claimed she would be without sufficient means to provide for her own support. The court appointed referee found that her inability to improve her earning capacity constituted a substantial change of circumstances and modified the award to one of permanent maintenance. The appeals panel reversed and remanded to the district court to address why the wife had failed to rehabilitate herself. The court found that she had failed to make any reasonable effort toward rehabilitation and attributed to her the income she could have been producing by reasonable effort. Even with the attributed income, however, she was unable to meet her monthly expenses and held that she was not precluded from receiving further maintenance if she failed to become self-supporting through her diligent efforts. It awarded her permanent maintenance to the extent of the difference between her monthly expenses and the attributed income.

A number of courts have held that when the payor's financial position greatly improves after divorce, the alimony recipient is entitled only to support at the level enjoyed during the marriage and will not be granted an increase in spousal support based solely on the payor's increased ability to pay.[106] Other courts, however, have held that the payor spouse's post-divorce wealth should be shared by the recipient spouse.[107] For example, in *Naylor v. Naylor*,[108] the Utah Supreme Court emphasized that the earnings and financial assets of the husband, who was a surgeon, had increased dramatically since the divorce, while the ex-wife's financial status and employment as a hairdresser had not changed. Although alimony had originally been ordered for only five years, the court relied on its statutory power to modify support, regardless of the parties' previous agreement or stipulation. It found that the parties' earlier expectations that the wife's income would increase had failed to materialize, and, along with increased costs of raising the parties' child, constituted a sufficient change of

---

[104] *See, e.g., Sistrunk v. Sistrunk*, 235 So. 2d 53 (Fla. Dist. Ct. App. 1970).

[105] 568 N.W.2d 705 (Minn. 1997).

[106] *See, e.g., In re Marriage of Hoffmeister*, 236 Cal. Rptr. 543 (Cal. Ct. App. 1987); *Irwin v. Irwin*, 539 So. 2d 1177 (Fla. Dist. Ct. App. 1990); *see also In re Marriage of Smith*, 274 Cal. Rptr. 911 (Cal. Ct. App. 1990) (increase of support to marital standard of living unwarranted where actual marital standard of living unreasonable).

[107] *See, e.g., In re Marriage of Geis*, 512 N.E.2d 1354 (Ill. App. Ct. 1987); *Lott v. Lott*, 302 A.2d 666 (Md. Ct.Spec. App. 1973).

[108] 700 P.2d 707 (Utah 1985).

circumstances to warrant a four-year extension of the alimony, as well as an increase in the amount.

If the payor's income substantially declines after the divorce, through no fault of his or her own, an alimony award may be reduced. [109] An involuntary loss of employment, a physical or mental handicap, or attainment of mandatory retirement age may be sufficient to authorize a decrease in an alimony obligation. [110] In *Rome v. Rome*, [111] the parties had stipulated that the husband would pay the wife $1000 a month spousal support when they ended their 32-year marriage. Three months later, the husband sought a reduction of support because he had lost his job. The trial court lowered the amount to $100 a month and established a sliding scale correlated to his future income for subsequent support. Although the husband's evidence that he had been fired without cause was undisputed, the appellate court questioned the sincerity of his efforts to find new employment and reversed the order because of the trial court's refusal to continue the matter for reassessment of the husband's efforts to obtain employment.

Nevertheless, if the payor voluntarily reduces his or her income by taking a lower paying job, or no job at all, many courts have held that modification of alimony is not justified. In *Ellis v. Ellis*, [112] both parties appealed after the trial court ordered a reduction of the husband's alimony obligation. After the parties' divorce, the husband had remarried, assumed financial responsibility for his new wife's mother, and voluntarily retired from his job. The Iowa Supreme Court held that the modification of alimony was improper in light of the husband's voluntary retirement and plans for the future, remarking that the husband "equates self-interest with good faith." [113] It declared:

> We do not dispute the sincerity of his wish to leave his employment and move to a warmer climate. We do not doubt his desire to see his present wife continue her education. Nor do we question his devotion to their child and his mother-in-law. Although the record indicates his health problems are not as serious as he makes them out to be, we do not think they are imaginary. However, he is not free to plan his future without regard to his obligation to his first wife. He cannot arbitrarily freeze her out of his future. Similar obligations in and apart from family life compel many persons to maintain employment which may be difficult, undesirable and even physically or mentally painful. [114]

The court reinstated the alimony to its original amount.

---

[109] *See, e.g., Smith v. Smith*, 419 A.2d 1035 (Me. 1980).

[110] *See, e.g., Marriage of Kowski*, 463 N.E.2d 840 (Ill. App. Ct. 1984).

[111] 167 Cal. Rptr. 351 (Cal. Ct. App. 1980).

[112] 262 N.W.2d 265 (Iowa 1978).

[113] *Id.* at 267.

[114] *Id.*

Voluntary retirement may be a factor, however, although not necessarily determinative, in deciding whether alimony should be reduced.[115] For example, In *Olsen v. Olsen*,[116] the husband petitioned for modification of alimony and child support when his earning declined after he retired from the active practice of medicine. The court denied his petition in consideration of the parties' correlative needs and abilities. The husband had income from Social Security, a pension, and a substantial amount from a trust fund, plus he admitted that he would return to active practice if necessary, while the wife's income was reduced due to mandatory retirement, which left her with insufficient means to meet her expenses even with the continued alimony. Similarly, the New Jersey Supreme Court, in *Deegan v. Deegan*,[117] denied the husband's motion to terminate alimony when he voluntarily retired at age 60 because of an attractive retirement package, a suspicion that he would soon be laid off due to lack of work, and his job and been increasingly difficult for him because of its physical demands. The court held that even if a former spouse retires in good faith, it must balance the advantage of a new life for the retiring party and the disadvantage to the payee spouse. Here, the wife relied on the alimony in order to survive. The court further cautioned that issues of early retirement or voluntary changes in life should be addressed at the time of divorce, and that "[n]o thoughtful matrimonial lawyer should leave an issue of this importance to chance and subject his or her client to lengthy future proceedings."[118]

In some circumstances, the courts may look not only at the payor's actual income, but potential earning capacity as well.[119] However, the payor should be left with sufficient income to pay his or her own reasonable needs.[120]

A payor spouse who wishes to make a career change to a lower paying job may continue to be burdened with alimony payments based on his or her previous higher salary. While some courts focus on the payor's motives and good faith and may allow modification under the circumstances,[121] others have held that the needs of the former spouse and children have priority and refuse to adjust support payments based on the lower pay,

---

[115] *See Pimm v. Pimm*, 601 So. 2d 534 (Fla. 1992) (retirement is a change in circumstance that may be considered by the court in deciding whether to modify an alimony obligation); *Smith v. Smith*, 419 A.2d 1035 (Me. 1980) (retirement of payor spouse for primary purpose of avoiding alimony does not of itself bring about substantial change in payor's circumstances needed to justify reduction in alimony).

[116] 557 P.2d 604 (Idaho 1976).

[117] 603 A.2d 542 (N.J.Super. Ct. App. Div. 1992).

[118] *Id.* at 546.

[119] *See, e.g., Schuler v. Schuler*, 416 N.E.2d 197 (Mass. 1981). *But see In re Marriage of Dixon*, 683 P.2d 803 (Colo. Ct. App. 1983).

[120] *Compare Payne v. Payne*, 363 S.E.2d 428 (Va. Ct. App. 1987) (MBA husband who worked as hospital administrator and family counselor) *with Butler v. Butler*, 227 S.E.2d 688 (Va. 1976) (neurosurgeon who worked in hospital staff position).

[121] *See, e.g., In re Meegan*, 13 Cal. Rptr. 2d 799 (Cal. Ct. App. 1992) (reduction of spousal support proper where former husband quit his job in good faith to become a priest).

effectively locking the payor into the position held at the time of the divorce. [122]

Courts have had mixed responses to petitions for reduction of spousal support based on the payor's remarriage and the additional expenses of a new family and children. [123] On the one hand, the obligor has new legal duties of support to the later family, who is equally deserving of protection; on the other, the changed circumstances are voluntary and the payor should not be able to manipulate unilaterally pre-existing obligations to a former spouse. [124]

Remarriage of the recipient former spouse usually results in an automatic termination of alimony, often dictated by statute. In the absence of a statute or a provision in the divorce decree, the payor generally will need to bring an action for modification or termination, although remarriage will often raise a prima facie case of changed circumstances sufficient to extinguish a former spouse's alimony obligation. The Massachusetts Supreme Court adopted this position in *Kelly v. O'Brien*, [125] reversing a trial court determination that because the wife was still in need of support, her remarriage did not constitute a material change of circumstances. The supreme court held that alimony is not automatically terminated upon remarriage, but remarriage does create a prima facie case of termination absent extraordinary circumstances. The mere fact that the wife was unable to continue her previous standard of living based on her new husband's income was insufficient to continue the alimony.

In *Peterson v. Peterson*, [126] the divorce decree required the husband to pay alimony to the wife of $1000 per month for seven years, and then $500 per month for ten years unless she were to die or remarry, at which time the alimony would cease. Two years after the divorce, the wife remarried and the husband petitioned to have his duty extinguished. The wife argued that the alimony provision required the husband to pay alimony for the first seven years regardless of her remarriage, that the alimony was an integral part of the property settlement of the divorce decree, and that extenuating circumstances existed in that her current husband was unable to support her. The South Dakota Supreme Court held that unless specified in a divorce decree to the contrary, spousal support will be extinguished upon remarriage. It further held that the ability of a new spouse to support the former recipient is not a factor which will justify continuation of alimony

---

[122] *See, e.g., Wolcott v. Wolcott*, 735 P.2d 326 (N.M. Ct. App. 1987) (voluntary career change, resulting in major reduction of income, not in good faith, thus not substantial change in circumstances justifying modification). *See generally* David Giacalone, *The Dropout Ex-Husband's Right to Reduce Alimony and Support Payments*, 1 Fam. L. Rep. 4065 (1975).

[123] *Compare Edwards v. Lowry*, 348 S.E.2d 259 (Va. 1986) (reduction of child support denied when husband discharged from employment for theft and responsibility to second family constituted voluntary change of circumstances) *with Lewis v. Lewis*, 248 P.2d 1061 (Idaho 1962) (responsibility to second family and to father properly considered in modification of child support).

[124] *See Berg v. Berg*, 359 A.2d 354 (R.I. 1976). *Compare infra* § 9.06[E].

[125] 652 N.E.2d 589 (Mass. 1995).

[126] 434 N.W.2d 732 (S.D. 1989).

payments, adding that "it is illogical and unreasonable that a spouse should receive support from a present spouse and a former spouse at the same time."[127]

Although remarriage of the recipient usually terminates that party's right to receive support or alimony from a former spouse,[128] many courts refuse to reinstate an alimony award if the later marriage is annulled.[129] The payor may have detrimentally relied on the appearance of the recipient's remarriage, not its validity, and should not be penalized by the former spouse's decision to seek its invalidation. Furthermore, many states now authorize alimony in annulment actions as well as in divorce cases.[130]

A number of states authorize modification or termination of spousal support if the recipient cohabits with a person of the opposite sex, sometimes additionally requiring that the cohabitation be "conjugal" or of a marriage-like relationship.[131] Although an unmarried cohabitant does not incur a legal duty of support, as a practical matter, cohabitants are likely to share living expenses. Further, some decisions appear to be based on moral judgments that an unmarried cohabitant no longer deserves continued support from a former spouse.[132]

Absent a governing statute, most states do not automatically regard cohabitation as a basis for modification or termination, but, instead, will weigh the economic impact of the living arrangement and its effect upon the recipient's continued need for support by the former spouse.[133] The court in *Gayet v. Gayet*[134] adopted an economic test to determine the effect of cohabitation on alimony. It examined the competing policies of terminating alimony upon remarriage and the former spouse's interest in "privacy, autonomy, and the right to develop personal relationship free from governmental sanctions."[135] It concluded that only the actual economic effect of

---

[127] *Id.* at 736.

[128] *See Woodward v. Woodward*, 229 N.W.2d 274 (Iowa 1975) (no single factor controls whether award constitutes alimony for purpose of termination on recipient's remarriage).

[129] *Compare Denberg v. Frischman*, 264 N.Y.S.2d 114 (N.Y. App. Div. 1965) (no revival of alimony upon annulment) *with DeWall v. Rhoderick*, 138 N.W.2d 124 (Iowa 1965) (resumption of alimony following annulment). *See also In re Cargill*, 843 P.2d 1335 (Colo. 1993) (adopting equitable middle position to determine reinstatement on facts and equities of each case). *See generally* Louanne Love, *The Way We Were: Reinstatement of Alimony After Annulment of Spouse's "Remarriage,"* 28 J. Fam. L. 289 (1989–90).

[130] *See, e.g.*, Cal. Fam. Code § 2254 (West 1994); Conn. Gen. Stat. Ann. § 46b-60 (West 1995).

[131] *See, e.g.*, Conn. Gen. Stat. § 46b-86 (West 1995 & Supp. 2000); N.Y. Dom. Rel. Law § 248 (McKinney 1986). Ala. Code § 30-2-55 (1989); *see also* Evan Langbein, *Post-Dissolution Cohabitation of Alimony Recipients: A Legal Fact of Life*, 12 Nova L. Rev. 787 (1988); Thomas Oldham, *Cohabitation by an Alimony Recipient Revisited*, 20 J. Fam. L. 615 (1981–82).

[132] *See, e.g.*, *Bentzoni v. Bentzoni*, 442 So. 2d 235 (Fla. Dist. Ct. App. 1983); *Bisig v. Bisig*, 469 A.2d 1348 (N.H. 1983).

[133] *See, e.g.*, *In re Marriage of Dwyer*, 825 P.2d 1018 (Colo. Ct. App. 1991); *Mitchell v. Mitchell*, 418 A.2d 1140 (Me. 1980); *Abbott v. Abbott*, 282 N.W.2d 561 (Minn. 1979).

[134] 456 A.2d 102 (N.J. 1983).

[135] *Id.* at 103.

cohabitation, and not the former spouse's conduct as a cohabitant, should determine the duration of support. The trial court should modify alimony either when a third party contributes to the dependent spouse's support or when a third party resides with the spouse without contributing to household expenses. That same court reaffirmed that principle in *Melletz v. Melletz*,[136] a case in which the parties had specified in their divorce settlement agreement that the wife's alimony would be suspended if the wife cohabited with an unrelated male. The appellate court applied the *Gayet* economic impact test to hold that the husband's attaching conditions to the alimony unrelated to her financial status undermined the very purpose of alimony, noting that matters of personal preference, residence, or occupation, insofar as they do not reflect changes in the income, expenses, or other matters of recognized mutual concern, simply are not the business of a former spouse.

The Supreme Court of Nevada addressed the question of cohabitation in *Gilman v. Gilman*,[137] which consolidated two cases, one in which the divorce decree made no reference to cohabitation and one in which the parties negotiated agreement, approved by the court, stipulated that spousal support would terminate upon the death or remarriage of the wife, and the court would consider the issue if the wife cohabitated with a man who significantly contributed to her support. The court, approving of what it referred to as the majority rule, adopted an economic needs test, which requires a showing that the recipient's financial needs actually have decreased because of the cohabitation. Finding neither former husband had proved such change of circumstances, the court upheld the trial court's denials of the modification petitions. One judge dissented with respect to decrees that do not mention cohabitation, arguing that a marriage type relationship should result in a rebuttable presumption of a change of circumstances.

When a non-cohabitation restriction is part of the parties' agreement, the courts have construed them more narrowly. For example, the Supreme Judicial Court of Massachusetts in *Bell v. Bell*[138] determined that a former husband's contractual obligation to pay alimony had ended upon the wife's cohabitation and dismissed a contempt complaint brought for his failure to make alimony payments. The parties' separation agreement provided that the husband would pay alimony for fifteen years or until the wife died, remarried or lived "with a member of the opposite sex so as to give the outward appearance of marriage."[139] The court interpreted the language to provide for termination of alimony if the wife lived as though she was married, despite additional provisions in the separation agreement that neither party would interfere with the personal liberty of the other and each would be free of any criticism or restraint by the other.

---

[136] 638 A.2d 898 (N.J. App. Div. 1994).

[137] 956 P.2d 761 (Nev. 1998).

[138] 468 N.E.2d 849 (Mass. 1984).

[139] *Id.* at 861.

Similarly, the court in *O'Connor Brothers Abalone Co. v. Brando*[140] construed a clause in an agreement pursuant to an annulment to determine whether support payments terminated upon the wife's cohabitation. The contractual provision stated that the obligation would terminate upon remarriage, which was defined to include without limitation Plaintiff's appearing to maintain a marital relationship with any person." The former wife allegedly began a relationship with another man who lived with her, used her address and her car, kept his clothing at her residence, and engaged in a sexual relationship with her. The court held that the characterization of a relationship as "marital" does not depend on whether third parties believe the parties are actually married; rather a common financial or economic relationship plus a strong probability of violating the intent of the agreement will suffice. It concluded that the appearance of living together constituted a reasonable interpretation of the terms of the agreement and warranted termination of the support payments.

Some courts have barred claims for past-due spousal support or alimony based on laches or waiver if the recipient unreasonably delayed bringing the action.[141] Most courts, however, have not been receptive to such defenses for two reasons: first, if the spousal support award was ordered by the court, the court has not waived its enforceability, even if the recipient arguably has; second, a long delay does not amount to laches unless the payor can clearly demonstrate detrimental reliance on the delay.[142]

Generally, only periodic alimony may be modified; lump sum alimony, like property division, is not modifiable. Although rehabilitative alimony resembles lump sum alimony to the extent that it is ordered as a liquidated sum for a specific period of time, some courts have allowed modification if the recipient has been unable to become self-supporting despite his or her best efforts.[143] Other courts have refused to permit modification of rehabilitative alimony.[144]

§ 9.06   Child Support and Maintenance

[A]   Basic Concepts

Child support has changed radically during the past two decades. Congress has mandated that states enact child support guidelines in order to receive federal funds, in attempt to make child support awards more

---

[140] 114 Cal. Rptr. 773 (Cal. Ct. App. 1974).

[141] *See, e.g., Clark v. Chipman*, 510 P.2d 1257 (Kan. 1973) (claim barred by laches after 5-year delay).

[142] *See, e.g., Brock v. Cavanaugh*, 468 A.2d 1242 (Conn. App. Ct. 1984) (6-year delay not barred by laches); *Richardson v. Moore*, 229 S.E.2d 864 (Va. 1976) (25-year delay not barred by laches).

[143] *See, e.g., In re Marriage of Morrison*, 573 P.2d 41 (Cal. 1978); *In re Marriage of Webb*, 156 Cal. Rptr. 334 (Cal. Ct. App. 1979).

[144] *See, e.g., Campbell v. Campbell*, 432 So. 2d 666 (Fla. Dist. Ct. App. 1983), *petition for review dismissed*, 453 So. 2d 1364 (Fla. 1984); *Cann v. Cann*, 334 So. 2d 325 (Fla. Dist. Ct. App. 1976).

uniform and to increase award levels and efficiency. Today, all states have enacted guidelines, although they differ considerably. Child support enforcement mechanisms have also been enacted by to increase collection, and both state and federal statutes have established new jurisdiction rules to stabilize jurisdiction disputes.

Although earlier common law imposed a primary duty of support on the father of a child, holding the mother only secondarily liable, states today regard the duty to support a child as gender neutral.[145] For example, in *Rand v. Rand*,[146] the Court of Appeals of Maryland held that the trial court's allocation of 92% of the child support obligation to the father was erroneous in light of the state's Equal Rights Amendment. The mother, who had sought an increase in child support to finance the child's college education, earned over $16,000, while the father's annual income exceeded $27,000. Faced with the mother's contention that she should be responsible only to the extent the father was financially incapable of providing support, the court held that the obligation of child support is now shared by both parents in a ratio corresponding to their financial resources.

Further, the law requires individuals to support their children regardless of whether the parents were ever married to each other.[147] The duty of child support commonly is codified under the subjects of divorce or dissolution and paternity,[148] although some states have a generalized family support statute.[149]

The common law imposed no duty of support on stepparents, except when the stepparent voluntarily assumes the duty of support when the child is assimilated into the stepparent's family.[150] Usually the voluntary assumption of supporting a stepchild may be terminated at will and does not extend beyond the end of the marriage to the child's parent,[151] except in unusual cases in which the stepparent is estopped from denying the duty because his or her conduct induced the child's reliance and dependence.[152] A number of states have enacted legislation that requires stepparents to support their spouses' children in certain circumstances.[153] The primary

---

[145] *See* Harry Krause, *Child Support In America: The Legal Prospective* 4 (1981); *see also Carole K. v. Arnold K.*, 380 N.Y.S.2d 593 (N.Y. Fam. Ct. 1976) (striking down statute requiring fathers, but not mothers, to pay child support); *In re Aguilar*, 145 Cal. Rptr. 197 (Cal. Ct. App. 1978)(imposing primary criminal liability upon father, but only secondary liability upon mother, for willful failure to support minor children violates equal protection guarantee of federal and state constitutions.

[146] 374 A.2d 900 (Md. Ct. Spec. App. 1977).

[147] *See, e.g., Mercer Cty. Dep't of Soc. Servs. v. Alf M.*, 589 N.Y.S.2d 288 (N.Y. Fam. Ct. 1992).

[148] *See, e.g.,* Unif. Marriage and Divorce Act § 309, 9A U.L.A. 147 (1998); Unif. Parentage Act § 15, 9B U.L.A. 333 (1987).

[149] *See, e.g.,* Cal. Fam. Code § 3900 (West 1994).

[150] *See* Homer Clark, *supra* note 7, at 264.

[151] *Id.*

[152] *See M.H.B. v. H.T.B.*, 498 A.2d 775 (N.J. 1985). *But see Knill v. Knill*, 510 A.2d 546 (Md. 1986); *NPA v. WBA*, 380 S.E.2d 178 (Va. Ct. App. 1989).

[153] *See, e.g.,* N.H. Rev. Stat. Ann. §§ 546A:1, 546A:2 (1997 & Supp. 2000); N.Y. Soc. Serv. Law § 101 (McKinney 1992 & Supp.2000); Utah Code Ann. § 40 (2000).

purpose of these statutes is usually to reduce or eliminate the child's eligibility for state welfare benefits.[154]

The Supreme Court of Washington has held that stepparent responsibility statutes may impose a duty of support on parties who were married prior to the enactment of the legislation In *Washington Statewide Organization of Stepparents v. Smith*.[155] The *Smith* decision also upheld the constitutionality of the statute, refuting claims that the statute violate equal protection principles by not imposing similar duties on unmarried cohabitants.

Traditionally, the amount of a person's child support obligation was determined on a case-by-case basis and took into account the particular needs of the child and the ability of the parents to provide for those needs. For example, the Uniform Marriage and Divorce Act directs courts to consider all relevant factors, except marital misconduct, in awarding child support, including:

    (1)   the financial resources of the child;

    (2)   the financial resources of the custodial parent;

    (3)   the standard of living the child would have enjoyed had the marriage not been dissolved;

    (4)   the physical and emotional condition of the child and his educational needs; and

    (5)   the financial resources and needs of the noncustodial parent.[156]

A broad range of a parent's financial resources may be considered in setting child support awards. Most types of assets and income are appropriate sources, including alimony payments,[157] income from overtime, bonuses, and night shift differential,[158] and rent due to a support obligor.[159] State child support guidelines often broadly define "income" for purposes of determining the amount of child support in an individual case.[160] In the absence of a statute, an appropriate definition of available "income" could include wages, salary, commissions, bonuses, payments to an independent contractor, dividends, capital gains, gifts, prizes, awards, partnership profits, disability benefits, workers' compensation benefits, veterans and social security benefits, annuities, awards in civil suits, interest, rents, royalties, real and personal property, insurance proceeds, trust income, inheritance rights, severance pay, unemployment compensation, and pension or retirement benefits.[161]

---

[154] *See* Homer Clark, *supra* note 7, at 263.

[155] 536 P.2d 1202 (Utah 1975).

[156] Unif. Marriage and Divorce Act § 309, 9A U.L.A. 147 (1998).

[157] *See Hyde v. Hyde*, 618 A.2d 206 (Pa. Super. Ct. 1992) *overruling Steinmetz v. Steinmetz*, 554 A.2d 83 (Pa. Super. Ct. 1989).

[158] *See In re Pins*, 19 Fam. L. Rep. (BNA) 1046 (Iowa Ct. App. Nov. 24, 1992); *In re Marriage of Pettit*, 493 N.W.2d 865 (Iowa Ct. App. 1992).

[159] *See Kipper v. Kipper*, 542 N.Y.S.2d 617 (N.Y. App. Div. 1989).

[160] *See, e.g.*, N.M. Stat. Ann. § 40-4-11.1(c) (Michie 1999); N.Y. Dom. Rel. Law § 240(1-b)(e) (McKinney 1999 & Supp. 2000).

[161] *See, e.g.*, Robert Horowitz, et al., *Remedies Under the Child Enforcement Amendments of 1984*, 112–130 (1985).

For some time, the courts were divided on the issue of whether a support obligor could be required to use disability payments to satisfy a support obligation.[162] In 1987, the United States Supreme Court held in *Rose v. Rose*[163] that federal law does not preempt a state's right to hold a disabled veteran in contempt for failure to pay support when his only means of payment were his disability payments from the Veteran's Administration for compensation relating to service-related injuries, despite express statutory provisions that the benefits were not subject to attachment or other forms of seizure.[164] The Court, although noting that the legislative history of the provisions was sparse, concluded that Congress intended the anti-attachment provisions to "avoid the possibility of the Veterans' Administration . . . being placed in the position of a collection agency" and to "prevent the deprivation and depletion of the means of subsistence of veterans dependent upon these benefits as the main source of their income."[165] The Court held that neither purpose would be frustrated by allowing a state court to hold a child support obligor in contempt for failing to pay child support:

> The contempt proceeding did not turn the Administrator into a collection agency; the Administrator was not obliged to participate in the proceeding or to pay benefits directly to appellee. Nor did the exercise of state-court jurisdiction over appellant's disability benefits deprive appellant of his means of subsistence contrary to Congress' intent, for these benefits are not provided to support appellant alone.[166]

The United States Supreme Court in *Bowen v. Gilliard*[167] held that AFDC eligibility may take into account payments made by a noncustodial parent. In 1970, the federal statute authorizing AFDC did not require all parents and siblings to be included in a filing unit for determining the amount of payments based on the number of family members. The statute was amended in 1975 to require that recipients of AFDC payments assign to the state their right to receive any child support for a family member included in the filing unit. The Deficit Reduction Act of 1984 established a requirement that the parents and siblings living with an eligible child must generally be included in the filing unit, reducing the amount of total income available to many families in the AFDC program, although another amendment provided that the first $50 of child support collected by the state would be paid directly to the family and not counted as income for

---

[162] *Compare In re Marriage of Robinson*, 651 P.2d 454 (Colo. Ct. App. 1982) (Social Security disability and retirement payments for minor children may be credited toward father's obligation to pay child support) *with Douglas v. Donovan*, 534 F. Supp. 191 (D.C. Cir. 1982), *vacated as moot*, 704 F.2d 1276 (1983) (Federal Employee's Compensation Act benefits are not subject to attachment or garnishment for enforcement of child support or alimony payments).

[163] 481 U.S. 619 (1987).

[164] 38 U.S.C. § 5301 (1992).

[165] 481 U.S. at 630.

[166] *Id.*

[167] 483 U.S. 587 (1987).

determining AFDC benefits. The Court rejected a recipient's argument that the statutory scheme violated her equal protection rights under the Fifth Amendment by interfering with a family's living arrangements. It held that Congress may allocate limited funds among the large class of needy recipients by reducing amounts available to those perceived to be less needy because of outside financial resources. It further concluded that AFDC benefits could be reduced generally and that assignments of child support obligations could be required without constituting a deprivation of property. The Court observed:

> The law does not require any custodial parent to apply for AFDC benefits. Surely it is reasonable to presume that a parent who does make such an application does so because she or he is convinced that the family as a whole — as well as *each* child committed to her or his custody — will be better off with the benefits than without. In making such a decision, the parent is not taking a child's property without just compensation; nor is the State doing so when it responds to that decision by supplementing the collections of support money with additional AFDC benefits. [168]

[B] Temporary Child Support *Pendente Lite*

Just as temporary alimony may be ordered prior to a final divorce decree, [169] child support orders *pendent lite* may be entered during the course of divorce litigation to assure that the children are provided for during the interim. [170] Because of the state's interest in protecting children, a court may order child support regardless of whether a parent seeks it in a divorce action. [171]

Many courts will also enter *pendente lite* child custody orders, temporary restraints on disposition of the parties' marital assets, and temporary non-molestation orders against a spouse who has made physical threats to the other spouse or children. [172] Because *pendente lite* orders are temporary, they are not binding in a subsequent divorce proceeding. [173]

[C] Statutory Child Support Guidelines

Because of the variety of factors that may be considered and the considerable extent of judicial discretion in the traditional case-by-case method of awarding child support, child support awards have lacked uniformity within individual states as well as between states and, overall, were generally considered to be inadequate. In response to the insufficiency in

---

[168] *Id.* at 608–9 (emphasis in original).

[169] *See supra* § 9.04[A].

[170] *See, e.g.*, Cal. Fam. Code §§ 3900, 3028, 4000 (West 1994); Ohio Rev. Code §§ 3103.03, 3109.05 (Anderson 1996 & Supp. 1999).

[171] *See* Homer Clark, *supra* note 7, at 711–712.

[172] *See, e.g.*, Cal. Fam. Code § 3011 (West 1994); N.Y. Dom. Rel. Law § 236 (McKinney 1999 & Supp. 2000).

[173] *See, e.g., Shepherd v. Shepherd*, 200 S.E.2d 893 (Ga. 1973).

child support amounts, inefficient determination of awards, and inconsistent treatment of similarly situated parties, Congress enacted legislation In 1984 to require all states to develop guidelines for determining child support.[174] States are not required to adopt any particular type of guideline; therefore, the standards and resulting orders continue to vary considerably from one state to another.[175] However, the guideline amount of child support must be presumptive, with a written finding of fact required to overcome that amount.[176] States are required to review their guidelines periodically.[177]

Despite variation among jurisdictions, several general formulas commonly have been adopted, including the flat percentage method, income share models, and the Delaware Melson formula.[178] Other formulas, such as an income equalization approach, have been proposed and have generated considerable commentary but have not been widely adopted.[179] Unique factors are considered in each approach, and different compromises between equity and simplicity have been reached.[180]

Flat percentage guidelines base the child support amount on the income of the obligor and the number of children, without consideration of the custodial parent's income or any extraordinary expenses of the child.[181] Percentage guidelines vary as to their definitions of the types of income available for child support. Unlike most flat percentage guidelines, the well-known Wisconsin percentage of income standard accounts for shared or split physical custody and later children of the obligor.[182]

The Supreme Court of North Dakota, in *Eklund v. Eklund*,[183] upheld its state's percentage guidelines, rejected the father's argument that the Department of Human Services had exceeded its delegated authority in adopting such guidelines. Despite the fact that an income shares model might be more fair, the percentage, or "obligor model," guidelines were

---

[174] Pub. L. No. 98-378, 42 U.S.C. 667 (1984). *See also infra* § 9.06[F][4].

[175] *See generally* Robert Williams, *Guidelines for Setting Levels of Child Support Orders*, 21 Fam. L.Q. 281 (1987); Linda Balisle, *New Formulas to Fairness*, 10 Fam. Advoc. 16 (Spring 1988); Diane Dodson, *A Guide to the Guidelines*, 10 Fam. Advoc. 4 (Spring 1988); Karen Getman, *Changing Formulas for Changing Families*, 10 Fam. Advoc. 46 (Spring 1988).

[176] 42 U.S.C. § 667(b) (1997).

[177] 42 U.S.C. § 667 (1997).

[178] *See* Nancy Thoennes, Patricia Tjaden, & Jessica Pearson, *The Impact of Child Support Guidelines on Award Adequacy, Award Variability, and Case Processing Efficiency*, 25 Fam. L.Q. 325 (1991).

[179] *See* Sharon Badertscher, *Ohio's Mandatory Child Support Guidelines: Child Support or Spousal Maintenance*, 42 Case W. Res. L. Rev. 297 (1992); Mark Connor, *Resolving Child Support Issues Beyond the Scope of AR 608–99*, 132 Mil. L. Rev. 67 (1991); Peter Leehy, *The Child Support Standards Act and the New York Judiciary: Fortifying the 17 Percent Solution*, 56 Brook. L. Rev. 1299 (1991).

[180] *See generally* Robert Williams, *supra* note 175.

[181] *See, e.g.,* Ill. Ann. Stat. ch. 40, para 505 (Smith-Hurd 1993 & Supp. 2000). *See generally* Nancy Thoennes, *supra* note 178, at 329.

[182] *See, e.g., Mdstad v. Mstad,* 535 N.W.2d 63 (Wis. App. 1995); *Prosser v. Cook,* 519 N.W.2d 649 (Wis. App. 1994).

[183] 538 N.W.2d 182 (N. Dak. 1995).

found to be less complex and more difficult to use, and in most cases resulted in little or no difference in child support awards.

The income shares model, variations of which have been adopted by a number of states,[184] accounts for the incomes of both parents, in an attempt to approximate the standard of living the child would have enjoyed if the parents had remained together.[185] Under this method, a basic child support obligation is calculated based on the parents' combined incomes and estimated child-rearing expenditures, and supplemented by actual child-care expenses and extraordinary needs of the specific children. The parents are required to contribute to that obligation on a pro-rata basis of their incomes, with the custodial parent simply retaining the amount assessed against him or her. Alterations may be made for split and shared custody arrangements, and the formula adapted to assure that the obligor has sufficient remaining funds for self-support, at least at the poverty level. Schedules can be varied to correspond to the ages of the children, based on the notion that the cost of raising a child increases as the child grows older.[186]

In *P.O.P.S. v. Gardner*,[187] the 9th Circuit Court of Appeals upheld the constitutionality of the Washington State Child Support Schedule, which applies an income shares approach. The plaintiffs, Parents Opposed to Punitive Support (P.O.P.S.) argued that the guideline amounts were so high that they effectively prevented some noncustodial parents from remarrying, and thus infringing on their fundamental right to marry. The court rejected this claim, noting that if a parent were so burdened, the court would be authorized to deviate from the formula. P.O.P.S. also argued that noncustodial parents become so frustrated by the schedule that they spend less time with their children. The court also rejected this claim, again noting the courts' power to deviate from guideline amounts, as well as the plaintiff's Equal Protection claim, holding that the schedule does not discriminate, and that, in any event, children of noncustodial parents are not a suspect class.

The Oregon Supreme Court approved a variation of the income shares model in *Smith v. Smith*,[188] calculating a parent's child support obligation as the fraction of the payor's income divided by the combined incomes of both parents, multiplied by the needs of the children. To determine the children's needs, the court must consider the standard of living they would have enjoyed but for the divorce, as well as the physical and emotional condition of the child, the child's educational needs and capacity, the child's age, and the child's own financial resources and earning ability. After calculating the obligation pursuant to this formula, the court must additionally consider the interrelationship of the child support with any awards of property and spousal support, indirect forms of child support, including

---

[184] *See, e.g.*, Colo. Rev. Stat. Ann. § 14-10-115 (West 1997).

[185] *See* Nancy Thoennes, *supra* note 178, at 327–328.

[186] *See* Me. Rev. Stat. Ann. tit. 1919-A c. 694 § B-1 (October 1997).

[187] 998 F.2d 764 (9th Cir. 1993).

[188] 626 P.2d 342 (Or. 1981).

medical care, insurance, and trusts, the income of each spouse's current domestic partner or spouse, each parent's assets, including equity in real or personal property, the existence of, and support obligations to, each parent's other dependents, and special hardships of each parent. Because of the variables involved, this form of an income shares model continues to require a case-by-case evaluation.

The Delaware, or Melson, formula is based on the principle that the basic needs of a person's children must be met before the parent should be allowed to retain any income beyond that necessary to satisfy the parent's minimum needs.[189] It further presumes that excess income should be shared to allow children to benefit from an absent parent's higher standard of living. Application of the Melson formula entails complex calculations of each parent's available incomes and deductions for the parent's own subsistence requirements, which varies upon whether the parent lives alone, is married, or cohabiting. Remaining income is applied to the child support obligation.

Child care and extraordinary medical expenses are encompassed into child support guidelines. Several different methods are utilized, including deducting the cost from the income of the parent who incurs the expense, adding the cost to the basic child support obligation and dividing proportionately between the parents, and considering the expenses a factor for deviating from the presumptive award.[190]

The Melson formula then requires calculation of the children's basic subsistence support requirements, based on the number of children, with adjustments for the custodial arrangement, and including necessary additional child-rearing expenses. This obligation is pro-rated between the parents, with a standard of living allowance awarded from any remaining income.[191]

The guidelines actually adopted by different states vary considerably in their details, regardless of the model upon which they are based. Guidelines vary in their definitions of applicable income;[192] some states have detailed statutory provisions defining income for child support purposes,[193] and case law has included as income such sources as deferred compensation,[194] disability payments,[195] personal injury awards,[196] retirement income,[197] and

---

[189] *See* Nancy Thoennes, *supra* note 178, at 328–329.

[190] *See* Laura Morgan, *Child Support Guidelines: Interpretation and Application* 3-21 (1997).

[191] *See generally* Robert Williams, *supra* note 175.

[192] *See* Laura Morgan, *Child Support Guidelines: Interpretation and Application* 2-10, 2-11 (1997)(noting that states are about evenly split as to whether net or gross income should be used).

[193] *See, e.g.,* Maryland Code Ann., Fam. L. § 12-201 (1997); Minn. Stat. Ann., Dom. Rel. § 518.551 (1997).

[194] *See Posey v. Tate,* 656 N.E.2d 222 (Ill. App. Ct. 1995).

[195] *See In re Callaghan,* 869 P.2d 240 (Kan. Ct. App. 1994); *Whitaker v. Colbert,* 442 S.E.2d 429 (Va. Ct. App. 1994).

[196] *See In re Fain,* 794 P.2d 1086 (Colo. Ct. App. 1990); *Tullock v. Flickinger,* 616 A.2d 315 (Del. 1992).

[197] *See In re Kelm,* 878 P.2d 34 (Colo. Ct. App. 1994).

Social Security benefits.[198]

Most states require a minimum amount of support to be paid.[199] However, because children generally are entitled to support consistent with the parents' ability to pay, questions concerning "reasonable" limits on child support obligations arise when a parent has an unusually large income. In *White v. Marciano*,[200] the California Court of Appeal held that when the child has a wealthy parent, "the child is entitled to, and therefore 'needs,' something more than the bare necessities of life." Although the non-custodial parent's standard of living, in addition to his or her income, is relevant, the court will not make a detailed inquiry into the parent's lifestyle.

Similarly, in *Voishan v. Palma*,[201] the Court of Appeals of Maryland refused to imply a cap on child support when the parents' combined income exceeds $10,000 a month. It held that the children should enjoy a standard of living comparable to that which they would have had the parents remained married, and refused to impose an artificial ceiling on child support awards.[202]

Some states set a maximum limit on child support, based on the theory that the child would not necessarily have received the benefit of the parent's excess income in an intact family. In *State v. Hall*,[203] the Minnesota Court of Appeals held that the trial court did not abuse its discretion in declining to deviate from statutory child support guidelines that provided for a maximum of $1000 monthly support when an obligor's net income is $4000 or above, despite the obligor's actual monthly income of $116,000 and the mother's meager resources. The court found that the child's actual personal expenses did not exceed $1000 a month and held that it would be inappropriate to increase the mother's own standard of living indirectly by means of child support. Other courts have held that when a parent's income exceeds the maximum listed in the guidelines, the court should use evidence of special circumstances, such as the realistic needs of the children, the obligor's ability to satisfy these needs, the financial condition of both parents, a parent's new spouse.[204]

A court may order child support in an amount that deviates from the statutory guidelines only upon express findings of fact in order to provide adequate support.[205] In *Kowalzek v. Kowalzek*,[206] the Minnesota Court of

---

[198] *See Forbes v. Forbes*, 610 N.E.2d 885 (Ind. Ct. App. 1994); *In re Lee*, 486 N.W.2d 302 (Iowa 1992).

[199] *See, e.g.,* Cal. Fam. Code § 4050. (Formula to establish minimum amount of support to be ordered.)

[200] 235 Cal. Rptr. 779 (Cal. Ct. App. 1987).

[201] 609 A.2d 319 (Ct. App. Md. 1992).

[202] *See also Mehra v. Mehra*, 819 S.W.2d 351 (Mo. 1991) (en banc); *Cassano v. Cassano*, 651 N.E.2d 878 (N.Y. 1995).

[203] 418 N.W.2d 187 (Minn. Ct. App. 1988).

[204] *See, e.g., Peterson v. Peterson*, 434 N.W.2d 732 (S.D. 1989). *See also Nash v. Mulle*, 846 S.W.2d 803 (Tenn. 1993) (placing burden of showing increased need on the recipient parent).

[205] Pub. L. 100-485, Title I, Subtitle A, § 103, 102 Stat. 2346 (1988) (effective October 13,

Appeals held that a mechanical calculation based solely on the child living with a parent and a mere general reference to "all the circumstances of this case" were insufficient to justify an order substantially below the guideline amount. The Illinois Appellate Court, in *In re Marriage of Bush*,[207] however, held that the guideline support amount of $30,000 a year, or 20% of the father's income, was excessive and that a deviation from that amount to 6%, or $800 per month was justified. The court remarked that the child support guidelines were "not intended to create windfalls but, rather, adequate support payments for the upbringing of the children."[208]

In *Estevez v. Superior Court*,[209] the California Court of Appeals held that in a case in which the father had an extraordinarily high income, it may not be necessary to compel discovery of all financial information to calculate the presumptive guideline amount of child support when such discovery would be unduly burdensome and oppressive, when the parent has stipulated that he is able and willing to pay any reasonable amount of child support based on his stipulated income.

If a parent voluntarily unemployed, or not employed to full earning capacity, the court may impute income based on the parent's capacity to earn rather than actual income. In *Henderson v. Smith*[210] the Supreme Court of Idaho examined when it is appropriate to impute income. In *Henderson*, the biological father of a child born outside of marriage, an attorney, was ordered to pay child support, under the state's guidelines based on the average income of attorneys in the area, rather than on his actual income. The court noted that "[t]he determination of income and expenses from an individual who is self employed should be carefully reviewed to determine the level of gross income to satisfy a child support obligation. This gross income for the self employed parent may differ from a determination of business income for tax purposes."[211] It held that a parent who is underemployed may have his income calculated by on his potential earnings, based on his employment history, qualifications, and opportunities and job availability in the community. Similarly, in *In re Marriage of Paulin*[212] the California Court of Appeals found that child support obligation of a mother who had remarried and voluntarily ended her employment could be based on her earning capacity, because she failed to produce documented efforts to find comparable employment. The court held that this indicated an unwillingness, rather than an inability, to work. The Supreme Judicial Court of Maine overturned a trial court's decision

---

1988, mandating that guidelines provide for a rebuttable presumption that guideline amounts of support are correct and requiring written of specific record finding that application of guidelines "would be unjust or inappropriate in a particular case" to rebut presumption); *see also Schmidt v. Schmidt*, 444 N.W.2d 367 (S.D. 1989).

[206] 360 N.W.2d 423 (Minn. Ct. App. 1985).

[207] 547 N.E.2d 590 (Ill. App. Ct. 1989).

[208] *Id.* at 597.

[209] 27 Cal. Rptr. 2d 470 (Cal. Ct. App. 1994).

[210] 915 P.2d 6 (Idaho 1996).

[211] *Id.* at 13.

[212] 54 Cal. Rptr. 2d 314 (Cal. Ct. App. 1996).

to modify a father's child support obligation based on his current actual income in *Harvey v. Robinson*,[213] when the father voluntarily retired from the National Guard and return to college, with aspirations of eventually attending medical school. Despite a conclusion that he had left his full-time employment in good faith, the court held that his good faith did "not ameliorate the dramatic effect on the children,"[214] which must be balanced against his decision. The court suggested that he could work full time and attend school part time in order to fulfill his parental responsibilities, and remanded for reconsideration of child support based on his current earning capacity. A strong dissent noted that consideration of earning capacity is not mandatory and that the trial court's decision should not be overturned absent an abuse of discretion.

In *Goldberger v. Goldberger*,[215] the Court of Special Appeals of Maryland dealt with imputing the income of a father of six who was a permanent Torah/Talmudic student, and had been throughout the entire marriage. He had been supported by donations from others for support, and the trial court based his earning capacity on the average of contributions for the previous three years. While agreeing that the father was "voluntarily impoverished," and that his child support obligation should be calculated on his earning capacity, the appellate court concluded that the trial court erred in assuming that his earning potential should be based on his ability to raise funds during the course of the custody litigation, and remanded to the trial court to hear testimony and make findings regarding his earning capacity, and then determine whether the amount presumed under the guidelines should be altered.

Other courts have held that participation in a strike is not a voluntary reduction of income,[216] and that incarceration alone is insufficient to demonstrate a parent's inability to pay child support.[217]

Courts frequently face the question of whether the income of a parent's new spouse or an obligation to support other children should be taken into account in determining child support. In *In re Marriage of Wood*[218] the California Court of Appeal held that recent amendments to the state's statute prohibiting consideration of the income a parent's subsequent spouse "except in the extraordinary case where excluding that income would lead to extreme and severe hardship to any child" prevented the trial court from examining the income of the mother's new husband, a wealthy man, although the earlier statute allowed consideration of a new spouse's income.[219] The court held that an impact on the former wife and children's standard of living was insufficient, and that the new spouse's income could only be considered when the children were negatively affected. Other courts

---

[213] 665 A.2d 215 (Me. 1995).

[214] *Id.* at 218.

[215] 624 A.2d 1328 (Md. App. 1993).

[216] *See, e.g., Rawlings v. Rawlings*, 460 S.E.2d 581 (Va. Ct. App. 1995).

[217] *See, e.g., Thomasson v. Johnson*, 903 P.2d 254 (N.M. Ct. App. 1995).

[218] 44 Cal. Rptr. 2d 236 (Cal. App. 1995).

[219] Cal. Civ. Code § 4057.5 (effective Jan. 1, 1994) (superseding § 4721).

have been willing to consider a new spouse's income, particularly when statutory authority to do so exists. [220] Some courts, however, flatly refuse to consider spousal income. [221] Income of a cohabitant seems even less relevant to a former spouse's child support obligation. [222]

All states consider the obligation to support other children in calculating child support, although different methods are applied. [223] Although the rationale for considering other support obligations is that all children are worthy of support, some states require or permit a deduction from the parent's income for child support paid for other children, [224] which generally results in a preference for first families. In *Feltman v. Feltman,* [225] the Supreme Court of South Dakota rejected a father's claim that the support guidelines violate the equal protection rights of children born in subsequent marriages by giving support priority to children of the first marriage. The court held that the guidelines survived a rational relationship standard of review, and that the guidelines prevented the standard of living of the children of a first marriage from suffering due to voluntary acts of the noncustodial parent, such as a subsequent remarriage and support of additional children from that marriage.

Other states regard the obligation to other children as a factor in deviating from the guideline amount, typically gives both families equal status. [226] The Supreme Court of Wyoming applied the latter standard in *Hasty v. Hasty,* [227] in which it concluded that although the presumptive amount of child support should be calculated only with respect to the child in question, the court then may consider the parent's responsibility to other children as a factor in deciding whether to deviate from the guideline amount.

The federal regulations also require states to adopt expedited judicial or administrative methods for establishing and enforcing child support awards. [228] States may delegate child support determinations to administrative hearing officers. The federal regulations further require that states periodically review their child support guidelines and adjust them to reflect current economic conditions. [229]

The use of guidelines has improved the efficiency of child support adjudication. Their implementation has increased voluntary settlement and

---

[220] *See, e.g., Flanagan v. Flanagan,* 673 So. 2d 894 (Fla. Dist. Ct. App. 1996); *LaForge v. La Forge,* 649 So. 2d 151 (La. Ct. App. 1995).

[221] *See, e.g., In re Marriage of Hardiman,* 889 P.2d 1354 (Or. Ct. App. 1995).

[222] *See, e.g., Jackson v. Jackson,* 907 P.2d 990 (Nev. 1995).

[223] *See* Laura Morgan, *Child Support Guidelines: Interpretation and Application* 3-37 (1997).

[224] *See, e.g., Flanagan v. Flanagan,* 673 So. 2d 894 (Fla. Dist. Ct. App. 1996).

[225] 434 N.W.2d 590 (S.D. 1989).

[226] *See, e.g., State ex rel. English v. Troisi,* 659 So. 2d 658 (Ala. Civ. App, 1995); *Burch v. Burch,* 916 P.2d 443 (Wash. Ct. App. 1996).

[227] 828 P.2d 94 (Wyo. 1992).

[228] 45 C.F.R. § 303.101 (1991); *see also infra* § 9.06[F][4].

[229] 45 C.F.R. § 303.4 (1991).

reduced court or agency time in resolving disputed cases because of increased predictability.[230]

[D] Duration of the Child Support Obligation

Absent a written agreement to the contrary, a parent's obligation to support his or her child usually ends when the child reaches the age of majority, commonly age 18.[231] In the past, some states specified a younger age of majority for females than for males, based on the notion that girls tend to mature and marry earlier and that boys needed a good education or training to prepare them for the eventual responsibility of supporting a family.[232] In the 1975 case of *Stanton v. Stanton*,[233] the Supreme Court declared such gender-based classifications unconstitutional on equal protection grounds.

The parent's duty of child support may end before the child attains the age of majority if the child becomes legally emancipated by validly marrying, entering the United States military service, or becoming otherwise self-sufficient.[234] If a child leaves home and becomes self-supporting, courts have the discretion to deem the child emancipated because of changed circumstances which justify modification of support.[235] Some states have statutes which establish a judicial procedure for emancipation.[236]

An emancipated child may become unemancipated, by termination of the minor child's marriage, for instance, and the parents' obligation of support may be reinstated.[237] Correspondingly, some courts have held that a minor child who wilfully places himself or herself out of the parents' control may lose the right to support.[238] In *Roe v. Doe*,[239] the New York Supreme Court held that a father was not required to continue supporting his daughter when she disobeyed her father's demands that she live in the college dormitory. The court held that where the minor is of an employable age and is in full possession of her faculties, voluntarily and without cause abandons the parent's home, against the will of the parent and for the purpose of avoiding parental control she or he forfeits the right to demand support.

---

[230] Robert Williams, *supra* note 175, at 324.

[231] *See, e.g., Hogue v. Hogue*, 561 S.W.2d 299 (Ark. 1978); *see also* Kathleen Horan, *Post-minority Support for College Education-A Legally Enforceable Obligation In Divorce Proceeding?*, 18 N.M. L. Rev. 153 (1988).

[232] *See Stanton v. Stanton*, 517 P.2d 1010 (Utah 1974), *rev'd*, 421 U.S. 7 (1975).

[233] 421 U.S. 7 (1975).

[234] *See, e.g.,* Va. Code Ann. §§ 16.1-333, 334 (Michie 1999 & Supp.2000).

[235] *See, e.g., In re Marriage of O'Connell*, 146 Cal. Rptr. 26 (Cal. Ct. App. 1978) (judicial decree of emancipation insufficient to end parental support obligation).

[236] *See, e.g.,* Cal. Fam. Code §§ 7050 (West 1994); N.M. Stat. Ann. § 28-6-4 (Michie 1995).

[237] *See Eyerman v. Thias*, 760 S.W.2d 187 (Mo. Ct. App. 1988) (annulment of daughter's marriage during her minority reinstated parent's duty of child support).

[238] *Compare Parker v. Stage*, 371 N.E.2d 513 (N.Y. 1977) *with Brunswick v. LaPrise*, 262 A.2d 366 (Me. 1970). *See In re Sandlin*, 831 P.2d 64 (Or. Ct. App. 1992) (child not ineligible to receive support because of cohabitation with man).

[239] 272 N.E.2d 567 (N.Y. 1971).

Either by statutory interpretation or by application of common law principles, most jurisdictions extend the legal duty of child support beyond the child's minority if the child is mentally or physically handicapped or disabled.[240] Some courts have revived the parental duty of support when a child becomes disabled after reaching the age of majority.[241] However, in a minority of states, the courts have refused to extend the parental obligation beyond the literal statutory language, despite the child's mental or physical incapacity. For instance, in *Baril v. Baril*,[242] the Maine Supreme Court held that it was powerless to extend a father's child support obligation beyond the eighteenth birthday of his handicapped daughter when the controlling statute merely described the parent's duty as extending until a child reaches the age of majority.

The duty of child support traditionally ended upon the death of either the child or the parent. In recent years, some statutes and judicial decisions have extended the parent's duty to support after his or her death.[243] In such cases, a support order may be entered against the estate of the deceased parent. Section 316 (c) of the Uniform Marriage and Divorce Act permits such child support to be modified, revoked, or commuted to a lump sum payment when appropriate.[244]

Life insurance is an appropriate vehicle for dealing with post-death support problems whether or not the jurisdiction recognizes survival of the child support obligation.[245] Parents can agree by contract that the supporting parent will maintain life insurance designating the child or custodial parent as the beneficiary. Absent a contract, some courts have held that a court may not order a parent to maintain life insurance.[246] In other jurisdictions, courts may order such policies as part of an overall support award.[247]

States are divided on the issue of whether a court may require a divorced parent to continue child support beyond the age of majority while the child continues his or her education or to pay for the cost of college if the parent has the financial ability to do so.[248] In *Childers v. Childers*,[249] the

---

[240] *See, e.g., Grapin v. Grapin*, 450 So. 2d 853 (Fla. 1984) (common law); *Brown v. Brown*, 474 A.2d 1168 (Pa. Super. Ct. 1984) (common law); *Miller v. Miller*, 660 P.2d 205 (Or. Ct. App. 1983) (statute); *Hight v. Hight*, 284 N.E.2d 679 (Ill. App. Ct. 1972) (statute). *See generally* Horan, *supra* note 231.

[241] *See Towery v. Towery*, 685 S.W.2d 155 (Ark. 1985).

[242] 354 A.2d 392 (Me. 1976).

[243] *See, e.g.,* Ill. Ann. Stat. ch. 40, para. 510(c) (Smith-Hurd 1993 & Supp. 2000); *Bailey v. Bailey*, 471 P.2d 220 (Nev. 1970). *But see Hirst v. Dugan*, 611 A.2d 616 (N.H. 1992) (no claim against estate of unwed father in absence of pre-existing support order).

[244] 9A U.L.A. 490 (1987).

[245] *See* Bratt, Note, *Child Support, Life Insurance and the Uniform Marriage and Divorce Act*, 67 Ky. L.J. 239 (1978).

[246] *See, e.g., Hudson v. Aetna Life Ins. Co.*, 545 F. Supp. 209 (E.D. Mo. 1982).

[247] *See Thomas v. Studley*, 571 N.E.2d 454 (Ohio Ct. App. 1989); *Kulmacz v. New York Life Ins. Co.*, 466 A.2d 808 (Conn. Super. Ct. 1983); *Wallace v. Wallace*, 371 S.W.2d 918 (Tex. Ct. App. 1989).

[248] *Compare Jones v. Jones*, 225 Cal. Rptr. 95 (Cal. Ct. App. 1986) (parent not obligated

Washington Supreme Court concluded that a parent may be required to support a child beyond the age of majority while the child pursues a college education. It construed its child support statute as basing its obligation on dependency, not minority, and ending the obligation at the child's emancipation, not majority. In determining that the facts indicated that the children in question remained dependent while they continued their college educations, the court declared, "[W]e think it reasonable to assume that a medical doctor, himself with years of higher education which brings him a higher than average income, would willingly treat his sons as dependents if they chose and showed an aptitude for college, but for the fact of the divorce."[250] The court noted that although married parents are not obligated to support their children through college, in fact, most "choose willingly to make financial sacrifices for their children's education," regardless of their age.[251] Children from divorced families deserve additional protection to compensate for the disadvantages they experience because of the divorce. Thus the parent's duty of support following divorce may include providing a college education if the child displays an aptitude and the parent will not suffer a significant hardship.

Another line of cases has refused to interpret similar statutes to require post-majority child support for children attending college.[252] In *In re Marriage of Plummer*,[253] the Colorado Supreme Court reversed a trial court's order requiring a father to continue supporting his twenty-one-year-old daughter who was in her third year of college. Although Colorado's statutory duty of support terminates upon the child's "emancipation," the court noted that emancipation generally is presumed to occur upon reaching the age of majority. When the child is incapable of self-support because of mental or physical handicap, the presumption is defeated. The court refused to extend that reasoning "to require an award of child support payments when a capable, able-bodied young adult chooses to attend college after reaching the age of majority."[254]

The Supreme Court of Pennsylvania recently held that a state statute allowing a court to order separated, divorced, or unmarried parents to provide equitably for their children's college educations was unconstitutional because it discriminated against children of intact marriages who may be in need of funds for post-secondary education.[255] A dissenting

---

to pay post-majority educational expenses when child unable to demonstrate need eligibility pursuant to statute) *with Hutchinson v. Hutchinson*, 397 A.2d 1218 (Pa. Super. Ct. 1979) (both parents required to assist child attending college). *See also Carr v. Carr*, 834 P.2d 970 (Okla. 1992) (child support may be continued until age 19 without showing changed circumstances while child attends high school).

[249] 575 P.2d 201 (Wash. 1978).

[250] *Id.* at 205.

[251] *Id.* at 207.

[252] *See, e.g., Blue v. Blue*, 616 A.2d 628 (Pa. Super. Ct. 1992) (duty to support child ends on later of child's 18th birthday or graduation from high school, repudiating nearly two decades of case law developed by lower state courts).

[253] 735 P.2d 165 (Colo. 1987).

[254] *Id.* at 167.

[255] *Curtis v. Kline*, 666 A.2d 265 (Pa. 1995).

opinion argued that the act was supported by a legitimate state interest, in that it sought to redress the negative effects of divorce on children. It urged that equal protection would not be compromised by an attempt to equalize the situations of children in intact families and non-intact families.[256]

Even in jurisdictions where the court has no power to award post-majority child support, most states permit the parents to extend the obligation contractually.[257] When contractual provisions for post-majority support or for payment of educational expenses are incorporated into a divorce decree, some jurisdictions allow those terms to be enforced as part of the court decree itself, even though the children have reached the age of majority.[258]

[E] Modification of Child Support

The traditional standard for modification of child support has been the changed circumstances test. Under this standard, a court may modify child support prospectively if material or substantial changed circumstances warrant an increase or decrease. Section 316(a) of the Uniform Marriage and Divorce Act adopts a higher standard for modification of child support awards, requiring that the changed circumstances be "so substantial and continuing as to make the terms unconscionable."[259] The changed circumstances which may justify a modification of support can affect the child, the supporting parent, the custodial parent, or a combination of the parties. A change in the child's circumstances frequently relates to increased need due to medical care, special education, or training. Some courts have held that the changed circumstances test is not applicable where there is no previous child support order.[260]

The non-custodial parent's substantial increase in income may authorize an increase in child support because of the theory that the child is entitled to share in the parent's standard of living. In *Graham v. Graham*[261] the court held that an increase in the parent's ability to pay child support may alone constitute a material change in circumstances justifying an increase in support. The *Graham* court rejected the view that the needs of the recipients must also increase to support an upward modification, reasoning that a decrease in the payor's income may support a downward modification. "To adopt such a distinction would mean that children would have to bear the burden of a lowered standard of living when their parent's income declined but could not share the benefit when that parent's resources grew."[262]

---

[256] *Id.* at 272.

[257] *See, e.g., H.P.A. v. S.C.A.*, 704 P.2d 205 (Alaska 1985); *Nichols v. Tedder*, 547 So. 2d 766 (Miss. 1989).

[258] *See Jameson v. Jameson*, 306 N.W.2d 240 (S.D. 1981).

[259] 9A pt.2 U.L.A. 102 (1998).

[260] *See Warren v. Hart*, 747 P.2d 511 (Wyo. 1987).

[261] 597 A.2d 355 (D.C. 1991).

[262] *Id.* at 358.

Similarly, a substantial decline in the supporting parent's income may justify a decrease in child support if the parent becomes unable to furnish the amount previously ordered.[263] However, a voluntary decrease in salary may be deemed insufficient to warrant a reduction of child support. In *Antonelli v. Antonelli*,[264] the Supreme Court of Virginia held that a father who changed employment which resulted in a reduction of income, was not entitled to reduce his child support obligation because he had failed to demonstrate that his current inability to pay was not brought about by his own voluntary act or neglect. Although it was not determined whether the father had changed employment to frustrate the feasibility or enforceability of the support obligation, the court held that he assumed the risk of not being able to pay when he moved from a salaried position to a commissioned one. Because a custodial parent's income is also a consideration in child support, changes in that parent's income or family circumstances may also warrant modification.

In the past, some courts allowed child support to be modified retroactively, to reduce the amount of arrearages, upon proof that it was impossible for the obligor to make the payments when they were due.[265] Under current federal law, states are not permitted to allow modification of past due support payments.[266] *Price v. Price*,[267] a decision of the Kentucky Supreme Court, illustrates that this rule may have harsh results. In *Price*, the mother was awarded custody of the couple's child in 1987 and the father was ordered to pay $1400 a month in child support. Three years later, the parents agreed to change the child's residence to the father's home because of behavioral problems the child was experiencing. When the child moved to the father's house, the father stopped paying child support. Over a year later, the mother filed a motion to compel the father to pay child support payments from the date of the child's move. The father filed for modification of child support and a legal change in custody. The trial court held that requiring the father to pay the arrearages would be unfair, and the decision was upheld by the court of appeals. The Kentucky Supreme Court held that the trial court had no power to relieve the father of his child support obligations because the child support statute provides that payments may be modified only as to installments due after the filing of a motion for modification. Furthermore, because the courts are without authority to forgive accrued child support, they cannot enforced a private oral agreement between the parties to do the same thing.

As discussed earlier in the section on establishing guideline support obligations,[268] career changes by a parent have generated much of the litigation concerning modification of child support. When an obligor parent

---

[263] See *Guyton v. Guyton*, 602 A.2d 1143 (D.C. 1992).

[264] 409 S.E.2d 117 (Va. 1991).

[265] See *In re C.S.S. (Grant)*, 18 Fam. L. Rep. (BNA) 1366 (N.Y. Fam. Ct. May 13, 1992); *Schoenfeld v. Marsh*, 614 A.2d 733 (Pa. Super. Ct. 1992).

[266] See 42 U.S.C. § 666(a)(9)(C) (1997).

[267] 912 S.W.2d 44 (Ky. 1995).

[268] *Supra* § 906[c].

voluntarily changes employment that substantially decreases his or her income, that party may seek a decrease in the child support obligation. Some courts find a voluntary career change which drastically reduces the parent's income a suspicious circumstance. [269] Others have emphasized that because a married parent has the option of changing the economic lifestyle of the family it would be inequitable for a divorced parent to be denied that same flexibility. [270]

In *Rome v. Rome*, [271] the Montana Supreme Court held that the appellant's change of jobs and remarriage did not sufficiently alter his ability to pay the previously ordered child support amount. It refused, however, to adopt a standard that would automatically foreclose modification when the payor voluntarily brings about the conditions that reduce the ability to pay. Instead, the judge should consider all the circumstances, including whether the change in income was intentional.

While courts are reluctant to effectively lock a parent into his or her job, they sometimes base the parent's obligation on the obligor's earning capacity rather than actual income. [272] In *Weiser v. Weiser* [273] the husband, a patent lawyer, left the law firm at which he had been employed shortly before the couple's separation and established a practice on his own, reducing his income by about one half. The wife appealed the sum awarded for support of her and the parties' three children, arguing that the husband's earning potential and the family's standard of living, rather than his current income should be considered. Acknowledging that there was no evidence that he had deliberately decreased his income to defeat his support obligation, the court observed that the husband had not reduced his own standard of living. It stated:

> Appellee's change in employment resulted in an income reduction of more than one half. It is also a fact that as a partner in the firm he could control the draw and his weekly income of $340 may not accurately reflect his new earnings. It is for these reasons that we feel the award is inadequate. Most certainly he has the right to establish his own business but not at the expense of his family whose life style he created based on $40,000 per year income which

---

[269] *See Devault v. Waller*, 494 N.W.2d 92 (Minn. Ct. App. 1992); *In re Marriage of McKeever*, 583 P.2d 30 (Or. Ct. App. 1978).

[270] *See, e.g., Schuster v. Schuster*, 586 N.E.2d 1345 (Ill. App. Ct. 1992) (career change by former husband not in good faith; no rehabilitative maintenance awarded to husband who was 32 yrs. old, possessed engineering and law degree but did not like engineering or law); *Antonelli v. Antonelli*, 409 S.E.2d 117 (Va. 1991) (when father chooses to pursue other employment, risk of his success at his new job was upon him, not upon children); *Curtis v. Curtis*, 442 N.W.2d 173 (Minn. Ct. App. 1989) (husband acted In bad faith in terminating his employment of more than 10 years; no reduction of support or forgiveness of arrears); *Daigre v. Daigre*, 527 So. 2d 9 (La. Ct. App. 1988) (father's voluntary change in circumstances in leaving real estate business and entering law school was reasonable and not an attempt to avoid support obligations, reduction in child support warranted.)

[271] 621 P.2d 1090 (Mont. 1981).

[272] *See, e.g., Wollschlager v. Veal*, 601 So. 2d 274 (Fla. Dist. Ct. App. 1992).

[273] 362 A.2d 287 (Pa. Super. Ct. 1976).

now must be changed to meet the new conditions while he continues to enjoy his usual standard.[274]

The court ordered a modification to increase the amount of the husband's support obligation.[275]

In *In re Marriage of McCord*,[276] the Colorado Court of Appeals held that the trial court could find that the father was voluntarily unemployed and imputed income to increase child support when the father had quit his job after winning the state lottery. It rejected the father's argument that the mother must show an increased need on the part of the child and that his decision to resign from his job was a good faith career choice.

The remarriage of either parent frequently prompts an action seeking modification of child support.[277] The income of a new spouse may increase the parent's ability to support the child and justify an adjustment of the parent's support obligation. In *Yost v. Yost*,[278] the Idaho Supreme Court concluded that the remarriage of the custodial parent requires consideration of the new marital community's financial resources, not merely the parent's individual income, because of the nature of community property in that state.

Courts are also divided on the effect of a parent's acquiring new family obligations. Some courts have held that obligations owed to later children justify a decrease in the supporting parent's previous child support responsibility because all children deserve equal support.[279] Other courts have expressed the conventional opinion that a supporting parent starts a new family at his or her own risk and have refused to reduce child support when new children arrive.[280] Some states' child support guidelines accommodate preexisting child support obligations by excluding those amounts actually paid from a parent's income.[281]

The problem is more complex when a support obligor adopts the children of a new spouse. In *Berg v. Berg*,[282] a father was found in contempt when he stopped making support payments to his first wife and two children after he adopted the three children of his new wife. The court ruled that although it was irrelevant whether the acquisition of new children resulted from birth or adoption, the trial court should examine the father's good faith

---

[274] *Id.* 290.

[275] *See also Van Offeren v. Van Offeren*, 19 Fam. L. Rep. (BNA) 1123 (Wis. Ct. App. 1992) (unnecessary to show bad faith in refusing to decrease child support when father shirked his obligation by leaving job in order to start new business).

[276] 910 P.2d 85 (Colo. Ct. App. 1995).

[277] *See generally*, Simon Fodden, *Poor Relations: The Effect of Second Families on Child Support*, 3 Can. J. Fam. L. 207 (June 1980).

[278] 735 P.2d 988 (Idaho, 1987).

[279] *See, e.g., In re Michael M.*, 561 N.Y.S.2d 870 (N.Y. Fam. Ct. 1990); *Martin v. Martin*, 430 N.E.2d 962 (Ohio Ct. App. 1980).

[280] *See, e.g., Meyers v. Bohner*, 176 So. 2d 3 (La. Ct. App. 1965); *Oregon ex rel. State of New York v. Hasbun*, 556 P.2d 166 (Or. Ct. App. 1976).

[281] *See, e.g.*, Col. Rev. Stat. Ann. § 14-10-115(3)(a) (1997).

[282] 359 A.2d 354 (R.I. 1976).

when considering the additional financial obligations he voluntarily incurred.[283]

When a new family includes stepchildren, the effect on previous child support obligations may depend on whether a stepparent has a legal obligation to those children. In *Ainsworth v. Ainsworth*,[284] the court concluded that courts have discretion to deviate from statutory child support guidelines in consideration of expenses associated with subsequent families even in the absence of court orders. In the absence of a legal duty for persons to support stepchildren, however, the court held that remarriage along with the acquisition of stepchildren does not necessarily justify a reduction in child support owed to a previous family, although the court must consider all relevant factors to avoid an inequitable result.[285]

Jurisdictions remain divided on the question of whether a support obligor's incarceration justifies a reduction in child support. Some courts have held that a parent's current inability to pay does not warrant modification when it results from voluntary conduct that led to imprisonment.[286] The majority of courts have held that modification is appropriate when the incarcerated obligor lacks assets from which the support obligation could be paid.[287]

Whether deviation from the guideline constitutes a sufficient change in circumstances has become a dominant issue under statutory child support guidelines. Federal rules require states to adopt provisions which make any inconsistency between the support order and the guideline grounds for modification.[288] States have adopted quantitative standards of ten to thirty percent, which allow modification to occur as soon as the deviation between an actual support order and the current guideline amount reaches that percentage.[289] Additionally, parties can include escalator clauses in their marital settlement agreements, which automatically increase the amount of support upon certain circumstances.

[F] Enforcement of Spousal and Child Support Orders

While obtaining a spousal support award or an adequate child support order can pose its own difficulties, enforcing an existing order can be even more problematic. It has been estimated that about one-third of the total child support owed is not paid, resulting in an annual deficit of approximately $5 billion.[290] Both the state and federal governments have

---

[283] *See also Mack v. Mack*, 749 P.2d 478 (Haw. Ct. App. 1988).

[284] 574 A.2d 772 (Vt. 1990).

[285] *See also Openshaw v. Openshaw*, 639 P.2d 177 (Utah 1981).

[286] *See In re Phillips*, 493 N.W.2d 824 (Iowa 1992).

[287] *See Pierce v. Pierce*, 412 N.W.2d 291 (Mich. Ct. App. 1987); *Foster v. Foster*, 471 N.Y.S.2d 867 (N.Y. App. Div. 1984).

[288] 45 C.F.R. § 303.8(d)(2).

[289] *See* Laura Morgan, *Child Support Guidelines: Interpretation and Application* 5-11, 5-12 (1997).

[290] U.S. Commission on Interstate Child Support, *Supporting Our Children: A Blueprint For Reform, summary reprinted In* 18 Fam. L. Rep. (BNA) 2105 (1992).

established a number of mechanisms for increasing the amount of support that actually reaches the hands of the intended recipients when the obligor does not voluntarily comply with the support obligation. While governmental interest in support enforcement has focused largely on child support, most of the same remedies are available for collection of spousal support as well.

[1] Support Arrearage Issues and Defenses

In most states, unpaid and past due installments of either alimony or child support are considered final judgments.[291] Support installments that are final judgments may not be modified retroactively and may be enforced by execution without further legal action.[292] In the past, a few jurisdictions permitted modification of accrued alimony installments,[293] and even fewer allowed retroactive modification of child support, although some states have permitted modification of past due payments in extreme circumstances when necessary to prevent severe hardship to the obligor.[294] This practice is now prohibited by federal law. In some states, if the child support obligation arose by contractual agreement between the parents, such as in a marital settlement agreement, the debt for arrearages must be reduced to judgment and then remedies available for non-payment of a debt are available for collecting the arrearages.[295] Therefore, good practice dictates that private settlement agreements be merged into the decree of divorce to give those support obligations the status of court orders. Even when reduction to judgment is required, the proceeding is generally regarded as a continuation of the original divorce action and no re-assertion of personal jurisdiction over the defendant is necessary.[296]

Once a support payment has become a final judgment, it accrues interest. States vary with respect to the applicable statute of limitations on past due child support,[297] and methods for collecting arrearages differ greatly among the states.

Inability to pay will not serve as a defense in an action for arrearages, although it may render such an action impractical. An obligor who becomes unable to pay spousal or child support because of loss of employment or other circumstances may not simply stop paying, but must bring an action to modify the support obligation due to changed circumstances. It may be worthwhile to initiate the enforcement process if there is a chance that the obligor may acquire money in the future. A debt for arrearages is

---

[291] *See, e.g., Britton v. Britton*, 671 P.2d 1135 (N.M. 1983).

[292] *See* Homer Clark, *supra* note 7 at 672, 725.

[293] *Id.* at 672.

[294] *Id.* at 725.

[295] *See Keltner v. Keltner*, 589 S.W.2d 235 (Mo. 1979).

[296] *See* Homer Clark, *supra* note 7 at 672–673.

[297] *See Carter v. Carter*, 611 A.2d 86 (Me. 1992) (statute of limitations for civil actions does not preclude claim for child support arrearages).

enforceable against the estate of a deceased obligor, and some states allow the estate of a deceased support recipient to collect arrearages.[298]

[2] State Enforcement Remedies

[a] Contempt Proceedings

Contempt proceedings are a common method of enforcing spousal and child support, available in almost all states once a support decree has been entered.[299] Decrees based on agreement are also subject to enforcement by contempt.[300] The court's contempt power may be statutory[301] or may stem from the court's equitable powers to enforce its orders and injunctions.

In *In re Marriage of Ramos*,[302] a former husband, a surgeon with an income over about $300,000 a year and assets over $20 million, was held in contempt for his failure to pay his ex-wife $175,000 due on a lump-sum maintenance award. On appeal, the Illinois Court of Appeals first concluded that a settlement agreement which is incorporated into a judgment is enforceable through contempt proceedings under state statutes and further noted that the availability of other means of support and alternative remedies for enforcement do not preclude a proceeding for contempt. It then held that the trial court's conclusion that the contempt was willful was supported by ample evidence of the appellant's assets and transactions, and was not rebutted by his general testimony that he was unable to pay.

The Wisconsin Supreme Court, in *Dennis v. Dennis*,[303] upheld a trial court's holding a father in contempt for his failure to seek work as ordered and his failure to make minimal child support payments. The supreme court noted that the trial court had not ordered the husband to take a different job, but only to seek other work in order to allow the court to make an accurate and informed finding as to his earning ability upon which to make a fair child support award.

Incarceration for non-payment of a support debt has been held exempt from state constitutional provisions prohibiting imprisonment for failure to pay a debt because a support debt derives from the duty of support, provides maintenance for the recipient, and fulfills public policy goals.[304] While failure to pay alimony or spousal support falls within the category of debts exempted from the constitutional ban, failure to make payments

---

[298] *See, e.g., Kay v. Vaughan*, 165 S.E.2d 131 (Ga. 1968); *In re Estate of Nielsen*, 445 N.W.2d 780 (Iowa 1989); *Spiliotis v. Campbell*, 431 N.E.2d 591 (Mass. App. Ct. 1982).

[299] *See, e.g.*, Cal. Fam. Code § 290 (West 1994); N.Y. Dom. Rel. Law § 245 (McKinney 1999 & Supp. 2000). *See also* Unif. Marriage and Divorce Act § 311(d), pt.III U.L.A. 14 (1998).

[300] *See, e.g., Keltner v. Keltner*, 589 S.W.2d 235 (Mo. 1979).

[301] *See, e.g.*, Cal. Fam. Code § 290 (West 1994); N.Y. Dom. Rel. Law § 245 (McKinney 1999 & Supp. 2000); Unif. Marriage and Divorce Act § 311(d), pt.III U.L.A. 14 (1998).

[302] 466 N.E.2d 1016 (1984), *cert. denied*, 471 U.S. 1017 (Ill. App. Ct. 1985).

[303] 344 N.W.2d 128 (Wis. 1984).

[304] *See, e.g., Bradley v. Superior Court*, 310 P.2d 634 (Cal. 1957); *McAlear v. McAlear*, 469 A.2d 1256 (Md. 1984); *West v. West*, 101 S.E. 876 (Va. 1920). *See Bradley v. Superior Court*, 310 P.2d 634 (Cal. 1957); *Seablom v. Seablom*, 348 N.W.2d 920 (N.D. 1984).

due under a property settlement provision generally are not punishable by contempt.[305] However, property division awards that assume the function of support sometimes have been held to be enforceable by contempt.[306] Contempt proceedings may also be brought to enforce counsel fees and court costs. Courts have also allowed attorneys' fees to be awarded against defendants in contempt actions brought for failure to pay support.[307]

Contempt proceedings may be either criminal or civil actions. Criminal contempt imposes a punishment for violation of a court order. Because of the criminal nature of the action, a defendant is entitled to constitutional protection guaranteed by the Due Process Clause. Civil contempt, on the other hand, is intended to enforce compliance with the support order and to collect arrearages by coercing the obligor to comply with the court order. If the obligor refuses to comply, he or she may be jailed; while the obligor is committed, a government agency often will provide support to the needy ex-spouse and children. If the obligor is unable to pay, imprisonment is impermissible; therefore, the key feature of civil contempt is that the obligor must have the ability to purge himself of the contempt by payment of the amount owed.[308] Ordinarily, this means that the obligor's inability to pay is an excuse for nonpayment, although it will not defeat an action to collect arrearages. Moreover, the court may hold the obligor in contempt for refusing to sell assets to satisfy the support obligation.

Because both forms of contempt actions relate to the non-payment of a support order and either may result in a fine or imprisonment, it is often difficult to distinguish between the two actions. The United States Supreme Court dealt with the problems of differentiating between civil and criminal contempt in *Hicks v. Feiock*[309] in the course of evaluating the constitutionality of a California contempt statute, deemed "quasi-criminal" in nature by the state courts. The statute required the defendant to prove his inability to pay the ordered support as a defense, rather than allocating the burden of proving ability to comply with the order to the state as an element of its case. The Court held that the substance of the action and the relief sought, rather than its label, should control whether the contempt is civil or criminal in nature and dictate the extent of the procedural safeguards necessary. It noted that civil contempt is brought for the benefit of the complainant, while criminal contempt seeks to vindicate the authority of the court. Further, if the defendant may be imprisoned until he performs some affirmative act, the action is civil, but if the sentence is for a definite period, it is criminal. If a fine is imposed, it is civil if it is remedial and payable to the complainant, but criminal if punitive and payable to the

---

[305] See *Bradley v. Superior Court*, 310 P.2d 634 (Cal. 1957); *Seablom v. Seablom*, 348 N.W.2d 920 (N.D. 1984).

[306] See, e.g., *McAlear v. McAlear*, 469 A.2d 1256 (Md. 1984); *Haley v. Haley*, 648 S.W.2d 890 (Mo. Ct. App. 1982); *Hall v. Hall*, 838 P.2d 995 (N.M. Ct. App. 1992), *cert. denied*, 838 P.2d 468 (N.M. 1992); *Hanks v. Hanks*, 334 N.W.2d 856 (S.D.1983).

[307] See, e.g., *Hartt v. Hartt*, 397 A.2d 518 (R.I. 1979).

[308] See *Mead v. Batchlor*, 460 N.W.2d 493 (Mich. 1990).

[309] 485 U.S. 624 (1988).

court. However, if the defendant may avoid paying the fine by performing some act, the contempt action is civil.

Civil contempt does not necessarily require all the due process protections afforded criminal defendants. The Michigan Supreme Court, in *Sword v. Sword*,[310] after setting out possible, non-exclusive factors that may determine the defendant's present ability to pay, held that a defendant in a civil contempt action for non-support does not have a constitutional right to court-appointed counsel. In determining that the action was civil rather than criminal, the court focused on the intention to compel the defendant to support his minor children, rather than to punish him or remove him from society, and the fact that he would be able to procure his own release upon payment. Furthermore, it found that the contempt proceeding is generally a relatively simple, informal hearing, establishing the arrearages and determining the reasons for non-payment. The *Sword* court similarly rejected the defendant's claim of entitlement to a jury trial. In a subsequent case, the Michigan Supreme Court reversed its position regarding the right to counsel in civil contempt proceedings because of the "indigent's fundamental interest in physical liberty," which would be curtailed by incarceration regardless of whether the proceeding is designated civil or criminal.[311] It noted that the federal circuit and district courts, as well as a large majority of state courts, had recently reached the same conclusion.[312]

[b] Other State Law Remedies

Most states authorize a broad range of other remedies for enforcing support obligations. These methods include discovery of assets, execution, liens on real property, attachment, garnishment, sequestration, and the appointment of a receiver. Courts traditionally have had the power to order the support obligor to provide security for future support in the form of a bond, insurance policy, cash, or other property. These security measures are becoming more common since federal law, discussed below, now encourages states to employ such methods.[313]

Imposing liens on the obligor's property is another common support enforcement procedure.[314] The courts are split as to whether a divorce decree containing a spousal or child support order automatically becomes a lien in the absence of any specific statutory authority.[315] Most courts

---

[310] 249 N.W.2d 88 (Mich. 1976), *overruled in part, Mead v. Batchlor*, 460 N.W.2d 493 (Mich. 1990).

[311] *Mead v. Batchlor*, 460 N.W.2d 493, 498 (Mich. 1990).

[312] *Id.* at 499–500. *See generally* Robert Monk, Note, *The Indigent Defendant's Right to Court Appointed Counsel In Civil Contempt Proceedings for the Nonpayment of Child Support*, 50 U. Chi. L. Rev.326 (1983).

[313] *See, e.g.*, Cal. Civ. Code § 4701.1 (West Supp. 1993) (allowing an obligee to apply for security for future payments when the obligor becomes 60 days overdue on child support payments).

[314] *See generally* Jeffrey Ball & Virginia Sablan, *Effective Use of Liens In Child Support Cases* (1990).

[315] *Compare Prior v. Prior*, 447 A.2d 1155 (R.I. 1982) *with In re Marriage of Daniel*, 639 S.W.2d 650 (Mo. Ct. App. 1982).

consider liens proper only when there is evidence that the obligor intends to be uncooperative or is likely to convey or conceal assets.[316]

A number of state statutes also provide for attachment of the obligor's property for non-payment of spousal or child support obligations.[317] Alternatively, an uncooperative support obligor may be required to provide some form of security assuring compliance with these obligations.[318]

Traditional garnishment procedures are available for enforcing spousal and child support obligations. Since the enactment of federal-state child support enforcement remedies in 1984 and 1985,[319] income withholding, or wage assignment, procedures have been streamlined.[320] Many of these expedited techniques may apply to spousal support, as well as child support collection, especially if the spousal support was intended, at least in part, to provide funds for children in the recipient's custody.

A number of states have enacted statutes authorizing the refusal, suspension, or revocation of state licenses of delinquent child support obligors. These statutes include any state license, including driver's, hunting and fishing, and professional licenses, such as membership in a state bar.[321]

[3] Interstate Enforcement

[a] Traditional Interstate Enforcement

Final judgments of one state are enforceable in all other states under the Full Faith and Credit Clause of the federal Constitution.[322] Finality, however, is essential to invoking full faith and credit; therefore, interstate enforcement of alimony and child support traditionally depended on whether the decree was final.

Although the Supreme Court held in *Barber v. Barber*[323] that periodic installments of alimony are entitled to full faith and credit as the installments mature, it later concluded in *Lynde v. Lynde*[324] that alimony payable in the future is not a final judgment for a fixed sum and does not qualify for the same recognition. In *Sistare v. Sistare*,[325] the Court elaborated, concluding that future alimony installments were entitled to full faith and credit to the same extent as arrearages if the recipient's right was "vested"

---

[316] *See, e.g., White v. White*, 429 So. 2d 730 (Fla. Dist. Ct. App. 1983).

[317] *See, e.g.*, N.C. Gen. Stat. § 50-16.7 (1999).

[318] *See, e.g.*, N.Y. Dom. Rel. Law § 243 (McKinney 1999); Va. Code Ann. § 20-114 (Michie 1995).

[319] Title IV-D of the Social Security Act, 42 U.S.C. §§ 651–665 (1993), and the Child Support Enforcement Amendments of 1984, 42 U.S.C. §§ 651–667 (1993).

[320] *See infra* § 9.06[F][4][a].

[321] *See, e.g.*, Tex. Fam. Code Ann. § 232.003 (1997).

[322] Art. IV, Sec. 1, 28 U.S.C. § 1738 (1988).

[323] 62 U.S. 582 (1859).

[324] 181 U.S. 183 (1901).

[325] 218 U.S. 1 (1910).

and could not be canceled or modified by the original court, even if the order was not reduced to a money judgment.

The Supreme Court later recognized the possibility that the court that originally ordered the alimony may have the authority to retroactively modify its award,[326] and therefore, a sister state need only give the order the same recognition that the state which issued the order would give it. Because child support orders are always prospectively modifiable, the full faith and credit requirement does not prevent another state from modifying an original decree, although the same inquiry regarding retroactive modification of arrearages arises in enforcement of child support arrearages.[327]

Historically, enforcement of a judgment for child support or alimony arrearages in another state required the cumbersome process of filing a suit on the judgment in the rendering state and establishing the judgment in the sister state. To facilitate enforcement of judgments, the majority of states have adopted the Uniform Enforcement of Foreign Judgments Act.[328] The Act establishes a simplified procedure for the registration of foreign judgments, which are defined as "any judgment, decree, or order of a court of the United States or of any other court which is entitled to full faith and credit in this state."[329] The court in which the judgment is registered then treats and regards the judgment in the same manner as it does its own judgments.

The Uniform Enforcement of Foreign Judgments Act has been held to be constitutionally applicable to periodic payments of support.[330] When a past-due support payment is regarded as a final judgment of the state that ordered the support, it is entitled to full faith and credit and may not be modified by a state in which the decree is later registered, although it may be modified prospectively upon showing of a sufficient change of circumstances.[331] A decree that was subject to retroactive modification in the state that entered the decree is not entitled to full faith and credit under the Act, however.[332]

In states that have not adopted the Uniform Enforcement of Foreign Judgments Act, the traditional method of enforcement must be used. In either case, multiple suits will be necessary to enforce arrearages as they accrue. The Uniform Reciprocal Enforcement of Support Act and its revisions has supplemented these traditional methods, and facilitates continued collection of support as well as arrearages.

---

[326] *Griffin v. Griffin*, 327 U.S. 220 (1946).

[327] *See, e.g., Elkind v. Byck*, 439 P.2d 316 (Cal. 1968); *Banton v. Mathers*, 309 N.E.2d 167 (Ind. Ct. App. 1974).

[328] Unif. Enforcement of Foreign Judgments Act, *Table of Jurisdictions*, 13 U.L.A. 149 (1986 & Supp. 2000).

[329] Unif. Enforcement of Foreign Judgments Act, *Table of Jurisdictions*, 13 U.L.A. 149 (1986 & Supp. 2000).

[330] *See, e.g., Willhite v. Willhite*, 546 P.2d 612 (Okla. 1976).

[331] *Holley v. Holley*, 568 S.W.2d 487 (Ark. 1978) (action to register Kansas divorce decree with vested alimony arrearages).

[332] *See Overman v. Overman*, 514 S.W.2d 625 (Mo. Ct. App. 1974) (action to register Tenn. divorce that could be retroactively modified).

[b] The Uniform Reciprocal Enforcement of Support Act

Prior to the enactment of the Uniform Reciprocal Enforcement of Support Act [URESA] of 1958 and its 1968 revision, the Revised Uniform Enforcement of Support Act [RURESA],[333] support obligors found it relatively easy to avoid payment of their support obligations by crossing state lines. Most recipients lacked the financial means to enforce interstate judgments. URESA and RURESA were enacted to simplify and expedite enforcement of spousal and child support payments owed by absent spouses or parents. Although the Acts were originally intended to apply to husbands and fathers, they have equal application to wives and mothers outside the jurisdiction who are not fulfilling their duties of support.[334]

Every state and territory of the United States, the District of Columbia, and several Canadian provinces enacted some version of URESA or RURESA, although variations of the statutory details and judicial interpretations frequently existed. URESA and RURESA were intended to provide a simple and inexpensive method of enforcing the duty of supporting dependent family members whenever the parties are in different states or in different counties within the same state. RURESA also extends to foreign jurisdictions which have enacted this or a substantially similar support enforcement law.[335]

RURESA was designed to assist the obligee, or a state agency providing support,[336] in enforcing a support obligation against an absent obligor without requiring the obligee to leave his or her own state of residence.[337] RURESA applies whether or not the parties are married, and regardless of whether a judicial order for support has been entered. An obligation of support, arising from the relationship of the parties, must exist in the state where the obligor is present, independent of URESA or RURESA, as the Acts are procedural rather than substantive statutes.[338]

The Nebraska Supreme Court clarified that it is unnecessary for a claimant to have an outstanding order for support to establish a support obligation under RURESA in *Iowa ex rel. Petersen v. Miner*.[339] Although an Iowa divorce decree had failed to provided specifically for support of one of the parties' children, a later request for modification of a RURESA petition was granted to include that child. The respondent father appealed, citing RURESA for the proposition that the Act "itself creates not duties

---

[333] Revised Unif. Reciprocal Enforcement of Support Act, 9B U.L.A. 381 (1987).

[334] *See generally* Jane Gorham, *Stemming the Modification of Child-Support Orders by Responding Courts: A Proposal to Amend RURESA's Antisupersession Clause*, 24 U. Mich. J.L. Ref. 405, 405–407 (1991).

[335] *See* Carl Gallageher, Note, *Uniform Reciprocal Enforcement of Support Act*, 20 Washburn L.J. 409 (1981).

[336] Revised Unif. Reciprocal Enforcement of Support Act, § 8, 9B U.L.A. 438 (1987).

[337] *Id.* § 4, 9B U.L.A. 412. RURESA also may be used when the parties reside in different counties of the same state. 9B U.L.A. 412 (1987).

[338] *See Elkind v. Byck*, 439 P.2d 316 (Cal. 1968).

[339] 412 N.W.2d 832 (Neb. 1987).

of family support but leaves this to the legislatures of the several states."[340] The court held that duties of support arising from the parent-child relationship, as well as those reduced to a specific monetary amount by another state, may be enforced through RURESA, and that the responding state may order support payments without a determination of the support obligation by the initiating state.

URESA and RURESA established two commonly used procedures, plus an extradition process which is rarely implemented. The first and most frequently employed procedure entails a two-state proceeding which may be instituted whenever a support obligation exists, whether or not that obligation has been reduced to a court order. The person or agency seeking support, the obligee, files a petition in his or her own state of residence, the initiating state.[341] Upon examination of the petition, if the court in the initiating state identifies a duty to support, it forwards the petition and supporting documentation to the state where the obligor currently resides, the responding state.[342]

The designated official of the responding state, usually a county district attorney, brings an action to enforce the support obligation against the obligor.[343] It summons the obligor into its courts and conducts a hearing de novo, under the laws of that state, to determine if a support obligation is owed in the responding state.[344] The obligor's defenses in an action brought under URESA or RURESA are limited, usually to circumstances that would negate a duty of support, such as non-paternity, or to proof of payment of the obligation.[345] If the obligor does raise evidence constituting a defense, the responding court must continue the hearing and allow the obligee the opportunity to present additional evidence, by deposition or appearance, before making its final determination.[346] If the court in the responding state finds a support obligation, it may order the obligor to pay support arrearages, as well as order a specific amount of support for the future. The payments are made to the designated official in the responding state.[347] This official collects the payments, monitors the obligor's compliance, and transmits the money to the initiating state where it is paid to the obligee.[348]

---

[340] *Id.* at 834, *quoting* Prefatory Note to the Revised Unif. Reciprocal Enforcement of Support Act, 9B U.L.A. 382 (1987).

[341] Revised Unif. Reciprocal Enforcement of Support Act, § 11, 9B U.L.A. 440–441 (1987).

[342] *Id.* § 14, 9B U.L.A. 450 (1987).

[343] *Id.* §§ 18, 19, 9B U.L.A. 461, 467 (1987).

[344] *See Stephens v. Stephens,* 331 S.E.2d 484 (Va. 1985) (responding court cannot make support determination unless obligor is within its jurisdiction).

[345] *See Virginia ex. rel. Halsey v. Autry,* 441 A.2d 1056 (Md. 1982) (In response to father's argument that New Jersey court terminated his obligation to pay support for his illegitimate child, court held that Act should be liberally construed to provide support between jurisdictions).

[346] *See Williams v. Williams,* 781 P.2d 1170 (N.M. Ct. App. 1989); Note, *Counterclaims and Defenses Under the Uniform Reciprocal Enforcement of Support Act,* 15 Ga. L.Rev. 143 (1980).

[347] Revised Unif. Reciprocal Enforcement of Support Act, § 24, 9B U.L.A. § 24, 487–488 (1987).

[348] *Id.* § 26, 9B U.L.A. 520 (1987).

Because the Acts confer jurisdiction only to determine and enforce duties of support, most courts will not allow any counterclaims concerning divorce, child custody or visitation, or other matters in a URESA or RURESA action.[349] In *State ex rel. McDonnell v. McCutcheon*,[350] the Minnesota Supreme Court addressed the question of collection of arrearages and the defense of wrongful removal of the child from the original jurisdiction in a RURESA action. In *McDonnell*, the parties divorced in New York, where the divorce court had ordered child support. The mother later moved to Colorado without obtaining permission of the father or the court and brought a RURESA action to enforce child support in Minnesota, where the father had subsequently moved. Although the father had made fairly regular payments of $100 a month, the mother sought arrearages of $24,717 under the terms of the New York decree. The Minnesota trial court ordered the father to pay $160 a month, purporting to cancel the arrearages on the basis of the mother's wrongful interference with the father's visitation rights. The Minnesota Supreme Court interpreted RURESA to mean that a foreign support order is evidence of the duty of support, but does not require a responding court to order the same amount of support. It reasoned that detailed inquiries into foreign state law would frustrate the expeditious and economical enforcement of support contemplated by RURESA and that the Act anticipated that the responding court would apply its own domestic law in setting the level of support for enforcement in an interstate action. However, under both Minnesota law and the provisions of RURESA itself, interference with custody or visitation is not a proper factor to apply in determining the level of a child support award. In light of other factors relating to the parties' financial positions, however, the court upheld the award of $160 a month. The *McDonnell* court emphasized that its decision did not eliminate or modify the arrearages, but simply deferred that determination to the New York court as a more appropriate forum. It noted that if the past-due amount was enforced by that court, the obligee would be able to enforce the judgment in Minnesota under a registration proceeding.

A minority of jurisdictions permitted certain counterclaims if there was a significant connection between the counterclaim and the duty of support.[351] In *Moffat v. Moffat*,[352] the former wife refused to allow the husband to exercise visitation that had been granted in the parties' divorce decree. The trial court excused the husband from paying spousal or child support until the wife complied with the visitation order. After the wife moved to Virginia, she initiated a RURESA action in that state. The Virginia court held that despite the fact that the wife was in contempt for denial of the husband's visitation rights, she was not estopped from pursuing a RURESA

---

[349] *See, e.g., State ex rel. Hubbard v. Hubbard*, 329 N.W.2d 202 (Wis. 1983) (despite mother's violation of court order by removing child from state, trial court erred in dismissing mothers URESA action; father's counterclaims for interference with custody and visitation rights are not proper considerations under URESA).

[350] 337 N.W.2d 645 (Minn. 1983).

[351] *See* Note, *supra* note 346 at 150–175.

[352] 612 P.2d 967 (Cal. 1980).

action. The responding California court ordered the husband to pay child support, but that state's supreme court reversed. It held that although no defense based on the custodial parent's conduct is recognized under RURESA, the husband's duty of support was suspended under the prior erroneous but effective order. Although the wife was free to seek a modification of that order, she could not collaterally attack it.

As the court in *McDonnell* noted, the responding court is not bound by an outstanding support order entered by another state and may decide to increase or decrease the support obligation pursuant to its own support criteria.[353] Nevertheless, unless the new decree expressly modifies the earlier decree, the original decree is still valid, and the obligee may recover any difference through traditional means of enforcement. A minority of states, however, prohibit any modification of a preexisting sister state support order.[354] Due to the uncertainty regarding modification and the collection of support arrearages, the obligee's attorney may decide to pursue an alternative or supplementary action in the obligee's own state, reduce the debt to judgment, and enforce it in the obligor's state.[355]

In *Taylor v. Vilcheck*,[356] the Nevada Supreme Court upheld the jurisdiction of the state district courts to enter child support orders in RURESA actions in smaller amounts than ordered in the original decrees. The court distinguished between ordering a lower support payment, due to the obligor's inability to pay the full original amount, and purporting to modify the child support order of another state. Construing the state's legislature's intention to preclude modification, however, it further held that the court was restricted from increasing the amount of support in a RURESA action; rather, the more complex questions concerning an increase in support were better dealt with in other, more formal proceedings.

RURESA affords an alternative mechanism that permits a support obligee to register a pre-existing support order in the obligee's state, where it will be enforced as though it were a judgment of the latter state.[357] A registered foreign support order is treated the same as an order originally issued by that state with respect to enforcement, procedures, defenses, and proceedings for reopening, vacating, or staying a support order.[358] If the obligor does not petition for the order to be vacated or for other relief within 20 days after the mailing of notice of the registration, the registered support order is confirmed.[359] At a hearing to enforce the registered support order,

---

[353] *See also, e.g., Thompson v. Thompson*, 366 N.W.2d 845 (S.D. 1985); *Bjugan v. Bjugan*, 710 P.2d 213 (Wyo. 1985). *See generally* Gorham, *supra* note 334.

[354] *See, e.g., Hamilton v. Hamilton*, 476 S.W.2d 197 (Ky. 1972).

[355] *See Sistare v. Sistare*, 218 U.S. 1 (1910) (support arrearages are final judgments for full faith and credit purposes); *Barrell v. Barrell*, 415 A.2d 579 (Md. 1980) (enforcement of sister state support order may utilize methods other than URESA and RURESA).

[356] 745 P.2d 702 (Neb. 1987).

[357] Revised Unif. Reciprocal Enforcement of Support Act, §§ 35-40, 9B U.L.A. 540-546 (1987). Comment, *Scott v. Sylvester*, 302 S.E.2d 30 (Va. 1983), *cert. denied*, 464 U.S. 961 (1983).

[358] *Id.* § 40(a), 9B U.L.A. 546 (1987).

[359] *Id.* § 40(b), 9B U.L.A. 546 (1987).

the obligor is limited to defenses that would be available in an action to enforce a foreign money judgment. [360] If the obligor requests and is granted a stay, based on limited statutory grounds, he or she must furnish security for the payment of the support ordered. [361] Under the registration procedure as well as the two-state enforcement procedure, the obligor's state collects and forwards actual support payments, thus the initiating and responding states both bear the financial burden of enforcing the support order under either procedure. [362]

In *Gibson v. Baxter*, [363] the Minnesota Court of Appeals held that Minnesota courts should apply the law of the state that entered the support order in an enforcement proceeding brought under RURESA's registration provisions. In *Gibson*, the parties had been married in Minnesota, were later divorced in Nebraska, where the husband was ordered to pay child support, and both had moved back to Minnesota. During the preceding thirteen years, the husband had made only sporadic child support payments, and had received a reduction of his support obligation on three occasions — twice from Colorado courts and once from a Minnesota court. The wife registered the Nebraska judgment and decree and sought enforcement in a Minnesota county court. The Minnesota court, trial judge, applying Nebraska law, ordered the husband to pay $26,600.32 in arrearages and interest. It further held that his obligation continued until the children reached the age of majority under Nebraska law. The appellate court agreed that RURESA subjects a registered foreign judgment "to the same procedures, defenses, and proceedings for reopening, vacating, or staying as a Minnesota judgment . . . [but does] not, however, require Minnesota courts to apply Minnesota substantive law in enforcing a foreign judgment." [364] It observed that RURESA was specifically intended to discourage or eliminate the type of forum shopping that had been engaged in by the husband.

Commentators have observed that URESA and RURESA have not been as successful as intended in actually providing inexpensive, expeditious enforcement of interstate support obligations. A major perceived defect has been an unwillingness of the prosecuting attorneys in responding states to perform the duties imposed on them by the Acts. Official inaction may occur because overworked district attorney's offices in the responding states often give low priority to claims under the Acts, perhaps due to fears that enforcement may deprive an obligor's new family of support and make them eligible for public assistance, lack of enthusiasm for clients they never see, and emphasis on more visible criminal convictions. The impact of local political considerations, combined with bureaucratic red-tape, may cause delay and difficulty in implementing the provisions of URESA and

---

[360] *Id.* § 40(c), 9B U.L.A. 546 (1987).

[361] *Id.*

[362] *See generally* William Fox, *The Uniform Reciprocal Enforcement of Support Act*, 12 Fam. L.Q. 113 (1978).

[363] 434 N.W.2d 486 (Minn. Ct. App. 1989).

[364] *Id.* at 488.

RURESA.[365] In practice, many have found that the Acts do not provide an effective mechanism for collecting support obligations.[366]

[4] The Uniform Interstate Family Support Act

A thorough revision of RURESA began in 1988 and ultimately became the Uniform Interstate Family Support Act [UIFSA]. The federal Personal Responsibility and Work Opportunity Reconciliation Act of 1996 [PRWORA] required all states to adopt UIFSA by January 1, 1998, or lose federal funding for state welfare programs.[367]

UIFSA expands personal jurisdiction to its constitutional limits, which allows a custodial parent or state agency attempting to establish or collect support the maximum opportunity to do so without resorting to the two-state proceedings of RURESA. It permits a state to exercise long-arm jurisdiction based on limited contacts relating to the child in question, including a child residing in the state as a result of the individual's acts or directives and an individual engaging in sexual intercourse in the state if the child may have been conceived by that act.[368] Although the two-state proceeding of RURESA is retained by UIFSA, it should be less necessary because of the expanded grounds for asserting personal jurisdiction.

UIFSA applies the law of the forum state, simplifying the more complicated approach of RURESA. When arrearages exist, the forum court may need to apply the law of other states.[369]

To eliminate the problem of conflicting support orders under RURESA, UIFSA applies a one-order system. One child support order is entered and that order maintains continuing validity. To control issues of conflicting orders, UIFSA severely limits when a petition can be filed in one state if a pleading has already been filed in another state.[370] A state has "continuing, exclusive jurisdiction over a child support order . . . as long as this State remains the residence of the obligor, the individual obligee, or the child."[371] The state issuing the initial order has jurisdiction to modify as long as the child and obligee are present.[372]

UIFSA actions may be brought by either state agencies[373] or private attorneys.[374] Interstate enforcement usually begins with registration of a support order in the state where enforcement is sought. After registration, it is enforced by a tribunal of the state where it is registered, applying either local support enforcement mechanisms or those imposed by UIFSA itself.[375]

---

[365] *See, e.g.,* William Fox, *supra* note 362, at 124–125.

[366] *See* Homer Clark, *supra* note 7, at 734–735.

[367] Pub. L. No. 104–193, 110 Stat. 2105 § 32, codified at 42 U.S.C. § 666(f).

[368] *See* UIFSA § 201.

[369] *Id.* at § 202.

[370] *Id.* at § 204.

[371] *Id.* at § 205.

[372] *Id.* at § 206.

[373] *Id.* at § 307(a).

[374] *Id.* at § 309.

[375] *Id.* at § 601–604.

A major feature of UIFSA is that modification by an enforcing state is extremely limited. The original jurisdiction has the exclusive power to modify unless that state has lost jurisdiction because the child and the custodial parent have left. If the issuing state loses jurisdiction, another state may modify the order if it has jurisdiction over both parties. Once another state has validly modified a support order under UIFSA, it becomes the only enforceable order.[376] The North Carolina Court of Appeals interpreted this section in *Welsher v. Rager*,[377] when it reversed a trial court decision that refused to continue child support under a New York order. The father had argued that his duty to support the children ended when they turned 18. However, under New York law, a child is not emancipated until age 21. The North Carolina appellate court held that, under UISFA, which the state had enacted, requires that a support order be interpreted according to the law of the state where it was issued; the father was bound by the New York law which requires him to support his children until they attain 21.

In *P.A.N. v. R..N.*,[378] the Delaware Family Court also interpreted the difference between URESA and UIFSA. In that case, the parties were divorced in New York and their separation agreement specified that child support would be paid at a set amount until the youngest child became emancipated. When the oldest child reached the age of majority, the father requested and was awarded a decrease in support payments. Upon the mother's petition for review de novo, the court noted that while under URESA it was possible to have two or more valid child support orders coexisting, UIFSA requires that an order issued by a court of the current home state must be recognized. Because the mother and children continued to reside in New York, the court held that the earlier New York order would be recognized rather than the subsequent Delaware order. However, because the mother had never requested Delaware registration of the New York order, the Delaware courts had no authority to enforce it. Once she filed to register her order in Delaware, that court would have the power of enforcement.

UIFSA contains streamlined enforcement features. It allows a support order to be mailed directly to an employer in another state, eliminating the need for a hearing unless the payor actively seeks one.[379] Further, a party seeking to enforce a support order or an income withholding order may send the necessary documents to the support enforcement officer of another state.[380]

UIFSA is enhanced by a federal law known as the Full Faith and Credit for Child Support Orders.[381] Under this law, full faith and credit must be

---

[376] *See id.* at § 205, 206, 605–608.

[377] 491 S.E.2d 661 (N.C. Ct. App. 1997).

[378] 1996 Del. Fam. Ct. LEXIS 139.

[379] *Id.* at § 501.

[380] *Id.* at § 502.

[381] Pub. L. No. 103-383, 108 Stat. 4064, codified at 28 U.S.C. § 1738B (1997).

given to support orders that are consistent with express standards, which are the same as those required for a valid order under UIFSA. It also prohibits modification of support orders of a state with continuing exclusive jurisdiction.

[5] Federally Mandated Support Enforcement Remedies

The federal government's involvement in child support has not been limited to requiring the adoption of child support guidelines. Over the past several decades, federal concern with child support has increased enormously. In addition to concern for the welfare of children, Congress was concerned about the enormous costs of welfare programs, which were incurred largely because of parents' failure to fulfill their child support obligations. These considerations led to federal legislation intended to directly confront the problem of child support enforcement. Lack of enforcement of child support awards had become a national crisis and a drain on public funds, prompting Congress to enact Title IV-D of the Social Security Act[382] in 1974 to coordinate federal and state processes for efficient collection of child support. Title IV-D created a federal-state program for establishing and enforcing child support to be administered by the federal Office of Child Support Enforcement, which requires states to establish plans for improved child support enforcement with partial funding by the federal government.

The original Act required states to establish specific child support enforcement plans in order to continue receiving federal funding for family assistance programs.[383] Under the Act, the states were required to establish programs administered by state IV-D agencies to use existing state mechanisms for proving paternity and setting and enforcing child support orders, both for families receiving AFDC benefits and others.[384]

Although child support collection improved under the original act, noncompliance remained high, and state efforts focused almost exclusively on collection from parents whose families received Aid to Families with Dependent Children [AFDC] benefits. To increase the effectiveness of the programs, Congress, a decade later, enacted the Child Support Enforcement Amendments of 1984 (CSEA).[385] These amendments required states to legislate specific mechanisms for improving their child support enforcement programs to intensify interstate enforcement and to equalize treatment of non-AFDC families with those receiving such benefits. In addition to mandating longer statutes of limitations on paternity actions, the CSEA

---

[382] 42 U.S.C. §§ 651–665 (1988 & Supp. 1989).

[383] *See generally* Diane Dodson & Robert Horowitz, *Child Support Enforcement Amendments of 1984: New Tools for Enforcement*, 10 Fam. L. Rptr. 3051 (BNA) (1984).

[384] *Id.*

[385] Pub. L. 98-378, § 1 Aug. 16, 1984, 98 Stat. 1305; *see also* Harry O'Donnell, Note, *Title I of the Family Support Act of 1988 — The Quest for Effective National Child Support Enforcement Continues*, 29 J. Fam. L. 149 (1990–91).

ordered states to adopt procedures for (a) mandatory income tax withholding, (b) offsets to state income tax refunds, (c) guarantees to assure support (such as liens, bonds, and securities), and (d) reporting arrearages to credit agencies, and federal income tax offsets in non-AFDC cases.[386] Many of the resulting state statutes apply to enforcement of spousal support as well as child support.

[a] Income Withholding

One of the most important enforcement techniques mandated by the CSEA is the provision for income withholding, an expedited form of the traditional remedy of garnishment. The CSEA requires all support orders issued or modified within a state to include a provision for wage withholding, at least on a conditional basis, when the support payments are in arrears.[387] Private settlement agreements that are not incorporated or merged into a court decree are exempt from this requirement, but such provisions may be voluntarily inserted. While the CSEA requires wage withholding, it also allows states to reach broader forms of income, which could include commissions, bonuses, disability and retirement benefits, and any other sources of income.[388] Withholding may be initiated as soon as the obligor is in arrears of an amount equal to one month's support.[389] Under the Child Support Act of 1988, states are required to include automatic wage assignments in all new or modified child support orders.[390]

The procedures for income withholding dictated by Congress are mandatory with respect to obligees represented by the state IV-D agency, but state legislatures may elect to apply the same system to privately represented or pro se obligees. The compulsory provisions allow the withholding action to be commenced without further court or administrative order, and notice need only be sent to the obligor once the withholding decision has been made. While the withholding must be accomplished in accordance with procedural due process, the obligor may contest only on the limited ground of "mistakes of fact," which includes errors in the amount of current support due or of arrearages or mistaken identity of the obligor.[391] Contested withholding actions must be resolved within 45 days. The CSEA contemplates that states will develop clearinghouse devises to monitor support payments and facilitate accounting, which would reduce the number of contested actions.[392]

Withholding is accomplished by sending notice to the obligor's employer or other source of income, directing that a specified amount be withheld from the employee's pay. The employer is liable for failure to comply and

---

[386] *Id.*

[387] 42 U.S.C. §§ 666(a)(8); (b)(2), (b)(3) (Supp. 1992).

[388] *See* Diane Dodson & Robert Horowitz, *supra* note 383, at 3054.

[389] 42 U.S.C.A. § 666(b)(3) (1994).

[390] Pub. L. No. 100-485, 102 Stat. 2343.

[391] H. Rep. No. 527 at 33.

[392] Diane Dodson & Robert Horowitz, *supra* note 383, at 3054.

is prohibited from taking retaliatory action against the employee on account of the withholding.

CSEA requires withholding of an amount equal to the current support obligation and an additional amount to be applied toward the arrearage, plus a fee paid to the employer. The Consumer Credit Protection Act [393] limits the amount that may be withheld to 50 to 65 percent of the employee's disposable earnings, depending on whether the obligor has a second family to support and on whether the arrearages arose more than twelve weeks previously. States must give child support withholding priority over the rights of other creditors. Except in limited, specified circumstances, the withholding continues once the arrearages have been paid in order to assure a reliable continuation of support. [394]

States must provide access to their withholding systems to enforcement agencies of other states to enable out-of-state support obligees to reach the earnings of obligors within the state. Child support enforcement agencies now have access to an obligor's social security number, [395] as well as numerous other tracing devices. Information regarding certain amounts of unpaid support obligations must be reported to credit reporting agencies on their request. [396]

[b]　Security for Payments

The CSEA further requires states to adopt procedures for securing support payments by liens, bonds, and other securities. These devices may be particularly useful when the obligor is self-employed or has income or assets that are otherwise inaccessible through the withholding provisions. [397] The judge or administrative agency has discretion as to the type and amount of security to require in an individual case.

[c]　Income Tax Refund Intercepts

The CSEA also broadened the scope of tax refund intercepts for collection of past-due child support. Under this mechanism, any federal income tax refund due an obligor may be sent directly to the obligee. Under the earlier act, the intercept was only available to AFDC recipients and was usually limited to the amount owed to state agencies. [398] The CSEA extends the intercept mechanism to non-AFDC recipients, but only the state IV-D agency may initiate the procedure; thus, private obligees must enlist the assistance of the agency. Only arrearages, not current support, may be collected through the intercept, and it may be used only after other remedies have been exhausted. However, the amount collected is not

---

[393] 15 U.S.C. § 1673(b) (1988).

[394] 42 U.S.C. § 666(b) (1988 & Supp. II 1990).

[395] 42 U.S.C. § 653(b) (1988).

[396] 42 U.S.C. § 666(a)(7) (1988).

[397] *See* Diane Dodson & Robert Horowitz, *supra* note 383, at 3055.

[398] *See id.* a 3056.

limited by the Consumer Credit Protection Act. The procedures for implementing the tax refund intercept are complex and require prior notice and procedural due process protections to the obligor and an opportunity to contest the amount owed. States which impose state income taxes are also required to develop state income tax refund intercept mechanisms.

The United States Supreme Court held in *Sorenson v. Secretary of the Treasury* [399] that the intercept device may be used to confiscate tax refunds due to the earned-income credit as well as overpayment of taxes, resolving a split of authority among the federal circuits. In *Sorenson*, the father who owed support arrearages, had remarried and had a new child. The father and his new wife, who brought the action because she had earned most of the family's income, were due a tax refund of about $1400, partly attributable to overpayment of taxes and partly to the earned-income credit. [400] The IRS notified the couple that $1100 of the refund was being paid to the State of Washington, which had been assigned the mother's right to the child support arrearages under the AFDC program. The Supreme Court acknowledged the important goals of the earned-income credit, [401] but concluded that Congress could deem that alleviating the "devastating consequences for children and the taxpayers' of the epidemic of nonsupport" was a more compelling objective and upheld the Ninth Circuit's view that the refund based on the credit could be intercepted. [402]

[d] Child Support Guidelines

The CSEA also required that all states establish specific child support guidelines, in the form of schedules or formulas, for determining basic child support obligations. A variety of guideline schemes have been adopted by various state legislatures, [403] and generally account for extraordinary medical or dental expenses and child-care costs due to employment of the custodial parent. Periodic review of the guidelines is performed by an appropriate state agency.

Congress again amended the Social Security Act in 1988 to require that each state's guidelines would be applied as a rebuttable presumption, requiring express findings of fact for a deviation from those guidelines if their application would be unjust or inappropriate in a given case. [404] The amendments also require that by 1990 a state's guidelines must be reviewed at least every four years to assure their continued appropriateness and, as of 1993, all individual child support awards must be reviewed at least every 36 months.

---

[399] 475 U.S. 851 (1986).

[400] The earned-income credit allows a person supporting a child living with him a tax credit of ten percent of the earned income for the taxable year, up to $5000, which, unlike other credits, is refundable. *Id.* at 855.

[401] The credit is intended to encourage low-income persons to work and to provide them relief from rising costs of living, as well as to stimulate the economy. 475 U.S. at 864 (Stevens, J., dissenting).

[402] *Id.* at 858–59.

[403] *See generally supra* § 9.06 [C].

[404] 42 U.S.C.A. § 667 (Supp. 1992).

[e] Parent Locator Service

State child support enforcement programs are required by federal law to operate a Parent Locator Service [PLS], interconnected with other state and federal PLS programs, to trace child support obligors who have deserted their families or moved to unknown location. The PLS accepts location requests from IV-D agencies in both AFDC and non-AFDC cases. Non-AFDC custodial parents or their private attorneys seeking federal location assistance may request the state PLS to obtain federal PLS location information for a small fee.[405]

Location requests forwarded to the federal PLS should state the following: the absent parent's full name; any last-name alias; the parent's social security number, if known; whether the parent is or has been a member of the armed forces, and the branch of service, if known; whether the parent is a federal employee; and whether the parent is receiving any federal compensation or benefits. If the parent's social security number is not known, the state PLS must send additional identifying data, including the absent parent's date and place of birth, mother's maiden name, and father's full name. Upon receipt of a location request, the federal PLS will conduct a computer search of federal departments and agencies to learn the absent parent's social security number, last known address, and place of employment.[406]

When attempting to locate an absent parent for child support purposes, the PLS may obtain new mailing addresses and information from the post office system,[407] credit bureaus,[408] previous employers,[409] public information on file with the state Department of Motor Vehicles, state employment commissions and law enforcement divisions, and the Internal Revenue Service.[410]

[f] The Child Support Recovery Act of 1992

The Child Support Recovery Act of 1992[411] [CSRA] creates a federal crime for willful failure to pay child support. The statute provides for a criminal penalty of imprisonment for up to six months for the first offense of two years maximum for one who "willfully fails to pay a past due support obligation with respect to a child who resides in another state."[412]

Support obligations that have been determined by a court order or by an administrative order that have been due for one year or over $5000 are subject to the statute.

---

[405] 42 U.S.C. § 654(8) (1988).

[406] *See* Robert Horowitz, Diane Dodson, & Margaret Haynes, Remedies Under the Child Support Enforcement Amendments of 1984, 112–130 (1985).

[407] 39 C.F.R. § 265.6(d)(1) (1984).

[408] 15 U.S.C. § 1681b(3)(A) (1988).

[409] 45 C.F.R. § 303.100(d)(3)(1)(I) (1984).

[410] 26 U.S.C. §§ 6103(1)(6)(A)(I) and (ii) (1988).

[411] 18 U.C.C. § 228.

[412] *Id.* at § 228(a).

The constitutionality of the statute was upheld by the Court of Appeals for the 10th Circuit in *United States v. Hampshire*. [413] The defendant in *Hampshire*, who conditionally pled guilty and was sentenced to two years probation and ordered to pay $38,804 in restitution, challenged his conviction on the basis that the Child Support Recovery Act violates the Commerce Clause. Noting that while several district courts have held the CSRA unconstitutional, a number have upheld the constitutionality on the basis that nonpayment of child support involves payment of a debts and constitutes economic activity or commerce, that nonpayment of child support in general has a substantial impact on commerce, and that the requirement that the delinquent parent and child live in different states provides an interstate nexus. The court held that Congress had a rational basis for concluding that the child support delinquencies have a substantial impact on interstate commerce and upheld the CSRA.

[g] The Personal Responsibility and Work Opportunity Reconciliation Act of 1996

The Personal Responsibility and Work Opportunity Reconciliation Act of 1996[414] [PRWORA] replaced AFDC entitlements with block welfare grants to the states and removed the federal guarantee for child welfare, shifting the primary responsibility to the states. At the same time, it provided important provisions for collecting child support. It established a national system for tracking employment which requires reporting of new hires, requires states to adopt the UIFSA, allows enforcement agencies access to governmental sources of information for tracking delinquent parents, and permits military persons to be located immediately. PRWORA affords enforcement agencies access to private records, applies modern case management techniques to child support enforcement, including computer matching, and requires states to adopt expedited procedures. [415]

§ 9.07 Federal Tax Consequences of Child and Spousal Support

The tax implications of divorce were greater under previous tax law when the uppermost marginal income tax rate was higher and there was a greater differential between the highest and lowest rates, and, thus more opportunity for income shifting from a spouse in a higher bracket to one in a lower bracket. Nevertheless, the tax implications of divorce continue to have a significant effect on divorcing parties and their influence should be considered in negotiating the structure of a separation agreement. [416]

---

[413] 95 F.3d 999 (10th Cir. 1996), *review denied*, 117 S. Ct. 753 (1997).

[414] Pub. L. No. 104–193, 110 Stat. 2105.

[415] *See* Linda D. Elrod, *Child Support Reassessed: Federalization of Enforcement Nears Completion*, 1997 U. Ill. L. Rev. 695 (1997).

[416] *See generally* Harold Wren., Leon Gabinet & David Clayton Carrad, Tax Aspects of Marital Dissolution (1987); Garrison Lepow, *Nobody Gets Married for the First Time Anymore-A Primer on the Tax Implications of Support Payments In Divorce*, 25 Duq. L. Rev. 43 (1986).

Furthermore, the tax ramifications of divorce are complex because many of the former tax provisions continue to apply to divorce decree entered prior to the enactment of the present tax laws, resulting in a "current divorce tax system [that] is a confusing conglomeration of four different models."[417] Family law practitioners thus must be familiar with both prior and present tax laws, and they must also keep abreast of proposed and anticipated changes in those laws.

[A] Alimony or Spousal Support Payments

Since 1942,[418] the Internal Revenue Code (IRC) has treated payments of alimony or spousal support as taxable income to the recipient spouse[419] and deductible from the gross income of the payor spouse,[420] provided that the payments comply with specific statutory qualifications. The payor spouse may deduct alimony payments even if that spouse uses the standard deduction.[421]

Prior to the 1984 Deficit Reduction Act, the IRC prevented property division payments which were disguised as alimony from qualifying as alimony for tax purposes. Under the old Code, the payment needed to stem from a duty of spousal support, not a division of property, under a divorce decree, separation decree, or written instrument incident to divorce.[422] The purported distinction between alimony and property division generated considerable litigation, especially as the difference between the two concepts blurred at the state family law level.

Furthermore, the payments had to be paid on "periodic" basic, although the Code failed to define that term.[423] Installment payments of a lump sum amount were viewed as periodic only if they were stretched out over a period of more than ten years;[424] alimony payable for a shorter time was periodic if it could be modified or terminated because of the death of either spouse, the remarriage of the recipient, or a change in circumstances.[425]

The Deficit Reduction Act of 1984[426] and Tax Reform Act of 1986[427] simplified the alimony rules and eliminated the support and periodicity

---

[417] Beverly Moran, *Welcome to the Funhouse: The Incredible Maze of Modern Divorce Taxation*, 26 Harv. J. on Legis. 117, 118 (1989) (examining the history of divorce taxation and its current implications). Moran, *Welcome to the Funhouse: The Incredible Maze of Modern Divorce Taxation*, 26 Harv. J. on Legis. 117, 118 (1989) (examining the history of divorce taxation and its current implications).

[418] *See* Eleanor Rich, *Alimony Taxation After the Tax Reform Act of 1986*, 6 B.U.J. Tax Law 67, 67–68 (1988) (examining the historical tax treatment of alimony payment).

[419] I.R.C. § 71 (2001).

[420] I.R.C. § 215.

[421] *See* I.R.C. § 62(a)(10).

[422] I.R.C. § 71 (1954) (amended In 1984).

[423] *Id.*

[424] Treas. Reg. § 1.71-1(d)(4) (1960).

[425] Treas. Reg. § 1.71-1(d)(3) (1960).

[426] Deficit Reduction Act of 1984, Pub. L. No. 98-369, 98 Stat. 494 (1984).

[427] Tax Reform Act of 1986, Pub. L. No. 99-514, 100 Stat. 2085 (1986).

requirements for qualification as alimony. In order for payments to be deductible to the payor and includable income to the payee, current IRC § 71 now requires the following:

(1) The payments must be in cash, not in other property.[428]

(2) The payments must be received by, or on behalf of, a spouse under a divorce decree or separation agreement.[429]

(3) The divorce or separation instrument must not expressly state that the payments shall *not* be treated as alimony for tax purposes.[430]

(4) The spouses may not be "members of the same household" when the payments are made.[431]

(5) The payments must terminate upon the death of the recipient, with no substitute payments imposed on the payor spouse after the recipient's death. Unless the payments were part of a court order and state law automatically terminates the payments on the recipient's death, the instrument must expressly provide for such discontinuation.[432]

(6) The spouses cannot file a joint income tax return.[433]

(7) The payments cannot represent child support.[434]

To prevent parties from "front loading," or disguising property settlement payments as alimony to obtain a large tax benefit in the years immediately following divorce, the 1984 Act further devised a "recapture" rule.[435] The recapture rule applied whenever annual payments exceeding $10,000 decreased by more than $10,000 during any year over the six-year period following divorce. If excess payments were recaptured, the payor was required to re-compute the over-payments as income and the recipient was granted a corresponding deduction.[436]

The Tax Reform Act of 1986 modified the recapture rule and related certain earlier limitations on qualification as alimony for tax purpose.[437] The provisions currently require payments exceeding $15,000 per calendar year to be spread out over a three year period.[438] If the payments in the

---

[428] I.R.C. § 71(b)(1). Checks and money orders qualify as cash payments, and rent or mortgage payments made on behalf the recipient may qualify as alimony. T.D. 7973, 1984-2, C.B. 174.

[429] I.R.C. § 71(b)(1)(A).

[430] I.R.C. § 71(b)(1)(B).

[431] I.R.C. § 71(b)(1)(C). If the payments are made pursuant to a separation agreement but the parties are not yet legally separated or divorced and one spouse is preparing to leave the household and does so within one month of the payments in question, the payments may qualify. I.R.C. § 71(f)(5)(A).

[432] I.R.C. § 71(b)(1)(D).

[433] I.R.C. § 71(e).

[434] *See infra* § 9.07[B].

[435] I.R.C. § 71(c)(2) (1984) (amended In 1986).

[436] *See* Eleanor Rich, *supra* note 418, at 69–70 (examples of operation of recapture rule).

[437] *See generally* Beverly Moran, *supra* note 417, at 158–161; Eleanor Rich, *supra* note 418, at 71–81

[438] I.R.C. § 71(f).

first year exceed the average payments in the second two years by more than $15,000, the excess amount is recaptured in the third year. Similarly, payments in the second year that exceed those in the third year by more than $15,000 are recaptured in the third year. The calculations are made under a statutory formula.[439]

The current recapture rules apply to payments under instruments executed after December 31, 1986, and to earlier instruments modified after that date for the express purpose of meeting the current requirements.[440] The recapture rules do not apply to temporary support orders,[441] to payments to extend for a minimum of six years that are calculated as a fixed percentage of income of the payor's property, business, or compensation for employment or self-employment,[442] or to payments that cease upon the recipient's death.[443]

[B] Child Support Payments

Child support payments are not deductible for the payor nor included as income to the recipient.[444] In the past, pursuant to *Commissioner v. Lester*,[445] child support payments could be treated as alimony if the instrument establishing the payments was carefully drafted to avoid fixing a sum certain as child support and by incorporating the child support into an alimony payment. The 1984 Act overruled *Lester* and greatly reduced the opportunity to structure child support as deductible alimony. The current law regards payments as nondeductible child support if the payments to the recipient will be reduced on the occurrence of an event or contingency relating to the child or at a time that clearly can be associated with such contingency.[446] Applicable contingencies include events such as the child's reaching a specific age, marrying, or leaving school.[447] If, however, the payments are reduced on contingencies unrelated to the child, such as the remarriage of the former spouse, the payments may be treated as alimony, if they otherwise qualify.[448]

Whether payments are alimony or child support continue to raise questions, especially when payments to a former spouse are made in an

---

[439] *Id.*

[440] The 1984 Act contained a six-year minimum term and subjected payments varying by more than $10,000 in earlier years to recapture under a more complex formula. These provisions continue to apply to instruments executed after December 31,1984 and before January 1, 1987, unless modified thereafter expressly to adopt the 1986 rules, although a special transition rule retroactively amended the 1984 provisions to apply for only the first three years of payments. Tax Reform Act of 1986, 26 U.S.C. § 1843(c)(2)(3) (1986).

[441] I.R.C. § 71(f)(5)(B).

[442] I.R.C. § 71(f)(5)(C).

[443] I.R.C. § 71(f)(1).

[444] *See* Eleanor Rich, *supra* note 418, at 73–75.

[445] 366 U.S. 299 (1961)

[446] I.R.C. § 71(c).

[447] *See* I.R.C. § 71(a)(2)(A); T.D. 7973, 1984-2, C.B. 176.

[448] *See supra* § 9.07[A].

undifferentiated lump sum. Because the taxpayer has the burden of proving that the tax commissioner's determinations are erroneous, results in an individual case may appear inconsistent. For example, in *Roosevelt v. Commissioner of Internal Revenue*,[449] the Tax Court held that an unallocated family allowance, which had no portion specifically designated as child support, was taxable to the former wife as alimony. However, in *Folberg v. Commissioner of Internal Revenue*,[450] the tax court held, under similar facts, that an unallocated payment to the former spouse was child support and, therefore, was not deductible to the husband.

[C] Dependency Exemption for Children

Prior to 1984, the parent providing more than fifty percent of a child's support was entitled to claim the child as a dependent.[451] If the divorce decree specified that the non-custodial parent would take the exemption and that parent furnished at least $600 of the child's support, the exemption could be allocated to that parent.[452] Similarly, if the non-custodial parent provided at least $1200 in child support and the custodial parent could not establish that he or she furnished a greater amount, the non-custodial parent received the exemption.[453]

The dependency exemption rules were simplified under the current Code, providing that the parent who has custody of a child for the majority of the calendar year is entitled to a dependency exemption if the child receives over half of his or her support from the divorced or separated parents.[454] In cases of joint custody, the actual residence of the child controls.

If the custodial parent signs a written statement disclaiming the right to the exemption for a specified year and the non-custodial parent attaches that statement to the tax return, the noncustodial parent may claim the exemption.[455] The waiver can be executed on a yearly basis or made applicable to all years until the child reaches the age of majority. The non-custodial parent also may claim the exemption under a pre-1985 divorce or separation agreement that allocated the exemption to that parent if the parent provided at least $600 in support for the child.[456]

Some jurisdictions have held that the divorce court may allocate the dependency exemption without the agreement of the parties and order a custodial parent to execute a waiver.[457] Other courts have concluded that

---

[449] 70 T.C.M. (CCH) 612, T.C.M. (RIA) 95,430 (1995).

[450] 64 T.C.M. (CCH) 1527, T.C.M. (RIA) 92,713 (1992).

[451] I.R.C. § 151(e)(1)(A) & (B) (1954)(amended In 1984).

[452] I.R.C. § 152(e)(2)(A) (1954)(amended In 1984).

[453] *Id.* at § 152(e)(2)(B).

[454] I.R.C. § 152(e)(1) (1992).

[455] I.R.C. § 152(e)(2) (1992).

[456] I.R.C. § 152(e)(4) (1992).

[457] *See Fenner v. Fenner*, 599 So. 2d 1343 (Fla. Dist. Ct. App. 1992); *Singer v. Dickenson*, 588 N.E.2d 806 (Ohio 1992). *See generally* David Benson, *The Power of State Courts to Award the Federal Dependency Exemption Upon Divorce*, 16 U. Dayton L. Rev. 29 (1990); Joseph Landenwich, *Divorce and Amended Section 152(e) of the Internal Revenue Code: Do State Courts Have the Power to Allocate Dependency Exemptions?*, 29 J. Fam. L. 901 (1990–91).

federal law has preempted that option.[458]

A parent may also be entitled to a child care credit for certain employment-related child care expenses for a qualified child who is under the age of 15 or is incapable of self-care, regardless of allocation of the dependency exemption.[459] Furthermore, both parents can treat a child as a dependent for purposes of deducting medical expenses as long as the parents have actually paid the medical expense and meet certain other criteria.

[D] Deductibility of Legal Fees

In general, attorney fees incurred in a divorce or divorce related action are not deductible expenses. Personal living expenses and family expenses are not deductible,[460] while expenses incurred for producing income or managing, preserving or maintaining property for the production of income are deductible.[461] Deductibility in a divorce case depends on which of these categories attorney fees are allocated to, and claims for alimony and property may overlap the two classifications. In *United States v. Gilmore*, the Supreme Court held that assignment of attorney fees to either of these categories depends on whether the fees "arise in connection with the taxpayer's profit-seeking activities," rather than the effect on the party's property.[462] If the nature of the claim or defense arises from the marital relationship, not from income producing activity, the fee is non-deductible.[463] However, fees for advice regarding the tax implications of divorce have been held to be deductible if they are segregated from the rest of the divorce services rendered by the attorney.[464]

[E] Other Divorce Related Taxation Issues

[1] Transfer of Property

Before 1984, transfer of appreciated property from one spouse to the other pursuant to a divorce settlement could trigger recognition of gains or losses. Under *United States v. Davis*,[465] a transfer made as part of a property division was treated as a taxable event, comparable to a sale of the asset in exchange for release of the transferee's marital claims. The transferor was required to pay tax on the difference between the tax basis of the asset and its fair market value. The recipient received a basis measured by the

---

[458] *See Varga v. Varga*, 434 N.W.2d 152 (Mich. Ct. App. 1988); *Eichle v. Eichle*, 782 S.W.2d 430 (Mo. Ct. App. 1989).

[459] I.R.C. § 21.

[460] I.R.C. § 262.

[461] I.R.C. § 212.

[462] 372 U.S. 39, 48 (1963).

[463] *See* Homer Clark, *supra* note 7, at 704–705.

[464] *See Mann v. United States*, 455 F.2d 1028 (Ct. Cl. 1972); Rev. Rul. 72-545, 1972-2 C.B. 179.

[465] 370 U.S. 65 (1962).

fair market value of the property at the time of transfer, but was not required to include its value as income. One commentator has noted:

> While the *Davis* decision made theoretical tax sense, it made no practical sense. It frequently imposed a heavy tax burden at the worst possible time-when a couple's finances were in disarray and every available dollar was needed to finance the transition from one household into two. The taxable transfer was essentially involuntary because it was compelled by marital property law. Finally, the transfer produced no cash with which to pay the tax.[466]

However, equal divisions of community property were not treated as taxable, and courts and legislatures in non-community property jurisdictions soon began to adopt measures to effectuate the same result in those states. The result was "[a] deplorable state of confusion and complexity" in both types of jurisdictions, often catching divorcing parties and their lawyers unaware.[467]

Current I.R.C. § 1041 was enacted in 1984 to provide that property transfers between spouses during marriage or between spouses or former spouses incident to divorce are nontaxable transactions. Therefore, the transferor incurs no gain or loss and the transferee maintains the previous or "carryover" basis, without including the value as income.[468] To qualify, the transfer must occur within one year after the marriage ends or must be "related to the cessation of the marriage,"[469] which Treasury Regulations have defined as occurring pursuant to a divorce or separation instrument within six years after the marriage ends.[470] Certain transfers to third parties on behalf of a spouse may also qualify for such treatment.[471] If the property has appreciated, the recipient spouse will be taxed on the gain upon making a taxable disposition, such as a sale, of the asset. Therefore, an attorney must also be attentive to future tax implications of property transfers between spouses on divorce.[472]

[2]   Head of Household Status

A divorced or separated parent who has custody of a child usually will be entitled to the status of "Head of Household," which permits that party to be taxed at a lower filing rate.[473] The parent may be entitled to Head of Household status regardless of the allocation of the dependency exemption. To qualify, the parent must pay more than half of the cost of

---

[466] Michael Asimow, *The Assault on Tax-Free Divorce: Carryover Basis and Assignment of Income*, 44 Tax L. Rev. 65, 67 (1988).

[467] *Id.* at 68.

[468] I.R.C. § 1041. The general rule does not apply where the transferor is a nonresident alien. I.R.C. § 1041(d).

[469] I.R.C. § 1041 (c).

[470] T.D. 7973, 1984-2, C.B. 172.

[471] Treas. Reg. § 1.1041-IT, A-9.

[472] *See generally* Roland Hjorth, *The Effect of Federal Tax Consequences on Amount of Property Allocated to Spouses In State Court Dissolution Proceedings*, 24 Fam. L.Q. 247 (1990).

[473] *See* I.R.C. § 1(B) (1999).

maintaining a household for himself or herself and a child or a specified other dependent. When the parents have more than one child and each parent has custody of at least one child, both parents may qualify for head of household status.[474]

An abandoned spouse may also claim head of household status without divorce. That spouse must file a separate return, the other spouse may not have resided in the same household for the last six months of the year, and the household must have been the primary residence of a dependent child.[475] Head of household status is also available if the residence is the principal home for a dependent married child or parent.[476]

[3] Joint Returns

Marital status is determined on the last day of the year for purposes of eligibility for filing joint income tax returns.[477] Divorce or legal separation, but not informal separation, terminates marital status for filing joint returns.

Parties who file joint returns are jointly and severally liable for the tax.[478] To alleviate the hardship that joint and several liability may impose when one spouse was unaware of the other's significant understatement of tax liability, the "innocent spouse" rule relieves a spouse who signed a joint return from liability for taxes, penalties, and interest on substantial omitted income of which he or she had no knowledge.[479]

[4] The Family Home

In 1997, the Taxpayer Relief Act made important changes in taxation of gain on the sale of family homes, perhaps most importantly by providing for a tax-free sale of most family's homes.[480] After May 7, 1997, gain on the sale of a family home is taxable only to the extent that gain exceeds $250,000 for an individual or $500,000 for a couple if the home is sold in a year during which the couple files a joint tax return.[481] Qualifying homes must have been the couple's principal residence for two of the preceding five years.[482] The act also applies when one spouse is granted the exclusive use of the house following a divorce. When the house is later sold and the proceeds divided, the spouse who did not have possession will be treated as having possession for purposes of the exclusion.[483] This exclusion may be used every two years.[484]

---

[474] I.R.C. § 2(b) (1999).
[475] See I.R.C. §§ 2(c), 7703(b) (1999).
[476] I.R.C. § 2(b)(1)(A) (2001).
[477] I.R.C. § 6013(d)(1)(A) (1992).
[478] I.R.C. § 6013(d)(3).
[479] I.R.C. § 6013(e).
[480] I.R.C. § 121.
[481] I.R.C. § 121 (a), (b)(2)(A).
[482] I.R.C. § 121 (a).
[483] I.R.C. § 121(d)(3)(B).
[484] I.R.C. § 121(b)(3)(A).

[5] Retirement Plans

When a pension benefit is assigned to a spouse following a divorce pursuant to a Qualified Domestic Relations Order, the payee is taxed in the same manner as the original participant would have been, and no additional tax liability is incurred because of the assignment.[485] Annuities are taxed at the time of distribution, and are taxed only to the extent they were not previously taxed.[486] Similarly, lump sum payments are not taxed on original non-deductible contributions, and special rules avoid some of the harsh tax consequences of a single year payment on a lump sum distribution.[487] Alternatively, lump sum payments can be rolled over into an IRA or another qualified tax deferred retirement plan.[488]

[6] Stock Transfers and Redemptions

The transfer of stocks and bonds incident to divorce does not trigger tax consequences, and capital gains tax will not be incurred until the time that the recipient sells the stock.[489] The original basis of the stock is carried over. The rule applies to transfers of stock in closely held corporations as well as publicly traded stock.

When a family business is awarded to the proprietor spouse, an offset award to the other spouse is not taxable, regardless of whether it is paid at the time of divorce with other assets or a note. If the business is a closely held corporation, the matter may be complicated if a buy out is accomplished with corporate funds, called a stock redemption. Courts continue to differ as to the tax consequences of a stock redemption, because the transfer is to the corporation, and is not a transaction between the spouses. In *Arnes v. United States [Arnes I]*,[490] the Court of Appeals for the 9th Circuit held that such a transfer did relieve the proprietor spouse of an obligation, comprising a benefit. Therefore, the transaction did not constitute a recognizable gain to the non-proprietor spouse. In *Arnes v. Commissioner [Arnes II]*,[491] the tax court held that the transaction was not taxable to the husband, either, as he had not received any dividend in the transaction.[492]

[7] Federal Estate and Gift Taxes

No gift tax is imposed on transfers made in connection with divorce actions if the transfer is ordered in the divorce decree, is made according

---

[485] *See* Marjorie A. O'Connell, *Taxation of Employee Benefits: Qualified and Nonqualified Retirement Plans and Deferred Compensation Arrangements*, 30 Fam. L.Q. 91 (1996).

[486] *See* I.R.C. § 72.

[487] *See* I.R.C. § 402(e)(1)(B).

[488] *See* I.R.C. § 402(c)(3).

[489] *See* I.R.C. § 1041.

[490] 981 F.2d 456 (9th Cir. 1992).

[491] 102 T.C. 522 (1994).

[492] *See* Paul J. Buser and Thomas S. White, *Stock Redemption In Marital Separation Agreements: Unsteady Steps for the Unprepared*, 30 Fam. L.Q. 41 (1996).

to the terms of a property settlement agreement, or provides child support.[493] The transfer must be made within a period two years prior to or one year after the divorce.[494]

Similar provisions effectuate the same result for estate tax purposes. A transfer from a deceased spouse's gross estate is entitled to an unlimited marital deduction if the transfer was made pursuant to a divorce decree or a separation agreement that has become part of the decree.[495] The estate tax deduction is authorized if the agreement complies with the provisions for avoiding the gift tax.[496]

§ 9.08   Bankruptcy

Because of the expenses of divorce and the inadequacy of income available for supporting two households instead of one after divorce, it is not uncommon for one or both of the former spouses to file a bankruptcy action shortly after a divorce. Bankruptcy may affect the post-divorce financial obligations between former spouses.[497]

A primary, underlying policy of bankruptcy law is to give an honest debtor a "fresh start." The Supreme Court has described the fresh start as "a new opportunity in life . . . unhampered by the pressure and discouragement of pre-existing debt."[498] Accordingly, one of the most important features of bankruptcy law is to grant the debtor a discharge of most pre-bankruptcy debts, releasing the debtor from continued liability on those debts and preventing credits from attempting to collect them.[499] However, countervailing policies, deemed superior to bankruptcy law's fresh start policy, demand that the debtor remain liable for certain debts after bankruptcy and those debts are excepted from discharge.[500] Protecting a debtor's present or former family members has long been regarded as one of those overriding policy-based exceptions from discharge.

[A]   Support Obligations

Until 1994, bankruptcy law protected only support debts from the obligor's bankruptcy. The exception from discharge for family support debts originally was formulated by the United States Supreme Court in a trilogy

---

[493] I.R.C. § 2516 (1992).

[494] *Id.*

[495] I.R.C. §§ 2043(b)(2), 2053 (1992).

[496] I.R.C. §§ 2043(b)(2), 2053(e), 2516 (1992).

[497] *See generally* Margaret McGarity, "Family Law and the Bankruptcy Code," *Basis of Bankruptcy and Reorganization 1992*, at 531 (PLI Com. Law & Practice Course Handbook Series No. 630, 1992); Janet Chubb, Richard Holley, & James Greene, *Divorce and Bankruptcy: A Dangerous Liaison*, 4 Am. J. of Fam. L. 339 (1990).

[498] *See Local Loan Co. v. Hunt*, 292 U.S. 234, 244 (1934).

[499] 11 U.S.C. § 524 (1982 & Supp. 1988).

[500] 11 U.S.C. § 523(a) (exceptions from discharge In Chapter 7 and Chapter 11 cases); § 1328 (exceptions from discharge In Chapter 13 cases).

of cases at the beginning of this century,[501] Congress codified the exception in 1903, and the language of the support exception remained essentially unchanged until the enactment of the current Bankruptcy Code in 1978.[502] The current Bankruptcy Code prevents discharge of debts owed:

> to a spouse, former spouse, or child of the debtor, for alimony to, maintenance for, or support of such spouse or child, in connection with a separation agreement, divorce decree or other order of a court of record, determination made in accordance with State or territorial law by a governmental unit or property settlement agreement, but not to the extent that—
>
> (A) such debt is assigned to another entity, voluntarily, by operation of law, or otherwise (other than debts assigned pursuant to section 402(a)(26) of the Social Security Act, or any such debt which has been assigned to the Federal Government or to a State or any political subdivision of such State); or
>
> (B) such debt includes a liability designated as alimony, maintenance, or support, unless such liability is actually in the nature of alimony, maintenance, or support.[503]

Thus, the debtor's obligation to pay spousal and child support, whether accrued arrearages or future payments, will not be affected by the bankruptcy. However, to be excepted from discharge under section 523(a)(5), the debt must be "actually in the nature" of support. Until Congress enacted section 523(a)(15) in 1994, which makes certain property related debts nondischargeable also, debts that were classified as property division rather than support were discharged and extinguished, except to the usually insignificant extent they are paid off in the bankruptcy action.[504]

Determination of whether a debt should be categorized as support or property division for bankruptcy purposes has posed difficult classification problems and continues to generate an enormous volume of litigation.[505] The determination must be made under federal bankruptcy law, not state law, because bankruptcy law requires that the underlying nature of the debt, not merely its characterization in a court decree or marital settlement agreement, resolve the issue of its dischargeability.[506] Because support is

---

[501] *Wetmore v. Markoe*, 196 U.S. 68 (1904); *Dunbar v. Dunbar*, 190 U.S. 340 (1903); *Audubon v. Schufeldt*, 181 U.S. 575 (1901).

[502] Bankruptcy Act, ch. 487, 32 Stat. 797, 798 (1903). Section 17a(2) (later § 17a(7)) excepted from discharge debts "for alimony due or to become due, or for maintenance or support of wife or child."

[503] 11 U.S.C. § 523(a)(5) (1993).

[504] The former spouse will be treated as an ordinary creditor and will be entitled to share pro rata with other creditors of the same class in the distribution of the bankruptcy estate. However, few, if any assets, typically are available for such distribution. *See* Douglas Baird, The Elements of Bankruptcy 13 (1992).

[505] *See generally* Sheryl Scheible, *Defining "Support" Under Bankruptcy Law: Revitalization of the "Necessaries" Doctrine*, 41 Vand. L. Rev. 1 (1988).

[506] *See Long v. West (In re Long)*, 794 F.2d 928(4th Cir. 1986); *Shaver v. Shaver*, 736 F.2d 1314, 1316 (9th Cir. 1984).

a creation of state law, however, no federal law of support exists and the federal courts agree that state law must guide them in creating a federal standard, but the extent of that guidance has been unclear.

The currently accepted rule is that state-law principles in general, rather than the law of the particular state where the debt was created, should control the categorization of a debt for bankruptcy purposes.[507] Thus, the bankruptcy court will consider factors most often considered relevant by state courts generally in determining whether to grant support.[508] Those factors include, but are not limited to:

> the nature of the obligations assumed (provision of daily necessities indicates support); the structure and language of the parties' agreement or the court's decree; whether other lump sum or periodic payments were also provided; length of the marriage; the existence of children from the marriage; relative earning powers of the parties; the adequacy of support absent the debt assumption; and evidence of the negotiation or other understandings as to the intended purpose of the assumption."[509]

Because the law of the state where the debt arose will not control classification of the debt for bankruptcy purposes, debts that are labeled property division or were created pursuant to a property division may still be categorized as support and not subject to discharge;[510] conversely, the fact that an obligation was labeled support would not necessarily shield it from discharge.[511] However, the courts disagree as to the extent to which the language of a divorce decree or separation agreement itself will affect the determination. The majority of courts hold that the language of a decree or agreement is not determinative, although some courts place considerable importance on clear and unambiguous language.[512]

Courts generally will look behind the labels to determine the true nature of a debt. For example, in *In re Singer*,[513] the Court of Appeals for the Sixth Circuit concluded that a debtor's agreement to pay his former wife $800 a month for five years, then $400 a month for the next five years was nondischargeable support, despite the fact that the parties' separation agreement labeled the payments a release of property rights. Even in situations in which alimony would not have been authorized under state

---

[507] *See, e.g., Harrell v. Sharp (In re Harrell)*, 754 F.2d 902 (11th Cir. 1985); *Long v. Calhoun (In re Calhoun)*, 715 F.2d 1103 (6th Cir. 1983); *Pauley v. Spong (In re Spong)*, 661 F.2d 6 (2d Cir. 1981); *Yeates v. Yeates (In re Yeates)*, 44 B.R. 575 (Bankr. D. Utah 1984), *aff'd*, 807 F.2d 874 (10th Cir. 1986).

[508] *See Long v. Calhoun (In re Calhoun)*, 715 F.2d 1103, 1107–08 (6th Cir. 1983).

[509] *Id.* at 1108, n.7; *see also Goin v. Rives (In re Goin)*, 808 F.2d 1391 (10th Cir. 1987).

[510] *See, e.g., Singer v. Singer (In re Singer)*, 787 F.2d 1033 (6th Cir. 1986).

[511] *See, e.g., Roberts v. Poole*, 80 B.R. 81 (Bankr. N.D. Tex. 1987).

[512] *See, e.g., Clark v. Clark (In re Clark)*, 113 B.R. 797 (Bankr. S.D. Ga. 1990); *see also Long v. West (In re Long)*, 794 F.2d 928 (4th Cir. 1986) (holding that when an debt is designated alimony, although the label is not controlling, that designation is a significant factor in classifying a litigated award).

[513] 787 F.2d 1033 (6th Cir. 1986).

law, the payments may be considered "in the nature" of alimony or support for bankruptcy purposes.[514] Similarly, where no state law duty to pay post-majority child support exists, contractual agreements to do so have been found to constitute nondischargeable support.[515] However, debts owed to persons who were never validly married to the debtor are dischargeable. Therefore, the exception to discharge does not apply to debts owed under "palimony" agreements or to putative spouses.[516]

Bankruptcy courts generally concur that they should apply some version of an "intent" test to determine the nature of a marital debt.[517] Although the exact formulation of the intent test is not yet uniform, the analysis requires the court to discern whether the parties themselves, in a negotiated settlement agreement, or the court, in a litigated case, intended the debt to constitute support.[518] Intent, however, is frequently ambiguous and disputed, so the bankruptcy courts commonly balance the recipient spouse's needs against the supporting spouse's ability to pay, with regard to the marital standard of living to determine the reasonableness of the payment in light of the spouses' circumstances at the time of the divorce. Thus, if a debt *functioned* as support, the bankruptcy courts generally conclude that the requisite intention was present.[519] Because support is based on relative need, every disputed case will require an individualized investigation.

When divorce-related debts are payable directly to a spouse or child, the bankruptcy court immediately can proceed to determine whether those debts are in the nature of support and are therefore non-dischargeable. Frequently, however, the debtor will have agreed to or been ordered to make payments to a third party. These cases raise a preliminary question of whether a debt owed to someone other than a spouse, former spouse, or child still may be exempt from discharge under section 523(a)(5).

The statutory exception itself is worded in terms of debts owed "to" the spouse or child. The Bankruptcy Code also states that the debt may not be assigned to another entity if it is to be deemed nondischargeable under

---

[514] *See Benich v. Benich (In re Benich),* 811 F.2d 943 (5th Cir. 1987); *Balvich v. Balvich (In re Balvich),* 135 B.R. 323 (Bankr. N.D. Ind. 1991). *See generally* Frank Staggs, *Bankruptcy After Divorce: Rights and Liabilities of Former Spouses In Texas,* 23 S. Tex L.J. 173 (1982), for an analysis of cases arising in Texas, where alimony is not allowed under state law.

[515] *See Harrell v. Sharp (In re Harrell),* 754 F.2d 902 (11th Cir. 1985); *Boyle v. Donovan,* 724 F.2d 681 (8th Cir. 1984).

[516] *See Niermeyer v. Doyle, (In re Doyle),* 70 B.R. 106 (Bankr. 9th Cir. 1986) (nonmarital relationship between creditor and debtor is not the type of family arrangement creating family duties entitled to protection under the Bankruptcy Code); *see also In re Magee,* 111 B.R. 359 (M.D. Fla. 1990) (debt for support of debtor's illegitimate children not dischargeable, despite fact that mother was not debtor's former spouse because discharge would frustrate congressional intent that debtor should not be able to avoid child support obligations); Madison Grose, *Putative Spousal Support Rights and the Federal Bankruptcy Act,* 25 U.C.L.A. L. Rev. 96 (1977).

[517] *See, e.g., Yeates v. Yeates (In re Yeates),* 807 F.2d 874, 878 (10th Cir. 1986); *Smith v. Smith (In re Smith),* 131 B.R. 959 (Bankr. E.D. Mich. 1991).

[518] *See, e.g., Marker v. Marker (In re Marker),* 139 B.R. 615 (Bankr. W.D. Pa. 1992).

[519] *See, e.g., Long v. Calhoun (In re Calhoun),* 715 F.2d 1103 (6th Cir. 1983); *Daulton v. Daulton (In re Daulton),* 139 B.R. 708 (Bankr. N.D. Ill. 1992).

the support exception.[520] A 1984 amendment clarified that specified governmental units are excepted from this provision, allowing assignment when required for purposes of receiving public benefits. Furthermore, the section has been narrowly interpreted to mean that it is not necessary that the former spouse directly receive payment from the debtor; rather, the debtor's obligations to pay third parties for the benefit of a dependent may constitute nondischargeable support.[521] Some bankruptcy cases have also concluded that the provision does not apply when an assignment was made solely for the purpose of collection.[522]

Obligations to make specified future payments to third parties for the direct benefit of the former spouse or children, such as medical, educational, and insurance expenses, or payment of specified living costs, such as rent, mortgage payments, and utility bills, are usually analyzed in the same manner as debts payable directly to the spouse. In this context, courts generally disregard the fact that the actual recipient of the payments is not a dependent under the statutory terms.[523] In *In re Osterberg*,[524] the court concluded that the former husbands assumption of marital debts was essential to the wife's economic security and were nondischargeable maintenance and support.

A court order or separation agreement also frequently obligates a divorcing person to pay a dependent spouse's divorce-related expenses. Typically, when the question of dischargeability arises regarding obligations to pay attorney's fees, bankruptcy courts apply the same criteria used to classify direct support obligations.[525] Because state courts generally award attorney's fees on the basis of the spouse's need, bankruptcy courts consider these fees sufficiently related to support to escape discharge.[526] Similarly, courts have found attorney's fees for drafting documents in pre-divorce support actions, for post-divorce enforcement of decrees, or for defending modification actions to be nondischargeable.[527]

Many of the same courts that refuse discharge of attorney's fees take a much narrower view of other divorce related debts. For example, bankruptcy courts have allowed discharge of psychologist's fees incurred in custody hearings and fees of accountants hired to evaluate spousal assets.[528] Such cases have justified discharge by classifying the debt as one

---

[520] 11 U.S.C. § 523(a)(5)(A) (1993).

[521] *See, e.g., Edwards v. Edwards (In re Edwards)*, 31 B.R. 113 (Bankr. N.D. Ga. 1983).

[522] *See Brodsky v. Daumit (In re Daumit)*, 25 B.R. 371 (Bankr. D. Md. 1982). *But see Crawford v. Crawford (In re Crawford)*, 8 B.R. 552 (Bankr. D. Kan. 1981) (court-ordered attorney's fees payable to wife, otherwise classified as support, dischargeable when assigned to attorney).

[523] *See Williams v. Holt (In re Holt)*, 40 B.R. 1009 (Bankr. S.D. Ga. 1984).

[524] 109 B.R. 938 (Bankr. D.N.D. 1990).

[525] *See, e.g., Marks v. Catlow (In re Catlow)*, 663 F.2d 960 (9th Cir. 1981); *Pauley v. Spong (In re Spong)*, 661 F.2d 6 (2d Cir. 1981); *Bodrey v. Bodrey (In re Bodrey)*, 31 B.R. 589 (Bankr. M.D. Tenn. 1983).

[526] *See Senkel v. Fahland (In re Fahland)*, 110 B.R. 431 (Bankr. E.D. Mo. 1990).

[527] *See, e.g., Porter v. Gwinn (In re Gwinn)*, 20 B.R. 233 (Bankr. 9th Cir. 1982).

[528] *See Harrod v. Harrod (In re Harrod)*, 16 B.R. 711, 714 (Bankr. W.D. Ky. 1982).

owed to a party other than a dependent. Other courts have considered the substance of the debt and its relationship to support without regard to the identity of the payee.[529]

Difficult analytical problems arise when a spouse has agreed to, or was ordered to, assume sole responsibility for a debt incurred jointly by the spouses during marriage. Both former spouses have a continuing legal obligation to the joint creditor irrespective of an agreement made at the time of divorce; the assumption of the debt by one spouse is a secondary agreement that does not alter the underlying joint obligation to the third party creditor. Absent the creditor's release of the spouse, the assumption by the debtor merely indemnifies the spouse.[530] Thus, two debts are involved in the bankruptcy action, the debt owed directly to the third-party creditor, which is likely to be discharged to the extent it is unsecured, and the debt owed to the former spouse, which must be classified as either a support or property division debt to determine its dischargeability.

Courts have little difficulty concluding that the debtor may not be relieved of continuing liability to the spouse for an assumption simply because the underlying debt is owed to a third party when an express "hold-harmless" or indemnity clause is present.[531] Consequentially, courts are virtually unanimous In analyzing a hold-harmless agreement In the same manner as a direct obligation.[532] The courts have differed, however, when the debt assumption fails to provide such a clause. While many cases simply have held that an assumption itself implies an agreement to indemnify the former spouse for liability,[533] a number of courts have refused to extend the exception further and have granted discharge in the absence of an express hold-harmless provision, regardless of the effect of the debt's discharge on the dependents.[534]

A spouse's assumption of a joint obligation will always contribute to some extent to the other spouse's support, even if the debt arose from a property division, because the assumption frees additional funds that may used for support. The fact that a debt furnishes *some* degree of support, however, will not determine its classification for bankruptcy purposes.[535]

---

[529] See, e.g., Peters v. Hennenhoeffer (In re Peters), 133 B.R. 291 (Bankr. S.D.N.Y. 1991) (guardian ad litem fee incurred in custody dispute nondischargeable).

[530] See Williams v. Williams (In re Williams), 703 F.2d 1055, 1057 (8th Cir. 1983); Stevens v. French (In re French), 19 B.R. 255 (Bankr. M.D. Fla. 1982); Sledge v. Sledge (In re Sledge), 47 B.R. 349, 352 (Bankr. E.D. Va. 1981).

[531] See Williams v. Williams (In re Williams), 703 F.2d 1055, 1057 (8th Cir. 1983); Stevens v. French (In re French), 19 B.R. 255 (Bankr. M.D. Fla. 1982); Sledge v. Sledge (In re Sledge), 47 B.R. 349, 352 (E.D. Va. 1981).

[532] See Williams v. Williams (In re Williams), 703 F.2d 1055, 1057 (8th Cir. 1983); Stevens v. French (In re French), 19 B.R. 255 (Bankr. M.D. Fla. 1982); Sledge v. Sledge (In re Sledge), 47 B.R. 349, 352 (E.D. Va. 1981).

[533] See, e.g., Lewis v. Lewis (In re Lewis), 39 B.R. 842 (Bankr. W.D.N.Y. 1984); Jensen v. Jensen (In re Jensen), 17 B.R. 537 (Bankr. W.D. Mo. 1982).

[534] See, e.g., Lineberry v. Lineberry (In re Lineberry), 9 B.R. 700 (Bankr. W.D. Mo. 1981).

[535] See Long v. Calhoun (In re Calhoun), 715 F.2d 1103, 1108–09 (6th Cir. 1983).

The Sixth Circuit, in *In re Calhoun*,[536] proposed a three-step test for determining the nature of debt assumptions. First, the court must ascertain the court's or the parties' intention in creating the obligation by considering any relevant evidence, including the traditional criteria used by state courts in awarding support. If the requisite intent is absent, the inquiry ends, and the debt is dischargeable.

Once the court has found an intent to create a support obligation, the second inquiry under the *Calhoun* test is to determine if the assumption of liability has the effect of providing for support necessary to ensure that the daily needs of the former spouse and any children of the marriage are satisfied. Support, under *Calhoun*, means the amount intended and actually required to provide for the dependents' means of survival.

Calhoun's third, and most controversial, step requires a court to determine the reasonableness of the amount of support provided by the debt assumption in order to accommodate bankruptcy's fresh start policy. This step entails balancing the needs of the former spouse against the debtor's ability to pay. Any amount exceeding the ability to pay will not be classified as support, otherwise the debtor would forfeit the non-waivable right to discharge in bankruptcy. Furthermore, according to the *Calhoun* court, if the debtor's circumstances have changed since the time of the initial agreement to the extent that the amount of support is currently inequitable, the court may consider the debtor's current ability to pay "insofar as it relates to the continuing obligation to assume the joint debts," and may terminate or reduce the obligation accordingly.[537]

While most of the *Calhoun* opinion today is considered standard doctrine, and is applicable to the analysis of direct obligations as well as assumptions, its examination of present circumstances remains highly controversial.[538] If the bankruptcy courts consider the circumstances existing at the time of bankruptcy, the result is a federal modification of a state support obligation. The appellate courts of several circuits have flatly denied that present circumstances have any relevancy in dischargeability determinations.[539] The viability of the present circumstances test remains uncertain in the other federal circuits.

[B] Property Division Debts

In 1994, the bankruptcy code was amended to add section 523(a)(15), which makes property division debts presumptively nondischargeable. In order to avoid discharge under § 523 (a)(15), a debt must arise out of a divorce related agreement or court order, but not constitute support. The

---

[536] 715 F.2d 1103 (6th Cir. 1983).

[537] *Id.* at 1110, n.11.

[538] *See generally* Sheryl Scheible, *Bankruptcy and the Modification of Support: Fresh Start, Head Start, or False Start?*, 69 N.C.L. Rev. 577 (1991).

[539] *See Gianakas v. Gianakas (In re Gianakas)*, 917 F.2d 759 (3d Cir. 1990); *Sylvester v. Sylvester*, 865 F.2d 1164 (10th Cir. 1989); *Forsdick v. Turgeon*, 812 F.2d 801 (2d Cir. 1987); *Draper v. Draper*, 790 F.2d 52 (8th Cir. 1986); *Harrell v. Sharp (In re Harrell)*, 754 F.2d 902 (11th Cir. 1985).

debt will be nondischargeable unless the debtor does not have the ability to pay or that the "benefit to the debtor . . . outweighs the detrimental consequences to the creditor, the former spouse, or child."[540] Although the exceptions seem to raise affirmative defenses to the nondischargeability, the courts remain conflicted as to where the burden of proof for each element should be allocated.[541] In *In re Patterson*,[542] the Court of Appeals for the 6th Circuit held that the bankruptcy court had not erred when it concluded that the debtor did not meet his burden of proving an inability to pay his debt to his former wife, despite his evidence that his expenditures and child support payments exceeded his income and that he had injured his hand, which restricted his work. The bankruptcy court had found the evidence regarding the injury unpersuasive, and found that the debtor currently had excess income and thus an ability to pay the court ordered debt. In analyzing the balancing of the detriments test, the court held that the debt should not be discharged if the debtor's standard of living would be greater than or approximately equal to the former spouse's if the debt is not discharged.

Some courts have responded to the balancing test necessary under § 523(a) (15) by allowing a partial discharge of the debt.[543] Other cases have rejected this approach, because the code does not mention the potential for partial discharge.[544] The addition of § 523(a) (15) has strengthened the hold harmless clause in marital settlement agreements, as the clause may protect other previously dischargeable obligations

[C] Marital Liens

Although the bulk of bankruptcy cases involving family law issues have addressed the classification of marital debts for dischargeability purposes, bankruptcy and family law overlap in other contexts as well.[545] Another controversial issue involves the effect of bankruptcy on liens imposed to secure debts originating in divorce.

The United States Supreme Court addressed the question of whether a judicial lien imposed upon the debtor's exempt property to secure an obligation owed to a former spouse may be avoided by the debtor in a bankruptcy action. In *Farrey v. Sanderfoot*,[546] the husband had been awarded title to the marital home and other assets in a litigated property division. To equalize the property division, the divorce court awarded the wife half the value

---

[540] § 523(a) (15).

[541] *See* Bernice B. Donald & Jennie D. Latta, *The Dischargeability of Property Settlement and Hold Harmless Agreements In Bankruptcy: an Overview of § 523(a) (15)*, 31 Fam. L. Q 409, 420–21 (1997).

[542] 132 F.3d 33 (6th Cir. 1997).

[543] *See, e.g., In re Greenwalt*, 200 B.R. 909, 914 (Bankr. W.D. Wash. 1996); *In re Comisky*. 183 B.R. 883, 884 (Bankr. N.D. Cal. 1995).

[544] *See, e.g., In re Haines*, 202 B.R. 586, 592 (Bankr. S.D. Cal. 1997); *In re Florez*, 191 B.R. 112, 115 (Bankr. N.D. Ill. 1995).

[545] *See generally* Janet Chubb, *supra* note 497, at 339.

[546] 111 S. Ct. 1825 (1991).

of the parties' net estate, $29,208.44 in cash, payable in two equal installments. The court ordered a lien placed on the house to secure this debt.

Several months after the divorce decree, the husband filed his Chapter 7 bankruptcy action. He claimed the home as exempt property and moved to avoid the lien on the house under a Bankruptcy Code provision which allows a debtor to avoid the fixing of judicial liens which impair an exemption.[547] The bankruptcy court denied his motion, but the district court reversed, and the Seventh Circuit affirmed the reversal.

The Supreme Court reversed, holding that the lien was not avoidable because it had not fixed on an interest of the debtor in the property. It reasoned that because the parties had conceded that the wife had a pre-divorce interest in the property because of Wisconsin's enactment of the Marital Property Act, the judicial lien thus attached to her prior interest, not to the husband's previous interest. Therefore, the lien did not fix "on an interest of the debtor" in the property as required for avoidance under the Bankruptcy Code.[548]

Thus, when a judicial lien is created concurrently with or prior to the debtor's obtaining an interest in the property on which the lien is imposed, the lien cannot be destroyed in the bankruptcy action.[549] Because timing is critical under the *Sanderfoot* rationale, judicial liens imposed as part of a divorce action still risk being avoided in bankruptcy if they attach to a pre-existing property interest of the debtor. The result may vary depending on the underlying state marital property law.[550]

[D] Automatic Stay

Family law issues also arise in the setting of the Bankruptcy Code's automatic stay provisions, which bar most debt collection actions and suspend law suits against the debtor during the bankruptcy action.[551] Enforcement of alimony and child support obligations, as well as determinations of paternity, are excepted from the stay to the extent that satisfaction

---

[547] 11 U.S.C. § 522(f)(1) (1993).

[548] 111 S. Ct. at 1831.

[549] *See generally* Phyllis Klein, Comment, *A Fresh Start With Someone Else's Property: Lien Avoidance, The Homestead Exemption and Divorce Property Division Under Section 522(f)(1) of the Bankruptcy Code*, 59 Fordham L. Rev. 423 (1990).

[550] *Compare In re Donovan*, 137 B.R. 547 (Bankr. S.D. Fla. 1992) (divorce attorney's lien attached prior to client's ex-wife's interest in marital home; not avoidable by debtor-wife) *and Brockman v. Brockman (In re Brockman)*, 143 B.R. 703 (Bankr. S.D. Iowa 1992) (award of debtor's interest in farm equipment and lien attached simultaneously; not avoidable) *with Wright v. Wright (In re Wright)*, 135 B.R. 871 (Bankr. W.D. Mo. 1992) (lien attached to property owned by debtor prior to marriage; avoidable) *and Parrish v. McVay (In re Parrish)*, 144 B.R. 349 (Bankr. W.D. Tex. 1992) (lien attaching to debtor's separate property; avoidable). *See generally* Brady Williamson & Timothy Nixon, *The Malpractice Trap in Divorce Court Liens*, 14 Fam. Advoc. 48 (Winter 1992).

[551] 11 U.S.C. § 362; *see also Robbins v. Robbins (In re Robbins)*, 964 F.2d 342 (4th Cir. 1992) (stay lifted to allow equitable distribution to proceed in state court). *See generally* Henry Sommer, *The Automatic Stay Packs a Punch*, 14 Fam. Advoc. 50 (Winter 1992); Michaela White, *Spousal and Child Support Payments in Chapter 13 Plans*, 16 Cap. U. L. Rev. 369 (1987).

of these support obligations is made from assets that are not property of the bankruptcy estate.[552] Because this exception to the stay also turns on classifying the obligation as support, if collection of support might violate the automatic stay, the recipient should seek relief from the stay in the bankruptcy court.[553]

[E] Exempt Property

Bankruptcy law and family law may also intersect when the recipient of divorce-related payments files a bankruptcy. For instance, the right to receive alimony, support, or maintenance "reasonably necessary for the support of the debtor and any dependent of the debtor" is exempt property and is not liable for payment of the debtor's debts in the bankruptcy case.[554] Although the problems of classification of debts owed to a debtor by a former spouse could also arise in the exemption context, virtually no litigation has occurred on the right to exempt such payments.

Family law attorneys should be informed about bankruptcy law so they are able to structure divorce settlements that anticipate the possibility of later bankruptcy and to deal with the many family law issues that arise when, in fact, bankruptcy occurs. Pre-divorce bankruptcy planning may also be valuable when financial problems and marital problems coincide.[555]

---

[552] 11 U.S.C. § 362(b)(2).

[553] 11 U.S.C. § 362(d)(1); *see Carver v. Carver*, 954 F.2d 1573 (11th Cir. 1992) (reversing $18,000 fine imposed on wife for violation of stay in husband's Chapter 13 action by pursuing contempt action in state court for failure to pay support).

[554] 11. U.S.C. § 522(d).

[555] *See* Jefferson Giles, *Till Debt Do Us Part: Prebankruptcy Planning for Your Divorce Client*, 14 Fam. Advoc. 23 (Winter 1992).

Chapter 10

EQUITABLE DISTRIBUTION OF PROPERTY

§ 10.01 Introduction

Prior to the widespread adoption of equitable distribution statutes throughout the United States, a spouse was entitled to receive the property held in his name upon dissolution of marriage. Simply stated, except for the small minority of states in which community property principles were in force, title to property was the controlling factor. A leading commentator has summarized the common law approach to property division upon marriage dissolution as follows:

> Under the common law no property rights arise during marriage by virtue of the marriage itself. Since the Married Women's Property Acts were enacted giving the wife control over her separate property, there has been a complete separation of assets.Only at death, through dower, curtesy and, more recently, statutory forced shares, does one spouse acquire any interest in the property of the other by operation of law. . . . At [the time of divorce] the common law recognized no property interests by virtue of the marriage alone. In the absence of a statute, the courts of many states . . . had no power to order transfers or divisions of property.[1]

Wirth v. Wirth[2] is frequently cited as a shocking illustration of the harshness and injustice of the common law approach to disposition of property acquired during the marriage through the joint efforts and mutual endeavors of the spouses. In *Wirth*, during twenty-two years of marriage the husband gave his earnings to the wife, who pooled them with her own to support the family, paid bills and made investments. In time, the husband started a savings program, telling the wife that it was for the two of them. During most of the marriage, the wife used her salary for household expenses and family support while the husband invested part of his earnings in his own name.

The court rejected the wife's claim, based on a constructive trust theory, to half ownership of the marital home, titled in the husband's name, and half of his life insurance. The court found that there was no promise or arrangement in the husband's stated intention to save for the two of them or in any of the parties' conduct thereafter during the marriage.

---

[1] Krauskopf, *A Theory for "Just" Division of Marital Property in Missouri*, 41 Mo. L. Rev. 165, 167–168 (1976) (citations omitted).

[2] 326 N.Y.S.2d 308 (N.Y. App. Div. 1971)

§ 10.02 Community Property Origins

Equitable distribution of property in the United States is an outgrowth of the systems of community property introduced into the Western Hemisphere by Spanish and French settlers.[3] A leading treatise describes the theory that underlies community property as follows:

> Equality is the cardinal precept of the community property system. At the foundation of this system is the principle that all wealth acquired by the joint efforts of the husband and wife shall be common property; the theory of the law being that, with respect to marital property acquisitions, the marriage is a community of which each spouse is a member, equally contributing by his or her industry to its prosperity, and possessing an equal right to succeed to the property after its dissolution.[4]

A community property system has long existed in eight states: Arizona, California, Idaho, Louisiana, Nevada, New Mexico, Texas, and Washington. Under community property law, the property that a spouse owned at the time of the marriage, together with property acquired during marriage by gift or inheritance, remained that person's separate property.[5] Also, unless there was an agreement to the contrary between the spouses, all property acquired during the marriage was the property of both spouses, regardless of whose effort had led to its acquisition.[6] This system grew out of the principle that "upon their marriage, the husband and wife become partners in future business transactions with each devoting his or her own time and talent, as joint entrepreneurs, in furtherance of that enterprise."[7]

In 1983, the National Conference of Commissioners on Uniform State Laws approved the Uniform Marital Property Act (UMPA).[8] The UMPA adopts a partnership concept of marriage, based on the principle of shared ownership of property during the marriage. Professor William S. Reppy, Jr., a distinguished scholar who has written extensively on community property law, describes the UMPA as a community property act, albeit not a typical one.[9] Wisconsin, by enacting the UMPA with minor modifications[10] has joined the ranks of community property states.

---

[3] Lay, *Community Property: Its Origin and Importance to the Common Law Attorney*, 5 J. Fam. L. 51 (1965).

[4] W. DeFuniak & M. Vaughn, Principles of Community Property 2–3 (1971).

[5] Lay, *supra* note 3, at 54–55.

[6] *Id.*

[7] *Id.*

[8] 9A ULA 97 (West 1987) (hereinafter UMPA).

[9] Reppy, *The Uniform Marital Property Act: Some Suggested Revisions for a Basically Sound Act*, 21 Hous. L. Rev. 679 (1984).

[10] Wis. Stat. Ann. §§ 766.001 to 766.97 (West Supp. 1988–1989).

§ 10.03   Characterizing Property for the Purpose of Equitable Distribution

In cases involving the equitable distribution of property upon dissolution of marriage, the courts face three basic tasks. First, they must undertake classification of assets, identifying those that are subject to distribution and those that will remain the separate property of each spouse. The second task is valuing those assets that are subject to distribution and, in some instances, those that will be assigned separately to one of the spouses. The third task is deciding on a distribution that will be equitable, just and fair.[11] In this section, we turn to the first of these subjects, characterization or classification.

The statutes of each state provide the rules for classifying property subject to distribution on dissolution of marriage. Equitable distribution statutes in a slim majority of states, and particularly those statutes most recently enacted, employ a dual property system for classification of assets. Dual property jurisdictions make a distinction between marital property, which is subject to distribution, and separate property, which is assigned to the spouse having title.[12]

[A]   Dual Property Equitable Distribution Jurisdictions

In dual property states, marital property is generally defined to include all property acquired by either spouse (or party) subsequent to or during the marriage. Property acquired before the marriage is generally defined as separate property. There is, however, considerable variation in statutory language. A basic variation lies in the approach to the definition of marital property.

The first most common statutory approach defines marital property and then lists exceptions. The second defines marital property and then explicitly defines separate or nonmarital property. Although the precise wording is different in these two types of dual property statutes, the substance or effect is the same. That is, both types of statutes limit distribution to marital property, and the exceptions listed in the first group of statutes are generally equivalent to the definitions of nonmarital or separate property in the second group. Also, although dual property statutes explicitly limit distribution to marital property, in a few jurisdictions the courts under some circumstances have included property acquired in contemplation of marriage as eligible for distribution.[13]

---

[11] See, e.g., Rothman v. Rothman, 320 A.2d 496, 503 (N.J. 1974); Lancellotti v. Lancellotti, 481 A.2d 7, 10 (R.I. 1984).

[12] See, e.g., Colo. Rev. Stat. § 14-10-113(2) (1989); Ill. Ann. Stat. ch. 40, para. 503(a) (Smith-Hurd Supp. 1985); Mo. Ann. Stat. § 452.330 (Vernon 1985); N.Y. Dom. Rel. Law § 236 pt. B (McKinney 1986).

[13] The decisions suggest that when the parties acquire property shortly before their marriage with the intent that it be used as the family residence, the courts are willing to divide the property on the theory that it was acquired in contemplation of marriage. The courts in most cases appear to be reluctant, however, to so classify and distribute property acquired during premarital cohabitation; in such cases, the courts generally adopt a literal interpreta-

Under either statutory approach in dual property jurisdictions, the most common categories of separate or nonmarital property are:

1. Property acquired by gift, bequest, devise, or descent;

2. Property acquired in exchange for separate property;

3. The increase in value (appreciation) of separate property;

4. Property excluded by a valid agreement between the parties;

5. Property acquired by a spouse after a decree of legal separation.

Whether a jurisdiction defines marital property and lists exceptions or contains a definition of marital property followed by explicit definitions of separate property, lawyers must carefully examine the applicable statute. Although most statutes include the items commonly listed as separate property, they are found in differing combinations with varying additions and omissions. The New York statute, for example, includes within the meaning of the term "separate property" compensation for personal injuries and excludes the increase in value of separate property attributable to the contributions or efforts of the other spouse.[14]

[B] All Property Equitable Distribution Jurisdictions

A slim minority of equitable distribution states do not distinguish between marital property and separate property for purposes of property distribution upon dissolution of marriage. Although there are substantial variations in the language of the statutes in those jurisdictions, the result is essentially the same. The Montana statute is illustrative. It provides in broad terms that the court must "finally equitably apportion between the parties the property and assets belonging to either or both, however and whenever acquired and whether the title thereto is in the name of the husband or wife or both."[15] The Connecticut statute, framed in somewhat more economical language, achieves the same result by providing that the court "may assign to either the husband or wife all or part of the estate of the other."[16] Interpreting Indiana's all property statute,[17] the state's

---

tion of the statutory definition of marital property. *See In re Marriage of Altman*, 530 P.2d 1012 (Colo. Ct. App. 1974) ("Where . . . a family residence is selected and acquired within a few days of the parties' marriage in contemplation of that marriage, and the equity accumulated therein results from contributions by both parties, . . . the court [may treat] the residence and all equity obtained therein as marital property." *Id.* at 513; *Stallings v. Stallings*, 393 N.E.2d 1065 (Ill. App. Ct. 1979) (Real estate, purchased in contemplation of marriage with the intent that it would be the family home, was marital property); *see also In re Marriage of Ohrt*, 507 N.E.2d 160 (Ill. App. Ct. 1987). Other courts, however, have declined to classify property acquired by a spouse during premarital cohabitation as marital property, finding their conclusions to be compelled by the applicable equitable jurisdiction statute. *See, e.g., Grishman v. Grishman*, 407 A.2d 9 (Me. 1979) ("We cannot expand the definition the Legislature has provided to encompass property to which the husband took title before this couple were married.") *Id.* at 12; *Cummings v. Cummings*, 376 N.W.2d 726 (Minn. Ct. App. 1985); *Wilen v. Wilen*, 486 A.2d 775 (Md. Ct. Spec. App. 1985).

[14] N.Y. Dom. Rel. Law § 236(B)(d)(2)-B(d)(3) (McKinney 1986).

[15] Mont. Code Ann. § 40-4-202(1) (1983).

[16] Conn. Gen. Stat. Ann. § 406-81(a) (West 1986).

[17] Ind. Code Ann. § 31-11.5-11(b) (West 1979).

intermediate appellate court held that the statute's "one pot theory . . . specifically prohibits the exclusion of any assets from the scope of the trial court's power to divide and award."[18]

Despite the fact that all property in these jurisdictions is subject to division upon dissolution of marriage, the lawyer who represents either party in a divorce proceeding must be aware of the nature and origins of the property to which each party holds title, and must be familiar with the statutory factors the court must consider in making an equitable distribution. These circumstances may influence the manner in which the property is distributed. In Montana, for example, although the statute provides for the distribution of all property, it lists a number of factors the court must consider in disposing of certain kinds of property that would in most cases be classified as separate property in a dual property jurisdiction. The kinds of property listed are property acquired prior to marriage or its increased value; property acquired by gift, bequest, devise, or descent or its increased value; and property acquired in exchange for such property or acquired subsequent to legal separation. In distributing such property, the court must consider certain contributions to the marriage by the other spouse.[19]

In addition to making the nature and origin of the property a relevant consideration in distribution, all property statutes typically contain other factors that the court must consider in dividing property between the spouses. Taken together, the statutes contain a dazzling array of factors in combinations that defy classification. Accordingly, it cannot be overemphasized that the lawyer or student must pay careful attention to the explicit statutory provisions in a given jurisdiction.[20]

§ 10.04   Characterizing Property as Marital or Separate: Change in Classification

A significant set of issues confronted by courts and practitioners in dual property jurisdictions concerns the circumstances, events, or transactions that may cause a change in the character of property from separate property to marital property, and on occasion from marital to separate. Generally, this change in character or classification affects property that was wholly or partly acquired prior to marriage.

---

[18] *In re Marriage of Dreflak*, 393 N.E.2d 773, 776 (Ind. Ct. App. 1979).

[19] *See* Mont. Code Ann. § 40-4-202(1) (1987).

[20] A few examples are illustrative. The North Dakota statute simply requires the court to "make such equitable distribution of the real and personal property of the parties as may seem just and proper . . . having regard to the circumstances of the parties respectively." N.D. Cent. Code § 14-05-24 (1981); the Hawaii statute requires the court to consider "the respective merits of the parties, the relative abilities of the parties, the condition in which each party will be left by the divorce, the burdens imposed upon either party for the benefit of the children of the parties, and all other circumstances of the case." Haw. Rev. Stat. § 580-47(a) (1985). The statute in Vermont lists twelve explicit relevant factors that the court may consider. Vt. Stat. Ann. title 15, § 751(b) (Supp. 1988).

[A] The Marital Property Presumption

The equitable distribution statutes of several states contain a presumption that all property acquired by either party during marriage is marital property, regardless of how title is held.[21] For the most part these statutes explicitly provide that the presumption may be overcome by a showing that the property was acquired by a method listed in the exceptions to the definition of marital property. The presence or absence of this presumption in a statute does not appear to affect the burden of proof, which rests upon the party who seeks to show that property is separate or nonmarital. Depending on the wording of the statute, the party must prove either that the property was acquired in a manner listed in an exception or that the property was acquired in a manner described in the definition of separate property.

The fact that the marital property presumption is not set out explicitly in the statute of a given jurisdiction does not necessarily mean that the courts of a given state have not adopted it. The Supreme Court of New Jersey, for example, judicially created the presumption without reliance on statutory authority.[22]

[B] Judicial Development of Classification Rules

To deal with issues of characterization and changes in characterization of property, the courts in equitable distribution jurisdictions with dual property statutes have adopted or developed several basic rules or theories. These include inception of title, source of funds, and transmutation.

[1] Inception of Title

The inception of title rule derives from community property law and currently prevails in community property states. According to inception of title, property is classified as of the time that title is first taken. A typical case involves the husband's purchase of real property prior to marriage, making a down payment and giving a note payable in installments and secured by a mortgage. During the marriage mortgage payments are made with funds that are marital property. The wife will have no cognizable claim to equitable distribution on divorce. Once the property acquires the status of separate property, that status does not change, regardless of the application of marital funds to satisfy indebtedness or eliminate an encumbrance.

Although the inception of title rule was adopted in a series of opinions by intermediate appellate courts in Missouri, it did not gain favor in other equitable distribution states. The Supreme Court of Missouri ultimately

---

[21] *See, e.g.,* Colo. Rev. Stat. § 14-10-113(3) (1989); Del. Code. Ann. tit. 13, § 1513(c) (1981 & Supp. 1992); Fla. Stat. Ann. § 61.075(5) (West Supp. 1992); Ill. Ann. Stat. ch. 40, para. 503(b) (Smith-Hurd Supp. 1980); Ky. Rev. Stat. Ann. § 403.190(3) (Michie/Bobbs Merrill 1984 & Supp. 1992); Minn. Stat. Ann. § 518.54(5) (West 1990 Supp. 1993); Mo. Ann. Stat. § 452.330(3) (Vernon 1986); 23 Pa. Cons. Stat. § 3501(b) (1991); Va. Code Ann. § 20-107.3(A)(2) (Michie Supp. 1992).

[22] *See Painter v. Painter,* 320 A.2d 484 (N.J. 1974).

rejected inception of title[23] and adopted the source of funds theory.[24] Inception of title continues to be of some significance for the practitioner in a dual property state. Conceptually, it is the point of departure for the development of the currently evolving source of funds approach for the characterization of property for the purposes of equitable distribution.

[2] Source of Funds

Courts in a number of dual property states have explicitly rejected the inception of title theory. Rather than classifying property in accordance with the time of obtaining title, these courts have looked to the source of each contribution as payments are made. The decision of the Maryland Court of Special Appeals in a leading case, *Harper v. Harper*,[25] is illustrative. The court in *Harper* framed the issue before it in two parts. The first question was whether a parcel of real property purchased by the husband under a land installment contract and paid for in part prior to the marriage and in part during marriage was marital property. The second question was whether the marital home erected on the property during marriage was marital property.

In a lengthy and scholarly opinion, the court reviewed decisions from Maine, Missouri and Illinois, as well as those from a number of community property states. Explicitly rejecting the inception of title and transmutation[26] theories, the court stated:

> We conclude that . . . the appropriate analysis to be applied is the source of funds theory. Under that theory, when property is acquired by the expenditure of both nonmarital and marital property, the property is characterized as part nonmarital and part marital. Thus, a spouse contributing nonmarital property is entitled to an interest in the property in the ratio of the nonmarital investment to the total nonmarital and marital investment in the property. The remaining property is characterized as marital property and its value is subject to equitable distribution. Thus, the spouse who contributed nonmarital funds, and the marital unit that contributed marital funds each receive a proportionate and fair return on their investment.[27]

In applying the source of funds theory, the Maryland court followed the teaching of the Supreme Judicial Court of Maine in *Tibbetts v. Tibbetts*,[28] defining the statutory term "acquired" to mean "the on-going process of making payment for property,"[29] making the classification of property dependent on the source of each contribution as payments are made, rather

---

[23] *See Hoffman v. Hoffman*, 676 S.W.2d 817 (Mo. 1984).

[24] *See infra* § 10.04[B][2].

[25] 448 A.2d 916 (Md. Ct. Spec. App. 1982).

[26] *See infra* § 10.04[B][3].

[27] *Harper*, 448 A.2d at 929.

[28] 406 A.2d 70 (Me. 1979).

[29] *Harper*, 448 A.2d at 929.

than the time of obtaining title. A number of other equitable distribution states have used similar reasoning in adopting the source of funds theory. [30]

[3] Transmutation

Like the inception of title rule, [31] the transmutation doctrine has its origins in the law of community property. Broadly stated, transmutation involves the process, based on the intent of the parties, by which separate property is altered in character and becomes marital or community property. Also, but less frequently, marital property may be transmuted to separate property. When the evidence shows the parties' intent to change the character of the property, the courts generally have reclassified the property based on this intent, often without explicit reference to "transmutation."

Courts faced with the task of distributing marital property in divorce proceedings frequently hold that separate assets may be so commingled with marital property that they do not retain their identity as separate, but are transmuted to marital property. The court's decision in *Jaeger v. Jaeger* [32] is both typical and illustrative. In *Jaeger*, the husband used the proceeds of sales of both separate and marital property to purchase new property. Addressing the question of whether the newly acquired property was marital, separate, or a mixture of the two, the court said:

> We believe that the proper result under the statute is that the newly acquired property so purchased constitutes marital property, irrespective of the state of title of the newly acquired asset. We reach this result relying on the presumption created by the statute that property acquired subsequent to the marriage is marital property. . . . In commingling his own assets with marital assets, the spouse has failed to sufficiently segregate his own property. Such commingling is indicative of an intent on the part of the owner of the pre-marriage property to contribute it to the marital estate. [33]

Transmutation may also be based on donative intent. In *Quinn v. Quinn* [34] for example, the Supreme Court of Rhode Island upheld the lower court's division of property based on transmutation, citing the transmutation doctrine as consistent with the partnership theory of marriage. The court classified as marital property the proceeds from the sale of real estate that the husband had inherited. The court justified its reasoning on the grounds that the proceeds had been placed into a joint account and that later some of the funds were used to purchase property in which the husband and wife held a joint tenancy. The court also held that investment

---

[30] *See, e.g., Gregg v. Gregg,* 474 So. 2d 262 (Fla. Dist. Ct. App. 1985); *Brandenberg v. Brandenberg,* 617 S.W.2d 871 (Ky. Ct. App. 1981); *Hoffman v. Hoffman,* 676 S.W.2d 817 (Mo. 1984); *Wade v. Wade,* 325 S.E.2d 260 (N.C. Ct. App. 1985).

[31] *See supra* § 10.04[B][1].

[32] 547 S.W.2d 207 (Mo. Ct. App. 1977).

[33] *Id.* at 211.

[34] 512 A.2d 848 (R.I. 1986).

securities, which were partly purchased with inherited funds, were marital property. The court held that "when marital and nonmarital assets are commingled and then exchanged for other property, the newly acquired asset is marital property."[35]

Divorce courts in recent years have accepted the transmutation doctrine with increasing frequency.[36] In *Smoot v. Smoot*,[37] for example, the Virginia Supreme Court construed that state's equitable distribution statute so as to adopt the transmutation theory and reject the source of funds approach. *Smoot* involved the source of the funds used for the construction of a home on property owned by the husband and wife as joint tenants. The funds for the construction consisted of a $25,000 construction loan and $20,000 contributed by the husband. The court's construction of the statute was based primarily on the explicit definition provided for "marital" and "separate" property, which, the court ruled, had effectively left no room for a hybrid of the two definitions. The court also relied on the marital property presumption contained in the statute and the provision that separate property must be maintained as separate property. These reasons led the court to conclude that when "a spouse fails to segregate and instead commingles, separate property with marital property, the chancellor must classify the commingled property as marital property subject to equitable distribution."[38]

[C] Tracing

A party may, in some jurisdictions, defeat the characterization of property as marital property by "tracing" separate property into assets acquired during the marriage. As one court has stated, "[t]he tracing of funds is a procedure which allows the court to find that property which would otherwise fall within the definition of marital property is actually nonmarital property under one of the exceptions."[39] Tracing is a difficult procedure, particularly in long marriages or where liquid assets rather than real property are involved. The party seeking to identify the property as separate has the burden to prove that separate property was given in exchange for marital assets. Tracing has been criticized as discouraging the partnership theory of marriage by rewarding the spouse who carefully accounts for what is his or hers. Courts that prefer to "expand the scope of divisible estates" can limit the success of tracing by finding that separate property has commingled with or transmuted into marital property.[40]

In *Chenault v. Chenault*[41] the Supreme Court of Kentucky Court of Kentucky rejected the assertion that a party seeking to prove through

---

[35] *Id.* at 853.

[36] *See, e.g., Umber v. Umber*, 591 P.2d 299 (Okla. 1979); *Kendall v. Kendall*, 367 S.E.2d 437 (S.C. Ct. App. 1988).

[37] 357 S.E.2d 728 (Va. 1987).

[38] *Id.* at 731; *see also Lambert v. Lambert*, 367 S.E.2d 184 (Va. Ct. App. 1988); *Marion v. Marion*, 401 S.E.2d 432 (Va. Ct. App. 1991).

[39] *In re Marriage of Scott*, 407 N.E.2d 1045 (Ill. App. Ct. 1980).

[40] *See* Oldham, *Tracing, Commingling and Transmutation*, 23 Fam. L.Q. 219, 249 (1989).

[41] 799 S.W.2d 575 (Ky. 1990).

tracing the nonmarital character of property must do so withe documentary evidence and with almost mathematical precision. The court observed:

> While such precise requirements for nonmarital asset-tracing may be appropriate for skilled business persons who maintain comprehensive records of their financial affairs, such may not be appropriate for persons of lesser business skills or persons who are imprecise in their record-keeping abilities. This problem is compounded in a marital union where one spouse is the recorder of financial detail and the other is essentially indifferent to such matters. Moreover, such a requirement may promote marital disharmony by placing a premium on the careful maintenance of separate estates. [42]

§ 10.05　Appreciation of Separate Property During Marriage

As discussed, in dual property states, property acquired before the marriage is generally defined as separate property. [43] Other categories of property may also be defined as separate under a variety of statutory provisions. [44] A number of dual property statutes deal with the question of whether the increase in value of property acquired before marriage, or otherwise classified as separate, is treated as separate property or marital property. In some states, the increase in value, or amount of appreciation, is classified as marital property. In others, the increase in value is treated as separate property. Even in these latter jurisdictions, however, the treatment accorded to appreciation may depend on whether or not the increase in value is attributable, in whole or in part, to the contribution of the nontitled spouse. Again, even if the applicable statute designates the increase in value of separate property as separate, some jurisdictions, applying the source of funds rule, have classified the appreciation as marital because of spousal contributions to separate property. [45]

When characterizing the increase in value of property, courts frequently make a critical distinction between active appreciation and passive appreciation. In *Rogers v. Rogers*, [46] the Supreme Court of Appeals of West Virginia, applying that state's equitable distribution statute, provided typical and serviceable definitions. The court defined passive appreciation of separate property as an increase "which is due to inflation or to a change in market value resulting from conditions outside the control of the parties," and which is not subject to equitable distribution. [47] Active appreciation, on the other hand, is an increase that "results from . . . an expenditure of funds which are marital property, including an expenditure of such funds which reduces indebtedness against separate property, extinguishes liens, or

---

[42] *Id.* at 578.

[43] *See supra* § 10.03[A].

[44] *Id.*

[45] *See, e.g., Hoffman v. Hoffman*, 676 S.W.2d 817 (Mo. 1984); *Hall v. Hall*, 462 A.2d 1179 (Me. 1984).

[46] 405 S.E.2d 235 (W. Va. 1991).

[47] *Id.* at 239; *see* W. Va. Code § 48-2-1(f)(6) (1986).

otherwise increases the net value of separate property, or . . . work performed by either or both of the parties during the marriage".[48] Active appreciation of separate property will be classified under this approach as marital property eligible for distribution on marriage dissolution. Accordingly, in *Rogers*, where the increase in value of separate property was attributable solely to illegal mining underneath the property, the court held that the appreciation was the result of market factors beyond the parties' control and, therefore, not distributable as marital property.

As we have noted, the characterization of the increase in value of property during marriage may also depend upon whether the appreciation is caused, in whole or in part, by contributions by the nontitled or non owning spouse. In several states, the applicable statute explicitly classifies as marital property appreciation attributable to the contributions or efforts of the nonowner.[49] Courts applying such statutes have not reached consistent results when determining whether a spouse's indirect contributions, such as homemaker services, will qualify. In *Brandenberg v. Brandenberg*,[50] for example, the court held that the only contributions to be considered with respect to the increase in value were marital funds or nonmarital funds of the nontitled spouse. Other efforts or contributions, such as homemaker contributions, although they were to be considered in dividing marital property, were not to be considered with respect to the increase in value of nonmarital property.

In *Price v. Price*,[51] a leading case, the New York Court of Appeals took a sharply different view with respect to contributions to the appreciation of separate property in the indirect form of homemaker services. *Price* involved a husband who received a large amount of stock in a family corporation by gift and subsequently became the sole owner of the corporation when its outstanding shares were redeemed. The wife gave up her outside employment upon the birth of their first child to devote all of her efforts to being a homemaker and parent. The dispute arose concerning the appreciation of the stock of the corporation.

Relying on the economic partnership theory of marriage, the court stated:

> The Equitable Distribution Law reflects an awareness that the economic success of the partnership depends "not only upon the respective financial contributions of the partners, but also on a wide range of non-remunerated services to the joint enterprise, such as homemaking, raising children and providing the emotional and moral support necessary to sustain the other spouse in coping with the vicissitudes of life outside the home" (*see* Governor's Memorandum, McKinney's Session Laws of N.Y., 1980, p. 1863).[52]

---

[48] *Id.*; *see* W. Va. Code § 48-2-1(e)(2) (1986).

[49] *See, e.g.*, Ky. Rev. Stat. Ann. § 403.190(2)(e) (Michie/Bobbs-Merrill Supp. 1986); NY Dom. Rel. Law § 236(B)(d)(3) (McKinney 1986); S.C. Code Ann. § 20-7-473(5) (Law. Co-op. 1986); Tenn. Code Ann. §§ 36-4-121(b)(2) (Supp. 1986); W. Va. Code § 48-2-1(e)(2) (1986).

[50] 617 S.W.2d 871 (Ky. Ct. App. 1981).

[51] 503 N.E.2d 684 (N.Y. 1986).

[52] *Id.* at 687.

In keeping with the active appreciation-passive appreciation distinction,[53] the court held:

> As a general rule, however, where the appreciation is not due, in any part, to the efforts of the titled spouse but to the efforts of others or to unrelated factors including inflation or other market forces, as in the case of a mutual fund, an investment in unimproved land, or in a work of art, the appreciation remains separate property, and the nontitled spouse has no claim to a share of the appreciation.[54]

Other courts have applied statutory provisions governing increases in value of separate property in the identical manner as the court in *Price*. In *Goderwis v. Goderwis*[55] for example, the husband devoted virtually all of his time during the course of an 18-year marriage to an auto repair business that he had started before the marriage. The Supreme Court of Kentucky affirmed a holding that the increase in value of the business during the marriage was marital property. After noting that increases in value due to general economic conditions are not marital property, the court held that the opposite is true when the increase is the result of the joint efforts of the parties. The court explicitly recognized indirect contributions of the nontitled spouse, stating: "The efforts of the parties may include the contribution of one spouse as a primary operator of the business and the other spouse as primarily a homemaker."[56]

The equitable distribution statutes of several states do not state directly whether the increase in value during marriage of separate property is to be treated as marital or separate. A number of court decisions in these states, however, have addressed the issue, reaching results generally consistent with the decisions discussed in this section that rely on explicit statutory provisions.[57] The Maryland Court of Appeals, for example, in *Harper v. Harper*,[58] has applied the source of funds theory[59] to appreciation of separate property. The court in *Harper* held that "a spouse contributing non-marital property is entitled to an interest in the property in the ratio of the non-marital investment to the total non-marital and marital investment in the property."[60] Accordingly, when the wife contributed her separate funds toward the improvement of the separate property of her husband, marital funds also having been contributed, she was entitled to

---

[53] *See supra* notes 46–48, and accompanying text.

[54] 503 N.E.2d at 687; *see also* S.C. Code Ann. § 20-7-473(5) (Law. Co-op. 1986) (includes in definition of nonmarital property "any increase in value of nonmarital property, except to the extent that the increase resulted directly or indirectly from efforts of the other spouse during marriage.").

[55] 780 S.W.2d 39 (Ky. 1989).

[56] *Id.* at 40.

[57] *See, e.g., Mol v. Mol*, 370 A.2d 509 (N.J. Super. Ct. App. Div. 1977); *Palmer v. Palmer*, 455 N.E.2d 1049 (Ohio Ct. App. 1982); *Templeton v. Templeton*, 656 P.2d 250 (Okla. 1982); *Plachta v. Plachta*, 348 N.W.2d 193 (Wis. Ct. App. 1984).

[58] 448 A.2d 916 (Md. 1982).

[59] *See supra* § 10.04[B][2].

[60] 448 A.2d at 929.

a percentage of the entire value of the property, including appreciation, represented by her contributions.

In *Cockrill v. Cockrill,*[61] the Supreme Court of Arizona, a community property state, rejected the husband's assertion that the increase in value of a farm operation that the husband owned before marriage was separate property, and also declined to classify it as community property. Refusing to accept the all or none doctrine from other jurisdictions, the court held that "when the value of separate property is increased the burden is upon the spouse who contends that the increase is also separate property to prove that the increase is the result of the inherent value of the property itself and is not the product of the work effort of the community".[62] Accordingly, the court remanded the case to the trial court for apportionment of the increase in value between the husband's separate property and the community property.

§ 10.06   Gifts and Inheritances

[A]   Statutory Approaches

Statutes in the vast majority of dual property states explicitly classify gifts and inheritances (generally, property acquired by bequest, devise or descent) as separate or nonmarital property. In a slight majority of all property jurisdictions the equitable distribution statutes are silent with respect to property acquired by gift or inheritance. Courts interpreting these statutes have permitted distribution of such property in a variety of circumstances.[63] In other all property jurisdictions, the typical statutory treatment of gifts and inheritances is to include them among the factors the court must consider in dividing the marital estate or to list their source of acquisition as a factor. The Indiana statute is illustrative of this latter approach, providing in pertinent part: "In determining what is just and reasonable, the court shall consider the following factors: . . . (2) the extent to which the property was acquired by each spouse prior to the marriage or through inheritance or gift."[64]

[B]   Judicial Treatment

Among a variety of issues the courts have addressed in connection with the characterization of gifts and inheritances, the most commonly encountered and significant involve (1) acquisition by gift or inheritance by either spouse from a third party, (2) transfers to the spouses jointly, (3) inter-spousal transfers, and (4) whether or not an asset is a gift.

---

[61] 601 P. 2d 1334 (Ariz. 1979).

[62] *Id.* at 1336.

[63] *See, e.g., Ahlo v. Ahlo,* 619 P.2d 112 (Haw. 1980); *In re Marriage of Jenks,* 656 P.2d 286 (Or. 1982); *Goehry v. Goehry,* 354 N.W.2d 192 (S.D. 1984).

[64] Ind. Code Ann. § 31-15-7-4(West 2001); Wyo. Stat. § 20-2-114 (1986) (requiring the court to consider" the party through whom the property was acquired").

[1] Gifts or Inheritances From a Third Party to Either Spouse

Under various statutory formulations, the courts have generally held that gifts or inheritances from a third party to one of the spouses are nonmarital or separate property. The Appellate Court of Illinois, for example, reached this result under a statute that contains the presumption, set out in a number of dual property statutes, that all property acquired by either spouse during the marriage is marital property.[65] The court concluded that acquisition of property by gift was a method of acquisition that overcomes the presumption of marital property.[66]

The decision of the Supreme Court of Alaska in *Julson v. Julson*[67] is also instructive, holding that an inheritance received during marriage was not distributable, even though the Alaska statute provides for "division between the parties of their property, whether joint or separate, acquired only during coverture. . .".[68] The court noted that the decision was consistent with its "view of equitable distribution in general, which recognizes the partnership theory of marriage and considers the mutual effort and tangible contributions of the parties rather than the mere existence of the marital relationship."[69] In *Gaulrapp v. Gaulrapp,*[70] the husband and wife each received gifts during the marriage. The Supreme Court of North Dakota held that it was error to exclude from the marital estate gifts to the wife that were in cash and not segregated from other marital assets. The court noted that both the length of the marriage and the origins of the property were relevant and that "redistribution of gifted property may often be equitable in long-term marriages."[71]

[2] To the Spouses Jointly

Almost invariably, the courts treat transfers to the spouses jointly through gift or inheritance as property eligible for equitable distribution upon marriage dissolution in both all property and dual property jurisdictions, reaching the same result under varying statutory formulations.[72] The

---

[65] *See supra* § 10.04[A].

[66] *In re Marriage of Cook*, 453 N.E.2d 1357 (Ill. App. Ct. 1983).

[67] 741 P.2d 642 (Alaska 1987).

[68] Alaska Stat. § 25.24.160(a)(4) (Supp. 1988).

[69] *Julson*, 741 P.2d at 642 (citations omitted); *see also Van Newkirk v. Van Newkirk*, 325 N.W.2d 832 (Neb. 1982).

[70] 510 N.W. 2d 620 (N.D. 1994).

[71] *Id.* at 62.

[72] *See, e.g., In re Marriage of Wendt*, 339 N.W.2d 615 (Iowa Ct. App. 1983) (holding that gift to both parties is jointly acquired property, divisible in the same way as other jointly held marital assets); *Van Newkirk v. Van Newkirk*, 325 N.W.2d 832 (Neb. 1982) (reaffirming earlier authority that gifts or inheritances acquired by one of the parties were ordinarily not part of the marital estate, but holding that a gift to both husband and wife is includable); *Darwish v. Darwish*, 300 N.W.2d 399 (Mich. Ct. App. 1981) (holding that wedding gifts that were to be enjoyed and used jointly should be considered the same as property purchased jointly by the spouses).

decision in *Forsythe v. Forsythe*,[73] a leading case, is illustrative. The trial court in *Forsythe* set aside to the wife property, the source of which was a gift from the wife's parents to the parties as husband and wife. Reversing, the Missouri Court of Appeals accepted the husband's claim that a gift to both husband and wife was marital property subject to distribution. The court noted that the Missouri statute defined marital property to mean "all property acquired by either spouse subsequent to the marriage," listing as one of the exceptions "property acquired by gift, bequest, devise, or descent."[74] The statute also contained a marital property presumption.[75] After reviewing the intent and purpose of the statute, the court concluded:

> The purpose of [the statutory provision] which by mention exempts from division only a gift to *either* spouse is to treat as marital property a gift to *both* spouses. From this we conclude that the integral Act intends for the court to divide and settle title to all property which has come to the spouses by virtue of the marriage relation.[76]

[3]   Interspousal Transfers

Cases addressing the transfer of property between the spouses contain a variety of approaches. Interspousal transfers are likely to result in the characterization of the transferred property as marital in cases where one spouse transfers property into joint tenancy or tenancy by the entirety.

A common statutory formulation explicitly characterizes such transfers as marital property. In *In re Marriage of Deem*,[77] the husband and wife took title as tenants by the entirety to property acquired during marriage with the wife's separate funds. Subsequently, the spouses transferred the property to the wife by warranty deed. The husband argued on appeal that there was insufficient evidence to prove that the transfer was a gift and, therefore, nonmarital property. The court, noting the marital property presumption in the Illinois statute, held that the party seeking to exclude property acquired during the marriage from distribution has the burden of proving by clear and convincing evidence that the property was a gift. Considering that the deed itself was not sufficient to prove a gift, the court ordered the property to be treated as marital on remand.[78]

In *Roig v. Roig*,[79] however, where the trial court included in the marital estate the value of jewelry and furs that the husband and his aunt had given to the wife, the Supreme Court of Appeals of West Virginia reversed. The court held that "it was obviously the intent of the legislature to allow one spouse to transfer property to the other spouse by irrevocable gift and

---

[73] 558 S.W.2d 675 (Mo. Ct. App. 1977), *aff'd*, 591 S.W.2d 222 (Mo. Ct. App. 1979).

[74] Mo. Rev. Stat. § 452.330(2)(1) (1986).

[75] Mo. Rev. Stat. § 452.330(3) (1986).

[76] *Forsythe*, 558 S.W.2d at 678 (emphasis in original).

[77] 463 N.E.2d 1317 (Ill. App. Ct. 1984).

[78] *See also In re Marriage of Severns*, 416 N.E.2d 1235 (Ill. Ct. App. 1981).

[79] 364 S.E.2d 794 (W. Va. 1988).

thereby remove assets so transferred from inclusion in the marital estate."[80] The court cautioned, however, that in every instance the spouse claiming the gift has the burden of proof.[81] In *O'Neill v. O'Neill*,[82] the husband presented jewelry and other personal items to his wife on her birthday, at Christmas, and on other occasions, all of which items were paid for from the husband's salary. The Kentucky Court of Appeals noted that classification turns on the pertinent facts in each case, including the source of the purchase money, the donor's intent, the status of the marriage and the like. Accordingly, because the husband had purchased the items as an investment, hoping that an increase in value could be turned to cash for the children's education, the items were not a gift.

The Supreme Judicial Court of Maine, in *Carter v. Carter*,[83] classified an interspousal transfer of the husband's separate property as marital property. In *Carter*, the husband conveyed to himself and his wife, by joint tenancy warranty deed, certain real property that he had acquired before marriage. The court held that the statutory gift exception to marital property was not applicable to transfers from one spouse to the spouses jointly. Absent clear and convincing evidence to the contrary, the conveyance demonstrated an intention to transfer the property to the marital estate.

Property acquired with marital funds is likely to be characterized as marital property, regardless of a subsequent interspousal transfer. In *McArthur v. McArthur*,[84] a case of first impression, the Supreme Court of Georgia held that property acquired during marriage remains marital property, despite any subsequent transfers between the spouses. In *McArthur*, the parties purchased with joint funds a house that became the marital home. The house was titled in the husband's name at the time of purchase. Subsequently, he deeded the property to the wife and title remained in her name.

The wife contended that the house was a gift to her and, therefore, separate property. The husband argued that he intended no gift, nor did he intend to give up his equitable interest in the home. Having reviewed the judicial treatment of interspousal gifts in several other jurisdictions, the court embraced the view of the District of Columbia Court of Appeals in *Hemily v. Hemily*,[85] looking "to the source of the money with which the 'gift' was purchased. Thus, if a gift from one spouse to another was purchased with marital funds, the 'gift' remains marital property subject to equitable division."[86]

The courts of Missouri and Pennsylvania, in varying factual contexts, have classified interspousal transfers as marital property. In *Dildy v.*

---

[80] *Roig*, 364 S.E.2d at 798.

[81] *See* W. Va. Code § 48-3-10 (1984).

[82] 600 S.W. 2d 493 (Ky. Ct. App. 1980).

[83] 419 A. 2d 1018 (Me. 1980).

[84] 353 S.E.2d 486 (Ga. 1987).

[85] 403 A.2d 1139 (D.C. 1979)

[86] *McArthur*, 353 S.E.2d at 488, n.3.

Dildy,[87] the Missouri Court of Appeals classified as marital property stocks that the husband transferred as an inter vivos gift to himself and his wife as joint tenants. Similarly, the Superior Court of Pennsylvania held, under a statute excepting gifts from distribution and containing a marital property presumption, that bonds placed by the husband in joint ownership with his wife were subject to distribution.[88] Again, in *Semasek v. Semasek*,[89] the Pennsylvania court affirmed the trial court's determination that jewelry was purchased by the husband with money from his salary, which was a marital asset. Although the purchase changed the form of the asset, it remained marital property includable for distribution.

[4] Was There a Gift?

In determining how transfers of property by gift should be classified for the purpose of equitable distribution, lawyers and courts must occasionally face the question of whether, as a matter of definition, a transfer is a gift at all.

McGlone v. McGlone[90] sharply presents the question. The case concerned a grant from the Veterans Administration (VA) to the husband, a totally disabled career serviceman who was confined to a wheelchair. The husband received the grant during marriage. The parties used the funds in part to defray the costs of constructing and designing special features of the marital residence to accommodate the husband's physical handicaps. The divorce court found that the grant was marital property subject to division. On appeal, the Supreme Court of Kentucky, having reviewed the federal statute that entitled the husband to the grant, concluded that the grant was not awarded for military service but was made pursuant to an authorization for the VA to make gifts to veterans with disabilities similar to the husband's. The court held that the grant was a gift within the meaning of the Kentucky statute and, accordingly, should have been classified as nonmarital property.

In the course of interpreting the New Jersey statute, which excepts gifts from equitable distribution, the Superior Court of New Jersey has identified the hallmarks of a gift. The court noted that "[a]'gift' is a transfer without consideration, . . . requiring an unequivocal donative intent on the part of the donor, actual or symbolic delivery of the subject matter of the gift, and an absolute and irrevocable relinquishment of ownership by the donor."[91] Consistent with this definition, the Missouri Court of Appeals has held that a conveyance of real property that was conditioned upon lifetime care for the decedent was a contract for services rather than a gift.[92]

---

[87] 650 S.W.2d 324 (Mo. Ct. App. 1983).

[88] *Madden v. Madden*, 486 A.2d 401 (Pa. Super. Ct. 1984).

[89] 479 A.2d 1047 (Pa. Super. Ct. 1984).

[90] 613 S.W.2d 419 (Ky. 1981).

[91] *Sleeper v. Sleeper*, 446 A.2d 1220, 1222 (N.J. Super. Ct. App. Div. 1982) (citations omitted).

[92] *Cochenour v. Cochenour*, 642 S.W.2d 402 (Mo. Ct. App. 1982).

§ 10.07   Personal Injuries and Workers' Compensation

[A]   Introduction

Equitable distribution jurisdictions have reached varying results in the treatment of compensation for personal injuries or workers' compensation benefits. In any given jurisdiction, however, for the most part, the courts afford these two types of assets similar treatment. Therefore, we treat them here as a single subject. Equitable distribution statutes generally contain no explicit reference to the treatment or characterization of personal injury claims and awards or workers' compensation. The New York statute is a notable exception. In its definition of "separate property," the statute includes "compensation for personal injuries."[93]

[B]   Approaches to Classification

There are two predominant approaches to the division of personal injury awards, commonly described as the mechanistic approach and the analytic or purpose approach. The analytic approach originated in community property states. Under this method of classification, recovery for lost wages and for medical expenses paid out of marital funds is deemed distributable marital property. Recoveries for pain and suffering or for the injury itself, on the other hand, are classified as nonmarital or separate property. The mechanistic approach was adopted in a number of the earlier decisions in dual property states. This method does not divide the personal injury claim or award into component parts.

The highest courts of several states have considered the characterization of personal injury and workers' compensation proceeds. The decisions suggest a trend toward preference for the analytic approach. The decision of the supreme Court of Appeals of West Virginia in *Hardy v. Hardy*[94] a case of first impression, is instructive. In *Hardy*, the husband and wife recovered separate judgments for injuries to the husband and for loss of consortium and nursing services by the wife. In the subsequent divorce proceeding, the wife asserted that the husband's personal injury award was marital property subject to equitable distribution.

The court noted that several early decisions in a number of states had concluded that a personal injury award was marital property. As the court observed, these decisions "were generally based upon a purely mechanical reading of statutory definitions of marital and separate property."[95] That is, under the mechanistic approach adopted in these decisions, if an award was acquired during the marriage and did not fall within an explicit

---

[93] N.Y. Dom. Rel. Law § 236(B)(1)(d)(2) (McKinney 1986).

[94] 413 S.E.2d 151 (W. Va. 1991).

[95] *Id.* at 154.

exception to the definition of marital property or within the definition of separate property, it was marital property.[96]

Ultimately rejecting the mechanistic approach, the court in *Hardy* observed that in recent years an increasing number of state courts "have classified personal injury settlements under a framework referred to as the analytical, or purpose, approach, which draws a distinction between the economic loss suffered by the marital partnership and the economic and personal loss suffered by each individual spouse and asks what a personal injury award was intended to replace."[97] Accordingly, the court in *Hardy* concluded that a personal injury recovery should be characterized based on its purpose. The court held:

> [To] the extent that its purpose is to compensate an individual for pain, suffering, disability, disfigurement, or other debilitation of the mind or body a personal injury award constitutes the separate nonmarital property of an injured spouse. However, economic losses, such as past wages and medical expenses, which diminish the marital estate are distributable as marital property when recovered in a personal injury award or settlement. The burden of proving the purpose of part or all of a personal injury recovery is on the party seeking a nonmarital classification.[98]

The Supreme Court of Oklahoma, consistent with the trend noted, followed the analytical approach with respect to a workers' compensation award, holding in *Crocker v. Crocker*[99] that the award was marital property "only to the extent to which it reimburses the couple for loss of income during the marriage."[100] It is separate property, however, insofar as it is compensation for loss of the injured spouse's post-divorce earnings, even though the injury occurred during marriage.[101]

§ 10.08 Licenses, Degrees and Enhanced Earnings

[A] Overview

The overwhelming majority of courts that have addressed the issue have concluded that a professional license or degree is not marital property. The

---

[96] *See, e.g., Clayton v. Clayton*, 760 S.W.2d 875 (Ark. 1988); *In re Marriage of Fjeldheim*, 676 P.2d 1234 (Colo. Ct. App. 1983); *In re Marriage of Burt*, 494 N.E.2d 868 (Ill. App. Ct. 1986); *Nixon v. Nixon*, 525 S.W.2d 835 (Mo. Ct. App. 1975); *Maricle v. Maricle*, 378 N.W.2d 855 (Neb. 1985); *Platek v. Platek*, 454 A.2d 1059 (Pa. Super. Ct. 1982); *Bero v. Bero*, 367 A.2d 165 (Vt. 1976); *Richardson v. Richardson*, 407 N.W.2d 231 (Wis. 1987).

[97] *Hardy*, 413 S.E.2d at 154.

[98] *Id.* at 156.

[99] 824 P.2d 1117 (Okla. 1991).

[100] *Id.* at 1118.

[101] *See also Bandow v. Bandow*, 794 P.2d 1346 (Alaska 1990) (applying analytic approach to annuity given in settlement of medical malpractice claim); *Weisfeld v. Weisfeld*, 545 So. 2d 1341 (Fla. 1989) (applying analytic approach to workers' compensation award); *Kirk v. Kirk*, 577 A.2d 976 (R.I. 1990) (applying analytic approach to personal injury settlements and workers' compensation benefits).

highest court of only one state, New York, has reached a contrary result, and panels of the Michigan Court of Appeals are split on the question. With these exceptions, the courts unanimously have declined to characterize a degree or license as property.

Many courts, however, using a variety of theories, have provided remedial relief in one form or another to the "non-degreed" or supporting spouse. The relief has generally consisted of reimbursement of funds spent for the education or support of the degree-earning spouse, or consideration of the spousal contribution in a maintenance award or in the division of marital property. Also, some courts have held, or recognized in dicta, that enhanced earning capacity is a appropriate consideration in the distribution of marital property on marriage dissolution.

[B] Statutory Treatment

For the most part, equitable distribution statutes are silent with respect to the characterization or treatment of professional licenses or degrees. There are a few exceptions. The North Carolina statute, in its definition of "separate property," provides: "All professional licenses and business licenses which would terminate on transfer shall be considered separate property."[102] The Indiana statute states, in pertinent part:

> (d) If the court finds there is little or no marital property, the court may award either spouse a money judgment not limited to the property existing at the time of final separation. However, this award may be made only for the financial contribution of one (1) spouse toward tuition, books, and laboratory fees for the higher education of the other spouse.[103]

In Ohio, among the factors that the court must consider in awarding spousal support is "the contribution of each party to the education, training, or earning ability of the other party, including, but not limited to, any party's contribution to the acquisition of a professional degree of the other party."[104]

[C] Degree or License Not Property

In re Marriage of Graham,[105] a landmark decision of the Supreme Court of Colorado, presents on its facts what has become virtually the paradigmatic case of the treatment of licenses and degrees for the purpose of the equitable distribution of property. In *Graham*, the parties were divorced after a relatively brief marriage (six years), during which they accumulated no significant marital assets. The husband attended school for about three and a half years of the marriage, earning a bachelor's degree and a master's degree while the wife worked full time. The wife contributed 70 percent

---

[102] N.C. Gen. Stat. § 50120(b)(2) (1984).

[103] Ind. Code Ann. § 31-15-7-6 (West 2001).

[104] Ohio Rev. Code § 3105.18(C) (1991).

[105] 574 P.2d 75 (Colo. 1978).

of the spouses' finances, which were devoted both to family expenses and to the husband's education. The trial court found that the husband's education was jointly held property in which the wife had a property right and valued the husband's MBA degree at $82,836. Of this, the court awarded the wife $33,134, payable in monthly installments of $100. The Colorado court of appeals reversed and remanded, and certiorari was granted.

Affirming the judgment denying the wife relief, the Supreme Court of Colorado observed in a passage so frequently quoted as to become the pervasive rationale in subsequent license or degree cases:

> An educational degree, such as an M.B.A., is simply not encompassed even by the broad views of the concept of "property." It does not have any exchange value or any objective transferable value on an open market. It is personal to the holder. It terminates on death of the holder and is not inheritable. It cannot be assigned, sold, transferred, conveyed, or pledged. An advanced degree is a cumulative product of many years of previous education, combined with diligence and hard work. It may not be acquired by the mere expenditure of money. It is simply an intellectual achievement that may potentially assist in the future acquisition of property. In our view, it has none of the attributes of property in the usual sense of that term.[106]

In a lengthy and carefully reasoned opinion, the Supreme Court of New Jersey, in *Mahoney v. Mahoney*,[107] stated a variety of reasons why the value of a professional degree (MBA) earned during marriage was not property for the purposes of equitable distribution. The court pointed out that although "New Jersey courts have subjected a broad range of assets and interests to equitable distribution including vested but unmatured pensions," the Supreme Court had "never subjected to equitable distribution an asset whose future monetary value is as uncertain and unquantifiable as a professional degree or license."[108]

Citing the decision in *Graham* with approval, the court observed that distribution of a professional degree would involve distributing the earning capacity relating to speculative future earnings. Further, valuation of the degree at the threshold of the holder's career "would involve a gamut of calculations that reduces to little more than guesswork."[109] Finally, miscalculation of the value of the license or degree would result in unfairness, with the finality of the property division precluding any remedy.[110] Accordingly, although the court enunciated several theories under which the supporting spouse might receive remedial relief,[111] it adopted the overwhelming majority view excluding a license of degree from equitable distribution.

---

[106] *Id.* at 77.

[107] 453 A.2d 527 (N.J. 1982).

[108] *Id.* at 531.

[109] *Id.* at 532.

[110] *Id.*

[111] *See infra* § 9.08[E].

The opinions of the highest courts of other jurisdictions, while often not as carefully or thoroughly reasoned as *Mahoney*, have not departed significantly from the principle enunciated in *Graham*, that a license or degree is not property.[112] In several states, where the issue of classification of a professional license or degree has not yet reached the highest court, trial courts and intermediate appellate courts have, with rare exceptions, reached the same conclusion, denying distribution of licenses or degrees.[113] The only dissent from this unanimous view among appellate courts is found in several decisions from Michigan, where panels of the Court of Appeals have taken contrary views on the question.[114]

[D]   Degree or License as Marital Property

In *O'Brien v. O'Brien*,[115] the New York Court of Appeals held that a medical license was marital property within the meaning of the state's equitable distribution statute and was, therefore, subject to equitable distribution. *O'Brien* is the first and only unequivocal holding to this effect by the highest court of any state.[116]

In *O'Brien*, after about two and a half years of marriage, the parties moved from New York to Guadalajara, Mexico, where the husband became

---

[112] *See, e.g., Nelson v. Nelson*, 736 P.2d 1145 (Alaska 1987); *Wilson v. Wilson*, 741 S.W.2d 640 (Ark. 1987); *In re Marriage of Francis*, 442 N.W.2d 59 (Iowa 1989); *Sweeney v. Sweeney*, 534 A.2d 1290 (Me. 1987); *Drapek v. Drapek*, 503 N.E.2d 946 (Mass. 1987); *Ruben v. Ruben*, 461 A.2d 733 (N.H. 1983); *Nastrom v. Nastrom*, 262 N.W.2d 487 (N.D. 1978); *Stevens v. Stevens*, 492 N.E.2d 131 (Ohio 1986); *Hubbard v. Hubbard*, 603 P.2d 747 (Okla. 1979); *Hodge v. Hodge*,520 A.2d 15 (Pa. 1986); *Helm v. Helm*, 345 S.E.2d 720 (S.C. 1986); *Wehrkamp v. Wehrkamp*, 357 N.W.2d 264 (S.D. 1984); *Martinez v. Martinez*, 818 P.2d 538 (Utah 1991); *Downs v. Downs*, 574 A.2d 156 (Vt. 1990); *Hoak v. Hoak*, 370 S.E.2d 473 (W. Va. 1988); *Haugan v. Haugan*, 343 N.W.2d 796 (Wis. 1984); *Grosskopf v. Grosskopf*, 677 P.2d 814 (Wyo. 1984).

[113] *See. e.g., Jones v. Jones*, 454 So. 2d 1006 (Ala. Ct. App. 1984); *In re Marriage of Wisner*, 631 P.2d 115 (Ariz. Ct. App. 1983); *Wright v. Wright*, 469 A.2d 803 (Del. Fam. Ct. 1983); *Hernandez v. Hernandez*, 444 So. 2d 35 (Fla. Dist. Ct. App. 1983); *In re Marriage of Weinstein*, 470 N.E.2d 551 (Ill. App. Ct. 1984); *Wilcox v. Wilcox*, 365 N.E.2d 792 (Ind. Ct. App. 1977); *Moss v. Moss*, 639 S.W.2d 370 (Ky. Ct. App. 1982); *Riaz v. Riaz*, 789 S.W.2d 224 (Mo. Ct. App. 1990); *Beeler v. Beeler*, 715 S.W.2d 625 (Tenn. Ct. App. 1986).

[114] *See infra* § 10.08[D].

[115] 489 N.E.2d 712 (N.Y. 1985).

[116] Panels of the Court of Appeals of Michigan are divided on the question of whether a license or degree may be distributed as a marital asset. In *Woodworth v. Woodworth*, 337 N.W.2d 332 (Mich. Ct. App. 1982), the court held that in some circumstances the spouse of a degree holder is "entitled to share in the fruits of the degree." *Id.* at 335. *But see Watling v. Watling*, 339 N.W.2d 505 (Mich. Ct. App. 1983) (distinguishing the facts in *Woodworth* and declining to award the supporting spouse any part of the husband's dentistry degree); *Olah v. Olah*, 354 N.W.2d 359 (Mich. Ct. App. 1984) (holding that a degree is not a marital asset, but awarding permanent alimony to wife who supported husband through medical school). More recent cases continue to reflect this apparent disagreement. The court cited *Woodworth* with approval in *Postema v. Postema*, 471 N.W.2d 912 (Mich. Ct. App. 1991); *Beckett v. Beckett*, 463 N.W.2d 211 (Mich. Ct. App. 1990); *Lewis v. Lewis*, 448 N.W.2d 735 (Mich.Ct. App. 1989); and *Wiand v. Wiand*, 443 N.W.2d 464 (Mich. Ct. App. 1989). Cases adopting the reasoning of *Wattling* include *Rickel v. Rickel*, 442 N.W.2d 735 (Mich. Ct. App. 1989); *Krause v. Krause*, 441 N.W.2d 66 (Mich. Ct. App. 1989); *Sullivan v. Sullivan*, 438 N.W.2d 309 (Mich. Ct. App. 1989).

a full-time medical student. While he completed three years of medical school, the wife worked at teaching and tutoring and contributed her earnings to meet the parties' expenses. They then returned to New York, where the husband completed his last two semesters of medical school and his internship and the wife returned to a former teaching position. The husband began a divorce proceeding two months after obtaining his license to practice medicine.

The trial court awarded the wife $188,000, representing 40 percent of the value of the husband's medical license, payable in eleven annual installments.[117] The intermediate appellate court, by a divided vote, determined that the husband's medical license was not marital property.[118]

Before the New York Court of Appeals, the husband did not argue that his medical license was separate property and excluded from equitable distribution for that reason. Rather, he asserted that the license was "not property at all, but represents a personal attainment in acquiring knowledge."[119] The court squarely rejected this argument, stating:

> Neither contention is controlling because decisions in other States rely principally on their own statutes and the legislative history underlying them, and because the New York Legislature deliberately went beyond traditional property concepts when it formulated the Equitable Distribution Law. . . . Instead, our statute recognizes that spouses have an equitable claim to things of value arising out of the marital relationship and classifies them as subject to distribution by focusing on the marital status of the parties at the time of acquisition. Those things acquired during marriage and subject to distribution have been classified as "marital property" although, as one commentator has observed, they hardly fall within the traditional property concepts because there is no common law property interest remotely resembling marital property.[120]

The court concluded: "The determination that a professional license is marital property is also consistent with the conceptual base upon which the statute rests."[121] Despite the decision in *O'Brien*, the law remains well settled elsewhere that a license or degree is not marital property. No court that has subsequently addressed the question has adopted the reasoning or reached the same result as the New York Court of Appeals. Courts in other states have, however, devised a variety of remedies designed to avoid the gross unfairness that a contrary result in *O'Brien* would have entailed.[122]

Trial courts and intermediate appellate courts in New York have applied the principle of *O'Brien* liberally, holding that a variety of licenses, degrees,

---

[117] *O'Brien*, 452 N.Y.S.2d 801 (N.Y. Sup. Ct. 1982).

[118] *O'Brien*, 485 N.Y.S.2d 548 (N.Y. App. Div. 1985).

[119] *O'Brien*, 489 N.E.2d at 715.

[120] *Id.*

[121] *Id.* at 716.

[122] *See infra* § 10.08[E].

and certificates are marital property.[123] Moreover, in *Elkus v. Elkus*,[124] the New York Supreme Court, Appellate Division, reversed a trial court determination that an opera singer's career or celebrity status was not marital property. The court found that "to the extent the [husband's] contributions and efforts led to an increase in value of the [wife's] career, this appreciation was a product of the marital partnership, and, therefore, marital property subject to equitable distribution."[125] Thus, at least until New York's highest court revisits the issue, *O'Brien* appears to make eligible for distribution anything that has value because it enhances the holder's earning capacity.

[E] Alternative Remedies for the Supporting Spouse

[1] Overview

The overwhelming majority of courts have determined that a professional license or degree is not marital property, or, indeed, property at all. Many courts have recognized, nevertheless, the inherent unfairness in a situation when one spouse contributes earnings to support the other spouse's professional education, only to be rewarded, shortly after graduation, with a divorce decree. Accordingly, the courts have devised several remedies for the supporting spouse. The most common forms of relief are reimbursement for funds expended for the education or support of the degree-holding spouse and consideration of the supporting spouse's contribution when a maintenance award of property distribution is determined.

Courts sometimes purport to compensate the supporting spouse in professional license or degree cases by taking that spouse's contribution into account as a factor either in awarding maintenance or in dividing property. Indeed, equitable distribution statutes in some states list the contributions of one spouse to the education of the other spouse among the factors the court must consider in making a property division. It is questionable whether this is an effective or satisfactory resolution of the problem. In these cases, the degree-holding spouse is typically at the threshold of a professional career and has limited income, and there is virtually no property available for distribution. Furthermore, depending on the circumstances of the case, the statute in a given jurisdiction may or may not authorize a maintenance award.

In some instances, courts have made a lump-sum award to the supporting spouse, hardly reflective of the value of the degreed spouse's education and

---

[123] *See, e.g., Savasta v. Savasta*, 549 N.Y.S.2d 544 (N.Y. Sup. Ct. 1989) (medical board certification); *Anderson v. Anderson*, 545 N.Y.S.2d 335 (N.Y. App. Div. 1989) (nursing home license); *Morimando v. Morimando*, 536 N.Y.S.2d 701 (N.Y. App. Div. 1988) (certificate as a physician's assistant); *McAlpine v. McAlpine*, 539 N.Y.S.2d 680 (N.Y. Sup. Ct. 1989) (fellowship in Society of Actuaries); *McGowan v. McGowan*, 535 N.Y.S.2d 990 (N.Y. App.Div. 1988) (master's degree).

[124] 572 N.Y.S.2d 901 (N.Y. App. Div. 1991).

[125] *Id.* at 901; *see also Golub v. Golub*, 527 N.Y.S.2d 946 (N.Y. Sup. Ct. 1988) (finding no rational basis for distinguishing between celebrity status and a degree, license or other income generating special skill).

enhanced earning capacity, or have declined to compensate the supporting spouse at all.

[2] Reimbursement or Rehabilitation

In the landmark case *In re Marriage of Graham*,[126] the Supreme Court of Colorado set out principles that courts in other jurisdictions have often followed, occasionally with variations. The court observed:

> A spouse who provides financial support while the other spouse acquires an education is not without a remedy. Where there is marital property to be divided, such contribution to the education of the other spouse may be taken into consideration by the court. . . . Further, if maintenance is sought and a need is demonstrated, the trial court may make an award based on all relevant factors. . . . Certainly, among the relevant factors to be considered is the contribution of the spouse seeking maintenance to the education of the other spouse from whom the maintenance is sought.[127]

This remedy did not apply in the *Graham* case itself, however, because the wife had not sought maintenance.

Almost ten years later, in *In re Marriage of Olar*,[128] the Supreme Court of Colorado considered whether it should overrule *Graham* or whether the wife should receive maintenance, taking into consideration her contribution to the husband's education. The court acknowledged the harsh and frequently unfair results under *Graham* when one spouse postpones educational and career goals to support and contribute to those of the other spouse. Nevertheless, after an extensive review of decisions in other jurisdictions, the majority of which follow the position in *Graham*, the court reaffirmed its holding in the earlier case that an educational degree is not marital property.

Having reaffirmed its *Graham* decision, even while recognizing the "potential for injustice" in this result, the court explored possible remedies for the supporting spouse under the maintenance statute, which permitted maintenance only for a spouse who "[l]acks sufficient property . . . to provide for his reasonable needs"[129] and [i]s unable to support himself through appropriate employment. . . ."[130] The court construed this language broadly and remanded the case to the trial court for reconsideration of a maintenance award.

The Supreme Court of Vermont in *Downs v. Downs*,[131] a case of first impression, agreed explicitly with the decision of the Colorado court in *Olar*,

---

[126] 574 P.2d 75 (Colo. 1978).

[127] *Id.* at 78 (citations omitted).

[128] 747 P.2d 676 (Colo. 1987).

[129] Colo. Rev. Stat. § 14-10-114(1)(a) (1987).

[130] *Id.* § 14-10-114(1)(b).

[131] 574 A.2d 156 (Vt. 1990).

construing similar statutory language to permit courts to consider the future value of a professional degree as a relevant factor for consideration in making an equitable maintenance award. Again the Supreme Court of Iowa, while adhering to earlier decisions that an advanced degree or professional license is not a divisible marital asset, held in *In re Marriage of Francis* [132] that the enhanced earning capacity resulting from the degree or license was a factor to be considered in dividing property and awarding alimony. [133] In *Lowery v. Lowery*, [134] the Supreme Court of Georgia reached the same conclusion. Consistent with this view, the Supreme Court of Pennsylvania in *Bold v. Bold*, [135] held that the supporting spouse should receive "equitable reimbursement to the extent that his or her contributions to the education, training or increased earning capacity of the other spouse exceeds the bare minimum legally obligated support. . . ." [136]

§ 10.09 Professional Goodwill

Closely held business interests, especially professional practices, frequently present problems of both characterization and valuation. This section will consider the various ways in which the courts have addressed characterization or classification questions, and then will address several approaches to valuation.

The courts have often struggled with the problem of whether to classify the goodwill of these enterprises as a marital asset subject to distribution upon dissolution of marriage. Generally, the courts have opted for one of three basic approaches. Some courts have declined to recognize goodwill as a marital asset. Others recognize goodwill and assign it a value, as difficult as the task may be. In a third group of cases, the courts hold that professional goodwill is divisible if it is independent of the individual practitioner.

[A] Goodwill: Definitions and Basic Concepts

Goodwill, an intangible asset of a business or professional practice, is often considered by the courts even though a precise definition does not exist. Early in the nineteenth century, Lord Eldon defined goodwill as "nothing more than the probability that the old customers will resort to the old place." [137] The most frequently cited modern definition of goodwill is that of Mr. Justice Story, who wrote:

> [G]ood-will may be properly enough described to be the advantage or benefit, which is acquired by an establishment, beyond the mere value of the capital, stock, funds, or property employed therein, in

---

[132] 442 N.W.2d 59 (Iowa 1989).

[133] *See also In re Marriage of Lalone*, 469 N.W.2d 695 (Iowa 1991).

[134] 413 S.E.2d 731 (Ga. 1992).

[135] 574 A.2d 552 (Pa. 1990).

[136] *Id.* at 556.

[137] *Cruttwell v. Lye*, 34 Eng. Rep. 129, 134 (Ch. 1810).

consequence of the general public patronage and encouragement, which it receives from constant or habitual customers, on account of its local position, or common celebrity, or reputation for skill or affluence, or'punctuality, or from other accidental circumstances or necessities, or even from ancient partialities or prejudices.[138]

Also frequently cited is Judge Cardozo's observation in *In re Brown*,[139] that "[m]en will pay for any privilege that gives a reasonable expectancy of preference in the race of competition. Such expectancy may come from succession in place or name or otherwise to a business that has won the favor of its customers. It is then known as good will."[140] Despite scholarly criticism of such definitions as confusing and unsound,[141] these or similar definitions persist in the case law and continue to be cited and relied upon by the courts.

[B]   Classification of Professional Goodwill

[1]   Community Property Influences

California courts have long held that professional goodwill should be considered an asset subject to division on divorce, and courts in Arizona and Washington have held to the same effect. The Texas courts, however, strongly reject this view. Courts in several equitable distribution jurisdictions have relied heavily on the reasoning and result reflected in one or the other of these conflicting judicial approaches.

In *Golden v. Golden*,[142] the California Court of Appeal decided the issue squarely and unequivocally, holding that the goodwill of the husband's medical practice was a community asset and should be considered in determining the award made to the wife. The court took pains to distinguish between the situation in divorce and that in which a firm is being dissolved and concluded:

> [I]n a matrimonial matter, the practice of the sole practitioner husband will continue, with the same intangible value as it had during the marriage. Under the principles of community property law, the wife, by virtue of her position of wife, made to that value the same contribution as does a wife to any of the husband's earnings and accumulations during marriage. She is as much entitled to be recompensed for that contribution as if it were represented by the increased value of stock in a family business.[143]

---

[138] J. Story, Commentaries on the Law of Partnerships § 99 at 170 (6th ed. Boston, 1868).

[139] 150 N.E. 581 (N.Y. 1926).

[140] *Id.* at 582 (citation omitted).

[141] *See, e.g.*, Friedman, *Professional Practice Goodwill: An Abused Value Concept*, 2 J. Acad. Matrimonial L. 23 (1986): "Publications by attorneys may accurately record and analyze case law development across the country, but case law generally is not grounded on sound economic theory or valid value concepts." *Id.*

[142] 75 Cal. Rptr. 735 (Cal. Ct. App. 1969).

[143] *Id.* at 735.

The court's observation has obvious applicability to the analogous principle, underlying the law of equitable distribution, of marriage as an economic partnership.[144]

Other courts in community property jurisdictions reject the proposition that professional goodwill is divisible on divorce as a community asset. In *Nail v. Nail*,[145] the Supreme Court of Texas held that the goodwill of the husband's practice could not be said to be a vested or earned property right that qualified as property divisible by a court decree. The court stated:

> It did not possess a value or constitute an asset separate and apart from his person, or from his individual ability to practice his profession. It would be extinguished in the event of his death, or retirement, or disablement, as well as in the event of the sale of his practice or the loss of his patients, whatever the case.[146]

[2] Classification of Goodwill for Equitable Distribution

In determining whether the goodwill of a professional practice is an asset eligible for distribution upon dissolution of marriage, the courts in equitable distribution jurisdictions often rely heavily on decisions in community property states. There are three conflicting views. The courts of one group of states have followed the lead of California and found professional goodwill to be distributable property. To the contrary, in a number of states the decisions are consistent with those of the Texas courts, holding that professional goodwill is personal to the holder and not distributable as a marital asset. In several other states, the courts have adopted still a third approach to the classification of goodwill, holding that goodwill may or may not be divisible, depending on its marketability.

[a] Professional Goodwill as Divisible Property

New Jersey was the first equitable distribution state to give extensive consideration to the classification of goodwill as a marital asset. In *Stern v. Stern*,[147] although classification was not in dispute, the Supreme Court of New Jersey acknowledged the existence of goodwill in a professional partnership. The court noted that although ethical considerations barred the sale of the goodwill of a law firm, its existence and value could be proved in a given case.[148] The goodwill of a lawyer in his solely owned professional corporation came directly before the Supreme Court of New Jersey in *Dugan v. Dugan*.[149] In a thorough and wide-ranging opinion, the court, citing authority from California and other jurisdictions, held that an

---

[144] *See also Marriage of Fleege*, 588 P.2d 1136 (Wash. 1979); *Mitchell v. Mitchell*, 732 P.2d 208 (Ariz. 1987).

[145] 486 S.W.2d 761 (Tex. 1972).

[146] *Id.* at 764; *see also Pearce v. Pearce*, 482 So. 2d 108 (La. Ct. App. 1986).

[147] 331 A.2d 257 (N.J. 1975).

[148] *Id.* at 261, n.5.

[149] 457 A.2d 1 (N.J. 1983).

attorney's goodwill in his wholly owned professional corporation was subject to equitable distribution.

The Colorado Court of Appeals in *In re Marriage of Nichols*,[150] a case of first impression in that state, held that the goodwill of the husband's dental practice was distributable on divorce. Setting out the rationale for this approach to the question, the court observed:

> Professional practices that can be sold for more than the value of their fixtures and accounts receivable have saleable goodwill. A professional, like any entrepreneur who has established a reputation for skill and expertise, can expect his patrons to return to him, to speak well of him, and upon selling his practice, can expect that many will accept the buyer and will utilize his professional expertise. These expectations are a part of goodwill, and they have a pecuniary value.[151]

In *Hanson v. Hanson*,[152] the Supreme Court of Missouri, after an extensive review of conflicting authorities in both equitable distribution and community property states, held that the goodwill of a professional practice is a marital asset that may be divided in a proceeding for dissolution of marriage. The court carefully distinguished professional goodwill from future earning capacity and the reputation or professional skill of the practitioner. The court stated: "We define goodwill within a professional setting to mean the value of the practice which exceeds its tangible assets and which is the result of the tendency of clients/patients to return and recommend the practice irrespective of the reputation of the individual practitioner."[153] The highest courts and intermediate appellate courts in the majority of jurisdictions that have confronted the question have come to the conclusion that professional goodwill is a divisible marital asset.[154]

In what appears to be the furthest extension of the recognition of professional goodwill, a New Jersey intermediate appellate court upheld the trial court's recognition of "celebrity goodwill" as marital property. In *Piscopo v. Piscopo*,[155] the court analogized the goodwill flowing from the husband's celebrity status to the professional goodwill that the state's Supreme Court had recognized in *Dugan v. Dugan*,[156] defined as ". . . essentially reputation that will probably generate future business."[157]

---

[150] 606 P.2d 1314 (Colo. Ct. App. 1979).

[151] *Id.* at 1315.

[152] 738 S.W.2d 429 (Mo. 1987).

[153] *Id.* at 434.

[154] *See, e.g., In re Marriage of Hull*, 712 P.2d 1317 (Mont. 1986); *Ford v. Ford*, 782 P.2d 1304 (Nev. 1989); *In re Marriage of Keyser*, 820 P.2d 1194 (Colo. Ct. App. 1991); *Russell v. Russell*, 399 S.E.2d 166 (Va. Ct. App. 1990); *Clark v. Clark*, 782 S.W.2d 56 (Ky. Ct. App. 1990); *Sorenson v. Sorenson*, 769 P.2d 820 (Utah Ct. App. 1989).

[155] 557 A.2d 1040 (N.J. Super. Ct. App. Div. 1989).

[156] 457 A.2d 1 (N.J. 1983).

[157] *Id.* Courts in New York also have recognized celebrity status as marital property. The New York decisions do not analogize to professional goodwill, but find celebrity status to be indistinguishable from the licenses or degrees involved in *O'Brien v. O'Brien*, 489 N.E.2d 712 (N.Y. 1985), and its progeny. *See Elkus v. Elkus*, 572 N.Y.S.2d 901 (N.Y. App. Div. 1991); *Golub v. Golub*, 527 N.Y.S.2d 946 (N.Y.Sup. Ct. 1988); *infra* § 10.08[D].

[b] Professional Goodwill Not Divisible

The leading case in an equitable distribution state holding that professional goodwill is not marital property is *Holbrook v. Holbrook*,[158] decided by the Wisconsin Court of Appeals. After reviewing myriad authorities from other jurisdictions, the court concluded:

> We are not persuaded that the concept of professional goodwill as a divisible marital asset should be adopted in Wisconsin. We are not obliged nor inclined to follow the twisted and illogical path that other jurisdictions have made in dealing with this concept in the context of divorce.
>
> The concept of professional goodwill evanesces when one attempts to distinguish it from future earning capacity. Although a professional business's good reputation, which is essentially what goodwill consists of, is certainly a thing of value, we do not believe that it bestows on those who have an ownership interest in the business, an actual, separate property interest. The reputation of a law firm or some other professional business is valuable to its individual owner to the extent that it assures continued substantial earnings in the future. It cannot be separately sold or pledged by the individual owners. The goodwill or reputation of such a business accrues to the benefit of the owners only through increased salary.[159]

The court in *Holbrook* then analogized professional goodwill to an educational degree or its increased earning capacity, which the court in an earlier case had held was not marital property.[160] Further, the court found "a disturbing inequity in compelling a professional practitioner to pay a spouse a share of intangible assets at a judicially determined value that could not be realized by a sale or another method of liquidating value."[161] Finally, the court noted that the goodwill or reputation of the husband's law partnership was reflected in the husband's salary and that to treat the law firm's goodwill as a separate, divisible asset would be "double counting."[162] The fact that he was a partner was, however, a proper factor for consideration in the division of assets or the determination of support.

The decision of the Wisconsin Court of Appeals in *Holbrook* continues to be enormously influential in cases in other states holding that professional goodwill is not a distributable marital asset. In *Powell v. Powell*,[163] for example, the Supreme Court of Kansas, having reviewed conflicting decisions from other jurisdictions, quoted *Holbrook* at length and held that a physician's professional practice does not have goodwill but is personal to and entirely dependent upon the professional. Similarly, and more

---

[158] 309 N.W.2d 343 (Wis. Ct. App. 1981).

[159] *Id.* at 354.

[160] *See De Witt v. De Witt*, 296 N.W.2d 761 (Wis. Ct. App. 1980).

[161] *Holbrook*, 309 N.W.2d at 355.

[162] *Id.*

[163] 648 P.2d 218 (Kan. 1982).

recently, the Supreme Court of Oklahoma in *Travis v. Travis*,[164] a case of first impression, quoted *Holbrook* with approval in holding that a law practice had no goodwill value for the purpose of dividing property at divorce.[165]

[c]   Professional Goodwill Divisible if Independent of Individual

Courts in a small but increasing minority of jurisdictions take a third approach to the characterization of professional goodwill, declining to adopt a rigid rule. The Supreme Court of Nebraska, in *Taylor v. Taylor*,[166] was the first court to adopt this approach. In *Taylor*, the court held that the husband's medical practice did not have goodwill as a divisible asset. Unlike other courts so holding, however, the Nebraska court declined to announce a firm and unvarying rule. The court concluded that to be distributable property, "goodwill must be a business asset with value independent of the presence or reputation of a particular individual, an asset which may be sold, transferred, conveyed, or pledged."[167] The court cautioned, however, that it was neither stating nor implying that a professional practice may never have goodwill as a salable business asset.

In a case in which the goodwill of the husband's medical practice was at issue, the Supreme Court of Arkansas in *Wilson v. Wilson*[168] noted approvingly the *Taylor* court's observations and concluded accordingly: "Thus, whether goodwill is marital property is a factual question and a party, to establish goodwill as marital property and divisible as such, must produce evidence establishing the saleability or marketability of that goodwill as a business asset of a professional practice."[169]

A Maryland court's decision in *Prahinski v. Prahinski*,[170] applying the approach in *Taylor* to the husband's law practice, is also instructive. The court in *Prahinski* defined "true goodwill" as "not simply a *possibility* of future earnings, but a *probability* based on existing circumstances"[171] and observed that "goodwill is a marketable and transferrable asset."[172] The court noted that even if the goodwill of a law practice cannot ethically be sold, it may still have value. The court concluded that "[i]f there is true goodwill in an attorney's practice, separable from his individual future earning capacity, then a value can be placed on it."[173] The court determined

---

[164] 795 P.2d 96 (Okla. 1990).

[165] *See also Zells v. Zells*, 572 N.E.2d 944 (Ill. 1991); *Donahue v. Donahue*, 384 S.E.2d 741 (S.C. 1989); *Sonek v. Sonek*, 412 S.E.2d 917 (N.C. Ct. App. 1992).

[166] 386 N.W.2d 851 (Neb. 1986).

[167] *Id.* at 858–59.

[168] 741 S.W.2d 640 (Ark. 1987).

[169] *Id.* at 647.

[170] 540 A.2d 833 (Md. Ct. Spec. App. 1988), *aff'd*, 582 A.2d 784 (Md. 1990) (lawyer's goodwill not marital property).

[171] *Id.* at 841 (emphasis in original).

[172] *Id.*

[173] *Id.*

that on the facts in the case before it, the wife could not make a showing that goodwill existed as an asset distinct from the husband's continued presence and reputation.

Since the decision of the Supreme Court of Nebraska in *Taylor*, courts in other jurisdictions increasingly have followed its commonsensical and persuasive approach and applied its teaching in a variety of circumstances. The Supreme Court of Alaska in *Richmond v. Richmond*,[174] for example, held that only marketable goodwill may be included in the marital estate, and that the goodwill of a sole practitioner was not marketable and, therefore, not an asset subject to distribution in a divorce proceeding. Again, the Supreme Court of Florida in *Thompson v. Thompson*[175] citing *Taylor* with approval, held that goodwill is divisible if it was developed during the marriage and exists separate and apart from the individual's reputation.[176] Holdings in a number of intermediate appellate courts reflect this trend toward recognition of professional goodwill as a divisible marital asset only if it is independent of the individual practitioner.[177]

[C] Valuation

Valuation of professional practices and other closely held business interests is without question one of the most difficult problems that courts and lawyers face in connection with the equitable distribution of property on dissolution of marriage. There are few principles that are uniformly or unvaryingly reliable. The form of the enterprise -whether a sole proprietorship, a partnership, or a closely held corporation -is generally not controlling and most often not of particular significance. In most cases, and certainly when the enterprise is financially or structurally complex, valuation requires the testimony of experts. This is not to suggest, however, that valuation involves valid and reliable scientific methods. All too frequently, well-qualified experts, purporting to use identical methods of valuation, reach widely variant conclusions as to the value of the same assets. There is as much conflict over the value of goodwill as there is with respect to its classification.[178] Nevertheless, appellate courts uniformly hold that the difficulty of establishing value does not relieve trial courts of the obligation to do so.

Valuation contemplates the determination of fair market value, commonly defined as "the price at which the property would change hands between a willing buyer and a willing seller when the former is not under any compulsion to buy and the latter is not under any compulsion to sell, both parties having reasonable knowledge of relevant facts."[179]

---

[174] 779 P.2d 1211 (Alaska 1989).

[175] 576 So. 2d 267 (Fla. 1991).

[176] *See also Ombres v. Ombres*, 596 So. 2d 956 (Fla. 1991).

[177] *See, e.g., Fexa v. Fexa*, 578 A.2d 1314 (Pa. Super. Ct. 1990); *McCabe v. McCabe*, 575 A.2d 87 (Pa. Super. Ct. 1990); *Hollander v. Hollander*, 597 A.2d 1012 (Md. Ct. Spec. App. 1991).

[178] *See supra* § 10.09[B].

[179] Rev. Rul. 59–60, 1959 -1 CB 237.

Determining the fair market value of a closely held corporation (and by analogy, other closely held business interests) is problematic. Because sales of such corporations are infrequent, no market of willing buyers and sellers exists.

The methods or approaches to valuation in the following discussion should be considered as representative or illustrative, not all-inclusive. As long as the method of valuation chosen by a trial court is fair and reasonable and is supported by the evidence, a reviewing court is unlikely to reject it.

[1] Book Value

A number of courts have expressed skepticism with respect to exclusive reliance on book value in valuing shares of closely held corporations. The Superior Court of New Jersey, in *Lavene v. Lavene*,[180] cogently described the limitations of book value as a method of valuation:

> There are probably few assets whose valuation imposes as difficult, intricate and sophisticated a task as interests in close corporations. They cannot be realistically evaluated by a simplistic approach which is based solely on book value, which fails to deal with the realities of the goodwill concept, which does not consider investment value of a business in terms of actual profit, and which does not deal with the question of discounting the value of a minority interest.[181]

The courts do not, however, categorically and without exception reject book value as the measure of value. The circumstances of the case may justify its acceptance.[182]

[2] Capitalization of Excess Earnings

There is widespread agreement that earnings are the most important factor in valuation of the stock of an operating company, and these are sometimes the sole factor used in determining value.[183] The courts generally accept the fact that "at least in the case of an operating company with consistent earnings, asset value has markedly less importance in valuation than does earnings,"[184] and occasionally, "earnings have been the only factor used to determine value."[185]

Earnings having been determined, capitalization of excess earnings is frequently employed as a method of valuation. This method involves

---

[180] 372 A.2d 629 (N.J. Super. Ct. App. Div. 1977), *cert. denied*, 379 A.2d 259 (N.J. 1977).

[181] *Id.* at 633; *see also Nehorayoff v. Nehorayoff*, 437 N.Y.S.2d 584 (N.Y. Sup. Ct. 1981).

[182] *See, e.g., In re Marriage of Messerle*, 643 P.2d 1286 (Or. Ct. App. 1982), *review denied*, 648 P.2d 853 (Or. 1982); *Whaley v. Whaley*, 436 N.E.2d 816 (Ind. Ct. App. 1982).

[183] Longnecker, *A Practical Guide to Valuation of Closely Held Stock*, 122 Tr. & Est. 32, 33 (Jan. 1983).

[184] *Id.* at 32 (citations omitted).

[185] *Id.* at 33.

applying to the earnings of the corporation a capitalization rate or multiplier that reflects the stability of past corporate earnings and the predictability of future earnings.[186]

Courts frequently adopt this approach in evaluating the goodwill of professional corporations. As the court noted in *Poore v. Poore*[187] in a frequently cited passage:

> Under this approach, the value of goodwill is based in part on the amount by which the earnings of the professional spouse exceed that which would have been earnings by a person with similar education, experience, and skill as an employee in the same general locale. . . . It has also been suggested that the value of goodwill be based on one year's average gross income of the practice or a percentage thereof. . . .[188]

The trial court should then determine and average the net income before taxes of the professional for approximately five years, compare this average with the employee norm and multiply the excess amount by an appropriate capitalization factor.

[3] Buy-Sell Agreements

A serviceable description of buy-sell agreements is as follows:

> A buy-sell agreement usually provides for the business entity or remaining principal's purchase of the withdrawing parties' shares at a predetermined price. Such an agreement is restrictive in nature as it alienates the transferability of the shares. Those agreements are usually entered into to meet the business-planning objectives such as protection from outsiders, prevention of changes in ownership, economic continuity and estate tax purposes.[189]

Such arrangements frequently appear as partnership agreements and in connection with other forms of closely held business interests. Generally, the courts take such agreements into account in arriving at a valuation of these interests but do not consider them as binding.[190]

[4] Discount for Minority Interest

Among the factors affecting the fair market value of the stock of closely held corporations is the size of the block of stock being valued. A minority

---

[186] *See* Hartwig, *Valuing an Interest in a Closely Held Business for the Purpose of Buy/Sell Agreements and for Death Tax Purposes*, 26 So. Cal. Tax Inst. 215, 256–264 (1974).

[187] 331 S.E.2d 266 (N.C. Ct. App. 1985).

[188] *Id.* at 272–273.

[189] Skoloff, *A Matrimonial Attorney's Alert: Beware of Buy-Sell Agreements*, 7 Nat'l. L.J., Sept. 10, 1984, at 16 (citing Desmond & Kelly, Business Valuation Handbook 239 (1980)).

[190] *See, e.g., Amodio v. Amodio*, 509 N.E.2d 936, 937 (N.Y. 1987); *Kaye v. Kaye*, 478 N.Y.S.2d 324, 328 (N.Y. App. Div. 1984) ("A bona fide buy-sell agreement which predates the marital discord, while not conclusive, may also prove an invaluable aid."); *Stern v. Stern*, 331 A.2d 257 (N.J. 1975).

interest in an enterprise that others control may be of significantly less value than the liquidation value of the shares. This lack of control significantly reduces the value of the minority shareholder's stock.[191] Accordingly, courts in a number of equitable distribution jurisdictions discount the value of a minority interest in valuing and distributing interests in closely held corporations upon marriage dissolution.[192]

§ 10.10   Pensions and Retirement Benefits

[A]   Overview

With the possible exception of the marital home, pensions or retirement benefits are the most significant asset available for distribution in many marriage dissolution proceedings. Consequently, there is a large body of cases dealing with the treatment of pensions. Courts have struggled to classify and value pensions, sometimes with little statutory guidance. The majority of courts in equitable distribution jurisdictions hold that all pensions, including military retirement benefits, are distributable as marital property. A few decisions, however, have treated pensions somewhat less expansively, distinguishing between vested and nonvested benefits.

The majority of equitable distribution statutes are silent with respect to the treatment of pensions and other forms of retirement benefits. Those statutes that do address the question reflect two basic approaches. They either classify pensions or retirement benefits as marital or separate property[193] or list these assets among the factors the divorce court must consider when making a property distribution.[194] The statutes offer no guidance with respect to the valuation or equitable distribution of these assets.

[B]   Basic Terms and Concepts

Pensions are generally either defined contribution plans or defined benefit plans. A defined contribution plan provides a separate account for each participating employee into which specified periodic contributions are made.[195] Interest in the invested assets and appreciation are allocated to each employee's account, and the employee, upon retirement, "is entitled to an amount equal to the cumulative value of his share."[196]

---

[191] *See* Feld, *The Implications of Minority Interest and Stock Restrictions in Valuing Closely Held Shares*, 122 U. Pa. L. Rev. 934, 934–936 (1974).

[192] *See, e.g., Eyler v. Eyler*, 485 N.E.2d 657 (Ind. Ct. App. 1986). *But see Redding v. Redding*, 372 N.W.2d 31 (Minn. Ct. App. 1985).

[193] *See, e.g.*, Fla. Stat. Ann. § 61.075(3)(a)(4) (West 1984); Kan. Stat. Ann. § 23-201(b) (1985); N.C. Gen. Stat. § 50-20(b)(1)(2) (1987).

[194] *See, e.g.*, Iowa Code Ann. § 598.21(1)(i) (West Supp. 1992).

[195] *See Rosenberg v. Rosenberg*, 497 A.2d 485, 493 (Md. Ct. Spec. App. 1985).

[196] *Id.* at 494.

Defined benefit plans provide a fixed monthly (or annual) amount for the employee upon retirement and for the rest of his or her life. The employer, under such plans, does not maintain a separate account for each employee. Most state retirement systems are defined benefit plans.

A further distinction involves whether a plan is contributory or noncontributory, terms that describe the method of the plan's funding. In a contributory plan, employees make payments into the plan, whereas under a noncontributory plan, the employer makes all the payments or contributions. Most commonly, both the employer and the employee, generally through payroll deductions, make contributions under the plan. Both defined contribution plans and defined benefit plans may be contributory or noncontributory, nominally funded by the employee, the employer, or both.

Valuation and distribution of pension benefits may be affected significantly by whether they are vested or nonvested and whether they are mature or nonmatured. Generally, pension benefits are said to be vested when the employee's discharge or voluntary termination of employment would not forfeit benefits.[197] Once pension benefits are vested, in order to receive them the employee need only survive until retirement age.[198] Nonvested pension benefits, on the other hand, "are contingent upon the employee continuing his employment with the employer or organization sponsoring the plan."[199] Pension benefits are said to be matured when the employee, upon retirement, has an unconditional right to receive payment.[200]

[C] Characterization of Pension Benefits

The overwhelming majority of courts that have addressed the issue hold that pensions, whether or not vested, are marital property insofar as the rights are acquired during the marriage. In some states, the courts have ruled only with respect to vested pensions.

[1] Majority View -All Pensions Marital Property

The leading case holding that pension benefits are marital property whether vested or nonvested is *In re Marriage of Brown*,[201] decided by the Supreme Court of California, a community property jurisdiction. Courts in a substantial number of equitable distribution jurisdictions have followed the result in Brown and often adopted its reasoning. Accordingly, the case warrants more than cursory attention.

The court in *Brown* overruled its own decision, some thirty years earlier in *French v. French*,[202] that nonvested pension rights were not property

---

[197] *See Damiano v. Damiano*, 463 N.Y.S.2d 477, 480 (N.Y. App. Div. 1983).

[198] *Id.*

[199] *Id.*

[200] *Id.*

[201] 544 P.2d 561 (Cal. 1976).

[202] 112 P.2d 235 (Cal. 1941).

but a mere expectancy and, therefore, not subject to division upon divorce as community property. The husband's employer in *Brown* maintained a noncontributory pension plan under which the employee could forfeit his rights if discharged before accumulating a minimum number of "points." The trial court held that because the husband's rights were not fully vested, they were not divisible as community property. Reversing, the Supreme Court of California noted that pension benefits were not merely an expectancy, but were a form of deferred compensation for service rendered and thus were property. In a frequently quoted passage, the court observed:

> We conclude that *French v. French*, and subsequent cases erred in characterizing nonvested pension rights as expectancies and in denying the trial courts authority to divide such rights as community property. The mischaracterization of pension rights has, and unless overturned, will continue to result in inequitable division of community assets. Over the past decades, pension benefits have become an increasingly significant part of the consideration earned by the employee for his services. As the date of vesting and retirement approaches, the value of the pension right grows until it often represents the most important asset of the marital community. . . . A division of community property which awards one spouse the entire value of this asset, without any offsetting award to the other spouse, does not represent the equal division of property contemplated by [the statute]. [203]

Since the California court's decision in *Brown*, the highest courts or intermediate appellate courts of several states have ruled to the same effect in a variety of circumstances. Although appellate courts in some jurisdictions have yet to decide the question, the clear trend is to hold that nonvested as well as vested pensions are marital property. In some cases, even when the pension benefits are vested, the language of the decisions and their reliance on *Brown* make clear their application to nonvested pensions as well. [204]

After surveying the law in a number of community property and equitable distribution jurisdictions, the New York Supreme Court, Appellate Division in *Damiano v. Damiano* [205] stated the generally prevailing view that "pension benefits belonging to either spouse attributable to employment during the marriage, whether those benefits are vested or nonvested, and whether the plan is contributory or noncontributory constitute marital property subject to distribution upon divorce." [206]

---

[203] *Brown*, 544 P.2d 561, 566 (Cal. 1976) (citation omitted).

[204] *See, e.g., Laing v. Laing*, 741 P.2d 649 (Alaska 1987); *Robert C.S. v. Barbara J.S.*, 434 A.2d 383 (Del. 1981); *Janssen v. Janssen*, 331 N.W.2d 752 (Minn. 1983); *Carpenter v. Carpenter*, 657 P.2d 646 (Okla. 1983).

[205] 463 N.Y.S.2d 477 (N.Y. App. Div. 1983).

[206] *Id.* at 481.

[2] Classification of Pensions -Minority View

A minority of courts have not explicitly accepted the teaching of the decision in *In re Marriage of Brown*.[207] The Supreme Court of South Carolina, for example, has consistently declined to characterize retirement pay as marital property,[208] and the Court of Civil Appeals of Alabama has held to the same effect.[209] Again, in *Kirkman v. Kirkman*,[210] the Supreme Court of Indiana declined to approve distribution of pension or retirement benefits that were not vested, having held in an earlier case that vested benefits were distributable property.[211]

[D] Valuation and Distribution of Pensions

There are three basic approaches to the division of pension benefits that have been characterized as marital property. The first, and the one the courts have usually preferred, is to determine the present value of the pension benefits, taking into account contingencies such as vesting, maturity, and mortality, and to award the nonemployee spouse a lump sum or other assets as an offset. Second, the court may award the nonemployee spouse a specific share or percentage of the pension benefits, if, as, and when received. Finally, the court may defer distribution, reserving jurisdiction until the time the employed spouse actually begins to receive benefits under the pension plan. This latter method usually eliminates the need for the court to value the pension during the course of the divorce proceeding.

The decision of the Superior Court of Pennsylvania in *Braderman v. Braderman*[212] provides an excellent overview of the selection and application of methodology for the valuation and distribution of retirement benefits. In *Braderman*, the husband was in receipt of monthly benefits from the State Employees Retirement System. After determining that the husband's vested and matured benefits were marital property, the court turned to the questions of valuation and distribution of those benefits.

The immediate offset method "divides the benefits at the time the equitable distribution order is entered by assigning a present value to them."[213] Having determined this present value, the court must calculate the portion earned during the marriage, and then proceed as follows.

> The present value must then be multiplied by the "coverture" fraction to reach the present value of the entitlement which was acquired during the marriage. The "coverture" fraction represents

---

[207] 544 P.2d 561 (Cal. 1976).

[208] *See, e.g., Carter v. Carter* 286 S.E.2d 139 (S.C. 1982) (holding that husband's civil service nondisability retirement pay is not subject to distribution but may be considered as factor in determining alimony); *Haynes v. Haynes*, 303 S.E.2d 429 (S.C. 1983) (applying same principles to military retirement pay).

[209] *Robinson v. Robinson*, 563 So. 2d 1054 (Ala. Ct. Civ. App.).

[210] 555 N.E.2d 1293 (Ind. 1990).

[211] *See In re Marriage of Adams*, 535 N.E.2d 124 (Ind. 1989).

[212] 488 A.2d 613 (Pa. Super. Ct. 1985).

[213] *Id.* at 619.

that portion of the value of the benefits attributable to the marriage. The numerator of the fraction reflects the total period of time the employee spouse participated in the plan during the marriage, and the denominator is the total period the employee participated in the benefits program. . . . Next, the court must determine how the sum available for equitable distribution should be apportioned between the spouses. . . . After determining the non-employee spouse's interest in the benefits, the court awards these benefits to the employee spouse and offsets this award by distributing other marital property or by ordering payment to the non-employee spouse.[214]

In some jurisdictions, while recognizing that present value is generally accepted as the proper test for determining the value of pension benefits, contingencies such as disability or early retirement cannot be accurately calculated under this rule. In *In re Rolfe v. Rolfe,*[215] the Supreme Court of Montana responded to such concerns, stating:

> The division of retirement benefits upon receipt is commonly known as the "time rule. . . ." Under this method, the marital interest is represented by a fraction, the numerator of which is the length of the employee's service during the marriage, and the denominator of which the employee's total length of service. This fraction is then applied to each benefit payment, lump or periodic, to determine the portion earned during the marriage. Although the extent of the marital interest is determined as of the date of the dissolution, the benefit factors to be applied to the pension credits earned during the marriage are those in effect at retirement. Thus, the non-employee spouse is entitled to increases or accruals on her interest because of the delay in receiving these payments[216]

Under the reserved jurisdiction (or deferred distribution) method of awarding pension benefits, the court retains jurisdiction until the pension benefits reach maturity or pay status. Under this method, as previously stated, it is not necessary to calculate the present value. Instead, "the'coverture' fraction is applied to the benefits when they enter pay status because there are too many variables projected into the future."[217]

A number of courts have expressed a preference for reducing pension benefits to present value and disposing of them in the course of the divorce proceeding.[218] The rationale for this preference is that it settles the pension

---

[214] *Id. See generally* Skoloff, *How to Evaluate and Distribute Employee Benefits in Divorce,* Nat'l. L.J., Feb. 13, 1984, at 25. *See also McDermott v. McDermott,* 14 Fam. L. Rep. (BNA) 1533 (Vt. Sup. Ct., No. 86-51 8/19/88) (holding that failure of trial court to use coverture fraction in calculating present value of husband's retirement benefits attributable to marriage was abuse of discretion).

[215] 766 P. 2d 223 (Mont. 1988).

[216] *Id.* at 226.

[217] *Braderman,* 488 A.2d at 619.

[218] *See, e.g., Morlan v. Morlan,* 720 P.2d 497 (Alaska 1986); *Diffenderfer v. Diffenderfer,* 491 So. 2d 265 (Fla. 1986); *Hodgins v. Hodgins,* 497 A.2d 1187 (N.H. 1985).

distribution question and avoids continued strife and hostility between the spouses. In *Moore v. Moore*[219] the Supreme Court of New Jersey cogently summarized the potential problems under an alternative method of distribution:

> Under the "deferred distribution" approach the parties, the court, and the employer of the pensioner may continue to be embroiled in controversy. On actual receipt of the benefits by the pensioner a determination of the proper percentage of each pension payment to be distributed to the non-employee spouse must be made. The non-employee spouse must keep contact with the employee spouse to determine the official date of retirement. Additionally, the non-employee spouse will have to be constantly vigilant to ensure that proper revised beneficiary forms are filed with the employer and that agreed proper benefits are chosen at retirement. For instance, if the employee spouse remarries and changes the beneficiary of the plan, his new wife may receive the benefit.[220]

Despite the frequently expressed judicial preference for reduction of pension benefits to present value and distribution at the time of the dissolution proceeding, the decisions generally make it clear that once pensions are characterized as marital property, their treatment is within the discretion of the court. The way in which this discretion is exercised depends on the facts of the case and the circumstances of the spouses.

[E] Disability Benefits

The courts in equitable distribution jurisdictions have not addressed the treatment of disability pensions with great frequency. Decisions in this area, compared with those involving retirement benefits, are relatively sparse. The courts take three basic and distinct approaches to disability benefits. Some courts hold that disability benefits are subject to equitable distribution and do not distinguish them, in this respect, from retirement benefits. Simply stated, these courts hold that disability payments are marital property, finding no meaningful distinction between annuities payable upon disability and those payable on longevity.[221]

Under a second approach, the nonpensioned spouse may be entitled to an equitable distribution of a disability pension only to the extent that the pension matches the benefits that the previously employed spouse would have received upon retirement. Courts adopting this approach view disability payments as subject to equitable distribution only to the extent that they represent what would be payable upon retirement and are, therefore, indistinguishable from a longevity retirement benefit.

The decision of the Superior Court of Pennsylvania in *Ciliberti v. Ciliberti*[222] is illustrative, holding that a true disability pension is not marital

---

[219] 553 A.2d 20 (N.J. 1989).

[220] *Id.* at 26.

[221] *See, e.g., Morrison v. Morrison*, 692 S.W.2d 601 (Ark. 1985); *Lookingbill v. Lookingbill*, 483 A.2d 1 (Md. 1984;) *Watson v. Watson*, 379 N.W.2d 588 (Minn. Ct. App. 1983).

[222] 542 A.2d 580 (Pa. Super. Ct. 1988).

property subject to equitable distribution. The court noted that the purpose of such benefits is the compensation of the employee spouse for lost earning capacity, replacing future income that the employee cannot earn because of disability. The court cautioned, however, that when a portion of the disability pension represents retirement benefits, that amount remains marital property subject to equitable distribution.[223]

The third approach holds that disability payments are not distributable as marital property.[224] In *Christmas v. Christmas*,[225] the Supreme Court of Oklahoma offered a persuasive rationale for this conclusion. The court observed that retirement pensions, which insure against survival beyond the age of retirement, function as substitutes for life savings. Absent retirement coverage, savings of the additional wages received would be joint property earned during marriage. Disability benefits, however, are insurance against wage losses from disability prior to superannuation, and when received after divorce "replace post-coverture wages that would be the earner's separate property."[226] Therefore, the court concluded, "while retirement pensions replace joint property, disability benefits replace separate property. This difference in the replacement nature of the benefits requires that disability benefits be classified as the disabled worker's separate property."[227]

[F] Federal Pensions

The Supremacy Clause of the United States Constitution forbids states from interfering with federal authority. Although family law traditionally has been a state matter for most purposes, the Supremacy Clause may still be invoked when a federal interest is at stake. Such a federal interest is involved in some federal pensions.

In *Hisquierdo v. Hisquierdo*,[228] for example, the Supreme Court struck down a state court ordered property division of a Railroad Retirement pension. The Court found that the state court order determining that the benefits were community property would do major damage to federal interests. The decision was based on the two provisions of the Act that stated that the benefits were not assignable and could not be anticipated.[229] Subsequently, *Hisquierdo* was overruled in part by a 1983 amendment that allows some railroad retirement benefits to be classified as either community or marital.

The remainder of benefits under the Railroad Retirement Act remain preempted and state courts cannot consider these benefits when making a property division.[230]

---

[223] *See also Mylett v. Mylett*, 558 N.Y.S.2d 160 (N.Y. App. Div. 1990).

[224] *See, e.g., Freeman v. Freeman*, 468 So. 2d 326 (Fla. Dist. Ct. App. 1985); *Sherman v. Sherman*, 740 S.W.2d 203 (Mo. Ct. App. 1987).

[225] 787 P.2d 1267 (Okla. 1990).

[226] *Id.* at 1268.

[227] *Id.*

[228] 439 U.S. 572 (1970).

[229] 45 U.S.C.A. § 231 (West 1986).

[230] *See Belt v. Belt*, 398 N.W.2d 737 (N.D. 1987).

[G] Qualified Domestic Relations Orders (QDROs)

State courts also must deal with the application of state domestic relations laws to private pensions that are regulated by the federal Employee Retirement Income Security Act of 1974 (ERISA).[231] As originally enacted, ERISA prohibited assignment or alienation of benefits under pension plans subject to the Act.

The Retirement Equity Act of 1984 (REA)[232] now provides that if a state court accepts a Qualified Domestic Relations Order (QDRO), the pension benefits may be assigned. A "qualified domestic relations order" is one "which creates or recognizes the existence of an alternate payee's right to, or assigns to alternate payee the right to, receive all or a portion of the benefits payable with respect to a participant under a [pension or retirement] plan."[233]

A QDRO must specify the name and last known mailing address of the participant and each alternate payee designated by the court order, and the amount or percentage of benefits each alternate payee is to receive when the benefits are to be distributed. The QDRO must also specify the number of payments or the period for which the order is effective, and identify which retirement or pension plan the order applies to. Upon receipt of a domestic relations order, the pension plan administrator must notify the participant and alternate payee, and if within 18 months the domestic relations order is determined to be a qualified domestic relations order (QDRO), the plan administrator will distribute the money to the alternate payee. If, however, the domestic relations order is found not to be a qualified domestic relations order, the plan administrator must pay the pension proceeds to the person who would have received the money if there had been no order in the first place.[234]

[H] Military Retirement Benefits

On June 26, 1981, the Supreme Court of the United States held, in *McCarty v. McCarty*,[235] that federal law bars state courts from dividing military retirement pay under state community property laws. Although the decision explicitly addressed division in community property states, its language and principles clearly apply to the division of marital property in equitable distribution states generally. The Court in *McCarty* posed the issue as "whether, upon the dissolution of a marriage, federal law precludes a state court from dividing military nondisability retired pay pursuant to state community property laws."[236] The Court concluded that the federal supremacy clause barred states from dividing or distributing military retirement benefits in divorce proceedings.

---

[231] 29 U.S.C.A. § 1003(a)(1) (West 1985).

[232] 29 U.S.C. § 1056 (1988).

[233] 29 U.S.C.A. § 1056(d)(3)(B)(i) (West Supp. 1988); Int. Rev. Code § 414(p)(1)(A) (1988).

[234] *See generally* I.R.C. § 414(p)(2)(7) (1988).

[235] 453 U.S. 210 (1981).

[236] *Id.* at 211.

In response to the decision in *McCarty*, Congress enacted the Uniformed Services Former Spouses Protection Act (USFSPA),[237] effective January 1, 1983. The effect of the act is to place state courts in the position they were in prior to the decision in *McCarty*, enabling them to apply state law in determining whether military retirement pay is divisible on divorce. The statute provides, in part:

> Subject to the limitations of this section, a court may treat disposable retired or retainer pay payable to a member for pay periods beginning after June 25, 1981, either as property solely of the member or as property of the member and his spouse in accordance with the law of the jurisdiction of such court.[238]

The USFSPA, then, permits state courts to treat military retirement benefits as property subject to distribution but it does not require them to do so. The determination is within the province of the state courts. A majority of state courts addressing the question hold that military retirement pensions are marital property. A small minority of courts have held that military retirement benefits are not distributable.

Military pensioners may be eligible to receive tax exempt disability benefits, but must waive a corresponding portion of their retirement payments to avoid double compensation. The Uniformed Services Former Spouse's Protection Act (Act) authorizes states to treat military retirement pay as divisible property excluding any amount waived in order to receive disability benefits.

In *Mansell v. Mansell*,[239] parties entered into a settlement agreement prior to the Act's passage. The agreement provided for the wife to receive 50% of the husband's military pension including the portion waived to receive veterans disability benefits. The husband's modification petition was denied by the lower and intermediate appellate courts. The Supreme Court reversed and remanded holding that states may not treat military pay waived to receive veteran's benefits as divisible property.

The Court noted that the Act exemplifies "one of those rare instances where Congress has directly and specifically legislated in the area of domestic relations."[240] The holding was based on a plain meaning reading of the Act and an interpretation by the Court that the legislature intended to create new benefits for spouses but also to limit the state court's discretion and thereby protect military retirees.

§ 10.11   Valuation of Assets: General Principles

Valuation of assets is a critical step in an equitable distribution proceeding. After the court has determined what property is eligible for

---

[237] 10 U.S.C. § 1408 (1988).

[238] 10 U.S.C. § 1408(c)(1) (1988).

[239] 490 U.S. 581 (1989).

[240] *Id.* at 587.

distribution, a value must be placed on that property so that an equitable allocation can be made between the spouses.[241]

There is a clear consensus among appellate courts that the valuation of assets is within the trial court's discretion and that those courts' findings will not be disturbed on appeal absent an abuse of that discretion. In *Hertz v. Hertz*,[242] the Supreme Court of Minnesota set out the basic principal in language that is typical and characteristic of the cases generally:

> Assigning a specific value to an asset is a finding of fact; disputes as to asset valuation are to be addressed to the trier of fact, and conflicts are to be resolved in that court. . . .

> Furthermore, valuation is necessarily an approximation in many cases, and it is only necessary that the value arrived at lies within a reasonable range of figures. Thus, the market valuation determined by the trier of fact should be sustained if it falls within the limits of credible estimates made by competent witnesses even if it does not coincide exactly with the estimate of any one of them.[243]

§ 10.12   Fair and Equitable Distribution

[A]   Introduction

Courts undertaking the equitable distribution of property pursuant to divorce face three tasks. The first task, classification or characterization, requires determination of which assets of the spouses are subject to division and distribution. Second, a trial court must place a value on the assets, both those that are distributable and those, if any, that remain the property of one spouse or the other. The final task, of course, is to make a fair division of the distributable assets.

Most equitable distribution statutes set out a list of factors that trial courts must consider when distributing property. In a few states, where the statutes do not contain factors, appellate courts have developed them for the guidance of trial courts. No particular factors are intended to be more important than any others. Thus, in the final analysis, judicial discretion is the hallmark of equitable distribution of property on divorce.

A much debated point is whether equal division is the most equitable.[244] The question is far from resolved and perhaps never will be. In a small minority of states, the statutes contain a presumption of equal division of marital property. In a few others, the courts have created a fifty-fifty starting point for division, even while rejecting a presumption of equal division. Some courts reject altogether both presumptions of equal division and starting points.

Also, with some frequency courts will decline to make substantial property distributions in marriages that are of short duration. In *Rose v.*

---

[241] *See Rothman v. Rothman*, 320 A.2d 496, 503 (N.J. 1974).

[242] 229 N.W.2d 42 (Minn. 1975).

[243] *Id.* at 44 (citation omitted).

[244] *See, e.g.*, Foster, *Commentary on Equitable Distribution*, 26 N.Y.L. Sch. L. Rev. 1 (1981).

Rose,[245] for example, the Supreme Court of Alaska adopted this approach, stating that "in marriages of short duration, where there has been no significant commingling of assets between the parties, the trial court may, without abusing its discretion, treat the property division as an action in the nature of recission, aimed at placing the parties in, as closely as possible, the financial position they would have occupied had no marriage taken place."[246]

[B]   Factors in Equitable Distribution

As noted, most equitable distribution statutes require that the trial court consider a variety of explicit factors in arriving at a fair and equitable division of marital property. Absent statutory factors, courts have enumerated factors similar to those that are statutorily mandated elsewhere. Generally, judicial application of the factors is mandatory, often with the additional requirement that the trial court set forth written reasons for its determinations on property distribution or to indicate the factors on which it relied.

Several states have adopted the provisions of the 1970 version of the Uniform Marriage and Divorce Act (UMDA) to control the disposition of property. The Act requires that the court consider all relevant factors, including:

(1)   contribution of each spouse to acquisition of marital property, including contribution of a spouse as homemaker;

(2)   value of the property set aside to each spouse;

(3)   duration of the marriage; and

(4)   economic circumstances of each spouse when the division of property is to become effective including the desirability of awarding the family home or the right to live therein for reasonable periods to the spouse having custody of any children.[247]

The UMDA factors are by no means exclusive or exhaustive, and additional factors appear in various combinations and with variations in language in statutes in the several jurisdictions. An additional factor in an increasing number of jurisdictions is the contribution of a spouse to the education, training, or increased earning power of the other spouse.[248] Also, in a considerable number of states, the list of factors concludes with a catchall provision, authorizing the court to consider any other factors deemed relevant, just, or proper, in addition to those expressed in the statute.[249]

---

[245] 755 P.2d 1121 (Alaska 1988).

[246] *Id.* at 1125.

[247] UMDA § 307, 9A U.L.A. 240 (1973).

[248] *See, e.g.,* Iowa Code § 598.21-e (1980); Pa. Stat. Ann. title 23, § 401(d)(4) (1980).

[249] *See, e.g.,* N.Y. Dom. Rel. Law § 236(B)(5)(d)(13) ("any other factor which the court shall expressly find to be just and proper").

[C] Equal Division and Starting Points

The statutes of several states contain a presumption that property subject to distribution shall be divided equally. The language of the Arkansas statute is illustrative, requiring that "marital property shall be distributed one-half (1/2) to each person unless the court finds such a division to be inequitable. In that event the court shall make some other division that the court deems equitable" after considering nine listed factors. [250]

In a number of other states, courts have held that the equal division of marital property is presumptively equitable or is an appropriate starting point when undertaking equitable distribution at divorce. These courts have so held without the benefit of statutory guidance or mandates to this effect. Most such courts caution, however, that the adoption of a fifty-fifty starting point by no means reflects a presumption of equal division. Rather, the determination of what distribution is fair, just, and equitable is a matter within the sound discretion of the trial court.

It is not uncommon for courts to abstain from significant property divisions in marriages of short duration. Typifying this approach is *Rose v. Rose.*

[D] Dissipation of Assets and Marital Misconduct

[1] Overview [251]

There is general agreement that dissipation of assets is a relevant factor in the equitable distribution of property. In fact, in most states, the equitable distribution statute lists dissipation among the factors the court is required to consider when making a property division. There is somewhat less agreement, however, about what conduct constitutes dissipation of assets. To establish dissipation, the burden of proof is generally on the party charged. Remedies for the adversely affected party range from inclusion of the value of the dissipated assets in the marital estate to consideration of a party's dissipation of assets as a factor in the ultimate property distribution.

There is considerably less agreement about the relevance in equitable distribution of marital misconduct or fault that is not economic in nature. In some jurisdictions, the statutes require that fault be considered, while others proscribe its consideration. In still other states, the statutes are silent and the courts decide the issue by applying general equitable principles.

[2] What Conduct Constitutes Dissipation?

The courts have not adopted a uniform definition of dissipation to determine what actions or inactions by a spouse that diminish the amount

---

[250] Ark. Stat. Ann. § 9-12-315 (2001).

[251] *See generally* Becker, *Conduct of a Spouse That Dissipates Property Available for Equitable Property Distribution: A Suggested Analysis*, 52 Ohio St. L.J. 95 (1991).

of property available for division are sufficient to affect the ultimate distribution. Whether or not a spouse's conduct constitutes dissipation depends on the facts of the particular case.[252] The Supreme Court of Illinois has detailed the elements that constitute dissipation of assets. Courts in other states frequently cite or rely on Illinois authority when addressing this issue. In *In re Marriage of O'Neill*,[253] the court stated: "[T]he term 'dissipation' . . . refers to the 'use of marital property for the sole benefit of one of the spouses for a purpose unrelated to the marriage at a time that the marriage is undergoing an irreconcilable breakdown. . . .'"[254]

The courts have departed on occasion from the general requirement that dissipation, to be cognizable as a factor in distribution, must occur during the breakdown of the marriage.[255] Also, a requirement of intent to dissipate assets is often implied or mentioned explicitly by courts. In *Robinette v. Robinette*,[256] for example, the Court of Appeals of Kentucky stated:

> We believe the concept of dissipation, that is, spending funds for a nonmarital purpose, is an appropriate one for the court to consider when the property is expended (1) during a period when there is a separation or dissolution impending, and (2) where there is a clear showing of intent to deprive one's spouse of his or her proportionate share of marital property.[257]

[3] Burden of Proof

The courts are in general agreement that the party against whom dissipation is charged has the burden of proving the legitimacy of his or her expenditure of marital funds. The opinion of the Appellate Court of Illinois in *In re Marriage of Smith*[258] presents a useful paradigm. In *Smith*, the trial court awarded the wife some 63 percent of the marital property, having concluded that the husband had dissipated marital assets.

On appeal, the husband asserted that the trial court's finding of dissipation was not supported by the evidence, implying that it was the wife's obligation to prove how the husband had spent the funds. Squarely rejecting this position, the court stated the following general principle: "[T]he person charged with dissipation is under an obligation to establish by clear and specific evidence how the funds were spent. General and vague statements that funds were spent on marital expenses or to pay bills are inadequate to avoid a finding of dissipation."[259]

---

[252] *In re Marriage of Sevon*, 453 N.E.2d 866 (Ill. App. Ct. 1983).

[253] 563 N.E.2d 494 (Ill. 1990).

[254] *Id.* at 498–499 (citation omitted).

[255] *See, e.g., In re Marriage of Kaplan*, 500 N.E.2d 612 (Ill. App. Ct. 1986).

[256] 736 S.W.2d 351 (Ky. Ct. App. 1987).

[257] *Id.* at 354; *see also Semasek v. Semasek*, 479 A.2d 1047 (Pa. Super. Ct. 1984).

[258] 471 N.E.2d 1008 (Ill. App. Ct.1984).

[259] *Id.* at 1013; *see also Manaker v. Manaker*, 528 A.2d 1170 (Conn. 1987); *Robinette v. Robinette*, 736 S.W.2d 351 (Ky. Ct. App. 1987); *In re Marriage of Roehrdanz*, 410 N.W.2d 359 (Minn. Ct. App. 1987).

[4]   Remedies for Dissipation

In seeking to compensate or make whole the innocent party in cases involving spousal dissipation of assets, the courts have not taken a uniform approach. Some courts hold that dissipation justifies including in the marital estate assets that are no longer in existence at the time when the equitable distribution of property is ordered. In other jurisdictions, however, the courts find such awards to be improper.

The Appellate Court of Illinois stated the commonly prevailing principle in *In re Marriage of Partyka*[260] as follows: "Where a party has dissipated marital assets, the court may charge the amount dissipated against his or her share of the marital property so as to compensate the other party."[261] In accordance with this principle, courts in several states have included in the marital estate dissipated assets no longer in existence.[262]

Not all courts find authority to include dissipated, and therefore nonexistent, assets in the marital estate. In *Lippert v. Lippert*,[263] for example, the Supreme Court of Montana held that although the state's equitable distribution statute required the court to consider dissipation, the power of the trial court did not extend to assets not in existence. As an alternative to the award of nonexistent assets, the court may take into account a party's dissipation of assets as a factor in the ultimate distribution of whatever marital property remains. Thus, in *In re Marriage of Merry*,[264] the Supreme Court of Montana affirmed a disproportionate division after a marriage of some twenty-three years. In light of the husband's dissipation of marital assets, the court approved a distribution of 70 percent to the wife and 30 percent to the husband.

[5]   Marital Misconduct or Fault

It is clear that dissipation of assets, a kind of economic fault, is invariably a factor that the courts consider when dividing property. One cannot say the same for marital misconduct, commonly referred to simply as fault. In the overwhelming majority of states, either spouse can have the marriage dissolved without proving marital fault on the part of the other spouse. With respect to the aspect of the divorce proceeding involving distribution of assets, however, there is no such clear consensus.

State legislatures generally take one of five basic approaches to the issue. Some states follow the approach of the Uniform Marriage and Divorce Ace (UMDA), which requires the division of the spouses' property "without regard to marital misconduct."[265] A number of states have adopted identical

---

[260] 511 N.E.2d 676 (Ill. App. Ct. 1987).

[261] *Id.* at 680.

[262] *See, e.g., Berish v. Berish,* 432 N.E.2d 183 (Ohio 1982); *A.I.D. v. P.M.D.,* 408 A.2d 940 (Del. 1979); *Sharp v. Sharp,* 473 A.2d 499 (Md. Ct. Spec. Ap. 1984).

[263] 627 P.2d 1206 (Mont. 1981).

[264] 689 P.2d 1250 (Mont. 1984).

[265] UMDA § 307, 9A U.L.A. 238 (1987).

language in their equitable distribution statutes.[266] Statutes in the second group explicitly command that the court consider "the conduct of the parties during the marriage"[267] or "the respective merits of the parties"[268] when making an equitable distribution of property.

A few states take a third approach, requiring trial courts to consider only misconduct that causes or leads to the breakdown of the marriage or to divorce.[269] Fourth, some statutes contain a so-called catchall factor. In New York, for example, the court must consider, in addition to twelve other listed factors, "any other factor which the court shall expressly find to be just and proper."[270] Under such formulations, the extent, if any, to which marital misconduct is a factor in property division is a matter for judicial interpretation. Accordingly, in *O'Brien v. O'Brien*,[271] New York's highest court stated:

> Except in egregious cases which shock the conscience of the court, . . . [marital fault] is not a "just and proper" factor for consideration in the equitable distribution of marital property. . . . That is so because marital fault is inconsistent with the underlying assumption that a marriage is in part an economic partnership and upon its dissolution the parties are entitled to a fair share of the marital estate, because fault will usually be difficult to assign and because introduction of the issue may involve the courts in time-consuming procedural maneuvers relating to collateral issues. . . .[272]

Finally, some statutes are silent with respect to marital misconduct or fault. Here, again, the courts must determine whether or not fault is relevant in dividing property. Interpreting such a statute in *Painter v. Painter*,[273] the Supreme Court of New Jersey held that marital fault is not an appropriate factor to consider in the equitable distribution of marital assets. The Supreme Court of Arkansas, on the other hand, in *Stover v. Stover*,[274] interpreting a statute in which fault was not a factor, approved the trial court's consideration of the fact that the wife was convicted of criminal conspiracy to cause her husband's murder.

[E] Marital Debts and Liabilities

In the strict sense, debts or liabilities of the spouses existing at the time of divorce are not assets or property. Nonetheless, legislatures and courts

---

[266] *See, e.g.,* Ill. Ann. Stat. ch. 40 § 503 (Smith-Hurd 1987 Supp.); Minn. Stat. Ann. § 518.18 (West Supp. 1987); Pa. Stat. Ann. title 23 § 401 (Purdon 1987 Supp.).

[267] *See, e.g.,* Mass. Gen. Laws Ann. ch. 208 § 34 (West Supp. 1987); Mo. Rev. Stat. § 452.325(4) (1986).

[268] *See, e.g.,* Vt. Stat. Ann. title 15 § 751(b)(12) (Supp. 1986).

[269] *See, e.g.,* Conn. Gen. Stat. Ann. § 46-6-81 (West 1986); Va. Code Ann. § 20-107-3-E-5 (Supp. 1987).

[270] N.Y. Dom. Rel. Law § 236B(5)(d)(13) (McKinney 1986).

[271] 489 N.E.2d 712 (N.Y. 1985).

[272] *Id.* at 719.

[273] 320 A.2d 484 (N.J. 1974).

[274] 696 S.W.2d 750 (Ark. 1985).

in many equitable distribution states generally analyze the characterization and distribution of debts in the same manner as they do assets. Most commonly, debts or liabilities are listed among the factors that the trial court is required to consider when making an equitable distribution of property.[275] In jurisdictions in which the statutes do not mention the subject, the courts must formulate principles to govern the treatment of debts and liabilities in order to ensure property divisions that are just and equitable.

Judicial decisions on the subject reflect two fundamental views. In a few states, appellate courts hold that the trial court must allocate debts and liabilities when making an equitable distribution of marital property.[276] In a greater number of states, the courts hold that although the allocation of debts and liabilities is not required, it is the better practice. As the Missouri Court of Appeals pointed out in *N.J.W. v. W.E.W.*:[277]

> A debt owed by the spouses does not constitute "property" owned by them. The failure of the decree to provide as to payment of debts is therefore not a fatal defect, although the better practice would be to do so and thereby reduce subsequent dispute and contention.

> The existence and extent of debts does, of course, affect the fairness of the way in which assets are divided.[278]

[F] The Marital Home

In many cases, perhaps most, the marital home, homestead, or family residence is the most valuable asset of the divorcing spouses. It is usually acquired during the marriage and clearly falls within the category of marital property. The overriding concern in cases concerning the marital home is what constitutes a fair and equitable distribution in light of statutory and other factors and the circumstances of the case and the parties. In approximately a third of the states, there is statutory treatment of the marital home. The statutes explicitly authorize trial courts to award exclusive use and possession of the marital home to the spouse having custody of any children.[279]

Decisions treating the marital home fall into two basic categories. In many cases, the courts order use and occupancy by the custodial spouse, followed by sale of the home and division of the proceeds when the child is emancipated or the custodial spouse remarries. In a second group of cases, the courts make an award of the marital home or order its sale and

---

[275] *See, e.g.*, Ark. Stat. Ann. § 9-12-315(a)(1)(A)(vii) (1987); Ill. Rev. Stat. ch. 40, para. 503(d)(7) (Smith-Hurd Supp. 1988); Minn. Stat. Ann. § 518.58 (West Supp. 1989); N.C. Gen. Stat. § 50-20(c)(1) (1987); Va. Code § 20-107-3(E)(7) (Supp. 1988).

[276] *See, e.g.*, *In re Marriage of Johnson*, 299 N.W.2d 466 (Iowa 1980).

[277] 584 S.W.2d 148 (Mo. Ct. App. 1979).

[278] *Id.* at 151.

[279] *See, e.g.*, Colo. Rev. Stat. § 14-10-113(1)(c) (1987) (including among the statutory factors in property division "[t]he economic circumstances of each spouse at the time the division of property is to become effective, including the desirability of awarding the family home or the right to live therein for reasonable periods to the spouse having custody of any children.").

an equitable division of the proceeds at the time of divorce. It is apparently within the courts' inherent equity powers to award possession of the marital home to the custodial spouse, whether or not there is explicit statutory authority. Such an award is also appropriate, when just and equitable, under the catchall factor listed in a number of equitable distribution statutes. By and large, as the Supreme Court of South Carolina remarked in *Herring v. Herring*,[280] "[t]he best interests and needs of the child are paramount."[281]

---

[280] 335 S.E.2d 366 (S.C. 1985).
[281] *Id.* at 369.

Chapter 11

CHILD CUSTODY AND VISITATION

§ 11.01 Introduction

The issues of child custody and visitation addressed in this chapter arise most frequently in the context of divorce, but also may occur in disputes between parents who have not married each other. Upon dissolution of a marriage, when there are children, the court ordinarily will award physical, or residential, custody to one of the parents. The noncustodial parent generally will be granted visitation rights. Visitation may be viewed as a limited form of custody, at least to the extent that the noncustodial parent has the authority to make decisions relating to the child during visitation.

In recent years, frequently in response to legislative mandates, courts have looked to joint custody as an alternative to the traditional award of sole custody with visitation. In principle, joint custody arrangements afford shared responsibility for major decisions relating to their children after divorce. As a practical matter, however, joint custody arrangements often resemble sole custody with visitation, in that one of the parents has primary physical custody of the child or children.

Whatever the form of custody, judicial discretion clearly is the hallmark of child custody decision making. A serviceable statement of the rationale for placing child custody decisions within the sound discretion of the trial court is that broad discretion "enables the court to explore every aspect of the litigants' circumstances so that its custody determination will reflect the child's best interests."[1] Such broad discretion obviously carries the potential for subjective decisions that may be tainted by personal bias or lack of understanding of child development.

§ 11.02 Child Custody Jurisdiction

Child custody jurisdiction refers to the authority of a court to resolve a custody dispute. Although child custody jurisdiction issues arise in a number of contexts, including adoption, neglect proceedings, and actions to terminate parental rights, most custody jurisdiction disputes develop during proceedings related to divorce. Moreover, although custody jurisdiction issues sometimes surface as part of an initial custody determination at the time of divorce, they most frequently arise when one party attempts to have a custody decree modified. The problem exists largely because custody decrees are not considered final judgments, but may be modified in order to safeguard the best interests of the child upon changed circumstances.

---

[1] *Berman v. Berman*, 270 N.W.2d 680 (Mich. Ct. App. 1978).

Interstate jurisdictional disputes constitute the most common dilemma, usually occurring when a court attempts to modify a custody order of another state. Such conflicts generally arise when a noncustodial parent seeks a modification of custody while the child is with that parent either legally, during visitation or with the consent of the custodial parent, or illegally, when the noncustodial parent refuses to return the child after visitation or abducts the child. Jurisdictional disputes ensue in these situations not only because of the natural desire of parents to have custody of their children, but also because of a strong tendency of state courts to assert their own jurisdictional power.

As in most areas of family law, jurisdiction to resolve child custody matters has always been the domain of the state courts, and state courts gradually expanded the limits of their own jurisdictional requirements for resolving custody matters. During this century, the increased mobility of the American population contributed to forum shopping and parental kidnapping, as disappointed parents attempted to obtain more favorable forums for their custody actions. In an attempt to discourage such behavior, considered detrimental to the children involved, both state and federal governments have responded over the past several decades by enacting legislation intended to give stability to custody decrees and to assure that custody litigation occurs in an optimal forum.

[A] Traditional Rules and Habeas Corpus Actions

Under the traditional view, reflected in the first Restatement of the Conflict of Laws, only a court of the state where a child was domiciled could enter a custody decree.[2] The domicile rule was based on the concept that only the state of the child's domicile had a sufficient relationship with the child to give the state a legitimate interest in regulating the status of custody. Although the domicile rule forestalled interstate custody disputes to the extent that a child could be domiciled in only one state at a time, such a rigid rule was severely criticized for the ease at which it could obscure a genuine inquiry into the best interests of children.[3]

In addition, the United States Supreme Court recognized few constitutional limitations on the states' jurisdiction to resolve custody jurisdiction disputes. The Court had earlier pronounced that the Full Faith and Credit Clause does not require a state to give a sister state judgment greater recognition than the original state would afford that judgment, nor does it preclude inquiry into the validity of the judgment.[4] In *New York ex rel. Halvey v. Halvey*,[5] the Court extended those principles to custody jurisdiction, concluding that because a custody decision is modifiable in the state

---

[2] Restatement, Conflict of Laws § 117 (1934).

[3] *See* Strumburg, *The Status of Children in Conflicts of Laws*, 8 U. Chi. L. Rev. 42 (1940); Stansbury, *Custody and Maintenance Across State Lines*, 10 Law & Contemp. Probs. 818 (1944).

[4] *Reynolds v. Stockton*, 140 U.S. 254 (1891).

[5] 330 U.S. 610 (1947).

where it was entered, the Full Faith and Credit Clause does not prevent modification by other states. The Court explained:

> [A] judgment has no constitutional claim to a more conclusive or final effect in the State of the forum than it has in the state where rendered. . . . Whatever may be the authority of a State to undermine a judgment of a sister State on grounds not cognizable in the state where the judgment was rendered, it is clear that the State of the forum has at least as much leeway to disregard the judgment, to qualify it, or to depart from it as does the State where it was rendered.[6]

The *Halvey* Court emphasized that because the welfare of the child and the parents' interest in the child's welfare are the primary considerations in custody determinations, a change in circumstances or facts not previously considered may justify a modification of a custody decree not only in the state that originally decided custody, but also in another state.

In light of *Halvey*'s apparent broad authorization for custody modification, many state courts began to exert their powers liberally, sometimes finding changed circumstances sufficient for adjusting custody rights based merely on the fact that the child was living in a different state. The result was a system in which a parent who did not receive a favorable custody award could simply take the child to another jurisdiction and seek to modify the award.[7] State courts developed additional grounds for asserting custody jurisdiction, including the domicile of one or both parents or the physical presence of the child, in addition to domicile of the child.[8]

Sampsell v. Superior Court[9] illustrates the development of a multi-factor approach to custody jurisdiction to replace the traditional domicile rule. In *Sampsell*, the parents and child had lived in California until the parents separated. The mother later moved to Nevada with the child, where she obtained a divorce decree, remarried, then moved to Utah with the child and her new husband. Before the Nevada divorce decree had been entered, the child's father brought a custody action in California, which the trial court dismissed for lack of jurisdiction. The father applied for a writ of mandamus to compel the California trial court to hear the custody case.

In granting the father's plea, Justice Traynor, writing for the Supreme Court of California, first noted:

> Several theories have been advanced with respect to the correct basis for jurisdiction over the subject matter of a child custody proceeding. According to one theory, jurisdiction over children's custody is based on *in personam* jurisdiction over the children's parents. . . . Another theory regards the question of custody as

---

[6] *Id.* at 615.

[7] For historical accounts of this period of the law, *see* Blakesley, *Child Custody Jurisdiction and Procedure*, 35 Emory L.J. 291 (1986); Coombs, *Interstate Child Custody: Jurisdiction, Recognition, and Enforcement*, 66 Minn. L. Rev. 711 (1982).

[8] *See* Coombs, *supra* note 7.

[9] 197 P.2d 739 (Cal. 1948).

simply one of status and as such subject to the control of the courts of the state where the child is domiciled. A third theory requires the child to be physically present within the state, on the ground that the basic problem before the court is to determine what the best interest of the child is, and the court most qualified to do so is the one having access to the child.[10]

Justice Traynor observed that the various theories were founded on inconsistent considerations which cannot be reconciled when all the parties are not domiciled in the same state, and that the question of recognizing custody decrees from other states had overshadowed the best interest of the child. Because a state's interest in children requires that custody decrees be modified when circumstances change or previously unknown facts are revealed, they are not final decrees. States need only treat an earlier custody decree entered by another state with the same respect that the original state would accord it. He noted that undue emphasis was placed on the finality of custody decrees. None of the existing theories, applied as an exclusive test for child custody jurisdiction, adequately protected the interests of the child.

Justice Traynor concluded that a state which has a substantial interest in the child's welfare or the preservation of the child's family may have jurisdiction over the custody dispute. Thus, more than one state may have jurisdiction over a specific child custody matter, although both states should not necessarily exercise that jurisdiction and reach conflicting results; rather, a state might defer to another state which has a more substantial interest in the case, and courts should give appropriate respect to the decision of a previous forum.

The Second Restatement of Conflict of Laws similarly incorporated the multiple basis approach to jurisdiction.[11] The inevitable result of this liberal view of jurisdiction was for states to assert jurisdiction whenever they concluded it would be in the child's best interest.[12] Increased forum shopping followed, not only for an initial custody decree, but also for the opportunity to change an unfavorable decision, because courts exhibited a strong tendency to prefer the parent who presented evidence of the child's contact with that forum.[13] The expansion of jurisdictional grounds greatly exacerbated the problem of interstate custody disputes.

The Supreme Court compounded the problem in 1953 when it concluded in *May v. Anderson*[14] that a state was not required to give Full Faith and Credit to a sister state's custody decree that was not based upon personal jurisdiction over the respondent. In *May*, the father had obtained an ex parte Wisconsin divorce decree, which granted him custody. He later attempted to enforce the decree in Ohio, where the mother resided, when

---

[10] *Id.* at 748–749.

[11] Restatement (Second) of Conflict of Laws, § 79 (1971).

[12] *See* Unif. Child Custody Jurisdiction Act, *Prefatory Note*, 9 U.L.A. 116, 117 (1988) [hereinafter UCCJA.].

[13] *See O'Neal v. O'Neal*, 329 N.W.2d 666 (Iowa 1983).

[14] 345 U.S. 528 (1953).

she refused to return the children after visitation. With analogy to cases dealing with property rights, the Supreme Court held that Ohio did not need to recognize the Wisconsin decree because it was entered without personal jurisdiction over the mother, although the parties had stipulated in the divorce action that the children were domiciled in Wisconsin. *May* generated additional confusion over the necessary basis for exercising jurisdiction in child custody disputes, and has been criticized for ignoring the interests of the child.[15]

The lack of an effective remedy for enforcing a legal right to custody further contributed to jurisdictional problems. Disputing parents used writs of habeas corpus to gain physical custody over their children. Traditionally, writs of habeas corpus were used to free a person who was being unlawfully detained. A writ of habeas corpus is a judicial directive to the party to produce the detained person before the court so that it may determine whether the detention is lawful.[16] The writ of habeas corpus applied to custody disputes because the retention of a child without a legal right to custody is comparable to an unlawful retention.[17]

The person with a legal right to the child's custody may file a habeas corpus petition to regain possession of the child. The petitioner must establish that the child is being unlawfully detained and that the petitioner has a superior legal right to custody. The respondent must appear before the court to support his or her retention of the child.[18] A party who refuses to comply with a writ of habeas corpus may be held in contempt of court.

Currently, state habeas corpus procedures are most appropriately employed when a speedy, simple remedy is required, such as when the noncustodial parent flees the state with the child. The writ may also be effective when a party having physical custody of a child does not have legal custody, such as when grandparents dispute custody rights[19] or when the child has been placed in a state institution such as a foster home or juvenile detention center.[20]

In interstate custody disputes, the legal right to custody may hinge on the validity of a custody decree under the Uniform Child Custody Jurisdiction Act and the Parental Kidnaping Act.[21] Because of the jurisdictional requirements of those Acts,[22] habeas corpus usually is not the most appropriate mechanism for determining custody, and the majority of courts

---

[15] *See* 1 Homer J. Clark, Jr., Law of Domestic Relations in the United States 461; Hazard, *May v. Anderson: Preamble to Family Law Chaos*, 45 Va. L. Rev. 379 (1959).

[16] 2 J. McCahey *et al., Child Custody & Visitation Law & Practice*, § 7.05 (1992).

[17] *Id.* § 7.02[1].

[18] *See, e.g., Matthews v. Matthews*, 232 S.E.2d 761 (Ga. 1977); *see also* Dobbs, *Tort Law — Tort Recovery for Intentional Interference with Custodial Rights in Minnesota — [Larson v. Dunn, 460 N.W.2d 39 (Minn. 1990)]*, 17 Wm. Mitchell L. Rev. 1159, 1164 (1991).

[19] *See Uhing v. Uhing*, 488 N.W.2d 366 (Neb. 1992).

[20] *See People ex rel. McKay v. Barbaro*, 310 N.Y.S.2d 650 (N.Y. Sup. Ct. 1970); *see also* John P. McCahey, *supra* note16, § 7.01[1].

[21] *Id.* § 7.02[2].

[22] *See infra* §§ 11.02[B], [C].

will not permit modification of an existing custody order through the use of habeas corpus.[23] Furthermore, if discovery, witnesses, or proof of the child's best interests will be necessary, the writ may not be an effective method of determining custody.[24] Because of its limitations, the writ is largely regarded as an ineffective remedy for enforcing child custody rights, and has been replaced to a significant extent by equitable remedies.[25]

The ultimate abuse of the traditional approach to custody jurisdiction and enforcement of custody decrees was a form of kidnapping by a parent who retained the child after visitation without the permission of the custodial parent or removed the child to another state in order to relitigate the custody issue. The incidence of such abuses led to legislative action by both the state and federal governments, which has significantly diminished, but not totally extinguished, the problem.

[B] The Uniform Child Custody Jurisdiction Act

The Uniform Child Custody Jurisdiction Act [UCCJA],[26] promulgated in 1968, has been adopted in some form by all states. Its purpose was not only to create uniformity in child custody jurisdiction practices among states, but also to "avoid jurisdictional competition and conflict with courts of other states in matters of child custody which have in the past resulted in the shifting of children from state to state with harmful effects on their well-being."[27] The Act's primary goals are to provide a uniform basis for child custody decisions that is not as inflexible as the previous standard based on domicile, and, at the same time, to discourage multiple litigation of custody matters which the multi-factor approach encouraged.

The drafters of the UCCJA envisioned it encompassing a wide variety of custody proceedings: initial custody, visitation, modification, and dependency in child neglect cases.[28] Some states have altered its scope, for instance, to exclude dependency actions,[29] although many courts have held it applicable to adoptions and other issues involving child placement.[30] The Act extends to properly rendered custody decrees of foreign countries as well, so long as all interested persons are given notice and the opportunity to be heard.[31]

---

[23] John P. McCahey, *supra* note 16, § 7.07.

[24] Id. § 7.02[3][b].

[25] *Id.*

[26] UCCJA, *supra* note 12. *See generally* Brigette M. Bodenheimer, *Progress Under the Uniform Child Custody Jurisdiction Act and Remaining Problems: Punitive Decrees, Joint Custody, and Excessive Modifications*, 65 Cal. L. Rev. 978 (1977).

[27] UCCJA, *supra* note 12, § 1(a)(1).

[28] *See id.* § 2(3) and Official Cmt.

[29] UCCJA, *supra* note 12, § 2 cmt., 135, 136 (listing the following states: Montana, New Hampshire, New Mexico and New York).

[30] *See, e.g., Weathersby v. Stubbs*, 833 P.2d 1297 (Or. Ct. App. 1992) (Oregon joins majority of states holding that UCCJA applies to adoptions); *see also* Bernadette W. Hartfield, *The Uniform Child Custody Jurisdiction Act and the Problem of Jurisdiction in Interstate Adoption: An Easy Fix?*, 43 Okla. L. Rev. 621 (1990).

[31] UCCJA, *supra* note 12, at § 23. Some states have omitted this provision from their versions of the UCCJA. UCCJA § 23 cmt. lists Missouri, New Mexico, Ohio and South Dakota.

The Act attempts to fulfill its comprehensive goals by promoting cooperation of various state courts through facilitating the exchange of information among courts to ensure that custody decisions are rendered in the state best equipped to determine the best interests of a particular child. To encourage custody litigation in the state with the closest connection to the child and the family, where the most evidence with respect to the child's welfare is likely to be available, the UCCJA recognizes alternate bases for assertion of custody jurisdiction. It sets out mechanisms for enforcing existing custody decrees and avoiding re-litigation to the extent feasible, and establishes guidelines for state courts to decline jurisdiction in deference to a more appropriate forum.

A tension exists between the UCCJA's goals of achieving stability of custody decrees, on the one hand, and creating a system with sufficient flexibility to accommodate the best interests of the child in a mobile society, on the other. Indeed, one court has commented, "A close reading of the Act discloses a schizophrenic attempt to bring about an orderly system of decision and at the same time to protect the best interests of the children who may be immediately before the court."[32]

[1]   Jurisdictional Prerequisites

The UCCJA contains four bases for jurisdiction in custody actions, which can be described as (1) "home state" jurisdiction, (2) "significant connection" jurisdiction, (3) "emergency" jurisdiction, and (4) "default" jurisdiction.

"Home state" jurisdiction is present when a court of otherwise competent jurisdiction is the home state at the time the action is commenced.[33] The Act defines "home state" as "the state in which the child immediately preceding the time involved lived with his parent, a parent, or a person acting as parent, for at least 6 consecutive months."[34] If the child is less than 6 months old, the state where the child lived from birth with any of the parties mentioned is considered the home state.[35] Temporary absence of any of the named persons counts toward the requisite time period.[36] Home state jurisdiction also exists when the state had been the home state within the previous six months and the child is absent from the state because he or she has been removed or retained by a person claiming custody, or for other reasons, and a parent or person acting as a parent still lives in the state.[37]

Home state jurisdiction is based on the theory that the usual residence of the child and a parent or a person acting as a parent is likely to have access to the most information regarding the proper custody of the child.[38]

---

[32] *In re Marriage of Settle*, 556 P.2d 962, 968 (Or. 1976).

[33] UCCJA, *supra* note 12, § 3(a)(1).

[34] *Id.* § 2(5).

[35] *Id.*

[36] *Id.*

[37] *Id.* § 3(a)(1).

[38] *See, e.g., In re B.R.F.*, 669 S.W.2d 240 (Mo. Ct. App. 1984).

The concept of "home state" establishes jurisdiction in the vast majority of custody decisions. In a sense, it serves as a less rigid substitute for domicile, while providing a firmer foundation for jurisdiction than mere physical presence.

The second jurisdictional ground, referred to as "significant connection" jurisdiction, provides the major alternative to the home state provision and adds flexibility to the Act. Significant connection jurisdiction exists if:

> [I]t is in the best interest of the child that a court of this State assume jurisdiction because (i) the child and his parents, or the child and at least one contestant, have a significant connection with this State, and (ii) there is available in this State substantial evidence concerning the child's present or future care, protection, training, and personal relationships. . . .[39]

Unlike the multi-factor approach, discussed earlier, significant connection jurisdiction requires more than a mere conclusion that the exercise of jurisdiction would be in the child's best interests; it additionally demands both a significant connection with the state and substantial evidence relating to the child available in the state.

> The framers of the Act cautioned that this section perhaps more than any other provision of the Act requires that it be interpreted in the spirit of the legislative purposes. . . . The paragraph was phrased in general terms in order to be flexible enough to cover many fact situations too diverse to lend themselves to exact description. But its purpose is to limit jurisdiction rather than to proliferate it. The first clause of the paragraph is important: jurisdiction exists only if it is in the child's interest, not merely the interest or convenience of the feuding parties, to determine custody in a particular state. The interest of the child is served when the forum has optimum access to relevant evidence about the child and family. There must be maximum rather than minimum contact.[40]

Unfortunately, although the significant connection provision is an alternative, not an exception to, the home state provision, it creates a dangerous loophole that potentially could be used whenever a parent desires to litigate outside the home state. If a parent assembles facts sufficient to establish a significant connection before the other parent brings a custody action in the home state, the forum court will have considerable discretion in asserting jurisdiction on this ground.[41] Much of the litigation arising under the UCCJA has resulted from the manner in which the court interprets the significant connection test. Some courts have taken an extremely broad view of that section, placing great emphasis on the substantial evidence

---

[39] UCCJA, *supra* note 12, § 3(a)(2).

[40] Commissioners' Note, 9 U.L.A. 144, 145, § 3 (1968).

[41] *See* Pomraning v. Pomraning, 682 S.W.2d 775 (Ark. Ct. App. 1985); *Allison v. Superior Ct.*, 160 Cal. Rptr. 309 (Cal. Ct. App. 1979); *Smith v. Superior Ct.*, 137 Cal. Rptr. 348 (Cal. Ct. App. 1977).

which is in the forum state,[42] although provisions of the PKPA may resolve those issues.[43]

The third jurisdictional basis, "emergency" jurisdiction, exists when the child is physically present in the state and has been abandoned or "it is necessary in an emergency to protect the child because he has been subjected to or threatened with mistreatment or abuse or is otherwise neglected [or dependent]."[44] Emergency jurisdiction should be exercised only in extraordinary circumstances, such as situations in which the child faces imminent harm.[45] Some courts have held that exercise of emergency jurisdiction is a temporary measure which exists only until the state with more substantial contacts is able to consider the custody question.[46]

Finally, when no other state would have jurisdiction under grounds substantially similar to one of the first three grounds, or when another state declines to exercise jurisdiction because it determines that the forum state is more appropriate, the forum state has jurisdiction if it is in the best interest of the child that it assume jurisdiction.[47] This provision may be viewed as a "default" basis of jurisdiction.

The physical presence of the child or a party is not, in itself, sufficient to confer custody jurisdiction under the UCCJA.[48] While the presence of the child is preferable, it is not required for jurisdiction over matters concerning custody, except under the emergency basis for jurisdiction.[49]

Nor does the UCCJA require personal jurisdiction over the respondent in a custody action. Although the Supreme Court's plurality opinion in *May v. Anderson*[50] literally stands for the proposition that a custody decree is not entitled to full faith and credit unless there is personal jurisdiction over the respondent and has been construed to mean that custody decrees are void without personal jurisdiction,[51] the Court's later opinion in *Shaffer v. Heitner*[52] carved an exception for cases determining status. The continued vitality of *May*'s holding appears doubtful[53] and many courts have either limited *May* or simply ignored it.[54] One way of circumventing the

---

[42] *See, e.g., Schlumpf v. Superior Ct.*, 145 Cal. Rptr. 190 (Cal. Ct. App. 1978); *Allison v. Superior Ct.*, 160 Cal. Rptr. 309 (Cal. Ct. App. 1979).

[43] *See* § 11.02[D], *infra.*

[44] UCCJA, *supra* note 12, at § 3(a)(3).

[45] See Greenlaw v. Smith, 840 P.2d 233 (Wash. Ct. App. 1992); *Swan v. Swan*, 796 P.2d 221 (Nev. 1990).

[46] *See, e.g., State ex rel. D.S.K.*, 792 P.2d 118 (Utah Ct. App. 1990).

[47] UCCJA, *supra* note 12, § 3(a)(4).

[48] *Id.* § 3(b).

[49] *Id.* § 3(c).

[50] 345 U.S. 528 (1952); *see supra* note 14 and accompanying text.

[51] *See Kulko v. Superior Ct.*, 436 U.S. 84 (1978), *reh. den.*, 438 U.S. 908 (1978).

[52] 433 U.S. 186 (1978).

[53] *See* Brigitte M. Bodenheimer & Janet Neeley-Kvarme, *Jurisdiction Over Child Custody and Adoption After Shaffer and Kulko*, 12 U.C. Davis L. Rev. 229 (1979).

[54] *See, e.g., In re Marriage of Leonard*, 175 Cal. Rptr. 903 (Cal. Ct. App. 1981); *Morrell v. Giesick*, 610 P.2d 1189 (Mont. 1980); *Goldfarb v. Goldfarb*, 268 S.E.2d 648 (Ga. 1980).

personal jurisdiction requirement is to regard custody actions as merely determinations of status, which do not require *in personam* jurisdiction.[55] However, some commentators have contended that dispensing with personal jurisdiction over a parent in a custody dispute deprives the parent of procedural due process.[56]

While more than one state may have statutory authority to decide a custody case under the UCCJA, only one state should exercise that jurisdiction. Ideally, that state will be the one with the most substantial connection to the child and the litigants. Courts often reach divergent conclusions regarding jurisdiction based upon similar facts under the UCCJA. Usually such discrepancies arise in the context of custody modification actions.[57]

[2] Restraints on Jurisdiction

The mere existence of a ground for custody jurisdiction is insufficient to justify a court's exercise of its authority. If a custody proceeding concerning a child is pending in a court which is exercising jurisdiction substantially conforming to the UCCJA, the Act forbids another court from asserting its jurisdiction unless the first court stays its action because the forum state is more appropriate or for other reasons.[58] The Act further directs the court to examine available information to determine whether proceedings may be pending in another state and to inquire of the officials of that state if has reason to believe such an action is pending.[59]

If the court learns of another pending custody action, it must stay the action and communicate with the other court to determine which state is the more appropriate forum.[60] The court must also inform the other court if it happens to make a custody decision before discovering another pending action or if it is informed of an action that was commenced in another state after it had assumed jurisdiction.[61]

The UCCJA further permits a court to decline jurisdiction on its own motion or upon motion of a party or representative of the child prior to entering a decree, if it determines that another state provides a more appropriate forum.[62] The Act lists factors that may be considered and provides for the exchange of information with the other court before deciding whether to retain jurisdiction or to dismiss or stay the action.[63]

---

[55] *See In re Marriage of Schuham*, 458 N.E.2d 559 (Ill. App. Ct. 1983); *see also* Brigitte M. Bodenheimer & Janet Neeley-Kvarme, *supra* note 53.

[56] *See* Helen Garfield, *Due Process Rights of Absent Parents in Interstate Custody Conflicts: A Commentary on In re Marriage of Hudson*, 16 Ind. L. Rev. 445 (1983).

[57] *See infra* § 11.06.

[58] UCCJA, § 6(a); *see also In re C.A.D.*, 839 P.2d 165 (Okla. 1992).

[59] UCCJA, § 6(b).

[60] *Id.* § 6(c).

[61] *Id.*

[62] *Id.* §§ 7(a), (b).

[63] *Id.* § 7(c)-(I).

[3]   Recognition and Enforcement of Custody Decrees under the UCCJA

The UCCJA requires states to recognize and enforce the properly rendered custody decrees of other states.[64] Relatedly, one of the most important provisions of the Act forbids states from modifying sister state custody decrees unless the forum court itself has jurisdiction under one of the four bases of the UCCJA *and* it appears to the forum court that the state which initially entered the custody order no longer has such jurisdiction or has declined to assume jurisdiction to modify its decree.[65] Modifying states are directed to give "due consideration" to the earlier proceedings.[66]

The modification provision does not require that the state which initially rendered the decree continue to possess the *same* basis for jurisdiction that it originally had, only that it continue to have *one* of the jurisdictional bases. The Supreme Court of Washington, in *Greenlaw v. Smith*,[67] held that it retained jurisdiction over its own custody decree even after the mother and children had moved from the state, because the child had consistently visited his father in Washington, the court had records extending over many years regarding the litigation between the parents, the child had extended family and a counselor in the state, and the child was 15 years old and had expressed the desire to live with his father. Thus, even though the forum state may otherwise fulfill the jurisdictional requisites, it may not exercise that jurisdiction to modify another state's custody decree unless the original state no longer has any basis for jurisdiction or has deferred to the new state as a more appropriate forum.

The modification provisions frequently have been misinterpreted or abused. Some courts have concluded that they may modify another state's custody decree once the forum state has become the home state and the children have established significant connections in that state, without thoroughly analyzing the original state's potential basis for continuing jurisdiction or communicating with that state to determine whether it would defer to the forum state.[68] More recent decisions indicate, however, that most states have recognized the distinction between original and continuing jurisdiction, and have correctly refused to modify the custody decree of another state in cases where that original state continues to have a significant connection with the children, usually because a parent remains a resident in that state and the children visit there on a somewhat regular basis.[69] The enactment of the PKPA has resolved some of these issues, and the UCCJEA should resolve others.[70]

---

[64] *Id.* § 13.

[65] *Id.* §§ 14(a)(1), (2).

[66] *Id.*

[67] 869 P.2d 1024 (Wash. 1994).

[68] *See, e.g., Liford v. Goodman*, 19 Fam. L. Rep. (BNA) 1071 (Iowa Ct. App. 1992) (concluding that because previous state, Indiana, was no longer home state of children, Indiana no longer had jurisdiction).

[69] *See, e.g., In re Hendricks*, 817 P.2d 1339 (Or. Ct. App.), *cert. denied*, 824 P.2d 417 (Or. 1992).

[70] *See* § 11.02[C], [D] *infra*.

[4]   Effect of a Party's Conduct on Jurisdiction

The UCCJA also contains provisions for a court to decline what would otherwise be appropriate jurisdiction because of a party's conduct in the custody dispute. If the petitioner for an *initial* custody decree has "wrongfully taken the child from another state or has engaged in similar reprehensible conduct" the court is authorized, but not required, to decline jurisdiction when it is "just and proper under the circumstances."[71] In an action to *modify* another state's custody decree, however, the court is prohibited from exercising its jurisdiction "if the petitioner, without consent of the person entitled to custody, has improperly removed the child from the physical custody" of that person or "has improperly retained the child after a visit or other temporary relinquishment of physical custody," unless the interests of the child require that the court exercise its jurisdiction.[72] The court may also decline to exercise its jurisdiction for other violations of any existing custody decree of another state, if it is "just and proper under the circumstances."[73] If a court dismisses an action because of wrongful conduct, it may assess "necessary travel and other expenses, including attorneys' fees, incurred by other parties or their witnesses" to the petitioner.[74]

The conduct provisions of the UCCJA have, on occasion, been applied by courts in a manner that circumvents the Act's other jurisdictional requisites. For example, in *In re Marriage of Settle*,[75] the Oregon Supreme Court was faced with a custody modification action which dealt with both the continuing jurisdiction of Indiana, the state which had rendered the earlier custody decree, and the effect of the mother's conduct in removing the children from that state and concealing them in Oregon. The mother in *Settle* had left Indiana with the couple's two children to accompany another man to Oregon; upon her later return to Indiana, she filed for divorce and was granted temporary custody pursuant to an agreement between the parties. Prior to the final hearing, the mother again returned to Oregon with the children, without informing the court or the father. The Indiana divorce court awarded the father custody solely on the basis of his evidence.

When the mother subsequently registered the Indiana decree in Oregon and petitioned for a change of custody to herself, the father filed a habeas corpus proceeding for their return, based on his Indiana decree. In light of evidence not presented to the Indiana court and the children's 20-month separation from their father, the Oregon trial court modified the decree and awarded custody to the mother. The Court of Appeals reversed, concluding that the trial court should have declined jurisdiction.

The Oregon Supreme Court reversed, finding sufficient jurisdiction, and ordered the modification decree reinstated. The court acknowledged that

---

[71] UCCJA, *supra* note 12, § 8(a).

[72] *Id.*

[73] *Id.* § 8(b).

[74] *See, id.* § 8(c).

[75] 556 P.2d 962 (Or. 1976).

absent Indiana's declining jurisdiction, the UCCJA permitted Oregon court to modify the Indiana custody decree only if Oregon had jurisdiction and if Indiana no longer had jurisdiction. Because the children had been in Oregon for more than six months, the court concluded that Oregon had home state jurisdiction; alternatively, because the children and their mother had a significant connection with Oregon and substantial evidence concerning the children's custody existed there, significant connection jurisdiction also existed. Without consulting the Indiana court, however, the Oregon court further concluded that because the children had been absent from Indiana for more than 18 months, Indiana not only had lost home-state jurisdiction, but no longer retained significant connection jurisdiction. The court then decided that the best interest of the children would be furthered by litigating their custody in Oregon.

Having found jurisdiction to modify, the *Settle* court next addressed the problem posed by the mother's wrongful removal of the children to Oregon. Conceding that the UCCJA incorporates a "clean hands" doctrine, the court found that, despite the mother's temporary custody decree, her actions of removing the children from Indiana were "just as culpable as if she had removed the children from the legal and physical custody of father or retained them after a visit. . . . It is the kind of act which the Act intended should preclude the exercise of jurisdiction — *unless the best interests of the children otherwise require*."[76] Faced with what it viewed as an "irreconcilable conflict," it concluded that the best interest of the children required the court to assume jurisdiction rather than to punish the mother for her wrongful behavior, because the Oregon proceeding was likely to be the only time all the relevant information was before any court.

By equating the time spent in the forum state with the children's best interest and declining to refuse jurisdiction acquired by wrongful conduct, the *Settle* decision fails to discourage the child snatching and forum shopping that the UCCJA was intended to remedy and subverts the jurisdictional bases for modification actions. Based on such considerations, the Oregon Supreme Court reconsidered its position in *In re Custody of Ross*.[77]

Ross involved a father who had abducted his infant daughter from Montana and concealed her in Oregon. A Montana court issued a custody decree in favor of the child's mother, who was unable to locate the child, although the father occasionally called to assure her of the child's safety. The mother ultimately traced the father to Oregon and filed suit to enforce the Montana decree; the father requested that the Oregon court assume jurisdiction and award custody to him. The trial court, following *Settle*, granted the father's petition and the Court of Appeals affirmed.

Faced with the consequences that the *Settle* decision rewarded the "successful long-term concealment following an abduction" by vesting of jurisdiction in the forum state,[78] Oregon's supreme court reversed. It found

---

[76] *Id.* at 967 (emphasis added).

[77] 630 P.2d 353 (Or. 1981)

[78] *Id.* at 358.

that, because the mother, the child's sister, and others who had been involved in the child's early upbringing continued to reside in Montana after the child's forcible removal, Montana still retained jurisdiction based on the child's significant connection with that state. Further, the court observed that if a state lost jurisdiction because of a unilateral removal of the child, both the Act and the child's best interests would be thwarted. The court conditioned its decision, however, noting "it is inescapable that, with the passage of each day, the relationship of the abducted child to the decree state becomes a little less substantial. Ultimately, perhaps, decree state jurisdiction would cease to exist. . . ."[79] While the court in *Ross* could have merely distinguished *Settle* on its facts, its decision to limit that earlier case may well reflect public dissatisfaction with parental abduction.

Although the UCCJA does not require an actual violation of a custody decree, or even the existence of a custody decree, for a court to decline jurisdiction based on a party's "wrongfully" taking the child from the other parent, courts have been somewhat reluctant to decline jurisdiction on this ground. In *Morgan v. Morgan*[80] the Supreme Court of Alaska decided to recognize as valid a Virginia custody decree entered in favor of a father who had removed the child from Washington before any custody action had been filed. The Alaska court reasoned that the father had not "wrongfully" transported the children from Washington to Virginia because both parents were equally entitled to custody prior to a court action.

A court's refusing to decline jurisdiction based on misconduct absent an outstanding custody decree may result in a case being decided in a less optimal forum. *Morgan*, however, may be distinguished on the basis that it merely refused to regard another state's custody decree as invalid because of that state's previous refusal to decline jurisdiction. The Alaska Supreme Court later held that its own state courts should refuse to decide a custody case brought by a father who had removed the children to Alaska after the mother had dismissed an earlier custody action in another state because she feared losing custody under a temporary order.[81]

[C] The Uniform Child Custody Jurisdiction and Enforcement Act

In the summer of 1997, the National Conference of Commissioners on Uniform State Laws completed a new version of the UCCJA called the Uniform Child Custody Jurisdiction and Enforcement Act (UCCJEA), which clarifies some of the inconsistencies between the UCCJA and the PKPA and takes into account the provisions of the Uniform Child Visitation Act[82]

---

[79] *Id.* at 361.

[80] 666 P.2d 1026 (Alaska 1983).

[81] *Stokes v. Stokes*, 751 P.2d 1363 (Alaska 1988).

[82] *See* Patricia M. Hoff, *The ABC's of the UCCJEA: Interstate Child-Custody Practice Under the New Act*, 32 Fam. L. Q. 267 (1998).

The UCCJEA adopts the position of the PKPA that states a preference for home state jurisdiction. The significant connection/substantial evidence test is to be used only when no home state exists. Further, it clarifies the issue of continuing jurisdiction by expressly providing that the state that made the initial custody determination should have continuing jurisdiction at least until all parties and the child no longer have a significant connection with that state.

The UCCJEA has also altered the emergency jurisdiction provision, which was a basis of jurisdiction in the UCCJA. The UCCJEA provides that a court may assert emergency jurisdiction over a child who has been abandoned in the state or when necessary to safeguard the child, a parent, or sibling from mistreatment or abuse.[83] It specifies that orders under this section are temporary, effective only until the court with appropriate jurisdiction under other sections can act.

[D] The Parental Kidnapping Prevention Act of 1980

Although the UCCJA marked an improvement over the traditional approach to custody jurisdiction, not all states had adopted the UCCJA by the end of the 1970s. Those which had enacted it as their state law frequently altered its provisions or interpreted it in a manner that undermined its purposes. As a result, forum shopping and parental kidnapping continued. Congress decided to intervene by enacting legislation that would specify which types of custody decrees must be afforded full faith and credit, as well as the circumstances that would allow states to modify an outstanding custody decree of another state.

The result was the 1980 Parental Kidnapping Prevention Act [PKPA]. While the Act also contains provisions which criminalize parental kidnapping[84] and employ parent locator services,[85] its major impact is to set federal standards for recognition of custody decrees.[86] To the extent that the PKPA and UCCJA conflict in this respect, the PKPA preempts state law.[87]

[1] Scope of Application

The PKPA is concerned only with interstate enforcement and recognition of decrees. The PKPA does not dictate the terms for exercising initial custody jurisdiction nor does it prohibit states from recognizing decrees that do not conform to the Act. Rather, it sets out criteria which, if complied with, will result in a custody decree that must be afforded full faith and credit. It further forbids states from modifying custody decrees of other states that were entered consistently with the PKPA, except under specified conditions. To constitute a custody determination that must be afforded full

---

[83] UCCJEA § 204.

[84] 18 U.S.C. § 1073.

[85] 42 U.S.C. § 663.

[86] 28 U.S.C. § 1738A; *see also Meade v. Meade*, 812 F.2d 1473, 1475–76 (4th Cir. 1987).

[87] *Id.*

faith and credit, the court entering the decree must have jurisdiction both under its owns laws, including the UCCJA, and under the PKPA.

[2] Similarities and Differences between the PKPA and the UCCJA

The relationship of the PKPA and the UCCJA is complex, and Congress failed thoroughly to consider the interrelationship of the two Acts.[88] The Acts correspond in many features, but differ in others.

The PKPA sets out four bases for jurisdiction modeled after the UCCJA.[89] However, the PKPA establishes a statutory preference for home state jurisdiction, and the three alternate bases, significant connection, emergency, and default jurisdiction, are to be exercised only if it is apparent that no other state has home state jurisdiction.[90] Unlike the UCCJA, the PKPA specifies an additional ground for continuing jurisdiction.[91]

The Washington Court of Appeals recently addressed this home state preference in *In re Marriage of Murphy*.[92] In *Murphy*, the parties had lived together with their two children in several states, until the husband abandoned the family in Arizona and moved to Ohio. The mother and children later moved to Washington. The husband subsequently filed for divorce in Ohio and requested that the Ohio court determine parental rights. Although the mother argued in a motion in the Ohio court that Ohio lacked jurisdiction because it was not the home state (which the husband conceded), the court denied her motion. The spouses entered into an agreement, which awarded the wife custody of the children, with liberal visitation in the husband, and stipulated jurisdiction in Ohio. The wife later claimed that she entered into this agreement under duress, in fear of losing custody of the children.

Subsequently, the mother returned to the Washington court seeking that court to assume jurisdiction, which the trial court denied. The Court of Appeals reversed and remanded, relying on the home state preference in the PKPA. The court concluded that although the PKPA did not give the home state exclusive jurisdiction in an initial custody hearing, if a home state exists, other states need not accord full faith and credit to a custody decree based on another jurisdictional ground. Because the jurisdictional ground for the Ohio decree was not evident from the record, the Washington court held that it was impossible to determine the basis for its assertion for jurisdiction, and remanded the case to the trial court for a determination of whether the decree was the type that must be recognized by the Ohio court. The court in *Murphy* apparently overlooked the fact that even if the PKPA did not require recognition of the Ohio decree, Washington's own

---

[88] *See* Homer J. Clark, Jr., *supra* note 15, at 477–78.

[89] The PKPA was amended in 1998 to apply to visitation as well as custody. H.R. 4164, amending 28 U.S.C. § 1738A.

[90] 28 U.S.C. § 1738A(c)(2)(B)(I).

[91] 28 U.S.C. § 1738A(c)(2)(E).

[92] 952 P.2d 624 (Wash. App. 1998).

version of the UCCJA would require recognition if the Ohio decree were based on *any* valid jurisdictional basis, not merely on home state jurisdiction.

Both the PKPA and the UCCJA contain provisions for notice and the opportunity to be heard.[93] Neither Act requires a court to have personal jurisdiction over a parent to determine child custody. Both Acts restrict courts from exercising custody jurisdiction when a custody proceeding is pending in another state which is exercising jurisdiction consistent with the provisions of the PKPA or UCCJA,[94] but the PKPA does not have a provision preventing the exercise of jurisdiction where the child has been wrongfully taken. The "clean hands" criteria for declining jurisdiction will still apply to state courts under the UCCJA, however, because the PKPA requires a court to have jurisdiction under its own state law, as well as federal law. Similarly, courts may apply the inconvenient forum provision of the UCCJA despite the lack of a similar provision in the PKPA.[95] The procedural mechanisms of the UCCJA are lacking in the PKPA, as are the provisions of the UCCJA that extend to custody decrees of foreign countries.

Like the terms of the UCCJA, the PKPA prohibits a court of another state from modifying a custody decree unless it has jurisdiction itself and the court of the original state either no longer has jurisdiction or has declined to exercise such jurisdiction to modify the decree.[96] Under the PKPA, the court that entered an initial custody determination consistently with the statute continues to retain jurisdiction as long as it has jurisdiction under its own laws, and the state "remains the residence of the child or of any contestant."[97] The UCCJA, however, does not specifically recognize continuing jurisdiction based on the continued residence of a party.

Where the PKPA and state law conflict, the PKPA preempts state law under the Supremacy Clause.[98] The Alaska Supreme Court explained this principle in *Murphy v. Woerner*,[99] in which a mother had obtained custody of the couple's two children under a 1981 Kansas divorce decree. After the mother and children moved to Alaska in 1982, the Kansas court modified the custody decree, awarding joint custody and designating specified visitation periods. The mother subsequently sought modification in Alaska and requested the Kansas court to relinquish jurisdiction; the Kansas court refused.

In holding that the PKPA prohibited Alaska from modifying the Kansas custody order, the *Murphy* court analyzed the interplay between the PKPA and the UCCJA. It stated,

---

[93] 28 U.S.C. § 1738A(e); UCCJA, *supra* note 12, § 4; *see also Lutes v. Alexander*, 421 S.E.2d 857 (Va. Ct. App. 1992).

[94] 28 U.S.C. § 1738A(g).

[95] *See Patricia R. v. Andrew W.*, 467 N.Y.S.2d 322 (N.Y. Fam. Ct. 1983).

[96] 28 U.S.C. § 1738A(f); *see also Walter v. Walter*, 589 N.Y.S.2d 104 (N.Y. App. Div. 1992).

[97] 28 U.S.C. § 1738A(d).

[98] *See* Russell M. Coombs, *supra* note 7, at 826–834.

[99] 748 P.2d 749 (Alaska 1988).

> The threshold question was whether the 1982 Kansas decree was made consistently with the PKPA. . . . [T]he Kansas decree conforms with the PKPA if Kansas had jurisdiction under its version of the UCCJA. When the initial decree was entered, Kansas had jurisdiction because it was the home state of the children. Kansas had continuing jurisdiction to modify in 1982 because Murphy continued to reside there and was the primary custodial parent. Therefore, the 1982 Kansas order was consistent with the PKPA.[100]

Consequently, the Alaska court could only modify that decree if Kansas no longer had jurisdiction or declined to assert it. The court concluded that, pursuant to other Kansas opinions asserting continuing jurisdiction after children had acquired a new home state, Kansas retained modification jurisdiction because the father remained a resident and the children maintained a significant connection through their visitations in Kansas. Thus, the PKPA prohibited modification by an Alaska court.

The Supreme Court of Washington arrived at the same conclusion in *Greenlaw v. Smith*,[101] holding that is own courts retained jurisdiction to modify a custody degree, despite the fact that the custodial mother and the son had been outside the state for over nine years while the mother was in the military and later when she attended law school in California. The father, who sought custody of the then-15-year-old child, had remained in Washington the entire period. The son had regularly visited his father there, had extended family of both parents in the state, and other connections. The court interpreted the UCCJA in conjunction with the PKPA to mean that modification jurisdiction continues with the decree-granting state so long as the original decree was properly entered, one of the parents or other contestants continue to reside there, and the child continues to have more than slight contacts with the decree state.

Because state courts are permitted to determine whether a sister state custody decree was or remains valid, problems arise when a state refuses to recognize another state's decree for its failure to comply with either UCCJA or PKPA principles. If the second state relitigates the custody issue, inconsistent custody decrees may result, with each parent asserting the validity of his or her decree, although these conflicts could be resolved by use of the inter-court communications provisions in the UCCJA.

Because state courts are permitted to determine whether a sister state custody decree was or remains valid, problems arise when a state refuses to recognize another state's decree for its failure to comply with either UCCJA or PKPA principles. If the second state relitigates the custody issue, inconsistent custody decrees may result, with each parent asserting the validity of his or her decree, although these conflicts could be resolved by use of the inter-court communications provisions in the UCCJA. The Supreme Court of Arkansas addressed such a conflict in *Atkins v. Atkins*,[102]

---

[100] *Id.* at 749-751.

[101] 869 P.2d 1024 (Wash. 1994).

[102] 823 S.W.2d 816 (Ark. 1992).

concluding that a Louisiana decree awarding custody to the mother was invalid because the parties had resided in Arkansas during the marriage, until the mother removed the children to Louisiana and filed for divorce there. In finding that the Louisiana custody decree was not entered in "substantial conformity" with the UCCJA, the court concluded that the provisions of the PKPA favoring home state jurisdiction, which apply directly only to modification proceedings, also indirectly govern initial custody determinations. Thus, the court held, "if a custody decree fails to conform to the requirements of the PKPA, it will not be entitled to full faith and credit in another state."[103]

In an attempt to determine which of two outstanding custody decrees is valid, parties sometimes have sought resolution in the federal courts. The United States Supreme Court denied litigants a federal forum as a tie-breaker for conflicting state court decrees in *Thompson v. Thompson*,[104] holding that the PKPA does not furnish an implied private cause of action to resolve a "jurisdictional stalemate."[105]

The *Thompson* case involved a California decree that modified its earlier award of joint custody to sole custody in the mother when she moved to Louisiana. The decree was to be effective only until the California court received a more detailed report from a court investigator. Before that occurred, the mother sought recognition and enforcement of the California decree in Louisiana, which granted her motion and awarded her sole custody. Subsequently, the California court awarded sole custody to the father based on its investigative report. The father eventually filed an action in federal district court seeking a declaration of validity of his California decree and invalidity and injunction of the Louisiana decree.

Upon dismissal by the district court and the Court of Appeals for the Ninth Circuit, the Supreme Court affirmed, finding that Congress did not intend to create a federal private cause of action when it enacted the PKPA, but, instead, had deliberately rejected the notion of extending diversity jurisdiction to enforcement of custody orders. Noting that "ultimate review remains available in the [Supreme] Court for truly intractable jurisdictional deadlocks," the Court refused to presume that either state was unable or unwilling to enforce the provisions of the Act. The Court concluded:

> State courts faithfully administer the Full Faith and Credit Clause every day; now that Congress has extended full faith and credit requirements to child custody orders, we can think of no reason why the courts' administration of federal law in custody disputes will be any less vigilant. Should state courts prove as obstinate as petitioner predicts, Congress may choose to revisit the issue. But any more radical approach to the problem will have to await further legislative action; we "will not engraft a remedy on a statute, no matter how salutary, that Congress did not intend to provide."[106]

---

[103] *Id.* at 819.

[104] 484 U.S. 174 (1988).

[105] *Id.* at 177.

[106] *Id* at 187 (citing *California v. Sierra Club*, 451 U.S. 287, 297 (1981)).

While proper application of both the PKPA and the UCCJA should prevent conflicting custody decrees, Professor Clark has noted that, "If anything, the injection of the PKPA into the continuing jurisdiction issue has amplified the confusion already evident under the UCCJA."[107] However, the UCCJEA should resolve some of that confusion.

Both the UCCJA and PKPA have been held by most courts which have addressed the issue to apply to adoptions and terminations of parental rights.[108] The UCCJEA, on the other hand, does not apply to adoptions, but defers to the Uniform Adoption Act.s[109] The UCCJEA, does, however, apply to neglect, abuse, dependency, wardship, guardianship, termination of parental rights and domestic violence cases.[110]

[3] Personal Jurisdiction

Neither the UCCJA, UCCJEA, nor the PKPA require personal jurisdiction over the respondent. Although the Supreme Court's 1952 plurality decision in *May v. Anderson*[111] literally stands only for the proposition that full faith and credit will not be given to a custody decree unless there is personal jurisdiction over the respondent, an implication of this case is that all custody decrees without such jurisdiction are void. This interpretation of *May* has been ignored by the framers of the UCCJA, UCCJEA, and PKPA, and the issue has never again been directly addressed by the Supreme Court. However, in 1990, in *Burnham v. Superior Court*,[112] Justice Scalia, writing for the plurality, perhaps inadvertently and in dictum, assumed that personal jurisdiction is necessary for child custody.[113] The unresolved personal jurisdiction question raises serious issues relating to the best interest of the child if the Court were to conclude that custody decisions or modifications could not be made if a parent were absent.

[E] The Hague Convention on International Child Abduction

Enforcement of child custody rights becomes even more complex when a child is taken to a foreign country or brought into the United States from another country. While the UCCJA's provisions apply to recognition of custody decrees of other countries,[114] the Act has no application to custody

---

[107] Homer J. Clark, Jr., *supra* note 15, at 485.

[108] *See, e.g., Souza v. Superior Court*, 193 Cal. App. 3d 1304, 238 Cal. Rptr. 892 (1987); *In re Baby Girl Clausen*, 502 N.W.2d 649 (Mich. 1993); *In re Adoption of Child by T. W. C.*, 636 A2d 1083 (N.J. Super.Ct. App Div. 1994). *But see State in re. R.N.J.*, 908 P.2d 345 (Utah App. 1995).

[109] UCCJEA § 103.

[110] *Id.* at § 102 (4).

[111] 345 U.S. 528, 533–34 (1952) (discussed *supra*, § 11.02[A]).

[112] 495 U.S. 604 (1990).

[113] *See* Barbara Ann Atwood, *Child Custody Jurisdiction and Territoriality*, 52 Ohio St. L.J. 369 (1991).

[114] UCCJA, *supra* note 12, § 23. (Cmt. lists Missouri, New Mexico, Ohio, and South Dakota as omitting this provision.)

disputes which are litigated in foreign forums. In response to the increasing problem of international child abductions, in 1988 the United States joined a number of nations as a party to the Hague Convention on the Civil Aspects of International Child Abduction [the Hague Convention].[115] In United States also has enacted the Interantional Parental Kidnaping Act, which creates a federal felony for a parent who wrongfully removes or retains a child outside the United States.[116]

The Hague Convention was intended to decrease the incidence of international child abduction. It provides for the prompt return of a child under 16 years old, who has been wrongfully removed or retained, back to the country of his or her habitual residence without an adjudication on the merits of the custody dispute.[117]

The Convention itself does not define "habitual residence," which has been developed by case law. In *Feder v. Evans-Feder*,[118] the United States Court of Appeals for the Third Circuit adopted "settled purpose" test for determining the child's habitual residence. In that case, the parties had lived with their son in Pennsylvania for the child's first three and a half years, until the father accepted a job in Australia. The mother reluctantly agreed to move to Australia, where they bought a house, enrolled the child in nursery school, and exhibited other indications of intent to remain in that country. The mother was unhappy, and decided to leave her husband and return to the States with their son after five months, but she told her husband she was going to visit her family. Within a month, the mother filed for divorce in Pennsylvania, seeking custody of the child, among other things, and the father was served with the complaint when he went to visit them while on a business trip to the States. Upon returning to Australia, the father received a declaration from the Family Court of Australia under the Hague Convention, which declared that the child and parents were habitual residents of Australia immediately before the mother retained the child in the United States, that the father had been exercising his rights to joint custody, and that the mother's retention of the child was wrongful under the Convention. The father then filed a petition pursuant to the Convention in the United States, requesting the child's return.

The U.S. District Court denied his petition, concluding that the father had failed to prove that the child's habitual residence had changed from the United States to Australia, focusing on the period of time that the child had lived in the United States prior to the move to Australia. The Court of Appeals reversed, agreeing that there must be a degree of settled purpose, either specific or general, but concluding that the father had demonstrated that purpose. The court reasoned:

---

[115] Hague Convention on the Civil Aspects of International Child Abduction, Oct. 25, 1980, 19 I.L.M. 1501, implemented by the International Child Abduction Remedies Act, 43 U.S.C. § 11601 *et seq.* [hereinafter Hague Convention].

[116] 18 U.S.C. § 1204 (1994).

[117] Hague Convention art. 1.

[118] 63 F.3d 217 (3d Cir. 1995).

[W]e believe that a child's habitual residence is the place where he
or she has been physically present for an amount of time sufficient
for acclimatization and which has a "degree of settled purpose" from
the child's perspective. We further believe that a determination of
whether any particular place satisfies this standard must focus on
the child and consists of an analysis of the child's circumstances
in that place and the parents' present, shared intentions regarding
their child's presence there.[119]

Consequently, the court concluded that both parents did what people who
intend to reestablish themselves and their children generally do. Despite
the mother's lack of intent to remain permanently in Australia, a settled
purpose to live as a family in that country was established.

The 6th Circuit Court of Appeals came to a similar conclusion in the
converse situation, in *Friedrich v. Friedrich*,[120] in which the child was born
in Germany to a German father and an American mother, where they lived
as a family until the mother removed the child to the United States. The
court concluded that the child's habitual residence was in Germany, despite
the mother's evidence that the child had United States citizenship, that his
permanent address for United States documentation was in Ohio, and that
the mother intended to return to the United States with the child upon her
discharge from the military.

The Hague Convention requires countries to establish a Central Authority to assist in locating and returning children who have been abducted
across international boundaries.[121] A pre-existing custody order is not
required if the petitioning party is the child's parent.[122]

The Central Authority must first seek a voluntary return of the child
before initiating legal action.[123] The obvious problem with this provision
is that the runaway parent is given notice that his or her whereabouts are
known and an opportunity to further conceal the child. If legal proceedings
occur, the court must find a breach of custodial rights; after this finding
is made, the Central Authority must return the child to the other country
immediately. However, if the proceeding to return the child is initiated
more than one year after the child's removal, the country may decline to
return the child if there is proof that the child has been integrated into
the new home.[124]

A country is not required to return the child if the parent seeking return
was "not actually exercising custody rights at the time of removal or
retention or had consented to or subsequently acquiesced in the removal
or retention" of the child.[125] Important exceptions to the Convention allow

---

[119] *Id.* at 224.

[120] 983 F.2d 1396, 1401 (6th Cir. 1993).

[121] The Department of State is the Central Authority in the United States. Exec. Order
No. 12,648, 53 Fed. Reg. 30,637 (1988).

[122] Hague Convention art. 3.

[123] Hague Convention arts. 7(c), 10.

[124] Hague Convention art. 12.

[125] Hague Convention art. 13(a).

the other country to retain the child if "there is a grave risk that his or her return would expose the child to physical or psychological harm or otherwise place the child in an intolerable situation"[126] or if the child's return "would not be permitted by the fundamental principles of the requested State relating to the protection of human rights and fundamental freedoms."[127] Another exception gives the foreign authority the discretion to defer to the child's wishes if the child is of sufficient age and maturity.[128] A conflicting custody order entered in the child's present location does not constitute a defense, however.[129] A decision to return is not a decision on the merits of the custody issue, although the authorities may initiate a legal action regarding visitation rights.[130]

The Hague Convention merely supplements existing procedures and does not preclude persons from pursuing alternate legal or administrative remedies. It does, however, require any court with notice of the unauthorized removal of a child to stay any custody action initiated by the alleged abductor until the matter has been resolved under the Convention's provisions.[131]

The United States declined to adopt a provision that the countries themselves bear the costs of actions without charge to the applicant, except the expense of private legal counsel and travel expenses.

In addition to the potential expense of invoking the Hague Convention, continuing problems include the inability of state authorities to locate the abducted children and removal to non-member countries.[132] Despite these inherent obstacles, the Hague Convention has been hailed as "remarkably successful in achieving its goals,"[133] although it is premature to draw decisive conclusions.

§ 11.03 Factors in Disputed Child Custody Cases

[A] The Best Interests of the Child

The generally prevailing standard in child custody adjudications is the best interest of the child. Modern statutes generally reflect this standard. In some jurisdictions, the legislature has provided little guidance to the courts, merely setting out the "best interest" standard in broad terms. The Arkansas statute governing the award of custody of children of the marriage on divorce, for example, simply requires that the award "shall be made

---

[126] Hague Convention art. 13(b); *see also* Caroline LeGette, *International Child Abduction and the Hague Convention: Emerging Practice and Interpretation of the Discretionary Exception*, 25 Tex. Int'l L.J. 287 (1990).

[127] Hague Convention art. 20.

[128] Hague Convention art. 13.

[129] Hague Convention art.17.

[130] Hague Convention art.16.

[131] Hague Convention art.16.

[132] Caroline LeGette, *supra* note 113, at 288–289.

[133] *Id.* at 287.

without regard to the sex of the parent but solely in accordance with the welfare and best interests of the children."[134]

In other states, reflecting an approach that is increasingly more typical, the statute sets out a detailed list of guidelines or relevant factors that define the best interests of the child, or that the trial court must consider in making its determination. The Minnesota statute is illustrative, requiring the court to consider and evaluate the following factors:

    (1)   the wishes of the child's parent or parents as to custody;

    (2)   the reasonable preference of the child, if the court deems the child to be of sufficient age to express preference;

    (3)   the child's primary caretaker;

    (4)   the intimacy of the relationship between each parent and the child;

    (5)   the interaction and interrelationship of the child with a parent or parents, siblings, and any other person who may significantly affect the child's best interests;

    (6)   the child's adjustment to home, school, and community;

    (7)   the length of time the child has lived in a stable, satisfactory environment and the desirability of maintaining continuity;

    (8)   the permanence, as a family unit of the existing or proposed custodial home;

    (9)   the mental and physical health of all individuals involved;

    (10)   the capacity and disposition of the parties to give the child love, affection, and guidance, and to continue educating and raising the child in the child's culture and religion or creed, if any;

    (11)   the child's cultural background; and

    (12)   the effect on the child of the actions of an abuser, if related to domestic abuse, . . . that has occurred between the parents.[135]

In *Maxfield v. Maxfield,*[136] the Supreme Court of Minnesota, affirming the award of the custody of three children to the mother, discussed in detail the way in which the enumerated statutory factors relate to the best interests of the child standard. The court stated:

> In applying the bests interests analysis, we recognize much must be left to the discretion of the trial court. Some statutory criteria

---

[134] Ark. Code Ann. § 9-13-101 (Michie 1987); *see also* Ala. Code § 30-3-1 (1975) (providing that on divorce the court may give custody of children of the marriage "to either father or mother, as may seem right and proper, having regard to the moral character and prudence of the parents and the age and sex of the children").

[135] Minn. Stat. Ann. § 518.17 (West 1990); (the statute also precludes the use of "one factor to the exclusion of all others," explicitly bars use of the primary caretaker factor as a presumption in determining best interests, and requires detailed findings on each factor and an explanation of how the factors led to the court's best interest determination. When the parties seek joint custody, the court must consider additional listed factors.) *Id.*

[136] 452 N.W. 2d 219 (Minn. 1990).

will weigh more in one case and less in another and there is rarely an easy answer. Yet,. . .the golden thread running through any best interests analysis is the importance, for a young child in particular, of its bond with the primary parent as this relationship bears on the other criteria, such as the need for "a stable, satisfactory environment and the desirability of maintaining continuity" and "mental and physical health of all individuals involved." Usually this relationship "should not be disrupted without strong reasons.[137]

* * *

[B] Doctrinal Presumptions

Just as state legislatures have enacted guidelines and factors in attempts to define the content of "best interests of the child," the prevailing standard in cases involving child custody,[138] the courts have struggled to enunciate factors in an attempt to give the concept a reliable and precise meaning. Over time, courts reviewing child custody cases have developed, and sometimes subsequently rejected, a number of presumptions intended to aid in determining best interests. Among the most common are the tender years presumption, the natural parent presumption, and the primary caretaker presumption. Preference for the natural parent has been attenuated to some extent by the acceptance of some courts of the concept of psychological parenthood.

[1] The Tender Years Presumption

Among the earliest presumptions that courts adopted in attempting to reach custody determinations consistent with the best interests of the child was the tender years doctrine, which favored placement of young children with their mothers. The court in *Freeland v. Freeland*[139] tersely stated the rationale underlying the doctrine: "Mother love is a dominant trait in even the weakest of women, and as a general thing surpasses the paternal affection for the common offspring, and, moreover, a child needs a mother's care even more than a father's."[140] Thus, the court noted judicial reluctance to deprive a mother of custody absent a clear showing that she is so unfit as to endanger her children's welfare.

While modern courts have largely rejected the tender years doctrine on constitutional and other grounds, some have done so grudgingly. In *De-Camp v. Hein*,[141] for example, the court considered a gender neutral amendment to the Florida custody statute requiring that fathers be given the same consideration as mothers in determining the child's primary residence, regardless of the child's age. The court rejected the trial court's view that

---

[137] *Id.* at 222.

[138] *See supra* § 11.03[A].

[139] 159 P. 698 (Wash. 1916).

[140] *Id.* at 699.

[141] 541 So. 2d 708 (Fla. Dist. Ct. App. 1989).

the statute had totally abolished the tender years doctrine. Rather, the court held that the statutory mandate to consider all relevant facts in custody matters required some consideration of the tender years doctrine. Accordingly, the court held that common sense required that girls aged one and three years should reside with their mother.

Although remnants of the tender years doctrine appear occasionally in contemporary decisions, it is now largely a historical anachronism, as are the stereotypical views that supported it. The opinion of the Supreme Court of Alaska in *Johnson v. Johnson* [142] is illustrative. The court in *Johnson* held that use of the tender years doctrine was not a permissible criterion for the state's trial courts to use. The court held that the age of children in a custody dispute is only one factor, to be weighed against others in making a best interests determination, and that the tender years doctrine was inconsistent with the statutory "best interests" requirement. [143]

While the court in *Johnson* found it unnecessary to reach the father's contention that the trial court's use of the tender years doctrine violated his right to equal protection, courts in other jurisdictions have invoked the 14th Amendment of the United States Constitution as a basis for rejecting the doctrine. In *Ex parte Devine*, the Supreme Court of Alabama undertook a detailed and thoughtful examination of the history of the tender years presumption and a reexamination of the doctrine in light of pronouncements relating to gender discrimination by the Supreme Court of the United States. [144] The court concluded that "the tender years presumption represents an unconstitutional gender-based classification which discriminates between fathers and mothers in child custody proceedings solely on the basis of sex." [145]

[2] The Natural Parent Presumption

Custody disputes between a child's natural or biological parent and another arise occasionally in divorce proceedings, but more often in other contexts. Generally, to overcome statutory or judicially created preferences for the natural parent will require circumstances such as unfitness, abandonment or the like, but the courts have not been entirely consistent in adhering to this standard. In *Bennett v. Jeffreys*, [146] the natural mother sought custody of an eight-year-old girl from a friend of the child's grandmother to whom she had entrusted the child shortly after birth. In the

---

[142] 564 P.2d 71 (Alaska 1977).

[143] *Id.* at 75; *see also In re Marriage of Bowen*, 219 N.W.2d 683 (Iowa 1974); *State ex rel. Watts v. Watts*, 350 N.Y.S.2d 285 (N.Y. Sup. Ct. 1973).

[144] The court reviewed the Supreme Court's holdings in *Reed v. Reed*, 404 U.S. 71 (1971) (striking down a provision of the Idaho probate code that gave men preference over women for appointment as estate administrators); *Frontiero v. Richardson*, 411 U.S. 677 (1973) (overturning a federal statutory presumption of dependency extended to spouses of male but not female members of the armed forces); and *Orr v. Orr*, 440 U.S. 268 (1979) (invalidating a state statute imposing the obligation to pay alimony on husbands, but not wives), among others.

[145] *Devine*, 398 So. 2d at 686; *see also Pusey v. Pusey*, 728 P.2d 117 (Utah 1986).

[146] 356 N.E.2d 277 (N.Y. 1976).

course of its opinion, New York's highest court ringingly endorsed its preference for the natural parent in disputed custody matters, stating:

> Absent extraordinary circumstances, narrowly categorized, it is not within the power of a court, or, by delegation of the Legislature or court, a social agency, to make significant decisions concerning the custody of children, merely because it could make a better decision or disposition. The state is *parens patriae* and always has been, but it has not displaced the parent in right or responsibility. Indeed, the courts and the law would, under existing constitutional principles, be powerless to supplant parents except for grievous cause or necessity. . . .[147]

The court noted, however, exceptions to parental rights "created by extraordinary circumstances, illustratively, surrender, abandonment, persisting neglect, unfitness, and unfortunate or involuntary disruption of custody over and extended period of time."[148] Only when such extraordinary circumstances are present may the court inquire into and base its custody determination on the best interests of the child. In the case before it, the court found that the mother's protracted separation from the child, lack of her own established household, her unwed state and the child's attachment to the custodian were extraordinary circumstances. Accordingly, the court remitted the case to the trial court for an inquiry into the best interests of the child.

On remand, the trial court awarded custody to the foster mother, basing its decision in large part on the testimony of a psychiatrist that a psychological parent-child relationship[149] had developed between the child and the foster mother.[150] Thus it would appear that in the view of at least some courts, a natural parent presumption or preference will be rebutted by proof that a third party has become the child's psychological parent.

In *Guardianship of Philip B.*,[151] the court elaborately described and applied the psychological parent concept in awarding custody to a third party over the objections of a child's natural parents. The child involved, born with Down's Syndrome, was placed by his parents in a residential facility for developmentally disabled children. Over time, the child developed a close and caring relationship with a volunteer worker at the facility and her family, while the natural parents simultaneously developed a pattern of physical and emotional detachment from their son. Describing the right of parents to custody of their children as fundamental, the court noted that a custody award to a nonparent required a finding that custody to the parent would be detrimental to the child and that custody to the nonparent would be in the child's best interests. Purporting to apply this standard, the court approved the trial court's finding that an award of

---

[147] *Id.* at 281.

[148] *Id.*

[149] *See* J. Goldstein, A. Freud & A. Solnit, Beyond the Best Interests of the Child (1973).

[150] *Bennett v. Marrow*, 399 N.Y.S.2d 697 (N.Y. App. Div. 1977).

[151] 188 Cal. Rptr. 781 (Cal. Ct. App. 1983).

custody to the child's natural parents would be harmful to the child "in light of the psychological or'de facto' parental relationship established between him and [the nonparents]."[152]

Although a few courts have expressly relied on psychological parenthood in reaching decisions in custody cases, the concept has by no means achieved universal approval, and some courts have explicitly rejected it.[153] In any event, well before the concept was enunciated, the courts often enough identified factors or circumstances that would overcome the presumption favoring a fit parent. In *Painter v. Bannister*,[154] for example, after the death of his wife, the father voluntarily gave custody of his son to the child's maternal grandparents. Four years later, the father was unsuccessful in his attempt to regain custody. The court acknowledged the presumption of parental preference, but nevertheless awarded custody to the grandparents, noting the child's positive development in their care, the stability and security of their home, and a father-son relationship that the child had established with his grandfather.

In sum, the decisions make clear that the preference for the natural parent in custody proceedings is a strong one, but that it may be rebutted in a variety of circumstances. Thus, when divorced parents voluntarily gave custody of children to the sister of the ex-husband, the court held that the parental preference doctrine was not applicable when the mother sought to regain custody after four and a half years, and failed to show that a change would promote the children's welfare.[155] Again, in a case in which the child's father died several years after his divorce from the child's mother, a Florida court noted that the right of a fit natural parent to custody in a dispute with a third party was "older than the common law itself," and awarded custody to the mother over the stepparent who had been married to the deceased father.[156] Conversely, the Supreme Court of Idaho held that where a child has a long-term relationship with a stepparent, the best interest test is appropriate and the natural parent presumption does not preclude its application.[157]

[3] The Primary Caretaker Presumption

As discussed, modern courts for the most part have rejected the tender years doctrine in favor of gender neutral decision making, either as a matter of policy or based on the view that the doctrine is violative of the right to equal protection under the United States Constitution.[158] The primary

---

[152] *Id.* at 789.

[153] *See generally* Crouch, *An Essay on the Critical and Judicial Reception of Beyond the Best Interests of the Child*, 13 Fam. L.Q. 49 (1979).

[154] 140 N.W.2d 152 (Iowa 1966).

[155] *In re Criqui*, 798 P.2d 69 (Kan. Ct. App. 1990).

[156] *Webb. v. Webb*, 546 So. 2d 1062, 1065 (Fla. Dist. Ct. App. 1989)

[157] *Stockwell v. Stockwell*, 775 P.2d 611 (Idaho 1989); *see also Prawdzik v. Hiner*, 454 N.W.2d 399 (Mich. Ct. App. 1990) (awarding custody of child to parental grandparents with whom child had lived for five years in preference to the child's mother).

[158] *See supra* § 11.03[B][1].

caretaker presumption, while gender neutral on its face, may compel the same results as would obtain under the tender years doctrine. Obviously, and as might have been anticipated, it is usually the mother of the child who will meet the definitional requirements of primary caretaker.

The decision of the Supreme Court of Appeals of West Virginia in *Garska v. McCoy*[159] is the leading articulation of the primary caretaker presumption. The case arose in the context of a legislative amendment eliminating gender based presumptions in awarding custody, which was enacted in response to an earlier case that had announced a strong maternal presumption for children of tender years.[160] The court held that "there is a presumption in favor of the primary caretaker parent, if he or she meets the minimum, objective of being a fit parent . . ., regardless of sex."[161]

Conceding the difficulty of enumerating all of the factors that will identify the primary caretaker parent, the court, nevertheless, listed certain criteria as requiring consideration, stating:

> In establishing which natural or adoptive parent is the primary caretaker, the trial court shall determine which parent has taken primary responsibility for, *inter alia*, the performance of the following caring and nurturing duties of a parent: (1) preparing and planning of meals; (2) bathing, grooming and dressing; (3) purchasing, cleaning and care of clothes; (4) medical care, including nursing and trips to physicians; (5) arranging for social interaction among peers, after school, *i.e.*, transporting to friends' houses or, for example, to girl or boy scout meetings; (6) arranging for alternative care, *i.e.*, babysitting, day-care, etc.; (7) putting child to bed at night, waking child in the morning; (8) disciplining, *i.e.*, teaching general manners and toilet training; (9) educating, *i.e.*, religious, cultural, social, etc; and (10) teaching elementary skills, *i.e.*, reading, writing and arithmetic.[162]

In *Burchard v. Garay*,[163] the Supreme Court of California sharply criticized a trial court's decision awarding custody to the father of an out of wedlock child because of his better economic position. The trial court also referred to the fact that the mother worked and placed the child in day care, while the father's new wife could care for the child at home. The reviewing court summarily rejected the unfair assumption that working mothers cannot provide care, nurturance and continuity of attention, particularly where the working mother has been the primary caregiver. The court found all of the grounds relied on by the trial court as insignificant, compared to the fact that the mother had been the child's primary caretaker from birth until the date of trial.

[159] 278 S.E.2d 357 (W. Va. 1981).

[160] *See J.B. v. A.B.*, 242 S.E.2d 248 (W. Va. 1978).

[161] *Id.* at 362.

[162] *Id.* at 363; *see also Pikula v. Pikula*, 374 N.W.2d 705, 713 (Minn. 1985).

[163] 724 P.2d 486 (Cal. 1986).

Consideration of the primary caretaker factor does not necessarily raise it to the level of a presumption. The Supreme Court of North Dakota in *Wolf v. Wolf*[164] noted that the best interests and welfare of the child remains the governing standard for trial courts in child custody determinations. Stating what would appear to be the rule in most jurisdictions, the court observed that "the primary caretaker factor is not a presumptive rule but only one of many considerations to be evaluated by the trial court in making its finding as to the best interest of the child."[165]

[C] The Effect of Parental Conduct on Custody Determinations

The conduct of a parent that will most often affect custody is sexual conduct, sometimes disguised by references to "lifestyle." Courts generally will consider a parent's heterosexual conduct outside of marriage or homosexual conduct as one factor to be considered in a custody determination, rather than as constituting unfitness *per se*. Nevertheless, cases involving lesbian or gay male custodians who maintain live-in or other relationships with persons of the same sex often enough provoke judicial high dudgeon.[166]

[1] Statutory Provisions Relating to Parental Conduct

In some states, the statutes governing custody explicitly identify parental conduct among the factors a court must consider in arriving at a determination reflecting the best interests of the child. The Minnesota statute, for example, contains a range of factors involving parental conduct, but directs that "[t]he court shall not consider the conduct of a proposed custodian that does not affect the custodian's relationship to the child."[167] In Alabama the court must consider, among other things, "the moral character and prudence of the parents."[168] In the District of Columbia, the statute identifies "race, color, national origin, political affiliation, sex or sexual orientation" as factors that alone should not be determinative of custody or visitation.[169] This language clearly does not preclude the trial judge from considering these factors.

[2] Judicial Approaches

Decisions that address the relevance of a parent's sexual conduct to fitness for custody often reflect varying judicial views of what constitute appropriate moral standards. The appellate court's framing of the question

---

[164] 474 N.W.2d 257 (N.D. 1991).

[165] *Id.* at 258.

[166] *See generally* Stone, *The Moral Dilemma: Child Custody When One Parent is Homosexual or Lesbian*, 23 Suffolk U. L. Rev. 711 (1989).

[167] Minn. Stat. Ann. § 518.17 (West 1990).

[168] Ala. Code § 30-3-1 (1975).

[169] D.C. Code Ann. § 16-914 (1981).

presented in *Feldman v. Feldman* [170] reflects an astute recognition of this truism. The court stated: "The issue presented is whether the [lower] court's determination, cloaked in the rubric 'best interests of the child,' was, in fact, based upon its subjective moral judgment rejecting and in effect severely punishing this sexually-liberated divorced woman for her life-style and personal beliefs." [171]

In *Feldman*, the court below transferred custody of two children, aged six and nine, from their mother, with whom they had lived since birth, to their father. At the hearing, it appeared that the mother had in the home a copy of "Screw," a sexually explicit magazine, together with letters with explicit photographs attached, solicited through an advertisement that the wife and her boyfriend had placed in the magazine. Evidence at the hearing also established that the mother's sex life did not affect the children, who were in a happy, cheerful, and comfortable home, and were well provided for emotionally and physically. Nevertheless, without finding the mother unfit, the hearing court awarded custody to the father based on its view that the mother's life-style indicated a "desire to experiment sexually." [172]

Awarding custody to the mother, the appellate court observed that "amorality, immorality, sexual deviation and what we conveniently consider aberrant sexual practices do not *ipso facto* constitute unfitness for custody." [173] The court also cited precedents that absolved sexually active unmarried men from moral censure and found no rational basis for imposing a more stringent standard on divorced women.

In *Jarrett v. Jarrett*, [174] however, the Supreme Court of Illinois was far less solicitous of the right of a divorced woman, engaged in a nonmarital sexual relationship, to retain custody of her three daughters. Despite the absence of any evidence whatsoever that the custodial mother's open cohabitation with a male had any adverse effect on the children, who were healthy and well cared for, the court affirmed the trial court's transfer of custody to the father. The court reasoned that the relevant standard of conduct was expressed in the provisions of the criminal code that sanctioned open and notorious cohabitation or sexual intercourse with a nonspouse as fornication. Accordingly, the court concluded:

> [The mother's] disregard for existing standards of conduct instructs her children, by example, that they, too, may ignore them . . ., and could well encourage the children to engage in similar activity in the future. That factor, of course, supports the trial court's conclusion that their daily presence in that environment was injurious to the moral well-being and development of the children. [175]

---

[170] 358 N.Y.S.2d 507 (N.Y. App. Div. 1974).

[171] *Id.* at 509.

[172] *Id.* at 509–510.

[173] *Id.* at 510.

[174] 400 N.E.2d 421 (Ill. 1979).

[175] *Id.* at 424 (citations omitted).

In sharp contrast to *Jarrett* is the opinion of the Supreme Court of Vermont in *Hansen v. Hansen*,[176] a case in which the trial court, at divorce, awarded physical custody of the parties' son and daughter, aged eight and five years, to the father. The trial court based its decision in part on the mother's continuing what had begun as an extramarital affair that had caused the breakup of the marriage. The reviewing court reversed the award and remanded for a new hearing. The court found an abuse of discretion by the trial court in basing its award on factors unrelated to the best interests of the children, in that the decision was not supported by any findings that the mother's misconduct affected them. Similarly, in *Hanhart v. Hanhart*,[177] the Supreme Court of South Dakota held that the trial court did not abuse its discretion in awarding custody to the child's adulterous mother, noting that the mother's affair had not had a deleterious impact on the children, and that fault is not relevant to custody determinations "except to the extent it is relevant to prove unfitness of the parent."[178]

The Supreme Court of Virginia in *Roe v. Roe*[179] posed the question of "whether a child's best interests are promoted by an award of custody to a parent who carries on an active homosexual relationship in the same residence as the child."[180] The court concluded not only that a custody award to such a parent was not in the child's best interests, but also that such an award constituted an abuse of judicial discretion.

When the parents in *Roe* were divorced, they agreed on custody to the mother. Some two years later, the father took over the child's care because of the mother's illness. Several years later the mother sought custody of the nine year old child, having learned that the father was living with a homosexual lover. The trial court granted joint legal custody to the parents, and provided that the child should live with the mother during summer vacation and with the father during the school year. The trial court found that the child was happy and well adjusted, and there was no evidence that the father's conduct had affected her adversely. Nevertheless, the order contained a condition that the father not share his bed or bedroom with any male friend or lover while the child was in residence.

The Virginia Supreme Court reversed and granted sole custody to the mother, relying on an earlier case that removed custody from an otherwise fit custodial mother who maintained an open, adulterous relationship with a male lover. Noting that sexual relations between homosexuals were punishable as a felony, the court concluded that "[t]he father's continuous exposure of the child to his immoral and illicit relationship renders him an unfit and improper custodian as a matter of law."[181] In addition to the change in custody, the court ordered that all visitation "in the father's home or in the presence of his homosexual lover" should cease.[182]

---

[176] 562 A.2d 1051 (Vt. 1989).

[177] 501 N.W. 2d 776 (S.D. 1993).

[178] *Id.* at 777.

[179] 324 S.E.2d 691 (Va. 1985).

[180] *Id.* at 691.

[181] *Id.* at 694.

[182] *Id.* at 694.

A decade later, in *Bottoms v. Bottoms,*[183] the court of Appeals of Virginia overturned a trial court's award to his grandmother on the ground that the child's parent was unfit because she was living in an open lesbian relationship with another woman and engaged in the illegal act of sodomy. The court held that the presumption favoring a natural parent over a third party, in this case the grandmother, was not rebutted merely because of the mother's lesbian relationship. On appeal, the Supreme Court of Virginia construed the facts differently and, without articulating a clear legal standard, reversed the judgment of the court of appeals.[184]

Although the approach of the Virginia Supreme Court in *Roe* was antagonistic to judicial recognition of the legitimacy of homosexual relationships, courts in other states have taken a more expansive position toward a custodial parent's intimate relationship with a person of the same sex. In *S.N.E. v. R.L.B.,*[185] for example, a father sought a change in custody from the mother, who was living with a female companion, on the grounds that she was a lesbian, was emotionally unstable, and held radical political views. The Supreme Court of Alaska emphasized that for parental conduct to be relevant to a custody award, an adverse effect on the child must result from the parental conduct. Citing *Palmore v. Sidoti,*[186] the court stated, "[s]imply put, it is impermissible to rely on any real or imagined social stigma attaching to Mother's status as a lesbian."[187]

Similarly, in *Conkel v. Conkel,*[188] the Court of Appeals of Ohio affirmed a trial court's order granting overnight visitation for a father who was living with a male friend with whom he maintained a sexual relationship. The child's mother argued that the children's sexual development could be influenced by the father's sexual orientation, that they might contract AIDS, and that they would "suffer the slings and arrows of a disapproving society."[189] Citing *Palmore*, the court stated, "[t]his court cannot take into consideration the unpopularity of homosexuals in society when its duty is to facilitate and guard a fundamental parent-child relationship."[190]

[D] Relative Considerations Between Fit Parents

[1] The Gender of the Parents

As discussed, the tender years presumption, favoring maternal custody of young children, no longer prevails.[191] In some states, statutes that

---

[183] 444 S.E. 2d 276 (Va. Ct. App. 1994), *reversed* 457 S.E. 2d 102 (Va. Ct. App. 1995).

[184] *See Bottoms v. Bottoms,* 457 S.E. 2d 102 (Va. 1995).

[185] 699 P.2d 875 (Alaska 1985).

[186] 466 U.S. 429 (1984) (concluding that the effects of racial prejudice did not justify removing a child from Caucasian custodial mother who had married a Black man); *see infra,* § 11.03[D][3].

[187] *S.N.E.,* 699 P.2d at 875.

[188] 509 N.E.2d 983 (Ohio Ct. App. 1987).

[189] *Id.* at 984.

[190] *Id.* at 987.

[191] *See supra* § 11.03[B][1].

govern child custody contain an explicit mandate that courts maintain an attitude of gender neutrality. The Arkansas statute, for example, provides that in divorce actions custody of the children "shall be made without regard to the sex of the parent but solely in accord with the welfare and best interests of the children."[192] Accordingly, in *Fox v. Fox*,[193] the Arkansas Court of Appeals reversed an award of custody to the mother in light of the trial court's view that young girls should be with their mothers. The court noted the statutory abolition of gender based presumptions and emphasized that custody questions must be determined on an individual basis.[194]

The Indiana statute includes "the age and sex of the child" among the factors that a trial judge must consider when determining custody.[195] In *Warner v. Warner*,[196] the Court of Appeals of Indiana affirmed the trial court's award of custody to the father of a four year old boy. The court took into account a psychologist's testimony that the father was able to provide the young child with the important "nurturing usually attributable to a mother."[197] The psychologist also stressed the importance of being able to identify with a parent of the same sex as a child gets older.[198] Accordingly, the court found no abuse of discretion in granting custody to the father.

[2] The Child's Preference in Custody Determinations

[a] Statutory Treatment

Taking a variety of approaches, a number of states have determined by statute the question of what role the child's preference plays in a custody determination. The Minnesota statute is illustrative, allowing the court to interview the child in chambers "to ascertain the child's preference as to custodian, if the court deems the child to be of sufficient age to express a preference."[199] The court is required to permit counsel to be present and to ask reasonable questions at the interview, either directly or through the court.[200]

The Illinois statute similarly allows the court to interview the child in chambers, with counsel present unless the parties agree otherwise, and requires the presence of a court reporter whose record of the interview is

---

[192] Ark. Code Ann. § 9-13-101 (Michie 1987); *see also* N.Y. Dom. Rel. Law § 240(1) (McKinney 1988) (enacting a "best interests of the child" standard and providing that "[i]n all cases there shall be no prima facie right to the custody of the child in either parent").

[193] 788 S.W.2d 743 (Ark. Ct. App. 1990).

[194] *See also Pusey v. Pusey*, 728 P.2d 117 (Utah 1986) (disavowing "those cases that continue to approve, even indirectly, an arbitrary maternal preference"). *Id.* at 120.

[195] Ind. Code Ann. § 31-17-2-8(1) (West 2001).

[196] 534 N.E.2d 752 (Ind. Ct. App. 1989).

[197] *Id.* at 754.

[198] *Id.*

[199] Minn. Stat. Ann. § 518.166 (West 1990).

[200] *Id.*

made a part of the record in the case.[201] The Georgia statute gives a child who is 14 or older the right to select the custodial parent, and the child's selection controls unless the parent selected is determined to be unfit for custody.[202]

[b]   Judicial Approaches

It is clear from the statutes that the trial court must first determine whether a child is mature enough to state a preference for one or the other parent. Also, the court must decide how much weight should be given to the child's preference, and how to determine it reliably. The Supreme Court of Rhode Island addressed these questions in *Goldstein v. Goldstein*.[203]

The child in *Goldstein* was a 9 1/2-year-old girl. The trial judge questioned the child in open court, where the child voiced difficulty in saying with which parent she wanted to live. Subsequently, in chambers, the child conceded that she preferred her father, but could not say so in the presence of her parents. The reviewing court held that there was no abuse of discretion in awarding custody to the father, and rejected the mother's contention that the trial court had allowed the child's preference to control its decision.

The court noted that the child was very intelligent for her age. Further, legislative policy setting 14 as the minimum age at which a child may nominate a preferred guardian was merely one factor among other relevant considerations weighed by the trial court. The court concluded that the factors favoring each parent were "so nearly in a state of equipoise" that the trial court did not abuse his discretion in giving substantial weight to the child's preference.[204]

The Supreme Court of Wyoming, in *Yates v. Yates*[205] neatly summarized the factors that the trial court should consider with respect to the child's preference in custody matters. Noting that as the child grows older, his preference should receive more weight, the court stated:

> In determining the weight to be given a child's preference several factors should be considered: the age of the child; the reason for the preference; the relative fitness of the preferred and non-preferred parent; the hostility, if any of the child to the non-preferred parent; the preference of other siblings; and whether the child's preference has been tainted or influenced by one parent against the other.[206]

An interview is not necessarily the only way or the best way for a court to determine a child's wishes with respect to custody. In *In re Marriage of Susen*,[207] the mother argued on appeal that the trial court's decision not

---

[201] *See* Ill. Ann. Stat. ch. 40 para. 604(a) (Smith-Hurd 1980).

[202] *See* Ga. Code Ann. § 19-9-1(a) (1991).

[203] 341 A.2d 51 (R.I. 1975).

[204] *Id.* at 53.

[205] 702 P. 2d 1252 (Wyo. 1985).

[206] *Id.* at 1255.

[207] 788 P.2d 332 (Mont. 1990).

to interview a child of kindergarten age was a violation of the statutory mandate that the court consider the child's wishes.[208] The court noted that while the statute requires consideration of the wishes of the child, it does not require that the court interview the child. In light of the testimony of all of the witnesses that the child loved and had a good relationship with both parents, the trial court's award of shared legal and physical custody was not an abuse of discretion.

In *Miller v. Miller,*[209] the Supreme Court addressed the custodial preferences of the three children of the parties to a divorce proceeding in a most unusual way. Having received a telephone call from one of the children, an attorney agreed to undertake pro bono representation of the child and his siblings. Construing statutory civil procedure requirements and having examined whether the children's claims were entitled to constitutional recognition, the court rejected the proposition that the children's preference should have primacy in a custody determination. To the contrary, the court observed,

> The best interest standard set forth in [the applicable statute] appropriately makes the preference of the child only one of many factors that the court must consider. The exclusion of children as parties in the divorce of their parents, and the related possibility that there will be no forceful advocacy for the custodial preference of the children, does not increase the risk of erroneous custody determinations that disserve the best interests of children. The guardian ad litem is already an advocate for the best interest of the children in all of its complex dimensions. The narrow focus of an attorney for the children, who would be obligated to carry out their preferences regardless of the wisdom of such a course, might well increase the likelihood of a custody determination that is not in the best interest of the children.[210]

[3] Race

Ordinarily, courts have broad discretion in making child custody awards and may consider a variety of factors, many of which are frequently delineated in statutes.[211] Subsequent to the decision of the United States Supreme Court in *Palmore v. Sidoti,*[212] however, it is clear that race may not be the determinative factor in awarding custody of children.

In *Palmore*, when the parties, both Caucasians, were divorced, a Florida court awarded custody of their three year old daughter to the mother. Subsequently, the court granted the father's petition to modify custody based on changed circumstances, in that the mother had first cohabited with and then married a Black man. The court found both parents fit.

---

[208] *See* Mont. Code Ann. § 40-4-212(1)(b) (1991).

[209] 677 A. 2d 64 (Me. 1996)

[210] *Id.* at 69 (citations omitted).

[211] *See supra* § 11.03[A].

[212] 466 U.S. 429 (1984).

Nevertheless, the court concluded that because the child would be vulnerable to peer pressure and social stigmatization as part of an interracial household, her best interests would be served by living with her father.

The Supreme Court rejected the Florida court's reasoning as impermissibly resting on race alone and, therefore, violative of the Equal Protection Clause. The Court concluded:

> The question . . . is whether the reality of private biases and the possible injury they might inflict are permissible considerations for removal of an infant child from the custody of its natural mother. We have little difficulty concluding that they are not. The Constitution cannot control such prejudices but neither can it tolerate them. Private biases may be outside the reach of the law, but the law cannot, directly or indirectly, give them effect.[213]

Thus, the Court concluded that the effects of racial prejudice would not justify a racial classification removing a child from a natural mother found to be an appropriate custodian.[214]

Subsequent to the decision of the Court in *Palmore*, state courts have become quite skittish about taking race into consideration at all in custody contests between fit parents. An exception is the judgment of the Supreme Court of South Dakota in *Jones v. Jones*.[215] In Jones, the mother of the child argued that the trial court had awarded the children to the husband because he, having suffered prejudice as a Native American, could better help the children, who were biracial with Native American features, to deal with the prejudice that they would encounter. The appellate court affirmed the custody award to the father, and concluded:

> To say, as [the mother] argues, that a court should never consider whether a parent is willing and able to expose to and educate children on their heritage, is to say that society is not interested in whether children ever learn who they are. *Palmore* does not require this, nor do the constitutions of the United States or the State of South Dakota.[216]

Accordingly, the court held "that it is proper for a trial court, when determining the best interests of a child in the context of a custody dispute between parents, to consider the matter of race as it relates to a child's ethnic heritage and which parent is more prepared to expose the child to it.[217]

[4] Religion

As is the case with race, consideration of religion in child custody determinations implicates constitutional issues. In *Pater v. Pater*,[218] the

---

[213] *Id.* at 433.

[214] *See* Perry, *Race and Child Placement: The Best Interests Test and the Cost of Discretion*, 29 J. Fam. L. 51 (1990–91), for an excellent discussion of *Palmore* and related questions.

[215] 542 N.W. 2d 119 (S.D. 1996).

[216] *Id.* at 123.

[217] *Id.* at 123–24.

[218] 588 N.E.2d 794 (Ohio 1992).

Supreme Court of Ohio described the impact of the Constitution on child custody determinations, observing that "a domestic relations court may consider the religious practices of the parents in order to protect the best interests of a child. . . . However, the United States Constitution flatly prohibits a trial court from ever evaluating the merits of religious doctrine or defining the contents of that doctrine."[219] Cases addressing the relevance of religion in child custody matters . . . generally adhere to this principle.

Illustrative is *Quiner v. Quiner*,[220] a leading case decided in California in 1967 that involved a custody dispute between the fit parents of a two-year-old boy. The parents were divorced following the wife's decision to remain affiliated with their religious group, which had become isolated to the greatest extent possible from the outside world and its influences.

At the time *Quiner* was decided, the statutory tender years presumption[221] in California would have placed the child with his mother, and the custodial parent was entitled to determine the child's religion. Having found that either parent would provide for the child's physical needs, the court examined the factor of mental welfare, defined to include "the opportunities for intellectual, character and personality growth, and the development of those social graces and amenities without which one cannot live comfortably or successfully in a complex, integrated society."[222]

After an exhaustive survey of ways in which the religious practices of the mother's group could adversely affect a young child's development by isolating him from the rest of society, the court concluded that custody in the mother was "more than likely to retard his mental growth and personality development, would be inimical to his welfare, and would severely handicap him in later years in his struggle to achieve his goals of social and economic attachment."[223] The court cited ample precedents to support the constitutionality of its decision, upholding the state's interest in protecting children's welfare and best interests over the parents' rights to control religious practices.

In *In re Marriage of Hadeen*,[224] the Court of Appeals of Washington considered whether religious acts could be a determinative factor in a custody award and if so, the required test for protection of both the children's interests and the parents' religious freedom. The parents in *Hadeen* belonged to a fundamentalist Christian sect that required of its members total loyalty and subservience; condoned strict discipline of children, including beating, fasting and isolation; and fostered hostility toward non-members. When the spouses separated, the father left the church. The trial court awarded him custody of the four youngest of five children, observing that custody in the mother would cut him off from the contact his children needed.

---

[219] *Id.* at 797.

[220] 59 Cal. Rptr. 503 (Cal. App. Dep't Super. Ct. 1967).

[221] *See supra* § 11.03[B][1].

[222] *Quiner*, 59 Cal. Rptr. at 527.

[223] *Id.* at 532.

[224] 619 P.2d 374 (Wash. Ct. App. 1980).

On appeal, the mother of the children argued successfully that the trial court's decision violated her right freely to exercise her religion under the First Amendment because there was no showing that her religion adversely affected the children's welfare. The appellate court reversed and remanded, stating that "religious decisions and acts may be considered in a custody decision only to the extent that those decisions or acts will jeopardize the temporal mental health or physical safety of the child."[225] This standard is met, the court held, by showing "a reasonable and substantial likelihood of immediate or future impairment" of the child's mental or physical well-being.[226]

The parents in *In re Marriage of Gershowitz*[227] agreed to a joint custody arrangement for their son. The trial court decided that when the boy reached school age he should reside primarily with one parent to avoid interruption of his education by multiple transfers of custody. The child's father objected to the trial court's selection of the mother as primary physical custodian, arguing that the child's continued upbringing in the Jewish faith and way of life would be undermined. The Supreme Court of Montana affirmed, holding that the trial court's decision correctly reflected the child's best interests and was constitutionally sound. Reflecting the conventional wisdom, the court observed:

> The First Amendment guarantees religious liberty, and the right of parents to direct the religious upbringing of their children. . . . [C]ourts will not debate the merits of different religions or show preference to any religious faith. However, courts will examine religious practices which interfere with the child's general welfare. . . . A question of religious education must be strictly limited to the context of the best interests of the minor child.[228]

The court noted that under the applicable Montana statute the custodial parent determines the child's religious training, and that in the case before it, "an award of custody for the purpose of religious education should not dominate other elements which comprise the best interests" of the child.[229]

In *In re Marriage of Wang,*[230] the Supreme Court of Montana considered another custody challenge related to one parent's religious beliefs. The court rejected the mother's assertion that the trial court was required to make specific findings with respect to the husband's church affiliation and how his religious involvement affected the child's best interest. Over a strong dissent, the court held that a review of the entire record demonstrated that

---

[225] *Id.* at 382.

[226] *Id.*

[227] 779 P.2d 883 (Mont. 1989).

[228] *Id.* at 885.

[229] *Id.*; *see also Pater v. Pater*, 588 N.E.2d 794, 801 (Ohio 1992) (adopting "the majority rule that a court may not restrict a non-custodial parent's right to expose his or her child to religious beliefs, unless the conflict between the parents' religious beliefs is affecting the child's general welfare").

[230] 896 P. 2d 450 (Mont. 1995

both parents were suitable and that the trial court's findings were supported by credible evidence.

In *Leppert v. Leppert,*[231] the Supreme Court of South Dakota reversed the trial court's award of custody of five children to their mother, despite a law guardian's report stating that because of her beliefs the mother's parenting was physically and emotionally extremely dangerous to the children. The court in *Leppert* clearly and cogently set out the reigning principle with respect to the impact of a parent's religion on the best interests of the child. The court observed:

> Although we agree with the district court that [the mother] must not be discounted from consideration as a custodial parent simply because of her religious *beliefs,* this does not mean her religiously motivated *actions,* which are emotionally and physically harmful to the children, should be ignored when determining the children's best interests. Such a holding would immunize from consideration all religiously motivated acts, no matter what their impact on the children.[232]

[5] Physical Condition of the Custodial Parent

The Uniform Marriage and Divorce Act includes among the factors a court shall consider in determining custody in accordance with the best interest of the child "the mental and physical health of all individuals involved."[233] Statutes in some states also include this factor.[234] Decisions involving the mental or emotional fitness of prospective custodians, primarily in intermediate appellate courts, are largely dependent on the unique facts in the individual cases.[235]

The decision of the Supreme Court of California in *In re Marriage of Carney*[236] is a paradigmatic case addressing the weight to be given to the physical disability of a parent seeking custody. The father in *Carney,* pursuant to a written agreement with the mother, had cared for their two boys for almost five years prior to the commencement of a marriage dissolution action. During this entire time the mother resided some 3,000 miles away in New York and neither visited the children nor contributed to their support. Shortly before the dissolution action began, the father was paralyzed as the result of injuries sustained in an automobile accident.

---

[231] 519 N.W. 2d 287 (N.D. 1994).

[232] *Id.* at 290.

[233] U.M.D.A. § 402(5), 9A U.L.A. 561 (1988).

[234] *See, e.g.,* Minn. Stat. Ann. § 518.17(9) (West 1990).

[235] *See, e.g., In re Marriage of Lewin,* 231 Cal. Rptr 433, 437 (Cal. Ct. App. 1986) (finding the mother's unfounded allegations that the father used drugs and sexually abused his daughter to be "outrageous conduct" supporting an award of custody to the father); *In re Marriage of Nordby,* 705 P.2d 277, 278 (Wash. Ct. App. 1985) (reversing award of custody to mother based on trial court's view that there would probably be a remission of her mental illness and holding that "[t]he test for fitness of custody should be the present condition of the mother and not any future or past conduct.").

[236] 598 P.2d 36 (Cal. 1979).

The trial judge awarded custody to the mother, noting that sports and other physical activities are an important aspect of a father-son relationship. The trial judge concluded that because the father could do nothing more for the children than talk to them and teach them, "[i]t wouldn't be a normal relationship between father and boys."[237] Reversing the award to the mother, the Supreme Court of California stated that while the health or physical condition of parents is relevant in determining the child's best interests, it is ordinarily a factor of minor importance. The court then set forth the following standard for evaluating the suitability for child custody of a physically disabled parent:

> [I]f a person has a physical handicap it is impermissible for the court simply to rely on that condition as prima facie evidence of the person's unfitness as a parent or of probable detriment to the child; rather, in all cases the court must view the handicapped person as an individual and the family as a whole. To achieve this, the court should inquire into the person's actual and potential physical capabilities, learn how he or she has adapted to the disability and manages its problems, consider how the other members of the household have adjusted thereto, and take into account the special contributions the person may make to the family despite — or even because of — the handicap. Weighing these and all other relevant factors together, the court should then carefully determine whether the parent's condition will in fact have a substantial and lasting adverse effect on the best interests of the child.[238]

Having rejected the trial court's "conventional sex-stereotypical thinking,"[239] the court pointed out that public policy, reflected in a number of legislative enactments, supports the total integration of disabled people into society. This includes participation in the "responsibilities and satisfactions of family life, [the] cornerstone of our social system."[240]

The decision of the Supreme Court of Idaho in *Moye v. Moye*[241] reflects an approach that is entirely consistent with that of the California court in *Carney*. Among the factors that an Idaho court must consider when making a custody determination is "[t]he mental and physical health and integrity of all individuals involved."[242] In *Moye*, the mother's epilepsy, somewhat controlled by medication, manifested itself in seizures, post-seizure lack of energy, migraine headaches and the need for nine to ten hours sleep each night.

The reviewing court found that this evidence did not sufficiently support the trial court's conclusion that the best interests of two pre-school children would be served by awarding custody to the father. The court observed that

---

[237] *Id.* at 41.

[238] *Id.* at 42.

[239] *Id.*

[240] *Id.* at 42.

[241] 627 P.2d 799 (Idaho 1981).

[242] Idaho Code § 32-717 (1983).

an abuse of discretion may occur not only when there is insufficient evidence to support the trial court's conclusion, but also when the court places undue emphasis on a single factor, such as the physical condition of a parent. In either case, the court fails to support its conclusion that a particular custody award serves the interests and welfare of a child.

With increasing frequency, courts face issues relating to custodial fitness of persons infected with human immunodeficiency virus (HIV), which causes acquired immune deficiency syndrome (AIDS).[243] The decision of the Court of Appeals of Indiana in *Stewart v. Stewart*[244] is illustrative. The father in *Stewart* sought a change of custody from the mother, alleging that she was not properly caring for their daughter.[245] After hearing testimony that the father tested positive for the HIV virus, the trial court terminated his visitation rights, ruling that he presented a physical danger to the child.

The Indiana Court of Appeals carefully reviewed medical evidence that no cases of transmission of the AIDS virus through "household contact" had been reported, even when the household member had developed AIDS.[246] Accordingly, the court held that termination of the father's visitation was an "extreme and unwarranted action."[247]

New York courts addressing this question have reached similar results. In *Doe v. Roe*,[248] the maternal grandparents sought custody of two minor children from their custodial father and moved for an order to compel him to submit to a test for AIDS. Citing the leading case of *Carney v. Carney*,[249] the court noted that the proper inquiry is whether a debilitating condition has a detrimental effect on the child. Further, the court observed, the potentially shortened life span of a person with AIDS would not justify removal of children from a long term caretaker with whom they have strong bonds of love and affection.[250]

§ 11.04   Joint Custody

[A]   Introduction and Overview

Traditional awards of sole custody, even with liberal visitation in the non-custodial parent, may result in, or at least have the appearance of elevating

---

[243] *See generally* Mahon, Note, *Public Hysteria, Private Conflict: Child Custody and Visitation Disputes Involving an HIV Infected Parent*, 63 N.Y.U. L. Rev. 1092 (1988).

[244] 521 N.E.2d 956 (Ind. Ct. App. 1988).

[245] *See infra* § 11.06 for a discussion of modification of child custody awards.

[246] 521 N.E.2d at 963–964.

[247] 521 N.E.2d at 965.

[248] 526 N.Y.S.2d 718 (N.Y. Sup. Ct. 1988).

[249] 598 P.2d 36 (Cal. 1979).

[250] *See also Anne D. v. Raymond D.*, 528 N.Y.S.2d 775 (N.Y. Sup. Ct. 1988) (holding that husband's allegations that wife engaged in a series of extra-marital affairs were not sufficient basis to require her to undergo HIV blood test for AIDS in connection with custody determination; *Steven L. v. Dawn J.*, 561 N.Y.S.2d 322 (N.Y. Fam. Ct. 1990) (holding that positive HIV test did not warrant change of custody from mother whose physical condition did not impair her caretaking ability of affect the child's physical or psychological well being).

the status of one parent over the other. Recently, courts and legislatures have looked to joint custody as an alternative that, at least in theory, permits parents to share responsibility and decision making on an equal basis. A reading of the cases reveals that there are those who question whether shared parenting arrangements between divorced couples actually fulfill the ideas embodied in the concept of joint custody.

As is the case with sole custody, the courts weigh various factors to determine whether joint custody is the preferable arrangement. The overall objective, however, is constant. It is the best interests and welfare of the child that forms the framework within which the factors are considered. The question is not whether a particular number of factors is present. Rather, each case turns on its individual facts and circumstances.

As the court in a leading case has accurately observed, "[t]he inability of courts and commentators to agree on what is meant by the term 'joint custody' makes difficult the task of distilling principles and guidelines from a rapidly growing body of literature and case law."[251] Although a precise definition has proved elusive, two concepts are embodied within the definition — legal custody and physical custody. In *Beck v. Beck*,[252] the Supreme Court of New Jersey has provided a useful articulation of these concepts:

> Under a joint custody arrangement legal custody — the legal authority and responsibility for making "major" decisions regarding the child's welfare — is shared at all times by both parents. Physical custody, the logistical arrangement whereby the parents share the companionship of the child and are responsible for "minor" day-to-day decisions, may be alternated in accordance with the needs of the parties and the children.[253]

Although the language of the decisions may vary, the conceptual difference between physical custody and legal custody is critical.

[B]   Statutory Joint Custody Provisions

State legislatures have taken a variety of approaches to joint custody. The scope and language of statutes governing the matter vary greatly from state to state. The examples below are illustrative of common approaches, but are by no means comprehensive or exhaustive.

Adopting a common approach, the Florida statute sets out a presumption in favor of joint custody, stating that "[t]he court shall order that the parental responsibility for a minor child be shared by both parents unless the court finds that shared parental responsibility would be detrimental to the child."[254] Similarly, the Louisiana statute contains a rebuttable presumption that joint custody is in the best interests of the child.[255]

---

[251] *Taylor v. Taylor*, 508 A.2d 964, 966 (Md. 1986).

[252] 432 A.2d 63 (N.J. 1981).

[253] *Id.* at 66.

[254] Fla. Stat. Ann. § 61.13.2 (West 1985 & Supp. 1993).

[255] La. Civ. Code Ann. art. 131 (West Supp. 1993).

In sharp contrast to the approach in Florida and Louisiana, Massachusetts reflects an entirely neutral approach with respect to the form of custody awards. The statute permits sole or shared awards of legal or physical custody, provides that absent misconduct the parents' rights are equal, and declares that "[t]here shall be no presumption either in favor of or against shared legal or physical custody at the time of the trial on the merits."[256]

The Iowa statute sets out a preference for a custody award that will maximize the child's opportunity for emotional and physical contact with both separated or divorced parents. To that end, the statute directs the courts to "consider the denial by one parent of the child's opportunity for maximum contact with the other parent, without just cause, a significant factor in determining the proper custody arrangement."[257] Although such "friendly parent" provisions are intended to encourage cooperation between the parents, it is obvious that they may also discourage a parent from opposing a joint custody arrangement out of fear of losing custody.

There is some evidence, admittedly scant, that the legislative tide in favor of joint custody may be turning. The legislatures of both California and Utah have repealed legislative joint custody presumptions that had been in effect in those states.[258]

[C] Judicial Treatment of Joint Custody

It is not possible to identify a universal standard that courts employ in deciding when joint custody is appropriate. As discussed, the child's best interests are paramount. In seeking to achieve this objective in joint custody, the courts generally consider the ability of the parents to communicate with each other and reach shared decisions affecting the child's welfare.

In *Beck v. Beck*,[259] the Supreme Court of New Jersey declined to establish a presumption in favor of joint custody, recognizing that such an arrangement would be appropriate infrequently. The initial inquiry is "whether the children have established such relationships with both parents that they would benefit from joint custody."[260] At a minimum, the court suggested, both parents must be fit, which means psychologically and physically able to fulfill the parental role. Further, each must be willing to accept custody, although the parents' opposition to joint custody does not preclude the court from ordering that arrangement. Finally, the trial court should examine such practical considerations as the parties' financial status, their geographical proximity, and the age and number of children,[261] and must

---

[256] Mass. Gen. Laws ch. 208 § 31 (Cum. Supp. 1990).

[257] Iowa Code Ann. § 598.41 (West 1992).

[258] *See* Utah Code Ann. § 30-3-10.2 (2001).

[259] 432 A.2d 63 (N.J. 1981).

[260] *Id.* at 71.

[261] *Id.* at 72.

accord due weight to the preference of children of "sufficient age and capacity."[262]

New York's highest court reviewed a joint custody determination in *Braiman v. Braiman*,[263] holding that joint custody is not appropriate when the parents are "embattled and embittered."[264] The court concluded:

> There are no painless solutions. In the rare case, joint custody may approximate the former family relationships more closely than other custodial arrangements. It may not, however, be indiscriminately substituted for an award of sole custody to one parent. Divorce dissolves the family as well as the marriage, a reality that may not be ignored.[265]

The view of Maryland's highest court, as set out in *Taylor v. Taylor*,[266] is not inconsistent with that of the New York court in *Braiman*. In the Maryland court's view, the parents' capacity to communicate and reach shared decisions affecting the child's welfare is clearly the most important factor in the determination of whether an award of joint legal custody is appropriate, and is relevant as well to a consideration of shared physical custody. Rarely, if ever, would joint legal custody be awarded in the absence of a record of mature conduct on the part of the parents evidencing an ability to effectively communicate with each other concerning the best interest of the child, and then only when it is possible to make a finding of a strong potential for such conduct in the future.[267]

Noting that no enumeration of appropriate factors in a joint custody is all-inclusive, the court considered as relevant factors, among others, fitness of the parents, the relationship between the child and each parent, the preference of a child of suitable age and discretion, the potential disruption of the child's school and social life, the geographical proximity of the parents' homes, the demands of parental employment, the number and ages of the children and the parents' financial status.[268]

In *Squires v. Squires*,[269] the Supreme Court of Kentucky considered "whether parties who are found to be good parents will endeavor to place the interest of their child uppermost should be denied joint custody due to their hostility and refusal to cooperate with one another."[270] The court in *Squires* noted that joint custody and sole custody do not require a significantly different analysis; in either case the court must look at all the relevant factors in order to determine a result that comports with the best interest of the child.

[262] *Id.* at 73.

[263] 378 N.E.2d 1019 (N.Y. 1978).

[264] *Id.* at 1021.

[265] *Id.* at 1022; *see also Dodd v. Dodd*, 403 N.Y.S.2d 401 (N.Y. Sup. Ct. 1978).

[266] 508 A.2d 964 (Md. 1986).

[267] *Id.* at 971

[268] *Id.* at 973–974; *see also In re Marriage of Weidner*, 338 N.W.2d 351, 355–358 (Iowa 1983).

[269] 854 S.W. 2d 765 (Ky. 1993).

[270] *Id.* at 767.

Thus, there is no requirement of agreement between the parties and willingness to cooperate at the time when the court determines custody. The court pointed out that such a requirement would permit the parent opposed to joint custody "to dictate the result by his or her own belligerence and would invite contemptuous conduct.

Accordingly, the court held that the trial court, after considering the application of statutory standards for a custody award must weigh the likelihood of future parental cooperation. The court continued:

> Thereafter, we believe a trial court should look beyond the present and assess the likelihood of future cooperation between the parents. I would be shortsighted to conclude that because parties are antagonistic at the time of their divorce, such antagonism will continue indefinitely. Emotional maturity would appear to be a dependable guide in predicting future behavior. By cooperation we mean willingness to rationally participate in decisions affecting the upbringing of the child. It should not be overlooked that to achieve such cooperation, the trial court may assist the parties by means of its contempt power and its power to modify custody in the event of a bad faith refusal of cooperation.[271]

The court in *Squires* took pains to point out that it was not endorsing a preference for joint custody, but that under current law "joint custody must be awarded the same dignity as sole custody and trial courts must determine which form would serve the best interest of the child.[272]

§ 11.05 Visitation

[A] Right of Noncustodial Parent to Visitation

In essence, under the traditional approach of awarding sole custody to one of the parents, visitation rights are a corollary to custody awards. Any number of issues may arise in connection with post-divorce disputes relating to visitation. Typical are questions that involve schedules, transportation costs, the impact on visitation of a custodial parent's relocation, and behavioral problems in children resulting from ongoing conflict between the parents.[273]

As in the case of an initial custody determination, trial courts have considerable discretion in determining visitation for noncustodial parents that is in the best interests of the child. As one court has cogently put it, "[a] noncustodial parent's right of visitation is a natural right and should be denied only under extraordinary circumstances, which would include, among other things, a showing that the visitation would harm the child."[274]

---

[271] *Id.* at 769.

[272] *Id.* at 768–69.

[273] *See Sterbling v. Sterbling*, 519 N.E.2d 673 (Ohio Ct. App. 1987).

[274] *Id.* at 676.

One example of parental conduct that may result in the denial of visitation is drug or alcohol addiction.[275] On occasion, courts have considered the visitation rights of noncustodial parents who are incarcerated. In *Suttles v. Suttles*,[276] for example, a father who was imprisoned for shooting his father-in-law and abducting his son requested reasonable visitation rights. The court held that although incarceration alone does not preclude visitation, it was inappropriate in this case in light of the father's violent behavior.[277]

[1]　Illustrative Statutes

State statutes that govern custody often contain explicit provisions relating to visitation rights of the noncustodial parent. The Colorado statute, for example, entitles the parent not granted custody of the child to reasonable visitation rights unless there is a finding by the court that visitation "would endanger the child's health or significantly impair his emotional development."[278] Curiously, the Colorado statute sets out a list of crimes which, if committed by the custodial parent, may result in divestment of visitation rights.

The statute governing custody in Illinois similarly provides that the parent not granted custody of a child is entitled to reasonable visitation rights unless a hearing reveals that visitation would seriously endanger the child physically, mentally, morally, or emotionally.[279] The statute also contains procedures for enforcing visitation where there has been "visitation abuse," meaning that one party has denied visitation rights to the other, or that a party has exercised visitation rights in a manner that is harmful to either the child or the child's custodian.[280]

---

[275] *See, e.g., Soltis v. Soltis*, 470 So. 2d 1250 (Ala. Civ. App. 1985) (denying visitation to mother who was addicted to ethyl alcohol and engaged in violent behavior in child's presence). *But see Roberts v. Roberts*, 371 A2d 689, 694 (Md. Ct. Spec. App. 1977) (reversing a decree that terminated a mother's visitation rights because of alcohol abuse, stating that even an "errant parent" has a right of reasonable access to a child in the absence of injury to the child's welfare).

[276] 748 S.W.2d 427 (Tenn. 1988).

[277] *See also In re Marriage of Brewer*, 760 P.2d 1225 (Kan. Ct. App. 1988) (rejecting claim that denial of visitation abridged father's constitutional rights and holding that although incarceration alone may not foreclose visitation rights, tender ages of children and lengthy estrangement from father made visitation in a prison setting contrary to their best interests). *But see McCurdy v. McCurdy*, 363 N.E.2d 1298 (Ind. Ct. App. 1977) (holding that visitation of imprisoned father with four-and seven-year-old children can mutually benefit parent and child in that children need to appreciate the reality of the situation, and visitation might have rehabilitative effect on father).

[278] Colo. Rev. Stat. § 14-10-129 (West 2001).

[279] 750 Ill. Comp. Stat. (2001).

[280] *Id.* at § 6607.1.

[2] Enforcement of Visitation

[a] Statutory Remedies

The statutes of some states contain explicit remedial provisions for failure to permit visitation or other disputes concerning visitation. In Colorado, for example, upon an allegation of noncompliance with a visitation order the court may set a hearing or require the parties to seek mediation. Upon proof of noncompliance, the court may impose additional terms or conditions, require the posting of a bond to assure future compliance, require makeup visitation, find the violator in contempt and impose a fine or jail sentence, or schedule a modification hearing. [281]

The Alaska statute creates a cause of action against the custodian for money damages of $200 for each wilful and inexcusable failure to permit court ordered visitation. [282] In Michigan, the statute sets out a highly structured and detailed makeup visitation policy, administered by the office of the friend of the court, in cases of wrongful denial of visitation to a noncustodial parent. [283]

[b] Judicial Remedies

A variety of remedies are available to the noncustodial parent whose visitation rights are thwarted by the parent who has custody of the child. In *Smith v. Smith*,[284] for example, the custodial mother appealed unsuccessfully from an order finding her in contempt and sentencing her to 5 days in a correctional facility for failing to abide by the father's visitation schedule established by the trial court. The appellate court rejected the mother's argument that all she need do to comply with the trial court's order was to encourage visitation with the father. The children, aged 5 and 8, were too young to "affirmatively and independently" refuse to have visitation with their father. [285] Under these circumstances, and absent evidence of harm to the children from visitation, the court found that the custodial parent had a duty to "follow the court order that she deliver the children to the [father] for purposes of visitation." [286]

Generally, in instances where the child's lack of cooperation results in frustration of the noncustodial parent's visitation rights, the courts will carefully scrutinize the child's unwillingness to visit in light of the possibility of influence by the custodial parent. Obviously, enforcement of visitation

---

[281] Colo. Rev. Stat. Ann. § 14-10-129.5 (West 1987).

[282] Alaska Stat. § 25.20.140 (1992).

[283] Mich. Comp. Laws Ann. § 552.642 (West 1988).

[284] 434 N.E.2d 749 (Ohio Ct. App. 1980).

[285] *Id.* at 752.

[286] *Id.*; *see also Prater v. Wheeler*, 322 S.E.2d 892, 894 (Ga. 1984) (holding that although 14-year-old may select custodian under Georgia law, visitation is parent's natural right. To permit children to refuse visitation "would permit, if not encourage, custodial parents to vent their spite for their former mates by pressuring, directly or indirectly their children to make such an election").

is likely to be difficult or nearly impossible when an older child refuses to cooperate.[287]

The custodial mother's persistent and extreme interference with her former husband's visitation rights resulted in a change of custody in *Egle v. Egle*.[288] The mother's conduct included physically evading the children's father and alienating them from him. The court observed that although, as a general rule, a change of circumstances is required before custody is changed, "[a] showing of sabotage or deliberate frustration of visitation rights provides an alternative ground for a change of custody and obviates the need to show a change of circumstances."[289] Accordingly, the court concluded that in such instances it would serve the best interests of the children to change their custody "to the parent who is more likely to honor the other parent's (and the children's) rights."[290]

In *Schutz v. Schutz*,[291] the Supreme Court of Florida addressed the assertion by the child's mother, the custodial parent, that the trial court's order that she do all that was in her power to create a loving feeling toward their father violated her first amendment rights. The court, purporting to "balance the mother's right to free expression against the state's parens patriae interest in assuring the well-being of the parties' minor children"[292] stated:

> [W]e read the challenged portion of the order at issue to require nothing more of the mother than a good faith effort to take those measures necessary to restore and promote the frequent and continuing positive interaction (e.g., visitation, phone calls, letters) between the children and their father and to refrain from doing or saying anything likely to defeat that end. There is no requirement that [the mother] express opinions that she does not hold, a practice disallowed by the first amendment..[293]

Conventional civil remedies may not always be available in connection with disputes involving visitation. In *Gleiss v. Newman*,[294] for example, a noncustodial mother sought to recover damages against her former husband for the tort of intentional infliction of emotional distress arising from his interference with her rights of visitation. Having looked to the law of other jurisdictions that have declined to recognize such claims, the court held that no such cause of action exists.

---

[287] *See, e.g., In re Two Minor Children*, 249 A.2d 743 (Del. 1969) (refusing to force 16-year-old to visit her mother, because enforcement would be impossible). *See generally* Novinson, *Post-Divorce Visitation: Untying The Triangular Knot*, 1983 U. Ill. L. Rev. 121 (1983).

[288] 715 F.2d 999 (5th Cir. 1983).

[289] *Id.* at 1016.

[290] *Id.* at 1017; *see also Rosenberg v. Rosenberg*, 504 A.2d 350 (Pa. Super. Ct. 1986) (holding that automatic transfer of custody is not an appropriate remedy for interference with visitation, and that normal means of enforcement is through contempt proceeding).

[291] 581 So. 2d 1290 (Fla. 1991).

[292] *Id.* at 1293.

[293] *Id.* at 1292.

[294] 415 N.W.2d 845 (Wis. Ct. App. 1987).

As the court noted, several reasons of public policy support its decision. Allowing suits of this kind may encourage claims for "petty infractions" before courts that are already overburdened with visitation disputes.[295] Further, there are other remedies available for interference with visitation rights, including contempt proceedings, proceedings to enforce visitation rights, and proceedings to modify custody. Finally, recognition of a claim for compensatory and punitive damages is contrary to the child's best interests. It "would alter the focus from determining visitation consistent with the child's best interests to parental compensation."[296]

[B] Restrictions on Visitation

There are occasions when the courts will approve restrictions on noncustodial parents' exercise of visitation rights. Disputes appear to arise most frequently with respect to the religious training of children and the noncustodial parent's sexual conduct. In *Zummo v. Zummo*,[297] a Pennsylvania appellate court vacated a trial court order barring a noncustodial parent from taking his children during visitation periods to religious services that were inconsistent with the custodial mother's faith. Refusing to impose restricted visitation, the court found that the parents' earlier agreement and practice of bringing up the children in the Jewish faith did not control. The court rejected the argument that inconsistent religious teachings would result in substantial physical or emotional harm to the children.

Based on similar reasoning, a New Jersey trial court in *Brown v. Szakai*[298] refused to require a father to observe Jewish dietary laws during visitation with his children. The court balanced the right of the custodian to control the religious upbringing of the children against the goal of promoting a good relationship with the father through "appropriate unrestricted visitation."[299] Citing with approval authority from other jurisdictions, the court concluded that absent a showing of harm to the children it would not impose on the noncustodial parent the burden of carrying out the custodial parent's religious instructions.[300]

As is the case with initial custody determinations,[301] courts from time to time have reviewed the sexual conduct of noncustodial parents in

---

[295] *Id.* at 846.

[296] *Id.* at 846–847.

[297] 574 A.2d 1130 (Pa. Super. Ct. 1990).

[298] 514 A.2d 81 (N.J. Super. Ct. Ch. Div. 1986).

[299] *Id.* at 83.

[300] *Id.* at 84. *But see LeDoux v. LeDoux*, 452 N.W.2d 1, 5 (Neb. 1990) (upholding an order prohibiting a Jehovah's Witness father from exposing the children during visitation to religious practices inconsistent with the custodial mother's Catholic faith. Noting that the children and the father-child relationship were being harmed by participation in the father's religion, the court stated that while the custodial parent ordinarily controls the children's religious training, it is constitutionally permissible for courts to restrict religious practices in the best interest of the children through narrowly tailored orders).

[301] *See supra*, § 11.03[C].

connection with visitation. In *DeVita v. DeVita*,[302] for example, a New Jersey appellate court in a questionable decision upheld a restriction that a father's weekend visitation with his seven children, aged eight to twenty, not take place in the presence of a female friend. The court conceded that there was no showing of harm to the children, but recognized "that in the mother's view the moral welfare of the child is possibly endangered if the trial judge's restriction is not upheld."[303] The court also observed "that her views are not contrary to those of a substantial body of the community."[304]

In a case with facts similar to those in *DeVita*, the court in *Kelly v. Kelly*,[305] adopted an arguably more enlightened view, purporting to distinguish *DeVita* and holding that the court must consider the best interests of the child, and not only a custodian's "moral outrage," when determining visitation arrangements. Taking note of the testimony of psychiatric experts, the court concluded that the children's welfare would be served by a continuation of overnight visitation with their father, despite the presence of his female companion.

Similarly, in *In re Marriage of Cabalquinto*,[306] the mother refused to allow the child visitation in the father's home out of state because the father resided with a homosexual lover. The court cited the rule in several states that "homosexuality in and of itself is not a bar to custody or to reasonable rights of visitation."[307] To hold otherwise would be to base visitation on a parent's sexual orientation rather than the best interests of the child.

[C] Visitation and Child Support

In most states, child support obligations and visitation rights are treated separately and one is not tied to the other. In a few states there is a statutory link between visitation and child support, while in others statutes explicitly bar the denial of visitation for failure to pay child support. Cases that address the issue generally take a similar approach.

[1] Illustrative Statutes

The Oregon statute is unusual, in that it links child support and visitation and enables the court to modify either provision when a person having custody of a child denies visitation rights.[308] The statute in Kentucky provides that when children entitled to support are receiving public assistance, neither parent may use matters concerning custody or visitation as a reason for failing to pay child support.[309] The Minnesota statute is an excellent example of a logical and principled approach to this issue:

[302] 366 A.2d 1350 (N.J. Super. Ct. App. Div. 1976).

[303] *Id.* at 1354.

[304] *Id.*

[305] 524 A.2d 1330 (N.J. Super. Ct. Ch. Div. 1986).

[306] 669 P.2d 886 (Wash. 1983).

[307] *Id.* at 888.

[308] Or. Rev. Stat. § 107.431(1) (2001).

[309] Ky. Rev. Stat. Ann. § 205.770 (Michie 1991).

Failure by a party to make support payments is not a defense to: interference with visitation rights; or without the permission of the court or the noncustodial parent removing a child from this state. Nor is interference with visitation rights or taking a child from this state without permission of the court or the noncustodial parent a defense to nonpayment of support. If a party fails to make support payments, or interferes with visitation rights, or without permission of the court or the noncustodial parent removes a child from this state, the other party may petition the court for an appropriate order. [310]

[2] Case Law

The cases that follow reflect quite typical fact patterns and judicial determinations with respect to the relationships between child support obligations and visitation rights. In *Kemp v. Kemp*, [311] after the custodial mother terminated all contact between her son and his father, the father discontinued support payments. The mother then sought suspension of visitation rights and a contempt citation against the father for nonpayment of child support, and the father sought to hold her in contempt for noncompliance with the visitation order. The trial court suspended both visitation and child support, and the intermediate appellate court reversed both determinations.

When the case reached the Maryland Court of Appeals, the court held that one and a half years having passed since the last hearing on visitation, changed circumstances required a new hearing on that issue. The court directed the trial judge on remand to base a visitation decision on the best interests of the child, cautioning that "he should . . . only deny visitation if the evidence clearly demonstrates the existence of extraordinary circumstances requiring such drastic action." [312]

In *Cooper v. Cooper*, [313] a noncustodial father sought termination of child support and relief from any obligation to pay for the college education of his two minor children, alleging that the children refused to visit him. The court reviewed allegations that the mother deliberately influenced the children to refuse visitation through behavior characterized as "psychological warfare." Remanding, the court held that termination was within the trial court's authority under extreme and unusual circumstances.

[D] Visitation by Third Parties

The common law rule, generally favoring natural parents in the absence of a showing of unfitness, did not provide for visitation by third persons.

[310] Minn. Stat. Ann. § 518.612 (West 2001). *See generally*, Taylor, *Note, Making Parents Behave: The Conditioning of Child Support and Visitation Rights*, 84 Colum. L. Rev. 1059 (1984) (criticizing courts that link child support and visitation for creating a remedy that adversely affects the parties involved).

[311] 411 A.2d 1028 (Md. 1980).

[312] *Id.* at 1031–1032 (citation omitted).

[313] 375 N.E.2d 925 (Ill. App. Ct. 1978).

In recent years, however, legislatures throughout the country have enacted statutes that permit courts to grant visitation rights to grandparents in a variety of circumstances. In some states, the statutes extend visitation rights to other third parties, including stepparents, siblings, so called de facto parents, and others who have established relationships with the child. Although grandparent visitation is the only species of third party visitation that the United States Supreme Court has addressed,[314] a number of courts have applied state constitutional provisions far more broadly.

[1] The Common Law Rule

The decision by a California appellate court in *Odell v. Lutz*[315] is illustrative of the common law rule regarding visitation by parties other than the parents. The plaintiff in this case sought to visit her 8-year-old granddaughter, her deceased daughter's child, over the objection of the child's father, who had remarried. The court held that while parental rights are not absolute and are subject to the state's power to protect the child from parental abuse, it would be unconstitutional to interfere with the "natural liberty of parents to direct the upbringing of their children."[316]

Again, in a decision typical of those addressing the question, the Court of Appeals of North Carolina adhered to the traditional rule that grandparents' love for a child does not give them the right to enforce visitation. Although ties of love and affection between children and grandparents are desirable, this is no justification for interference with the parent-child relationship.

[2] Third Party Visitation Statutes

A dazzling variety of legislative enactments across the country currently provide for visitation by grandparents, and in not a few instances other third parties are also authorized to seek visitation. The California statute is among the most liberal. It directs the court to order reasonable visitation rights to the noncustodial parent in the absence of detriment to the child, and also gives the court discretion to award visitation to "any other person having an interest in the welfare of the child."[317] Similarly, the Connecticut statute authorizes the trial court to grant visitation rights "to any person, upon an application of such person."[318]

The Oregon provision is also broad in scope, although it contains some limiting language, authorizing petitions for visitation rights to any person "who has established emotional ties creating a parent-child relationship or an ongoing personal relationship with a child. . . ."[319] The right to petition

---

[314] 530 U.S. 57 (2000).

[315] 177 P.2d 628 (Cal. Dist. Ct. App. 1947).

[316] *Id.* at 629.

[317] Cal. Fam. Code § 3100(a) (West 2001).

[318] Conn. Gen. Stat. Ann. § 46b-59 (West 1986).

[319] Or. Rev. Stat. § 109.119 (1999).

extends but is not limited to stepparents, foster parents, grandparents and relatives by blood or marriage.

In some states, the statutory right of third parties to petition for visitation is more limited. In both Louisiana and New Jersey, for example, the right is afforded only to siblings and grandparents of children whose parents are deceased, divorced or legally separated. [320] Similarly, the Alaska statute allows visitation by a grandparent or other person when one or both parents of the child are deceased. [321]

[3] Grandparent Visitation

Grandparents generally enjoy a statutory right to petition for visitation. [322] The reported cases reflect varying degrees of success when custodial parents have challenged this right. In *Kudler v. Smith*, [323] for example, a Colorado appellate court affirmed the trial court's termination of visitation with the grandparents of the children's deceased mother. Observing that the grandparents had maligned, criticized and undermined the father during visits with the children, the court held that termination of visitation was in the children's best interest.

In *In re Visitation of Gasteau*, [324] the child's divorced father, after the mother's remarriage, voluntarily terminated his parental rights to allow adoption by the stepfather. The Court of Appeals of Indiana reversed the lower court's order dismissing the grandmother's visitation petition on the ground that termination of the father's parental rights also terminated the grandmother's derivative rights. The court held that the legislature, in enacting the Grandparent Visitation Rights Act, [325] intended that grandparents' visitation rights survive adoption of the child by a stepparent.

Recent cases in some jurisdictions have subjected grandparent visitation statutes to constitutional scrutiny. In *King v. King*, [326] for example, the Supreme Court of Kentucky upheld the constitutionality of a statute upon which the trial court relied in ordering visitation by a child's grandfather over the objection of the married parents of the child. In the course of an extensive disquisition in support of its judgment, the court stated:

> This statute seeks to balance the fundamental rights of the parents, grandparents and the child. At common law, grandparents had no legal rights to visitation. However, the [legislature] . . .determined that, in modern day society, it was essential that some semblance of family and generational contact be preserved. If a grandparent

---

[320] *See* La. Rev. Stat. Ann. § 344 (West 2001); N.J. Stat. Ann. § 9:2-7-1 (West 1993).

[321] Alaska Stat. § 25.24.150 (1992).

[322] *See supra* § 11.05[D][2]. *See generally* McCrimmon & Howell, *Grandparents' Legal Rights to Visitation in the Fifty States and the District of Columbia*, 17 Bull. Am. Acad. Psychiatry & L. 355 (1989).

[323] 643 P.2d 783 (Colo. Ct. App. 1981).

[324] 585 N.E.2d 726 (Ind. Ct. App. 1992).

[325] *See* Ind. Code § 31-1-11.7 (Supp. 1992).

[326] 828 S.W. 2d 630 (Ky. 1992).

is physically, mentally and morally fit, then a grandchild will ordinarily benefit from contact with the grandparent. . .*The grandparent can be invigorated by exposure to youth, can gain an insight into our changing society, and can avoid the loneliness which is so often a part of an aging parent's life. These considerations by the state do not go too far in intruding into the fundamental rights of parents.* [327]

A dissenting opinion in *King* described the court's opinion as "mak[ing] little pretense of constitutional analysis," depending on "the sentimental notion of an inherent value in visitation between grandparent and grandchild," and worst of all, reaching the "conclusion that a grandparent has a 'fundamental right' to visitation wit a grandchild." [328] Nevertheless, the Supreme Court of Missouri, in *Herndon v. Tuhey,* [329] upheld the that state's grandparent visitation statute with copious comments from and in full agreement with *King.*

Some state courts, however, have invalidated grandparent visitation statutes under the applicable state constitutions or the federal constitution.. In *Hawk v. Hawk,* [330] for example, the Supreme Court of Tennessee held that the state's grandparent visitation statute was unconstitutional. The court in *Hawk,* reviewed a number of Supreme Court decisions, stated that although it is "often expressed as a 'liberty' interest, the protection of 'childrearing autonomy' reflects the Court's larger concern with privacy rights for the family. [331] Also, the court was not persuaded by the grandparents' argument that a finding that visitation is in a child's best interest creates a compelling state interest. Rather, the court concluded that under both the Tennessee and federal constitutions, state interference with the right of a parent to raise a child must be based on a showing of harm to the welfare of the child. [332]

In *Troxel v. Glanville,* [333] the United States Supreme Court held, in a plurality opinion, that the Washington grandparent visitation statute was unconstitutional. Finding the statute "breathtakingly broad," the plurality found that, as applied, the statute ignored the decision making authority of the parents and unconstitutionally infringed on the parent's fundamental right to make decisions relating to the child's care, custody, and rearing.

[4] Stepparent Visitation

There is a relative paucity of reported cases that involve visitation rights of stepparents. Not all courts have been persuaded, however, that allowing visitation by stepparents "opens the door to the butcher, the baker and the

---

[327] *Id.* at 632 (citation omitted) (emphasis added).

[328] *Id.* at 633 (Lambert, J., dissenting).

[329] 857 S.W. 2d 203 (Mo. 1993).

[330] 855 S.W. 2d 573 (Tenn. 1993).

[331] *Id.* at 578

[332] *Id.* at 580–81.

[333] 530 U.S. 57 (2000).

candlestick maker to a right to a hearing on visitation' rights."[334] Thus, in *Evans v. Evans*,[335] Maryland's highest court rejected a lower court decision limiting statutory visitation rights to biological parents, adoptive parents and grandparents. The court also held that in loco parentis status need not be established for stepparent visitation to be granted, although it may be a relevant factor in determining the best interests of the child.

More typically, however, state courts have held that in loco parentis status is a significant factor when a stepparent seeks to be awarded visitation rights. In *Spells v. Spells*,[336] for example, perhaps the first reported appellate case to apply the in loco parentis doctrine to favor a stepparent seeking visitation over the biological parent's objection, the Pennsylvania Superior Court stated:

> [W]hen a stepparent is "in loco parentis" with his stepchildren, courts must jealously guard his rights to visitation. Of course, the paramount concern in any child custody or visitation dispute is the welfare and best interests of the child. But the hearing court must permit a stepparent to establish what his relationship to the child is and to demonstrate that his interest in visitation should be protected.[337]

The former stepparent in *Simmons v. Simmons*[338] was ineligible to petition for visitation under a Minnesota statute that permits reasonable visitation rights when a child has resided with a person for at least two years.[339] Although the petitioner had lived with his stepson for only 18 months before divorcing the child's mother, he was successful, nevertheless, in establishing his right to visitation. The court held that a former stepparent who was in loco parentis to his former stepchild may have a common law right to visitation, and that nothing in the statute specifically repealed, restricted, or abridged a non-parent's common law rights of visitation.

[5] "De facto parent" Visitation

The claims that the California Court of Appeal addressed in *Nancy S. v. Michele G.*[340] are typical of those asserted by persons who seek legal recognition as "de facto parents" or "co-parents" for the purpose of obtaining rights to visitation. The court declined to recognize any of the theories under which the lesbian former partner claimed visitation rights with two children.

---

[334] *Simpson v. Simpson*, 586 S.W.2d 33, 36 (Ky. 1979) (Stephenson, J., dissenting).

[335] 488 A.2d 157 (Md. 1985).

[336] 378 A.2d 879 (Pa. Super. Ct. 1977).

[337] *Id.* at 883; *see also Carter v. Broderick*, 644 P.2d 850 (Alaska 1982); *Bryan v. Bryan*, 645 P.2d 1267 (Ariz. 1982); *Wills v. Wills*, 399 So. 2d 1130 (Fla. 1981); *Collins v. Gilbreath*, 403 N.E. 2d 921 (Ind. 1980); *Simpson v. Simpson*, 586 S.W.2d 33 (Ky. 1979); *Hickenbottom v. Hickenbottom*, 477 N.W.2d 8 (Neb. 1991); *Looper v. McManus*, 581 P.2d 487 (Okla. Ct. App. 1978); *Gribble v. Gribble*, 583 P.2d 64 (Utah 1978); *Paquette v. Paquette*, 499 A.2d 23 (Vt. 1985).

[338] 486 N.W.2d 788 (Minn. Ct. App. 1992).

[339] *See* Minn. Stat. § 257.022 (1990).

[340] 279 Cal. Rptr. 212 (Cal. Ct. App. 1991).

The children were conceived through artificial insemination during the parties' relationship. After the parties separated and came to disagree about a custody arrangement, the biological mother, Nancy S., sought a declaration under the Uniform Parentage Act that her former partner was not a parent and was, therefore, entitled to visitation only if the biological mother consented. Michele G. then sought an order for shared custody and visitation which the court denied, holding that Michele lacked standing to pursue visitation and awarding sole custody to Nancy.

Michele then argued that she was a de facto parent, defined as one who assumes the role of parent from day to day and fulfills the child's physical and psychological needs. While conceding that Michele might be a de facto parent under California law, the court ruled that this status does not give one the right to visitation over the objection of the biological parent. The court similarly rejected Michele's theory that the common law in loco parentis doctrine gave her rights to seek custody and visitation equal to those of the biological parent, declining to extend the doctrine to give a nonparent the same rights as a parent in a custody dispute. Lastly, after finding the doctrine of equitable estoppel inapplicable, the court concluded:

> [E]xpanding the definition of a "parent" in the manner advocated by appellant could expose other natural parents to litigation brought by child-care providers of long standing, relatives, successive sets of stepparents or other close friends of the family. . . . By deferring to the Legislature in matters involving complex social and policy ramifications far beyond the facts of the particular case, we are not telling the parties that the issues they raise are unworthy of legal recognition. To the contrary, we intend only to illustrate the limitations of the courts in fashioning a comprehensive solution to such a complex and socially significant issue.[341]

In *Alison D. v. Virginia M.*,[342] the parties shared child care and support duties toward a child conceived by artificial insemination pursuant to their agreement. After the women separated, the biological mother eventually ended all contact between her former companion and the child. The New York Court of Appeals held that the petitioner was not a parent within the meaning of the applicable statute and, therefore, lacked standing to petition for a hearing regarding visitation. The court noted that the petitioner had no right to "limit or diminish the right of the concededly fit biological parent to choose with whom her child associates."[343] The court further observed:

> Traditionally, in this State it is the child's mother and father who, assuming fitness, have the right to the care and custody of the child, even in situations where the nonparent has exercised some control over the child with the parent's consent. To allow the courts to award visitation-a limited form of custody-to a third person would necessarily impair the parents' right to custody and control.[344]

---

[341] *Id.* at 219.

[342] 572 N.E.2d 27 (N.Y. 1991).

[343] *Id.* at 29; *see also In re Interest of Z.J.H.*, 471 N.W.2d 202 (Wis. 1991).

[344] *Id.* at 29 (citations omitted).

Courts in other jurisdictions have rendered decisions similar to that of New York's highest court in *Alison D.* More recently, however, a number of courts have rejected an approach that strictly construes the applicable statute. In *In re Custody of H.S.H.-K.,* [345] for example, the Supreme Court of Wisconsin, departing from its own decision in an earlier case, recognized visitation rights for lesbian partners of legal parents. Even thought the Wisconsin visitation statute did not apply to the case before it, the court concluded that the legislature did not intend that the visitation statute "to be the exclusive provision on visitation," nor that it "supplant or preempt the courts' long standing equitable power to protect the best interest of a child by ordering visitation *in circumstances not included in the statute."*[346]

Similarly, in *E.N.O. v. L.M.M.,* [347] the Supreme Judicial Court of Massachusetts reached the same result. Even though there was no statutory authority to award visitation, and even though the court recognized the amorphousness of the best interest of the child standard, the court concluded that the authority to award visitation could be found in the equity jurisdiction of the trial court. Adopting a similar line of reasoning, the Supreme Court of New Jersey in *V.C. v. M.J.B.* [348]

§ 11.06   Modification of Child Custody

[A]   Introduction and Overview

A change in child custody almost invariably involves the potential for conflict between two important principles. The need for finality of judgments or decrees complements the desire for continuity and stability in child custody arrangements. At the same time, however, it is essential that ongoing custody arrangements continue to provide for the best interests of the child. The standard that generally governs modification of child custody, requiring a showing of materially changed circumstances and that modification is in the best interest of the child, reflects these ostensibly competing principles. [349]

The Colorado statutory provisions governing modification of sole custody and joint custody are illustrative, taking into account both the need for continuity and stability, and concern for the child's best interests. In this jurisdiction, once a motion to modify a custody decree is filed, whether it is granted or not, no subsequent modification motions may be filed unless the court finds that the child's emotional or physical well-being is endangered. [350] Further, the court may not modify a prior sole custody absent

---

[345] 533 N.W. 2d 419, 420 (Wis. 1995).

[346] *Id.* at 424–25 (emphasis supplied).

[347] 711 N.E. 2d 886 (Mass. 1999).

[348] 748 A. 2d 539 (2000).

[349] *See generally* Wexler, *Rethinking the Modification of Child Custody Decrees,* 94 Yale L.J. 757 (1985) (discussing the standards for modification of custody decrees and proposing a more restrictive standard for modification and greater use of social science data).

[350] Colo. Rev. Stat. Ann. § 14-10-131 (West 1987).

a finding, based on facts that have arisen since the prior decree or were unknown at the time of its issuance, that there has been a change in circumstances and that modification will serve the child's best interests. [351] Additionally, a prior custody arrangement will not be disturbed unless the custodian agrees or the child has been "integrated into the family of the petitioner" and the custodian consents to that arrangement, or the present arrangement poses a danger to the child's emotional or physical welfare such that the potential harm of a custody change is less than the potential benefit to the child. [352]

Modification or termination of a joint custody decree must be in the best interest of the child and the potential benefit of a "change in environment" must be greater than the harm likely to result from the change. [353] Regardless of the disposition of a prior motion for modification of joint custody, no such motion may be filed within two years, unless the court finds cause for a hearing or the parties stipulate to the change. [354] The party seeking modification must prove by a preponderance of the evidence that the change is indicated. [355]

[B] Judicial Standards for Modification of Custody Decrees

In *Burchard v. Garay*, [356] the mother of a child born out of wedlock cared for the child for two years while the father denied paternity and neither visited the child nor furnished support. After the mother established paternity in a court proceeding, both parents filed petitions for exclusive custody. The trial court awarded custody to the father, in accordance with its view of the child's best interests.

On appeal, the Supreme Court of California examined the function of the changed circumstance rule in child custody cases. The court concluded that the rule does not require a change of circumstances where no prior custody decree exists, but affirmed "the importance of stability in custody arrangements, placing the burden upon the person seeking to alter a long-established arrangement." [357] The court noted that in most cases the result will be the same whether the court applies a changed circumstance or a best interest test because of the importance of the child's need for stability and continuity.

The Supreme Court of New Hampshire, in *Perrault v. Cook*, [358] provided elaborate reasons for the importance of requiring a substantial and material

---

[351] *Id.*

[352] *Id.*

[353] Colo. Rev. Stat. Ann. § 14-10-131.5 (West 1987).

[354] *Id.*

[355] *Id.*

[356] 724 P.2d 486 (Cal. 1986).

[357] *Id.* at 804.

[358] 322 A.2d 610 (N.H. 1974).

change of circumstances before altering an existing custody arrangement. The court observed:

> In a custody proceeding . . . the focus is on the welfare of the child. The stability of family relationships is recognized as an essential ingredient in nurturing the healthy psychological development of a child. . . . The shuffling of a child back and forth between a father and mother can destroy his sense of security, confuse his emotions, and greatly disrupt his growth as an individual. . . . Accordingly, the party to whom custody of a child has been given pursuant to a divorce decree has a much higher interest in maintaining the status quo for the purpose of protecting the child from psychological injury. The relationship established by the custody award should not be disturbed unless the moving party demonstrates that the circumstances affecting the welfare of the child have been so greatly altered that there is a strong possibility the child will be harmed if he continues to live under the present arrangement. [359]

With the increasing emphasis on joint custody, [360] courts must now consider with some frequency petitions seeking modification of this arrangement. In *King v. King*, [361] for example, when the child was eight years old, the divorce court awarded joint physical custody, with primary residence in the mother's home. Four years later, the trial court granted the father's motion to amend the decree and award him sole custody. In its affirmance, the Supreme Court of Rhode Island held that the child's substantially increased age at a critical time of his life was a sufficient change of circumstances to warrant reopening the prior custody order. In *In re Marriage of Birnbaum*, [362] however, California court held that the trial court's change of the child's joint custody residential arrangement was not a change in custody. Therefore, no showing of a change in circumstances was required.

§ 11.07 Relocation of Custodial Parent

[A] Statutory Restrictions

Statutes in a number of states, of which the following are illustrative, impose residential restrictions on custodial parents. The New Jersey statute prohibits removal of a child who is a native of New Jersey or who has resided there for five years without the consent of both parents or a court order issued upon good cause. [363] In Indiana, the statute requires a custodial parent who intends to move out of state or one hundred miles from the county of residence to file a notice of that intent with the court, and a copy with the noncustodial parent. [364] Either party is then entitled

---

[359] *Id.* at 612.

[360] *See supra* § 11.04.

[361] 333 A.2d 135 (R.I. 1975).

[362] 260 Cal. Rptr. 210 (Cal. Ct. App. 1989).

[363] N.J. Stat. Ann. § 9:2-2 (West 1993).

[364] Ind. Code Ann. § 31-17-2-4 (West 2001).

to a hearing to review and modify when appropriate prior custody, visitation, and support orders.[365] The statute in Nevada provides that a parent having custody or joint custody must petition the court for permission to move out of the state if the other parent does not consent to the move; noncompliance may be a factor if the noncustodial parent or other joint custodial parent requests a change of custody.

[B] Court Ordered Limitations on Relocation by a Custodial Parent

In *Schwartz v. Schwartz*,[366] the Supreme Court of Nevada, in a case of first impression interpreted that state's "anti-removal" statutory provisions.[367] The child's father, the residential custodian, sought the court's permission to move from Nevada to Pennsylvania to be near his family, where he could provide better care for the child. In establishing guidelines for the removal of children from the state, the court relied heavily on the criteria adopted by the Chancery Division of the Superior Court of New Jersey in *D'Onofrio v. D'Onofrio*,[368] a leading and frequently cited case in the area.

The court required that the custodial parent show that both the children and the custodial parent would realize an "actual advantage" in moving so far from the current residence as virtually to preclude weekly visitation.[369] Once this requirement is met, the court must weigh several additional factors, including (1) the extent to which it is likely that the move will improve the children's and the custodial parent's quality of life; (2) whether the custodial parent has honorable motives, not intended to impede visitation rights; (3) whether the custodial parent will comply with the court's visitation orders after removal; (4) whether the noncustodian's motives in resisting removal are honorable, and not designed to obtain financial advantages; and (5) whether reasonable visitation can be accomplished at the distance contemplated. When alternative reasonable visitation is possible and removal affords a clear advantage, the court will not deny relocation solely to preserve weekly visitation.

In *DeCamp v. Hein*,[370] a Florida court similarly adopted the New Jersey relocation test set out in *D'Onofrio*. In *DeCamp*, the children's mother physically separated from her husband and moved from Florida to her birthplace

---

[365] *Id.*

[366] 812 P.2d 1268 (Nev. 1991).

[367] *See supra* § 11.07[A].

[368] 365 A.2d 27 (N.J. Super. Ct. Ch. Div.), *aff'd.*, 365 A.2d 716 (N.J. Super. Ct. App. Div. 1976).

[369] *Schwartz*, 812 P.2d at 1271. In *Cooper v. Cooper*, 491 A.2d 606 (N.J. 1984), the New Jersey Supreme Court required that a custodial parent must establish, inter alia, a real advantage from a move. The court modified this requirement in *Holder v. Polanski*, 544 A.2d 852, 855 (N.J. 1988) (holding that "a custodial parent may move with the children of the marriage to another state as long as the move does not interfere with the best interests of the children of the visitation rights of the non-custodial parent").

[370] 541 So. 2d 708 (Fla. Dist. Ct. App. 1989).

in New Jersey to be near her relatives, and there secured employment and housing. In a subsequent Florida divorce decree, the court granted custody to the mother, but required that the children reside in Florida near their father. The appellate court found these requirements incompatible and, relying on the guidelines in *D'Onofrio*, held that the wife could retain custody of the children and move to New Jersey.

As the court in *DeCamp* observed, in deciding the children's best interest in cases involving the relocation of a custodial parent, "[t]here can be no bright line test," and the court must examine all the facts and circumstances. [371] Thus, in *Lozinak v. Lozinak* [372] the Pennsylvania Superior Court affirmed an award of physical custody to the mother on the condition that she remain in Pennsylvania, with the father to have custody if she moved to Iowa. The court found that the mother offered no reasons, "economic, educational, religious, health or emotional," to justify moving a child from Pennsylvania, where the child had an extended family, the time and attention of both parents and an excellent environment. [373]

Similarly, in *Carpenter v. Carpenter*, [374] the Supreme Court of Virginia affirmed an order enjoining a custodial mother from moving from Virginia to New York, where she would be near to her family and anticipated substantially improved employment opportunities. The court accepted the lower court's conclusions that removal to New York would not be in the children's best interests because they benefited from the care of both parents in Virginia, and the mother's employment plans were entirely speculative. Also, "the cultural and educational advantages in New York City were not significantly greater than the cultural, educational and recreational advantages in Tidewater Virginia." [375]

For many years, the New York courts applied a different and arguably stricter rule in determining whether to permit removal of a child to another jurisdiction. In *Aldrich v. Aldrich*, [376] the court stated that "[i]t is now hornbook law that exceptional circumstances must exist before the visitation rights of a noncustodial parent may be diminished or denied." [377] In *Tropea v. Tropea*, [378] the New York Court of Appeals departed from this long standing approach to the custodial parent's relocation. The court held "that each relocation request must be considered on its own merits with due consideration of all the relevant facts and circumstances and with predominant emphasis being placed on what outcome is most likely to serve the best interests of the child." [379] The court was careful to point out that

[371] *Id.* at 712.

[372] 569 A.2d 353 (Pa. Super. Ct. 1990).

[373] *Id.* at 355.

[374] 257 S.E.2d 845 (Va. 1979).

[375] *Id.* at 848.

[376] 516 N.Y.S.2d 328 (N.Y. App. Div. 1987).

[377] *Id.* at 329.

[378] 665 N.E. 2d 145 (N.Y. 1996).

[379] *Id.* at 150.

among the significant factors that must be considered are the rights of custodial and non custodial parents. But "it is the rights and needs of the children that must be accorded the greatest weight, since they are innocent victims of their parents decision to divorce and are the least equipped to handle the stresses of the changing family situation." [380]

In *Burgess v. Burgess,* [381] the Supreme Court of California also overruled prior law created by the appellate courts that favored noncustodial parent. The court stated:

> [I]n a matter involving immediate or eventual relocation by one or both parents, the trial court must take into account the presumptive right of a custodial parent to change the residence of the minor children, so long as the removal would not be prejudicial to their rights or welfare. . . .The showing required is substantial. We have previously held that a child should not be removed from prior custody of one parent and given to the other "unless the material facts and circumstances occurring subsequently are of a kind to render it essential or expedient for the welfare of the child that there be a change." [382]

The decisions in *Tropea* and *Burgess,* rendered by the highest courts of New York and California respectively, may well signal a trend toward near universal acceptance of the best interest of the child standard in cases involving relocation by the custodial parent.

§ 11.08　Interference With Child Custody

[A]　State Criminal Sanctions

Statutes in many states provide for punishment for the act of interference with custody by a noncustodial parenst. The statutes, of which the following are illustrative examples, generally supplement criminal kidnapping provisions.

In Colorado, the offense of violation of custody, a felony, is committed when a person, including a natural parent or foster parent who knows he "has no privilege to do so," takes or entices a child from the parent or legal guardian or violates a custody order with the intent of depriving the parent or legal custodian of custody. [383] The offender's reasonable belief that the conduct was necessary to protect the child is an affirmative defense. [384] The California statute similarly contains criminal sanctions against a person having a custodial right to a child. It punishes maliciously taking the child with the intent to deprive another of custody rights without good cause

---

[380] *Id.*

[381] 913 P. 2d 473 (Cal. 1996).

[382] *Id.* at 478, 482.

[383] Colo. Rev. Stat. § 18-3-304 (West 2001).

[384] *Id.*

relating to the child's protection. [385] Violation of the provision carries fines of $1000 to $10,000 or imprisonment from one year in the county jail to three years in state prison. [386]

In Arizona, the status of the person who interferes with custody or visitation determines the level of the offense. That is, a parent or a parent's agent who violates the statute commits a felony of a lower grade than a parent who engages in the same conduct. [387] Again, if the parent or the parent's agent safely returns the child before being arrested, the offense is a misdemeanor. [388]

The definition of "simple kidnapping" in the Louisiana Criminal Code includes:

> The intentional taking, enticing or decoying away and removing from the state, by any parent of his or her child, from the custody of any person to whom custody has been awarded by any court of competent jurisdiction of any state, without consent of the legal custodian, with intent to defeat the jurisdiction of the said court over the custody of the child. [389]

Simple kidnapping is punished by a fine up to $5,000, imprisonment for up to five years, or both. [390] In Louisiana, interference with child custody is an offense separate and distinct from simple kidnapping, and is punishable by a fine of up to $500, six months imprisonment, or both. [391]

[B] Tortious Interference With Custody

In *Wood v. Wood*, [392] the Supreme Court of Iowa recognized a cause of action for tortious interference with custody. [393] In so doing, the court pointed out that it was joining the majority of jurisdictions that had considered the question in following the Restatement of Torts, which provides that "[o]ne parent may be liable to the other parent for the abduction of his own child if by judicial decree the sole custody of the child has been awarded to the other parent." [394] A strong dissent in *Wood* argues vigorously against

---

[385] Cal. Penal Code § 277 (West 2001).

[386] *Id.*

[387] Ariz. Rev. Stat. Ann. § 13-1302 (1989). A person commits custodial or visitation interference under the statute "if, knowing or having reason to know that he has no legal right to do so, such person knowingly takes, entices or keeps from lawfuls custody or specified visitation any child less than eighteen years of age or incompetent, entrusted by authority of law to the custody of another person or institution." *Id.*

[388] *Id.*

[389] La. Rev. Stat. Ann. § 14:45(A)(4) (West 1986).

[390] La. Rev. Stat. § 14:45(B) (1992).

[391] La. Rev. Stat. § 14:45.1 (1992).

[392] 338 N.W.2d 123 (Iowa 1983).

[393] *See generally* Campbell, *Note, The Tort of Custodial Interference-Toward A More Complete Remedy to Parental Kidnappings*, 1983 U. Ill. L. Rev. 229 (1983) (arguing that tort liability for custodial interference, because it is the only remedy that gives compensation to the custodial parents, is an important component in solving the problem of kidnapping).

[394] Restatement (Second) of Torts § 700 (1977); *see also Fenslage v. Dawkins*, 629 F.2d 1107,

establishment of a cause of action in tort for interference with custody. The dissent asserts that the decision of the court will generate excessive litigation for already overburdened courts, and that pursuit of a tort remedy will be contrary to the best interests of children and their families as a "new weapon for the arsenal of litigants engaging in marital or post-marital warfare."[395]

Arguably, the court's decision in *Kajtazi v. Kajtazi*[396] verifies the dissenter's dire predictions in *Wood*. In *Kajtazi*, the child's father, with help from his other relatives, removed his child from the country without the consent or knowledge of the mother, who was the temporary custodian. The court held the defendants liable to the child for false imprisonment and intentional infliction of emotional distress, and awarded punitive damages based on the defendants' malicious and intentional disregard of the child's rights. The mother recovered damages for "loss of services of the child, the parent's wounded feelings and for the expenses incurred in attempting to recover the child," together with punitive damages and compensation for intentional infliction of emotional distress.

§ 11.09 Mediation of Child Custody Disputes

As alternative dispute resolution has increasingly taken hold in connection with matrimonial and family issues,[397] a number of state legislatures have enacted provisions authorizing mediation of custody and visitation matters. In Kansas, for example, the statute permits the court to order mediation of contested child custody or visitation questions upon the motion of either party or on its own motion.[398] If mediation is ordered, the statute directs that the court or hearing officer take into account the parties' choice of a specific mediator, whether the proposed mediator has relationships with the parties or any interests that might result in a conflict of interest or bias, and the proposed mediator's training and experience, including knowledge of child development, community resources, and relevant state law.[399]

The California Civil Code contains what are perhaps the most elaborate and comprehensive custody mediation provisions of any jurisdiction. In custody or visitation matters, the statute mandates that mediation be scheduled prior to or concurrently with the setting a hearing.[400] The provision states explicitly that its purpose is to "reduce acrimony" between the parties and to encourage an agreement that will assure "close and

1109 (5th Cir. 1980) (awarding compensatory and punitive damages to a custodial mother against the child's father and others who conspired to keep the child from the mother, and noting that the Texas Supreme Court would follow the Restatement's principles).

[395] *Id.* at 127.

[396] 488 F. Supp. 15 (E.D.N.Y. 1978).

[397] *See supra*, § 8.08.

[398] Kan. Stat. Ann. § 23-602 (2000).

[399] *Id.*

[400] Cal. Fam. Code § 31-15-9.4-2 (West Supp. 2001).

continuing contact" between parents and their children.[401] The mediator must strive for a settlement that is in the children's best interests, and has the authority to exclude counsel from the proceeding, interview the children, and meet separately with the parties.[402]

---

[401] *Id.*

[402] *Id.*

TABLE OF CASES

[Principal cases appear in capital letters, with page references in italics. Other cases are those cited or discussed by the author.]

[Principal cases appear in capital letters, with page references in italics. Other cases are those cited or discussed by the author.]

[Principal cases appear in capital letters, with page references in italics. Other cases are those cited or discussed by the author.]

[Principal cases appear in capital letters, with page references in italics. Other cases are those cited or discussed by the author.]

[Principal cases appear in capital letters, with page references in italics. Other cases are those cited or discussed by the author.]

[Principal cases appear in capital letters, with page references in italics. Other cases are those cited or discussed by the author.]

[Principal cases appear in capital letters, with page references in italics. Other cases are those cited or discussed by the author.]

[Principal cases appear in capital letters, with page references in italics. Other cases are those cited or discussed by the author.]

I

J

[Principal cases appear in capital letters, with page references in italics. Other cases are those cited or discussed by the author.]

[Principal cases appear in capital letters, with page references in italics. Other cases are those cited or discussed by the author.]

M

[Principal cases appear in capital letters, with page references in italics. Other cases are those cited or discussed by the author.]

[Principal cases appear in capital letters, with page references in italics. Other cases are those cited or discussed by the author.]

N

O

[Principal cases appear in capital letters, with page references in italics. Other cases are those cited or discussed by the author.]

[Principal cases appear in capital letters, with page references in italics. Other cases are those cited or discussed by the author.]

[Principal cases appear in capital letters, with page references in italics. Other cases are those cited or discussed by the author.]

[Principal cases appear in capital letters, with page references in italics. Other cases are those cited or discussed by the author.]

[Principal cases appear in capital letters, with page references in italics. Other cases are those cited or discussed by the author.]

[Principal cases appear in capital letters, with page references in italics. Other cases are those cited or discussed by the author.]

[Principal cases appear in capital letters, with page references in italics. Other cases are those cited or discussed by the author.]

INDEX

[References are to page numbers.]

[References are to page numbers.]

[References are to page numbers.]

[References are to page numbers.]

[References are to page numbers.]

[References are to page numbers.]

[References are to page numbers.]

[References are to page numbers.]

[References are to page numbers.]

[References are to page numbers.]

[References are to page numbers.]

[References are to page numbers.]

[References are to page numbers.]

[References are to page numbers.]

[References are to page numbers.]

[References are to page numbers.]

[References are to page numbers.]

[References are to page numbers.]

[References are to page numbers.]

[References are to page numbers.]

[References are to page numbers.]

[References are to page numbers.]

[References are to page numbers.]

[References are to page numbers.]

W

WAIVER
Spousal support claims . . . 312

WASTE OF MARITAL ASSETS (See EQUITABLE DISTRIBUTION OF PROPERTY)

WORKERS' COMPENSATION
De facto spouses . . . 41-42
Equitable distribution of property 386-387
Nonmarital child bringing action . . 117

WRONGFUL BIRTH
Cause of action . . . 148
Damages . . . 203

WRONGFUL CONCEPTION
Cause of action . . . 148

WRONGFUL DEATH
Consortium, loss of . . . 86
De facto spouses . . . 41
Nonmarital child bringing action . . 117
Unborn child as person . . . 203

WRONGFUL LIFE
Generally . . . 204
Cause of action . . . 148
Damages . . . 204

Z

ZONING
Unmarried cohabitants and single family residence zoning . . . 42